"This book fills a lacuna in evangelical scholarship. Rarely does academic specialization in canon studies converge with thorough commitment to biblical authority. In this work, close evaluation of the history of approaches to the canon is matched by a richly theological interpretation of what it means to call Scripture our 'canon.' Careful, accessible, and wise in his explorations, Michael Kruger has given us a gift that will keep on giving for generations to come."

Michael S. Horton, J. Gresham Machen Professor of Systematic Theology and Apologetics, Westminster Seminary California

"The Christian canon of Scripture is under fire now more than ever. Sadly, even as so much of this fire has been issuing from academic quarters, we are left with more smoke than light. Stepping into the gap with a fresh synthesis is Michael Kruger's *Canon Revisited*. Gracefully uniting theology and history, Kruger invokes the chief Reformed argument for canon and gives it fresh wings."

Nicholas Perrin, Franklin S. Dyrness Professor of Biblical Studies, Wheaton College Graduate School

"Of all the recent books and articles on the canon of Scripture, this is the one I recommend most. It deals with the critical literature thoroughly and effectively while presenting a cogent alternative grounded in the teaching of Scripture itself. Michael Kruger develops the historic Reformed model of Scripture as self-authenticating and integrates it with a balanced appreciation for the history of the canon and the role of the community in recognizing it. This is the definitive work on the subject for our time."

John M. Frame, J. D. Trimble Chair of Systematic Theology and Philosophy, Reformed Theological Seminary, Orlando, Florida

"Michael Kruger has written the book on the canon of Scripture that has been much needed for a long time. His focus is not on the process, but on the vitally important question of how Christians can know that they have the right books in their canon of Scripture. The question is an excellent one and needs to be addressed honestly and competently. Kruger does just that. This excellent book goes a long way toward clearing up confusion and misguided theories. I highly recommend it."

Craig A. Evans, Payzant Distinguished Professor of New Testament, Acadia Divinity College and Acadia University

"Here, finally, is what so many pastors, seminary professors, and students have long been waiting for: a clear, well-informed, and scripturally faithful answer to the question of how Christians should account for the New Testament canon. Perhaps not since Ridderbos's *Redemptive History and the New Testament Scriptures* has there appeared such a valuable single source on the New Testament canon that is both historically responsible and theologically satisfying (and this book improves on Ridderbos in many ways). Michael Kruger's work will help readers get a handle on what may seem like a myriad of current approaches to canon, whether ecclesiastical or critical. This book will foster clearer thinking on the subject of the New Testament canon and will be a much referenced guide for a long time to come."

Charles E. Hill, Professor of New Testament,
Reformed Theological Seminary, Orlando, Florida

"Michael Kruger has written an important and comprehensive treatment of the New Testament canon. As an advocate of the self-authenticating view, he goes to great lengths to argue his case, but he also delves deeply into the variety of historical and community-based positions. He provides an insightful treatment of epistemological grounds for belief, and debates the positions in a rigorous way not often found in such discussions. I am sure friend and foe alike will learn from this valuable volume."

Stanley E. Porter, President, Dean, and Professor of New Testament,
McMaster Divinity College;
author, *Verbal Aspect in the Greek of the New Testament*

"*Canon Revisited* is a well-written, carefully documented, and helpful examination of the many historical approaches that have been written to explain when and how the books of the New Testament were canonized. The author's interest, however, is to move beyond the historical to the theological, concluding that the concepts of a self-authenticating canon and its corporate reception by the church are ultimately how we know that these twenty-seven books belong in the New Testament."

Arthur G. Patzia, Senior Professor of New Testament,
Fuller Theological Seminary; author, *The Making of the New Testament*

CANON
REVISITED

Also by Michael J. Kruger

The Heresy of Orthodoxy: How Contemporary Culture's Fascination with Diversity Has Reshaped Our Understanding of Early Christianity, coauthored with Andreas J. Köstenberger

CANON REVISITED

Establishing the Origins and Authority
of the New Testament Books

MICHAEL J. KRUGER

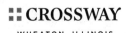

WHEATON, ILLINOIS

Canon Revisited: Establishing the Origins and Authority of the New Testament Books
Copyright © 2012 by Michael J. Kruger
Published by Crossway
      1300 Crescent Street
      Wheaton, Illinois 60187

Cover design: Studio Gearbox
Cover image(s): Photos.com
Interior design and typesetting: Lakeside Design Plus

First printing 2012
Printed in the United States of America

All English translations of the apostolic fathers, unless otherwise noted, are from Bart D. Ehrman, *The Apostolic Fathers*. 2 vols. Cambridge, MA: Harvard University Press, 2003.

Unless otherwise noted, English translations cited as Eusebius, *Hist. eccl.* are from *Ecclesiastical History*. Translated by Kirsopp Lake. Loeb Classical Library. Harvard: Harvard University Press, 1926.

English translations cited as Origen, *Princ.* are from *On First Principles*. Translated by G. W. Butterworth. Gloucester, MA: P. Smith, 1973.

English translations of other church fathers, unless otherwise indicated, are from *The Ante-Nicene Fathers*. Edited by Alexander Roberts and James Donaldson, vol. 1. 1885. Repr. Peabody, MA: Hendrickson, 1994.

Unless otherwise indicated, Scripture quotations are from the ESV® Bible (*The Holy Bible, English Standard Version*®), copyright © 2001 by Crossway. Used by permission. All rights reserved.

All emphases in Scripture quotations have been added by the author.

Hardcover ISBN:	978-1-4335-0500-3
ePub ISBN:	978-1-4335-3081-4
PDF ISBN:	978-1-4335-3079-1
Mobipocket ISBN:	978-1-4335-3080-7

Library of Congress Cataloging-in-Publication Data
Kruger, Michael J.
    Canon revisited : establishing the origins and authority of the New Testament books / Michael J. Kruger.
        p. cm.
    Includes bibliographical references and index.
    ISBN 978-1-4335-0500-3 (hc)
        1. Bible. N.T.—Canon. I. Title.
BS2320.K78 2012
225.1'2—dc23
                                            2011050116

Crossway is a publishing ministry of Good News Publishers.

SH	24	23	22	21	20	19	18	17	16	15
14	13	12	11	10	9	8	7	6	5	4	3

To my students

CONTENTS

PREFACE

The most enjoyable books to write are those that answer questions you yourself have been asking. This is one of those books. For many years I have been fascinated with the origins of the New Testament and have devoted my research to the production and transmission of early Christian texts (both canonical and apocryphal). However, the core question I was asking never seemed to be addressed. I was interested not only in when and how these books were recognized as canonical, but also in *how we know* these books are canonical. My concerns were not only historical but also epistemological (and theological). Of course, I had a broad idea of how to address these epistemological issues, but my thinking needed more precision. After all, the canon is a complex topic with a seemingly endless number of loose ends that never seemed to get tied up. And the existing resources on canon—regardless of how proficiently they answered the historical questions—never quite seemed to scratch my epistemological and theological itch (at least not in a way that was satisfying).

This question reached a head as I started to teach my elective at Reformed Theological Seminary on the origins of the New Testament canon. Like me, the students in my class were not satisfied with just learning when and how the canon was received; they too wanted to know whether Christianity had adequate grounds to claim that these twenty-seven books were the right ones. That is the question that critics of the faith are always asking. And my students were looking for answers. This issue, then, is the motivation for this book. I have written it not so much to answer the question about whether the Christian belief in the canon is true, but to answer the question about whether the Christian belief in the canon is intellectually justified. As we shall see below, those are two different questions. My hope is that this book will provide some preliminary answers, though it certainly will not be (nor is it intended to be) the final word on the subject. No doubt my students will let me know whether it has adequately done the job. It is to them, and their inquisitive minds, that I dedicate this book.

Needless to say, projects like this are never individual affairs. Though I was the lone author, I was not an author who was alone. Many deserve thanks and appreciation for their support and help as I wrote this volume. I am grateful to the Lilly Foundation and the Association of Theological Schools for the Lilly Theological Research Grant, which helped fund my research sabbatical to Cambridge, England, in 2009. It was there that I enjoyed the impressive library and warm fellowship of Tyndale House and did the foundational research for this project. In addition, I benefitted greatly from my time at St Edmund's College of Cambridge University and the opportunity to study there as a visiting scholar. I am thankful to Reformed Theological Seminary for granting my 2009–2010 sabbatical leave, and to the generosity of Dr. and Mrs. Randy Randall. In addition, I am grateful to my home church, Uptown Church (PCA) in Charlotte, North Carolina, for their generous support and encouragement of my sabbatical. In particular, Bill and Kristin Macurda and Peter Barwick are owed a special debt of gratitude.

Beyond institutions, I owe a special thanks to individuals who had a hand in this volume. I am grateful to James Anderson, Michael Horton, Chuck Hill, and many others, for their helpful feedback and reflections. No doubt this is a better piece with their input (though I am still accountable for its shortcomings). I am thankful for Al Fisher at Crossway for his keen interest in this project—he and the entire Crossway staff have been a delight. And thanks to Crossway for allowing some portions of *The Heresy of Orthodoxy* (coauthor Andreas Köstenberger, 2010) to be reused at various points in this volume. My teaching assistants, Jordan Olshefski, Crawford Stevener, and Alan Gay, have worked tirelessly helping me edit and proof this volume—not to mention chasing down random footnotes at the last minute. Most of all, I thank my wife, Melissa, and my children, Emma, John, and Kate. They have sacrificed much as I have spent countless hours on this project, and have always done so with joy and thankfulness. It could not have happened without them.

Charlotte, North Carolina
Easter, 2011

ABBREVIATIONS

ABD	*Anchor Bible Dictionary*. Edited by D. N. Freedman. 6 vols. New York: Doubleday, 1992
AJP	*American Journal of Philology*
ANET	*Ancient Near Eastern Texts Relating to the Old Testament*. Edited by James B. Pritchard. 3rd ed. Princeton, NJ: Princeton University Press, 1969
ANRW	*Aufstieg und Niedergang der römischen Welt: Geschichte und Kultur Roms im Spiegel der neueren Forschung*. Edited by H. Temporini and W. Haase. Berlin: de Gruyter, 1972–
APF	*Archiv für Papyrusforschung*
AThR	*Anglican Theological Review*
BA	*Biblical Archaeologist*
BBR	*Bulletin for Biblical Research*
BJRL	*Bulletin of the John Rylands University Library of Manchester*
CBQ	*Catholic Biblical Quarterly*
CI	*Critical Inquiry*
CurTM	*Currents in Theology and Missions*
EvQ	*Evangelical Quarterly*
ETL	*Ephemerides theologicae lovanienses*
EvT	*Evangelische Theologie*
HBT	*Horizons in Biblical Theology*
HeyJ	*Heythrop Journal*
HS	*Hebrew Studies*
HTR	*Harvard Theological Review*
ICC	International Critical Commentary
Int	*Interpretation*
JBL	*Journal of Biblical Literature*
JEA	*Journal of Egyptian Archaeology*
JECS	*Journal of Early Christian Studies*
JEKT	*Jahrbuch für evangelikale Theologie*
JETS	*Journal of the Evangelical Theological Society*
JJS	*Journal of Jewish Studies*
JR	*Journal of Religion*
JSNT	*Journal for the Study of the New Testament*
JSOT	*Journal for the Study of the Old Testament*

JTS	*Journal of Theological Studies*
LLC	*Literary and Linguistic Computing*
LXX	Septuagint
MT	*Modern Theology*
Neot	*Neotestamentica*
NICNT	New International Commentary on the New Testament
NIGTC	New International Greek Testament Commentary
NovT	*Novum Testamentum*
NTS	*New Testament Studies*
Presb	*Presbyterion*
ProEccl	*Pro ecclesia*
PTR	*Princeton Theological Review*
RAC	*Reallexikon für Antike und Christentum.* Edited by T. Kluser et al. Stuttgart: Hiersemann, 1950–
RB	*Revue biblique*
RHA	*Revue hittite et asianique*
RTR	*Reformed Theological Review*
SE	*Studia evangelica*
SecCent	*Second Century*
SJT	*Scottish Journal of Theology*
SNTSU	*Studien zum Neuen Testament und seiner Umwelt*
SPCK	Society for Promoting Christian Knowledge
ST	*Studia theologica*
StPatr	*Studia patristica*
TNTC	Tyndale New Testament Commentaries
TDNT	*Theological Dictionary of the New Testament.* Edited by G. Kittel and G. Friedrich. Translated by G. W. Bromiley. 10 vols. Grand Rapids: Eerdmans, 1964–1976
Them	*Themelios*
TrinJ	*Trinity Journal*
TS	*Theological Studies*
TU	Texte und Untersuchungen
TynBul	*Tyndale Bulletin*
VC	*Vigiliae christianae*
VT	*Vetus Testamentum*
WBC	Word Biblical Commentary
WCF	Westminster Confession of Faith
WTJ	*Westminster Theological Journal*
ZAC	*Zeitschrift für Antikes Christentum*
ZAW	*Zeitschrift für die alttestamentliche Wissenschaft*
ZNW	*Zeitschrift für die neutestamenliche Wissenschaft und die Kunde der älteren Kirche*
ZPE	*Zeitschrift für Papyrologie und Epigraphik*
ZTK	*Zeitschrift für Theologie und Kirche*

INTRODUCTION

No one has come up with a satisfactory solution as to how we
determine which books should be in the canon.

ERNEST BEST

This book is about a very specific problem confronting the Christian
faith. It is certainly not a new problem (though there are plenty of those)
but is perhaps one of the oldest. For the infant church, it was one of its
earliest and most potent challenges. It continued to be a serious point
of contention even during the time of the Reformation. And still today
it endures as one of the perennial questions faced by any believer in our
modern (and postmodern) age. It is what D. F. Strauss has called the
"Achilles' heel" of Protestant Christianity.[1] It is what many still consider
to be, as Herman Ridderbos has observed, the "hidden, dragging illness
of the Church."[2] It is the problem of canon.

The problem of canon (at least as we are using the phrase here) refers
to the fundamental question of how we, as Christians, can *know* that
we have the right twenty-seven books in our New Testament.[3] Why not
twenty-six books? Or twenty-eight? Of course, such a question would not
be asked if the New Testament were like most other books, formed (more

---

[1]D. F. Strauss, *Die christliche Glaubenslehre in ihrer geschichtlichen Entwicklung und im Kampfe
mit der modernen Wissenschaft*, 2 vols. (Tübingen: Osiander, 1840), 1:136. See discussion in
G. C. Berkouwer, "The Testimony of the Spirit," in *The Authoritative Word*, ed. Donald K.
McKim (Grand Rapids: Eerdmans, 1983), 155–81, esp. 156.
[2]Herman Ridderbos, "The Canon of the New Testament," in *Revelation and the Bible:
Contemporary Evangelical Thought*, ed. C. F. H. Henry (Grand Rapids: Baker, 1958), 198.
[3]The Old Testament canon also raises important and interesting questions, but that will not be
the focus of this volume. For a helpful overview of the Old Testament canon, see R. T. Beckwith,
The Old Testament Canon of the New Testament Church, and Its Background in Early Judaism
(Grand Rapids: Eerdmans, 1986).

or less) all at the same time, in the same place, by a single author. Instead, within the boundaries of the New Testament we are faced with a rather complex array of different books, authors, geographical settings, theological perspectives, and historical contexts that are all brought together into one unified volume. What do all these books share in common? What was the process by which they were brought together? And why should the results of that process be considered normative for the modern church? Moreover, what are we to make of disputes within the early church over some of these books? What of the abundance of apocryphal literature that has been discovered? And what would we do if we discovered, say, a lost epistle of Paul? When faced with this plethora of questions we are tempted to agree with Ernest Best when he declared, "No matter where we look there are problems and it may therefore be simpler at this stage to cut our losses and simply dispense with the concept of canon."[4]

Despite these problems, these many questions deserve (and require) an answer from biblical Christianity. For, if Christians cannot adequately answer these questions about the canonical boundaries of the New Testament, then on what grounds could they ever appeal to the *content* of the New Testament? Certainly, there can be no New Testament theology if there is no such thing as a New Testament in the first place.[5] Thus, questions about the canon can take on more foundational significance than other types of questions. It is one thing for a person to question the meaning of a given passage (and whether it says what we think it says), or to question whether a particular passage is historically or factually accurate, but it is quite another to question whether that passage belongs in the Bible in the first place. The question of the canon, therefore, is at the very center of how biblical authority is established. Unless a coherent response can be offered to such questions, then Strauss may be all too right—the canon issue could become the single thread that unravels the entire garment of the Christian faith.

Critics of biblical Christianity have long recognized the significance of the canon question and have therefore focused much of their scholarly energies on that very issue. Although it has been more than two centuries since Johann Semler offered one of the earliest attacks on the origin of the New Testament canon, *Treatise on the Free Investigation of the Canon*

---

[4]Ernest Best, "Scripture, Tradition, and the Canon of the New Testament," *BJRL* 61 (1979): 275.
[5]Ernst Käsemann, "The Problem of a New Testament Theology," *NTS* 19 (1973): 235–45; Christine Helmer and Christof Landmesser, eds., *One Scripture or Many?* (Oxford: Oxford University Press, 2004).

(1771–1775), the question is still hotly contested in the modern day.[6] Kurt Aland, in his well-known work *The Problem of the New Testament Canon*, declared that the "question of Canon will make its ways to the centre of the theological and ecclesiastical debate" because "the question is one which confronts not only the New Testament scholar, but every Christian theologian."[7] Indeed, Aland has been proved right as modern scholars have continued to press their critique of the biblical canon, offering new challenges and proposals, and keeping the canon question at the center of much of modern biblical scholarship. Willi Marxsen argued that the church made mistakes when it originally chose the canon, and therefore it is "subject to revision"; and when it comes to Hebrews and 2 Peter, "we should remove both writings from the canon."[8] David Dungan has suggested that advances in biblical scholarship will "precipitate a massive series of changes regarding the shape and content of the Bible which should rival for creativity the Reformation period, if not the second through fifth centuries."[9] Robert Funk agrees that developments in modern scholarship have "opened the door to a reconsideration of what ancient documents the Christian Scriptures ought to contain"; and he adds, "It will be a great tragedy if we do not seize the opportunity to revamp and revise."[10] Bart Ehrman joins his voice to this chorus of modern criticisms of the canon and declares it to be an "invention" of the dominant Christian factions of early Christianity designed to suppress (or oppress) other factions of the church with different theological convictions.[11]

This continued interest in (and critique of) the New Testament canon can be attributed to several factors. First, modern critical scholarship has continued to raise doubt about the authorship and date of numerous New Testament books, attributing many of them to later, pseudonymous

---

[6]For a more thorough survey of the history of publications on the canon, see Bruce M. Metzger, *The Canon of the New Testament: Its Origin, Development, and Significance* (Oxford: Clarendon, 1987), 11–36.

[7]Kurt Aland, *The Problem of the New Testament Canon* (London: Mowbray, 1962), 31. Aland offers his own critique of canon, suggesting that the church should be willing to reduce its canon in order to eliminate the embarrassing books that all agree are not genuinely canonical (2 Peter, Revelation, etc.).

[8]Willi Marxsen, *The New Testament as the Church's Book* (Philadelphia: Fortress, 1972), 19, 25.

[9]David Dungan, "The New Testament Canon in Recent Study," *Int* 29 (1975): 339.

[10]Robert W. Funk, "The Once and Future New Testament," in *The Canon Debate*, ed. Lee Martin McDonald and James A. Sanders (Peabody, MA: Hendrickson, 2002), 555. Funk goes on to suggest that we need a "new New Testament, indeed, a new Bible" (ibid.). For more on Funk and the Jesus Seminar's attempt to modify the existing canon, see Jeffrey Sheler, "Cutting Loose the Holy Canon: A Controversial Re-Examination of the Bible," *U.S. News & World Report* 15, no. 18 (1993): 75.

[11]Bart D. Ehrman, *Lost Christianities: The Battles for Scripture and the Faiths We Never Knew* (New York: Oxford University Press, 2002), 229–46.

authors.[12] Not only are the traditional authors of the canonical Gospels rejected, but the Pauline letters of Colossians, Ephesians, and the Pastoral Epistles are deemed to be inauthentic, along with books like 2 Peter, Jude, and others.[13] Of course, if a New Testament book were to be exposed as a later forgery, then the inevitable question would arise about whether it has a legitimate claim on canonical status. Second, the last century and a half have been filled with sensational discoveries of apocryphal materials that have raised new questions about which books should be included in the canon. Most notable are the discoveries of apocryphal gospels such as the *Gospel of Peter*,[14] P.Oxy. 840,[15] the Nag Hammadi codices (including the *Gospel of Thomas*),[16] P.Egerton 2,[17] the *Secret Gospel of Mark*,[18] and most recently, the *Gospel of Judas*.[19] Such discoveries have spurred all

---

[12]For an example of modern critical approaches to pseudonymity, see David Meade, *Pseudepigrapha and Canon* (Tübingen: Mohr, 1986), and, most recently, Bart D. Ehrman, *Forged: Writing in the Name of God—Why the Bible's Authors Are Not Who We Think They Are* (New York: HarperOne, 2011). For an evangelical perspective, see D. A. Carson, "Pseudonymity and Pseudepigraphy," in *The Dictionary of New Testament Background*, ed. Craig A. Evans and Stanley E. Porter (Downers Grove, IL: InterVarsity, 2000), 856–64; Thomas D. Lea, "Pseudonymity and the New Testament," in *New Testament Criticism and Interpretation*, ed. David Alan Black and David S. Dockery (Grand Rapids: Zondervan, 1991), 535–59; and, to some extent, Bruce M. Metzger, "Literary Forgeries and Canonical Pseudepigrapha," *JBL* 91 (1972): 3–24.

[13]For general discussions see Robert A. Spivey and D. Moody Smith, *Anatomy of the New Testament* (New York: Macmillan, 1989); and Bart D. Ehrman, *The New Testament: A Historical Introduction to the Early Christian Writings* (New York: Oxford University Press, 1997).

[14]M. G. Mara, *Évangile de Pierre: Introduction, text critique, traduction, commentaire, et index* (Paris: Éditions du Cerf, 1973); H. B. Swete, *The Akhmîm Fragment of the Apocryphal Gospel of St. Peter* (London: Macmillan, 1893); Thomas J. Kraus and Tobias Nicklas, *Das Petrusevangelium und die Petrusapokalypse* (Berlin: de Gruyter, 2004); and most recently Paul Foster, *The Gospel of Peter: Introduction, Critical Edition and Commentary* (Leiden: Brill, 2010).

[15]See Michael J. Kruger, *The Gospel of the Savior: An Analysis of P.Oxy. 840 and Its Place in the Gospel Traditions of Early Christianity* (Leiden: Brill, 2005). A survey of prior literature on P.Oxy. 840 can be found in the introduction, 1–16.

[16]Robert M. Grant, *The Secret Sayings of Jesus* (Garden City, NY: Doubleday, 1960); J. A. Fitzmyer, "The Oxyrhynchus Logoi of Jesus and the Coptic Gospel According to Thomas," *TS* 20 (1959): 505–60; Roderick Dunkerley, "Oxyrhynchus Gospel Fragments," *HTR* 23 (1930): 30–35; and C. Taylor, "The Oxyrhynchus and Other Agrapha," *JTS* 7 (1906): 546–62.

[17]G. Mayeda, *Das Leben-Jesu-Fragment Papyrus Egerton 2 und seine Stellung in der urchristlichen Literaturgeschichte* (Bern: Paul Haupt, 1946); Jon B. Daniels, "The Egerton Gospel: Its Place in Early Christianity" (PhD diss., Claremont Graduate School, 1990); C. H. Dodd, "A New Gospel," *BJRL* 20 (1936): 56–92; and H. I. Bell and T. C. Skeat, *Fragments of an Unknown Gospel and Other Early Christian Papyri* (London: Trustees of the British Museum, 1935).

[18]Morton Smith, *Clement of Alexandria and a Secret Gospel of Mark* (Cambridge: Harvard University Press, 1973). Many now believe that *Secret Mark* was a hoax; e.g., Stephen C. Carlson, *The Gospel Hoax: Morton Smith's Invention of Secret Mark* (Waco, TX: Baylor University Press, 2005). See my review of Carlson, in *JETS* 49 (2006): 422–24.

[19]Herbert Krosney, *The Lost Gospel: The Quest for the Gospel of Judas Iscariot* (Hanover, PA: National Geographic Society, 2006); James M. Robinson, *The Secrets of Judas: The Story of the Misunderstood Disciple and His Lost Gospel* (San Francisco: HarperSanFrancisco, 2006); and Bart D. Ehrman, *The Lost Gospel of Judas Iscariot: A New Look at Betrayer and Betrayed* (New York: Oxford University Press, 2006).

sorts of publications with provocative titles that raise questions about the state of the canon; for example, *The Five Gospels*, *Lost Scriptures*, and *Forgotten Scriptures*.[20] Third, the continued influence of Walter Bauer's book *Orthodoxy and Heresy in Earliest Christianity* (1934) has kept the canonical issue open.[21] Bauer argued that early Christianity was originally very diverse and varied, with no clear orthodox or heretical camp. What would later be called "orthodoxy" was simply the beliefs of the one group that had triumphed over all the others. Thus, the books of the New Testament canon are simply the books of the "winners" of the early church power struggles, but do not necessarily represent "original" Christianity and should not be considered normative for Christians. The resurgence of interest in Bauer's thesis—and the subsequent interest in canon—is due in no small part to the degree to which it fits with postmodern worldviews that argue that there is no "right" or "wrong" version of any religious system.[22] Thus, according to Bauer, apocryphal books have just as much validity as any other Christian books.

It is these types of challenges that have led to the epistemological crisis faced by so many Christians today. If the early church was a theological quagmire, if apocryphal books are as valid as so-called canonical books, and if scholars are convinced the New Testament is filled with forgeries,

---

[20]Robert W. Funk, *The Five Gospels: What Did Jesus Really Say?* (New York: Polebridge, 1993); Bart D. Ehrman, *Lost Scriptures: Books That Did Not Make It into the New Testament* (New York: Oxford University Press, 2003); Lee McDonald, *Forgotten Scriptures: The Selection and Rejection of Early Religious Writings* (Louisville: Westminster John Knox, 2009).

[21]German title, *Rechtgläubigkeit und Ketzerei im ältesten Christentum* (Tübingen: Mohr, 1934). Bauer's thesis has been recently promoted on a number of fronts, including Helmut Koester, "Apocryphal and Canonical Gospels," *HTR* 73 (1980): 105–30; and Ehrman, *Lost Christianities*, 159–257. For a survey of its reception, see Daniel J. Harrington, "The Reception of Walter Bauer's *Orthodoxy and Heresy in Earliest Christianity* During the Last Decade," *HTR* 77 (1980): 289–98. Of course, Bauer has been challenged over the years: see H. E. W. Turner, *The Pattern of Christian Truth: A Study in the Relations Between Orthodoxy and Heresy in the Early Church* (London: Mowbray, 1954); Thomas Robinson, *The Bauer Thesis Examined: The Geography of Heresy in the Early Christian Church* (Lewiston, NY: Mellen, 1989); James McCue, "Orthodoxy and Heresy: Walter Bauer and the Valentinians," *VC* 33 (1979): 118–130; and I. Howard Marshall, "Orthodoxy and Heresy in Earlier Christianity," *Them* 2 (1976): 5–14. For a more recent critique of Bauer, see A. J. Köstenberger and M. J. Kruger, *The Heresy of Orthodoxy: How Modern Culture's Fascination with Diversity Has Reshaped Our Understanding of Early Christianity* (Wheaton, IL: Crossway, 2010).

[22]Helmut Koester, *Ancient Christian Gospels: Their History and Development* (London: SCM, 1990), draws heavily on Bauer's thesis and sounds quite postmodern when he argues that terms like *heresy* and *orthodoxy* should not be used because they reflect "discrimination" and "dogmatic prejudice" in favor of the canonical Gospels (xxx). Similarly, Ehrman, in *Lost Christianities*, shows his postmodern inclinations when he repeatedly chides orthodox Christianity (or "proto-orthodox," as he calls it) for being too "intolerant" of other religious systems (254–57). For a more thorough discussion (and critique) of postmodernity and its effects on Christianity, see D. A. Carson, *The Gagging of God: Christianity Confronts Pluralism* (Grand Rapids: Zondervan, 1996).

then on what possible basis can Christians have confidence that they have the right twenty-seven books? How can Christians ever *know* such a thing? It is here that we come to the precise question this book is designed to answer. This volume is concerned with the narrow question of whether Christians have a rational basis (i.e., intellectually sufficient grounds) for affirming that only these twenty-seven books rightfully belong in the New Testament canon. Or, put differently, is the Christian belief in the canon *justified* (or warranted)?[23] Of course, critics of biblical Christianity have roundly argued that Christians have no rational basis for holding such a belief about the canon. Christians can believe such a thing if they want to, it is argued, but it is irrational and intellectually unjustifiable. It must be taken on "blind faith."

Now this sort of objection to the canon—which this volume is concerned to address—should be carefully distinguished from other sorts of objections to the canon. For instance, one might offer what is called a *de facto* objection.[24] This objection argues that the Christian belief in the canon is intellectually unacceptable on the grounds that it is a *false* belief. *De facto* objections are quite common in modern canonical studies and have taken a variety of forms: for example, these books cannot be from God because they contradict each other, or because they are forgeries, or because they are merely the choice of the "winners" of early theological battles. Regardless of the specific form of the *de facto* objection, the overall claim is the same—the Christian belief in the canon should be rejected because it isn't true. In contrast, this book is addressing what might be called the *de jure* objection to the Christian belief in the canon. This objection has similarities to the *de facto* objection but is different in some important ways. The *de jure* objection argues not so much that Christian belief in the canon is false, but that Christians have no rational basis for thinking they could ever know such a thing in the first place. Given the chaos of early Christianity and the various disagreements over books—not to mention scholarly claims that some of these books are pseudonymous—it would be irrational for Christians to claim that they

---

[23]For the sake of simplicity, this volume will not delve into all the philosophical minutiae of what proper epistemic conditions are necessary for true belief to become knowledge (whether it be "justification" or "warrant"). Instead, this volume will operate in more general biblical terms, rather than philosophical ones (though this does not deny the validity of handling these issues at a more philosophical level). For more on the justification of knowledge, see William P. Alston, *Epistemic Justification: Essays in the Theory of Knowledge* (Ithaca, NY: Cornell University Press, 1989); and Alvin Plantinga, *Warrant and Proper Function* (New York: Oxford University Press, 1993).

[24]For further discussions of *de facto* and *de jure* objections, see Alvin Plantinga, *Warranted Christian Belief* (New York: Oxford University Press, 2000), viii–ix.

know these twenty-seven are the right ones.[25] Thus, on the *de jure* objection, the problem with the Christian belief in canon is something other than its truth or falsehood, but has to do with whether Christians have adequate grounds for holding such a belief.

Because this volume is designed to address the *de jure* objection and not the *de facto* objection (at least not directly), we must be clear about what it is not trying to accomplish. First, this volume is not attempting somehow to "prove" the truth of the canon to the skeptic in a manner that would be persuasive to him. Our goal here is not to find some neutral common ground from which we can demonstrate to the biblical critic that these books are divinely given. As desirable as that might sound to some readers (leaving aside its feasibility), this volume is not nearly so ambitious. Second, our concern here is not merely to explore how a Christian (for the first time) comes to believe that the canon is from God. Such knowledge can be legitimately acquired in a number of ways—even through something as simple as the testimony of another Christian[26]—and an individual may not even be consciously aware of the process that led to such a belief.[27] Instead, the issue that concerns us here is not about our having knowledge of canon (or proving the truth of canon) but *accounting* for our knowledge of canon.[28] It is about whether the Christian religion provides sufficient grounds for thinking that Christians can know which books belong in the canon and which do not.

Now, if this volume is concerned with whether the Christian religion can account for its knowledge of canon, then much of this volume will be about, well, the Christian religion. And, therefore, it particularly will

---

[25]Sometimes *de facto* objections and *de jure* objections can appeal to the same evidence. Thus, the disagreements among early Christians about canonical books can be used as an argument that the canon is not true (*de facto*), or it can be used as an argument that Christians are irrational in believing the canon to be true, whether or not it is true (*de jure*). See ibid., ix.

[26]Belief based on the testimony of another person can be justified (or warranted) if that other person's own knowledge is itself justified (or warranted). See ibid., 376–77.

[27]C. Stephen Evans, *The Historical Christ and the Jesus of Faith: The Incarnational Narrative as History* (New York: Oxford University Press, 1996), 277. A person can know something without knowing *how* he knows it or even *that* he knows it. Awareness that one's beliefs are justified (or warranted) is not necessary for those beliefs to be, in fact, justified (or warranted). As will be seen below, a person can come to know the truth of Scripture by simply apprehending its divine qualities with the help of the internal testimony of the Spirit (and may not be consciously aware of this process).

[28]Evans understands this sort of question as dealing with what he calls "second-level knowledge," namely, how we *know* that we know the Bible is true. He contrasts this with "first-level knowledge," which is just a person's knowing the Bible is true. It is one thing to know the Bible is true (first-level); it is another thing to give an *account* of how we know the Bible is true (second-level). Second-level knowledge inevitably requires the use of the Bible itself when we give an account of how we know that we know it. See discussion in Evans, *The Historical Christ and the Jesus of Faith*, 274–82.

be about the *Christian* conceptions of canon, God, history, revelation, knowledge, and more. Thus, the reader should not expect to find here a purely historical account of canon (whatever that means) void of theological categories and considerations. Aside from whether a purely historical account of canon is even possible, this volume will be unashamedly theological in its approach. Indeed, this is unavoidable if we are dealing with the *de jure* objection. How can the Christian religion account for its knowledge of the canon without talking about the Christian understanding of the way knowledge is acquired? It is important to note, however, that this does not mean this volume is disinterested in historical matters. On the contrary, much attention will be given to the key historical issues. We shall argue that the canon can only be rightly understood (and defended) when both history and theology are taken into account. They should be in a dialogical relationship with one another—as allies, not adversaries.

Of course, it is quite unfashionable these days to suggest that theological issues may play a role in historical (or biblical) studies. The quest for purely "objective" history is still firmly entrenched in the psyche of the modern academy.[29] Lessing's ditch is as deep as it ever was.[30] Yet, the interconnectivity between these two areas is beginning to be acknowledged more and more.[31] Iain Provan makes the point that "all the great giants of biblical study in the last 200 years have worked within certain dogmatic and philosophical positions."[32] Francis Watson has pressed the case that biblical theology can only really be done when both categories (Bible *and* theology) are given their due: "Theological concerns should have an acknowledged place within the field of biblical scholarship."[33] Stephen Chapman has also affirmed the relationship between theology and history.

---

[29]For an example, see Paul Davies, *Whose Bible Is It Anyway?* (Sheffield: Sheffield Academic, 1995), esp. 51–52; also John Collins, "Is a Critical Biblical Theology Possible?," in *The Hebrew Bible and Its Interpreters*, ed. W. Propp (Winona Lake: Eisenbrauns, 1990), 1–17.

[30]G. E. Lessing (1729–1781) argued that there was an impassable barrier (a "big, ugly ditch") between "accidental truths of history" and "necessary truths of reason." This argument, however, is based on a view where history is investigated neutrally and autonomously with no consideration for theological norms.

[31]See the helpful overview in M. G. Brett, "Canonical Criticism and Old Testament Theology," in *Text in Context: Essays by Members of the Society for Old Testament Study*, ed. A. D. H. Mayes (Oxford: Oxford University Press, 2000), 63–85; also F. Watson, *Text, Church and World: Biblical Interpretation in Theological Perspective* (Edinburgh: T&T Clark, 1994), and Watson, *Text and Truth: Redefining Biblical Theology* (Grand Rapids: Eerdmans, 1997).

[32]Iain Provan, "Canons to the Left of Him: Brevard Childs, His Critics, and the Future of Old Testament Theology," *SJT* 50 (1997): 23. See also Provan, "Ideologies, Literary and Critical: Reflections on Recent Writings on the History of Israel," *JBL* 114 (1995): 585–606.

[33]Watson, *Text and Truth*, 3. See also F. Watson, "Bible, Theology and the University: A Response to Philip Davies," *JSOT* 71 (1996): 3–16.

Classic presuppositional, circular argument. Theology based on 'sola scriptura' is to determine the validity of the canon.

Theological concerns are deeply related to questions of historical reconstruction and cannot simply be avoided. Confessional categories are always
present, even (or perhaps especially) when they go unacknowledged. It is a
mistake therefore to pretend that differences in historical reconstruction turn
solely on data and methodology or that historical proposals are unrelated
to theological positions.[34]

Thus, as we press forward in our study of canon, we do well to remember
the simple observation of Kevin Vanhoozer: "History alone cannot answer
the question of what the canon finally is; theology alone can do that."[35]

Now that we have a better understanding of the question at hand—
whether Christians have adequate grounds for thinking they can know which
books are canonical—we turn our attention to how it will be answered in the
chapters to come. The book will be divided into two large sections, the first
of which is "Determining the Canonical Model." In this section we begin
our taxonomy of canonical models, explaining and critiquing how each of
them seeks to authenticate the twenty-seven books of the New Testament.
Chapter 1 explores what we are calling "community-determined" models
of canon, in which the canon is, in some sense, determined by its reception
or recognition by individuals or the church. Canon exists when there is
a *response* from the community. In chapter 2, which is much briefer, we
engage what we are calling "historically determined" models of canon. As
the title suggests, these models argue that canon is determined not so much
by community reception as by the historical merits of each of the canonical
books (or portions thereof). If historical investigations can show a book to
contain authentic Jesus tradition or apostolic content, then it is regarded
as canonical. With these canonical models as a backdrop, chapter 3 lays
forth the case for the "self-authenticating" model, which will become the
foundation for the entire volume. Here we shall argue that God has created
the proper epistemic environment wherein a Christian's belief in the New
Testament canon can be reliably formed. Or, put differently, we shall argue
that Christians have adequate grounds for regarding their belief in canon
to be justified (or warranted).

The second part of the book is "Exploring and Defending the Canonical
Model." In this section we unpack the self-authenticating model of canon
in greater detail and examine some potential "defeaters" to the Christian
belief in the canon. Are there objections to the canon that have such merit

---

[34]Stephen B. Chapman, "The Old Testament Canon and Its Authority for the Christian Church,"
Ex auditu 19 (2003): 126.
[35]Kevin J. Vanhoozer, *The Drama of Doctrine: A Canonical-Linguistic Approach to Christian
Theology* (Louisville: Westminster John Knox, 2005), 146.

that they could bring doubt upon the grounds of our belief? Chapter 4 explores the divine qualities of canonical books and whether supposed contradictions between canonical books present an insurmountable problem for the Christian view of canon. Chapter 5 dives deeper into the issue of the apostolic origins of these books and whether the first-century environment was well suited for the emergence and growth of a new collection of canonical documents. The last three chapters—6 through 8—examine the lengthy historical process by which each of these twenty-seven books was recognized and received as canonical Scripture by early Christians. In particular, these chapters explore whether divisions and disagreements within the early church provide reasons to abandon the belief that these twenty-seven books are the right ones.

The overall structure of this volume highlights what is (hopefully) its distinctive contribution to the study of canon. Most prior studies of the canon have provided precious little by way of the theology of canon and have focused almost exclusively on historical questions. If theological (and epistemological) questions of canon are raised at all, they are typically done at the end of the study, after the historical investigations are already completed.[36] As noted above, however, this volume is committed to addressing *both* the theology of canon and the history of canon in an integrated fashion. The theology of canon is viewed not as an "epilogue" to be addressed only after the formal investigation of the historical evidence is complete, but instead as the paradigm through which the historical evidence is investigated in the first place. For this reason, this volume begins by analyzing and critiquing canonical models—which are, in essence, various canonical theologies—and only then turns to the historical evidence. Such an approach is bound to disappoint some readers who might have wished more time could have been spent analyzing the historical data (and the author wishes the same!). In a larger volume, perhaps more of this could have been done. However, this balance between theology and history is fitting with the overall goal of this study because (as I hope to show) it offers a more adequate answer to the *de jure* objection to canon and thus provides much-needed assurance to Christians about their belief in these books. With such a perspective in mind, we now turn to the following chapters to take the first steps toward accomplishing that goal.

---

[36]E.g., H. Y. Gamble, *The New Testament Canon: Its Making and Meaning* (Philadelphia: Fortress, 1985), 82ff.; Metzger, *The Canon of the New Testament*, 251ff.; F. F. Bruce, *The Canon of Scripture* (Downers Grove, IL: InterVarsity, 1988), 255ff.; David G. Dunbar, "The Biblical Canon," in *Hermeneutics, Authority, and Canon*, ed. D. A. Carson and John D. Woodbridge (Grand Rapids: Zondervan, 1986), 342ff.

PART 1

DETERMINING
THE CANONICAL MODEL

1

THE CHURCH'S BOOK

Canon as Community Determined

The decision[s] to collect a group of chosen books and form
a "Scripture," are all human decisions.

JAMES BARR

In 1979, Brevard Childs was able to say that "much of the present confusion over the problem of canon turns on the failure to reach an agreement
regarding the terminology."[1] Unfortunately, the situation has not changed
much since that time. Canonical studies still finds itself so mired in ongoing
discussions and disagreements about canonical semantics[2]—what canon
"is" and how that should affect our historical reconstructions—that there

---

[1]B. Childs, *Introduction to the Old Testament as Scripture* (Philadelphia: Fortress, 1979), 51.
[2]Our discussions about canonical semantics will largely focus upon the *concept* of canon, not
the etymology and use of the term κανών in early Christianity. For a variety of reasons there
seems to be a fascination in modern scholarship with the latter. In fact, Alexander Souter, *The
Text and Canon of the New Testament* (London: Duckworth, 1954), says, "The word 'Canon'
has had a history unsurpassed in interest, perhaps, by any other word in the Greek language"
(141). For studies on the word itself, see Hermann Beyer, "κανών," in *TDNT* 3:596–602; Bruce
Metzger, *The Canon of the New Testament: Its Origin, Development and Significance* (Oxford:
Clarendon, 1987), 289–93; H. Oppel, *KANΩN. Zur Bedeutungsgeschichte des Wortes und seiner
lateinischen Entsprechungen (regula-norma)* (Leipzig: Dietrich'sche Verlagsbuchhandlung, 1937);
and E. Ulrich, "The Notion and Definition of Canon," in *The Canon Debate*, ed. Lee Martin
McDonald and James A. Sanders (Peabody, MA: Hendrickson, 2002), 21–35.

appears to be no end in sight.[3] And while the issue of terminology is certainly an important and necessary one to address in any study of the canon, the indefatigable focus upon it has unfortunately prevented even larger (and arguably more vital) questions from being addressed. In particular, too little attention has been given to understanding overarching *canonical models* that often determine one's definition of canon in the first place. A canonical model is just a way of describing a particular canonical system, if you will, which includes the broader methodological, epistemological, and, yes, even theological frameworks for how canon is understood, and, most importantly, how canon is authenticated. Everyone who studies the origins of the canon has such a system, or process, (whether clearly thought out or not) by which he or she distinguishes a canonical book from a noncanonical book. Thus, a canonical model is not to be equated simply with one's historical conclusions about when and how these books became authoritative, but instead it describes the broader methodological approach that led to those conclusions. It is not just about the date of canonicity (or even its definition), but the *grounds* of canonicity—how does one go about determining which book, or which set of books, belongs in the canon? A canonical model, then, is one's canonical "worldview." Once the issue of canonical models is put on the table, then the scholarly obsession with topics like the definition and date of canon proves to be somewhat myopic. It is not that these topics are unimportant (they are critical), but it is simply that they are derivative. They stem from other prior and broader commitments.

Before us, then, is not simply a choice between historical positions on the New Testament canon (e.g., a late date or early date), but a choice

---

[3]Some recent studies include J. Barton, *The Spirit and the Letter: Studies in the Biblical Canon* (London: SPCK, 1997), 1–34; Stephen B. Chapman, *The Law and the Prophets: A Study in Old Testament Canon Formation* (Tübingen: Mohr Siebeck, 2000), 71–110; Stephen B. Chapman, "How the Biblical Canon Began: Working Models and Open Questions," in *Homer, the Bible, and Beyond: Literary and Religious Canons in the Ancient World*, ed. Margalit Finkelberg and Guy G. Strousma (Leiden: Brill, 2003), 29–51; J. Webster, "'A Great and Meritorious Act of the Church'? The Dogmatic Location of the Canon," in *Die Einheit der Schrift und die Vielfalt des Kanons*, ed. John Barton and Michael Wolter (Berlin: de Gruyter, 2003), 95–126; Ulrich, "The Notion and Definition of Canon," 21–35; E. Ulrich, "Qumran and the Canon of the Old Testament," in *The Biblical Canons*, ed. J.-M. Auwers and H. J. de Jonge (Leuven: Leuven University Press, 2003), 57–80; J. Z. Smith, "Canons, Catalogues, and Classics," in *Canonization and Decanonization*, ed. A. van der Kooij and K. van der Toorn (Leiden: Brill, 1998), 295–311; Kendall W. Folkert, "The 'Canons' of 'Scripture,'" in *Rethinking Scripture: Essays from a Comparative Perspective*, ed. Miriam Levering (Albany: State University of New York Press, 1989), 170–79; J. A. Sanders, *Torah and Canon* (Philadelphia: Fortress, 1972), 91ff.; G. T. Sheppard, "Canon," in *Encyclopedia of Religion*, ed. Lindsay Jones, vol. 3 (Detroit: Thomson Gale, 1987), 62–69; John C. Peckham, "The Canon and Biblical Authority: A Critical Comparison of Two Models of Canonicity," *TrinJ* 28 (2007): 229–49; John Goldingay, *Models for Scripture* (Grand Rapids: Eerdmans, 1994), 85–197.

But what is the point of discussing models if the concept of canon is not clear by its existence is not the model derivative?

But who says there is such a thing as 'canon'?

between canonical models (one overarching system or another). It is the purpose of the chapters in this section to categorize and describe these various models—a canonical "taxonomy" if you will—and then offer a brief critique and response. Then, the final chapter in this section will briefly outline the canonical model being advocated in this volume, allowing it to be seen against the backdrop of all the other approaches already reviewed. This model will provide the methodological and theological infrastructure for the entire volume and will guide us as we delve deeper into the origins of the New Testament canon.

Before we begin our survey, we need to recognize from the outset how notoriously difficult it is to categorize scholars (and their approaches) into various camps. Not only are there countless variables to consider, but each scholar has his own distinctive nuances and often has aspects of his approach that could legitimately be placed into multiple categories. Moreover, approaches could be categorized on the basis of varying criteria: definition of canon, date of canon, function of canon, and so forth. With such complexities in mind, some caveats are in order: (1) We will be categorizing the various models not on the basis of date or definition of canon (as is commonly done), but in regard to the method of *authenticating* canon. In other words, on what grounds does one consider a book to be canonical? Or, put differently, on what basis does one know that a book belongs (or does not belong) in the New Testament? (2) If we categorize models on this basis, then it is possible that some scholars who are grouped into the same overall model (on the basis of how they authenticate books) may still have differences in other areas (such as definition and date of the canon). Although there is typically a correlation between these things, it is not always uniform or predictable. In order to avoid confusion, the basis of categorization must be kept in mind. (3) The description of these models cannot (and will not) be exhaustive and thus will inevitably be vulnerable to charges of generalizing. Nevertheless, we shall do our best here to summarize the large sweep of approaches to canonical studies, recognizing that while a broad road map cannot capture every detail, it still remains a very helpful (and necessary) enterprise if we hope to understand the overall landscape through which we all must eventually navigate.

The various canonical models will be divided into two large categories, *community determined* and *historically determined*. This chapter will cover the first of these. As a general description, community-determined approaches view the canon as something that is, in some sense, established or constituted by the people—either individually or corporately—who have received these books as Scripture. Canonicity is viewed not as something inherent to any set of books, but as "something officially or authoritatively imposed upon certain literature."[4] Thus, a "canon" does not exist until there is some sort of *response* from the community. Simply put, it is the result of actions and/or experiences of Christians. Specific examples of the community-determined model, as will be seen below, can vary quite widely. Some view the canon as somewhat of a historical accident (the historical-critical model); some view it as the result of the inspired declarations of the church (the Roman Catholic model); and others view it as an "event" that takes place when the Spirit works through these books and impacts individuals (the existential/neoorthodox model). But all share this in common: when asked how one knows which books are canonical, they all find the answer in the response of the Christian community.

I. Historical-Critical Model

A. Description

Since the rise of historical criticism during the period of the Enlightenment, scholars have argued that the idea of a canon, with its particular boundaries, is simply (or largely) the product of human activities within the church during the early centuries of Christianity. As the historical investigations of canon throughout the eighteenth and nineteenth centuries continued to reveal the disputes and controversies over books within the early church, the "human" element in the canonical process continued to be emphasized and placed at the forefront of scholarly discussions.[5] James Barr epitomizes this approach: "The decision[s] to collect a group of chosen books and form a 'Scripture,' are all human decisions."[6]

Since the canon is viewed as merely the product of normal human processes—a trend that Webster calls the "naturalization" of canon[7]—scholars have subsequently sought to explain the existence of the canon

---

[4]J. A. Sanders, "The Issue of Closure in the Canonical Process," in McDonald and Sanders, *The Canon Debate*, 252.

[5]E.g., J. S. Semler, *Abhandlung von freier Untersuchung des Canon*, 4 vols. (Halle, 1771–1775; repr., Gütersloh: Mohn, 1967); Adolf von Harnack, *Das Neue Testament um das Jahr 200* (Freiburg: Mohr, 1889); Harnack, *Origin of the New Testament and the Most Important Consequences of a New Creation* (London: Williams & Northgate, 1925); J. Leipoldt, *Geschichte des neuetestamentlichen Kanons* (Leipzig: Hinrichs Buchhandlung, 1907).

[6]James Barr, *The Bible in the Modern World* (New York: Harper & Row, 1973), 120. Elsewhere Barr refers to the canonization process strictly as the "decision of the later church" and therefore without authority; see James Barr, *Beyond Fundamentalism* (Philadelphia: Westminster, 1984), 50. See also, Schubert Ogden, "The Authority of Scripture for Theology," *Int* 30 (1976): 252; and Willi Marxsen, *The New Testament as the Church's Book* (Philadelphia: Fortress, 1972), 15–16.

[7]Webster, "The Dogmatic Location of Canon," 101.

on the basis of specific historical phenomena. Harnack famously laid
the impetus for the New Testament canon at the feet of Marcion, arguing that the canon is a "creative act" of the church in response to his
heretical teachings.[8] Others have suggested that the canon is simply a
sociocultural concept that reflects the relationship between a religious
society and its texts.[9] Thus, canon is just a social phenomenon that arises
when a community desires to express its identity.[10] As Kelsey notes, canon
is the church's "self-description."[11] From this perspective, to say a text is
canonical is not so much to speak of the text at all, but to speak about
the function of the text within a particular religious community.[12] And
still others have understood canon as a political construct, an ideological
instrument, created to wield power and control.[13] One cannot under-

---

[8]Adolf von Harnack, *History of Dogma*, vol. 2 (New York: Dover, 1961), 62n1. See also Hans
von Campenhausen, *The Formation of the Christian Bible* (London: A&C Black, 1972); German
title: *Die Entstehung der christlichen Bibel* (Tübingen: Mohr, 1968). For other assessments of
Marcion's influence on the canon, see R. Joseph Hoffmann, *Marcion: On the Restitution of
Christianity: An Essay on the Development of Radical Paulinist Theology in the Second Century*
(Chico, CA: Scholars Press, 1984); Barton, *The Spirit and the Letter*, 35–62; and Robert Grant,
The Formation of the New Testament (New York: Harper & Row, 1965), 126.

[9]Smith, "Canons, Catalogues, and Classics," 295–311; H. J. Adriaanse, "Canonicity and
the Problem of the Golden Mean," in van der Kooij and van der Toorn, *Canonization and
Decanonization*, 313–30; A. Assmann and J. Assmann, eds., *Kanon und Zensur, Archäologie
der literarischen Kommunikation II* (Munich: Wilhelm Fink Verlag, 1987); and Paul Davies,
Whose Bible Is It Anyway? (Sheffield: Sheffield Academic, 1995), 17–27.

[10]Paul Ricoeur, "The 'Sacred' Text and the Community," in *The Critical Study of Sacred Texts*,
ed. W. D. O'Flaherty (Berkeley: Graduate Theological Union, 1979), 271–76. A number of
recent studies of canon have taken on a *comparative* dimension, showing how other religions,
groups, and communities have their own sorts of "canons." E.g., Margalit Finkelberg and
Guy G. Strousma, eds., *Homer, the Bible and Beyond* (Leiden: Brill, 2003); Tomas Hägg, "Canon
Formation in Greek Literary Culture," in *Canon and Canonicity: The Formation and Use of
Scripture*, ed. Einar Thomassen (Copenhagen: Museum Tusculanum Press, 2010), 109–28; W. C.
Smith, *What Is Scripture? A Comparative Approach* (London: SPCK, 1993); L. Alexander,
"Canon and Exegesis in the Medical Schools of Antiquity," in *The Canon of Scripture in Jewish
and Christian Tradition*, ed. P. S. Alexander and K. Jean-Daniel (Lausanne: Éditions du Zèbre,
2007), 115–53; Armin Lange, "Oracle Collection and Canon: A Comparison Between Judah
and Greece in Persian Times," in *Jewish and Christian Scripture as Artifact and Canon*, ed. C. A.
Evans and H. Daniel Zacharias (London: T&T Clark, 2009), 9–47; and many of the essays in
Anders-Christian Jacobsen, ed., *Religion and Normativity*, vol. 1, *The Discursive Fight over
Religious Texts in Antiquity* (Aarhus: Aarhus University Press, 2009).

[11]D. H. Kelsey, *The Uses of Scripture in Recent Theology* (Philadelphia: Fortress, 1975), 106.

[12]Webster, "The Dogmatic Location of Canon," 98–101; J. Nissen, "Scripture and Community
in Dialogue," in Auwers and de Jonge, *The Biblical Canons*, 651–58.

[13]On this general topic, see A. K. Bowman and G. Wolf, eds., *Literacy and Power in the Ancient
World* (Cambridge: Cambridge University Press, 1994); George Aichele, *The Control of Biblical
Meaning: Canon as Semiotic Mechanism* (Harrisburg, PA: Trinity, 2001); James E. Brenneman,
Canons in Conflict: Negotiating Texts in True and False Prophecy (New York: Oxford University
Press, 1997), 52–80; Robert P. Coote and Mary P. Coote, *Power, Politics, and the Making of
the Bible* (Minneapolis: Fortress, 1990); Gerald L. Bruns, "Canon and Power in the Hebrew
Scriptures," *CI* 10 (1984): 462–80; K. Haines-Eitzen, *Guardians of Letters: Literacy, Power,
and the Transmitters of Early Christian Literature* (Oxford: Oxford University Press, 2000);
and David L. Dungan, *Constantine's Bible: Politics and the Making of the New Testament*

stand canon without understanding what it was designed to combat, suppress, or refute.[14] This approach is most aptly seen in the work of Walter Bauer and his modern adherents.[15] Bauer argues that there was no "orthodoxy" or "heresy" within earliest Christianity, but rather there were various "Christianities," each competing for dominance. Thus, says Bauer, the New Testament canon we possess is nothing more than the books chosen by the eventual theological winners—a historical accident, so to speak.

Regardless of the particular version of the historical-critical[16] approach one may hold, all versions share a core belief that the canon is a fundamentally human construct that can be adequately accounted for in purely natural terms. How then does one know which book should be in the canon? For the historical-critical approach this is the wrong question to ask. The issue is not about which books *should* be in the canon, but simply which books *are* in the canon. Since the canon is an entirely human creation, all we can do is simply describe what happened in history. The canon has no metaphysical or intrinsic qualities that need to be accounted for—"canon" is not something that describes the quality of a book, but is something that is *done* to books.[17] Hugo Lundhaug embodies such an approach: "Canonical status is not an intrinsic quality of a text, but a status bestowed upon it by a community of interpreters."[18] Thus, often

---

(Philadelphia: Fortress, 2006). In response to the idea that canons always represent those in power, see Willie van Peer, "Canon Formation: Ideology or Aesthetic Quality?," *British Journal of Aesthetics* 36 (1996): 97–108.

[14]Max Weber, *The Sociology of Religion* (Boston: Beacon, 1993), 68; David Brakke, "Canon Formation and Social Conflict in Fourth Century Egypt: Athanasius of Alexandria's Thirty-Ninth Festal Letter," *HTR* 87 (1994): 395–419; and George Aichele, "Canon, Ideology, and the Emergence of an Imperial Church," in Thomassen, *Canon and Canonicity*, 45–65.

[15]Walter Bauer, *Orthodoxy and Heresy in Earliest Christianity*, ed. Robert Kraft and Gerhard Krodel, trans. Paul J. Achtemeier (Philadelphia: Fortress, 1971). For an overview of Bauer and a modern critique, see A J. Köstenberger and M. J. Kruger, *The Heresy of Orthodoxy: How Modern Culture's Fascination with Diversity Has Reshaped Our Understanding of Early Christianity* (Wheaton, IL: Crossway, 2010).

[16]Admittedly, the use of this term *historical-critical* can be confusing because scholars from various canonical models would claim to use the historical-critical method. Moreover, there are various versions of the historical-critical method; see Anthony C. Thiselton, "Canon, Community, and Theological Construction," in *Canon and Biblical Interpretation*, ed. Craig Bartholomew et al. (Carlisle: Paternoster, 2006), 4. Nevertheless, even with these limitations, this still seems to be the most fitting term to capture this canonical model, as long as the imprecision of the term is kept in mind.

[17]Smith, *What Is Scripture?*, 237. It needs to be noted that not all in the historical-critical camp think that every *book* in the canon (or portion of a book) is merely a human creation, but their view is that the canon *as a whole* is a human creation. Thus, inevitably, aspects of this approach will overlap with the "canon within a canon" approach discussed below. Such overlap is impossible to avoid in any canonical taxonomy.

[18]Hugo Lundhaug, "Canon and Interpretation: A Cognitive Perspective," in Thomassen, *Canon and Canonicity*, 68.

the real concern for adherents of the historical-critical model is not to declare which books are the "right" ones, but to make sure that no one else declares which books are the "right" ones. Such distinctions, argues Helmut Koester, are simply the result of "deep-seated prejudices."[19] No book should be privileged over another. All books are equal.[20]

Consequently, as the historical-critical model continues to redefine canon and push it further into the realm of church history—more the result of human than of divine activity—the critical question ceases to be about the boundaries of the canon (which books), but now is about the very legitimacy of the canon itself (should there be one at all). H. Y. Gamble declares, "It ought not to be assumed that the existence of the NT is a necessary or self-explanatory fact. Nothing dictated that there should be a NT at all."[21] James Barr makes a similar claim: "Jesus in his teaching is nowhere portrayed as commanding or even sanctioning the production of a . . . written New Testament. . . . The idea of a Christian faith governed by Christian written holy Scriptures was not an essential part of the foundation plan of Christianity."[22] Thus, we see again that the historical-critical model rejects any intrinsic value to these texts and places the impetus for canon entirely within the realm of later church decisions.

Such a canonical model inevitably has an impact on the date and definition of canon. If canon is something that is created and constituted by the community, and there is nothing inherent in these books to make them canonical, then a canon cannot exist before the community formally acts.[23] Thus, it is not unusual for the historical-critical approach to have a fairly late date for canon and to insist on a strict semantic distinction between Scripture and canon.[24] In this regard, appeal is often made to the

---

[19]Helmut Koester, "Apocryphal and Canonical Gospels," *HTR* 73 (1980): 105.

[20]This trend is vividly seen in the recent concern to make sure apocryphal literature is treated with equal regard and that the terms *apocryphal* and *noncanonical* are understood to be anachronistic. E.g., H. Koester, *Ancient Christian Gospels: Their History and Development* (London: SCM, 1990), xxx; R. W. Funk, "The Once and Future New Testament," in McDonald and Sanders, *The Canon Debate*, 554–55; and Bart D. Ehrman, *Lost Christianities: The Battles for Scripture and the Faiths We Never Knew* (New York: Oxford University Press, 2002), 4.

[21]H. Y. Gamble, *The New Testament Canon: Its Making and Meaning* (Philadelphia: Fortress, 1985), 12.

[22]James Barr, *Holy Scripture: Canon, Authority and Criticism* (Philadelphia: Westminster, 1983), 12.

[23]W. Wrede, *The Origin of the New Testament*, trans. J. S. Hill (New York: Harper, 1909), 138–39.

[24]Not every scholar who makes a sharp distinction between Scripture and canon is representative of the historical-critical model. Moreover, not every scholar in the historical-critical model would adopt this sharp distinction between Scripture and canon. Most notably, Harnack was willing to call a book canonical if it was cited as Scripture by the early Christian communities; the canon did not have to be closed before it could be called such. See discussion in Barton, *The Spirit and the Letter*, 1–33. Nevertheless, the sharp distinction between these two terms has become quite fashionable in recent years; e.g., G. M. Hahneman, "The Muratorian Fragment and the

work of A. C. Sundberg, who insists that we cannot speak of the idea of canon until at least the fourth century.[25] Sundberg employs an *exclusive* definition of canon, arguing that it is a fixed, final, closed list of books, and therefore we cannot use the term *canon* to speak of any second- (or even third-) century historical realities.[26] To do so would be "anachronistic." Although Scripture would have existed prior to this time period, Sundberg argues that we must reserve the term *canon* until the end of the entire process. Thus, simply marshaling evidence of a book's scriptural status in the early church—as is so often done in canonical studies—is not enough to consider it canonical. The book must be part of a list from which nothing can be added or taken away.

B. Evaluation

Limitations of space allow for only brief evaluations of each canonical model in this chapter (and the next). However, further responses will be offered throughout the rest of this volume as appropriate. In regard to the historical-critical model, only a few observations can be made here. On a positive note, it must be acknowledged that the historical-critical model is correct to remind us of the role of the Christian community in the formation of the New Testament canon. Indeed, the canon did not drop from the sky on golden tablets, fully formed and complete—it had a long (and sometimes complicated) historical development, and human beings played a role in that development. This important aspect of canon is occasionally forgotten by some approaches (as we shall see below).

That being said, however, the fundamental problem with the historical-critical model is not its affirmation that the church played a role, but rather its insistence that the church played the determinative and decisive role. Quickly swept aside are any claims that these books contain any intrinsic

---

Origins of the New Testament Canon," in McDonald and Sanders, *The Canon Debate*, 405–15; L. M. McDonald, *The Biblical Canon: Its Origin, Transmission, and Authority* (Peabody, MA: Hendrickson, 2007), 20–69; J. Barton, "Canonical Approaches Ancient and Modern," in Auwers and de Jonge, *The Biblical Canons*, 199–209; Gamble, *The New Testament Canon*, 18–19; James Barr, *The Scope and Authority of the Bible* (Philadelphia: Westminster, 1980), 120; Kelsey, *The Uses of Scripture in Recent Theology*, 104–5; and Craig D. Allert, *A High View of Scripture? The Authority of the Bible and the Formation of the New Testament Canon* (Grand Rapids: Baker Academic, 2007), 44–47.

[25] A. C. Sundberg, "Towards a Revised History of the New Testament Canon," *SE* 4 (1968): 452–61; Sundberg, "The Making of the New Testament Canon," in *The Interpreter's One-Volume Commentary on the Bible* (Nashville: Abingdon, 1971), 1216–24.

[26] Chapman, "How the Biblical Canon Began," 34–35, uses the term *extrinsic* instead of *exclusive*. The term *extrinsic* was also used by Smith, "Canons, Catalogues, and Classics," 297ff. But Chapman does use *exclusive* in "The Canon Debate: What It Is and Why It Matters," (presented at the Society of Biblical Literature, San Diego, 2007).

authority that might have been a factor in their reception. The canon is instead explained as merely the result of the "contingent"[27] choices of the church. Such an approach provides us with a merely human canon stripped of any normative or revelational authority and thereby unable to function as God's word to his people. Thus, the historical-critical approach does not really construct a positive model of canon, per se, but rather *deconstructs* the canon entirely, leaving us with an empty shell of books.[28]

Although most adherents of the historical-critical model would not likely view such a deconstruction as problematic, it does raise the question of how they establish that the canon is a solely human enterprise in the first place. How does one demonstrate this? One not only would have to rule out the possibility that these books bear intrinsic qualities that set them apart, but also would need to show that the reception of these books by the church was a purely human affair. Needless to say, such a naturalistic position would be difficult (if not impossible) to prove. Appeal could be made to evidence of human involvement in the selection of books, such as discussions and disagreements over books, diversity of early Christian book collections, the decisions of church councils, and so forth.[29] But simply demonstrating some human involvement in the canonical process is not sufficient to demonstrate *sole* human involvement. The fact that proximate, human decisions played a role in the development of the canon does not rule out the possibility that ultimate, divine activity also played a role. The two are not mutually exclusive. It appears, then, that the insistence on a human-conditioned canon may not be something that can be readily proved—or even something that its adherents regularly try to prove—but is something often quietly assumed. It is less the conclusion of the historical-critical model and more its philosophical starting point.

presupposition!

C. Sundberg's Definition of Canon

Before we leave our discussion of the historical-critical model, it is important that we consider Sundberg's exclusive definition of the canon as a final, fixed, closed list. Although this definition is not the sole property

[27]Gamble, *The New Testament Canon*, 83.

[28]Of course, attempts have been made to salvage some "authority" for these books even in the midst of their entirely human character. For a review and critique of such attempts, see Webster, "The Dogmatic Location of Canon," 101–7.

[29]E.g., for Ehrman, *Lost Christianities*, 1–11, diversity is early Christianity's most decisive characteristic and the backbone of his argument that the canon is a human invention of the proto-orthodox. For more on the issue of diversity in early Christianity, see Köstenberger and Kruger, *The Heresy of Orthodoxy*, 41–67.

of the historical-critical model, it is commonly employed by this model and therefore warrants a brief assessment and response here.[30] We should acknowledge from the outset that much of the impetus behind Sundberg's definition is commendable. Certainly we would agree that the church's role in receiving these books is a critical aspect of canonicity and one that Sundberg's definition certainly captures. Moreover, we would agree that "Scripture" and "canon" are not synonymous in every way, and distinctions between them can be helpful at points (though the kind of distinctions and their severity need to be further clarified). However, there does not appear to be any compelling historical requirement to adopt this definition, despite the confident assertions of some that it creates historical anachronisms.[31] On the contrary, a number of residual concerns about this definition raise questions about whether it is really the best way to capture the historical phenomenon of canon.

Although the strict demarcation between Scripture and canon may seem clear to Sundberg, it seems difficult to imagine these two concepts being separated within the minds of, say, second-century Christians. In order to recognize a certain book to be Scripture in the first place, an early Christian would have needed to be able to say another book in his library was *not* Scripture. And as soon as Christians began to declare which books are, and which books are not, Scripture, how was this materially different from declaring which books are in, or not in, a canon? Thus, it seems that the term *Scripture* already implies exclusion and limitation to some degree, making a sharp distinction between Scripture and canon more difficult to sustain.[32] We might even say that collections of scriptural books are, in some sense, "closed" simply because they include some books and not others.

One wonders, then, whether the sharp Scripture-canon distinction really brings greater clarity to our understanding of the canon's development (as advocates of that distinction maintain), or whether it runs the risk of imposing artificial either–or categories upon it. Was the state of

---

[30]Sundberg is not the first, or the only, scholar to propose a sharp distinction between Scripture and canon. Its roots can be traced to W. Staerk, "Der Schrift- und Kanonbegriff der jüdischen Bibel," *Zeitschrift für systematische Theologie* 6 (1929): 101–19; G. Hölscher, *Kanonisch und Apocryph: Ein Kapitel aus der Geschichte des altestamentlichen Kanons* (Naumburg: Lippert, 1905); and arguably back to Semler's original critique of canon, *Abhandlung von freier Untersuchung des Canon*. See discussion in Iain Provan, "Canons to the Left of Him: Brevard Childs, His Critics, and the Future of Old Testament Theology," *SJT* 50 (1997): 9–11; and Chapman, *The Law and the Prophets*, 34.

[31]Allert, *A High View of Scripture?*, 49–50; Barton, *The Spirit and the Letter*, 158ff.; L. M. McDonald, "The Integrity of the Biblical Canon in Light of Its Historical Development," *BBR* 6 (1996): 104.

[32]Provan, "Canons to the Left of Him," 9–10.

the canon so very different in the fourth century that we are obligated to use different terminology when discussing any prior time period? Such a rigid division seems hard to justify historically. After all, before this time most of the New Testament books had already been functioning with sacred authority for generations, and their place in the New Testament corpus was fully secure.[33] The supposed closing of the canon in the fourth century neither changed their status nor increased their authority—it was already as high as it could be.[34] In regard to the function of these books, one could rightly say there was already a canon, or at least the category of a canon, well before the fourth century.[35] Sundberg's definition is so focused on the final stage of the canon's development that it misses the fact that it is, after all, a *stage*—and therefore is intimately connected to, and dependent on, what has come before. As we shall argue below, the concept of canon cannot be reduced to a single point of time. It is best conceived of as a continuum—less like a dot and more like a line.

Moreover, the fourth century does not appear to provide the decisive and formal "closing" of the canon, as Sundberg's definition would require. If one is looking for a time when the boundaries of the canon are absolutely fixed with no exceptions, then it will not be found in the fourth century—nor even in the modern day, for that matter.[36] If the "closing" of the canon refers to a formal, official act of the New Testament church, then we are hard-pressed to find such an act before the Council of Trent in the sixteenth century.[37] The challenge for Sundberg's definition, then, is that it never fully corresponds to any historical reality.[38] To insist that we have a canon only when there is an officially closed list with no exceptions is to insist on a canon that never existed. Ironically, then, it is the exclusive definition of *canon* that appears to be, at least at some points, "anachronistic."

---

[33]H. Gamble, "The New Testament Canon: Recent Research and the Status Quaestionis," in McDonald and Sanders, *The Canon Debate*, 271.

[34]Barton, *The Spirit and the Letter*, 18.

[35]Sheppard, "Canon," 62–69, would define this approach as what he calls "canon 2."

[36]E.g., the modern-day lectionary of the Syrian Orthodox Church still operates on the twenty-two-book canon of the Peshitta, and the modern-day Ethiopian church appears to have a broader New Testament canon, though the exact number is unclear. For further discussion see Metzger, *The Canon of the New Testament*, 218–28.

[37]H. Gamble, "Christianity: Scripture and Canon," in *The Holy Book in Comparative Perspective*, ed. Frederick M. Denny and Rodney L. Taylor (Columbia: University of South Carolina Press, 1985), 46–47. Gamble argues that church councils like Laodicea (360) were local, not ecumenical, and therefore had no binding authority. McDonald agrees: "There was never a time when the church as a whole concluded that these writings and no others could help the church carry out its mission in the world" ("The Integrity of the Biblical Canon," 131–32).

[38]Chapman, *The Law and the Prophets*, 108.

For these reasons, the exclusive definition of canon seems particularly vulnerable to misunderstanding. Insisting that the early church *only* had "Scripture" prior to the fourth century not only gives the misleading impression (unwitting or not) that the state of the canon in these earlier stages must have been radically different, but can also give the impression that, in some sense, the church actually constitutes or creates the canon. But this seems to confuse the reception of the canon with the existence of the canon. Why could there not be a canon prior to its reception by the church? Indeed, if one views the canon as Christians have historically understood it, namely, as the product of God's divine covenant-making activity (as we shall discuss further below), then there is no reason to think that we should reserve the term *canon* to refer only to the end of the entire process, as Sundberg suggests. Indeed, from the perspective of God's revelational activity, a canon exists as soon as the New Testament books are written—the canon is always the books God has given to the corporate church, no more, no less.

With these considerations in mind, we can agree with M. G. Brett when he states, "Attempts to draw a sharp distinction between Scripture and canon are of limited value."[39] Although Sundberg's definition rightly captures certain aspects of canon, it does not adequately account for others. While this is true of every definition (to one degree or another), we hope to make progress below in crafting a more balanced definition that can more adequately capture the various historical phenomena surrounding canon.

II. Roman Catholic Model

A. Description

On the surface it may seem that the Roman Catholic model is quite the opposite of the historical-critical model we just described—and in many ways this is true. However, in regard to the overall category of "canon as community determined" we shall see that these two models share a common methodology in regard to how canon is authenticated. At the core of the Roman Catholic view of canon is Rome's view of the authority of Scripture. Roman Catholicism denies that ultimate authority exists in the Scriptures alone (*sola scriptura*) and has consequently adopted the well-

---

[39]M. G. Brett, "Canonical Criticism and Old Testament Theology," in *Text in Context: Essays by Members of the Society for Old Testament Study*, ed. A. D. H. Mayes (Oxford: Oxford University Press, 2000), 67. Of course, as noted above, there are *some* ways that canon and Scripture are different, but just not the way Sundberg suggests. See discussion below in chap. 3.

known trifold authority structure that includes Scripture, tradition, and the Magisterium (the church's teaching authority).[40] The key component in this trifold authority is the Magisterium itself, which is the authoritative teaching office of the Roman Catholic Church, primarily manifested in the pope and his bishops.[41] Although the Magisterium is presented as only one of three sources of authority, it is distinguished by the fact that it alone has the right to interpret Scripture and tradition, and, more importantly, it has the sole authority to define what writings constitute Scripture and tradition in the first place.[42] Thus, as we shall discuss further below, questions are raised about whether the authority within the Roman Catholic system is really equally divided among these three sources, or whether it functionally resides in the church (or Magisterium) itself.[43]

The implications of this approach on the question of canon become immediately clear. When faced with the dilemma of how we know which books should be in or out of the canon, the Roman Catholic model claims a quite simple solution. As H. J. Adriaanse observes, "Catholic Theology . . . has solved the canon problem with a plea to the authority of the Church."[44] Thus, the canon is ultimately community determined. The fundamental challenge from Roman Catholicism is that in order to

---

[40]*Dei Verbum*, 2.9–10. See Walter M. Abbott, ed. *The Documents of Vatican II* (New York: America Press, 1966). For a helpful discussion about new developments in Vatican II, see G. C. Berkouwer, *The Second Vatican Council and the New Catholicism* (Grand Rapids: Eerdmans, 1965); and A. Dulles, *The Craft of Theology: From Symbol to System* (New York: Crossroad, 1992), 96ff.

[41]The conciliar document, *Lumen Gentium*, from Vatican II, refers to the pope as having "infallible teaching" (3.18), as does the document *Pastor Aeternus*, from Vatican I, which declares the pope's teaching to be "infallible" and "irreformable" (Jaroslav Pelikan and Valerie R. Hotchkiss, eds., *Creeds and Confessions of Faith in the Christian Tradition*, 4 vols. [New Haven, CT: Yale University Press, 2003], 3:358). For discussion, see John H. Armstrong, *A View of Rome: A Guide to Understanding the Beliefs and Practices of Roman Catholics* (Chicago: Moody, 1995), 73–82; Keith A. Mathison, *The Shape of Sola Scriptura* (Moscow, ID: Canon, 2001), 210–25; and Mark E. Powell, "Canonical Theism and the Challenge of Epistemic Certainty," in *Canonical Theism: A Proposal for Theology and the Church*, ed. William J. Abraham, Jason E. Vickers, and Natalie B. Van Kirk (Grand Rapids: Eerdmans, 2008), 195–209.

[42]*Dei Verbum* declares that it is through sacred tradition, which the Magisterium defines, that the "full canon of sacred books is known" (2.8). Moreover, it states, "The task of authentically interpreting the Word of God, whether written or handed on, has been entrusted exclusively to the living teaching office of the Church" (2.10).

[43]It should be noted that the Roman Catholic Church insists that the Scripture is always superior to the Magisterium. *Dei Verbum* adds, "This teaching office is not above the Word of God, but serves it" (2.10), and the Catholic Catechism says, "Yet, this Magisterium is not superior to the word of God, but its servant" (86); see *Catechism of the Catholic Church* (San Francisco: Ignatius, 1994). Despite these qualifications, one still wonders how Scripture can be deemed the ultimate authority if the Magisterium is able to define, determine, and interpret the Scripture in the first place. Even with these declarations from Rome, residual concerns remain about whether the Magisterium *functionally* has authority over the Scriptures.

[44]Adriaanse, "Canonicity and the Problem of the Golden Mean," 318.

have an infallible Scripture, we need to have an infallible guide (namely, the church) to tell us what is, and what is not, Scripture.[45] As Karl Rahner asserts, "[Scripture] exists because the church exists."[46] Thus, it is argued, the Protestant claim of *sola scriptura* is inevitably hollow—you cannot have Scripture as the ultimate authority if you have no certain way of knowing what Scripture is.[47] One needs an external source of authority, outside of the Bible, in order to know what should be included in the Bible. Karl Keating declares, "The Catholic believes in inspiration because the Church tells him so."[48] The sixteenth-century Roman Catholic cardinal Stanislaus Hosius, papal legate to the Council of Trent, put it more bluntly: "The Scriptures have only as much force as the fables of Aesop, if destitute of the authority of the Church."[49]

As for the formal definition of the term *canon*, this model does not produce uniformity across Roman Catholic writers. Though one might expect Sundberg's definition of canon as a final, closed list to be particularly attractive to the Roman Catholic model, the term *canon* is often used simply to refer to the books that functioned as an authoritative "norm" or standard for the Christian community, that is, as Scripture. Since Catholics more readily acknowledge the inspiration of these books—in contrast with the historical-critical view above—they are often more willing to view the canon as something that existed, in some sense, earlier than the fourth century. Thus, Joseph Lienhard is quite comfortable declaring that "about 180, there is a New Testament," and "a New Testament exists when a collection of Christian writings is generally accepted in the church as equal in authority to the Jewish Scriptures."[50]

---

[45]This argument is the cornerstone for modern Roman Catholic apologetics. E.g., Scott Hahn and Kimberly Hahn, *Rome Sweet Home* (San Francisco: Ignatius, 1993); David Currie, *Born Fundamentalist, Born Again Catholic* (San Francisco: Ignatius, 1996); Patrick Madrid, ed. *Surprised by Truth* (San Diego: Basilica, 1994).

[46]Karl Rahner, *Foundations of Christian Faith: An Introduction to the Idea of Christianity* (New York: Crossroad, 1997), 362.

[47]Recent Catholic critiques of *sola scriptura* include Robert A. Sungenis, ed., *Not by Scripture Alone: A Catholic Critique of the Protestant Doctrine of Sola Scriptura* (Santa Barbara: Queenship, 1997); and Mark Shea, *By What Authority?* (Huntington, IN: Our Sunday Visitor, 1996).

[48]Karl Keating, *Catholicism and Fundamentalism* (San Francisco: Ignatius, 1988), 127.

[49]Confutatio Prolegomenon Brentii, *Opera*, 1.530. English translation from Francis Turretin, *Institutes of Elenctic Theology*, trans. George Musgrave Giger, ed. James T. Dennison Jr., 3 vols. (Phillipsburg, NJ: P&R, 1992–1997), 1:86 (2.6.2).

[50]J. T. Lienhard, *The Bible, the Church, and Authority* (Collegeville, MN: Liturgical, 1995), 27, 28. Farkasfalvy also shares this definition of canon; see W. R. Farmer and D. M. Farkasfalvy, *The Formation of the New Testament Canon* (New York: Paulist, 1976), 102. Rahner acknowledges that both definitions play a role; see K. Rahner, *Inspiration in the Bible* (New York: Herder & Herder, 1961), 28n18, 29–30. Hoffman would lean toward Sundberg's definition; see Thomas A. Hoffman, "Inspiration, Normativeness, Canonicity, and the Unique Sacred Character of the Bible," *CBQ* 44 (1982): 447–69.

B. Evaluation

It should be noted from the outset that, like the historical-critical approach above, the Roman Catholic model rightly captures certain aspects of canon. Indeed, the church's historical reception of these books plays an important role in our conviction that they are from God (though there are differences in how that role is construed). Moreover, the willingness of Roman Catholics to acknowledge that the canonical process is not entirely human, but involves divine activity, is a refreshing alternative to the naturalistic approach so common in the historical-critical model. That said, a number of historical and theological concerns about the Roman Catholic model remain, which we will attempt to briefly outline here.

We begin by noting that there are different conceptions of the church-canon relationship within the Catholic model, which are too often twisted together and left undifferentiated. Thus, we must be careful to "untwist" them if we hope to make some progress. One Catholic conception of the church-canon relationship views the church not as creating or constituting the canon, but merely as recognizing the authority of the canon that was already there. On this conception, the church's role is primarily episte-mological—it is the sole and fundamental means by which we infallibly *know* which books belong in the canon. It is only in this sense that one could say that the canon is dependent upon the church.[51] We see this approach even in Vatican I, as the *Dogmatic Constitution on the Catholic Faith* declared, "These books the church holds to be sacred and canonical not because she subsequently approved them by her authority . . . but because, being written under the inspiration of the Holy Spirit, they have God as their author."[52] Lienhard similarly states, "No Catholic would want to say that the authority of the Bible derives simply from the decree of a council. Trent recognized the Bible; it did not create it. The Bible is in the Church, but *not from the Church*."[53]

If these last two statements were the extent of Catholic formulation, there might be little to disagree with here (though there are still some problem areas, as we shall see). Unfortunately, there have been more

---

[51]R. Murray, "How Did the Church Determine the Canon of Scripture?," *HeyJ* 11 (1970): 115–26, discusses how this less stringent Catholic position is much closer to the classic Protestant approach.

[52]Norman P. Tanner, ed., *Decrees of the Ecumenical Councils*, 2 vols. (Washington, DC: Georgetown University Press, 1990), 2:806.

[53]Lienhard, *The Bible, the Church, and Authority*, 72, emphasis mine. For a similar view, see George H. Tavard, *Holy Writ or Holy Church* (New York: Harper, 1959), 66. The words of Augustine could also be added, "I would not believe in the Gospel if the authority of the Catholic Church did not move me to do so" (Augustine, *Fund.* 1.6). Calvin's understanding of this statement can be found in his *Institutes*, 1.7.3.

stringent expressions of the church-canon relationship. Another Catholic approach views the church not simply as the means by which the canon is infallibly recognized (although it does affirm this), but as, in some sense, the foundation or the grounds for the canon. As Rahner puts it, we "derive the essence of the Scripture from the essence of the church,"[54] and therefore the Scripture is "derivative"[55] from the church and "an act of the Church."[56] This sentiment is echoed by Peter Kreeft, who argues that the church "caused" the canon because it preceded the canon: "The first generation of Christians did not even have the New Testament."[57] Hans Küng states it more directly: "Without the Church there would be no New Testament."[58]

Although these two approaches are distinguished here, it is important to keep in mind that they are often bundled together without distinction in many treatments of Catholic theology, and often by Catholic writers themselves. Our evaluation, then, will attempt to address both of these views. As for the first approach, the fundamental claim of the Roman Catholic model is that *sola scriptura* is untenable because, without some external infallible authority, there is no way to know which books are to be included in the canon.[59] This epistemological challenge, in the words of Catholic author Patrick Madrid, is that Christians do not have an "inspired table of contents" that reveals "which books belong and which books do not."[60] If only Christians had this inspired table of contents, then we would not need the authoritative rulings of the Roman Catholic Church to authenticate the canon. Although such an argument is made repeatedly within Catholic writings, it proves to be problematic upon closer examination.

Imagine for a moment that God had inspired another document in the first century that contained this "table of contents" and had given it to the church. We will call this the twenty-eighth book of the New Testament

---

[54]Rahner, *Foundations of Christian Faith*, 373.

[55]This is Rahner's term (ibid., 371).

[56]Rahner, *Inspiration in the Bible*, 75 (cf. 36).

[57]Peter Kreeft, *Catholic Christianity* (San Francisco: Ignatius, 2001), 20.

[58]H. Küng, *The Council in Action: Theological Reflections on the Second Vatican Council*, trans. C. Hastings (New York: Sheed and Ward, 1963), 187.

[59]On this point, see the impressive volume by Nicolaus Appel, *Kanon und Kirche: Die Kanonkrise im heutigen Protestantismus als kontroverstheologisches Problem* (Paderborn: Bonifacius-Druckerei, 1964). For a helpful summary and response to Appel, see David G. Dunbar, "The Biblical Canon," in *Hermeneutics, Authority, and Canon*, ed. D. A. Carson and John D. Woodbridge (Grand Rapids: Zondervan, 1986), 350–52.

[60]Patrick Madrid, "*Sola Scriptura*: A Blueprint for Anarchy," in *Not by Scripture Alone: A Catholic Critique of the Protestant Doctrine of Sola Scriptura*, ed. Robert A. Sungenis (Santa Barbara: Queenship, 1997), 22.

canon. Would the existence of such a book have satisfied the Catholic concerns? Would this allow Catholics to affirm *sola scriptura* and deny the need for an infallible church? Not at all. Instead, they would simply ask the next logical question: "On what basis do you know that *this* twenty-eighth book comes from God?" And even if it were argued that God had given a twenty-ninth book saying the twenty-eighth book came from God, then the same objection would still apply: "Yes, but how do you know the twenty-ninth book came from God?" And on it would go. The Catholic objection about the need for a "table of contents," therefore, misses the point entirely. Even if there were another document with such a table, *this document would still need to be authenticated as part of the canon.* After all, what if there were multiple table-of-contents–type books floating around in the early church? How would we know which one was from God? In the end, therefore, the Roman Catholic objection is to some extent artificial. Such a "table of contents" would never satisfy their concerns, even if it were to exist, because they have already determined, *a priori*, that no document could ever be self-attesting. In other words, built into the Roman Catholic model is that any written revelation (whether it contains a "table of contents" or not) will require external approval and authentication from an infallible church.

This insistence that canonical books, by definition, require external validation raises questions about whether the Catholic model pays adequate attention to the intrinsic authority built into these books and how that intrinsic authority could play a role in their authentication. Ironically, then, the Catholic model, at least at this point, is quite similar to the historical-critical model above. Both so overemphasize the reception by the Christian community that they overlook, at least in practice, the internal qualities of the books themselves. Although the Catholic model would not formally deny that these books bore intrinsic authority prior to their formal canonization, such an approach unwittingly downgrades their intrinsic authority during this period by portraying it as virtually unknowable without the help of formal church declarations.[61] Rahner

---

[61]Bernard Ramm, *The Witness of the Spirit* (Grand Rapids: Eerdmans, 1959), 109–10. It is here that the classic Roman Catholic distinction is made between the authority of Scripture with respect to itself (*quoad se*), and the authority of Scripture with respect to us (*quoad nos*). This distinction is designed to argue that the Scriptures are still the ultimate authority in respect to themselves, but they are known to us only through the authority of the church. Bavinck offers the appropriate response to this idea when he contends: "This distinction [between *quoad se* and *quoad nos*] cannot be applied here. For if the church is the final and most basic reason why I believe the Scripture, then the church, and not the Scripture, is trustworthy in and of itself (αὐτόπιστος)" (*Reformed Dogmatics*, vol. 1, *Prolegomena*, ed. John Bolt, trans. John Vriend [Grand Rapids: Baker, 2003], 457). See also, Turretin, *Institutes*, 1:86ff. (2.6.2).

does this very thing when he states, "[Canonicity] cannot be established, it seems, from the books themselves."[62] The problem, then, is not that the church plays a role in identifying canonical books (Protestants would agree with this), but the Catholic insistence that it plays the *only* and *definitive* role.

In regard to the more stringent Catholic approach to the church-canon relationship, the idea that the canon is "derivative"[63] from the church or "caused"[64] by the church also raises a number of concerns: (1) Although the New Testament was not completed all at once, the apostolic teaching was the substance of what would later become the New Testament.[65] And it was this apostolic teaching, along with the prophets, that formed the foundation for the church, rather than the other way around.[66] As Ephesians 2:20 affirms, the church was "built on the foundation of the apostles and prophets."[67] The church is always the *creatura verbi* ("creation of the Word").[68] Chapman sums it up: "The biblical canon is not a creation of the church, the church is instead a creation of the biblical canon."[69] (2) The earliest Christians *did* have a canon, namely, the Old Testament itself (Rom. 15:4; 1 Cor. 10:6; 2 Tim. 3:15–16), which seems

---

[62]Rahner, *Inspiration in the Bible*, 25. Hoffman goes even further when he declares, "It is the church's decision, and this alone, not some inherent component of inspiration or normativeness, that is the ultimate reason why a book is or is not canonical" ("Inspiration," 463).

[63]Rahner, *Foundations of Christian Faith*, 371.

[64]Kreeft, *Catholic Christianity*, 20.

[65]Turretin declares, "Although the church is more ancient than the Scriptures formally considered (and as to the mode of writing), yet it cannot be called such with respect to the Scriptures materially considered (and as to the substance of doctrine) because the Word of God is more ancient than the church itself, being its foundation and seed" (*Institutes*, 1:91 [2.6.16]).

[66]Calvin wrote, "The Church is, as Paul declares, founded on the doctrine of Apostles and Prophets; but these men [of the Roman Catholic Church] speak as if they imagined that they mother owed her birth to the daughter." See John Calvin, *Tracts and Treatises*, ed. Thomas F. Torrance, trans. Henry Beveridge (Grand Rapids: Eerdmans, 1958), 267.

[67]William Hendriksen, *Ephesians* (Grand Rapids: Baker, 1967), 142; Richard B. Gaffin, *Perspective on Pentecost* (Phillipsburg, NJ: P&R, 1979), 93–95; and others, argue that "prophets" here is a reference not to the Old Testament, but to a revelatory office within the first-century church (cf. Eph. 4:11). Even if that is the case, however, it does not affect the overall argument here that the revelational deposit given to God's spokesmen (which is preserved in the New Testament), is not the result of the church's activity, but the foundation for the church's activity. Those who view "prophets" as a reference to the Old Testament writers include John Calvin, *Commentaries on the Epistles of Paul to the Galatians and Ephesians* (Grand Rapids: Baker, 1993), 243; Chrysostom, Theodoret, Ambrosiaster, and Beza; see Ernest Best, *A Critical and Exegetical Commentary on Ephesians*, ICC (Edinburgh: T&T Clark, 1998), 282. In addition, Polycarp seems to make an allusion to Eph. 2:20 and understands "prophets" in the Old Testament sense (*Phil.* 6.3).

[68]M. S. Horton, *People and Place: A Covenant Ecclesiology* (Louisville: Westminster John Knox, 2008), 37–71; and J. Webster, "The Self-Organizing Power of the Gospel of Christ: Episcopacy and Community Formation," in *Word and Church* (Edinburgh: T&T Clark, 2001), 191–210.

[69]Stephen B. Chapman, "The Old Testament Canon and Its Authority for the Christian Church," *Ex auditu* 19 (2003): 141.

to have existed just fine prior to the founding of the church.[70] There are no reasons to think that the Israel of Jesus's day had any infallible revelation from God that helped it choose the books of the Old Testament canon. (3) From the very earliest days, believers received Paul's letters as Scripture (1 Thess. 2:13), Paul clearly intended them to be received as Scripture (Gal. 1:1–24), and even other writers thought they were Scripture (2 Pet. 3:16). Thus, the Scriptures themselves never give the impression that their authority was "derivative"[71] from the church, or from some future ecclesiastical decision. (4) It was not until the Council of Trent in 1546 that the Roman Catholic Church ever made a formal and official declaration on the canon of the Bible, particularly the Apocrypha.[72] In light of this scenario, what can we make of the Roman Catholic claim that "without the Church there would be no New Testament"?[73] Are we to believe that the church had no canon for over fifteen hundred years, until the Council of Trent? The history of the church makes it clear that the church did, in fact, have a functioning canon long before the Council of Trent (or even the fourth-century councils). J. I. Packer sums it up well: "The Church no more gave us the New Testament canon than Sir Isaac Newton gave us the force of gravity. God gave us gravity . . . Newton did not create gravity but recognized it."[74]

From all of this it is clear that there is some confusion in the Catholic model (at least in its more stringent versions) regarding human agency and divine agency. For example, Kreeft's argument that the church "caused" the Bible is based on the fact that the Bible was written by "apostles and saints."[75] Although Kreeft is technically correct that the Bible was written by human beings—human beings who were part of the "church"—to say that they are the "cause" of the Bible is obscurant at best. Surely, we must distinguish between ultimate and proximate causes. Although human beings are no doubt the proximate cause of the Bible, the ulti-

---

[70]Of course, the state of the Old Testament in the first century has been challenged; e.g., Albert C. Sundberg, "The 'Old Testament': A Christian Canon," *CBQ* 30, no. 2 (1968): 143–55. For more on this topic, see n. 55 in chap. 4.

[71]Rahner, *Foundations of Christian Faith*, 371.

[72]Early councils such as Laodicea (363), Hippo (393), and Carthage (397) produced canonical lists, but these were regional councils, and there were disagreements among them, as well as scattered disagreements even after the councils were over. E.g., Augustine was more favorable to the books of the Apocrypha (*Civ.* 18.36), but also admitted that they were not accepted by the Jews into their canon (*Civ.* 19.36–38). In contrast, Jerome was decidedly against them (see prologue to *Expl. Dan.*). See standard discussion in Bruce M. Metzger, *The Canon of the New Testament*, 209–47, and *An Introduction to the Apocrypha* (New York: Oxford University Press, 1977).

[73]Küng, *The Council in Action*, 187.

[74]J. I. Packer, *God Has Spoken: Revelation and the Bible* (Grand Rapids: Baker, 1993), 109.

[75]Kreeft, *Catholic Christianity*, 20.

mate cause is none other than God himself. It is God's activity to inspire the biblical authors that produced the Scriptures. He, not the church, determined what would be inspired and what would not. Kreeft has confused the *instruments* God used to produce the Bible (human beings) and the ultimate cause of the Bible (God himself). Or, put differently, he has confused the historical order of church and canon (church is "first") with the theological order (canon is "first"). N. T. Wright describes this confusion in the Catholic view.

> This makes the rather obvious logical mistake analogous to that of a soldier who, receiving orders through the mail, concludes that the letter carrier is his commanding officer. Those who transmit, collect and distribute the message are not in the same league as those who write it in the first place.[76]

It is this confusion that leads Catholics to regularly claim that the Bible is a product of the church, instead of acknowledging that it is really a product of God's activity, only to be recognized and obeyed by the church.[77] Here again we see commonalities with the historical-critical model above. Both so overemphasize the role of the community that the divine origins of these books are either denied or overlooked.

Of course, all these concerns simply lead up to the most fundamental concern, namely, whether the Roman Catholic model, in some sense, makes the Scripture subordinate to the church. The answer to that question is revealed when we ask another question: How does the Roman Catholic Church establish its *own* infallible authority? If the Roman Catholic Church believes that infallible authorities (like the Scriptures) require *external* authentication, then to what authority does the church turn to establish the grounds for its own infallible authority? Here is where the Roman Catholic model runs into some difficulties. There are three options for how to answer this question.

(1) The church could claim that its infallible authority is authenticated by (and derived from) the Scriptures. But this proves to be rather vicious circular reasoning. If the Scriptures cannot be known and authenticated

---

[76]N. T. Wright, *The Last Word: Beyond the Bible Wars to a New Understanding of the Authority of Scripture* (San Francisco: HarperSanFrancisco, 2005), 63.

[77]There are additional problems with Kreeft's argument. Even if Kreeft were right and human beings ("apostles and saints") could rightly be considered the cause of the Bible, this would still not prove an ongoing infallibility for the church. Simply because certain *members* of the church were used by God to produce the Bible does not mean that the church as an institution bears the attribute of infallibility. And even if it did, there is no reason to think that such infallibility would be a perpetual and ongoing attribute throughout the existence of the church. In the end, therefore, Kreeft's "cause-and-effect" argument proves to be problematic.

without the authority of the church, then you cannot establish the authority of the church on the basis of the Scriptures. You cannot have it both ways. Moreover, on an exegetical level, one would be hard-pressed to find much scriptural support for an infallible church (but we cannot enter into this question here).[78]

(2) The church could claim that its infallible authority is authenticated by external evidence from the history of the church: the origins of the church, the character of the church, the progress of the church, and so forth.[79] However, these are not *infallible* grounds by which the church's infallibility could be established. In addition, the history of the Roman Church is not a pure one—the abuses, corruption, documented papal errors, and the like do not naturally lead one to conclude that the church is infallible regarding "faith and morals."[80]

(3) It seems that the only option left to the Catholic model is to declare that the church's authority is self-authenticating and needs no external authority to validate it. Or, more bluntly put, we ought to believe in the infallibility of the Roman Catholic Church because it says so.[81] The

---

[78]For discussion of the key Roman Catholic proof text in this regard, Matt. 16:18, see D. A. Carson, *Matthew: Chapters 13–28*, The Expositor's Bible Commentary (Grand Rapids: Zondervan, 1995), 368ff.; Robert H. Gundry, *Matthew: A Commentary on His Handbook for a Mixed Church under Persecution*, 2nd ed. (Grand Rapids: Eerdmans, 1994), 334; and Leon Morris, *The Gospel According to Matthew* (Grand Rapids: Eerdmans, 1992), 422–24.

[79]Rahner, *Foundations of Christian Faith*, 346–59. Rahner seems to argue on *historical* grounds that the Catholic Church is the true church (and therefore rightly bears authority). He states that Roman Catholicism is the true church because "it possesses in the concrete a closer, more evident and less encumbered historical continuity with the church of the past" (357). However, if our assurance of the church's authority is only as certain as the historical evidence, then how is that an improvement over those Protestants who claim that the extent of the canon can also be determined by historical evidence (as opposed to being determined by the church)? Are not both claims as certain as the historical evidence? How then can it be claimed that only Roman Catholicism avoids the problem of uncertainty regarding the extent of the canon?

[80]This language of "faith and morals" comes right from Vatican II's *Lumen Gentium*, or "Dogmatic Constitution on the Church," and also from the *Catechism of the Catholic Church*, par. 891. The history of papal errors has been well documented. Examples include Pope Liberius, who signed an Arian confession condemning Athanasius; Pope Honorius, who was condemned by the Third Council of Constantinople for the heresy of being a monothelite; Pope Boniface VIII, who declared salvation to be impossible outside of Rome, but then the opposite was taught by Vatican II (*Unitatis Redintegratio* 1.2–3, makes this clear), and on it goes. For more, see Hans Küng, *Infallible? An Unresolved Inquiry* (Edinburgh: Continuum, 1994); and Loraine Boettner, *Roman Catholicism* (Philadelphia: Presbyterian and Reformed, 1962), 248–53. Of course, the Roman Catholic Church attempts to mitigate some of these errors by suggesting that the pope is infallible only in a very narrow sphere, that is, when he speaks *ex cathedra* (*Catholic Catechism*, par. 891). Since the Roman Catholic Church has no infallible list of *ex cathedra* statements, however, one wonders how the church can know which statements of the pope hold infallible authority and which do not (Powell, "Canonical Theism" 202–3).

[81]Indeed, the essence of this very option is taken by Kreeft, *Catholic Christianity*, when he argues that "The Church is infallible because she is faithful" (102). The problem with this claim is obvious: Who determines that faithfulness is the standard for deeming something to be infallible?

Catholic Church, then, finds itself in the awkward place of having chided the Reformers for having a self-authenticating authority (*sola scriptura*), when all the while it has engaged in that very same activity by setting itself up as a self-authenticating authority (*sola ecclesia*). On the Catholic model, the Scripture's own claims should not be received on their own authority, but apparently the church's own claims should be received on their own authority. The Roman Catholic Church, functionally speaking, is committed to *sola ecclesia*.

If so, then this presents challenges for the Catholic model. Most pertinent is the question of how there can be a canon at all—at least one that can genuinely challenge, correct, and transform the church—if the validation structure for the canon, in effect, already presupposes that the church bears an authority that is even higher? On the Catholic system, then, the canon's authority is substantially diminished. What authority it does have must be construed as purely derivative—less a rule over the church and more an arm of the church, not something that determines the church's identity but something that merely expresses it.[82] Even Lienhard, when discussing Rahner's expression of the Roman Catholic view, expresses his discomfort with its implications: "For Rahner, the Church produces the Bible; *it is difficult to see how the Church is not primary, the Scriptures secondary.*"[83]

III. Canonical-Criticism Model

A. Description

As we continue our survey of community-determined models, we turn now to a relatively new perspective on the canon that has emerged in the last thirty years, known as canonical criticism. This new approach to canon originally arose in discussions among Old Testament scholars—Brevard Childs and James Sanders primarily—and thus went largely unnoticed within New Testament circles for a period of time.[84] But Childs expanded

---

And who decides the definition of "faithful"? The answer, as seen above, is the church itself. Thus, we again see that the authority of the Roman church is essentially self-authenticating.

[82]Farkasfalvy even refers to the canon as the church's "act of self definition" (Farmer and Farkasfalvy, *The Formation of the New Testament Canon*, 103).

[83]Lienhard, *The Bible, the Church, and Authority*, 84, emphasis mine.

[84]Brevard Childs, *Biblical Theology in Crisis* (Philadelphia: Westminster, 1970); Childs, *Introduction to the Old Testament as Scripture*; Childs, *The New Testament as Canon: An Introduction* (London: SCM, 1984); James A. Sanders, *Torah and Canon*; Sanders, *Canon and Community: A Guide to Canonical Criticism* (Philadelphia: Fortress, 1984); Sanders, "Adaptable for Life: The Nature and Function of Canon," in *Magnalia Dei: The Mighty Acts of God*, ed. Frank Moore Cross, Werner E. Lemke, and Patrick D. Miller (New York: Doubleday, 1976), 531–60; Sanders, *From Sacred Story to Sacred Text* (Philadelphia: Fortress, 1987); and R. W.

his work also into the arena of the New Testament, and thus we will be focusing our discussions here primarily on his approach to canonical criticism.[85] This new approach has been driven largely by Childs's frustration and dissatisfaction with how the historical-critical approach to Scripture has hampered biblical theology. Childs argues that the meaning of the biblical text is not best found by trying to discover its earliest "layer" via form criticism, source criticism, or redaction criticism—the standard tools of modern critical scholarship—but the meaning of a text is bound up with how the text functions within its larger canonical context. In other words, contrary to popular perceptions, the text is best understood not at its earliest stage of literary development (after the scholar peels back the various layers), but in its latest stage of literary development, when it has taken its final shape.[86] The endless critical quest for the "original" text that underlies the final canonical form is misguided, argues Childs, because it is "prone to abstraction and speculation" and is unable to provide a normative text for the Christian community.[87] Thus, the central tenet of canonical criticism (at least according to Childs) is that only the final canonical form of the text embraced by the early church is the proper ground for biblical theology and exegesis. Childs declares, "The traditional scope of the New Testament provides an established context which has been received by the Christian church as faithfully reflecting the full dimensions of the gospel. The canon provides this point of standing from which one's identity with the church universal is made."[88]

Wall and E. E. Lemcio, *New Testament as Canon* (Sheffield: Sheffield Academic, 1992). For a helpful summary of canonical criticism, see Mikeal C. Parsons, "Canonical Criticism," in *New Testament Criticism and Interpretation*, ed. David Alan Black and David S. Dockery (Grand Rapids: Zondervan, 1991), 255–94; Paul R. Noble, *The Canonical Approach: A Critical Reconstruction of the Hermeneutics of Brevard S. Childs* (Leiden: Brill, 1995); John Barton, "Canonical Approaches Ancient and Modern," in Auwers and de Jonge, *The Biblical Canons*, 199–209; Bartholomew et al., *Canon and Biblical Interpretation*; multiple authors in *HBT* 2 (1980): 113–211; and Frank W. Spina, "Canonical Criticism: Childs Versus Sanders," in *Interpreting God's Word for Today*, ed. Wayne McCown and James Earl Massey (Anderson, IN: Warner, 1982), 165–94.

[85]It is important to note that Childs himself does not prefer the term *canonical criticism* (*Introduction to the Old Testament as Scripture*, 82), but that term has been used to refer to this approach since it was coined by Sanders (see *Torah and Canon*, ix–xx).

[86]Of course, Childs acknowledged that understanding the prehistory of the text still has *some* value in our exegetical task; see discussion in Barton, "Canonical Approaches Ancient and Modern," 201; Noble, *The Canonical Approach*, 145–86; and Stephen B. Chapman, "Reclaiming Inspiration for the Bible," in Bartholomew et al., *Canon and Biblical Interpretation*, 176.

[87]Childs, *The New Testament as Canon*, 43. Sanders disagrees with Childs here and is less concerned about only considering the final form of the text; he is more open to considering earlier forms of the text and how it changed over time—the "canonical process" as Sanders calls it (*Canon and Community*, 21–45). See discussion in Lee M. McDonald, *The Formation of the Christian Biblical Canon* (Peabody, MA: Hendrickson, 1995), 302–4; and Spina, "Canonical Criticism," 183–86.

[88]Childs, *The New Testament as Canon*, 30.

Driving Childs's insistence that only the final form of the New Testament is normative are two factors. (1) Childs argues that it is only the final form of the New Testament canon that brings together the divergent (and often contradictory) streams of early Christianity and provides a larger framework in which they can be understood and even harmonized.[89] In other words, the theological struggle among the early factions of Christianity is what shaped, formed, and molded the canon as we know it; to ignore the final form of the canon in favor of its earliest layer is to ignore all the factors that went into shaping it and thus is to ignore the real "historical" aspect of canon. (2) The final form of the New Testament should be normative because the final redactors who put the New Testament together intentionally shaped the material into a medium that would allow it to be transmitted to future generations. As Childs explains, this canonical shaping was done "precisely to loosen the text from any one given historical setting, and to transcend the original addressee."[90] If one approaches the text only on the basis of historical-critical methodologies, then meaning is restricted to the original context that produced that sublayer of tradition and has no lasting significance for the ongoing ecclesiastical community.[91] Thus, argues Childs, the final canonical form should be used because it provides a "flexible framework" for interpretation that is otherwise distorted by the "historicist's rigid model."[92] R. W. Wall agrees: "The tools of historical criticism misplace Scripture's theological reference point with a historical one, freezing its normative meaning in ancient worlds that do not bear upon today's church."[93]

---

[89]Ibid., 27–29; McDonald, *The Formation of the Christian Biblical Canon*, 301. Childs's assessment of diversity within the early church is quite similar to that of Bauer, *Orthodoxy and Heresy in Earliest Christianity*; James D. G. Dunn, *Unity and Diversity in the New Testament: An Inquiry into the Character of Early Christianity* (London: SCM, 1990); and G. T. Sheppard, "Canonization: Hearing the Voice of the Same God Through Historically Dissimilar Traditions," *Int* 34 (1982): 21–33. Watson is skeptical about whether the final canonical form really accomplishes this goal of unifying the divergent Scriptures and resolving interpretive conflict (F. Watson, *Text, Church and World: Biblical Interpretation in Theological Perspective* [Edinburgh: T&T Clark, 1994], 43–45).

[90]Childs, *The New Testament as Canon*, 23. Childs remains fairly vague on exactly how this material is transformed so that it is normative for future generations, but he says that "there was no one hermeneutical device used" (23).

[91]Gerald T. Sheppard, "Canon Criticism: The Proposal of Brevard Childs and an Assessment for Evangelical Hermeneutics," *Studia Biblica et Theologica* 4 (1974): 3–17. Sheppard notes, "To the degree that historical-grammatical or historical-critical exegesis is successful in reviving a 'lost' historical context, it effectively de-canonizes the literature by putting it in some other context than the canonical" (13).

[92]Childs, *The New Testament as Canon*, 24.

[93]R. W. Wall, "Canonical Context and Canonical Conversations," in *Between Two Horizons: Spanning New Testament Studies and Systematic Theology*, ed. Joel Green (Grand Rapids: Eerdmans, 2000), 166.

Child's approach, then, would reject the historical-critical notion that the idea of a canon is merely "a late, ecclesiastical activity, external to the biblical literature itself, which was subsequently imposed on those writings."[94] On the contrary, Childs would affirm that the church's "canonical consciousness" was there from the beginning and "lies deep within the New Testament literature itself."[95] Likewise, Childs's approach would reject any sort of "canon within a canon" model (see discussion in chap. 2) because it fragments and distorts a canon that is the final result of many generations of development and progress among the early Christian communities and thereby fails to provide a coherent and unified basis from which to declare a gospel message that has abiding significance to the modern-day church.[96]

By now it is clear how Childs's canonical-criticism model determines which books should be included in the canon. It consists of the books (and the shape of those books) finally settled upon and received by the early church as the basis for their understanding of the gospel. Even so, Childs does not restrict the technical term *canon* to only this final stage (as Sundberg's exclusive definition would do). Since Childs recognizes the importance of the canonical "process" by which the books were "collected, ordered, and transmitted,"[97] and the way the canon still functioned authoritatively during this time, then he is quite willing to use the term to refer to the interval before the canon reached its final shape.[98] Thus, he rejects the sharp distinction between Scripture and canon, saying that they are "very closely related, indeed often identical."[99] Childs plays a significant role, then, in establishing what we will call a *functional* definition of the term *canon* that provides an

---

[94]Childs, *The New Testament as Canon*, 21.

[95]Ibid. See Watson's helpful discussion on this point in *Text, Church and World*, 37ff.

[96]E.g., Childs criticizes Jeremias for his claim that "the authoritative form of the gospel for the Christian church is to be located in the reconstructed *ipsissima verba* of Jesus" (*The New Testament as Canon*, 537). Sanders disagrees with Childs at this point and is more open to a "canon within a canon" approach. See discussion in Parsons, "Canonical Criticism," 268–69; and Provan, "Canons to the Left of Him," 3–4.

[97]Childs, *The New Testament as Canon*, 25.

[98]Though this is Childs's most core definition, admittedly he uses the term *canon* or *canonical* in so many different ways that it can become quite confusing for the reader. For example, while some would understand "canonical process" as the gradual *recognition* of books by the believing community, Childs uses the phrase to refer to the way the books were changed, edited, and modified by the believing community, a process that normally would be associated with *redaction criticism* and not canon. Metzger, *The Canon of the New Testament*, 36n84, observed that the word *canonical* modifies over thirty different words in Childs's work.

[99]B. S. Childs, "On Reclaiming the Bible for Christian Theology," in *Reclaiming the Bible for the Church*, ed. C. E. Braaten and R. W. Jenson (Grand Rapids: Eerdmans, 1995), 9.

alternative to Sundberg's.[100] Instead of merely denoting a closed list, Childs and others have suggested that the term can refer to a collection of books that constitutes a religious norm for a community (regardless of whether the collection is "open" or "closed").[101] A canon would exist, on this definition, when there is evidence that books are functioning as Scripture. James Sanders agrees: "Canon as *function* antedates canon as *shape*."[102]

B. Evaluation

A number of positive things are certainly worth noting about the approach of canonical criticism. Most notably, Childs's willingness to allow theology back into the world of biblical studies is to be commended. His approach "takes as its primary task the disciplined theological reflection of the Bible in the context of the canon."[103] Also, the fact that Childs argues that exegesis ought to be done on a canonical level, considering the contribution of all twenty-seven (or sixty-six) books and the way they interact, is a refreshing change within the world of modern scholarship. Indeed, it has to be acknowledged that the meaning of any given text, or any given book, is related to how it fits with other texts and other books.[104] Lastly, Childs's critique of modern critical methodologies and the manner in which they splinter and fracture the canonical text is also a welcome feature of his work (and all too rare among those in modern biblical scholarship). However, a number of concerns remain.

Childs has argued that our canonical texts have undergone significant development throughout the canonical process as successive Christian generations not only chose writings, but have shaped, modified, and redacted these writings. Such a view broadens the activity of inspiration by moving it beyond its traditional locale—in the "apostles and prophets"—and

---

[100]Chapman, "How the Biblical Canon Began," 34–35, uses the term *intrinsic* instead of *functional*. The term *intrinsic* was also used by Smith, "Canons, Catalogues, and Classics," 297ff. Chapman uses *inclusive* in "The Canon Debate: What It Is and Why It Matters."
[101]See also Sanders, *Torah and Canon*, 56; Chapman, *The Law and the Prophets*, 106–10; P. R. Ackroyd, *Continuity: A Contribution to the Study of Old Testament Religious Tradition* (Oxford: Blackwell, 1962), 13–14; S. J. P. K. Riekert, "Critical Research and the One Christian Canon Comprising Two Testaments," *Neot* 14 (1981): 21–41; and Sheppard, "Canon," 62–69.
[102]James Sanders, "Canon: Hebrew Bible" in *ABD* 1:843, emphasis his.
[103]Childs, *Biblical Theology in Crisis*, 122; see also B. S. Childs, "Interpretation in Faith: The Theological Responsibility of the Old Testament Commentary," *Int* 18 (1964): 432–49.
[104]D. M. Smith, "John, the Synoptics, and the Canonical Approach to Exegesis," in *Tradition and Interpretation in the New Testament*, ed. G. F. Hawthorne and O. Betz (Grand Rapids: Eerdmans, 1987), 166–80. See also, Robert H. Gundry, *The Old Is Better: New Testament Essays in Support of Traditional Interpretations* (Tübingen: Mohr, 2005), 1–17.

expanding it to include the overall ecclesiastical community.[105] Chapman describes Childs's view of inspiration as something that happens "through various *communal* media."[106] Of course, there is not space here to enter into a full discussion of different models of inspiration, but Childs's view encounters a number of difficulties that we can briefly mention.

(1) Childs is hard-pressed to justify a sociological view of inspiration from the Scriptures themselves. The variety of biblical texts on the subject (and we cannot engage them here) give no indication that inspiration is a community affair, but rather view it as operative in key individuals and at key junctures in redemptive history.[107] Robert Gnuse observes, "The biblical tradition does not seem to give a direct affirmation to the social model of group inspiration; rather the group always seems to be addressed or led by a chosen individual."[108]

(2) There is also no indication that the early church viewed itself as bearing the same degree of inspiration as the apostles, or as bearing the authority to add, change, or modify the Scriptures (either Old Testament or New).[109] Based on the Old Testament precedents of Deuteronomy 4:2 (cf. 12:32) and Proverbs 30:5–6, as well as Josephus and other Jewish texts,[110] the reoccurring integrity formula "you shall neither add nor take away" is picked up in the New Testament context by Revelation 22:18–19, *Didache* 4.13, Papias (Eusebius, *Hist. eccl.* 3.39.15), *Barnabas* 19.11, Dionysius of Corinth (*Hist. eccl.* 4.23.12), Irenaeus (*Haer.* 5.13.1),

---

[105]Childs, *Biblical Theology in Crisis*, 104. Childs has been accused of rejecting the concept of inspiration; see David M. Williams, *Receiving the Bible in Faith: Historical and Theological Exegesis* (Washington, DC: Catholic University of America Press, 2004), 25–26. However, it would be more accurate to say he has a different view of inspiration that corresponds more closely to a "social construal of revelation" (Chapman, "Reclaiming Inspiration for the Bible," 172n24).

[106]Chapman, "Reclaiming Inspiration for the Bible," 180.

[107]Childs's view of inspiration is similar to that of Norbert Lohfink, "Über die Irrtumlosigkeit und die Einheit der Schrift," *Stimmen der Zeit* 174 (1964): 31–42; Paul J. Achtemeier, *Inspiration and Authority: Nature and Function of Christian Scripture* (Peabody, MA: Hendrickson, 1999); and J. L. McKenzie, "The Social Character of Inspiration," *CBQ* 24 (1962): 115–24. The essence of this view is critiqued by I. H. Marshall, *Biblical Inspiration* (London: Hodder & Stoughton, 1982), 37ff.

[108]R. Gnuse, *The Authority of the Bible: Theories of Inspiration, Revelation, and the Canon of Scripture* (Mawhaw, NJ: Paulist, 1985), 60.

[109]The frequent Patristic discussions of apostolic authority and its uniqueness is adequate to make this point here; for a helpful example, see C. E. Hill, "Ignatius and the Apostolate," in *StPatr*, vol. 36, ed. M. F. Wiles and E. J. Yarnold (Leuven: Peeters, 2001), 226–48. Childs's allowance for modifications to Scripture is seen by his argument that the text of any book should not be the original autograph but the earliest "received text," though he does not define what this is (*The New Testament as Canon*, 518–30, esp. 529).

[110]Josephus, *Ag. Ap.* 1.42; *Aristeas* 310–11; *1 Enoch* 104:9–10; *1 Macc.* 8:30; 11QTemple 54:5–7; *b. Meg.* 14a.

and others.[111] The church understood its role as the preserver of inspired texts, not the editor of them.[112]

(3) If the canonical documents can be continually shaped by successive Christian communities, what is significant about the fourth-century community that gives it permanent normative status?[113] Why should that particular community be the point where the shape of the canon is "frozen"? The apparently arbitrary nature of this stopping place led Frank Spina to ask, "Is canon being accorded too lofty a position when its existence may simply be the result of a historical accident?"[114] If the canonical documents were revisable for the first four centuries of the Christian church, then there seems to be no reason offered by Childs for why the canonical documents would not continually be open to revision even up to the present day.[115] If so, then there can be no "final form" of the canon from which Childs can do his biblical theology.

(4) If the response to this problem is that the Christian community has the authority not only to shape, mold, and change the canonical documents, but also to decide when to stop the "canonical process" and create a final canonical version, then it is difficult to avoid the implication that the church bears more authority than the canon itself.[116] Thus, canoni-

---

[111]David E. Aune, *Revelation 17–22*, WBC (Nashville: Thomas Nelson, 1998), 1208–16; W. C. van Unnik, "De la régle μήτε προσθεῖναι μήτε ἀφελεῖν dans l'histoire du canon," *VC* 3 (1949): 1–36; and M. J. Kruger, "Early Christian Attitudes Towards the Reproduction of Texts," in *The Early Text of the New Testament*, ed. C. E. Hill and M. J. Kruger (Oxford: Oxford University Press, forthcoming).

[112]For more on the early church's view of Scripture, see John D. Woodbridge, *Biblical Authority: A Critique of the Rogers/McKim Proposal* (Grand Rapids: Zondervan, 1982).

[113]It is important to note that the objection to Childs here is not precisely the same as the one made by John Barton, *Reading the Old Testament: Method in Biblical Study* (London: Darton, Longman, and Todd, 1996), 91–94. Barton argues that there is no way to determine which canon should be received by the church because there was disagreement over canonical *books* within early Christianity. This question has been addressed by others; see Provan, "Canons to the Left of Him," 11–25; and Christopher Seitz, "The Canonical Approach and Theological Interpretation," in Bartholomew et al., *Canon and Biblical Interpretation*, 58–110. Instead, the objection here pertains to the idea that the early church had communal inspiration to make *textual* changes or additions prior to the fourth century but not after.

[114]Spina, "Canonical Criticism," 183.

[115]James A. Sanders, "Canonical Context and Canonical Criticism," *HBT* 2 (1980): 173–97, has a more consistent position here than does Childs. He agrees that the Christian community can (and does) modify the text of the canon, but believes that it still has the right to do so today (187).

[116]Chapman, "Reclaiming Inspiration for the Bible," attempts to avoid the ecclesiological implications here by suggesting that Childs's view does, in fact, honor the "prophetic-apostolic witness" (179). However, Chapman's explanation that "for Childs the prophetic-apostolic witness is more than simply what individual prophets originally said and wrote" proves to be rather thin (179). It is unclear how this solves the problem because, again, the authority still shifts from the original apostles-prophets to the subsequent community, who adds their own inspired material. Simply to *call* this community revelation the "prophetic-apostolic witness" does not alleviate the problem. Chapman himself seems to recognize this when he says that

cal criticism finds itself in a very similar place as the Roman Catholic model above.[117] Carl Henry, critiquing Childs's position, puts it well: "If the canon represents a judgment by the community of faith . . . does not the community really constitute an authority just as ultimate, and even more so, than the canon?"[118] In the end, the canonical-criticism approach provides us with another canon derivative from, and dependent upon, the Christian community and thus unable to genuinely rule over it as the *norma normans* (the norm that norms).

This particular problem is brought into sharper relief when Childs's own approach to Scripture is considered. Although his critique of modern critical methodologies (form, source, and redaction criticism) may give the impression that he repudiates these methodologies, such is not the case.[119] Childs recognizes that some people might think he is proposing a "return to a traditional pre-Enlightenment understanding of the Bible," but he reassures the reader that "such an endeavor is not only wrong in concept but impossible in practice."[120] Childs quite readily accepts the conclusions of these methodologies, including suggestions that the text reflects the influence of redactional activity, pseudonymous authors, internal and historical contradictions, ancient myth, political infighting, and the like. Consequently, Childs's determination that a book belongs in the New Testament canon does not constitute a judgment that it is historically accurate or written by an apostle. These are not the issues that matter to Childs (and they have already been rejected by his commitment to the critical conclusions of modern scholarship).[121] Rather, to say that a book

---

Childs's model, in the eyes of those who hold a more traditional view of inspiration, "may still concede too much to tradition and ecclesiology" (180).

[117]Chapman even offers the canonical model as something that "provides new opportunities for conversation and rapprochement between Protestants and Catholics" ("Reclaiming Inspiration for the Bible," 174).

[118]Carl F. H. Henry, "Canonical Theology: An Evangelical Appraisal," *Scottish Bulletin of Evangelical Theology* 8 (1990): 99.

[119]Provan, "Canons to the Left of Him," 26–30, argues that there is a tension in Childs over his acceptance of modern critical methodology, and he argues that Childs should be more critical (!) of its validity.

[120]Childs, *The New Testament as Canon*, 35.

[121]Childs, of course, would object: "It is a basic misunderstanding of the canonical approach to describe it as a non-historical reading of the Bible. Nothing could be further from the truth!" (*Introduction to the Old Testament as Scripture*, 71). Indeed, it is this interest in "history" that distinguishes Childs from the approach of literary criticism (to which he is often compared). And in this regard, Barton's criticism is misguided (*Reading the Old Testament*, 102). Childs's objection aside, it is clear that he continues to view the Bible as a book full of historical errors, mistakes, political maneuvering, and other problems. Thus, Childs is able to declare that "a general hermeneutic is inadequate to deal with the particular medium through which this experience [of historical Israel] has been mediated" (71). In other words, since this "particular medium" is full of historical problems and contradictions, we must approach the book with a different hermeneutic that can allow God to still "speak" through such a book. Childs is

belongs in the canon is simply to say that these books, and not others, are what the church has chosen as the best summary of what constitutes the Christian faith and the Christian gospel.

Thus, it is here that we come to the crux of the canonical-criticism model. The canon is "authoritative" not because it is historically true or derived from the apostles; it becomes authoritative when a particular community embraces it in faith. Incredibly, then, the canonical-criticism approach has a strong component of existentialism built into it, leading many to draw comparisons to Barth's and Bultmann's view of Scripture.[122] What is most important is not whether the content of the text actually happened, but that "the text itself actually influenced a living community."[123] There must be a reception by a community before the canon has any religious or normative function—which makes the authority of the canon, to some extent, dependent upon human ratification. For canonical criticism, "revelation is channeled not into objective truth, but rather into experiential dynamic."[124] In many ways, then, canonical criticism is an ironic overreaction to the modern critical methods that Childs is so eager to refute. While the modern critical methods may have overlooked the final text for the sake of getting to the historical reality "behind" it, Childs's canonical criticism has overlooked the historical reality behind it for the sake of focusing on the final text.[125] He has retained literary context, but has lost the historical context. We are left simply with words that have little connection to the real world.

---

more frank elsewhere: "The Canonical context makes different uses of historical material. At times the context *hangs very loosely on history* as it bears witness to a *representative reality* which transcends any given historical situation" (Brevard S. Childs, "A Response," *HBT* 2 [1980]: 204, emphasis mine). Childs is free to insist that this is a "historical" approach, but one wonders whether his use of the term is entirely fair. If one is to suggest that the Bible only "hangs very loosely on history" and instead offers a "representative reality," then at least the term *historical* should be qualified to reflect such an approach.

[122] Connections between Childs and the existentialism of Barth and Bultmann are noted by many scholars: McDonald, *The Formation of the Christian Biblical Canon*, 304; M. G. Brett, "Against the Grain: Brevard Childs' Biblical Theology of the Old and New Testaments: Theological Reflections on the Christian Bible," *MT* 10 (1994): 281–87; David Dickermann, ed., *Karl Barth and the Future of Theology: A Memorial Colloquium Held at the Yale Divinity School, January 28, 1969* (New Haven, CT: YDS Association, 1969), 33; Roy A. Harrisville, "What I Believe My Old Schoolmate Is Up To," in *Theological Exegesis: Essays in Honor of Brevard S. Childs*, ed. Christopher Seitz and Kathryn Greene-McCreight (Grand Rapids: Eerdmans, 1999), 7–25; and Noble, *The Canonical Approach*, 4.

[123] Spina, "Canonical Criticism," 179. Spina offers a helpful discussion of the "existential" problems of Childs's view on 181–82.

[124] Henry, "Canonical Theology," 104.

[125] Only a view of Scripture that takes *both* the history behind the text and the text itself seriously can overcome this problem. Modern critical methods and canonical criticism have each opted for only one of these.

In the end, despite its positives, the canonical-criticism model reduces the canon to those books that the Christian community has determined are the basis for their religious encounter with God. Largely missing in this model is that the canonicity of these books is in any sense connected to the fact that they bear (and have always borne) intrinsic authority, or that they derive from the apostolic era and bear a historically accurate apostolic message. This overemphasis on community reception, once again, creates a canon that is, in some sense, dependent upon the community it is intended to rule.

C. Childs's Definition of Canon

As noted above, Childs (as well as others inside and outside canonical criticism) has offered an alternative to Sundberg's *exclusive* definition of canon by suggesting a *functional* one. Canon exists not when there is a final, closed list, but when books function as authoritative Scripture for the community—and this happened well before the fourth century.[126] There is much in this functional definition of canon that is welcome. In particular, it more accurately captures the historical reality that early Christians did possess a functioning canon even by the second century, though the borders were still fuzzy.[127] Thus, this definition does not run

---

[126]Harnack argued that a book could be considered canonical only if it were expressly called γραφή or introduced with γέγραπται. In contrast, Zahn argued that a book could be canonical without these formulaic markers, as long as there are indications that it enjoyed authoritative use. Barton, *The Spirit and the Letter*, makes a clear distinction between Zahn's view and Harnack's (1–14). However, we should be careful not to exaggerate the differences between Harnack and Zahn. Although they disagreed about *how* to determine a book's scriptural status (formulaic markers or authoritative use), they did agree that a book's canonicity was determined by its scriptural status (or function), as opposed to being a part of a final, closed list. In this sense, Harnack and Zahn essentially held the same view.

[127]Some might raise the question of how the functional definition accounts for books that were considered Scripture by some early Christian groups but never were received into the final canon (e.g., *1 Clement, Shepherd of Hermas*). What shall we call these books? Both Allert (*A High View of Scripture?*, 171) and McDonald (*Forgotten Scriptures: The Selection and Rejection of Early Religious Writings* [Louisville: Westminster John Knox, 2009], 23–25) argue against the functional definition because it would force us to regard these other books as canon. The exclusive definition, they argue, avoids this very sort of imprecision. However, two responses are in order: (1) This objection seems confused about what the functional definition is trying to do. The functional definition is simply saying that we should be allowed to call these twenty-seven books canon when they are being used as authoritative Scripture in the life of the church. Just because some other books were occasionally used as Scripture does not negate this approach, nor does it mean we are obligated to call these other books canon. The only way we would be obligated to call them canon is if we believed that the mere use of a book *makes* it canonical (more on this below). (2) Allert and McDonald argue that the functional definition is negated by the fact that there were disagreements over what was Scripture. If so, then the exclusive definition should be negated for the same reason. As discussed above, well after the fourth century there continued to be disagreements about which books belonged on

the danger of downplaying the authoritative nature of these books during this period, as the exclusive definition does. In addition, this definition seems less prone to unduly inflate the role of official church declarations about the canon—as if those declarations somehow "created" or "established" the authority of these books.[128]

Even with these positives, however, the functional definition of canon suffers from one of the same weaknesses as the exclusive definition. Whether one defines canon as final reception (exclusive), or as authoritative use (functional), neither of these definitions fully accounts for the divine origins of the canon. Put differently, both of these definitions largely overlook the ontology of the canon—what it *is* apart from what it does. As noted above, if one takes the historic Christian position that the canon was given by God—and does not just "become" a canon at a later point—then the canon can also be defined simply as the scriptural books that God gave the corporate church. We shall call this the *ontological* definition. On this definition, one could have a canon, in principle, even before it was used authoritatively (functional) and certainly before it was formally received by the church (exclusive). God's books are authoritative prior to anyone using them or recognizing them. Surely, the existence of canon and the recognition of canon are two distinguishable phenomena. Why, then, should the term *canon* be restricted to only the latter? This distinction is critical because it reminds us that neither the church's use of these books (functional definition) nor the church's final reception of these books (exclusive definition) is what *makes* them canonical. They are canonical by virtue of what they *are*, namely, God's books.

Given that the ontological definition of canon is, from one perspective, the most concrete—we have a canon when these God-given books *exist*—it is not difficult to imagine that a case could be made that the term *canon* should be used only in this sense. Perhaps one could argue the *opposite* position of Sundberg, namely, that canon only means the books given by God and therefore cannot be used to refer to the later, drawn-out recognition process. But this too would be mistaken. If we are

---

the church's canonical list. All this reminds us that a degree of imprecision is inevitable in all definitions of canon.

[128]Even though Childs generally uses this functional definition, his insistence that only the final form of the canon is normative (because it has been changed all along the way) implies that the church, in some sense, determines the canon (as argued above). Thus, there is a tension in Childs's system between his preferred definition of canon and his insistence that only the final form is ultimately normative.

to be balanced, it seems we need *three* aspects to our definition of canon: canon as reception (exclusive), canon as use (functional), and canon as divinely given (ontological).[129] As we shall discuss further below, we are not forced to choose between these three, but can recognize that each of them captures true aspects of canon. When all three are considered in tandem, their weaknesses can be balanced out, and a more well-rounded understanding of canon can emerge.

IV. Existential/Neoorthodox Model

A. Description

Whereas the models above have authenticated canon primarily through the collective and corporate "community," the existential/neoorthodox model tends toward a more individualistic and experiential approach.[130] The locus of authority is found not in the Scriptures themselves but ultimately in the individual who engages with them.[131] Authority exists when (and only when) an individual experiences God's word and responds to it in faith. The classical existential approach is best known through Karl Barth, Emil Brunner, Rudolph Bultmann, and other dialectical theologians. Although they differed extensively from one another—and certainly are not all "existential" in the same way or to the same degree[132]—we shall need to

---

[129]Each of these definitions can *roughly* correspond with dates for the canon's emergence. The exclusive definition typically leads to a fourth-century date, the functional typically leads to a second-century date (though arguably books function as authoritative prior to this period), and the ontological would lead to a first-century date.

[130]Even though the existential model is more individualistic, we still include it under the "community-determined" category because ultimately canon is still determined by *human reception.*

[131]Gnuse, *Authority of the Bible*, 75–86.

[132]The differences (and conflicts) among these three are well documented: e.g., Cornelius Van Til, *The New Modernism: An Appraisal of the Theology of Barth and Brunner* (Philadelphia: Presbyterian and Reformed, 1947), 188–221; Karl Barth, "Rudolf Bultmann: An Attempt to Understand Him," in *Kerygma and Myth*, ed. Hans-Werner Bartsch (London: SPCK, 1962), 83–132; and Herman Ridderbos, *Bultmann* (Philadelphia: Presbyterian and Reformed, 1960), 15–16. Despite the differences between these three, they all share a "dialectical" theology and thus, in regard to the issue of canon, they best fit together under this heading we call "existential." On the similarities between Barth's and Bultmann's views of Scripture, see David Congdon, "The Word as Event: Barth and Bultmann on Scripture," in *The Sacred Text*, ed. Michael Bird and Michael Pahl (Piscataway, NJ: Gorgias, 2010), 241–65. Although we could easily have added Schleiermacher to this category of "existential," we must limit ourselves to just Barth, Brunner, and Bultmann. For a look at Schleiermacher's view of the canon, see Christine Helmer, "Transhistorical Unity of the New Testament Canon from Philosophical, Exegetical, and Systematic-Theological Perspectives," in *One Scripture or Many?*, ed. Christine Helmer and Christof Landmesser (Oxford: Oxford University Press, 2004), 13–50.

group them together under one heading here.[133] Barth (or Barthianism[134]) believed that the Scriptures are not the word of God, per se, but merely a *witness* to the word of God (Jesus Christ).[135] Revelation is not a propositional statement about God; rather it is an event (*Ereignis*), an encounter, something that "happens" to an individual.[136] Thus, the Scriptures are not the word of God in a static sense, but "become" the word of God when an existential experience occurs.[137] Barth contends, "Again it is quite impos-

---

[133] As a result, the individual nuances of these theologians cannot be fully addressed or adequately appreciated in this brief treatment (nor does each aspect of the existentialist model described below always apply to all three). Particularly difficult in this regard are the varied and contradictory opinions about Karl Barth and his doctrine of Scripture. Helpful overviews of this issue can be found in John D. Morrison, "Barth, Barthians, and Evangelicals: Reassessing the Question of the Relation of Holy Scripture and the Word of God," *TrinJ* 25 (2004): 187–213; and G. W. Bromiley, "The Authority of Scripture in Karl Barth," in Carson and Woodbridge, *Hermeneutics, Authority, and Canon*, 271–94.

[134] In recent years, some "neo-Barthian" scholars have argued that virtually all prior assessments of Barth's understanding of Scripture have been mistaken and that he is, in fact, more orthodox than has been realized. Prior critics of Barth's doctrine of Scripture include Cornelius Van Til, *Karl Barth and Evangelicalism* (Philadelphia: Presbyterian and Reformed, 1964), 14ff.; and C. F. Henry, *God, Revelation and Authority*, 6 vols. (Waco, TX: Word, 1979), 1:203–12, 2:40–48, 4:257–71. More sympathetic (and recent) opinions include Kevin J. Vanhoozer, "A Person of the Book? Barth on Biblical Authority and Interpretation," in *Karl Barth and Evangelical Theology*, ed. Sung Wook Chung (Grand Rapids: Baker, 2006), 26–59; and Bruce L. McCormack, "The Being of Holy Scripture Is in Becoming: Karl Barth in Conversation with American Evangelicalism," in *Evangelicals and Scripture: Tradition, Authority and Hermeneutics*, ed. Vincent Bacote, Laura C. Miguelez, and Dennis L. Okholm (Downers Grove, IL: InterVarsity, 2004), 55–74. While Barth has no doubt been misunderstood by some (Van Til, at points, was guilty of this), it is difficult to believe that he has been universally misread—even by the likes of T. F. Torrance—and that only now is he understood for the first time. In disagreement with McCormack is Mark D. Thompson, "Witness to the Word: On Barth's Doctrine of Scripture," in *Engaging with Barth: Contemporary Evangelical Critiques*, ed. David Gibson and Daniel Strange (Nottingham: Apollos/IVP, 2008), 168–97. Nevertheless, portions of this section can be read as a critique of "Barthianism" if one does not believe Barth actually held these views.

[135] Karl Barth, *Church Dogmatics*, trans. G. W. Bromiley and T. F. Torrance, 2nd ed. (Edinburgh: T&T Clark, 1975), I/1:88–111. See also, Klaas Runia, *Karl Barth's Doctrine of Holy Scripture* (Grand Rapids: Eerdmans, 1962). Because Barth always sees revelation as an "event," he is unclear about the degree to which Scripture is still, in some sense, the "word of God" apart from the Spirit's use of it. At times, Barth seems to say that it is not (I/1:107, 112, 124), and other times, that it is (I/1:120, 121).

[136] T. F. Torrance, *Karl Barth: An Introduction to His Early Theology, 1910–1931* (Edinburgh: T&T Clark, 2000), 98–105; Roger Nicole, "The Neo-Orthodox Reduction," in *Challenges to Inerrancy: A Theological Response*, ed. Gordon Lewis and Bruce Demarest (Chicago: Moody, 1984), 121–44; Paul K. Jewett, *Emil Brunner: An Introduction to the Man and His Thought* (Chicago: InterVarsity, 1961), 22–23.

[137] Barth, *Church Dogmatics*, I/1:110–11. Robert L. Reymond, *A New Systematic Theology of the Christian Faith* (Nashville: Thomas Nelson, 1998), objects to the idea that neoorthodox theology teaches that the Bible "becomes" the word of God (12n22). Instead, he says that neoorthodox theology teaches that "the Bible becomes the instrument that reproduces the 'Christ event' in one subjectively" (ibid.). Although Reymond's clarification is welcome, the phrase "becomes" still seems to accurately capture the essence of the neoorthodox belief. No one suggests the term "becomes" *exhaustively* captures this position, but that it accurately communicates (1) the revelation-as-event character of neoorthodoxy, and (2) how the neoorthodox understand scriptural authority in "functional" terms. See Henry, *God, Revelation and Authority*, 84–85;

sible that there should be a direct identity between the human word of Holy Scripture and the Word of God."[138] Consequently, there is a division between issues of history and issues of faith in existential/neoorthodox thinkers. According to Barth, it doesn't matter that the Scriptures contain historical mistakes; God can still use the fallible records of men to speak meaningfully to his church.[139] Brunner also allowed for God to speak in the midst of contradictions within the Scripture: "God can speak to us His single, never contradictory word through . . . the contradictory accounts of Luke and Matthew."[140] Likewise, Bultmann's famous article "New Testament and Mythology" declares the New Testament not to be historically accurate, but to be mythologically conditioned in a manner incompatible with the modern scientific age.[141] Moreover, Bultmann argues that it does not matter whether the New Testament reflects real history; the thing that matters is not the historical cross but the "preached cross."[142] For Barth, Brunner, and Bultmann, what matters is the existential connection made with God through the Scriptures, not whether the Scriptures are historically "true."

The implications of this approach upon canon are immediately evident. If a particular document only "becomes" the word of God during an existential experience, then the canon is defined as those books through which the church encounters the living voice of God. Barth declares, "Discovery of the canon . . . is to be understood only as an event."[143] Avery Dulles notes, "For Barth himself, the canon was charismatically determined. In certain books the church heard God speaking; in others it did not."[144] For the existentialist, historical questions are not germane to the issue of canon in the first place; form criticism, source criticism, and investigations into

---

Kelsey, *The Uses of Scripture in Recent Theology*, 39–50; and Mary Kathleen Cunningham, "Karl Barth," in *Christian Theologies of Scripture*, ed. Justin S. Holcomb (New York: New York University Press, 2006), 183–201.

[138]Barth, *Church Dogmatics*, I/2:499. A very similar statement can be found in E. Brunner, *Dogmatics*, vol. 1, *The Christian Doctrine of God*, trans. O. Wyon (Philadelphia: Westminster, 1950), 15.

[139]Barth, *Church Dogmatics*, I/1:509; Nicole, "The Neo-Orthodox Reduction," 125–26; Henry, *God, Revelation and Authority*, 196–200, 272–89.

[140]Emil Brunner, *The Divine-Human Encounter*, trans. W. Amandus Loos (Westport, CT: Greenwood, 1980), 173; Robert L. Reymond, *Brunner's Dialectical Encounter* (Philadelphia: Presbyterian and Reformed, 1967), 10–15.

[141]Rudolph Bultmann, *New Testament and Mythology and Other Basic Writings*, trans. Schubert Ogden (Philadelphia: Fortress, 1984), 1–43. See also, Bultmann, ed., *Kerygma and Myth: A Theological Debate* (New York: Harper, 1961), 1–44.

[142]For a helpful discussion of Bultmann in this regard, see R. B. Strimple, *The Modern Search for the Real Jesus* (Phillipsburg, NJ: P&R, 1995), 103–26.

[143]Barth, *Church Dogmatics*, I/1:109.

[144]Avery Dulles, "Scripture: Recent Protestant and Catholic Views," in *The Authoritative Word: Essays on the Nature of Scripture*, ed. Donald K. McKim (Grand Rapids: Eerdmans, 1983), 241.

the authorship or date of books are not the means by which one decides whether a book is part of Scripture.[145] Christians do not experience God in the Scriptures because they are canonical; rather they are "canonical" because Christians experience God in them.[146]

When it comes to questions of the canon, Barth appears quite committed to the idea that the sixty-six books of our canon are the only books that God uses to actively speak to his church.[147] However, his downplaying of historical matters and his focus on existential matters prevent him from being able to provide any real basis for why we should be restricted to these certain books. Consequently, Barth "affirms the sixty-six books are the canon, but he leaves the door open to extensions."[148] As Dulles notes:

> The decision concerning the canon, for Barth, . . . is not irrevocable. In the sixteenth century, Barth admits, the Reformation churches changed the canon by excluding certain books (the deuterocanonicals) that had previously been accepted. Conceivably the church might decide to change the limits of the canon again at some future time.[149]

Brunner takes advantage of this door opened by Barth and walks right through it, arguing that the borders of the canon are not fixed.

---

[145]E.g., Emil Brunner, *Revelation and Reason* (Philadelphia: Westminster, 1946), 168–69, attacks any position that seeks to establish canonicity/authority on the basis of historical conclusions about a book's authorship. Referring to this approach he declares, "And on what a quaking ground has the Church of the Reformation, and its 'orthodox' perversion, placed both itself and its message! We owe a profound debt of gratitude to the historical criticism that has made it quite impossible to maintain this position" (168). In other words, we can base a book's authority not on historical investigations, but on existential encounter.

[146]This statement should sound quite similar to Bultmann's famous maxim, "The saving efficacy of the cross is not derived from the fact that it is the cross of Christ: it is the cross of Christ because it has this saving efficacy" (Bultmann, *Kerygma and Myth*, 41). Brunner says something similar: "Not because I believe in the Scriptures do I believe in Christ, but because I believe in Christ I believe in the Scriptures" (*Revelation and Reason*, 170).

[147]Barth, *Church Dogmatics*, I/1:101.

[148]Nicole, "The Neo-Orthodox Reduction," 133. Barth, in an effort to affirm the sovereignty and freedom of God, wants to make sure that we do not "lock up" the work of the Holy Spirit by imprisoning it in Scripture. But the unfortunate outcome of this effort is that Barth implies that the Spirit can move through books other than Scripture: "We recognize that the fact that Jesus Christ is the one Word of God does not mean that in the Bible, the Church and the world there are not *other words* . . . and *other revelations* which are quite real" (*Church Dogmatics*, IV/3:97, emphasis mine). Kimlyn J. Bender, "Scripture and Canon in Karl Barth's Early Theology," in *From Biblical Criticism to Biblical Faith*, ed. William H. Brackney and Craig A. Evans (Macon, GA: Mercer University Press, 2007), 164–98, notes that "Barth is quite ambivalent about questions of canonical boundaries" (179) and documents a letter from Barth to Harnack in which Barth expresses that there is "no *a priori* impossibility" of God speaking through noncanonical books (180). See further discussion in Gabriel Fackre, "Revelation," in Chung, *Karl Barth and Evangelical Theology*, 6–8; and Runia, *Karl Barth's Doctrine of Holy Scripture*, 38.

[149]Dulles, "Scripture," 241.

The question of the canon has never, in principle, been definitely answered, but is continually being reopened. Just as the church of the second, third, and fourth centuries had the right to decide . . . what was "Apostolic" and what was not, on their own responsibility as believers, so in the same way every church, at every period in the history of the church, possesses the same right and the same duty.[150]

The implications of Brunner's comments are clear. Which books are considered "apostolic"—and therefore in the canon—is determined by each generation's *experience* with those books. Thus, the canon of Scripture has "fluid edges"[151] and will change from generation to generation. But Brunner goes even further and suggests what Barth only implied, namely, that God could speak to his church in books *outside* the Bible.[152] After all, if truth is mediated through personal experience, who is to say that a person cannot hear God's voice in another book? Is God restricted by the Bible? Brunner simply takes his existential approach to its logical conclusion. Likewise, Bultmann also affirms that the "word of God" is not to be equated with the Scripture, but he is even more radical in his existential approach to the Christian faith than are Barth and Brunner, causing some to criticize Bultmann for denying that a religious encounter requires *any* connection to a historical Jesus.[153] Thus, Bultmann also leaves the door wide open to the possibility that such an encounter could happen through other books outside the canon.[154] Indeed, many of Bultmann's more radical successors (Karl Jaspers, Fritz Buri, and Van Austin Harvey) continued to make the case that existential fulfillment need not have anything to do with Christ at all, but could occur through other historical figures worthy of emulation—thus eliminating any need to consider the New Testament books as a unique source of revelation.[155]

---

[150]Brunner, *Revelation and Reason*, 131.

[151]Jewett, *Emil Brunner*, 35.

[152]Emil Brunner, *Our Faith* (New York: Scribner's, 1926), 10–11; Nicole summarizes Brunner's view: "Somehow it is God's voice, too, in the Koran or the Vedas" ("The Neo-Orthodox Reduction," 141). Also implying the same thing is Brunner's statement, "God can, if he so wills, speak his Word to a man even through a false doctrine and correspondingly find in a false Credo-credo the right echo of his Word"; Emil Brunner, *Truth as Encounter* (Philadelphia: Westminster, 1943), 137.

[153]See Brunner's critique of Bultmann in *Truth as Encounter*, 41–49; G. E. Ladd, *Rudolf Bultmann* (Chicago: InterVarsity, 1964), 35.

[154]Morris Ashcraft, *Rudolf Bultmann* (Waco, TX: Word, 1972), 73–76.

[155]Strimple, *The Modern Search*, 128–34. These followers of Bultmann claimed they were only being consistent with Bultmann's own statements, such as, "Anyone who asserts that to speak of God at all is mythological language is bound to regard the idea of an act of God in Christ as a myth" (*Kerygma and Myth*, 33–34). If Bultmann is correct, then why does "revelation" from God have to be connected to the historical Jesus at all?

B. Evaluation

We begin by affirming a number of commendable aspects of the existential/neoorthodox model. As with all the community-determined models, it rightly recognizes that the reception of these books by the Christian community is an important aspect of canon. There is undoubtedly an existential component to how the canon is authenticated, and it is important to be reminded of that reality (though there is not *only* an existential component). In addition, we would agree with Barth, as he appeals to Calvin, that the "Bible constitutes itself the Canon. It is the Canon because it imposed itself upon the church as such."[156] Barth seems to recognize some aspect of the self-authenticating nature of Scripture here, though we shall register disagreements later about the specific way that is understood. For this reason, we also can appreciate Barth's understanding of the relationship between the church and the Scripture, where he always affirmed the priority of the latter over the former (even if one might view such a position as inconsistent with other parts of his thinking). These many positives aside, however, there are still substantial concerns with this overall model that need to be mentioned.

The most fundamental concern pertains to the existential model's unfortunate separation of the authority of God and the authority of Scripture. The Scripture has no intrinsic authority, but is "contingent" upon whether God decides to use it.[157] For Barth, "the texts are authoritative *not in virtue of any property they may have.*"[158] Consequently, these texts must be considered canonical on *other* grounds, namely, "in virtue of a function they fill in the life of the Christian community."[159] But this leads to three problematic areas. First, if the boundaries of the canon are determined solely by the existential experience of the community, then the boundaries of the canon are fluid and ever changing.[160] And a perpetually uncertain canon is unable to function as an authoritative norm for the church. If the canon is regarded as an entirely personal and existential "event," then

---

[156]Barth, *Church Dogmatics*, I/1:107.

[157]Donald G. Bloesch, *Holy Scripture: Revelation, Inspiration, and Interpretation* (Downers Grove, IL: InterVarsity, 1994), does the same thing when he says, "The Bible is not in and of itself the revelation of God but the divinely appointed means and channel of this revelation" (57).

[158]Kelsey, *The Uses of Scripture*, 47, emphasis mine.

[159]Ibid.

[160]In response to critiques that his position is subjectivism, Barth emphasizes the *objective* nature of revelation by saying that revelation is really found in the person of Jesus himself (*Church Dogmatics*, IV/3:175–80). Though such a Christocentric clarification is welcome, it still does not solve the problem of subjectivism, because how does one have access to this Jesus apart from the scriptural testimony about him? And since Scripture is itself not revelation, then its value remains solely in its subjective appropriation by a community. For more discussion, see Fackre, "Revelation," 2–4.

there can never be a "right" canon, but simply the "current" canon—the canon that the church is now using. Henry observes:

> [On the Barthian view] the idea of a fixed scriptural canon collapses. Only isolated fragments of the Bible that "impose" themselves become the Word of God, and these cease to be the Word of God when not self-imposing. What is Word of God for some need not be Word of God for others—or can be, or not, at different times and places.[161]

Thus, the neoorthodox canon is reduced to a human-determined document that bears no real authority in and of itself.

Second, if Scripture does not bear authority in itself and is contingent upon reception by the community, then the community begins to take on authority equal to (if not greater than) that of Scripture. Stanley Grenz and John Franke run into this very problem when they make what is arguably a "Barthian" distinction between the authority of God and the authority of Scripture: "Ultimate authority [is located] only in the action of the triune God. If we must speak of a 'foundation' of the Christian faith at all, then, we must speak of neither Scripture nor tradition in and of themselves."[162] Thus, they declare, "neither Scripture nor tradition is inherently authoritative," and therefore both are "contingent on the work of the Spirit."[163] With this distinction in hand, Grenz and Franke are able to place church tradition and Scripture on equal footing. While acknowledging that in some sense the canon constitutes the church, they also declare that "canonical Scripture . . . is itself derived from that [Christian] community and its authority."[164] Just as in the Roman Catholic and canonical-criticism models above, it is unclear how this position is able to establish a canon that can function as an authority over the church.[165]

Third, if the existentialist model is correct that there is nothing distinctive about the biblical books, then the very *concept* of a canon is in jeopardy. We noted above that Barth (along with others) argues that the New Testament contains contradictions and historical mistakes (and for Bultmann, outright myth), but that God can speak through these documents anyway—that is, what matters is not history, but faith. But if accu-

---

[161]Henry, *God, Revelation and Authority*, 259–60.
[162]Stanley J. Grenz and John R. Franke, *Beyond Foundationalism: Shaping Theology in a Postmodern Context* (Louisville: Westminster John Knox, 2001), 117.
[163]Ibid.
[164]Ibid.
[165]Ironically, Barth himself was much clearer about the Scripture being an authority over church tradition. See *Church Dogmatics*, I/2:574, and discussion in Vanhoozer, "A Person of the Book?," 43ff.

rately recounting God's historical acts does not matter—nor anything else inherent in these books—then why should we have any concern about the extent of the canon at all? If God can supernaturally speak through any book (in his sovereignty and power), then what difference does it make which books ended up in the canon? In this regard, Bultmann's extreme approach may prove to be the most consistent. If there is nothing distinctive about these books (in and of themselves), then canonical boundaries are nonsensical. And therefore a canon is nonsensical.

In summary, the existential/neoorthodox view suffers from some of the same overall weaknesses of the other community-determined models. In its overemphasis on the subjective reception of these books, it does not adequately account for the intrinsic authority of these books or their historical and apostolic origins.

V. Conclusion

This chapter has been devoted to a variety of canonical models that see canon as community determined: historical-critical, Roman Catholic, canonical criticism, and existential/neoorthodox. Though they vary to one degree or another, they all authenticate the canon by appealing to its reception by the Christian community (either corporately or individually). Although these models rightly recognize the importance of community reception as an aspect of canon, they have absolutized this aspect so that it becomes the defining characteristic of canon. This has created an imbalanced approach to canon that is problematic not so much for what it affirms, but for what it leaves out. Largely overlooked in the above models are (1) the intrinsic authority and internal attributes of these books that makes them authoritative and (2) the historical origins of these books and the fact that they stem from the apostolic age and accurately capture the redemptive activities of God in Jesus Christ. As a result of these omissions, these models are left with a canon that is derived from and established by the church, and thus is unable to rule over the church. In effect, the canon has so much become the church's book that it is unable to be God's book.

2

TRACING THE ORIGINS

Canon as Historically Determined

It is a most assured result of biblical criticism that every one
of the twenty-seven books which now constitute our New
Testament is assuredly genuine and authentic.

B. B. WARFIELD

We now turn our attention to the second major category of canonical
models, those that view canon as *historically determined*. These models
deny that the Christian community's reception of the canon is definitive
in establishing its authority and instead seek to establish it by critically
investigating the historical merits of each of the canonical books. Contrary
to the models above that downplayed historical concerns or regarded them
as virtually irrelevant to a book's authority (e.g., canonical criticism),
the models here put a premium on the historical *origins* of a book (or
its component parts). If a book can be shown to contain authentic Jesus
tradition or can be shown to be apostolic, then it is considered part of the
genuine canon of Scripture. Specific examples of the historically determined models reach very different conclusions, ranging from a rejection
of most of the twenty-seven books (canon-within-the-canon model) to an
acceptance of all the twenty-seven books (criteria-of-canonicity model).

But the methodology is the same: canon is authenticated via historical investigation into these books.[1]

I. Canon-within-the-Canon Model

A. Description

In 1962, Kurt Aland published the now famous article "The Problem of the New Testament Canon," in which he argued that the formation of the canon was so laden with "imperfections and uncertainties" that its final shape clearly includes books (and portions of books) that are problematic.[2] Thus, the only way forward is to discover the "canon within the canon"[3] by reducing the New Testament to its core truths and selecting the parts that will bring "unity to the faith."[4] How is this to be done? By an investigation into the "historical development" of these books to determine which parts are genuine and which are not.[5] Aland's approach, then, is representative of the canon-within-the-canon model we will be exploring in this section. Like the historical-critical model above, this model often shares the critical methodologies that arose during the Enlightenment and views the New Testament collection as a largely human construct.[6] The difference, however, is in how each model responds to the human nature of the canon. While the historical-critical model is focused on the *reception* of these books and the natural causes for their selection by the early Christian community (Marcion, political power play, etc.), the canon-within-the-canon model is intent on exploring the *origins* of these books and finding the "core" material that could be considered genuine.[7]

---

[1]The community-determined models above also involve historical investigation in one sense as they explore the way the Christian community received these books. However, the historically determined models are different in that the historical investigations typically focus on the *books themselves* and their origins.

[2]Kurt Aland, *The Problem of the New Testament Canon* (London: Mowbray, 1962), 24. Aland's essay was in response to Käsemann's famous article, E. Käsemann, "Begründet der neutestamentliche Kanon die Einheit der Kirche?," *EvT* 11 (1951): 13–21.

[3]Aland, *The Problem of the New Testament Canon*, 29.

[4]Ibid., 33.

[5]Ibid., 31.

[6]There are notable exceptions to this trend, as will be shown below with Luther's approach to the canon.

[7]Of course, there is substantial overlap between these two models, and many scholars could rightly be placed in both of them. After all, one could view the canon as merely the books picked by the theological winners in the early church and *also* want to investigate the books themselves to discover the "core" truths they might contain. In addition, there is a good deal of overlap with other community-determined models. For example, Marxsen argues that the true canon is the earliest layer of Jesus material ("canon within the canon"), but also that the true canon is that which is existentially satisfying for the reader (existential/neoorthodox). See

Typically, this quest for the inner canon of the New Testament is pursued through the standard higher-critical investigations that attempt to discover the "historical" Jesus or the "real" message of Christ.[8] Semler advocated that we accept as canonical whatever contributes to "moral improvement" since that, he argued, was the main concern of the historical Jesus—thus setting the stage for later Ritschlian liberalism.[9] Marxsen suggests that the real canon is the earliest apostolic tradition we can uncover within the New Testament.[10] Similarly, Schubert Ogden argues that the true canon of the New Testament "must now be located in what form critics generally speak of as the earliest layer of the Synoptic tradition";[11] this will tell us about the real Jesus. In addition, there are myriads of other "lives of Jesus" that have been written and have attempted to strip away the accretions in the New Testament texts, hoping to recover the genuine christological focus and thereby find the inner canon.[12]

However, as these historical investigations seek to peel back the layers and find the real Jesus, inevitably philosophical and theological concerns get mixed in. Finding the real Jesus is not as simple as employing the techniques of, say, form or redaction criticism, but often involves the historian's own beliefs about what Jesus *should* be like or what message he *should* have preached. Thus, for feminist scholars, the only portions of the Bible that can be considered the real canon are often those that promote an egalitarian agenda.[13] Or for liberation theologians, the core canon would include only those teachings consistent with relieving the suffering of the oppressed.[14] A more orthodox version of this tendency

---

W. Marxsen, *Introduction to the New Testament: An Approach to Its Problems* (Philadelphia: Westminster, 1968), 282–83.

[8]For an overview of the various criteria used for canon-within-the-canon models, see W. Schrage, "Die Frage nach der Mitte und dem Kanon im Kanon des Neuen Testaments in der neueren Diskussion," in *Rechtfertigung: Festschrift für Ernst Käsemann zum 70*, ed. J. Friedrich, W. Pöhlmann, and P. Stuhlmacher (Tübingen: Mohr Siebeck, 1976), 415–42.

[9]See a helpful discussion on Semler's approach to canon in W. G. Kümmel, *The New Testament: The History of the Investigation of Its Problems* (Nashville: Abingdon, 1972), 62–69.

[10]W. Marxsen, *The New Testament as the Church's Book* (Philadelphia: Fortress, 1972), 28–29.

[11]S. Ogden, "The Authority of Scripture for Theology," *Int* 30 (1976): 258.

[12]Examples of such "lives of Jesus" (from Schleiermacher to Baur to Harnack) are too many to mention. For more discussion, see Robert Gnuse, *The Authority of the Bible: Theories of Inspiration, Revelation, and the Canon of Scripture* (Mawhaw, NJ: Paulist, 1985), 89.

[13]For an overview of a feminist approach, see Elisabeth Schüssler Fiorenza, *Bread Not Stone: The Challenge of Feminist Biblical Interpretation* (Boston: Beacon, 1995); and Fiorenza, *In Memory of Her: A Feminist Theological Reconstruction of Christian Origins* (New York: Crossroad, 1983). Fiorenza asserts, "Biblical revelation and truth are given *only in those texts* . . . that transcend critically their patriarchal frameworks" (*In Memory of Her*, 30, emphasis mine).

[14]A helpful overview of liberation theology can be found in Christopher Rowland, ed., *The Cambridge Companion to Liberation Theology* (Cambridge: Cambridge University Press, 2007).

is found in a number of scholars (many Lutheran) who view the gospel message itself as the determining factor for what constitutes the true canon.[15] Luther famously argued that the canon should be determined by "was Christum treibt" (whatever preaches Christ), and he therefore was highly critical of the books of James, Hebrews, and Revelation.[16] Werner Kümmel, agreeing with Luther, advocated that we should accept whatever books engender faith in Christ.[17] Theodore Zahn, in a similar manner, argues that we should receive those New Testament books which faithfully preach the gospel.[18] Likewise, Ernst Käsemann, while arguing for vast diversity and contradiction within the New Testament,[19] teaches that the gospel, particularly "justification" in Christ, is the determining factor for canon.[20] James Dunn suggests that the center of the canon—

---

[15]Ogden, "Authority," 242–61, is an example of how the historical and theological issues get mixed together. On the one hand, he argues that the earliest layer of Jesus tradition is the real canon, and, on the other hand, he maintains that the real canon is determined by the gospel message of the "Jesus-kerygma" (258).

[16]Although Luther was critical of these books in his earlier years (calling James an "epistle of straw"), his criticisms seemed to lessen later in his life. While Luther was vastly more orthodox than most others taking the historical-critical approach to canon (e.g., Semler, Barr), he nevertheless laid the groundwork for many later critical scholars who would appeal to his methodology for their approach to canon. At the same time, it must be stated that Luther's criticism of James (and other books) is not grounds for suggesting that he had a low view of inspiration, as some critical scholars have suggested; e.g., Willem Jan Kooiman, *Luther and the Bible* (Philadelphia: Muhlenberg, 1961). Rather, we must remember to distinguish between the nature of the canon and the extent of the canon; the question for Luther was not whether canonical books were inspired (he believed they were), but which books belonged in the canon in the first place. For a more thorough discussion, see John Warwick Montgomery, "Lessons from Luther on the Inerrancy of Holy Writ," in *God's Inerrant Word*, ed. John Warwick Montgomery (Minneapolis: Bethany, 1974), 63–94; and Francis Pieper, *Christian Dogmatics*, 4 vols. (St. Louis: Concordia, 1950–1957), 1:276–98.

[17]W. G. Kümmel, "Notwendigkeit und Grenze des neutestamentlichen Kanons," *ZTK* 47 (1960): 277–313; and Kümmel, *The New Testament*, 503–10.

[18]Theodore Zahn, *Die bleibende Bedeutung des neutestamentlichen Kanons für die Kirche* (Leipzig: Deichert, 1890); see fuller discussion of Zahn in Herman N. Ridderbos, *Redemptive History and the New Testament Scripture* (Phillipsburg, NJ: P&R, 1988), 4–5.

[19]Käsemann, "Begründet der neutestamentliche Kanon die Einheit der Kirche?," 13–21; English translation, "The Canon of the New Testament and the Unity of the Church," in *Essays on New Testament Themes* (London: SCM, 1964), 95–107; Ernst Käsemann, "The Problem of a New Testament Theology," *NTS* 19 (1973): 235–45.

[20]Ernst Käsemann, "Kritische Analyse," in *Das Neue Testament als Canon*, ed. Ernst Käsemann (Göttingen: Vandenhoeck & Ruprecht, 1970), 368–69. Käsemann is a good example of someone difficult to categorize. Given his similarities to Bultmann and other dialectical theologians, one could argue that he should be in the existential camp (see above). However, he has been placed here for two reasons: (1) Käsemann was much more concerned than Bultmann to make sure that faith in Jesus had *some* connection to real history, thus separating himself from his mentor (see Käsemann, "The Problem of the Historical Jesus," in *Essays on New Testament Themes*, 15–47); (2) others who have analyzed patterns in canonical studies have placed Käsemann in the "canon within a canon" camp: e.g., Lee Martin McDonald and James A. Sanders, eds., *The Canon Debate* (Peabody, MA: Hendrickson, 2002), 3; Joseph T. Lienhard, *The Bible, the Church, and Authority* (Collegeville, MN: Liturgical Press, 1995), 91; and Geoffrey Wainwright, "The New Testament as Canon," *SJT* 28 (1975): 564.

the only portion with real authority—is where the various books of the New Testament agree: "The unifying strand [is] Jesus himself" and "the significance of his death and resurrection."[21]

The canon-within-the-canon model also brings a new dimension to the definition of the term *canon*. When the historical development of the canon is being discussed, the term is used by this model in the standard exclusive and functional senses (as discussed above). But when discussion shifts to the inner core of the New Testament, the term *canon* becomes virtually synonymous with *true* or *real*.[22] In this sense, the term does not involve the *reception* of these books at all (as both the exclusive and functional definitions do), but is simply a way of speaking of the authentic portions of these books.

B. Evaluation

Compared with the community-determined models examined above, the positive of the canon-within-the-canon model is that it returns historical matters to their proper place. It *does* matter whether the books of the New Testament contain genuine teachings and activities of Jesus, and thus our historical investigations into these books play a role in their canonical status. However, a number of concerns remain that must be noted here.

The fundamental problem with the canon-within-the-canon approach is that it subjects the Scripture to a standard outside itself, namely, whatever criteria scholars set up to evaluate its truthfulness. As noted in the introduction, historical investigations are not neutral affairs but are guided by a variety of theological commitments. Thus, to allow the canon to be "edited" according to what seems reasonable or credible to us will leave us with nothing but a human book. The canon cannot function as a norm over the church if the church gets to decide which portions of the canon it will accept and which it will reject. H. J. de Jonge describes the problem with the canon-within-the-canon approach: "Individual Christians are not obliged to accept the entire New Testament as canonical; they are free to look in the New Testament

---

[21]James D. G. Dunn, *Unity and Diversity in the New Testament: An Inquiry into the Character of Early Christianity* (London: SCM, 1990), 376. Although Dunn argues that the center of the New Testament is Jesus, unfortunately, he leaves the details of this center rather vague. Does the center include a theological description of who Jesus is, what he has done, and what that means for Christians? Apparently, once a person tries to fill in the details, he quickly goes beyond the agreed-upon center and therefore enters areas that are nonnormative and nonbinding. For a more updated look at Dunn's thesis, see James D. G. Dunn, "Has the Canon a Continuing Function?," in McDonald and Sanders, *The Canon Debate*, 558–79.

[22]See discussion in B. M. Metzger, *The Canon of the New Testament: Its Origin, Development, and Significance* (Oxford: Clarendon, 1987), 275–82.

for what they themselves regard as authoritative and, in a way, to select their own canon."[23] Given the grand variety of external criteria used to evaluate the New Testament (e.g., feminism, liberation theology, what preaches Christ), each person's private canon will be entirely subjective and ever changing. Indeed, Barr even argues that all attempts to find a "center" to the canon should be "on a tentative, temporary, and perhaps even personal basis only."[24] If so, then what keeps people from having their own private Bibles? And what keeps those Bibles from always being in flux? This model flips the entire concept of canon on its head. In effect, humans become their own "canon"—they are the standard for truth.

In addition, the idea that the tools of modern biblical criticism—form criticism, source criticism, and redaction criticism—can reliably peel back the layers of Scripture and uncover the real historical Jesus, and thus the center of the canon, has been vigorously challenged over the years. Ever since Schweitzer's critical review of the Jesus Quest, it is clear that higher-critical methodologies provide few certain historical results, but are often contradictory and subjective, frequently producing a Jesus made in the image of those conducting the investigation.[25] Childs offers an extended critique of the effectiveness of these modern historical-critical methodologies (although he does not abandon them entirely),[26] as does Stanley Porter,[27] and the effectiveness of the Jesus Quest is critiqued by N. T. Wright, I. Howard Marshall, L. T. Johnson, Craig Evans, and others.[28] Moreover, Alvin Plantinga offers a more philosophical critique of modern biblical criticism, exposing how it rests on anti-Christian foundations.[29] Ironically, even J. D. Crossan, a founding member of the Jesus Seminar, laments the wild diversity of conclusions of the Jesus Quest: "[This] stunning diversity is an academic embarrassment. It is impos-

[23]H. J. de Jonge, "The New Testament Canon," in *The Biblical Canons*, ed. J.-M. Auwers and H. J. de Jonge (Leuven: Leuven University Press, 2003), 309.

[24]J. Barr, *The Bible in the Modern World* (New York: Harper & Row, 1973), 161.

[25]Albert Schweitzer, *The Quest of the Historical Jesus* (New York: Macmillan, 1968); and Martin Kähler, *The So-called Historical Jesus and the Historic, Biblical Christ* (Philadelphia: Fortress, 1964).

[26]B. S. Childs, *The New Testament as Canon: An Introduction* (London: SCM, 1984), 34–47.

[27]Stanley E. Porter, *The Criteria for Authenticity in Historical-Jesus Research* (Sheffield: Sheffield Academic, 2000).

[28]N. T. Wright, *Jesus and the Victory of God* (Minneapolis: Fortress, 1996); I. Howard Marshall, *I Believe in the Historical Jesus* (Grand Rapids: Eerdmans, 1977); L. T. Johnson, *The Real Jesus: The Misguided Quest for the Historical Jesus and the Truth of the Traditional Gospels* (San Francisco: HarperCollins, 1996); and Craig A. Evans, *Fabricating Jesus: How Modern Scholars Distort the Gospels* (Downers Grove, IL: InterVarsity, 2008).

[29]Alvin Plantinga, *Warranted Christian Belief* (New York: Oxford University Press, 2000), 374–421.

sible to avoid the suspicion that historical Jesus research is a very safe place to do theology and call it history, to do autobiography and call it biography."[30] Thus, to rest the authentication of the New Testament canon solely upon the conclusions of the historical-critical method is to rest it upon a tendentious foundation indeed.[31]

Even the criterion of the gospel message, which sounds more biblical, does not really provide a coherent foundation for establishing an authoritative canon. After all, how does Luther establish the fact that "what preaches Christ" should guide our decisions about what should be included in the canon? And by what standard does he determine if something "preaches Christ"? If he claims that Scripture provides the "what preaches Christ" standard, then that means that Luther has *already* established the extent of canonicity so that he knows which books provided this standard. But if he already knows which books are canonical and which are not, then why does he need to establish a criterion for canonicity in the first place? In reality, the "what preaches Christ" principle does not come from Scripture at all, but rather it comes from *his* Scripture—the books he already deems to be authentic in the first place (on some other grounds). But the question is, what are these other grounds? On what standard does he receive the books that give him the "what preaches Christ" principle? That is the key question that is never answered. It is not entirely cogent to choose certain books to be canonical (on some unnamed criterion), use those books to establish the new criterion of "what preaches Christ," and then turn around and use that criterion to decide which books are canonical.

In the end, the canon-within-the-canon model serves not to establish the authoritative boundaries of the canon, but to remove them and replace them with the boundaries determined by the conclusions of critical historical investigation. Once one allows external criteria (whether the gospel message or the conclusions of historical criticism) to determine the extent of the canon, then the biblical canon, at least in any authoritative sense, ceases to exist.

II. Criteria-of-Canonicity Model

A. *Description*

For many of those in the evangelical community, the prior models do not offer a viable basis for the authority of the canon. The community-

---

[30]J. D. Crossan, *The Historical Jesus: The Life of a Mediterranean Jewish Peasant* (San Francisco: HarperCollins, 1991), xxviii.

[31]As we shall see below, this does not mean that historical investigation cannot lead to knowledge. Rather, we are arguing against a particular version of historical investigation that is committed to modern critical methodologies and Enlightenment assumptions.

determined models above prove to be either too subjective (existential/ neoorthodox) or too focused on the church's reception or approval (Roman Catholic and canonical criticism). And the canon-within-a-canon model is no option because it simply results in a truncated, man-made New Testament. How then can it be shown that these (and only these) twenty-seven books belong in the New Testament? A number of evangelicals have sought an answer in the "criteria of canonicity."[32] These criteria—apostolicity, orthodoxy, usage, etc.—are thought to be the characteristics that define a canonical book.[33] Thus, the criteria-of-canonicity model argues that the authority of the canon can be established by doing a rigorous *historical investigation* of the New Testament books and showing how they meet these criteria. Ironically, then, this model shares much in common with the canon-within-a-canon model above. Although these two models reach radically different conclusions—one has a stripped down canon and the other a complete twenty-seven-book canon—they use the same overall methodology, namely, an appeal to the historical origins of these books. Paul Helm refers to this overall approach as "externalism," which is committed to the idea that "external data are required to validate the Scriptures as the Word of God."[34]

---

[32]Of course, evangelicals are not the only ones who discuss the criteria of canonicity. Virtually every academic treatment of canon addresses these criteria; e.g., H. Y. Gamble, *The New Testament Canon: Its Making and Meaning* (Philadelphia: Fortress, 1985), 67–72. In most critical treatments of canon, however, the criteria are mentioned only as the methods used by the early church and not necessarily the way the canon can (or should) be authenticated today; e.g., K.-H. Ohlig, *Die theologische Begründung des neutestamentlichen Kanons in der alten Kirche* (Düsseldorf: Patmos, 1972). It is primarily evangelicals who move beyond simply *observing* the early church's use of the criteria to suggesting that these are the *norms* by which a book's canonicity ought to be decided.

[33]Numerous criteria have been suggested over the years, and scholars have not always had the same list. F. F. Bruce, *The Canon of Scripture* (Downers Grove, IL: InterVarsity, 1988), 255–69, includes apostolicity, antiquity, orthodoxy, and usage by the early church. Similarly, Metzger argues for three criteria: the rule of faith, apostolicity, and usage (*The Canon of the New Testament*, 251–54). Geisler also suggests multiple criteria to determine canonicity: if it is authoritative (claims to be from God), prophetic (written by an apostle/prophet), authentic (orthodox and without error), dynamic (transformative for the reader), and accepted (received by the early church); see Norman L. Geisler and William E. Nix, *From God to Us: How We Got Our Bible* (Chicago: Moody Press, 1974), 67–71. A number of other popular evangelical books follow Geisler's lead: e.g., Paul Little, *Know What and Why You Believe* (Minneapolis: World Wide Publications, 1980), 193–94; Josh McDowell, *Evidence That Demands a Verdict*, vol. 1 (San Bernardino: Here's Life, 1991), 29–38; R. C. Sproul, *Now That's A Good Question!* (Wheaton, IL: Tyndale, 1996), 78–82.

[34]Paul Helm, "Faith, Evidence, and the Scriptures," in *Scripture and Truth*, ed. D. A. Carson and John D. Woodbridge (Grand Rapids: Zondervan, 1983), 303–20. "Externalism" is quite similar to the standard evidentialist approach to defending the authority of the Scriptures. For a description of evidentialism, see Kenneth D. Boa and Robert W. Bowman Jr., *Faith Has Its Reasons: An Integrative Approach to Defending Christianity* (Colorado Springs: NavPress,

A number of evangelical scholars expressly state that this historical methodology for establishing the authority of the canon is the same as for any other ancient book. Warfield is quite direct when he declares, "It is a most assured result of *biblical criticism* that every one of the twenty-seven books which now constitute our New Testament is assuredly genuine and authentic."[35] John Warwick Montgomery is also confident that the New Testament's authenticity can be demonstrated "on the basis of the accepted canons of historical method"[36] or, as he puts it elsewhere, "the tests of reliability employed in general historiography."[37] Gary Habermas argues that we can reach "sturdy conclusions" about the truth of Christianity, and therefore the truth of the canonical books, if we use the methodology contained within "the canons of historical research."[38]

Owing to the variety of criteria of canonicity that have been suggested over the years, this model naturally overlaps, at points, with other models that we have already discussed. For example, inasmuch as one focuses on the usage and/or reception of these books as a criterion of canonicity, then the model can begin to look like one of the community-determined models above. Out of all of these suggested criteria, however, the apostolicity of a book has emerged as the primary or dominant one. C. Stephen Evans argues that all the other criteria of canonicity either involve or imply apostolicity.[39] Thus, he maintains, "Apostolic authority is not simply one criterion among many, as many historical treatments of the formation of the canon imply, but is essentially linked to the notion of canon as the central criterion."[40] A. A. Hodge held this view: "We determine what books have a place in this Canon or divine rule by an examination of the evidences that show that each of them, severally, was written by the

---

2001), 159–248; and G. Habermas, "Evidential Apologetics," in *Five Views on Apologetics*, ed. S. B. Cowan (Grand Rapids: Zondervan, 2000), 92–121. The term *externalism* used by Helm should not be confused with externalism as an epistemological model that says true belief becomes knowledge when it is formed on proper grounds (Alston) or under the right epistemic circumstances (Plantinga). The latter stands in contrast to internalism, which says that a person must not only have adequate grounds but also know what they are (and that they are adequate). See discussions of epistemological externalism and internalism in C. Stephen Evans, *The Historical Christ and the Jesus of Faith: The Incarnational Narrative as History* (New York: Oxford University Press, 1996), 218–30; and Alvin Plantinga, *Warrant: The Current Debate* (Oxford: Oxford University Press, 1993), 3–29.

[35]B. B. Warfield, *The Inspiration and Authority of the Bible* (Philadelphia: Presbyterian and Reformed, 1948), 429, emphasis mine.

[36]John Warwick Montgomery, *History and Christianity* (Downers Grove, IL: InterVarsity, 1965), 43.

[37]Ibid., 26.

[38]Habermas, "Evidential Apologetics," 95.

[39]C. Stephen Evans, "Canonicity, Apostolicity, and Biblical Authority: Some Kierkegaardian Reflections," in *Canon and Biblical Interpretation*, ed. Craig Bartholomew et al. (Carlisle: Paternoster, 2006), 150.

[40]Ibid.

inspired prophet or apostle whose name it bears."[41] Warfield's seminal work also argued that apostolicity is the central criterion for canonicity, and a book should be accepted only if it bears "authenticating proof of its apostolicity."[42] R. Laird Harris follows in Warfield's footsteps and also insists that the apostolic authorship (or authorship by an apostolic companion) was the fundamental test for canonicity employed by the early church.[43]

As for the definition of the term *canon* in the criteria-of-canonicity model, there are a variety of different uses, depending on the author and the particular aspect of canon under discussion. However, the functional definition (canon as the books used as scriptural authority) and the onto-logical definition (canon as the books given by God) are quite common, reflecting the evangelical belief that these books have a divine origin. For example, Harris uses the functional definition when he declares that in the second century the Gospels and Pauline Epistles were "fully accepted as canonical."[44] Warfield employs the ontological definition when he says, "The Canon of the New Testament was completed when the last authoritative book was given to any church by the apostles, and that was when John wrote the apocalypse, about A.D. 98."[45]

B. Evaluation

As with the canon-within-the-canon model above, the criteria-of-canonicity model rightly is concerned with the historical origins of the canonical books and whether they really do relay authentic information about the historical Jesus. Indeed, one of the strengths of this approach is the careful collection and presentation of important historical evidence that bolsters these books' historical credibility. This model has also accurately identified apostolicity as a key component of canonicity—a fact that has been largely overlooked in many of the other models. There is no doubt that the redemptive-historical role of the apostles is foundational to our

---

[41]A. A. Hodge, *A Commentary on the Confession of Faith* (Philadelphia: Presbyterian Board of Publication, 1869), 51–52.

[42]B. B. Warfield, "The Formation of the Canon of the New Testament," in Warfield, *The Inspiration and Authority of the Bible*, 415. Warfield nuances what he means by the term *apostolic*. It includes not only books written directly by apostles, but also books that the apostles approved of and commended to the church as authoritative. A good example of his defense of apostolicity can be seen in Warfield, "The Canonicity of 2 Peter," in *Selected Shorter Writings of Benjamin B. Warfield*, ed. John E. Meeter, vol. 2 (Nutley, NJ: Presbyterian and Reformed, 1973), 49–79.

[43]R. Laird Harris, *Inspiration and Canonicity of the Bible* (Grand Rapids: Zondervan, 1978), 219–35.

[44]Ibid., 202.

[45]Warfield, "The Formation of the Canon," 415.

understanding of canon (more on this in chap. 5). A final positive of this model would be the degree to which the divine origins of the canon are taken seriously and given their due authority as Scripture (something that is not true of every canonical model). Even in the midst of these strengths, however, there are some residual areas of concern that need to be addressed.

1. "Neutral" Historical Investigations

Of primary concern is the degree to which this model insists that the canon must be authenticated solely through "the assured result(s) of biblical criticism"[46] or the "accepted canons of historical method."[47] No doubt such an approach is driven by the belief that all historical investigations should be conducted according to neutral standards that are accessible (and agreeable) to the Christian and non-Christian alike.[48] On the surface, this seems eminently reasonable. If scholars have various (and contradictory) worldviews, then historical investigations ought to be done in a fashion that is worldview-neutral. While reasonable, however, it also runs the danger of being overly simplistic. Are scholars really able to check their worldviews at the door so easily? Do these "accepted canons" of research really involve no worldview at all? Do they not require *some* ontological assumptions? It seems that the criteria-of-canonicity model does not fully recognize that historical methodologies are not (and cannot be) really

---

[46]Ibid., 429, emphasis mine.

[47]Montgomery, *History and Christianity*, 43.

[48]We see this trend in some evidentialist apologists; e.g., Dennis McCallum, *Christianity: The Faith That Makes Sense* (Wheaton, IL: Tyndale, 1992), argues that when we are doing our historical investigations, we ought to take a "neutral posture" (11). Boa defines evidentialism as that which supports "content-neutral methods" and "seeks to employ methods that are in principle acceptable to non-Christians" (Boa and Bowman, *Faith Has Its Reasons*, 182). Harold A. Netland, "Apologetics, Worldviews, and the Problem of Neutral Criteria," in *The Gospel and Contemporary Perspectives*, ed. Douglas Moo (Grand Rapids: Kregel, 1997), 138–52, argues that there are in fact neutral criteria to which apologists should appeal when proving the authority of the Bible. Netland argues that things like the laws of logic (in particular, the law of noncontradiction), can function "neutrally" as a criterion of truth. He even argues that the laws of logic are "independent" of any given worldview, including the Christian worldview (147–48). If this were the case, however, would the laws of logic exist even if God did not? Presumably, Netland would have to say yes (after all, the laws of logic presuppose no particular worldview). But this raises a couple of problems: (1) On what basis do immaterial, transcendent, and absolute laws of thought (which the laws of logic are) exist within an atheistic world? There is nothing within an atheistic system that would suggest anything like the existence of immaterial transcendent laws. In fact an atheistic universe—a universe that is entirely material and where random chance reigns—would make us expect the exact opposite. (2) To imply that the laws of logic could exist without God is to imply that the laws of logic are, in some way, more basic to the world than God is. According to Netland, one has to have the laws of logic to have rationality, but apparently one does not need God to have rationality (because a person can have logic in a world *without* God). But this does not seem to do justice to the biblical teaching on God as the foundation for correct thinking (Prov. 1:7; Matt. 22:37; 1 Cor. 1:20; 2 Cor. 10:5; Col. 2:3).

neutral; they are founded upon, and presuppose, some philosophical-religious system. As noted above, Plantinga, Evans, Alston, and others have critiqued modern historical methodologies and have demonstrated that they are largely founded upon non-Christian and Enlightenment assumptions.[49]

The reason there is no religiously neutral approach to historical study is that there is no religiously neutral approach to anything. Roy Clouser demonstrates that the Bible's own epistemological position is that "there is no knowledge or truth that is neutral with respect to God."[50] He appeals to a number of scriptural passages that show that how individuals think about God affects their ability to have knowledge. In Luke 11:52 Jesus says that when you take away the law of God, you "have taken away the key to knowledge." And there is no reason to think only *religious* knowledge is intended. Likewise, in 1 Corinthians 1:5 Paul reminds his readers that "in every way you were enriched in him in all speech and all knowledge." Other texts such as Colossians 2:3 affirm the same principle: "[In Christ] are hidden all the treasures of wisdom and knowledge." And Psalm 36:9 declares, "In [God's] light do we see light," showing that knowledge of God is the key to acquiring other kinds of knowledge. Clouser concludes, "The cumulative effect of these texts is to teach that no sort of knowledge is religiously neutral."[51]

---

[49]Plantinga, *Warranted Christian Belief*, 374–421; Evans, *The Historical Christ and the Jesus of Faith*, 170–202; William P. Alston, "Historical Criticism of the Synoptic Gospels," in *"Behind" the Text: History and Biblical Interpretation*, ed. Craig Bartholomew (Grand Rapids: Zondervan, 2003), 151–80. Ernst Troeltsch highlighted the three main principles of Enlightenment historiography as (1) the principle of methodological doubt, (2) the principle of analogy, and (3) the principle of correlation (Ernst Troeltsch, "Historical and Dogmatic Method in Theology," in *Religion in History* [Minneapolis: Fortress, 1991], 11–32). See helpful discussion and critique in Evans, *The Historical Christ and the Jesus of Faith*, 27–34, 184–202; and R. B. Strimple, *The Modern Search for the Real Jesus* (Phillipsburg, NJ: P&R, 1995), 6–11. In the modern era, scholars have also devised "criteria" for determining authentic historical events (and sayings) within the life of Jesus. Such criteria include, (1) the criterion of independent attestation, (2) the criterion of dissimilarity, and (3) the criterion of contextual credibility; cf. Bart D. Ehrman, *Jesus: Apocalyptic Prophet of the New Millennium* (New York: Oxford University Press, 1999), 85–101. These criteria have been roundly critiqued by evangelical scholars; e.g., Darrell L. Bock, "The Words of Jesus in the Gospels: Live, Jive, or Memorex?," in *Jesus Under Fire*, ed. Michael J. Wilkins and J. P. Moreland (Grand Rapids: Zondervan, 1995), 74–99. For further discussion of these principles see Robert L. Webb, "The Historical Enterprise and Historical Jesus Research," in *Key Events in the Life of the Historical Jesus*, ed. Darrell L. Bock and Robert L. Webb (Tübingen: Mohr Siebeck, 2009), 9–93.

[50]Roy A. Clouser, *The Myth of Religious Neutrality: An Essay on the Hidden Role of Religious Belief in Theories* (Notre Dame: University of Notre Dame Press, 2005), 94. Clouser demonstrates that there are clear religious presuppositions in every area of thought, including mathematics, psychology, physics, politics, and more. For further discussions of a Christian epistemology along the lines of Clouser, see J. M. Frame, *The Doctrine of the Knowledge of God* (Phillipsburg, NJ: P&R, 1987).

[51]Clouser, *The Myth of Religious Neutrality*, 95.

The lack of neutrality among scholars raises questions about the effectiveness of purportedly neutral historical arguments to authenticate the canon. Even though many scholars (myself included) find the historical evidence for the apostolicity of the New Testament books to be quite persuasive, it is clear that many other scholars do not. Arguments that Christians find compelling often prove entirely unconvincing to the skeptic. Indeed, much of modern critical scholarship has rejected the apostolicity of many of the New Testament books and is quite confident that they are pseudonymous forgeries (more on this below). This has led Evans (and others) to observe rightly that such evidentialist-style arguments, ironically, have a substantial degree of *subjectivity* involved in them.[52] Despite the claim that these types of arguments are more objective, and therefore presumably more acceptable, that has not proved to be the case. Their effectiveness is always dependent upon the worldview of the one evaluating the evidence.

Of course, many evangelicals in the criteria-of-canonicity model have recognized the bias in modern historical methodologies and rightly sought to challenge it. But often the challenge itself is still wedded to the Enlightenment ideal of neutral, objective history. Habermas, recognizing that bias can easily seep into these "canons of historical research," offers the rather simple solution that "we just must be careful not to read biases into the [historical] accounts."[53] Likewise, Warfield argues that we need to make sure our historical research is done "apart from presuppositions" and that it is just "an unprejudiced collection and examination of the facts."[54] But these responses not only imply that a neutral method of historical research really exists, which we can strive to meet (or at least come close to); they also imply that Christian scholars *ought* to think neutrally when they engage in historical research. In other words, the solution to the problem of bias is simply to push people further toward neutral thinking. Such a position stands in tension with the above scriptural passages, which suggest that the pursuit of neutrality is not a biblical virtue.

But this quest for a neutral historical methodology leads to greater concerns. To authenticate the canon on the basis of a supposedly independent,

---

[52]Evans, *The Historical Christ and the Jesus of Faith*, 241–43.
[53]Habermas, "Evidential Apologetics," 95. Likewise, Montgomery also seems to rightly recognize "prejudice" within modern methodologies. But, again, the issue is not simply whether one acknowledges it, but how the problem is to be solved. Montgomery's solution, like Habermas's, is simply to eliminate as much prejudice as possible within modern historical methodologies (*History and Christianity*, 89). See also, John Warwick Montgomery, *The Shape of the Past: A Christian Response to Secular Philosophies of History* (Minneapolis: Bethany, 1975), 73–74, 265.
[54]Warfield, *Inspiration and Authority of the Bible*, 429.

neutral standard ultimately subjects the canon to an authority outside itself. It allows autonomous human assessment of historical evidence to become an external authority over God's Word. How can the Scriptures be the ultimate standard of truth if their reception is dependent upon some *other* (presumably more certain) standard? For this reason, the challenge for the criteria-of-canonicity model is not all that different from the challenge faced by some of the community-determined models or even the canon-within-the-canon model. All of these, in the end, subject the canon's authority to some standard outside itself—whether the Roman Catholic Church or autonomous historical investigations or something else. Ironically, the Catholic model is in a slightly better position because at least it purports to rest the canon on divine revelation (through the infallible pope and church), whereas the criteria-of-canonicity model rests the canon on "neutral" human assessments of historical evidence.

Once we hitch our canonical wagon to the supposedly neutral "assured result(s) of biblical criticism," then we are in effect creating a canon that is always in flux. After all, modern biblical criticism proves to be a fickle partner. What happens when "the assured results of biblical criticism" shift or change? Does the canon change along with them? Although modern scholars may consider the book of Galatians to be written by Paul, what would happen if the consensus of biblical scholarship changed? Do we remove the book of Galatians from the canon?[55] Willi Marxsen, although not from the evangelical camp, understands the implications of connecting canonicity solely with modern historical investigations. While acknowledging (along with many evangelicals) that "apostolicity" should be the central criterion of canonicity, he contends:

> The ancient church wanted to canonize what was apostolic, but in the process error slipped in. If we intend to remain obedient to the ancient church . . . we have to accept its criteria but not its conclusions, since in several places they have turned out to be incorrect. For this reason the limits of the canon as set by the ancient church remain in question.[56]

---

[55]William Lane Craig, "Classical Apologetics," in Cowan, *Five Views on Apologetics*, 35–38, would note here that new historical evidence would *not* change his beliefs about things like the canon because the testimony of the Holy Spirit makes him sure that such beliefs are correct regardless of changes in the evidence. I would agree with Craig's position here. However, if Craig is committed to believing in the canon, regardless of new historical evidence, then he is not engaging in his historical research neutrally but proceeding on the basis of the truth of Christian theism. Such an approach, I would argue, is perfectly biblical, but its lack of neutrality simply needs to be acknowledged.

[56]Marxsen, *The New Testament as the Church's Book*, 27.

Marxsen is only being consistent here. If autonomous historical investigations alone determine canonicity, then what if these investigations claim the early church's decisions were mistaken? Marxsen states, "If better methods for historical study are available to us today . . . then we come face-to-face with the demand—not merely the permission—to apply them once again to determine what is canonical."[57] In other words, the canon can change as each generation's scholars reconsider the evidence for themselves.

Of course, these concerns about the criteria-of-canonicity model do not mean that the historical evidence for the apostolicity of these books is somehow lacking or inadequate. On the contrary, the evidential case put forth by the criteria-of-canonicity model is strong and ought to be used in our defense of the canon. Rather, the issue is simply that this historical evidence is not self-interpreting. It cannot stand alone. It authenticates the twenty-seven-book canon only when it is understood correctly—that is, when it is given a *Christian* interpretation. Thus, we shall argue below that historical evidence for the apostolicity of the New Testament books is an effective means of authenticating canon only when it is viewed as a means provided by the Scriptures and governed by the Scriptures, along with the internal testimony of the Holy Spirit.

2. The Criteria of Canonicity

In addition to this model's dependence on modern (and purportedly neutral) biblical criticism, there are also other concerns. In particular, there are problems with the very concept of "criteria of canonicity"—a concept that has been roundly critiqued in recent years and rightly so.[58] This does not mean that the criteria of canonicity are not founded on some important truths (e.g., apostolicity *was* important to early Christians), but it does mean that the manner in which these criteria are often understood and used needs some adjustment. One significant area of misunderstanding is the role played by the criteria of canonicity in the early church. The term *criteria* can give the impression that the early church consciously developed some set of standards for what constituted a canonical book and then expressly went out to find books that met those criteria—almost like a search committee would determine the profile of the ideal candidate

---

[57]Ibid., 25.
[58]E.g., Morwenna Ludlow, "'Criteria of Canonicity' and the Early Church," in *The Unity of Scripture and the Diversity of Canon*, ed. John Barton and Michael Wolter (Berlin: de Gruyter, 2003), 69–93; L. M. McDonald, "Identifying Scripture and Canon in the Early Church: The Criteria Question," in McDonald and Sanders, *The Canon Debate*, 416–39; and R. Gaffin, "The New Testament as Canon," in *Inerrancy and Hermeneutic* (Grand Rapids: Baker, 1988), 165–83.

prior to the formal interview process.[59] However, in the early stages of the development of the New Testament, the canonical process was not so much about the early church *choosing* books on the basis of some formal criteria as it was a matter of early Christians *receiving* what had been handed down to them from the very start. Any express discussions of "criteria" within the early church were, more often than not, after-the-fact justifications for the books that had long been recognized as canonical.[60] It was the church's attempt to explain what it already had, rather than the process of deciding what to have. This is not to suggest that early Christians were mistaken about why these books mattered (as if they attributed books to apostles in an *ad hoc* manner). Rather, it simply needs to be pointed out that such "criteria" were not always formally employed prior to these books being received as authoritative. In short, the very concept of "criteria of canonicity" unduly inflates the church's active role in the development of the canon.[61]

In addition, there are concerns about the adequacy of some of these criteria for authenticating canonical books. While orthodoxy played a key role within the development of the canon (as we shall discuss more extensively in chap. 4), it is hardly sufficient, in and of itself, to identify canonical books. Obviously, there were many books within early Christianity that were deemed to be orthodox but not canonical (e.g., the *Shepherd of Hermas, 1 Clement*). It is a necessary but not sufficient characteristic of canonical books. Thus, the concept of orthodoxy cannot stand alone; it needs to find its significance within a larger framework for how to think of canon. Likewise, mere usage of a book was not a sufficient indicator of canonicity.[62] Many noncanonical books were quite popular (again, the *Shepherd of Hermas*), and many canonical books received little attention (e.g., 2 and 3 John). The antiquity or date of a book also was not definitive. Books like *1 Clement* appear to be as old as some canonical books (e.g., Revelation), but were not regarded as canonical. The only so-called criterion of canonicity that seems to be adequate to identify a canonical

---

[59]Ludlow, "'Criteria of Canonicity' and the Early Church," 70.

[60]An example of one who defends the use of "criteria" of canonicity, in contradistinction to Gaffin, is Klyne Snodgrass, "Providence Is Not Enough," *Christianity Today* 32 (1988): 33–34. However, it seems that in many ways the view being put forth here is not all that different than that of Snodgrass. He too recognizes the after-the-fact usage of criteria of canonicity: "The usual 'criteria' of canonicity are ex post facto explanations why these books were accepted into the canon. That is, they were explanations offered *after* the books were already accepted as authoritative" (34, emphasis mine).

[61]Ludlow, "'Criteria of Canonicity' and the Early Church," 69–71.

[62]Some scholars equate *usage* of a book with the *reception* of a book as canonical. Obviously, the latter is very important (as I shall argue below), but I am making a distinction between these two terms for the sake of our discussion here.

book is apostolicity—but we shall explore and defend that concept in greater detail in chapter 5.[63]

Now we come to the most fundamental problem for the criteria of canonicity—one that often goes unobserved. If the criteria of canonicity, as the name suggests, provide some sort of norms or standards by which we determine whether a book comes from God, then where do the criteria themselves come from? How do we know that these "tests" are the way a divine book is identified? Put differently, what are the criteria that determine these criteria? When faced with this question, we have several options. First, we could argue that the criteria of canonicity are determined by what seems reasonable to us. The tests of a divine book could come from our sense of what a divine book *ought* to look like. But where do we get the authority to decide the standards for divine revelation? And how do we know divine revelation when we see it? Helm points out the problem.

> But who is to decide what this standard is? . . . [and] to what body of evidence is appeal being made when it is said that it is reasonable that anything counting as the Word of God must meet certain standards? We have not had experience of other revelations from God that would enable us to form a rule of generalization in the light of which we might judge that the next revelation has occurred.[64]

Second, we could argue that we get these criteria from the early church, claiming that these are the tests that early Christians used. But even if such a thing could be historically demonstrated, this simply raises the next question of whether the early church was correct in using these criteria. Why should we think that the church's criteria are necessarily the right way to identify a divine book? Is the practice of the early church normative? If the criteria of canonicity are defended solely on these grounds, then this approach simply morphs into a community-determined model of canon.

Third, some have argued that the criteria of canonicity, particularly apostolicity, can be derived from neutral historical arguments. Versions of this argument are found in Richard Swinburne, R. L. Harris, and R. C. Sproul.[65] Although there are differences between the particular formula-

---

[63]Concerns about "lost" apostolic books and books written by nonapostles (e.g., Mark and Luke) will be explored at that time.

[64]Helm, "Faith, Evidence, and the Scriptures," 306.

[65]Richard Swinburne, *Revelation: From Metaphor to Analogy* (Oxford: Oxford University Press, 2002); Harris, *Inspiration and Canonicity of the Bible*, 219; R. C. Sproul, J. Gerstner, and A. Lindsley, *Classical Apologetics* (Grand Rapids: Zondervan, 1984), 141ff.

tions of this type of argument,[66] it generally goes as follows: (1) the New Testament can be proved to be generally reliable history (but not inspired); (2) the New Testament testifies to the miracle of the resurrection; (3) the resurrection authenticates Jesus as the Son of God; (4) Jesus appointed twelve apostles to be his authoritative witnesses; (5) therefore, books by apostles should be received as authoritative.

There are a number of problems here, particularly with the first three premises. In regard to premise (1), this argument runs into the same problems noted above, namely, most of modern critical scholarship would simply *not* grant that the New Testament documents are generally reliable. Only on certain interpretations of the historical evidence would premise (1) stand. As for premise (2), we again run into problems with what other scholars are willing to accept. Even if one grants that the New Testament is generally reliable, there are very few who are willing to concede a miracle like the resurrection. This shows again that this argument works only if a person already has a certain worldview that is amenable to the Christian system (e.g., the existence of God, the possibility of miracles, and the like). When we come to premise (3), things are no better. Why should one assume that the resurrection of Jesus authenticates him as the Son of God? Even if the critic grants the fact of the resurrection (which is unlikely), why give the resurrection *that* interpretation? The idea that the resurrection shows Jesus to be the divine Son of God is a *biblical* interpretation of the resurrection that imports all sorts of other scriptural content (particularly from the Old Testament) about what miracles mean and the way God typically authenticates his messengers. What keeps the critic from offering a different interpretation of the resurrection, say, a *nonmiraculous anomaly* that has no bearing on the identity of Jesus at all?[67]

On top of all of these issues, the more fundamental challenge for this kind of argument is whether it provides a sufficiently sturdy foundation upon which to place our convictions about the validity of the canon. This is a multilayered argument that is open to challenge at numerous stages,

---

[66]E.g., Harris (*Inspiration and Canonicity of the Bible*) argues that the criterion of apostolicity should come from the books "that were never doubted" by early Christians (219). But why should this be the source for any criterion of canonicity? Where does he get this principle? In Harris's quest for the criteria of canonicity it seems that he *already* has a criterion that has gone unacknowledged. When he argues that we should derive the criteria of canonicity from books "that were never doubted" by the church, he is presuming the criterion of usage or reception by the early church even as he makes his argument. In fact, later he defends apostolicity as the correct criterion on the grounds that it was the preferred criterion of the early church (236–45). Thus, it seems the *real* criterion of canonicity for Harris is church usage or reception. But this criterion is itself never justified.

[67]See discussion in J. A. Cover, "Miracles and Christian Theism," in *Reason for the Hope Within*, ed. Michael J. Murray (Grand Rapids: Eerdmans, 1999), 345–74.

presupposes numerous antecedent beliefs (existence of God, miracles, etc.), and is out of step with much of the modern scholarship it professes to follow. Thus, at best, it provides an argument for canon based only on *probability*.[68] If the Christian is left with only this probabilistic argument as a reason to believe these books are from God, then some may legitimately question whether it can provide the necessary basis for the conviction of true religious faith. After all, Christians are asked to totally commit their lives to God on the basis of these books. Evans asks, "Can this kind of passionate, all-or-nothing, costly commitment be rooted in a tentative judgment of probability?"[69]

We are left, then, with what appears to be the only viable option, and that is to abandon the notion that the criteria of canonicity provide an independent, neutral Archimedean principle by which the canonical books can be tested. Instead, the criteria of canonicity are best understood as the way in which the Scripture sets the terms for how its own origins are to be investigated and explored. We derive the principle of apostolicity not from probabilistic historical investigations, but from the Scriptures themselves. After all, who has the authority to tell us what constitutes a divine book? Only God himself. And where would God tell us such a thing? In the Scriptures. Thus, apostolicity is not something that we *derive* from our historical investigations; rather it is a principle that *guides* our historical investigations. As we shall discuss further below, there is nothing inappropriate about doing historical work on a scriptural foundation (indeed, all historical work is done on some religious foundation).

By now it is evident that the entire concept of "criteria of canonicity" needs to be reworked. If so, we shall want to reconsider the phrase itself—for it gives the unfortunate impression (intentional or not) that God's books should be judged by some outside, and presumably more certain, standard. Perhaps a phrase like "*attributes* of canonicity" would be an appropriate alternative (but more on this below).[70]

3. The Priority of Historical Evidence

A final concern for the criteria-of-canonicity model is that it puts such a high priority on the role of evidences and historical investigation that one could (and often does) get the impression that this is the only (or at

---

[68]In particular, Plantinga refers to the "Principle of Dwindling Probabilities" where each stage has less and less probability; see Alvin Plantinga, "Two (or More) Kinds of Scripture Scholarship," in Bartholomew et al., "*Behind" the Text*, 19–57.

[69]Evans, *The Historical Christ and the Jesus of Faith*, 255.

[70]R. P. C. Hanson, *Tradition in the Early Church* (London: SCM, 1962), 213, suggested "norms of canonicity."

least the best) means by which the canon can be authenticated. No doubt very few in the criteria-of-canonicity camp would want to take the hard-line evidentialist position of William Clifford: "It is wrong always, every-where, and for everyone, to believe anything upon insufficient evidence."[71] And some scholars in this camp expressly discuss the internal testimony of the Holy Spirit as a means of knowing the truth of the Scriptures— one thinks here of the helpful clarifications from William Lane Craig[72] and Habermas.[73] Nevertheless, the unequivocal emphasis on the role of historical investigation can unwittingly communicate that there are no other God-given means by which Christians can have assurance about the boundaries of the canon. Largely overlooked in this regard are the *internal* characteristics of the canonical books that testify to their intrinsic authority. Helm's advice is helpful: "It is wrong to decide such questions [about the origin and authority of the Scriptures], either for or against, without considering the content of the Scriptures themselves."[74]

But the concerns go beyond the limited attention given to the inter-nal attributes of Scripture. There is also limited attention given to the role the church might play in the authentication of the canonical books. Understandably, evangelicals are hesitant to lean too heavily on the church's role in authenticating these books, lest it seem they have adopted a Roman Catholic position (or some other community-determined model). However, one wonders if perhaps the evangelical community has overcorrected by providing virtually no role for the church in how we know which books come from God. In the next chapter we shall put forth a model that seeks to recover the ecclesiastical dimension of canon while (hopefully) avoiding a number of the pitfalls of the community-determined models.

In summary, the criteria-of-canonicity model has a number of areas of concern that require careful reflection and consideration. It needs to be reiterated, however, that the concerns with this approach are not simply that it uses historical evidences in the discussion of canon. The use of historical evidence and the investigation of the history of the canon are entirely legitimate. Rather, the concern here is the *manner* in which such historical investigation is often pursued. The quest for a neutral historical methodology and the lack of sufficient means for identifying the criteria of canonicity present a number of theological and practical problems that

---

[71]William K. Clifford, "The Ethics of Belief," in *Classics of Philosophy*, vol. 2, *Modern and Contemporary*, ed. Louis J. Pojman (Oxford: Oxford University Press, 1998), 1047–51.
[72]Craig, "Classical Apologetics," 35–38.
[73]G. Habermas, "The Personal Testimony of the Holy Spirit to the Believer and Christian Apologetics," *Journal of Christian Apologetics* 1 (1997): 49–64.
[74]Helm, "Faith, Evidence, and the Scriptures," 310.

can eventually undermine the authority of the very canon we are setting out to defend. Nevertheless, the many positives of the criteria-of-canonicity model should not be forgotten. This model has rightly focused on aposto-licity as a key component of canonicity and has taken tremendous steps forward in gathering historical evidences to support this claim.

III. Conclusion

This chapter has been devoted to models that view canon as historically determined: canon-within-the-canon and criteria-of-canonicity. Though these models can, at times, differ greatly with one another, they authenti-cate canon in a similar manner, namely, by engaging in a rigorous historical investigation of these books to see if they are authentic. Although they rightly recognize the importance of the historical dimension—canonical books are fundamentally connected to history—they so absolutize this dimension that other important areas are often minimized or ignored. Most notably, these models tend to downplay the intrinsic characteristics of these books and the ecclesiastical reception of these books as factors in their authentication as canon. As a result, these models are often left with a canon that is so conditioned by historical investigations that its very dignity and authority are inevitably dependent upon these investigations. The canon ceases to be a norm that *guides* our historical investigations, but becomes merely the *product* of our historical investigations.

3

My Sheep Hear My Voice

Canon as Self-Authenticating

He swore by himself.

Hebrews 6:13

The prior chapters have attempted to offer a taxonomy of canonical models, along with some reflection and critique (as difficult as that is in so little space). Throughout this analysis it has become clear that these models vary from one another in many different ways—for example, date of the New Testament, definition of *canon*, doctrine of Scripture, role of the church, and more. In the midst of such diversity, however, it has also become clear that all these models share one core characteristic. They all ground the authority of the canon in something outside the canon itself. It is this appeal to an external authority that unites all of these positions. As we have already noted, the insistence that the canon can be authenticated only by some external authority raises a host of theological and biblical questions. Richard Gaffin notes that such an approach is in danger of "subjecting the canon to the relativity of historical study and our fallible human insight. That is, it would destroy the New Testament as canon, as absolute authority."[1] Ridderbos also expresses concern about such

---

[1] R. Gaffin, "The New Testament as Canon," in *Inerrancy and Hermeneutic*, ed. Harvey M. Conn (Grand Rapids: Baker, 1988), 170.

approaches. He notes that "problems arise whenever the Scriptures are no longer regarded as the exclusive principle of canonicity, when something else is substituted."[2] For these models, "the final decision as to what the church deems to be holy and unimpeachable does not reside in the canon itself. Human judgment . . . is the final court of appeal."[3]

What is needed, then, is a canonical model that does not ground the New Testament canon in an external authority, but seeks to ground the canon in the only place it could be grounded, its own authority. After all, if the canon bears the very authority of God, to what other standard could it appeal to justify itself? Even when God swore oaths, "he swore by himself" (Heb. 6:13). Thus, for the canon to be the canon, it must be *self-authenticating*. A self-authenticating model of canon would take into account something that the other models have largely overlooked: the *content* of the canon itself. Rather than looking only to its reception (community determined), or only to its origins (historically determined), this model would, in a sense, let the canon have a voice in its own authentication. But this raises a number of questions. What exactly do we mean when we say that the canon is self-authenticating? And does a self-authenticating canon mean that we cannot use external data?

It is the purpose of this chapter to lay forth a canonical model that addresses these questions. An overview of the model will be offered here and the full details of the model will be developed throughout the remaining chapters of the book.

I. The Concept of a Self-Authenticating Canon

The idea of a self-authenticating canon is certainly not new. The hallmark teaching of the Reformers—and the foundation for the doctrine of *sola scriptura*—is the self-authenticating (*autopistic*) nature of the canon.[4] John Calvin notes, "God alone is a fit witness of himself in his Word. . . . Scripture is indeed self-authenticated."[5] Francis Turretin agrees: "Thus Scripture, which is the first principle in the supernatural order, is known by itself and has no need of arguments derived from without to prove

---

[2]H. N. Ridderbos, *Redemptive History and the New Testament Scripture* (Phillipsburg, NJ: P&R, 1988), 7.

[3]Ibid.

[4]This teaching did not start with the Reformers and can be traced back to the early Patristic period, most notably in Augustine (*Conf.* 6.5; 11.3). See discussion in F. H. Klooster, "Internal Testimony of the Holy Spirit," in *Evangelical Dictionary of Theology*, ed. W. Elwell (Grand Rapids: Baker, 1984), 564–65.

[5]John Calvin, *Institutes of the Christian Religion*, ed. John T. McNeill, trans. Ford Lewis Battles (Philadelphia: Westminster, 1960), 1.7.4–5.

and make itself known to us."[6] Herman Bavinck reminds us that the church fathers understood Scripture this way: "In the church fathers and the scholastics . . . [Scripture] rested in itself, was trustworthy in and of itself (αὐτόπιστος), and the primary norm for church and theology."[7] Therefore, Bavinck argues, an ultimate authority like Scripture (what he calls a "first principle") must be "believed on its own account, not on account of something else."[8] He says elsewhere, "Scripture's authority with respect to itself depends on Scripture."[9]

But what exactly do we mean when we say that the canon authenticates itself? Upon first glance, a self-authenticating canon may seem to refer to the fact that the canon *claims* to be the Word of God (e.g., 2 Tim. 3:16; 2 Pet. 1:21; Rev. 22:18–19), implying that all we can do is accept or reject that claim.[10] Although Scripture's testimony about itself is an important aspect of biblical authority (and will be discussed more below), we will not be arguing that the canon is authenticated simply by virtue of the fact that it says so. That is not how the phrase will be used here. Others may hear the phrase "self-authenticating" and recognize it as a reference to the traditional Reformed view that the books of Scripture bear evidence in themselves of their own divinity. As a result, some may assume that a self-authenticating canon means that our model will be concerned only with the internal qualities of these books and that external data or evidence plays no role in the authentication process. While we certainly agree that these books do bear internal marks of their divinity (indeed, this will be a core component of the model put forth below), this does not mean that outside information has no place in how the canon is authenticated. We shall argue that when it comes to the question of canon, the Scriptures themselves provide grounds for considering external data: the apostolicity of books, the testimony of the church, and so forth. Of course, this external evidence is not to be used as an independent and neutral "test" to determine what counts as canonical; rather it should always be seen as something warranted by Scripture and interpreted by Scripture.

---

[6]Francis Turretin, *Institutes of Elenctic Theology*, trans. George Musgrave Giger, ed. James T. Dennison Jr., 3 vols. (Phillipsburg, NJ: P&R, 1992–1997), 1:89 (2.6.11).

[7]Herman Bavinck, *Reformed Dogmatics*, vol. 1, *Prolegomena*, ed. John Bolt, trans. John Vriend (Grand Rapids: Baker, 2003), 452.

[8]Ibid., 458.

[9]Ibid.

[10]For a good article that describes the Scripture's own claims, see W. Grudem, "Scripture's Self-Attestation and the Problem of Formulating a Doctrine of Scripture," in *Scripture and Truth*, ed. D. A. Carson and J. D. Woodbridge (Grand Rapids: Baker, 1992), 19–59; this type of self-attestation was also the major focus of B. B. Warfield, *The Inspiration and Authority of the Bible* (Philadelphia: Presbyterian and Reformed, 1948).

Thus, for the purposes of this study, we shall be using the phrase *self-authenticating* in a broader fashion than was typical for the Reformers.[11] We are not using it to refer only to the fact that canonical books bear divine qualities (although they do), but are using it to refer to the way the canon itself provides the necessary direction and guidance about how it is to be authenticated. In essence, to say that the canon is self-authenticating is simply to recognize that one cannot authenticate the canon without appealing to the canon. It sets the terms for its own validation and investigation. A self-authenticating canon is not just a canon that claims to have authority, nor is it simply a canon that bears internal evidence of authority, but one that guides and determines how that authority is to be established.

Of course, for some who are used to a more foundationalist epistemology, the idea of a self-authenticating canon of Scripture might seem a bit strange.[12] We tend to think that we are not justified in holding a belief unless it can be authenticated on the basis of *other* beliefs. But as we have already noted, this approach overlooks the unique nature of the canon. The canon, as God's Word, is not just true, but the criterion of truth. It is an *ultimate* authority. So, how do we offer an account of how we know that an ultimate authority is, in fact, the ultimate authority? If we try to validate an ultimate authority by appealing to some other authority, then we have just shown that it is not really the ultimate authority. Thus, for ultimate authorities to be ultimate authorities, they have to be the standard for their own authentication. You cannot account for them without using them.

Although this whole line of thought can sound a bit circular to some, that is inevitable given the nature of the question being asked. We must

---

[11]E.g., Calvin often drew a *contrast* between the self-authenticating marks of Scripture and the evidence from the external world (*Institutes*, 1.7.4; 1.8.1). This is not to suggest that Calvin was opposed to the use of evidence; on the contrary he called such evidences "useful aids" (1.8.1). Rather, the point here is simply that, for Calvin, the *term* "self-authenticating" would have referred to only the divine marks of Scripture.

[12]Classical foundationalism, roughly speaking, argues that belief in Christianity and the Bible is not warranted unless it is first based on other beliefs; either ones that have an evidentiary basis or ones that are considered self-evident or basic (laws of logic, causality, etc.). A standard example of this position is John Locke, who believed that all beliefs we hold must be based on the evidence supplied by *other* facts we know that are certain. See discussion in Nicholas Wolterstorff, "Tradition, Insight and Constraint," *Proceedings and Addresses of the American Philosophical Association* 66 (1992): 43–57. Classical foundationalism has been roundly critiqued as fallacious by modern philosophers, primarily because belief in classical foundationalism itself cannot meet its own standards (there is no evidential or self-evident basis for it) and therefore is unwarranted (Alvin Plantinga, *Warranted Christian Belief* [New York: Oxford, 2000], 81–99). For further critique, see also Plantinga, "Reason and Belief in God," in *Faith and Rationality: Reason and Belief in God*, ed. Alvin Plantinga and Nicholas Wolterstorff (Notre Dame: University of Notre Dame Press, 1984), 16–93.

remember that we are not asking simply how a person (for the first time) comes to believe that the Scripture is true—that can happen in a number of different ways, and a person may not even consciously recognize the epistemological process that allows him to acquire such knowledge.[13] Nor, as we discussed in the introduction, are we attempting to somehow "prove" to the skeptic (in a way that would satisfy him) that these books are indeed from God. Rather, the question before us is whether the Christian faith, with its twenty-seven-book New Testament, can give an adequate account for how it can be known that these books are canonical. Do Christians, as the *de jure* objection contends, lack sufficient grounds for thinking that they can know which books belong in the canon and which do not? The question is not about our *having* knowledge of canon, but *accounting* for our knowledge of canon.[14] But that question can only be answered on the basis of the Christian faith itself, that is, what Christianity actually teaches about God, the Scriptures, the nature of Christian knowledge, and so on. After all, how can the Christian account of knowledge be explained and defended without appealing to the Christian account of knowledge?

William Alston agrees that a certain degree of circularity is required in our justification of our knowledge of Scripture.

> If we want to know whether, as the Christian tradition would have it, God guarantees the Bible . . . as a source for fundamental religious beliefs, what recourse is there except to what we know about God, His nature, purposes, plans and actions. And where do we go for this knowledge? In the absence of any promising suggestions to the contrary, we have to go to the very sources of belief credentials which are under scrutiny.[15]

This sort of circularity is not a problem but simply part of how foundational authorities are authenticated. For instance, let us imagine that we want to determine whether sense perception is a reliable source of belief. If I see a cup on the table, how do I know my sense perception is accurate? How would I test such a thing? I could examine the cup and table more closely to make sure they are what they seem to be (hold

---

[13]C. Stephen Evans, *The Historical Christ and the Jesus of Faith: The Incarnational Narrative as History* (New York: Oxford University Press, 1996), 277. For those aware of contemporary epistemological debates, it should be clear that this volume presupposes an "externalist" account of knowledge. A person can know something without knowing *how* he knows it or even *that* he knows it. Awareness that one's beliefs are justified (or warranted) is not necessary for those beliefs to be, in fact, justified (or warranted). For more, see Alvin Plantinga, *Warrant: The Current Debate* (Oxford: Oxford University Press, 1993).

[14]Evans, *The Historical Christ and the Jesus of Faith*, 274–82.

[15]William Alston, "Knowledge of God," in *Faith, Reason, and Skepticism*, ed. Marcus Hester (Philadelphia: Temple University Press, 1992), 42.

them, touch them, etc.). I could also ask a friend to tell me whether he sees a cup on the table. But in all these instances I am still assuming the reliability of my sense perception (or my friend's) even as I examine the reliability of my sense perception. Or, as another example, let us imagine that we wanted to inquire into whether our rational faculties would reliably produce true beliefs. How could we examine the evidence for the reliability of our rational faculties without, at the same time, actually using our rational faculties (and thereby presupposing their reliability)? Alston sums it up, "There is no escape from epistemic circularity in the assessment of our fundamental sources of belief."[16]

If so, then when it comes to authenticating the canon, we are not so much proving Scripture as we are using Scripture. Or, even better, we are *applying* Scripture to the question of which books belong in the New Testament. Perhaps this is a more tangible way to think of a self-authenticating canon because it is not all that different (in principle) from the way we apply the teaching of Scripture to any other question before us, whether politics, science, the arts, or anything else. And whenever the Scripture is applied to an issue, it is perfectly appropriate (and necessary) to use extrabiblical "facts." For example, if we want to apply the teachings of Scripture to, say, the field of bioethics (stem-cell research, human cloning, etc.), then we cannot just read the Bible only; the Bible does not speak *directly* of these things. It does not tell us what cloning is and what it entails. We actually have to acquire some outside information about these bioethical issues before we can reach biblical conclusions about them. So it is when it comes to applying the Scriptures to the question of canon.

But just because our conclusions required extrabiblical data does not mean the conclusions themselves are unbiblical or uncertain. We can still have biblical *knowledge* even with extrabiblical *data*. John Frame argues at length that a sharp distinction should not be made between the meaning of the Bible and the application of the Bible—we do not really understand the meaning until we can apply it correctly to the world around us.[17] Thus, he declares, "applications of Scripture are as authoritative as the specific statements of Scripture. . . . Jesus and others held their hearers responsible if they failed to apply Scripture properly."[18] The Westminster Confession affirms a similar idea when it says that authority belongs not only to those teachings "expressly set down in Scripture" but also to that which "by good and necessary consequence may be deduced from

---

[16]Ibid., 41.
[17]J. M. Frame, *The Doctrine of the Knowledge of God* (Phillipsburg, NJ: P&R, 1987), 81–85.
[18]Ibid., 84.

Scripture" (1.6). Similarly, even though the Scripture does not *directly* tell us which books belong in the New Testament canon (i.e., there is no inspired "table of contents"), we can account for that knowledge if we apply Scripture to the question. Again, where else would we turn to understand the Christian basis for receiving these books?

When we do apply the Scripture to the question of which books belong in the canon, we shall see that it testifies to the fact that God has created the proper epistemic environment wherein belief in the New Testament canon can be reliably formed. This epistemic environment includes three components:

- *Providential exposure.* In order for the church to be able to recognize the books of the canon, it must first be providentially exposed to these books. The church cannot recognize a book that it does not have.
- *Attributes of canonicity.* These attributes are basically characteristics that distinguish canonical books from all other books. There are three attributes of canonicity: (1) divine qualities (canonical books bear the "marks" of divinity), (2) corporate reception (canonical books are recognized by the church as a whole), and (3) apostolic origins (canonical books are the result of the redemptive-historical activity of the apostles).
- *Internal testimony of the Holy Spirit.* In order for believers to rightly recognize these attributes of canonicity, the Holy Spirit works to overcome the noetic effects of sin and produces belief that these books are from God.

These three components must all be in place if we are to have knowledge of the canon. We cannot know canonical books unless we have access to those books (providential exposure); we need some way to distinguish canonical books from other books (attributes of canonicity); and we need to have some basis for thinking we can rightly identify these attributes (internal work of the Spirit). We now turn our attention to these components.

II. The Components of a Self-Authenticating Canon

A. Providential Exposure

If the covenant community is to rightly recognize God's covenant books, it will need more than just attributes of canonicity and the work of the Holy Spirit. In addition, the covenant community will need to be collectively exposed to the canonical books. To state the obvious, the church cannot respond (positively or negatively) to a book of which it has no knowledge.[19] Christ's promise that his sheep will respond to his voice pertains only to books that have had their voice *actually heard* by the sheep (John 10:27). If God intended to give a canon to his corporate church—and not just to an isolated congregation for a limited period of time—then we have every reason to believe that he would providentially preserve these books and expose them to the church so that, through the Holy Spirit, it can rightly recognize them as canonical. As Evans has argued, the fact that certain books are lost "provides reason to think that God did not desire those writings to be included in the authorized revelation."[20]

The inclusion of the "providential exposure" component in the self-authenticating model is not only obvious (how could the church recognize books it was not familiar with?), but also critical if we are to claim that the Christian's epistemic environment is able to lead *reliably* to a knowledge of the canon. If God did not bring about the condition of corporate exposure to the church, then we would have no basis for thinking that the complete canon could actually be known. There could always be an unknown number of books left out of the canon—not because the church rejected them, but because they were lost before they could even be evaluated. Fortunately, we have good biblical grounds for affirming God's intent in giving his Word to his church (Rom. 15:4; 2 Tim. 3:16–17) and God's sovereign ability to accomplish it (Ps. 135:6; Dan. 4:35; Acts 17:25–28; Eph. 1:11; Heb. 1:3).

If so, then this has implications for how we are to think of books that the apostles may have written that were not preserved—such as Paul's *other* letter to the Corinthians (1 Cor. 5:9).[21] No doubt such letters, if written in an apostle's authoritative role, would have been inspired by the Holy Spirit. But since God did not providentially allow these books to be exposed to the corporate church (apparently they were known only to a limited group and then lost or forgotten), then we have no reason to think that they are relevant for our discussion about which books are canonical. Again, how can we recognize a book's canonicity unless we actually *have* that book? If the authentication of the canon is inherently

---

[19]By "knowledge" we mean not merely that the church was aware of the *existence* of these books, but also that the church actually had corporate *exposure* to these books and was familiar with them.

[20]C. Stephen Evans, "Canonicity, Apostolicity, and Biblical Authority: Some Kierkegaardian Reflections," in *Canon and Biblical Interpretation*, ed. Craig Bartholomew et al. (Carlisle: Paternoster, 2006), 157.

[21]Cf. Phil. 3:1; Col. 4:16. On the former text, J. B. Lightfoot, *St. Paul's Epistle to the Philippians* (Peabody, MA: Hendrickson, 1995), has a brief discussion of this passage entitled, "Lost Epistle to the Philippians?" (138–42).

about which books the church should accept or reject (and it is), then lost books, by definition, can play no role. Therefore, the self-authenticating model we are putting forth here can only be used to evaluate books that God has allowed the collective church to be exposed to, such as 1 Peter, the *Shepherd of Hermas, 1 Clement,* and the Gospel of John.

Of course, there is still the complex question of what terminology is appropriate for these "lost" apostolic books. What shall we call them? Although we certainly could use the term *canon* to refer to these books (at least in regard to the functional definition), that seems only to confuse matters. If God providentially intended some apostolic books to serve as permanent foundational books for the corporate church (e.g., John's Gospel), and other apostolic books to serve a temporary, one-time purpose after which they were lost or forgotten (e.g., Paul's other letter to the Corinthians), then our terminology ought to reflect such a distinction.[22] If so, then it seems best to refer to these lost apostolic writings as "inspired books" or perhaps even as "Scripture." In regard to the latter term, this would be the one instance, contra Sundberg, where there is a legitimate distinction between Scripture and canon.[23] But this distinction is only applicable to the narrow foundational and redemptive-historical period of the apostles and driven by their God-given function as caretakers and founders of the church. During this unique apostolic phase, canonicity was a subset of Scripture—all canonical books were Scripture, but not necessarily all scriptural books were canonical.[24]

Given this distinction, the term *canon* may be used for books *before* they are corporately recognized (e.g., John ten minutes after it was written), but not for books that were *never* corporately recognized (e.g., lost letters of Paul).[25] Such terminological distinctions, of course, are inevitably retrospective in nature. John was really canon when the ink was still wet on the autograph, but the church would have realized this only at a later point, after being exposed to John and recognizing it as canonical. The church could then *look back,* as we do, and realize that a canon really did

---

[22]Abraham Kuyper argues that God's preservation of some books and not others stems from the fact that we have a "predestined Bible" or a "preconceived form of the Holy Scripture" that existed in the mind of God before it came to pass in history (*Encyclopedia of Sacred Theology: Its Principles* [New York: Scribner, 1898], 474). For more discussion, see R. B. Gaffin, "Old Amsterdam and Inerrancy?," *WTJ* 44 (1982): 250–89, esp. 256–58.

[23]Sundberg insisted on a sharp distinction between Scripture and canon until the fourth century, when there was a final, closed list of books affirmed by the church. See A. C. Sundberg, "Towards a Revised History of the New Testament Canon," *SE* 4 (1968): 452–61.

[24]See Richard B. Gaffin, *Perspectives on Pentecost* (Phillipsburg, NJ: P&R, 1979), 100.

[25]This is not suggesting that the church's recognition of a book *makes* it canonical. No, the church recognizes it because it is canonical; it is not canonical because the church recognizes it.

exist in the first century even though at the time the church was not yet fully aware of it. Likewise, Paul's other Corinthian letter was not canon in the first century, but this would not have been known at the time by the limited groups acquainted with it. Only later, when it was lost or forgotten, would it become clear that it was not canonical.

Therefore, canonical books, as we have defined them here, cannot be lost. If they are lost, then they were never canonical books to begin with. So, even if we were to discover Paul's lost letter in the desert sands today, we would not place it into the canon as the twenty-eighth book. Instead, we would simply recognize that God had not preserved this book to be a permanent foundation for the church. Putting such a letter into the canon now would not change that fact; it could not make a book foundational that clearly never was.[26]

B. Attributes of Canonicity and the Holy Spirit

The above discussion has laid the appropriate groundwork for our canonical model. It is now clear that we are only dealing with (and can only deal with) the books we have available to us. And in this regard, we trust in the providence of God that the books available to us are the ones he intended. But, of course, this is just the very first step. Next, we must distinguish among these books available to us. How do we know which are canonical? The answer lies in the attributes of canonicity and the role of the Holy Spirit, to which we now turn.

1. Divine Qualities

Because the canonical books were constituted by the revelatory activity of the Holy Spirit, we would expect that there would be some evidence of that activity in the books themselves—the "imprint" of the Spirit, if you will. Thus, the first attribute of the canon's self-authenticating nature is that it bears the divine qualities or divine character of a book from God.[27]

---

[26]If a canonical book, as we have defined it, cannot be "lost," then one might wonder about Old Testament texts, like 2 Kings 22:8, that seem to speak of canonical books being lost and then found again under the reign of King Josiah. Moreover, one might wonder if this text would give warrant to the reception of a lost epistle of Paul, were it discovered. Two considerations: (1) A close reading of this text indicates that the Book of the Law was not so much lost but *ignored*. It had been a part of the life of Israel for generations but had sat unused and unread in the temple (22:8) while Israel was pursuing idols and false gods. (2) Another important distinction is that the Book of the Law was not being discovered for the *first* time by God's collective covenant community (as would be the case if a lost letter of Paul were discovered). The "Book of the Law" (likely Deuteronomy) had been recognized and received much earlier by the covenant people when God originally gave the Pentateuch as foundational books for Israel.

[27]Richard A. Muller, *Post-Reformation Dogmatics*, vol. 2, *Holy Scripture* (Grand Rapids: Eerdmans, 1993), 270–302; J. I. Packer, *Fundamentalism and the Word of God* (Grand Rapids: Eerdmans, 1992), 115–25.

John Murray reasons, "If . . . Scripture is divine in its origin, character, and authority, it must bear the marks or evidences of that divinity."[28] These "marks" (or *indicia*) can include a variety of things, but traditionally include the Scripture's beauty, efficacy, and harmony (which we will discuss further in a later chapter).[29] Calvin himself understood that there were objective qualities evident within the canonical books that show they are from God: "It is easy to see that the Sacred Scriptures, which so far surpass all gifts and graces of human endeavor, breathe something divine."[30] Elsewhere he states, "Indeed, Scripture exhibits fully as clear evidence of its own truth as white and black things do of their color, or sweet and bitter things do of their taste."[31] And again, Calvin reaffirms the internal divine qualities of Scripture.

> As far as Sacred Scripture is concerned . . . it is clearly crammed with thoughts that could not be humanly conceived. Let each of the prophets be looked into: none will be found who does not far exceed human measure. Consequently, those for whom prophetic doctrine is tasteless ought to be thought of lacking taste buds.[32]

As the Westminster Confession of Faith notes, these divine qualities are considered to be objective means "whereby [Scripture] doth abundantly *evidence itself* to be the Word of God."[33] Thus, all books that are canonical will bear these divine qualities.

In many ways the divine qualities of Scripture are analogous to the way the natural world attests to God as Creator. Christians have historically argued that we know the natural world is from God because it bears his "marks" and his "imprints." The beauty, excellency, and harmony of creation testify to the fact that God is its author. As Psalm 19:1 states,

> The heavens declare the glory of God,
>   and the sky above proclaims his handiwork.

---

[28] John Murray, "The Attestation of Scripture," in *The Infallible Word*, ed. Ned B. Stonehouse and Paul Woolley (Philadelphia: Presbyterian and Reformed, 1946), 46.

[29] WCF 1.5.

[30] Calvin, *Institutes*, 1.8.1. There has been dispute over the years concerning whether Calvin bases the authority of Scripture on objective internal evidence or on the internal testimony of the Holy Spirit. Edward A. Dowey Jr., *The Knowledge of God in Calvin's Theology* (Grand Rapids: Eerdmans, 1994), argues for the latter position, but seems to have misunderstood how Calvin distinguishes the internal evidence of Scripture itself from the internal testimony of the Holy Spirit that helps us apprehend those internal evidences. For more discussion, see John Murray, "Calvin and the Authority of Scripture," in *Collected Writings of John Murray*, vol. 4, *Studies in Theology* (Edinburgh: Banner of Truth, 1982), 176–90.

[31] *Institutes*, 1.7.2.

[32] *Institutes*, 1.8.2.

[33] WCF 1.5, emphasis mine.

And, similarly, Romans 1:20 explains, "For his invisible attributes, namely, his eternal power and divine nature, have been clearly perceived, ever since the creation of the world, in the things that have been made. So they are without excuse." If the created world (general revelation) is able to speak clearly that it is from God, then how much more so would the canon of Scripture (special revelation) speak clearly that it is from God? Murray draws this same connection: "If the heavens declare the glory of God and therefore bear witness to their divine creator, the Scripture as God's handiwork must also bear the imprints of his authorship."[34]

It is here that we see clearly how the doctrine of Scripture shapes one's canonical model. The *method* by which the canon is authenticated is correlative with the *nature* of the canon being authenticated. The two must be consistent with one another. Because a number of models deny that the canon bears such inherent divine qualities—historical-critical, canonical criticism, existential/neoorthodox, and canon-within-the-canon models—then they must appeal to criteria outside the canon in order to authenticate it. On these models, the canon is not *able* to authenticate itself, so it has to be justified on other grounds (experience, historical evidence, etc.). Thus, once again, we see that canonical models do not (and cannot) approach the question of canon with theological neutrality. All models have prior theological convictions about what Scripture is (or is not), and this in turn determines the manner in which canon is authenticated. But where do these prior theological convictions about Scripture come from if not from Scripture itself? Ironically, then, each model must know what Scripture is before determining how it is to be authenticated. There cannot be a theologically neutral approach to canon.

Of course, once we start talking about these divine qualities contained in the canonical books, we must also discuss the means God has provided that allows them to be reliably recognized. After all, if these marks are really there in the canonical books, then how is it that so many people do not receive them or acknowledge them? If they are objectively present, why do so many reject the Bible? The answer is that, because of the noetic effects of sin, the effects of sin on the mind (Rom. 3:10–18), one cannot

---

[34]Murray, "The Attestation of Scripture," 46. A very similar argument can be found in Turretin, 1:63, and John Owen, "The Divine Original: Authority, Self-Evidencing Light, and Power of the Scriptures," in *The Works of John Owen*, vol. 16, *The Church and the Bible*, ed. William H. Goold (repr., Edinburgh: Banner of Truth, 1988), 297–421. In the latter work, Owen states, "As God in the creation of the world . . . hath left such characters of his eternal power and wisdom in them and upon them . . . so in the giving out of his Word . . . [He] implanted in it and impressed on it such characters of his goodness, power, wisdom, holiness, love to mankind, truth, faithfulness, with all the rest of his glorious excellencies and perfections, that at all times and in all places . . . it declares itself to be his, and makes good its authority from him" (312).

recognize these marks without the *testimonium spiritus sancti internum*, the internal testimony of the Holy Spirit.[35] The Holy Spirit not only is operative within the canonical books themselves (providing the "marks" of divinity noted above), but also must be operative within those who receive them. The *testimonium* is not a private revelation of the Spirit or new information given to the believer—as if the list of canonical books were whispered in our ears—but it is a work of the Spirit that overcomes the noetic effects of sin and produces the belief that the Scriptures are the word of God.[36] The reason some refuse to believe the Scriptures is not that there is any defect or lack of evidence in the Scriptures (the *indicia* are clear and objective) but that those without the Spirit do not accept the things from God (1 Cor. 2:10–14).

---

[35]Calvin, *Institutes*, 1.7.4–5; 3.1.1–3; 3.2.15, 33–36. The role of the *testimonium* in the establishing of the canon has been acknowledged by a number of Reformed confessions, including the Belgic Confession, the French Confession of Faith, the Scots Confession, and the Helvetic Confession. Helpful treatments of the *testimonium* include Bernard Ramm, *The Witness of the Spirit* (Grand Rapids: Eerdmans, 1959); Plantinga, *Warranted Christian Belief*, 241–89; R. C. Sproul, "The Internal Testimony of the Holy Spirit," in *Inerrancy*, ed. N. L. Geisler (Grand Rapids: Zondervan, 1980), 337–54; and J. M. Frame, "The Spirit and the Scriptures," in *Hermeneutics, Authority, and Canon*, ed. D. A. Carson and John D. Woodbridge (Grand Rapids: Zondervan, 1986), 217–35. It is also important to note that there has been some confusion in some writers regarding (1) whether the *testimonium* determines the canonicity of Scripture or just its divinity and (2) whether it applies to individual books or only to the Scripture as a whole. For instance, see discussion in B. B. Warfield, *Calvin and Augustine* (Philadelphia: Presbyterian and Reformed, 1956), 74–87; G. C. Berkouwer, "The Testimony of the Spirit," in *The Authoritative Word* (Grand Rapids: Eerdmans, 1983), 155–81; and Ridderbos, *Redemptive History*, 10–11. However, these distinctions do not seem compelling for the following reasons: (1) There is no hard distinction between the divinity of Scripture and its canonicity. If a book is divine and given by God, it should be regarded as canonical. If this distinction is merely designed to acknowledge that some apostolic books were inspired but never were considered canonical, then the distinction is granted (but there are better ways to account for this distinction, as we noted above). If this distinction is trying to argue that the Spirit testifies merely to the *content* of a book's teaching and not the book itself, this too seems like a difficult distinction to maintain. Plantinga argues that the Spirit can testify to *both* the book and the content; indeed they are not separable (*Warranted Christian Belief*, 380). (2) There is also no hard distinction between the Scripture "as a whole" and the individual books within it. Granted, a twenty-six-book canon would still have divine qualities. But there is no reason an individual book, like Romans, would not also have divine qualities. After all, the earliest Christians recognized divine qualities in individual books before they even knew about the completed canon. Owen says it well: "On these suppositions I fear not to affirm that there are on every *individual book of the Scripture*. . . . those divine characters and criteria which are sufficient to difference them from all other writings whatever, and to testify their divine authority unto the minds and consciences of believers" (*The Works of John Owen*, vol. 4 [repr., Edinburgh: Banner of Truth, 1991], 107, emphasis his). (3) Some of these scholars may make these distinctions merely because they are concerned that some people may mistakenly think that if the *testimonium* determines the extent of the canon, then it must bring new and fresh revelation, like a canonical "list." However, the *testimonium* need not be understood this way in order for it to have a bearing on canonicity, as the discussion below will demonstrate.

[36]Calvin, *Institutes*, 1.19.1. For this reason, the term *testimony* has been confusing and led some to think that the Spirit is telling us some new revelation. Aquinas uses the more helpful "inward *instigation*" of the Holy Spirit (*Summa theologica* II-II, q. 2, a. 9, reply ob. 3, emphasis mine). See discussion in Plantinga, *Warranted Christian Belief*, 249ff.

Jesus himself affirmed this reality when he declared, "My sheep [i.e., those with the Spirit] hear my voice, and I know them, and they follow me" (John 10:27). Likewise, he said of his sheep, "A stranger they will not follow, but they will flee from him, for they do not know the voice of strangers" (John 10:5). Put simply, canonical books are received by those who have the Holy Spirit in them. When people's eyes are opened, they are struck by the divine qualities of Scripture—its beauty, harmony, efficacy—and recognize and embrace Scripture for what it is, the word of God. They realize that the voice of Scripture is the voice of the Shepherd.[37]

It is here that we see both similarities and differences with a number of the community-determined models above. The self-authenticating model is similar to these models in that they all recognize a legitimate place for the subjective response of Christians in the authentication of the canon. The difference, however, is that the community-determined models make the subjective response foundational to the canon's authority and, in some instances, that which constitutes the canonical authority. For example,

---

[37] J. W. Wenham, *Christ and the Bible* (Downers Grove, IL: InterVarsity, 1972), 125, objects to the efficacy of the *testimonium* in that it is not able to determine textual variants like Mark 16:9–20. But did the Reformers understand the *testimonium* as something that would solve textual variants? There is not space in this volume to treat issues of textual criticism at length, but we can make some brief observations in reply: (1) We need to recognize that the historical process of the church's recognizing canonical books is simply not parallel to the historical process of textual transmission. In the former, the shape of the canon is determined by the conscious and intentional actions of the corporate church as it receives these books. In the latter, the shape of the text is *not* determined by conscious and intentional actions of the church, but is determined by a myriad of causes during the transmission process, the most common of which is unintentional copying mistakes by individual scribes. Put simply, the canon is the result of the church's corporate response; the individual textual variations are not. Thus, there is no reason to think that the final shape of the text is necessarily connected to the internal testimony of the Holy Spirit or that the majority reading is necessarily the original one. See John H. Skilton, "The Transmission of the Scriptures," in Stonehouse and Woolley, *The Infallible Word*, 137–87. (2) Although we have indications that the early church certainly cared about textual variations and even discussed them, they viewed this as a very different question than which books should be included in the canon in the first place. Metzger indicates that for the church fathers, "the question of the canonicity of a document apparently did not arise in connection with discussion of variant readings" (B. M. Metzger, *The Canon of the New Testament: Its Origin, Development, and Significance* [Oxford: Clarendon, 1987], 269). Thus, we should not view the church's acceptance of a book as an endorsement of a particular version of that book. (3) It is a caricature to argue that a self-attesting canon means that even the smallest portions of Scripture, down to even a single word, can be immediately identified by Christians as divine. Such a caricature is built on the presumption that the Spirit simply tells Christians which words are from God and which are not. But the Spirit, as noted above, does not deliver private revelations to Christians as they read a text (or do textual criticism), but simply allows them to see the divine qualities of Scripture that are already objectively there. Since such qualities are bound up with the broader meaning, teaching, and doctrine communicated by a book, they are not as applicable to individual textual variations (which, on the whole, tend to be quite small and change very little of the overall meaning). As a result, two different copies of the book of Galatians, though they would differ at minor points, would *both* still communicate divine qualities.

in the existential/neoorthodox model the Scripture does not bear divine qualities in and of itself, but functions as the Word of God only when the Spirit decides to use it. In this sense, the authority of Scripture is utterly contingent on the subjective experience of those who receive it. The Spirit becomes the *grounds* of the canon's authority, not the *means* to recognizing it.[38] In contrast, the self-authenticating model understands the *testimonium* not as something that stands by itself, but as something that always stands in conjunction with the objective qualities of Scripture noted above.[39] The two always go together. Indeed, they are two aspects of the same phenomenon, not to be unduly separated.[40] Bavinck notes, "Scripture and the testimony of the Holy Spirit relate to each other as objective truth and subjective assurance . . . as the light and the human eye."[41] Thus, when a Christian embraces the Scriptures as the word of God, his actions are fully rational and warranted because they rest on the most sure basis possible—the divine attributes of Scripture.[42] So, while there is a subjective *aspect* to the self-authenticating model, it is not *subjectivism*.[43]

Of course, some may still object: "But how do I know I am experiencing the internal testimony of the Holy Spirit? How do I know it isn't, say, heartburn?" The problem with this objection is that it assumes we can only know that the Scriptures are from God if we can properly identify

---

[38]For this reason, the *testimonium* has become a synonym for inspiration in many neoorthodox thinkers. E.g., see E. Brunner, *Revelation and Reason* (Philadelphia: Westminster, 1946), 168–71; Karl Barth, *The Holy Ghost and the Christian Life* (London: Muller, 1938), 23; and further discussion in Frame, "The Spirit and the Scriptures," 222–25. In addition, seeing the Spirit's work as the *grounds* for the canon's authority is similar to the Mormon understanding of how the Book of Mormon is authenticated via a "burning in the bosom."

[39]C. Wistar Hodge, "The Witness of the Holy Spirit to the Bible," *PTR* 11 (1913): 41–84, esp. 52–54; Ramm, *The Witness of the Spirit*, 31–34.

[40]The connection between Word and Spirit is analogous to the connection between sacrament and Spirit. It is only through the work of the Spirit that the sacrament can be efficacious. The two belong together. But if someone does not embrace the sacraments in faith, this does not mean there is something wrong with the sacrament—it is still an objective means of grace regardless of whether it is ever received. Likewise, the Word needs the Spirit to become efficacious in the hearts of the hearer. But if that Word is rejected, that does not imply that it is somehow deficient. It is still the objective revelation of God regardless of whether it is ever received. For discussion, see M. S. Horton, *Covenant and Eschatology: The Divine Drama* (Louisville: Westminster John Knox, 2002), 211.

[41]Bavinck, *Reformed Dogmatics*, 598.

[42]Frame, "The Spirit and the Scriptures," 229–35.

[43]D. F. Strauss, *Die christliche Glaubenslehre in ihrer geschichtlichen Entwicklung und im Kampfe mit der modernen Wissenschaft*, 2 vols. (Tübingen: Osiander, 1840), was thus mistaken when he argued that the self-attestation of Scripture in Protestant theology could be reduced to subjectivism (1:136). He understood the *testimonium* as the grounds for Scripture's authority, rather than the means by which Christians apprehend the Scripture's authority. See discussion in Hodge, "The Witness of the Holy Spirit to the Bible," 52–53; and G. C. Berkouwer, "The Testimony of the Spirit," in *The Authoritative Word*, ed. Donald K. McKim (Grand Rapids: Eerdmans, 1983), 155–81, esp. 156.

the *testimonium*. But this would be true only if the *testimonium* were itself the grounds for our belief—as if we argued to ourselves, "Because I am having this experience of the Spirit, therefore, on that basis, the Scripture is true." But as we have maintained, the ground for our belief is the apprehension of the divine qualities of Scripture itself, not the *testimonium* or our experience with it.[44] Thus, we need not be consciously aware of the work of the Spirit for the Spirit to be, in fact, working.[45] It seems, then, that our belief in the truth of Scripture via the work of the Spirit is best construed not as an inductive inference from some aspect of our experience (whether the Spirit or something else),[46] but, as Jonathan Edwards noted, as a more "immediate" or "intuitive" belief.[47]

2. Corporate Reception

In all of this discussion, we would be mistaken to think of the recognition of the canon as happening only on a personal and individualistic level (which is perhaps partly why it has seemed subjective to some).[48] There are good biblical reasons to think that the *testimonium* would also result in a corporate, or covenantal, reception of God's Word. By this we mean not that the church would have *absolute* unity regarding the canon—there would still be portions or subgroups with differing opinions—but that the church as a whole, both in the present and throughout the ages, would experience *predominant* unity.[49] If so, then we have biblical grounds for

---

[44]For some scholars, the *testimonium* quickly reduces to an argument from experience; e.g., F. Schleiermacher, *The Christian Faith* (Edinburgh: T&T Clark, 1928), 597–611. As a result, subjective experience becomes the ultimate authority and functions as an external standard that judges the truth of Scripture.

[45]Evans, *The Historical Christ and the Jesus of Faith*, 276–77.

[46]Hodge, "The Witness of the Holy Spirit to the Bible," 52–53.

[47]Jonathan Edwards, *The Works of Jonathan Edwards*, vol. 2, *Religious Affections*, ed. John E. Smith (New Haven, CT: Yale University Press, 2009), 298; and Plantinga, *Warranted Christian Belief*, 258–60, 330. There is an ongoing debate about whether belief grounded in the divine qualities is inferential or noninferential. Some will argue that the divine qualities are the *occasion* of someone's belief but need not involve any inferential argument (such as "because the Bible displays such and such quality, *therefore* it is inspired"). However, while some sort of inferential argument is surely not necessary for such knowledge, the existence of inferential arguments does not appear to be problematic. After all, if the Scriptures are God's word, then this is a rational and warranted inference. Such reasoning is so informal that, if guided by the Spirit, it does not appear to be incompatible with understanding our knowledge of Scripture as still, in some sense, immediate. For more discussion, see Frame, "The Spirit and the Scriptures," 229–35.

[48]It is on this point that Plantinga's contribution to the internal testimony of the Spirit could be improved. Although Plantinga does not deny that the *testimonium* has a corporate dimension (and we have every reason to think he would affirm it), he devotes nearly all his attention to explaining it only on an individual level.

[49]The question of how to identify the "church" seems of little concern because exact precision is not required. Even if the church is conceived of in the broadest of terms—perhaps defined as those bodies that believe "what is common to the great creeds" of the Christian faith (Plantinga, *Warranted Christian Belief*, vii)—there is still an overwhelming consensus around

thinking that the consensus of the church is a reliable indicator of which books are canonical.

Several considerations suggest that we should expect the canon to be received on a corporate-covenantal level. First, God's redemptive pattern has not been simply to redeem individuals, but to redeem a people, a church, for himself (Acts 15:14; Titus 2:14; 1 Pet. 2:9). And when God, by his redemptive activity, creates a covenant community, he then gives them covenant documents that testify to that redemption.[50] For these reasons, Meredith Kline and others have argued that canonical books are ultimately, and primarily, *covenantal* books. The biblical witness indicates that it is God's corporate people—not as individuals but as a covenant whole—who are "entrusted with the oracles of God" (Rom. 3:2). As Kline has argued, God gives the covenant documents with the intent that those documents become a "community rule."[51] The implications of this are clear: if God's canonical books ultimately have a corporate purpose, then we have every reason to think that the *testimonium* ultimately has a corporate purpose. The canon cannot rule a community unless it is received by that community. Evans argues for precisely this biblical logic.

> It seems highly plausible, then, that if God is going to see that an authorized revelation is given, he will also see that this revelation is recognized. . . . On this view, then, the fact that the church recognized the books of the New Testament as canonical is itself a powerful reason to believe that these books are indeed the revelation God intended humans to have.[52]

Second, if we affirm the efficacy of the *testimonium* on an individual level, why should we be less willing to affirm its efficacy on the corporate-covenantal level? If the *testimonium* can reliably lead an individual to

---

these twenty-seven books. Even so, we still have good biblical grounds for thinking that Christians can rightly identify the true church (at least in a manner that is sufficient for our purposes here). At its core, the church is marked by the true preaching of the gospel (John 8:31–47; 14:23; 1 John 4:1–3; 2 John 9) and the right administration of the sacraments that Christ gave his church (Matt. 28:19; Acts 2:42; 1 Cor. 11:23–30). Added to this can be a variety of other things, including Jesus's own teachings that true Christians are identified by their love for one another (John 13:35; cf. 1 John 4:7–8; 5:1). For more on the marks of the church, see Calvin, *Institutes*, 4.2.1–3; and Edmund P. Clowney, *The Church* (Downers Grove, IL: InterVarsity, 1995), 99–115. The distinction between the true church and the false church reminds us that not every community's reception of books holds the same weight. For instance, even though Mormons *claim* to be followers of Christ, we would not accept their canon (composed of the twenty-seven New Testament books plus the *Book of Mormon*) because they are not part of the true church.

[50] M. G. Kline, *The Structure of Biblical Authority*, 2nd ed. (Eugene, OR: Wipf and Stock, 1997), 76–93.

[51] Ibid., 89.

[52] Evans, "Canonicity, Apostolicity, and Biblical Authority," 155. J. W. Wenham, *Christ and the Bible*, 162–63, makes a very similar argument.

belief in the canon, there seems little reason why we should not affirm such reliability for the church as a whole. On the contrary, one might even argue that there are biblical reasons to be *more* confident in the role of the *testimonium* on a corporate level. After all, we have additional biblical testimony that we should heed "an abundance of counselors" (Prov. 11:14) and run the same path as the "great cloud of witnesses" (Heb. 12:1) that have gone before us. Moreover, it is the church, and not just the individual, that is given the Spirit: the church is God's house (1 Tim. 3:15), also called a "spiritual house" (1 Pet. 2:5), and is a body with one Spirit (1 Cor. 12:13). All of this suggests that if we doubt the *testimonium* on a corporate level, we would be compelled to doubt it equally on an individual level.

Third, the covenantal-corporate aspect of the *testimonium* has been historically affirmed by Reformed scholars. Bavinck declares,

> Subsumed under this heading of the testimony of the Holy Spirit is the witness the Spirit has borne to Scripture in the church throughout the centuries; and this witness is . . . directly [embodied] in the united confession of the believing community throughout the centuries that the Scripture is the word of God.[53]

Likewise, Abraham Kuyper argues that the testimony of the Holy Spirit ultimately works corporately and thereby creates a "communion of consciousness not merely with those round about us, but also with the generation of saints from former ages . . . [through which] the positive conviction prevails, that we have a graphically inspired Scripture."[54] Roger Nicole contends that we can know which books belong in the canon by appealing to "the witness of the Holy Spirit given corporately to God's people and made manifest by a nearly unanimous acceptance of the NT canon in the Christian churches."[55] Ned Stonehouse makes a similar connection.

> Although the church lacks infallibility, its confession with regard to the Scriptures, represents not mere opinion but an evaluation which is valid as derived from, and corresponding with, the testimony of the Scriptures to their own character. The basic fact of canonicity remains, then, the testimony which the Scriptures bear to their own authority. But the historian of the canon must recognize the further fact that the intrinsic authority

---

[53]Bavinck, *Reformed Dogmatics*, 597.
[54]Kuyper, *Encyclopedia of Sacred Theology*, 561–62.
[55]R. Nicole, "The Canon of the New Testament," *JETS* 40 (1997): 204.

established itself in the history of the church through the government of its divine head.[56]

It is here that we begin to see the proper role of the church in the authentication of canon. The books received by the church inform our understanding of which books are canonical not because the church is infallible or because it created or constituted the canon, but because *the church's reception of these books is a natural and inevitable outworking of the self-authenticating nature of Scripture*. Viewing the role of the church in the context of a self-authenticating Bible can bring fresh understanding to the complex church-canon relationship and may serve as a corrective to some extreme positions in the other canonical models. The Catholic model insists that the church's reception of these books is the sole grounds for the canon's authority. In the self-authenticating model, however, the church's reception of these books proves not to be evidence of the church's authority to create the canon, but evidence of the *opposite*, namely, the authority, power, and impact of the self-authenticating Scriptures to elicit a corporate response from the church. Jesus's statement that "my sheep hear my voice . . . and they follow me" (John 10:27) is not evidence for the authority of the sheep's decision to follow, but evidence for the authority and efficacy of the Shepherd's voice to call.[57] After all, the act of hearing is, by definition, derivative not constitutive.[58] Thus, when the canon is understood as self-authenticating, it is clear that the church did not choose the canon, but the canon, in a sense, chose itself.[59] As Childs has noted, the content of these writings "exerted an authoritative *coercion* on those receiving their word."[60] Barth agrees: "The Bible constitutes itself the Canon. It is the Canon because it *imposed itself* upon the Church."[61] In this way, then, the role of the church is like a thermometer, not a thermostat. Both instruments provide information about the temperature in the room—but one determines it and one reflects it.

---

[56]N. B. Stonehouse, "The Authority of the New Testament," in Stonehouse and Woolley, *The Infallible Word*, 135–36.

[57]John Calvin, *Tracts and Treatises*, trans. Henry Beveridge (Grand Rapids: Eerdmans, 1958), 267.

[58]J. Webster, *Holy Scripture: A Dogmatic Sketch* (Cambridge: Cambridge University Press, 2003), 45; see also C. Schwöbel, "The Creature of the Word: Recovering the Ecclesiology of the Reformers," in *On Being the Church: Essays on the Christian Community*, ed. C. Gunton and D. W. Hardys (Edinburgh: T&T Clark, 1989), 110–55.

[59]James D. G. Dunn, *Unity and Diversity in the New Testament: An Inquiry into the Character of Early Christianity* (London: SCM, 1990), xxxi.

[60]Brevard S. Childs, "The One Gospel in Four Witnesses," in *The Rule of Faith: Scripture, Canon, and Creed in a Critical Age*, ed. Ephraim Radner and George Sumner (Harrisburg, PA: Morehouse, 1998), 53, emphasis mine.

[61]Karl Barth, *Church Dogmatics*, trans. G. W. Bromiley and T. F. Torrance, 2nd ed. (Edinburgh: T&T Clark, 1975), I/1:107, emphasis mine.

On the other extreme, some approaches have been so intent on avoiding the mistakes of Roman Catholicism that they have virtually ignored the role of the church altogether, creating a just-me-and-God type of individualism where canon is determined entirely outside any ecclesiastical or corporate considerations.[62] As Kline observed, "Traditional formulations of the canon doctrine have not done full justice to the role of the community."[63] For example, Charles Briggs, while affirming the church's role at some points, still viewed the internal testimony of the Holy Spirit so individualistically that he could declare that every man should "make up his own mind," and the canon is a "question between every man and his God."[64] Although such an approach is often practiced under the heading of *sola scriptura*, it is ironic that the Scriptures themselves provide no basis for a purely "private" approach to the canon but, as noted above, consistently view the books of the canon as a covenantal (and therefore corporate) reality. Bavinck corrects this type of individualism, "The testimony of the Holy Spirit is not a private opinion but the witness of the church of all ages, of Christianity as a whole."[65]

In many ways, the fact that the corporate church, as a whole, would naturally recognize the canonical books is analogous to the way justification naturally leads to good works. Just because we believe that justification inevitably produces good works in an individual does not mean Christians live a perfect life. You can imagine someone objecting to the relationship between justification and good works on the grounds that they know many Christians who commit heinous sins. However, the belief that good works follow justification does not rule out such sins, or even periods of backsliding, but is merely a claim that, through the work of the Spirit, the overall, collective direction of one's life is one that bears fruit. Likewise, the biblical teaching that Christ's sheep hear his voice does not require perfect reception by the church with no periods of disagreement or confusion, but simply a church that, by the work of the Holy Spirit, will collectively and corporately respond. But the analogy goes even further. The belief that justification inevitably leads to good works does not imply that good works are the grounds of, or the cause

---

[62]Craig D. Allert, *A High View of Scripture? The Authority of the Bible and the Formation of the New Testament Canon* (Grand Rapids: Baker Academic, 2007), 68–86, provides a helpful reminder that the corporate church plays an important role in the reception of the canon.
[63]Kline, *The Structure of Biblical Authority*, 90.
[64]Charles A. Briggs, *Church Unity: Studies of Its Most Important Problems* (New York: Scribner, 1909), 161. See his fuller discussion of canon in Briggs, *General Introduction to the Study of Holy Scripture* (New York: Charles Scribner, 1899), 117–68.
[65]Bavinck, *Reformed Dogmatics*, 599, emphasis mine.

of, justification—that would be a grand misunderstanding of the doctrine. Likewise, simply because the church, through the internal witness of the Spirit, will collectively respond to the voice of Christ in these books does not make the voice of Christ in these books somehow dependent on the church. Books are not canonical because they are recognized; they are recognized because they are already canonical. It is this critical distinction that sets the self-authenticating model apart from many of the community-determined models discussed above.[66]

Thus, we have every biblical reason to believe that the Spirit's work within the hearts of his people (both individually and corporately) is effectual and that Christ makes good on his promise that "my sheep hear my voice . . . and they follow me" (John 10:27). Ridderbos sums it up: "Christ will establish and build His church by *causing the church to accept just this canon* and, by means of the assistance and witness of the Holy Spirit, to recognize it as his."[67] Again, this does not mean that we should expect to find perfect unity among the church, but it does mean that we should expect to find a corporate or covenantal unity—which is precisely what we do find.[68]

3. Apostolic Origins

So far, we have seen that canonical books are characterized by two attributes: they bear the marks of divinity (divine qualities) and are recognized by the church as a whole (corporate reception). But when we read the Scriptures, there is more to the concept of canon than just these two attributes. Indeed, if only these two attributes were considered, one might erroneously get the impression that canonical books are abstract

---

[66]One further distinction should be made here between the self-authenticating model and community-determined models, particularly Roman Catholicism. Roman Catholics consider the church's reception of these books as the *only* means by which a person can know the canon. However, the self-authenticating model considers the church's reception of these books as just *one* means of knowing the canon. As addressed in the introduction, there are a variety of ways that individuals can come to know the canonical books for the first time, such as observing the divine qualities of the books through the help of the Holy Spirit. One does not need the church. However, when it comes to the issue of *authenticating* the canon—i.e., not how an individual gains canonical knowledge for the first time but how the Christian religion can provide an account for how it knows these are the right books—then we are free to employ multiple means for how we have knowledge of the canon. The self-authenticating model, then, argues that the church's reception is one of three attributes of canonicity that provide knowledge of the canon, not that the church's reception is *required* for an individual to come to knowledge of the canon.

[67]Ridderbos, *Redemptive History*, 37, emphasis mine.

[68]Wenham, *Christ and the Bible*, 129, objects to the efficacy of the *testimonium* on the grounds that Scripture was not "always recognized as such immediately by all true believers." But why should we expect recognition to be *immediate*, or even without disagreement? Where does that requirement come from? We shall argue below in chap. 6 that we have scriptural warrant for *not* expecting absolute uniformity among believers.

revelation from God, utterly ahistorical and timeless—something quasi-gnostic that just drops down from heaven to be given again and again throughout the life of the church. But the Scriptures do not present the canon as abstract revelation, but as *redemptive* revelation.[69] Canonical books derive from particular redemptive epochs where God has acted in history to deliver his people. This redemptive-historical aspect of the canon is clearly visible in the fact that the two main covenants of Scripture—the old (Sinaitic) covenant and the new covenant—both are established in written form *after* God's special (and powerful) redemptive work was accomplished (e.g., Ex. 20:2; John 20:31).

In regard to the establishment of the new covenant, the message of redemption in Jesus Christ was entrusted to the apostles of Christ, to whom he gave his full authority and power: "The one who hears you hears me, and the one who rejects you rejects me" (Luke 10:16). The apostles are the link between the redemptive events themselves and the subsequent announcement of those events.[70] Not only did the apostles themselves write many of these New Testament documents, but, in a broader sense, they presided over the transmission of the apostolic deposit and labored to make sure that the message of Christ was firmly and accurately preserved for future generations, through the help of the Holy Spirit (Luke 1:1–4; Rom. 6:17; 1 Cor. 11:23; 15:3; Gal. 1:9; Phil. 4:9; Col. 2:6–8; 1 Thess. 2:13–15; 1 Tim. 6:20; 2 Tim. 1:14; 2 Pet. 2:21; Jude 1:3). Thus, the New Testament canon is not so much a collection of writings by apostles, but a collection of apostolic writings—writings that bear the authoritative message of the apostles and derive from the foundational apostolic era (even if not directly from their hands).[71] As John Webster puts it,

> Canonization is recognition of apostolicity, not simply in the sense of the recognition that certain texts are of apostolic authorship or provenance, but, more deeply, in the sense of the confession that these texts [are] "grounded in the salvific act of God in Christ which has taken place once and for all."[72]

Thus, we come to the third attribute of canonicity, namely, that all canonical books are apostolic books. This attribute reminds us that the authentication of canon has a strong retrospective component; it is to

---

[69]See discussions in Geerhardus Vos, *Biblical Theology* (Edinburgh: Banner of Truth, 1975), 299–304.
[70]Ridderbos, *Redemptive History*, 12–14; Vos, *Biblical Theology*, 303.
[71]The concept and definition of apostolicity will be explored in greater detail in chap. 5.
[72]Webster, *Holy Scripture*, 64. Webster is quoting from E. Schlink, *Ökumenische Dogmatik Grundzüge* (Göttingen: Vandenhoeck & Ruprecht, 1983), 635.

look backward to a particular historical epoch in which God has acted in Jesus Christ and to recognize that these books provide the authoritative apostolic interpretation of those actions.[73] But it is more than that. It is not just the claim that these books are *about* Christ's redemptive work in history, but it is the claim that these books are the *product* of Christ's redemptive work in history—that they are the outworking of the authority Christ gave to his apostles to lay down the permanent foundation for the church.[74] This is why canonical books are not only marked by divine qualities and corporate reception. They are not just instances of generic revelation that God offers the church in the present and might continue to offer in the future, but are the final and complete stage of revelation offered once and for all in the past.[75]

The early church fathers certainly understood this connection between apostolicity and canonical books. Ignatius, Bishop of Antioch, recognized the unique role of the apostles: "I am not enjoining [commanding] you as Peter and Paul did. They were apostles, I am condemned."[76] Likewise, the book of *1 Clement* not only encourages its readers to "take up the epistle of that blessed apostle, Paul,"[77] but also offers a clear reason why: "The Apostles received the Gospel for us from the Lord Jesus Christ, Jesus the Christ was sent from God. The Christ therefore is from God and the Apostles from the Christ."[78] In addition the letter refers to the apostles as "the greatest and most righteous pillars of the Church."[79] Apostolic origins were also central to early discussions about potential canonical books; for example, the Muratorian fragment rejected the so-called Pauline epistle to the Laodiceans because it was not really written by Paul. The church fathers understood a book as having apostolic origins even if it was not directly written by an apostle but nevertheless bore apostolic content and derived from the foundational period of the church. It is for this reason that Tertullian regarded Mark and Luke as "apostolic men."[80]

Of course, if one of the attributes of canonicity is a book's apostolic origins, then this entails an appeal to some external historical evidences to establish whether a book is apostolic. Needless to say, we do not have

---

[73] Webster, *Holy Scripture*, 64.
[74] Thomas F. Torrance, *God and Rationality* (New York: Oxford University Press, 2000), 152.
[75] Vos, *Biblical Theology*, 302–4.
[76] *Rom.* 4.4. For more on Ignatius's extensive discussion of apostolic authority, see C. E. Hill, "Ignatius and the Apostolate," in *StPatr*, vol. 36, ed. M. F. Wiles and E. J. Yarnold (Leuven: Peeters, 2001), 226–48.
[77] *1 Clem.* 47.1–3.
[78] *1 Clem.* 42.1–2.
[79] *1 Clem.* 5.2.
[80] *Marc.* 4.2.

space in this volume to address the historical evidence for the apostolicity of each of the canonical books; that has been adequately done in the major commentaries and New Testament introductions (however, we will touch broadly on these historical questions at some points below). It should be noted here, however, that exploring the apostolic origins of these books not only works positively (showing they are apostolic), but also works negatively (showing that *other* books are not). Indeed, given that there are very few extant Christian writings outside the New Testament that can reasonably be dated to the first century, there simply are not many other potential candidates for canonicity.[81] This fact alone eliminates most contenders for a spot in the canon.

But this raises questions about the use of historical evidences within the self-authenticating model. Does the use of evidences to show apostolic origins not make the same mistake as the criteria-of-canonicity model above and subject the canon to the uncertainties of modern biblical criticism? Not at all. The key difference is that in the self-authenticating model the external evidence does not stand *alone* as an independent standard to which Scripture must measure up. Consider the following.

a. *External evidence is part of the application of Scripture.* As already noted above, whenever we apply Scripture to any issue, it will inevitably involve external evidence from the world around us. But the use of such evidence is not inconsistent with the self-authenticating model because it does not stand alone but is interpreted and understood by the norm of Scripture. Indeed, the only reason we even know to look for "apostolic" books in the first place (as opposed to other kinds of books) is that Scripture is guiding our investigations. Even the earliest Christians would have used extrabiblical data as they sought to apply their understanding of the role of the apostles to their particular situation. Such data may have included simple things like whether the courier who delivered an apostolic letter was a known companion of the apostle who wrote it (e.g., Tychicus and Onesimus delivered Colossians and Philemon, Col. 4:7–9; Philem. 1:12), knowledge of a personal visit from an apostle himself where he delivered or mentioned a letter (which is information that does not come from the text of the letter!), or awareness of when or where a book was written. The latter reason was the basis for the Muratorian fragment's rejection of the *Shepherd of Hermas.*[82]

---

[81]The only extant work of any popularity dated to the first century is *1 Clement* (c. 96), and even that date has been challenged. More discussion on *1 Clement* will be offered below.

[82]The *Shepherd of Hermas* was rejected as a canonical book by the Muratorian fragment because it was known to be written "very recently, in our own times" (line 74). The meaning of this

b. *External evidence can provide adequate grounds for a belief through the work of the Holy Spirit.* C. S. Evans has rightly argued that although one does not *need* external evidence to have grounds for a belief, it would "be a mistake to argue that the Holy Spirit could not operate by means of evidence."[83] He declares, "There is no need to claim that beliefs are produced in only one manner. The Holy Spirit might produce the beliefs as basic ones, or they might be the outcome of a process that involves reflection on the evidence."[84] Thus, it is entirely appropriate for a single canonical model to have attributes that are more immediately or intuitively known (the divine qualities of a book) and attributes that are known through some awareness of external evidence (apostolic origins of a book).[85] Whether a belief is basic or based on evidence, we have adequate grounds for affirming that belief if it is produced by the Holy Spirit.

c. *Apostolicity is not the only attribute of canonicity.* In the self-authenticating model, as opposed to the criteria-of-canonicity model, the historical evidence for apostolicity does not stand alone but stands in conjunction with the other attributes of canonicity, divine qualities and corporate reception. We have not yet explored the relationship between these three attributes, but we shall argue below that each of the three serves to confirm and reinforce the other two. For instance, since all apostolic books also bear divine qualities (by virtue of their inspiration), then divine qualities, in one sense, can function as evidence for apostolicity.

The criteria-of-canonicity model above encounters problems at precisely these points. It seeks to use extrabiblical data not in the process of applying Scripture, but in order to determine what should be Scripture in the first place. Apostolicity is not viewed as a principle supplied by the canonical books, but is viewed as an independent and external test of what constitutes a canonical book and what does not. As a result, the criteria-of-canonicity model finds itself in the unenviable position of being *solely* dependent on historical data and with no divine norm through

---

phrase has recently been disputed by G. M. Hahneman, *The Muratorian Fragment and the Development of the Canon* (Oxford: Clarendon, 1992), 34–72. See response from Charles E. Hill, "The Debate over the Muratorian Fragment and the Development of the Canon," *WTJ* 57 (1995): 437–52.

[83] Evans, *The Historical Christ and the Jesus of Faith*, 285–86.

[84] Ibid., 287–88. For this reason, Evans argues that the use of evidence is not incompatible with an "externalist" epistemology.

[85] To a lesser degree one could also include the corporate reception of these books as something that must be ascertained through some level of external evidence. One would need to have at least some awareness of the historical church's affirmation of these twenty-seven books.

which to interpret it and no *testimonium* to help understand it.[86] Thus, the warning of Ridderbos is fitting: "Historical judgment cannot be the final and *sole* ground for the church's accepting the New Testament as canonical. To accept the New Testament on that ground would mean the church would ultimately be basing its faith on the results of historical investigation."[87]

C. Summary

The argument of the self-authenticating model so far is that we can know which books are canonical because God has provided the proper epistemic environment where belief in these books can be reliably formed. This environment includes not only providential exposure to the canonical books, but also the three attributes of canonicity that all canonical books possess—divine qualities, corporate reception, apostolic origins—and the work of the Holy Spirit to help us recognize them. Thus, contra the *de jure* objection, Christians do have adequate grounds for affirming their belief in the canon.

By way of example, if we want to know whether, say, 1 John is canonical, then we can apply the various components of the model. Obviously, since 1 John has been providentially exposed to the corporate church, then it is a book that the model can address. When it is examined, we can see that John's first letter bears the attributes of canonicity.

- It bears *divine qualities*: for example, it is a powerful writing, bears the beauty of the gospel message, and also stands in harmony with other scriptural books (this latter point has to do with the issue of "orthodoxy," which will be discussed more below).
- It has clear *apostolic origins*: for example, we have good historical reasons to date it to the redemptive-historical time period and to link it to the apostle John (including textual similarities to both the Gospel of John and Revelation).
- It has been *received by the corporate church*. Not only has it been widely affirmed throughout the history of the church, but it was also recognized at the earliest stages in the development of the canon and was even included in the second-century Muratorian fragment.

---

[86] As noted in the prior chapter, some advocates of the criteria-of-canonicity model recognize the importance of the role of the Holy Spirit; e.g., Habermas, "The Personal Testimony of the Holy Spirit to the Believer and Christian Apologetics," *Journal of Christian Apologetics* 1 (1997): 49–64; C. H. Pinnock, *Set Forth Your Case* (Chicago: Moody, 1971), 119–25; William Lane Craig, "Classical Apologetics," in *Five Views on Apologetics*, ed. S. B. Cowan (Grand Rapids: Zondervan, 2000), 28–38.

[87] Ridderbos, *Redemptive History*, 32–33, emphasis mine.

- And in all of these attributes, the Spirit is at work helping the believer rightly recognize their presence and validity.

Of course, this is a very quick overview of the way the model would work and would obviously be applied (in greater detail) to all twenty-seven books of the New Testament, as well as other potential candidates (e.g., *1 Clement, Shepherd of Hermas, Gospel of Thomas*).[88] But it is important to remember that the goal of the model is not to *prove* the authenticity of the canon to the skeptic. Rather, as discussed above at numerous points, our goal here is to ask whether the *Christian* has sufficient grounds for knowing which books God has given. Or, put differently, is the Christian's belief about the canon justified (or warranted)?

It is also worth mentioning that this model does not imply that Christians can have some sort of infallible, incontrovertible certainty about the canon (in a Cartesian sense). Even though canonical books necessarily bear these attributes, one can always raise doubts about whether we are accurately identifying the divine qualities, reading the evidence for apostolicity correctly, and so forth. But if the model does not entail that Christians can have infallible certainty about the canon, that does not mean Christians cannot have *knowledge* of the canon. Most epistemologists have rejected the idea that we must have that level of certainty in order to know something—otherwise we would have very few instances of knowledge. Consider, again, our own sense perception. Does my seeing a cup on the table provide *infallible* certainty that a cup is indeed on the table? No, because I could be hallucinating or dreaming, or I could be a brain in a vat somewhere and electrical impulses could be making me think I see a cup on the table. But this does not require me to reject my sense perception as a reliable means of knowledge.[89] In this same manner, just because a person could be mistaken about whether a book has divine qualities does not mean divine qualities are not a reliable means of identifying canonical books. Again, one can know something even if it does not rise to the level of absolute, incontrovertible certainty.

III. Implications of a Self-Authenticating Canon

Now that we have examined the major components of the self-authenticating model, we turn our attention to some implications of this model for the

---

[88]Someone might ask, "But how do you know there isn't another canonical book out there that you do not know about?" Again, they would need to be reminded that the model, as discussed above, deals only with *known* books.

[89]See helpful discussion in Plantinga, *Warranted Christian Belief*, 333–35.

study of canon. We shall argue here that this model is distinctive in that (1) the attributes of canonicity relate to each other in a mutually reinforcing manner, and (2) it provides a basis for affirming multiple and complementary definitions of canon.

A. *Attributes of Canonicity as Mutually Reinforcing*

What is distinctive about the self-authenticating model is not just that it has three attributes of canonicity, but the way the three attributes relate to one another. These are not three independent and disconnected qualities that canonical books happen to possess, but each attribute implies and involves the other two. Thus, you cannot really speak of one attribute without, in a sense, speaking of the others. They are all bound together. Divine qualities exist only because a book is produced by an inspired apostolic author. And any book that has an apostolic author, due to the inspiration of the Holy Spirit, will inevitably contain divine qualities. In addition, any book with divine qualities (and apostolic origins) will impose itself on the church and, via the work of the *testimonium*, be corporately received. And if any book is corporately received by the church, then that book must possess the divine qualities that would cause the church to recognize the voice of Christ in it (again through the *testimonium*).[90] Thus, if a book is examined that has one of these attributes, then that implies that the book also has the other two.

Because these three attributes imply one another, they work together as a unit—as *a web of mutually reinforcing beliefs*. Any given attribute not only implies the other two, but is also confirmed by the other two. So, apostolic origins not only imply divine qualities and corporate reception, but divine qualities and corporate reception are part of the way we know a book has apostolic origins.[91] Likewise, corporate reception not only implies the existence of apostolic origins and divine qualities, but is confirmed by the existence of apostolic origins and divine qualities. And divine qualities do not simply imply apostolic origins and corporate reception, but apostolic origins and corporate reception are part of how we know a book has divine qualities. What this means is that the self-authenticating model, at its core, is both self-supporting and self-correcting. One attribute not only gets support from the other two, but can also be corrected by

---

[90]We should remember that Christ says of his sheep, "A stranger they will not follow, but they will flee from him, for they do not know the voice of strangers" (John 10:5).

[91]For example, one of the reasons (but not the only reason) we think that a book like 1 John is apostolic is its early reception by the church as apostolic; thus, corporate reception is evidence for apostolic origins.

the other two (e.g., a person may think he recognizes divine qualities in a book, say the *Shepherd of Hermas*, but this is corrected by the lack of apostolic origins and corporate reception).[92]

The core strength of the self-authenticating model of canon, then, is the fact that it is three-dimensional. In contrast, the other models above tend to be one-dimensional and seek to authenticate canon by appealing to only a single attribute. These models are to be commended for correctly identifying attributes of canonicity, but the problem is that these attributes, biblically speaking, are not meant to work in isolation. When the three attributes are split apart, distortions are inevitable. If we only consider corporate reception in isolation, we might get the impression that canon is merely a discussion about the church and its desires and decisions— canon is just the books we prefer. If we only consider apostolic origins, we might think that the canon is all about history, facts, and historical processes. In the end, we are just left holding a bag of raw data. And if we only consider divine qualities, we might get the impression that the canon is just an instance of generic revelation given straight from heaven, with no historical manifestation at all. This not only would ignore the historical process of canonization, but would leave us with a canon that does not connect to (or come from) the real world.

The dangers inherent in absolutizing only one attribute of canonicity are apparent in Luther's approach to canon. In his preface to James, Luther declared, "What does preach Christ is apostolic, even if Judas, Annas, Pilate, or Herod does it."[93] In this statement, it is clear that Luther is concerned foremost about a book's orthodoxy ("what preaches Christ"). As we shall see below, orthodoxy is one of the divine qualities of Scripture. Thus, Luther has absolutized the divine qualities of canon in a manner that completely overrides a book's apostolic origins. He is even willing to call Herod and Pilate "apostolic" as long as they preach Christ. Although it is true that orthodoxy (divine qualities) plays a role in whether we consider a particular book to be "apostolic," it is likewise true that the apostolic origins of a book play a role in whether we consider it to be orthodox. After all, it is often a book's connection with the apostles that gave its early readers (and now gives us) confidence that its doctrine is to

---

[92]This model would also allow certain communities with a truncated canon to correct themselves. For example, the Syriac church has a twenty-two-book canon. Those twenty-two books are sufficient for supplying the individual components of the self-authenticating model and if applied properly would show the Syriac church that they are out of step with biblical principles and have an incomplete canon.

[93]Martin Luther, "Prefaces to the New Testament," in *Luther's Works*, vol. 35, *Word and Sacrament I*, ed. E. Theodore Bachmann (Philadelphia: Fortress, 1960), 396.

be received as "orthodox." Thus, books from Judas or Pilate or Herod, regardless of their content, would *not* be considered canonical. So, it is overly simplistic to argue that orthodoxy always determines apostolicity, or to argue that apostolicity always determines orthodoxy—both interact with one another and, in a sense, need one another.

A helpful historical example of the intertwined nature of orthodoxy and apostolicity is that of Serapion, Bishop of Antioch (c. 200). Upon examination of the *Gospel of Peter*, which was being read by some at the church at Rhossus, Serapion determined that Peter did not write it and said, "We receive both Peter and the other apostles as Christ, but the writings which falsely bear their names we reject."[94] Although Serapion's concern for apostolic authorship here is fairly clear, some have attempted to show that Serapion's rejection of the *Gospel of Peter* was only because it was promoting false doctrine (probably docetism), not because it was not written by Peter.[95] In this particular historical scenario, however, it seems evident that *both* authorship (apostolic origins) and orthodoxy (divine qualities) were in play, one affecting the other.[96] J. A. T. Robinson sums it up well: "Though the *motive* of [Serapion's] condemnation of [the *Gospel of Peter*] was the docetic heresy that he heard it was spreading, the *criterion* of his judgment, to which he brought the expertise in these matters that he claimed, was its genuineness as the work of the apostle."[97]

In the end, the self-authenticating model of canon actually serves to unite the various canonical models by acknowledging that no one attribute is ultimate. Because these three attributes are so interdependent, one can look at the entire question of canon through the lens of just one attribute. Thus, in a sense, all three attributes are about apostolic origins. Apostolic origins are not only about the historical background of a book, but also about the qualities produced by apostolic origins and how it leads to corporate reception in the church. Likewise, all three attributes are, in a sense, about divine qualities. Divine qualities are not only about the internal marks of a book, but also about where the divine qualities come from and the impact those qualities have on the church. And, in a sense,

---

[94]Eusebius, *Hist. eccl.* 6.12.2.

[95]William R. Farmer, "Some Critical Reflections on Second Peter: A Response to a Paper on Second Peter by Denis Farkasfalvy," *SecCent* 5 (1985–1986): 31–46.

[96]Other examples of the interplay between orthodoxy and apostolicity/authenticity can be found in H. J. de Jonge, "The New Testament Canon," in *The Biblical Canons*, ed. J.-M. Auwers and H. J. de Jonge (Leuven: Leuven University Press, 2003), 309–19.

[97]J. A. T. Robinson, *Redating the New Testament* (Philadelphia: Westminster, 1976), 188, emphasis mine.

all three attributes are about corporate reception. Corporate reception is not only about the response of the church to a book, but also about those things that make that response possible, namely, the divine qualities and apostolic origins of a book. Thus, all three attributes are critical if we are to have a biblical understanding of canon.

In sum, we can diagram the self-authenticating model of canon as shown in figure 1.

Figure 1. The self-authenticating model

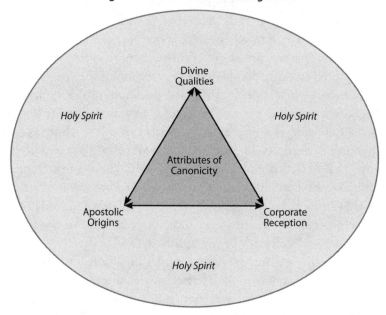

B. Balanced Definition of Canon

Once the self-authenticating model is understood, it can shed new light on the ongoing debate over the formal definition of canon. We noted above that canon can be defined in three different ways: exclusive (canon as reception), functional (canon as use), and ontological (canon as divinely given). These three definitions for canon generally correspond to the three attributes of canonicity in the self-authenticating model. If one looks at the canon from the perspective of corporate reception, then canon is most naturally defined as the books received and recognized by the consensus of the church (exclusive).[98] If one looks at the canon from the perspective

---

[98]However, there is a key difference between Sundberg's exclusive definition of canon and the one being used here. Sundberg insisted that the exclusive definition required near absolute uniformity, whereas our understanding of corporate reception requires only a predominant consensus.

of divine qualities, then canon is most naturally defined as those books that are used as authoritative revelation by a community (functional). And if one looks at the canon from the perspective of apostolic origins, then the canon is most naturally defined as those books given by God as the redemptive-historical deposit (ontological). The self-authenticating model, then, accommodates *all three* definitions of canon and acknowledges that each of them has appropriate applications and uses. Biblically speaking, there is no need to choose between these definitions (and their corresponding dates) because each of them captures a true attribute of canon and also implies the other two. It is only when certain canonical models absolutize just one of these three definitions (e.g., Sundberg's exclusive definition) that distortions can arise.

As noted in prior chapters, these three definitions of canon also have implications for the historical date assigned to the origins of the canon. When did the New Testament books become canonical according to the self-authenticating model? It depends upon which definition one uses. On the exclusive definition, we do not have a canon until the third or fourth century. On the functional definition, the extant evidence suggests that we certainly have a canon by the mid-second century (if not before). On the ontological definition, a New Testament book would be canonical as soon as it was written, giving a first-century date for the canon. When these three dates are viewed as a whole, they nicely capture the entire flow of canonical history: (1) God gives his books through his apostles; ➤ (2) the books are recognized and used as Scripture by early Christians; ➤ (3) the corporate church achieves a consensus around these books. The fact that these three dates are linked in such a natural chronological order reminds us that the story of the canon is indeed a *process*, and therefore it should not be artificially restricted to one moment in time. Put differently, the story of the canon is less like a dot and more like a line. If so, perhaps we should consider a shift in terminology. Rather than a myopic focus on the "date" of canon (and the ensuing debates that creates), perhaps it would be better to focus on the "stage" of canon. The former term suggests that canon can mean only one thing, whereas the latter term suggests that canon has a multidimensional meaning.

These three definitions of canon can be further illuminated by modern discussions in speech-act philosophy.[99] Speaking (and therefore divine

---

[99]Kevin J. Vanhoozer, *First Theology: God, Scripture and Hermeneutics* (Downers Grove, IL: InterVarsity, 2002), 159–203; Nicholas Wolterstorff, *Divine Discourse: Philosophical Reflections on the Claim That God Speaks* (Cambridge: Cambridge University Press, 1995); William P. Alston, *Illocutionary Acts and Sentence Meaning* (Ithaca, NY: Cornell University Press, 2000);

speaking) can take three different forms: (1) *locution* (making coherent and meaningful sounds or, in the case of writing, letters); (2) *illocution* (what the words are actually doing; e.g., promising, warning, commanding, declaring, etc.); and (3) *perlocution* (the effect of these words on the listener; e.g., encouraging, challenging, persuading).[100] Any speaking act can include some or all of these attributes. These three types of speech-acts generally correspond to the three definitions of canon outlined in the self-authenticating model. The ontological definition of canon refers to the actual writing of these books in redemptive history and thus refers to a *locutionary* act. The functional definition refers to what the canonical books do as authoritative documents and thus refers to an *illocutionary* act. And the exclusive definition refers to the reception and impact of these books on the church and thus envisions a *perlocutionary* act.

Speech-act theory helps clarify, once again, that the disagreements over the definition of canon often prove to be a matter of emphasis in any given canonical model. For example, the community-determined models tend toward viewing canon as a perlocutionary act and, therefore, often resist calling something canon until there is an impact or response from the believing community. This goes a long way, for example, toward explaining the existential/neoorthodox model of canon, particularly in its Barthian manifestation. As noted above, Barth's doctrine of Scripture emphasizes revelation as an "event" that happens to individuals when the Spirit illumines them and they experience the word of God. Thus, it is no surprise that canon exists only when there is a response from the community. Although there are residual concerns about Barth's doctrine of Scripture (as discussed earlier), he is correct on this important point: canon has a perlocutionary dimension to it.[101]

With these considerations in mind, if we are to offer a formal definition of canon for the self-authenticating model, it would be as follows: The New Testament canon is *the collection of apostolic writings that is regarded as Scripture by the corporate church*. Of course, as we use the word *canon*

J. L. Austin, *How to Do Things with Words* (Oxford: Oxford Paperbacks, 1976); and John R. Searle, *Speech Acts: An Essay in the Philosophy of Language* (Cambridge: Cambridge University Press, 1970).

[100] Austin, *How to Do Things with Words*, 100–103; Horton, *Covenant and Eschatology*, 126–27; Wolterstorff, *Divine Discourse*, 1–36.

[101] Kevin J. Vanhoozer, "A Person of the Book? Barth on Biblical Authority and Interpretation," in *Karl Barth and Evangelical Theology*, ed. Sung Wook Chung (Grand Rapids: Baker, 2006), 26–59. In this article, Vanhoozer offers a helpful discussion of how speech-act theory can help us understand Barth's doctrine of Scripture better (though I am not as optimistic as Vanhoozer that Barth's doctrine is consistent with that of Calvin or the Reformers). See also David Gibson, "The God of Promise: Christian Scripture as Covenantal Revelation," *Them* 29 (2004): 27–36.

throughout this study, we may focus upon just one of the three aspects of this definition at any given time. Therefore, it is important that the reader carefully note the following: while all canonical books (eventually) have all three attributes of canonicity, the term *canon* can still be used for a book *before* it has all three attributes of canonicity. For example, the Gospel of John was "canon" ten minutes after it was written even though it was not yet received by the corporate church. Again, the self-authenticating model is not arguing that the corporate reception of the church *makes* a book canonical. This stands in contrast with the community-determined models, which often make a book's canonicity contingent on corporate reception. Instead, this model argues that a book can be canonical prior to corporate reception, but cannot be canonical if it never has corporate reception.

IV. Potential Defeaters of a Self-Authenticating Canon

The essence of the self-authenticating model is that Christians have a rational basis (or warrant) for affirming the twenty-seven books of the New Testament canon because God has created the proper epistemic environment wherein belief in the canon can be reliably formed. However, that is not all that needs to be said. Even if one has a rational basis for holding to a belief, that belief still faces the possibility of epistemic defeat by other beliefs that one might come to hold. Such "defeaters" are the kind of beliefs that would challenge or undercut a prior belief, giving one reason to think that the prior belief is false.[102] For example, imagine John wakes up in the morning, and after seeing that his alarm clock says 9:00 a.m., he forms the belief that he is late for work. But as he scrambles to get ready, his wife informs him that their three-year-old daughter was playing with the alarm clock the night before and likely changed the time. This new information would serve as a defeater for John's prior belief that he was late for work, even though that prior belief was entirely justified.

Likewise, when it comes to our belief in the New Testament canon, there are potential defeaters that might serve to bring doubt upon the grounds of our belief. In a volume this size it is not possible to mention all potential canonical defeaters, so we will focus upon the primary ones. These primary defeaters are usually designed to challenge the attributes of canonicity discussed above and whether these attributes really provide a means of identifying canonical books. The three main defeaters are the following:

---

[102]Plantinga, *Warranted Christian Belief*, 357–73.

- *The challenge to divine qualities: apparent disagreements and/or contradictions between New Testament books.* This defeater is designed to argue against the existence of divine qualities in these books. If New Testament books are inconsistent with one another—as many scholars have claimed—then how could they really be from God? How could canonical books bear internal marks of their divinity if they prove to be a disparate collection of writings with different theologies and different doctrines?
- *The challenge to apostolic origins: a number of New Testament books were not written by apostles.* Although we have argued here that all canonical books are apostolic, much of modern scholarship argues that a number of our New Testament books are pseudonymous forgeries. For instance, of all of Paul's epistles, only seven are widely regarded as authentic (Romans, 1 and 2 Corinthians, Galatians, Philippians, 1 Thessalonians, and Philemon). In the face of such claims, how can we claim that all canonical books are apostolic?
- *The challenge to corporate reception: there was widespread disagreement in the early church that lasted well into the fourth century (and beyond).* In this chapter we have argued that the consensus of the corporate church is part of how we identify canonical books because such books would have imposed themselves on the church via the work of the Holy Spirit. But is the significance of the consensus of the church not called into question when we recognize the widespread disagreement and confusion that existed in early Christianity about the extent of the canon? If the church experienced disarray over canonical books from the very start, should this not raise doubts about whether the Spirit was really at work? Moreover, there are segments of the church still today that have a different New Testament canon (e.g., the Syrian Orthodox Church has a twenty-two-book canon). Are we to think that these churches do not have the Spirit?

These potential defeaters raise important questions about the canon that, unfortunately, cannot be addressed adequately in a single volume. Nevertheless, we will attempt to provide at least a preliminary response to each of them throughout the remaining chapters. In addition to responding to these defeaters, the rest of this volume will also probe deeper into each of the three attributes of canonicity and how they help us understand the origins and development of the New Testament.

PART 2

EXPLORING AND DEFENDING
THE CANONICAL MODEL

4

THE DIVINE QUALITIES
OF THE CANON

> All things the Divine Scripture says are utterances of the
> Holy Spirit.
>
> GREGORY OF NYSSA

Of all the attributes of canonicity, the divine qualities of Scripture are the least discussed in modern canonical studies. Most scholars prefer to devote their energies to the corporate reception of these books, or perhaps to their apostolic origins, but attention is rarely given to their divine qualities. This neglect is largely because a number of canonical models do not even acknowledge that such qualities *exist* in the canonical books. For the historical-critical model, the reason one book became canon and not another has less to do with the intrinsic qualities of the books themselves and more to do with the preferences and purposes of the early church that chose them. They are canonical not because of what they are but because of what the church is.[1] Likewise, the existential/neoorthodox model also denies that there is anything distinctive or intrinsic in the books themselves that sets them apart. For Barth, "The texts are authoritative not in virtue of any property they may have."[2] Instead, what sets them apart is that the Spirit uses them, despite their ordinariness, to speak to

---

[1] H. Y. Gamble, *The New Testament Canon: Its Making and Meaning* (Philadelphia: Fortress, 1985), 58–59.
[2] D. H. Kelsey, *The Uses of Scripture in Recent Theology* (Philadelphia: Fortress, 1975), 47.

the church. In addition, even certain versions of the criteria-of-canonicity model largely overlook the content of the book and focus solely on the book's apostolic origins.[3]

But this was not the approach of the early church fathers. Origen, for instance, was quite convinced that divine qualities played a central role: "If anyone ponders over the prophetic sayings . . . it is certain that in the very act of reading and diligently studying them his mind and feelings will be touched by a divine breath and he will recognize the words he is reading are not utterances of man but the language of God."[4] The Reformers were no different.[5] The Belgic Confession argues that these books are identified as canonical not so much by the testimony of the church but because "the Holy Spirit testifies in our hearts that they are from God, and also because they *prove themselves* to be from God."[6] And, as seen in the prior chapter, these same views were held by Calvin, Owen, Turretin, Bavinck, and many others. Such a conviction flows naturally from the belief that the canonical books are constituted by the Holy Spirit.[7] As Richard Muller has noted, "There must be some evidence or imprint of the divine work of producing Scripture in the Scriptures themselves."[8]

But what exactly is it about the content of these books that gives us good reasons to think they are from God? The Westminster Confession of Faith provides some clarity in this regard.

> The heavenliness of the matter, the efficacy of the doctrine, the majesty of the style, the consent of all the parts, the scope of the whole, (which is to give all glory to God), the full discovery it makes of the only way of man's salvation, the many other incomparable excellencies, and the entire perfection thereof, are arguments whereby [Scripture] doth abundantly *evidence itself* to be the Word of God.[9]

Within the WCF, we can observe three categories of divine qualities: (1) the beauty and excellency of Scripture, (2) the efficacy and power

---

[3]E.g., The divine qualities of the canonical books are largely overlooked in R. L. Harris, *Inspiration and Canonicity of the Bible* (Grand Rapids: Zondervan, 1978).

[4]*Princ.* 4.1.6. For Origen, all Scriptures were considered "prophetic sayings."

[5]For a fuller discussion, see Richard A. Muller, *Post-Reformation Dogmatics*, vol. 2, *Holy Scripture* (Grand Rapids: Eerdmans, 1993), esp. 270–302; and John Owen, "The Divine Original: Authority, Self-Evidencing Light, and Power of the Scriptures," in *The Works of John Owen*, vol. 16, *The Church and the Bible*, ed. William H. Goold (repr., Edinburgh: Banner of Truth, 1988), 297–421.

[6]Belgic Confession 5.2, emphasis mine.

[7]Muller, *Holy Scripture*, 270–302; J. I. Packer, *Fundamentalism and the Word of God* (Grand Rapids: Eerdmans, 1992), 115–25.

[8]Muller, *Holy Scripture*, 270.

[9]WCF 1.5, emphasis mine.

of Scripture, and (3) the unity and harmony of Scripture. The first two qualities will be addressed briefly, and the bulk of this chapter will be spent on the third. Of course, we must not draw too sharp a distinction between these categories. In many ways they overlap and interact with one another.[10]

I. The Beauty and Excellency of Scripture

The first category to be noted here is that the canonical Scriptures bear evidence of their divine origins by their beauty, excellence, and perfection. As the WCF notes, the Scriptures stand out due to "the heavenliness of the matter . . . the majesty of the style . . . the many other incomparable excellencies, and the entire perfection thereof." In other words, the Scriptures, being from God, bear the very attributes of God himself.[11] After all, how does a person know when he has encountered God? Does God need some external authority to confirm his identity? When men encounter God, they are vividly aware of his beauty, majesty, and perfection and need no further "evidence" that he is God (Pss. 27:4; 50:2; 96:6; Isa. 6:1–7; Rev. 1:12–17; 4:3). In addition, Scripture itself is described over and over again throughout the Bible as bearing these very same attributes. The psalmist declares of God's word:

> The law of the LORD is perfect. (19:7)

> The commandment of the LORD is pure. (19:8)

> How sweet are your words to my taste,
>   sweeter than honey to my mouth! (119:103)

> Your testimonies are wonderful. (119:129)

Thus, one knows the Scriptures are from God because they bear the beauty and perfection of God.

It should be noted that the Confession's understanding of the "majesty of the style" is not a reference to rhetorical or literary qualities that would appeal to modern man. The beauty of Scripture, then, is a *spiritual*

---

[10]Obviously, part of the beauty and excellency of a book can be its harmony and unity or even its power and efficacy. Nonetheless, it is still helpful to distinguish between these categories.

[11]John M. Frame, *Perspectives on the Word of God: An Introduction to Christian Ethics* (Phillipsburg, NJ: P&R, 1990), 13–15; see also Frame, *The Doctrine of the Word of God* (Phillipsburg, NJ: P&R, 2010), 297–315.

beauty, not just an aesthetic one. For this reason, Calvin acknowledges that the classics (Cicero, Plato, Aristotle) have rhetorical force, but that the Scripture "clearly is crammed with thoughts that could not be humanly conceived."[12] As Paul himself says, "And my speech and my message were not in plausible words of wisdom, but in demonstration of the Spirit and of power, so that your faith might not rest in the wisdom of men but in the power of God" (1 Cor. 2:4–5).[13] We are reminded, then, that the beauty and excellency of Scripture is primarily due to the manner in which it puts forth the beauty and excellency of Christ. G. C. Berkouwer observes, "The Spirit's witness begins by binding us to the center of Scripture, namely Jesus Christ."[14] No doubt this is why the Confession considers one of the internal evidences of Scripture to be "the full discovery it makes of the only way of man's salvation" (1.5).

We see this very approach evident in the early church fathers as they assessed the authority of the canonical books. For example, we read in the prologue to Jerome's commentary on Philemon that he defended the epistle on the grounds that it is "a document which has in it so much of the beauty of the Gospel," which is the "mark of its inspiration."[15] Chrysostom declares that in the Gospel of John there is "nothing counterfeit" because the Gospel is "uttering a voice which is sweeter and more profitable than that of any harp or any music . . . something great and sublime."[16] Origen defends the canonicity of the book of Jude because "it is filled with the healthful words of heavenly grace,"[17] and he defends the canonical Gospels because of their "truly venerable and divine contents."[18] Right before citing Matthew 4:17 and Philippians 4:5, Clement of Alexandria says that you can distinguish the words of men from the words of Scripture because "no one will be so impressed by the exhortations of any of the saints, as he is by the words of the Lord Himself."[19] Origen defends the canonicity of the book of Hebrews on the ground that "the ideas of the epistle are magnificent [θαυμάσιά]."[20] Tatian explains, "I was led to put faith in these [Scriptures] by the unpre-

---

[12]John Calvin, *Institutes of the Christian Religion*, ed. John T. McNeill, trans. Ford Lewis Battles (Philadelphia: Westminster, 1960), 1.8.2.
[13]Origen appeals to this very passage in his defense of the quality of Scripture (*Cels.* 1.62).
[14]G. C. Berkouwer, *Studies in Dogmatics: Holy Scripture,* trans. Jack Rogers (Grand Rapids: Eerdmans, 1975), 44.
[15]Prologue to *Comm. Phlm.*
[16]*Hom. Jo.* 1.2.
[17]*Comm. Matt.* 10.17.
[18]*Cels.* 3.21.
[19]*Protr.* 9.
[20]Eusebius, *Hist. eccl.* 6.25.12, translation mine.

tending cast of the language, the inartificial character of the writers, the foreknowledge displayed of future events, the excellent quality of the precepts."[21]

Even though we have been talking about how the "beauty and excellency" of Scripture leads to its acceptance, there is a parallel even within nonbiblical literature. Why is it that some secular writings are received with more popularity and regarded as classics, while others languish in obscurity? Is it always due to political pressures from the publisher, the shameless self-promotion of the author (or lack thereof), or some other *external* cause? No, sometimes it is a book's *internal qualities* that lead to its acceptance. Some books are just better than others. And the readers are quite able to notice the difference. Willie van Peer makes this case persuasively regarding the popularity of Shakespeare's 1593 version of *Romeo and Juliet*.[22] An earlier version of the story—with the same general plot and characters, but a very different ethos and ending—was published by Arthur Brooke in 1562. Why did Shakespeare's version gain such universal appeal, while Brooke's has been almost entirely forgotten? It certainly cannot be because Shakespeare's play fit with the political and moral climate that was dominant in Elizabethan England. On the contrary, Brooke's version was the one that upheld the dominant views of the day, and Shakespeare's was in many ways subversive to the status quo. In the end, it was the *content* of Shakespeare's work—and the way that content resonated with the masses—that led to its acceptance. Van Peer concludes that the Shakespeare example "falsifies the claim . . . that the canon is made up of only works that are in the interests of those in power."[23]

The reality that a book's own internal qualities might lead to its acceptance has also been observed by Old Testament scholars. While not acknowledging that Old Testament books possessed "divine qualities" in the way we have here, Shemaryahu Talmon still recognizes that the cause of their final acceptance was not official declarations of some authoritative

---

[21]*Address to the Greeks*, 29. Although Tatian is referring here to the Old Testament Scriptures, we have no reason to think that he would not have ascribed these same qualities to the New Testament Scriptures. Bruce M. Metzger, *The Canon of the New Testament: Its Origin, Development, and Significance* (Oxford: Clarendon, 1987), 115, declares, "[Tatian's] *Diatessaron* supplies proof that all four Gospels were regarded as authoritative, otherwise it is unlikely that Tatian would have dared to combine them into one gospel account." See also R. M. Grant, "Tatian and the Bible," in *StPatr*, vol. 1, = TU 63 (Berlin, 1957), 297–306; and K. L. Carroll, "Tatian's Influence on the Developing New Testament," in *Studies in the History and Text of the New Testament in Honor of Kenneth Willis Clark*, ed. B. L. Daniels and M. J. Suggs (Salt Lake City: University of Utah Press, 1967), 59–70.

[22]Willie van Peer, "Canon Formation: Ideology or Aesthetic Quality?," *British Journal of Aesthetics* 36 (1996): 97–108.

[23]Ibid., 107.

body, but their popularity with the people.[24] Talmon declares, "There is no explicit or implicit statement in the Hebrew Scriptures which can give reason to think that in the biblical period a council of any kind, at any time, ever debated the establishment of a corpus of authoritative writings, or enacted the inclusion of a book in such a corpus."[25] On the contrary, "public acclaim was the decisive factor"[26] in determining which books were in and which books were out. Simply put, "compositions which *earned* popular acclaim were transmitted."[27]

In these ways, we can see that a book's acceptance is not always a result of being chosen by the powers that be. Instead, a book often finds acceptance through a process not unlike the survival of the fittest.[28] The "strongest" books are the ones that prevail. In this way, a book really can choose itself.

II. The Power and Efficacy of Scripture

A second way the canonical Scripture testifies to itself is the way it functions in the life of the reader. Its divine origins are evident not only from what it *says*, but also from what it *does*. The teachings of Scripture prove to bring wisdom (Ps. 119:98; 2 Tim. 3:16), give joy to the heart (Neh. 8:8–12; Ps. 119:111), provide "light" to the dark paths of life (Ps. 119:105), give understanding to the mind (Ps. 119:144), give peace and comfort (Ps. 119:50), expose sin and guilt (2 Kings 22:11–13; Acts 2:34–37; Heb. 4:12–13), and lead to prosperity and blessing (Ps. 1:1–3). The WCF, cited above, refers to this particular line of internal evidence when it mentions "the efficacy of the doctrine." In other words, the teachings of Scripture not only bear the attributes of beauty and perfection (as noted above), but also prove to be powerful and effective. Paul Helm picks up on this same line of thought.

> It is not simply that the Scriptures say that they are the revelation of God that is the evidence for their being so, but also that they *function* as the Word of God. . . . One element [of Scripture functioning as the word of God] is the idea that the Bible purports to give an analysis or diagnosis of

---

[24]S. Talmon, "The Crystallization of the 'Canon of Hebrew Scriptures' in the Light of the Biblical Scrolls from Qumran," in *The Bible as Book: The Hebrew Bible and the Judaean Desert Discoveries*, ed. E. D. Herbert and E. Tov (London: The British Library, 2002), 5–20.
[25]Ibid., 9.
[26]Ibid., 10.
[27]Ibid., emphasis mine.
[28]C. E. Hill, *Who Chose the Gospels? Probing the Great Gospel Conspiracy* (Oxford: Oxford University Press, 2010), 226–29.

the reader. . . . Connected with this is the power of the Scriptures to raise
and satisfy certain distinctive needs in the reader. . . . Connected with this
is the displaying in Scripture of excellent moral standards. . . . And connected with this is the provision of new motivations to reach out for the
newly set standards.[29]

Of course, Helm's comments here are just a sampling of all that could
be said about the efficacy and actions of Scripture.[30] The fundamental
point to be realized here is that the Scriptures are powerful and dynamic,
making an impact on the reader in a way that testifies to their distinctive
origins and authority. As N. T. Wright has observed, "Those who read
these writings discovered, from very early on, that the books themselves
carried the same power, the same *authority in action*, that had characterized the initial preaching of the 'word.'"[31]

In the language of historical Reformed theology, this divine quality
can be summed up by saying that the Scriptures are a "means of grace."[32]
Scriptures do more than pass along propositional information (as important as that is); they are "living and active . . . piercing to the division
of soul and spirit, of joints and marrow" (Heb. 4:12). Returning to our
earlier discussion of speech-act theory, to say that the canon is a means
of grace is to say that the canon, when attended by the Holy Spirit, has
a *perlocutionary* effect; it changes, shapes, and transforms its reader or
hearer. The canon is not something to be judged as much as it is the thing
that does the judging. When this attribute of the canon is appreciated,
once again, we can see how the canon is not so much shaped by the community of faith, but a means of shaping the community of faith. Or in
the words of Martin Luther, "Ecclesia non facit Verbum sed fit Verbo."[33]

Such a construal of canon is emphasized in the work of William
Abraham, particularly his book *Canon and Criterion in Christian
Theology*.[34] Abraham argues that much of modern Christendom has mis-

---

[29]P. Helm, "Faith, Evidence, and the Scriptures," in *Scripture and Truth*, ed. D. A. Carson and
John Woodbridge (Grand Rapids: Zondervan, 1983), 310.

[30]For more on this point, see Francis Turretin, *Institutes of Elenctic Theology*, trans. George
Musgrave Giger, ed. James T. Dennison Jr., 3 vols. (Phillipsburg, NJ: P&R, 1992–1997), 1:63–64;
and E. J. Young, *Thy Word Is Truth* (Edinburgh: Banner of Truth, 1991), 33–34.

[31]N. T. Wright, *The Last Word: Beyond the Bible Wars to a New Understanding of the Authority
of Scripture* (San Francisco: HarperSanFrancisco, 2005), 51, emphasis his.

[32]Westminster Larger Catechism, questions 155–60; Louis Berkhof, *Systematic Theology* (Grand
Rapids: Eerdmans, 1941), 610–15.

[33]Martin Luther, "The Misuse of the Mass," in *Luther's Works*, vol. 36, *Word and Sacrament
II*, ed. A. R. Wentz (Philadelphia: Fortress, 1959), 144–45: "The church does not constitute the
word, but is constituted by the word."

[34]William J. Abraham, *Canon and Criterion in Christian Theology: From the Fathers to Feminism*
(New York: Oxford University Press, 2002); see also William J. Abraham, Jason E. Vickers, and

understood the function of the canon by using it as a doctrinal *norm*—an epistemic criterion for determining true from false beliefs—when believers should have been using it as a means of grace that can transform people's lives. Abraham's concern that the canon not become just an instrument to arbitrate doctrinal disputes is a valid one; indeed it is one that Reformed theology (and its emphasis on the Word as a means of grace) has long affirmed. However, Abraham's helpful reminder goes further than it should when he insists that the canon functions *only* as a means of grace and not as a doctrinal norm. As Vanhoozer has noted, "Why must it be one or the other? Jesus was full of grace *and* truth (John 1:14). . . . Doctrine's direction serves both epistemic and pastoral purposes."[35] Abraham has rightly recognized an important reason why canonical books impacted the early church—because they were a powerful means of grace—but he fails to realize that the canonical books bear *other* divine attributes as well.[36]

The early church fathers also recognized that the canonical books were distinctive because of their power and efficacy. Justin defends Christianity by declaring, "I shall prove to you as you stand here that we have not believed empty fables, or words without any foundation but words filled with the Spirit of God, and big with power, and flourishing with grace."[37] In addition, referring to the words of Christ, Justin says, "For they possess a terrible power in themselves, and are sufficient to inspire those who turn aside from the path of rectitude with awe; while the sweetest rest is afforded those who make a diligent practice of them."[38] In the *Apology of Aristides* (c. 130), the author invites the emperor to read "the Gospel" because "you also if you read therein, may perceive the power which belongs to it."[39] Clement of Alexandria reminds his listeners that transformation and sanctification come not by the words of men but by "those letters [of Scripture] that sanctify," and he proceeds to cite numerous New Testament books.[40] Irenaeus defends the fourfold Gospel on the grounds that these Gospels are always "breathing out immortality on every side, and vivifying men afresh."[41] Origen, defending the Gospels against the

---

Natalie B. Van Kirk, eds., *Canonical Theism: A Proposal for Theology and the Church* (Grand Rapids: Eerdmans, 2008).

[35]Kevin J. Vanhoozer, *The Drama of Doctrine: A Canonical-Linguistic Approach to Christian Theology* (Louisville: Westminster John Knox, 2005), 145.

[36]For further critique of Abraham, see J. Webster, "Canon and Criterion: Some Reflections on a Recent Proposal," *SJT* 54 (2001): 67–83.

[37]*Dial.* 9.1.

[38]*Dial.* 8.2.

[39]2.4 (Syriac).

[40]*Protr.* 9.

[41]*Haer.* 3.11.8.

criticisms of Celsus, declares that the words of Jesus contained therein are "accompanied with divine power" that transforms its hearers in regard to "their dispositions and their lives."[42]

III. The Unity and Harmony of Scripture

The third category of divine qualities is the remarkable internal harmony and consistency borne throughout the canonical books. The WCF, noted above, acknowledges this component when it refers to "the consent of all the parts." It is clear from the Scriptures themselves that God is a God of harmony and unity, always consistent with himself and never contradicting himself (Ps. 89:35; Prov. 14:5; Titus 1:2; Heb. 13:8). Therefore, we would expect any document purporting to be the word of God to be consistent with other revelation from God.[43] The early church fathers agree. Irenaeus says, "All Scripture, which has been given to us by God, shall be found by us perfectly consistent . . . and through the many diversified utterances [of Scripture] there shall be heard one harmonious melody in us, praising in hymns that God who created all things."[44] Tertullian echoes this sentiment in regard to the Gospels: "Never mind if there does occur some variation in the order of their narratives, provided that there be agreement in the essential matter. . . . And here I might now make a stand, and contend that a work ought not to be recognized . . . which exhibits no consistency."[45] Justin states this plainly: "I am entirely convinced that no Scripture contradicts another [Scripture]."[46]

Of course, concepts like harmony or consistency can be fairly vague and undefined. When we say that God's revelation is consistent with itself, what exactly do we mean? Consistent in regard to what? There are three different categories in which this consistency and unity can be expressed: doctrinal, redemptive-historical, and structural. Again, these categories overlap with one another and, to some extent, presuppose one another, so we should not make too sharp of a distinction between them.

A. Doctrinal Unity

The most obvious type of unity exhibited in the Scriptures is doctrinal unity. When the various parts of the Scriptures are examined, it is evident that there is unity on a complex array of theological issues, such as the

---

[42]Cels. 1.62.
[43]Muller, Holy Scripture, 293; Owen, The Divine Original, 342–43.
[44]Haer. 2.28.3.
[45]Marc. 4.2.
[46]Dial. 65.1.

nature of God, the make-up of man, the nation of Israel, the purpose and structure of the church, the person and work of Christ, the message of forgiveness and redemption, the importance of holiness, the role and function of the sacraments, eschatology and the last days, and so on. Whenever we speak of a canonical book's doctrinal unity with other divine revelation, that is just another way of saying that book is *orthodox*.[47] The subject of orthodoxy is common in modern studies of the canon and is often presented as one of several "criteria of canonicity."[48] As noted above, however, the very concept of canonical criteria raises a host of theological and epistemological challenges that should give us pause. Thus, instead of viewing orthodoxy as some sort of external, independent standard, outside of God's revelation, by which one can "test" a book's canonical status, we should view it simply as a way that God's revelation *confirms itself*. This very practice is exemplified in Scripture when a prophet's inspired words are confirmed on the basis of prior inspired revelations of God (Deut. 18:20), or when the Bereans search the Scriptures to see whether Paul's inspired teaching is consistent with the Old Testament inspired teaching (Acts 17:10ff.). That said, it may be useful to examine the issue of orthodoxy from two different perspectives: first, from the perspective of the earliest Christians as they worked with an *incomplete* New Testament canon and sought to recognize (for the first time) the books that God had given, and second from our modern day as we work with a *complete* New Testament canon and ask whether there are sufficient grounds for thinking that these books are indeed from God.

1. Orthodoxy and an Incomplete New Testament Canon

In the earliest phases of the Christian faith, before the canon was complete, the orthodoxy of a book often played a critical role in how canonical books were recognized.[49] Even though orthodoxy was not sufficient in and of itself to show that a book was canonical—many books circulating in

---

[47]Broad studies on the themes of heresy and orthodoxy include Alister McGrath, *Heresy: A History of Defending the Truth* (New York: HarperCollins, 2009); Robert M. Bowman, *Orthodoxy and Heresy* (Grand Rapids: Baker, 1992); Harold O. J. Brown, *Heresies: Heresy and Orthodoxy in the History of the Church* (Peabody, MA: Hendrickson, 1988); R. Williams, ed., *The Making of Orthodoxy: Essays in Honor of Henry Chadwick* (Cambridge: Cambridge University Press, 1989).

[48]General discussions of this issue can be found in Lee M. McDonald, *The Formation of the Christian Biblical Canon* (Peabody, MA: Hendrickson, 1995), 232–36; Bruce M. Metzger, *The Canon of the New Testament: Its Origin, Development, and Significance* (Oxford: Clarendon, 1987), 251–53; and F. F. Bruce, *The Canon of Scripture* (Downers Grove, IL: InterVarsity, 1988), 260–61.

[49]See helpful discussion of the role of orthodoxy in H. J. de Jonge, "The New Testament Canon," in *The Biblical Canons*, ed. J.-M. Auwers and H. J. de Jonge (Leuven: Leuven University Press, 2003), 309–19.

early Christianity were regarded as orthodox and yet were not necessarily considered canonical (e.g., the *Shepherd of Hermas*)—it was nevertheless an important and necessary step in that direction. In essence, orthodoxy functioned as the *sine qua non* of canonical books. A book could not be canonical without it. The classic example of the role of orthodoxy is the well-known account of Serapion, bishop of Antioch (c. 200), which we discussed above. Though Serapion also had concerns about the authorship of the *Gospel of Peter*, he condemned the gospel because it led the church into a "hole of heresy."[50] Likewise, the Muratorian canon rejects the pseudonymous epistle of Paul to the Laodiceans on the grounds that it contained "Marcionite heresy" and "it is not fitting that poison should be mixed with honey."[51] In both of these examples, the heretical nature of the book played a role in determining its noncanonical fate.

Of course, the idea that orthodoxy could be a reliable guide in the early church's recognition of the New Testament canon has been fundamentally challenged by Walter Bauer.[52] In *Orthodoxy and Heresy in Earliest Christianity*, Bauer argued that orthodoxy could not have been a reliable guide in the development of the canon because there was no uniform standard for orthodoxy until the fourth century. Before that time there was no Christianity per se, but rather a wide variety of Christianities (plural), each with its distinctive doctrinal beliefs and each vying to be the dominant version. It was only after the canon was complete, and the theological "winners" had been determined, that one could meaningfully speak of orthodoxy in early Christianity. Thus, the canon was not so much the result of orthodoxy, but the cause of it. Sure, the later Christians who finally picked the New Testament books *claimed* these books were consistent with the original teachings of Jesus. But, argues Bauer, such a claim was simply an after-the-fact justification of the choices they had already made. In the modern day, it would be like entering a route into your car's GPS system only *after* traveling that route and arriving at your destination (while claiming that it was the very thing that led you there).

In many ways, Bauer's thesis is the first "defeater" we shall examine regarding the divine qualities of Scripture (particularly regarding

---

[50]Eusebius, *Hist. eccl.* 6.12.2. It should be noted that there is no indication that the church at Rhossus actually regarded the *Gospel of Peter* as Scripture; rather it appears that they were just using the gospel as a helpful and edifying book. Either way, the incident helps illustrate the critical role of orthodoxy in the discussion of early Christian writings.

[51]Muratorian fragment, line 67.

[52]Walter Bauer, *Orthodoxy and Heresy in Earliest Christianity*, ed. Robert Kraft and Gerhard Krodel, trans. Paul J. Achtemeier (Philadelphia: Fortress, 1971); original German: Walter Bauer, *Rechtgläubigkeit und Ketzerei in ältesten Christentum* (Tübingen: Mohr, 1934).

Scripture's unity and orthodoxy). As we do so, we should acknowledge from the outset that Bauer is certainly correct at a number of points. Most notably, he rightly observes that early Christianity was quite a diverse affair—heresies emerged very early, as is evident from many of the New Testament writings themselves and the false teachings they were designed to oppose (e.g., Gal. 6:12; Col. 2:11–13; 2 Pet. 2:1; 1 John 2:19; Jude 4–8; Rev. 2:6, 15). And this diversity certainly continued into the later centuries of Christianity, as is evident from groups like the Ebionites, the Marcionites, the Valentinians, and so on.[53] However, the other aspects of Bauer's thesis have been challenged and roundly (some say decisively) critiqued.[54] Although there is not space here to revisit these critiques, we can briefly comment upon the heart of Bauer's argument. The sticking point for Bauer is whether there was a reliable standard by which a book's orthodoxy could be measured in this earliest phase of Christianity. No doubt various groups *believed* they were orthodox (everyone believed that), but is there any reason to think that one of the groups could have got it right? Was there an available and trustworthy basis by which they could have distinguished true teachings from false? We shall argue that early Christians had access to three sources by which orthodoxy could be measured.

a. *The Old Testament.* Routinely overlooked by those in the Bauer camp—ironically in a Marcionite fashion—is the decisive role the Old Testament played among the earliest Christians. M. F. Wiles once declared, "There was never a time when the Church was without written Scriptures. From the beginning she had the Old Testament and it was for her the oracles of God."[55] Aside from the numerous examples of Old Testament

---

[53]For an account of this diversity in the spirit of Walter Bauer, see B. D. Ehrman, *Lost Christianities: The Battles for Scripture and the Faiths We Never Knew* (New York: Oxford University Press, 2002); and J. D. G. Dunn, *Unity and Diversity in the New Testament: An Inquiry into the Character of Early Christianity* (London: SCM, 1990).

[54]For an overview and critique of Bauer's thesis, see A. J. Köstenberger and M. J. Kruger, *The Heresy of Orthodoxy: How Modern Culture's Fascination with Diversity Has Reshaped Our Understanding of Early Christianity* (Wheaton, IL: Crossway, 2010).

[55]M. F. Wiles, "Origen as Biblical Scholar," in *The Cambridge History of the Bible: From the Beginnings to Jerome*, ed. P. R. Ackroyd and C. F. Evans (Cambridge: Cambridge University Press, 1993), 454. In contrast, Sundberg has argued that "the church did not inherit a canon of Scriptures from Judaism. The church was forced to determine her OT for herself" (A. C. Sundberg, "The 'Old Testament': A Christian Canon," *CBQ* 30 [1968]: 152). Obviously, this is not the place to take up a full defense of the state of the Old Testament canon in early Christianity, but Sundberg's claim has been challenged by Stephen B. Chapman, "The Old Testament Canon and Its Authority for the Christian Church," *Ex auditu* 19 (2003): 125–48; Christopher Seitz, *The Goodly Fellowship of the Prophets: The Achievement of Association in Canon Formation* (Grand Rapids: Baker Academic, 2009); Andrew E. Steinmann, *The Oracles of God: The Old*

usage within the New Testament itself, quotations from the Old Testament are abundant within the writings of the apostolic fathers and other early Christian texts.[56] Thus, right from the outset, certain "versions" of Christianity would have been ruled as out of bounds. For example, any quasi-gnostic version of the faith that suggested that the God of the Old Testament was not the true God but a "demiurge"—as in the case of the heretic Marcion—would have been deemed unorthodox on the basis of these Old Testament canonical books alone. As Ben Witherington has observed, "Gnosticism was a non-starter from the outset because it rejected the very book the earliest Christians recognized as authoritative—the Old Testament."[57] So the claim that early Christians had no Scripture on which to base their declarations that some group was heretical and another orthodox is simply mistaken. The Old Testament books would have provided that initial doctrinal foundation.[58]

b. *"Core" New Testament books*. Although all New Testament books are orthodox, not all of them needed to have this expressly established prior to their recognition by the early church (or at least portions thereof). As we shall discuss further in subsequent chapters, some New Testament books, especially Paul's major epistles and the four Gospels, would have been recognized as authoritative from a very early time. They were received not so much because they measured up to some standard of orthodoxy but primarily on the basis of their obvious apostolic origins—these were the books that were "handed down" from the apostles.[59] Gamble notes, "The letters of Paul and the Synoptic Gospels . . . had been valued so long and so widely that their orthodoxy could only be taken for granted: it

---

Testament Canon (St. Louis: Concordia Academic Press, 1999); and R. T. Beckwith, *The Old Testament Canon of the New Testament Church, and Its Background in Early Judaism* (Grand Rapids: Eerdmans, 1986). Even if there is not an Old Testament canon in the first century in terms of the *exclusive* definition, there definitely seems to be an Old Testament canon in terms of the *functional* definition. The threefold structure of the Hebrew Old Testament seems well established by the turn of the century, even if the exact makeup of the writings was still in flux (e.g., Luke 24:44; Sir. 39:1; 4QMMT [95–96]; Philo, *Contempl. Life*, 25).

[56] John Barton, *The Spirit and the Letter: Studies in the Biblical Canon* (London: SPCK, 1997), 74–79; Larry W. Hurtado, *Lord Jesus Christ: Devotion to Jesus in Earliest Christianity* (Grand Rapids: Eerdmans, 2003), 496; Pheme Perkins, "Gnosticism and the Christian Bible," in *The Canon Debate*, ed. Lee Martin McDonald and James A. Sanders (Peabody, MA: Hendrickson, 2002), 355–71; Harry Gamble, "Literacy, Liturgy, and the Shaping of the New Testament Canon," in *The Earliest Gospels*, ed. Charles Horton (London: T&T Clark, 2004), 27–39.

[57] Ben Witherington, *The Gospel Code: Novel Claims About Jesus, Mary Magadelene, and Da Vinci* (Downers Grove, IL: InterVarsity, 2004), 115.

[58] C. H. Dodd, *According to the Scriptures: The Substructure of New Testament Theology* (London: James Nisbet, 1952), 127ff.

[59] Hill, *Who Chose the Gospels?*, 231–34.

would have been nonsensical for the church to have inquired, for example, into the orthodoxy of Paul!"[60]

Thus, there appears to have been a collection of core New Testament writings that would have functioned as a norm for apostolic doctrine at quite an early point. This explains why the vast majority of later "disagreements" about the boundaries of the New Testament canon appear to be focused narrowly on only a handful of books; apparently the core of the New Testament was intact from a very early stage. Barton also observes this pattern: "Astonishingly early, the great central core of the present New Testament was already being treated as the main authoritative source for Christians. There is little to suggest that there were any serious controversies about the Synoptics, John, or the major Pauline epistles."[61] If Barton is correct, then these core books would have provided a theological and doctrinal foundation for analyzing the orthodoxy of peripheral books such as 2 Peter, Jude, and 3 John. This entire scenario reminds us that in the earliest centuries of Christianity the internal quality of orthodoxy did not play an equal role in the reception of all the New Testament books (though the New Testament books are all equally orthodox). Instead, it played its primary role in the discussions about books whose status was disputed or uncertain.[62]

c. *The "rule of faith."* In the next chapter we shall discuss the role of apostolic tradition within early Christianity and how that provided the doctrinal norm for the earliest Christians (and how the New Testament books are, in essence, the written embodiment of that tradition). This apostolic tradition came to be summarized and known by a number of names, such as the *regula fidei* ("rule of faith"), ὁ κανὼν τῆς ἀληθείας ("the canon of truth"), and ὁ κανὼν τῆς ἐκκλησίας ("the canon of the church").[63] The fact that this summary of apostolic tradition was a key

---

[60]Gamble, *The New Testament Canon*, 70.
[61]Barton, *The Spirit and the Letter*, 18.
[62]Gamble, *The New Testament Canon*, 69–70.
[63]For more on this topic, see John Behr, *Formation of Christian Theology*, vol. 1, *The Way to Nicaea* (Crestwood, NY: St Vladimir's Seminary Press, 2001), 11–48; L. W. Countryman, "Tertullian and the Regula Fidei," *SecCent* 2 (1982): 208–27; W. R. Farmer, "Galatians and the Second Century Develoment of the Regula Fidei," *SecCent* 4 (1984): 143–70; Albert C. Outler, "Origen and the Regula Fidei," *SecCent* 4 (1984): 133–41; Catherine Gonzalez, "The Rule of Faith: The Early Church's Source for Unity and Diversity," in *Many Voices, One God: Being Faithful in a Pluralistic World*, ed. Walter Brueggemann and George W. Stroup (Louisville: Westminster John Knox, 1988), 95–106; Paul M. Blowers, "The Regula Fidei and the Narrative Character of Early Christian Faith," *ProEccl* 6 (1997): 199–228; Bryan Litfin, "The Rule of Faith in Augustine," *ProEccl* 14 (2005): 85–101; Paul Hartog, "The 'Rule of Faith' and Patristic Biblical Exegesis," *TrinJ* 28 (2007): 65–86; and most recently, R. W. Jenson, *Canon and Creed* (Louisville: Westminster John Knox, 2010).

weapon in the early church's battle against heresy is evident in the works of Dionysius of Corinth, Hippolytus, Irenaeus, Clement of Alexandria, Tertullian, and Origen.[64] This rule of faith was a particularly effective weapon because it was oral (in a mostly illiterate world),[65] it was relatively brief (and therefore easily employed),[66] and it was widespread (and thus available to a broad range of churches).[67]

Although the *regula fidei* is a type of "tradition," it is important to distinguish it from later ecclesiastical tradition. In Irenaeus's battle with the heretics, he refers to the *regula fidei* not as something that derives from the church but as something that derives from the apostles themselves—the church merely preserves it.[68] He declares, "We refer [the heretics] to that tradition from the apostles which is preserved through the succession of presbyters in the churches."[69] In this sense, the rule of faith did not contain new teachings or doctrines that were not found in the Scriptures, nor was it unduly separated from the Scriptures as if they were two entirely independent sources for orthodox teaching.[70] Instead, it was understood to be "a summary of Scripture's own story line"[71] or "the principle and logic of Scripture itself."[72] Or, as Irenaeus put it, the rule is "the order and the connection of the Scriptures."[73] This was certainly true in regard to the way the rule related to the Old Testament. Far from being something entirely separate, the rule expounded on the Old Testament and revealed

---

[64]Eric Osborn, "Reason and the Rule of Faith in the Second Century AD," in Williams, *The Making of Orthodoxy*, 40–61.

[65]Hartog, "The 'Rule of Faith,'" 82–85.

[66]Osborn, "Reason and the Rule of Faith," 48–49. The classic summaries of the rule can be found in Irenaeus, *Haer.* 1.10.1; Tertullian, *Praescr.* 13, *Virg.* 1, *Prax.* 2; and Origen, *Princ.*, preface 4–10.

[67]Irenaeus in particular emphasizes its universality by declaring that "the churches which have been founded in Germany do not believe or hand down anything else; neither do those founded in Spain or Gaul or Libya or in the central regions of the world" (*Haer.* 1.10.2; cf. 3.3.1).

[68]J. N. D. Kelly, *Early Christian Doctrines* (San Francisco: HarperCollins, 1978), 36–39.

[69]*Haer.* 3.2.2; cf. 3.3.1.

[70]E. Flesseman-van Leer, *Tradition and Scripture in the Early Church* (Assen: Van Gorcum, 1954), 127.

[71]Vanhoozer, *The Drama of Doctrine*, 206; O. Cullmann, "The Tradition," in *The Early Church* (London: SCM, 1956), 59–99; B. Hägglund, "Die Bedeutung der 'regula fidei' als Grundlage theologischer Aussagen," *ST* 12 (1958): 1–44; Osborn, "Reason and the Rule of Faith," 48.

[72]John J. O'Keefe and R. R. Reno, *Sanctified Vision: An Introduction to Early Christian Interpretation of the Bible* (Baltimore: Johns Hopkins University Press, 2005), 120. Paul L. Gavrilyuk, "Scripture and the *Regula Fidei*: Two Interlocking Components of the Canonical Heritage," in Abraham, Vickers, and Van Kirk, *Canonical Theism*, 27–42, draws too sharp a distinction between the Scriptures and the rule of faith, declaring that the latter "is not a summary of Scripture" (34).

[73]*Haer.* 1.8.1; see discussion in Behr, *The Way to Nicea*, 36. Tertullian declares that the Scriptures "indeed furnish us with our Rule of faith" (*Prax.* 11), and Origen also affirms that the rule of faith is that which is "discovered in holy Scripture" (*Princ.*, preface 10).

its relationship to the redemptive work of Christ. Christopher Seitz makes this point: "The rule of faith in the early church fathers is a correlating of the gospel with the stable and authoritative claims of the Scriptures of Israel, seen now as a first testament and crucial foundational witness."[74] Clement of Alexandria affirms this same connection: "The ecclesiastical canon is the concord and harmony of the law and the prophets in the covenant delivered at the coming of the Lord."[75]

Likewise, the rule can be understood as a summary of the message contained in the New Testament writings. Although the *regula fidei* certainly would have played a role in the church's recognition of those New Testament books that were disputed or uncertain (as discussed above), at the same time it would have undoubtedly been shaped by those core New Testament books that had already been used from an earlier time. Moreover, it is important to remember that the New Testament books are the written embodiment of the oral apostolic tradition (as we shall discuss in chapter 5). So, inasmuch as the rule of faith is itself a summary of that oral apostolic tradition, it is thereby also a summary of the New Testament writings—even those writings that had not yet been formally recognized by the church. There is therefore a "symbiotic,"[76] mutually affirming, and even "circular"[77] relationship between the *regula fidei* and the New Testament. Not only was the rule of faith used to "validate" canonical books, but the canonical books were also used to "validate" the content of the rule of faith.[78] Either way, we can understand these interactions as instances of the biblical message validating itself.

Because the rule of faith is a summary of scriptural teaching, Irenaeus makes sure his readers understand that this sort of tradition does not change or develop: "[The church] carefully guards this preaching and this faith, which she has received. . . . Neither will any of those who preside in the churches, though exceedingly eloquent, say anything else."[79] John Behr comments, "It is clear, then, that for Irenaeus 'tradition' is not alive . . . it cannot change, grow, or develop into something else."[80] Irenaeus

---

[74]Seitz, *The Goodly Fellowship of the Prophets*, 36; see also Kelly, *Early Christian Doctrines*, 34.
[75]*Strom.* 6.15.3.
[76]Daniel H. Williams, *Retrieving the Tradition and Renewing Evangelicalism: A Primer for Suspicious Protestants* (Grand Rapids: Eerdmans, 1999), 95.
[77]Gamble, *The New Testament Canon*, 70.
[78]Ibid., 69. See T. F. Torrance, "The Deposit of Faith," *SJT* 36 (1983): 1–28, particularly the discussion on 13.
[79]*Haer.* 1.10.2.
[80]Behr, *The Way to Nicea*, 38. Of course, this does not mean that the rule of faith cannot be adjusted or molded to fit particular needs and particular situations. See Williams, *Retrieving the Tradition and Renewing Evangelicalism*, 94; and Blowers, "The Regula Fidei," 226.

contrasts this approach with the heretics who are always listening to the "living voice," such as Valentinus, Marcion, or Cerinthus.[81] For Irenaeus (and other early Fathers), the church must not look to such a "living voice" in the present but must always be *looking back* to the apostolic voice in the past (which is found in Scripture and summarized in the rule of faith).[82] In other words, Irenaeus understands the apostolic deposit about Jesus in its proper redemptive-historical context—it is once and for all, unchangeable, and unrepeatable.

In the end, the use of the rule of faith by the early church fathers tells us something critical about their understanding of the internal qualities of Scripture. It demonstrates that they viewed Scripture not as a disjointed patchwork of divergent theological concepts, but as a unified and corporate story with overarching themes that are able to be summarized and captured. No doubt the rule, in some sense, *brings* harmony and homogeneity to the biblical text—it is a framework of reading the Bible rightly.[83] At the same time, however, it must be remembered that the Fathers did not view this harmony as artificial, as if the various parts were being forced into a man-made edifice. The rule of faith worked to bring harmony precisely because there was harmony *already* there that could be summarized and expressed. It was this conviction about the internal qualities of Scripture that helped guide the church fathers in their reception of the canon.

2. Orthodoxy and a Complete New Testament Canon

We have seen that orthodoxy would have played an important role in the initial recognition of the New Testament books by the earliest Christians. However, we cannot consider the orthodoxy of the New Testament books only from this perspective. We must remember that the question about how we recognize the canon is not just a historical one (how it happened in the early church), but also an epistemological one (whether the

---

[81]*Haer.* 3.2.1. Papias uses "living voice" to refer not to oral tradition but to his preference for *eyewitness testimony* from the disciples of Jesus Christ (Eusebius, *Hist. eccl.* 3.39.3–4). Since eyewitnesses to the life of Jesus were all dead by the time of Irenaeus, he can say that there is no longer a valid "living voice" available in his day (despite the claims of heretics like Valentinus and Marcion). Thus, Irenaeus argued that we must now depend on the apostolic deposit given in the Scriptures (and summarized in the *regula fidei*). For more on the concept of the "living voice," see R. Bauckham, *Jesus and the Eyewitnesses: The Gospels as Eyewitness Testimony* (Grand Rapids: Eerdmans, 2006), 21–30; and L. Alexander, "The Living Voice: Skepticism Toward the Written Word in Early Christian and Graeco-Roman Texts," in *The Bible in Three Dimensions*, ed. D. J. A. Clines, S. E. Fowl, and S. E. Porter (Sheffield: JSOT, 1990), 221–47.

[82]G. W. H. Lampe, "Scripture and Tradition in the Early Church," in *Scripture and Tradition*, ed. F. W. Dillistone (London: Lutterworth, 1955), 41.

[83]O'Keefe and Reno, *Sanctified Vision*, 120–21.

Christian religion has sufficient grounds for thinking that these twenty-seven books are given by God as canonical). And when we answer the latter question, we can do so by considering the New Testament canon *as a completed whole*. When this is done, the issue of orthodoxy takes on additional dimensions. Although the orthodoxy of an individual book is not sufficient to demonstrate its canonicity, the fact that all twenty-seven books share doctrinal harmony with each other (and with the thirty-nine books of the Old Testament) proves to be a compelling argument for the New Testament's divine origins. When one considers the vastness of the Scripture, the variety of authors, the diversity and complexity of topics, and different geographical locations, backgrounds, and time periods—combined with the fact that the canon was not assembled by a single individual or group who could have imposed such unity—it becomes all the more noteworthy that there is such remarkable theological harmony throughout these books. Indeed, this is the very argument used by the WCF when it refers to "the consent of all the parts" and "the scope of the whole" (1.5). This demonstrates the important fact that some divine qualities can be seen and appreciated only when the Scripture is viewed on a canonical level and not simply in a piecemeal fashion. In this sense, the canon is *synergistic* in nature: the whole is greater than the sum of the parts.[84]

Of course, the theological unity of the New Testament books has also not gone unchallenged.[85] Whereas Walter Bauer challenged the existence of orthodoxy in the early church, F. C. Baur has challenged the existence of orthodoxy across the spectrum of the completed New Testament canon. Baur argued that each New Testament book was constructed as a "party document" and motivated by a particular theological agenda, or *Tendenz*. Some books were Jewish-Christian (Matthew, James), some were Gentile-Christian (Pauline Epistles), and some were a synthesis (Acts, Hebrews, John).[86] Baur's ideas have been picked up (in varying forms) by modern

---

[84] In this regard, the excellent work of Brevard Childs has rightly highlighted the degree to which the scriptural books illumine one another and enhance one another when read canonically. In other words, the unity of Scripture becomes clearer when the books are read together. For more, see Brevard S. Childs, *The New Testament as Canon: An Introduction* (London: SCM, 1984).

[85] E.g., Heikki Räisänen, *Beyond New Testament Theology: A Story and a Program* (London: SCM, 1990); Dunn, *Unity and Diversity in the New Testament*; and Franz Overbeck, *On the Christianity of Theology*, trans. John Elbert Wilson (San Jose, CA: Pickwick, 2002).

[86] F. C. Baur, *Paul, the Apostle of Jesus Christ, His Life and Work, His Epistles and Teachings* (London: Williams and Norgate, 1873–1875), 1:113–16. The influence of Baur is felt in a number of more modern works suggesting that Paul was the real founder of Christianity and at odds with the historical Jesus: A. Loisy, *The Gospel and the Church*, trans. C. Home (London: Isbister, 1903); J. Weiss, *Paulus and Jesus* (Berlin: Verlag von Reuther & Reichard, 1909); Hyam Maccoby, *The Mythmaker: Paul and the Invention of Christianity* (London: Weidenfeld and

scholars such as Dunn and also Robinson and Koester—who speak of different "trajectories" within the New Testament.[87] Käsemann, in his famous essay "The New Testament Canon and the Unity of the Church," contends that "this variability [of doctrine] is already so wide in the New Testament that we are compelled to admit the existence not merely of significant tensions, but, not infrequently, of irreconcilable theological contradictions."[88] Lee Martin McDonald, noting that many scholars appeal to orthodoxy in their discussion of the canon, rejects this idea on the grounds that the New Testament has many theological positions that are "difficult to reconcile."[89] Ernest Best, having argued for "contradictions within Scripture," states that "a generation ago it was customary to speak of *the* theology of the New Testament, now it is more customary to speak of a number of theologies within the New Testament."[90]

Such objections constitute a second potential defeater to the divine qualities of Scripture and certainly cannot be dismissed lightly. Indeed, the New Testament writings are not always easy to understand and can, at times, prove challenging and difficult (2 Pet. 3:16). We must acknowledge that there is a substantial amount of diversity even within the pages of the New Testament itself. The Synoptics do not always tell the story of Jesus in the same manner or with the same words—raising endless discussions about potential contradictions.[91] John is quite different from the

---

Nicholson, 1986); Joseph Klausner, *From Jesus to Paul* (New York: Macmillan, 1943); and M. Casey, *From Jewish Prophet to Gentile God* (Cambridge: Clarke, 1991). For a response to this idea, see Eberhard Jüngel, *Paulus und Jesus: Eine Untersuchung zur Präzisierung der Frage nach dem Ursprung der Christologie* (Tübingen: Mohr [Siebeck], 1962); A. J. M. Wedderburn, *Paul and Jesus: Collected Essays* (Sheffield: JSOT, 1989); and David Wenham, *Paul: Follower of Jesus or Founder of Christianity?* (Grand Rapids: Eerdmans, 1995). For more on the differences between Jewish and Hellenistic Christianity, see Martin Hengel, *Judaism and Hellenism: Studies in Their Encounter in Palestine During the Early Hellenistic Period* (Philadelphia: Fortress, 1974).

[87] James M. Robinson and Helmut Koester, *Trajectories Through Early Christianity* (Philadelphia: Fortress, 1971); Dunn, *Unity and Diversity in the New Testament*, 1–8.

[88] Ernst Käsemann, "The Canon of the New Testament and the Unity of the Church," in *Essays on New Testament Themes* (London: SCM, 1964), 100. See also Ernst Käsemann, "The Problem of a New Testament Theology," *NTS* 19 (1973): 235–45.

[89] Lee Martin McDonald, "Identifying Scripture and Canon in the Early Church: The Criteria Question," in McDonald and Sanders, *The Canon Debate*, 428, emphasis his.

[90] Ernest Best, "Scripture, Tradition, and the Canon of the New Testament," *BJRL* 61 (1979): 272, emphasis his.

[91] Supposed theological contradictions among the Synoptics have been discussed more since the rise of redaction criticism. E.g., H. Conzelmann, *Theology of St. Luke* (New York: Harper & Row, 1960), famously argued that Luke was written to explain the delay of the parousia; and G. Bornkamm, "The Stilling of the Storm in Matthew," in *Tradition and Interpretation in Matthew*, ed. G. Bornkamm, G. Barth, and H. J. Held (Philadelphia: Westminster, 1963), 52–57, argued that Matthew changed Mark's version of the stilling of the storm to portray the disciples as having more faith. For more on contradictions in the Synoptics, see C. Blomberg, *The Historical Reliability of the Gospels*, 2nd ed. (Downers Grove, IL: InterVarsity, 2007), 152–95.

Synoptics, not only including original stories and events (e.g., the miracle at Cana, healing of the man born blind, raising of Lazarus), but also leaving out core elements of the life of Jesus (e.g., exorcisms and parables).[92] Paul's own letters often seem quite different from one another in both tone and content (e.g., Galatians and Romans vs. the Pastorals).[93] And, of course, Paul's theological concerns can, at times, seem opposed to the concerns of James.

Even in the midst of all these issues, however, it must not be assumed (though it often is) that differences necessarily entail genuine contradictions. We can affirm the multiplicity of theological perspectives while also recognizing that they share a common end. In addition, it is not clear that these objections are always as decisive as they are often made out to be. For one, many of the particular arguments have been answered by various scholars over the years who have labored to demonstrate the theological unity of these writings (though there is not space to revisit those works here).[94] These studies have made a solid case that many of these supposed factions are often overplayed and that time and time again apparent theological disagreements prove to be just that, apparent.[95] Take as a brief example the supposed division between Paul and James. Although there were certainly actual historical disagreements between Paul and men "from James" (Gal. 2:12) over the ongoing function of the

---

[92]A helpful survey of historical criticisms of John's Gospel (and some response to these criticisms) can be found in Paul Anderson, *The Fourth Gospel and the Quest for Jesus: Modern Foundations Reconsidered* (London: T&T Clark, 2006).

[93]A helpful overview of some of these issues can be found in Stanley E. Porter, "Pauline Authorship and the Pastoral Epistles: Implications for Canon," *BBR* 5 (1995): 105–23.

[94]For these types of works, see C. H. Dodd, *The Apostolic Preaching and Its Developments* (New York: Harper, 1949); Floyd Filson, *One Lord, One Faith* (Philadelphia: Westminster, 1943); A. M. Hunter, *The Unity of the New Testament* (London: SCM, 1952); P. Balla, *Challenges to New Testament Theology: An Attempt to Justify the Enterprise* (Peabody, MA: Hendrickson, 1998); David Wenham, "Unity and Diversity in the New Testament," appendix to George Eldon Ladd, *A Theology of the New Testament* (Grand Rapids: Eerdmans, 2001), 684–719; D. A. Carson, "Unity and Diversity in the New Testament: The Possibility of Systematic Theology," in Carson and Woodbridge, *Scripture and Truth*, 65–95; I. Howard Marshall, *New Testament Theology* (Downers Grove, IL: InterVarsity, 2004), 17–48; E. E. Lemcio, "The Unifying Kerygma of the New Testament," *JSNT* 33 (1988): 3–17; Lemcio, "The Unifying Kerygma of the New Testament, pt 2," *JSNT* 38 (1990): 3–11; Scott Hafemann and Paul House, eds., *Central Themes in Biblical Theology: Mapping Unity in Diversity* (Grand Rapids: Baker Academic, 2007); Walter C. Kaiser, *Recovering the Unity of the Bible: One Continuous Story, Plan, and Purpose* (Grand Rapids: Zondervan, 2009); and C. Blomberg, "The Legitimacy and Limits of Harmonization," in *Hermeneutics, Authority, and Canon*, ed. D. A. Carson and John D. Woodbridge (Grand Rapids: Zondervan, 1986), 135–74. A helpful summary can be found in Thomas Schreiner, *New Testament Theology: Magnifying God in Christ* (Grand Rapids: Baker Academic, 2008), 867–88.

[95]A. J. Köstenberger, "Diversity and Unity in the New Testament," in *Biblical Theology: Retrospect and Prospect*, ed. Scott Hafemann (Downers Grove, IL: InterVarsity, 2002), 144–58.

ceremonial law[96]—and, no doubt, such disagreement continued on into the early church[97]—it is not at all clear that different New Testament books actually put forth contradictory teaching on the matter.[98] Paul himself acknowledged that James was a "pillar" of the church and that he (Paul) was received by him with the "right hand of fellowship" (Gal. 2:9). In addition, Acts 15 makes it clear that although some differences in practice may have remained between the two "camps," Paul and James were unified around the gospel message going to the Gentiles and the nature of law observance they were expected to maintain (15:22–29), with Paul even being called "beloved" (15:25). Indeed, Paul even gathered a special collection for the saints in Jerusalem, demonstrating his ongoing care and affection for them (Rom. 15:26). As for the overplayed passage in James 2, many scholars have noted that upon closer examination there is no real disagreement with Paul's understanding of justification.[99] When the reader

---

[96]What exactly the meal dispute in Galatians 2 entails is still a matter of discussion. James D. G. Dunn, "The Incident at Antioch (Gal. 2:11–18)," *JSNT* 18 (1983): 3–57, argues that it is a dispute over whether ritual purity laws should be enforced at the common meal; D. R. Catchpole, "Paul, James, and the Apostolic Decree," *NTS* 23 (1976–1977): 428–44, maintains that the men from James are only concerned with upholding the decrees of the Jerusalem council (Acts 15) and not the oral laws of ritual purity; G. Howard, *Paul: Crisis in Galatia* (Cambridge: Cambridge University Press, 1979), argues that the men from James are seeking to have the Gentiles circumcised and to become full proselytes; E. D. W. Burton, *The Epistle to the Galatians* (Edinburgh: T&T Clark, 1952), claims that the dispute at Antioch is over Peter's willingness to eat unclean foods; Dieter Lührmann, "Abendmahlsgemeinschaft? Gal 2:11ff.," in *Kirche: Festschrift für Günther Bornkamm*, ed. Dieter Lührmann and Georg Strecker (Tübingen: Mohr, 1980), 271–86, contends that the meal in Gal. 2:11–14 is really the Lord's Supper. Those in agreement with Lührmann include, F. F. Bruce, *The Epistle to the Galatians: A Commentary on the Greek Text* (Grand Rapids: Eerdmans, 1982), 129; and Ernst Haenchen, "Petrus-Probleme," *NTS* 7 (1961): 187–97.

[97]There is no doubt that historically there were Jewish-Christian groups, like the Ebionites, who would have been pro-James and anti-Paul (Dunn, *Unity and Diversity in the New Testament*, 235–66). However, this is categorically different than suggesting that New Testament books *themselves* promote such teaching. For more on the Ebionites, see S. M. Mimouni, *Le judéo-christianisme ancien: Essais historiques* (Paris: Éditions du Cerf, 1998), 257–86; H. J. Schoeps, "Ebionite Christianity," *JTS* 4 (1953): 219–24; Schoeps, *Jewish Christianity: Factional Disputes in the Early Church* (Philadelphia: Fortress, 1969), esp. 38–117; J. A. Fitzmyer, "The Qumran Scrolls, the Ebionites and Their Literature," in *The Semitic Background of the New Testament* (Grand Rapids: Eerdmans, 1997), 435–80; J. L. Teicher, "The Dead Sea Scrolls—Documents of the Jewish-Christian Sect of the Ebionites," *JJS* 2 (1950–1951): 67–99; Georg Strecker, "Ebioniten," *RAC* 4 (1959): 487–500; David F. Wright, "Ebionites," in *Dictionary of the Later New Testament and Its Development*, ed. Ralph P. Martin and Peter H. Davids (Downers Grove, IL: InterVarsity, 1997), 313–17; and F. Stanley Jones, *An Ancient Jewish-Christian Source on the History of Christianity: Pseudo-Clementine Recognitions 1.27–71* (Atlanta: Scholars Press, 1995), especially the review of prior research on 1–38.

[98]Wenham, "Unity and Diversity in the New Testament," 690–97.

[99]See discussion in Ralph P. Martin, *James*, WBC (Waco, TX: Word, 1988), civ–cix; Douglas J. Moo, *The Letter of James* (Grand Rapids: Eerdmans, 2000), 37–43; T. Laato, "Justification According to James: A Comparison with Paul?," *TrinJ* 18 (1997): 47–61; and D. O. Via, "The Right Strawy Epistle Reconsidered: A Study in Biblical Ethics and Hermeneutic," *JR* 49 (1969): 253–67.

recognizes that the two authors are asking very different questions—Paul is concerned to deal with how a person can acquire right standing before a holy God (Rom. 3:19–31), whereas James is dealing with the situation of someone who claims to have faith but has no fruit (James 2:14)—then the supposed disagreement tends to evaporate.[100] Thus, we can agree with David Wenham when he declares that "ideas of a radical split between Paul and Jerusalem are exaggerated."[101]

Aside from these specifics, there is an additional (and broader) challenge for those who claim that the New Testament is a mix of contradictory and embattled theological camps. If Walter Bauer's reconstruction of early Christianity is correct, we are supposed to believe that the canon is composed of books that reflect the preferences of the theological "winners." Indeed, Ehrman raises the provocative question, "What if some other form of Christianity had become dominant, instead of the one that did?"[102] He answers that we would likely have "an entirely different set of books."[103] Our current canon therefore represents a loss of "the great diversity of the early centuries of Christianity."[104] But there is a problem here. If the current form of the canon includes the preferred books of the theological winners and thereby represents a *loss* of great diversity, how, at the same time, can one claim that the canon is composed of contradictory books that reflect great diversity? If the "winners" determined the canon, then why would they pick books from various and contradictory theological camps? One cannot argue that the canon is the "invention"[105] of the proto-orthodox designed to suppress the opposition and then turn around and argue that the canon is a cacophony of diverse theological viewpoints that stand in opposition. Which one is it? The problem is that one cannot believe Bauer is right and also believe the New Testament canon is a theological disaster area. It is one or the other.[106]

In all of these discussions it is important to remember that assessing the theological harmony of the New Testament involves more than simply following the standard academic steps. Indeed, this is the problem with most discussions of the New Testament's harmony—they assume that

---

[100]Childs, *The New Testament as Canon*, 443.
[101]Wenham, "Unity and Diversity in the New Testament," 691.
[102]Ehrman, *Lost Christianities*, 5.
[103]Ibid., 6.
[104]Ibid., 4.
[105]Ibid., 229.
[106]It should be noted that a unified canon does not thereby prove Bauer's theory. There is another explanation for the canon's theological unity that does not entail appeals to early church conspiracies, namely, that these books all have the same ultimate, divine author.

theological understanding is an entirely *human* affair.[107] Ironically, some seek to understand the theology of the New Testament while, at the same time, they reject its own teachings about how theological understanding actually occurs. One does not come to understand the New Testament in precisely the same way one understands the works of Plato or Tacitus. The New Testament claims to be, at its core, a divine book that has been constituted by the activity of the Holy Spirit. Thus, Paul reminds his readers, "The natural person does not accept the things of the Spirit of God, for they are folly to him, and *he is not able to understand them because they are spiritually discerned*" (1 Cor. 2:14). Childs affirms a similar principle when he argues—along with Dulles, Ebeling, and others—that the historical and theological aspects of biblical theology should not be sharply divided.[108] Discovering the theology of the Bible is more than a descriptive task; it is not just a *religionsgeschichtliche* (history-of-religions) discussion.[109] Thus, argues Childs, biblical theology is a "confessional" enterprise that acknowledges that the Bible is "Scripture" and thus is "pointing beyond itself to a divine reality."[110]

It is here, then, that we come to the crux of the matter. Should Christians abandon their commitment to the canon's authority because biblical critics, who view scriptural interpretation as merely a human enterprise, claim to have discovered theological incongruities? No, because Christians have no grounds for thinking that those without the Spirit can rightly discern such things—indeed, Christians have good grounds for thinking they cannot. One might as well ask whether Joshua Bell, world-renowned violinist, should abandon his musical career because his concert in a Washington, DC metro station (on a 3.5-million-dollar Stradivarius) was met with disinterest and boredom.[111] The answer depends on whether we have reason to think that the average pedestrians in the DC metro station can identify

---

[107]K. Stendahl, "Biblical Theology, Contemporary," in *The Interpreter's Dictionary of the Bible: An Illustrated Encyclopedia*, ed. G. A. Buttrick et al. (Nashville: Abingdon, 1962), 422, argues that both believer and agnostic can equally do biblical theology. See also Räisänen, *Beyond New Testament Theology*, 95–96.

[108]Brevard S. Childs, *Biblical Theology of the Old and New Testaments: Theological Reflection on the Christian Bible* (Philadelphia: Augsburg Fortress, 1993), 8. See also Childs, "Interpretation in Faith: The Theological Responsibility of the Old Testament Commentary," *Int* 18 (1964): 432–49. For an approach similar to that of Childs, see Peter Stuhlmacher, *Biblische Theologie des Neuen Testaments*, 2 vols. (Göttingen: Vandenhoeck & Ruprecht, 1992, 1999).

[109]P. Stuhlmacher, "Biblische Theologie des Neuen Testaments—eine Skizze," in *Eine Bibel— zwei Testamente. Positionen biblischer Theologie*, ed. C. Dohmen and T. Söding (Paterborn: Schöningh, 1995), 275–89, esp. 281ff.

[110]Childs, *Biblical Theology of the Old and New Testaments*, 9.

[111]For this true story, see Gene Weingarten, "Pearls Before Breakfast," *Washington Post*, April 8, 2007.

musical genius when they hear it. Apparently they cannot. When all was done, Bell had not drawn a crowd, was never given a single instance of applause, and left with a paltry $32.17.

At this point, the critic of the New Testament might respond by saying that this whole affair sounds suspiciously circular. After all, it is no surprise that Christians "conclude" that the New Testament is harmonious—they *already* believe in the truth of the New Testament from the outset! Therefore, it is not proper (it is argued) to allow those who believe the New Testament to be the final judges of its theological harmony.[112] However, this argument cuts both ways. If the Christian assumes the truth of the New Testament while arguing for its unity, then it is clear that the non-Christian assumes the falsity of the New Testament while arguing for its disunity. He assumes that (at least) 1 Corinthians 2:14 is mistaken and that New Testament theology *can* be understood rightly by those without the Spirit.[113] Thus, one could ask why we should allow those who have *already* rejected the New Testament to be the final judges of its theological harmony? Again, keeping with the music analogy, that would be like allowing a person who is tone-deaf (and thus rejects this whole concept of being "on key") to judge a singing contest. If the tone-deaf person were kept from judging, he might object and claim that this whole "on key" thing is a sham run by musical insiders who claim to have a special ability to hear such things. But despite all the protests, the truth of the matter would remain: there is such a thing as being on key whether the tone-deaf person hears it or not.

B. Redemptive-Historical Unity

It is not simply doctrinal unity that is present in the biblical canon, but there is also redemptive-historical unity (though these two categories clearly overlap). Indeed, many have noted that the Scripture, from Genesis to Revelation, is telling the same overarching redemptive story of God reconciling fallen humanity to himself through the person of Jesus Christ.[114] The issue for early Christians was not only whether the New Testament books agreed with the Old Testament books on any given doctrine (as

---

[112]Räisänen, *Beyond New Testament Theology*, 110–11.

[113]Indeed, a number of critical scholars make the *opposite* argument of 1 Cor. 2:14, namely, that the Scriptures can be rightly understood only when all prior faith commitments are abandoned. E.g., John Van Seters, *The Edited Bible: The Curious History of the "Editor" in Biblical Criticism* (Winona Lake, IN: Eisenbrauns, 2006), esp. 371–76.

[114]Wright, *The Last Word*, 63; N. T. Wright, *The New Testament and the People of God* (Minneapolis: Fortress, 1992); R. L. Brawley, "Canonical Coherence in Reading Israel's Scriptures with a Sequel," in Auwers and de Jonge, *The Biblical Canons*, 627–34; and H. H. Rowley, *The Unity of the Bible* (London: Carey Kingsgate Press, 1953).

important as that was), but whether the New Testament books actually *completed the story* begun by the Old Testament. Wright notes, "The Jews of the period did not simply think of the biblical traditions atomistically, but were able to conceive of the story as a whole, and to be regularly looking for its proper conclusion."[115] What made the New Testament books compelling was that the overall story of Israel, begun in the Old Testament, had reached its rightful conclusion in them. Robert Brawley observes that the "New Testament bears the character of a sequel . . . [it] presumes the continuation of the same story, and through the continuation, Israel's national story becomes universal."[116] As Wright observes again, it is in the Jesus of the New Testament books that "Israel's history has reached its climax."[117]

Thus, the unity between the Old Testament books and the New Testament books is such that they are not just a collection of individual stories on a variety of topics, but combine together to form one overarching story of salvation. It is this overall unified story that shows the Old Testament and New Testament to be, in fact, *one book*, clearly connected by the divine origins of its constituent parts. Wright has gone to great lengths to show (and his study cannot be repeated here) how various books and sections of the New Testament canon reflect this overall redemptive theme of Christ as the climax of Israel's story.[118] In a similar manner, D. Moody Smith has argued that the Gospels in particular would have been recognized as the clear continuation of the one biblical story of Jesus Christ.[119] Likewise, David Aune notes that Luke sees his writings as a "continuation of the scriptural story."[120] It is precisely for this reason (among others) that books like the *Gospel of Thomas* must be rejected. As Smith observes, "*Thomas* is not a narrative; it could not, I think by intention, be construed as continuing the biblical story."[121]

It is here that we can begin to fully appreciate one of the primary divine qualities present in the New Testament books: their *Christocentric nature*. Early Christians were able to recognize the canonical books because these were (among other things) the books that fully exalted Jesus Christ as the long-awaited resolution to the problem of sin and rebellion articulated

---

[115]Wright, *The New Testament and the People of God*, 218.
[116]Brawley, "Canonical Coherence," 629–30.
[117]Wright, *The New Testament and the People of God*, 401.
[118]Ibid., 371–417.
[119]D. Moody Smith, "When Did the Gospels Become Scripture?," *JBL* 119 (2000): 8–9.
[120]David E. Aune, "Luke 1:1–4: Historical or Scientific *Prooimion*?," in *Paul, Luke and the Graeco-Roman World*, ed. A. Christopherson et al. (Sheffield: Sheffield Academic, 2002), 138.
[121]Smith, "When Did the Gospels Become Scripture?," 13.

throughout the Old Testament books.[122] Again, the WCF observes this very reality when it declares that the divinity of Scripture is evident by "the full discovery it makes of the only way of man's salvation" (1.5). We see, then, that canonical books are not only books where Christ is the *speaker* (through the apostles), but also books where Christ is the *subject*.[123] Or, we could say that canonical books are those that have both apostolic origins (from Christ) and divine qualities (speak of Christ). Of course, this not only applies to New Testament books; the Old Testament books were also understood to be Christocentric in their core message (Luke 24:44). Indeed, it can be rightly said that *the* unifying factor for all canonical books is Jesus Christ. He is what makes the Bible one book.

C. Structural Unity

Because the Old and New Testaments form one overall book, we would expect to see evidence of this not only in a unified story but also in a unified structure. Thus, part of the internal evidence for the authenticity of the New Testament canon is demonstrated through the way these twenty-seven books fit together as the structural completion of the thirty-nine books of the Old Testament. This "structural" unity can be manifested in a number of different ways that we can only mention in a cursory manner here.

1. Covenantal Structure

We shall argue in the next chapter that both Old and New Testament documents reflect the overall structure of extrabiblical treaties in the ancient world. Thus, at the core of these documents is an impressive structural unity centered on the covenantal concept.[124] This means that the New Testament documents take on covenantal functions that parallel their Old Testament counterparts. Kline argues, for instance, that the canonical Gospels parallel the historical narratives of the Pentateuch, each functioning as the "historical prologue," where the great salvific acts of

---

[122]It is here that we see the major difference between the canonical Gospels and books like the *Gospel of Thomas. Thomas*, being just a list of 114 sayings (many of which appear to have a Gnostic flavor, though this has been challenged) presents Jesus, but does not present Jesus as the salvific resolution of the story begun in the Old Testament.

[123]J. H. Roberts and A. B. D. Toit, *Guide to the New Testament*, vol. 1, *Preamble to New Testament Study: The Canon of the New Testament* (Pretoria: N. G. Kerkboekhandel Transvaal, 1979), 130–34.

[124]This is not an argument that covenant is the primary theme of the Bible or the "center" of biblical theology. Rather, it is an argument that the whole Bible shares a covenantal structure; see Scott Hafemann, "The Covenant Relationship," in Hafemann and House, *Central Themes in Biblical Theology*, 23.

God are recited.[125] The parallels are particularly acute when the Gospels are compared to the book of Exodus: each includes (1) the inauguration of the covenant through a core salvific event; (2) a disproportionate amount of space devoted to the salvific event itself;[126] (3) a combination of both narrative and didactic portions;[127] (4) a focus on the life and death of the covenant mediator;[128] and (5) a giving of the law/teachings of the covenant and/or covenant mediator. These connections are amplified by the impressive amount of Moses-Jesus typology throughout the Gospel accounts.[129]

As for the book of Acts, both Kline and Walter Vogels argue that it fills the same canonical function as the historical books since they both highlight the time the covenant people enter into new lands immediately after the death of the covenant mediator (Josh. 1:2; Acts 1:8).[130] In addition, Kline and others have argued that the New Testament Epistles fulfill a similar function as the Old Testament prophetic books in that they are designed to apply and uphold the terms of the covenant laid forth in the prior historical accounts.[131] Gerald Sheppard agrees.

> In the [Hebrew Bible], the prophets whose books often predate the present Torah are, nonetheless, put after the Torah as though they are a commentary on it. So, in the New Testament, the letters of Paul which were written before are placed after the Gospels as theological commentary on the same subject.[132]

Indeed, the similarities between the Prophets and the Epistles continue in that they both function as "covenant lawsuits" against the people of God who have rejected the stipulations of the covenant and pursued false

---

[125]M. G. Kline, *The Structure of Biblical Authority*, 2nd ed. (Eugene, OR: Wipf and Stock, 1997), 172–203; see also Kline, "The Old Testament Origins of the Gospel Genre," *WTJ* 38 (1975): 1–27. Making a similar observation is Walter Vogels, "La structure symétrique de la Bible chrétienne," in Auwers and de Jonge, *The Biblical Canons*, 299.

[126]The covenantal inauguration takes up the bulk of Exodus, covering chaps. 19–40, and the extended passion narratives of the Gospels have been long observed, most notably by Martin Kähler.

[127]There has been a longstanding attempt to explain how the Gospels have both "deed" and "sayings" material; see J. M. Robinson and H. Koester, *Trajectories Through Early Christianity* (Philadelphia: Fortress, 1971), 158–204.

[128]Vogels, "La structure symétrique de la Bible chrétienne," 299–300.

[129]See Vern S. Poythress, *The Shadow of Christ in the Law of Moses* (Phillipsburg, NJ: P&R, 1991), and Kline, "The Old Testament Origins of the Gospel Genre," 1–27. For a broader look at images of Moses in the New Testament, see John Lierman, *The New Testament Moses* (Tübingen: Mohr Siebeck, 2004).

[130]Vogels, "La structure symétrique de la Bible chrétienne," 300; Kline, *The Structure of Biblical Authority*, 71–72.

[131]Kline, *The Structure of Biblical Authority*, 72–73.

[132]Gerald T. Sheppard, "Canonization: Hearing the Voice of the Same God through Historically Dissimilar Traditions," *Ex auditu* 1 (1985): 112.

gods.[133] And Revelation continues the Old Testament pattern of using apocalyptic literature to expound on the eschatological curses and blessings that will fall upon covenant breakers and covenant keepers, even ending in the standard inscriptional curse, "If anyone adds . . . and if anyone takes away . . ." (Rev. 22:18–19; cf. Deut. 4:2). In all these ways, it is clear that the New Testament canon is a genuine continuation of (and is integrally connected to) the Old Testament canon and therefore rightly regarded as a "new covenant" (2 Cor. 3:6).

2. Canonical Structure

While it is certainly positive that recent studies of the canon have tended to focus on the final canonical form of the text,[134] it is worth noting that the overall structure of the Old and New Testament canons has been largely overlooked.[135] Walter Brueggemann laments this oversight in regard to Childs's approach to the Old Testament: "Childs approaches biblical books one at a time. That is problematic because one never gets a sense of the whole of the Bible or the whole of the Old Testament."[136] However, other scholars have begun to observe more macrostructural features of both the Old and New Testament canons.[137] While examples of such features can only be briefly mentioned here, they are an important dimension of the overall harmony and unity of the canon and remind the reader that the Bible, in essence, is to be understood as a single book.

In regard to the Hebrew Old Testament, many scholars affirm that a threefold division—the Law, the Prophets, and the Writings—was likely

---

[133]E.g., W. L. Lane, "Covenant: The Key to Paul's Conflict with Corinth," *TynBul* 33 (1982): 3–29; C. Roetzel, "The Judgment Form in Paul's Letters," *JBL* 88 (1969): 305–12; and J. L. White, "Introductory Formulae in the Body of the Pauline Letter," *JBL* 90 (1971): 91–97.

[134]In regard to both the Old Testament and the New, Childs has rightly focused on the final form (or canonical form) of the text; see B. Childs, *Introduction to the Old Testament as Scripture* (Philadelphia: Fortress, 1979); Childs, *The New Testament as Canon*.

[135]Macrostructural features of the canon (order of books, textual divisions, book titles, etc.) are also known as "paratext" or "con-textuality." See Greg Goswell, "The Order of the Books in the Hebrew Bible," *JETS* 51 (2008): 673; and John H. Sailhamer, *Introduction to Old Testament Theology: A Canonical Approach* (Grand Rapids: Zondervan, 1995), 213.

[136]Walter Brueggemann, *Creative Word* (Philadelphia: Fortress, 1982), 5. See further discussion in Stephen G. Dempster, "An 'Extraordinary Fact': Torah and Temple and the Contours of the Hebrew Canon, Part I," *TynBul* 48 (1997): 32ff.

[137]E.g., O. H. Steck, "Der Kanon des hebraischen Alten Testament," in *Vernunft und Glauben*, ed. J. Rohls (Göttingen: Vandenhoeck & Ruprecht, 1988), 231–52; R. E. Clements, *Prophecy and Tradition* (Atlanta: John Knox, 1975); Joseph Blenkinsopp, *Prophecy and Canon: A Contribution to the Study of Jewish Origins* (Notre Dame: University of Notre Dame Press, 1986); Sheppard, "Canonization," 106–14; D. N. Freedman, *The Unity of the Hebrew Bible* (Ann Arbor: University of Michigan Press, 1991); Beckwith, *The Old Testament Canon of the New Testament Church*, 165ff.; E. Earle Ellis, *The Making of the New Testament Documents* (Leiden: Brill, 2002); and D. Trobisch, *The First Edition of the New Testament* (Oxford: Oxford University Press, 2000).

established by the time of Jesus and the apostles.[138] Of course, there
are some who argue that the specific content of the third division may
have still been in flux during this period (at least among some groups),[139]
but nonetheless the threefold division itself is generally not in dispute.[140]
Stephen Dempster has observed that the shape of this tripartite canon
is confirmed by textual markers at the beginning and end of each of the
three sections that focus on the theme of the divine word (torah) and
divine presence (temple).[141] The markers indicate "an exceedingly rich
intertextuality in which there are many linguistic and conceptual echoes
throughout Scripture. Later biblical books consciously echo and imitate
events, concepts, and language in earlier books."[142] Although the third
canonical section, the Writings, exhibits more fluidity in the order of
books, Dempster argues that we have a number of intersecting factors
that suggest this section likely began with the Psalms and ended with
Chronicles.[143] Thus, the three sections of the Hebrew Bible each end with
a major prophetic figure: the Torah ends with Moses (Deut. 34:12), the
Prophets end with Elijah (Mal. 4:5–6), and the Writings end with a renewed
Davidic hope that the temple will be (re)built in Jerusalem (2 Chron.

---

[138]Luke 24:44; Sir. 39:1; 4QMMT (95–96); Philo, *Contempl. Life*, 25. For discussion, see
Rolf Rendtorff, *Theologie des Altens Testaments: Ein kanonischer Entwurf* (Neukirchen-
Vluyn: Neukirchener Verlag, 1999), 4ff.; Beckwith, *The Old Testament Canon of the New
Testament Church*, 110–80; D. A. Carson and Douglas J. Moo, *An Introduction to the New
Testament* (Grand Rapids: Zondervan, 2005), 727–32; Chapman, "The Old Testament Canon
and Its Authority for the Christian Church," 125–48; Seitz, *The Goodly Fellowship of the
Prophets*, 97ff.

[139]Craig A. Evans, "The Scriptures of Jesus and His Earliest Followers," in McDonald and
Sanders, *The Canon Debate*, 185–95; and Julio C. Trebolle Barrera, "Origins of a Tripartite
Old Testament Canon," in McDonald and Sanders, *The Canon Debate*, 128–45.

[140]Others have downplayed the importance of the order of the canonical books; e.g., J. Barr,
Holy Scripture: Canon, Authority and Criticism (Philadelphia: Westminster, 1983), 57; and John
Barton, *Oracles of God: Perceptions of Ancient Prophecy in Israel After the Exile* (London:
Darton, Longman, and Todd, 1985), 83–91; Steinmann, *The Oracles of God: The Old Testament
Canon*, 182–85; and, in reference to the Writings, Childs, *Introduction to the Old Testament
as Scripture*, 502–3.

[141]Dempster, "An 'Extraordinary Fact': Part I," 23–56; and Stephen G. Dempster, "An
'Extraordinary Fact': Torah and Temple and the Contours of the Hebrew Canon, Part II,"
TynBul 48 (1997): 191–218. Although Dempster has rightly identified textual/thematic markers,
he seems too quick to attribute their cause solely to later redactional activity by a canonical
editor.

[142]Stephen G. Dempster, *Dominion and Dynasty: A Biblical Theology of the Hebrew Bible*
(Downers Grove, IL: InterVarsity, 2003), 31–32. By way of example, the Prophets section
concludes with (1) a reference back to the Torah ("the law of my servant Moses") in Mal. 3:4;
(2) a reference to the beginning of the Prophets with the unique phrase "Moses, my servant,"
which occurs only in Josh. 1:1–2 and Mal. 4:4; and (3) an anticipation of further prophetic
activity with the return of "Elijah before that great and terrible day of the Lord comes" (Mal.
4:5). See discussion in Dempster, "An 'Extraordinary Fact': Part I," 191–200.

[143]E.g., Luke 24:44 (cf. 11:51); *b. B. Bat.* 14b; Josephus, *Ag. Ap.* 1.37–42; 4QMMT (95–96);
Philo, *Contempl. Life*, 25.

36:23).[144] Such organizational structure—moving from Moses to Elijah to David—indicates a canonical consciousness among the biblical authors and "an awareness that the individual books of the Bible belonged to a larger whole."[145]

Of course, one does not have to read the Old Testament in its tripartite structure to appreciate its unity and coherence.[146] But when this canonical structure is considered, the manner in which the New Testament books complete the story that began in the Old Testament becomes even more evident. Ending the Old Testament canon with Chronicles is a reminder to the reader that Israel's return from exile documented in Ezra-Nehemiah is not the full story—it is only a physical return, not a spiritual one. The hearts of the people still needed to be changed. Israel remained in spiritual exile.[147] Such an ending places the reader in an eschatological posture, *looking ahead* to the time when the Messiah, the son of David, will come to Jerusalem and bring full deliverance to his people.[148] The Davidic focus of Chronicles is also borne out by its extensive genealogies, with David's ancestors at the very center (2 Chron. 3:1–24). With such an eschatological and Davidic posture in mind, it is noteworthy that the first book of the New Testament begins with a genealogy with David at the center: "The book of the genealogy of Jesus Christ, the son of David, the son of Abraham" (Matt. 1:1). The fact that both of these books (and only these books) begin with genealogies led D. Moody Smith to declare, "In doing so, Matthew makes clear that Jesus represents the restoration of that dynasty and therefore the history of Israel and the history of salvation. Thus, Jesus continues the biblical narrative."[149] The Gospels' focus on David is matched by its equal focus on the figures of Elijah and

---

[144]Dempster, "An 'Extraordinary Fact': Part I," 214. Additional evidence for canonical "seams" at Deuteronomy/Joshua and Malachi/Psalms is put forward by Sailhamer, *Introduction to Old Testament Theology*, 239–352; and Barrera, "Origins of a Tripartite Old Testament Canon," 133–34.

[145]Dempster, *Dominion and Dynasty*, 30.

[146]Goswell, "The Order of the Books in the Hebrew Bible," 677, rightly cautions against making the threefold structure of the canon "determinative for Old Testament theology."

[147]For discussion of Israel as still in exile, see Wright, *The New Testament and the People of God*, 268–79; C. A. Evans, "Aspects of Exile and Restoration in the Proclamation of Jesus and the Gospels," in *Exile: Old Testament, Jewish, and Christian Conceptions*, ed. James M. Scott (Leiden: Brill, 1997), 299–328; C. A. Evans, "Jesus and the Continuing Exile of Israel," in *Jesus and the Restoration of Israel*, ed. C. C. Newman (Downers Grove, IL: InterVarsity, 1999), 77–100; and Dempster, *Dominion and Dynasty*, 224–27.

[148]Nahum Sarna, "Bible," in *Encyclopedia Judaica*, vol. 3, edited by Fred Skolnik (Detroit: Macmillan Reference and Keter, 2006), 832.

[149]Smith, "When Did the Gospels Become Scripture?," 7. Although Genesis does not begin with a genealogy, the fact that the first and last books of the Old Testament contain genealogies is further evidence of its structural unity.

Moses—so much so that the transfiguration narratives even have Moses, Elijah, and the son of David in conversation with one another (Matt. 17:1–8; Mark 9:2–8; Luke 9:28–36). In many ways, then, the Moses-Elijah-David structure of the Old Testament canon is recapitulated and fulfilled in the motifs of the New Testament Gospels.

Additional connections between the Testaments are evident when the structure of the New Testament canon is considered. David Trobisch has demonstrated that the New Testament in the early church was divided into four clear subsections—Gospels, Praxapostolos (Acts and Catholic Epistles), Pauline Epistles, and Revelation—as can be seen from the uniform witness of the manuscript collections themselves.[150] Thus, the entire biblical canon (Hebrew and Greek), when viewed as a whole, contains seven sections. Given the biblical usage of the number seven as representative of completeness or wholeness,[151] a sevenfold canonical structure would speak to the overall unity of the biblical canon and provides further reason to think that the New Testament canon we possess is the proper conclusion to the original books of the Old Testament. In addition, it should be noted that in both the first book (Genesis) and the last book (Revelation) the number seven plays a significant role. The seven days of creation are the archetypal foundation for all of Scripture, governing mankind's own seven-day workweek, and demonstrating the sense of completeness and wholeness to God's creative activity. The number seven is also foundational to the book of Revelation. Not only is the book itself divided into seven sections, but there are seven churches, seven angels, seven seals, seven trumpets, seven bowls, seven plagues, and so on.[152] Thus, in effect, the first and last books of the canon form an *inclusio* of sevens, functioning as appropriate bookends to the overall sevenfold canonical structure—with Revelation as an appropriate "sabbath."[153]

---

[150]E.g., this structure is attested by the major codices Sinaiticus (א), Vaticanus (B), Alexandrinus (A), and Ephraemi Rescriptus (C). See discussion in Trobisch, *The First Edition of the New Testament*, 26.

[151]G. K. Beale, *The Book of Revelation*, NIGTC (Grand Rapids: Eerdmans, 1999), 58–59; A. Y. Collins, "Numerical Symbolism in Jewish and Early Christian Apocalyptic Literature," in *ANRW* 2.21.2 (1984): 1221–87.

[152]William Hendriksen, *More Than Conquerors* (Grand Rapids: Baker, 1994), 16–19.

[153]The first six days of creation build toward, and anticipate, the seventh and final day, which stands out by itself as distinctive. In a similar manner, the overall canonical structure contains six sections, followed by a seventh and final section consisting only of the book of Revelation, standing alone as an epilogue. Notably, the glories of heaven so aptly displayed in the book of Revelation are even referred to elsewhere as God's "Sabbath rest" (Heb. 4:9–11). That Heb. 4:9–11 refers to heaven is shown by Philip Edgcumbe Hughes, *A Commentary on the Epistle to the Hebrews* (Grand Rapids: Eerdmans, 1990), 191; F. F. Bruce, *The Epistle to the Hebrews* (Grand Rapids: Eerdmans, 1990), 109–10; Richard B. Gaffin, "A Sabbath Rest Still Awaits the People of God," in *Pressing Toward the Mark: Essays Commemorating Fifty Years of the*

The connections between Genesis and Revelation, and thus the existence of this macro *inclusio*, could be developed even further.[154] Genesis begins with the creation of the "heavens and earth" (1:1ff.); Revelation ends with re-creation and the new "heaven and earth" (21:1). Genesis begins with the theme of paradise in the garden (2:8ff.); Revelation ends with the paradise of heaven (21:4). Genesis begins with the theme of marriage (2:8); Revelation ends with the great wedding of the Lamb (21:9). Genesis begins with a focus on the serpent's deception (3:1ff.); Revelation ends with the serpent's destruction (20:10). Genesis begins with the curse being put upon the world (3:14ff.); Revelation ends with the curse being lifted (22:3). Genesis begins by describing the creation of day, night, and the oceans (1:3, 10, 14); Revelation ends with no more need for day (sun), or night, or oceans (21:1; 22:5). Genesis begins with the "tree of life" among the people of God (2:9); Revelation ends with the "tree of life" among the people of God (22:2). Genesis begins with God dwelling with his people (2:8; 3:8); Revelation ends with God finally dwelling with his people again (21:3).

The degree to which Genesis and Revelation provide appropriate canonical bookends is enhanced when it is recognized that they form the ends of a larger narrative chiasm centered upon Jerusalem. The narrative of the Old Testament canon clearly moves from the broad, overall creation in Genesis to a focus on a single city (Jerusalem) and a single person (the Davidic king) in the book of Chronicles. The New Testament narrative picks up where the Old left off—focused on the Davidic kingship returning to Jerusalem—but it does not stay in Jerusalem. Instead it begins to fan out into Samaria, Judea, and Asia Minor, and ultimately ends with a focus on all creation, Jews and Gentiles together (Acts 1:8; 8:4–5; Col. 1:23). Indeed, in the book of Revelation, the global focus is complete as we see people "from every nation, from all tribes and peoples and languages" (Rev. 7:9) joined together in God's ultimate re-creation. This macro chiasm shows that the New Testament canon is the reverse structure of the Old Testament and thereby forms its proper conclusion.[155]

Even within the New Testament itself, there are structural indicators that speak to its overall unity—what we might call cross-references between

---

Orthodox Presbyterian Church, ed. Charles G. Dennison and Richard C. Gamble (Philadelphia: Committee for the Historian of the Orthodox Presbyterian Church, 1986), 33–51.

[154]For more on this theme, see Paul Sevier Minear, *Christians and the New Creation: Genesis Motifs in the New Testament* (Louisville: Westminster John Knox, 1994).

[155]Dempster, *Dominion and Dynasty*, 231–32.

books that suggest that they belong together. For example, Lührmann, Trobisch, Ellis, Nienhuis, and others have noted that the order of the "pillars" mentioned by Paul in Galatians 2:9—James, Peter, and John—corresponds with the order of these same authors in the Catholic Epistles.[156] Even if the order of these names is "coincidence,"[157] Trobisch suggests that these names still prompt the reader to draw connections between key New Testament writings. Likewise, Ellis has argued that Galatians 2:9, regardless of the specific order, reflects the entire New Testament structure, which is built around the missions of these apostolic men: Paul, James, Peter, and John.[158] As another example, Trobisch argues that the book of 2 Peter includes a number of cross-references to other canonical books:[159] (1) Second Peter 1:4 would naturally connect the reader to John 21:18 as Peter predicts his death.[160] (2) Second Peter 1:16 would lead the reader to the accounts of the transfiguration in the Synoptic Gospels.[161] (3) Second Peter 3:15–16 is an obvious reference to the letters of Paul. And (4) the extensive overlap between 2 Peter and Jude functions as a cross-reference between these two books.[162] We could add further "intra-canonical" links—such as how the book of Acts functions as an introduction of sorts to the rest of the New Testament authors[163]—but space prohibits us from going further.

All these structural connections suggest that there is a grand unity not only between the Old Testament and the New Testament, but also within the New Testament itself. Although the skeptic may quickly dismiss such unity as coincidental or irrelevant, it is, nevertheless, precisely what we would expect from a divine book. Moreover, it is the

---

[156]D. Lührmann, "Gal 2, 9 und die katholischen Briefe: Bemerkungen zum Kanon und zur regula fidei," ZNW 72 (1981): 65–87; Trobisch, The First Edition of the New Testament, 57–59; Ellis, The Making of the New Testament Documents, 33; David R. Nienhuis, Not by Paul Alone: The Formation of the Catholic Epistle Collection and the Christian Canon (Waco, TX: Baylor University Press, 2007), 7–19.

[157]F. F. Bruce, The Epistle to the Galatians: A Commentary on the Greek Text (Grand Rapids: Eerdmans, 1982), 121. It is noteworthy that the standard order of the Catholic Epistles does not proceed according to length (as is typical), but follows the order in Gal. 2:9.

[158]Ellis, The Making of the New Testament Documents, 33.

[159]Such cross-references do not necessarily require a dating where 2 Peter is written late. Our argument is simply that these passages naturally lead a reader to other canonical passages that serve to link these books together. Peter himself may not have been aware of all these connections when he wrote his letter (though he would have clearly been aware of some).

[160]Trobisch, The First Edition of the New Testament, 87.

[161]Ibid., 57–59.

[162]Ibid.

[163]See, e.g., R. W. Wall and E. E. Lemcio, The New Testament as Canon: A Reader in Canonical Criticism (Sheffield: JSOT, 1992), 161–207; and, more recently, Wall, "The Jerusalem Council (Acts 15:1–21) in Canonical Context," in From Biblical Criticism to Biblical Faith, ed. William H. Brackney and C. A. Evans (Macon, GA: Mercer University Press, 2007), 93–101.

scope of the unity that is the compelling factor—such intricate connections, covering such a vast amount of literature, authors, and time
periods, suggest that the canon is not merely a human construct. And
one need not agree with all of Dempster's and Trobisch's arguments
(some are more compelling than others) to appreciate the way the two
Testaments fit together and the way canonical books cross-reference
themselves. Many of these structural features are still visible even when
the order of the canonical books differs (as it often did).[164] Of course,
many of these connections are apparent only when we view the canon
as a whole, and they therefore would not have been as accessible to the
earliest Christians, who did not yet possess a completed canon. This
fact reminds us again that some qualities of canonicity are *synergistic*—the whole can be greater than the constituent parts. It is like the
"fifth voice" of a barbershop quartet; you hear it only when all four
voices are joined together in harmony.

IV. Conclusion

Central to the self-authenticating model of canon is the conviction that
canonical books are recognized not only by their historical authenticity
(apostolic origins) or their ecclesiastical acceptance (corporate reception),
but fundamentally by the nature of their *content* (divine qualities). If these
books are constituted by the work of the Holy Spirit, then Christians,
who are filled with the Holy Spirit, should be able to recognize that fact.
In most prior studies of the New Testament canon, this aspect of canonicity has received far too little attention. This chapter has attempted to fill
in some of the blanks by arguing that the attributes of Scripture can be
understood in three different categories: beauty and excellency, power and
efficacy, and unity and harmony. Although critics have suggested some
potential defeaters to the divine qualities of Scripture (particularly Bauer

---

[164]In particular, some may object that some of these connections would not be as apparent for
those early Christians who used a Greek Old Testament (and many of them did). However,
simply because some connections would not be visible in certain translations does not mean they
do not exist. One does not have to read the Old Testament in the Hebrew order, but when it is
read in the Hebrew order these connections become visible and meaningful. Moreover, many
of these connections—macro *inclusio* of Genesis/Revelation, overall chiastic structure of the
biblical narrative, etc.—would still be visible even on a Greek ordering of the Old Testament
canon. For more on the significance of the Septuagint and the canon, see R. Glenn Wooden,
"The Role of the 'Septuagint' in the Formation of the Biblical Canons," in *Exploring the Origins
of the Bible: Canon Formation in Historical, Literary, and Theological Perspective*, ed. C. A.
Evans and E. Tov (Grand Rapids: Baker, 2008), 129–46; and Marvin Sweeney, "Tanak versus
Old Testament: Concerning the Foundation for a Jewish Theology of the Bible," in *Problems in
Biblical Theology: Essays in Honor of Rolf Knierim*, ed. Henry T. C. Sun et al. (Grand Rapids:
Eerdmans, 1997), 353–72.

and Baur), there proves to be little reason to abandon the Christian belief in canon on these grounds. Not only did early Christians have a basis for assessing orthodoxy, but the New Testament books exhibit impressive unity with one another and also with the Old Testament. All these features combine to suggest that the New Testament canon, by virtue of its divine qualities, genuinely speaks for itself.

5

THE APOSTOLIC ORIGINS
OF THE CANON

The Apostles received the Gospel for us from the Lord Jesus
Christ, Jesus the Christ was sent from God. The Christ therefore is from God and the Apostles from the Christ.

1 CLEMENT

Having focused on the internal, divine qualities of the canon in the prior
chapter, we now turn our attention to the origins of the canon. Where
did the idea of a New Testament come from? What was the impetus for
having a canon at all? Even a brief survey of modern scholarly opinion
reveals that the canon is often regarded as something that derives from
the period of early church history. For many scholars, particularly from
the historical-critical model, the idea of a canon arose well after the
books of the New Testament were written—and thus was retroactively
imposed upon books originally composed for another purpose.[1] Thus, it
is argued, the existence of a New Testament canon could not have been
anticipated or expected ahead of time, but finds its roots squarely in the
theological and political machinations of later Christian groups.[2] Koester

---

[1]D. Moody Smith, "When Did the Gospels Become Scripture?," *JBL* 119 (2000): 3–20,
acknowledges that there is a widespread conviction among scholars that the New Testament
books were not written to be Scripture: "The presumption of a historical distance, and consequent
difference of purpose, between the composition of the NT writings and their incorporation into
the canon of Scripture is representative of our discipline" (3).

[2]Harry Y. Gamble, *The New Testament Canon: Its Making and Meaning* (Philadelphia: Fortress,
1985), 12; James Barr, *Holy Scripture: Canon, Authority and Criticism* (Philadelphia: Westminster,
1983), 12.

argues that "the impelling force for the formation of the canon" was the second-century heretic Marcion.[3] In order to counter Marcion, the "New Testament canon of Holy Scripture . . . was thus essentially *created* by Irenaeus."[4] For reasons such as this, McDonald argues that "no conscious or clear effort was made by these [New Testament] authors to produce Christian Scriptures,"[5] and Gamble contends that "nothing dictated that there should be a NT at all."[6] Barr is even more direct: "The idea of a Christian faith governed by Christian written holy Scriptures was not an essential part of the foundation plan of Christianity."[7]

But are we to really think that "the impelling force for the formation of the canon" goes no further back than the second century? We shall argue that the historical-critical model has been myopically focused on the time after the writing of the New Testament books and, as a result, has overlooked the critical time before and during the writing of these books, particularly the significance of the redemptive-historical epoch from which they came. In short, it has been preoccupied with corporate reception of these books and has neglected their *apostolic origins*. It is here, then, that we come to the second of our three attributes of canonicity. The apostolic character of these books reminds us that their authority—indeed their very existence—does not depend on the actions of the later church but is rooted in the foundational role played by the apostles as "ministers of the new covenant" (2 Cor. 3:6). They are not regarded as canon because the church receives them; the church receives them because they are *already* canon by virtue of their apostolic authority.

---

[3]Helmut Koester, *Introduction to the New Testament*, vol. 2, *History and Literature of Early Christianity* (Philadelphia: Fortress, 1982), 8. The idea that Marcion was responsible for the origins of the New Testament canon can be found most notably in A. von Harnack, *Marcion: Das Evangelium von fremden Gott* (Leipzig: Hinrichs, 1924); H. von Campenhausen, *The Formation of the Christian Bible* (London: A&C Black, 1972); and J. Knox, *Marcion and the New Testament: An Essay in the Early History of the Canon* (Chicago: University of Chicago Press, 1942). However, Marcion's role in the formation of the canon has been minimized in recent years; e.g., John Barton, "Marcion Revisited," in *The Canon Debate*, ed. Lee Martin McDonald and James A. Sanders (Peabody, MA: Hendrickson, 2002), 341–54; John Barton, *The Spirit and the Letter: Studies in the Biblical Canon* (London: SPCK, 1997), 35–62; Franz Stuhlhofer, *Der Gebrauch der Bibel von Jesus bis Euseb: Eine statistische Untersuchung zur Kanonsgeschichte* (Wuppertal: Brockhaus, 1988), 73ff.; D. L. Balás, "Marcion Revisited: A 'Post-Harnack' Perspective," in *Texts and Testaments: Critical Essays on the Bible and the Early Church Fathers*, ed. W. E. March (San Antonio: Trinity University Press, 1980), 95–107; and R. Grant, *The Formation of the New Testament* (New York: Harper & Row, 1965), 126.
[4]Koester, *History and Literature of Early Christianity*, 10, emphasis mine. In agreement about the role of Irenaeus is Elaine Pagels, *Beyond Belief: The Secret Gospel of Thomas* (New York: Random House, 2003).
[5]Lee M. McDonald, *The Formation of the Christian Biblical Canon* (Peabody, MA: Hendrickson, 1995), 142.
[6]Gamble, *The New Testament Canon*, 12.
[7]Barr, *Holy Scripture*, 12.

The purpose of this chapter, then, is to explore the apostolic origins of these books in greater detail (while addressing a potential "defeater" to apostolic origins along the way). But we cannot begin there. The foundational role of the apostles must be understood within its proper context. Thus, we first want to examine the historical and theological matrix of the first century that gave birth to these books. Was this an environment in which canonical books would have naturally sprouted? Were the theological and historical conditions favorable for a new scriptural deposit to emerge? What do we know about early Christian beliefs, and how would they have affected their expectation of a new revelation from God? Although there are many ways to address these questions, we shall argue that there were two key factors in the historical context: (1) there was a structural framework for canon already in place: covenant; (2) and there was a clear and powerful rationale for canon: redemption. After this historical context has been established, we will then address the role of the apostles as the "agents" of the canon. When these three factors (covenant, redemption, and apostolicity) are viewed together, it will become clear that the idea of a canon was not an after-the-fact development with roots in church history, but rather a natural, early, and inevitable development with roots in redemptive history.

I. The Structural Framework for Canon: Covenant

If we are to understand the redemptive-historical environment that gave birth to the canon, we must begin with an issue that has too often been neglected in prior studies: the overarching covenantal backdrop of the New Testament itself. It is here that we discover that early Christians *already* had the macrostructural categories for understanding what a canon is and how it functions in the economy of God's unfolding redemptive plan. They understood this because they emerged from within the larger covenantal context laid down by the Old Testament.[8]

---

[8]Some helpful studies on covenant include O. Palmer Robertson, *The Christ of the Covenants* (Phillipsburg, NJ: P&R, 1980); Robertson, *Covenants: God's Way With His People* (Philadelphia: Great Commission, 1978); Meredith G. Kline, *Treaty of the Great King* (Grand Rapids: Eerdmans, 1963); Kline, *Kingdom Prologue: Genesis Foundations for a Covenantal Worldview* (Overland Park, KS: Two Age Press, 2000); Thomas Edward McComiskey, *The Covenants of Promise: A Theology of the Old Testament Covenants* (Grand Rapids: Baker, 1985); William J. Dumbrell, *Covenant and Creation* (Grand Rapids: Baker, 1984); Steven L. McKenzie, *Covenant* (St. Louis: Chalice, 2000); and most recently, Michael Horton, *God of Promise: Introducing Covenant Theology* (Grand Rapids: Baker, 2006).

A. The Concept of Covenant

Simply put, a covenant (בְּרִית) is an arrangement or contract between two parties that includes the terms of their relationship, covenant obligations (stipulations), and blessings and curses. Although covenants are made between humans in Scripture (1 Sam. 18:3; 20:16), the dominant biblical concept of covenant focuses on the relationship between God and man (Gen. 15:18; 17:2; Ex. 34:28; Isa. 55:3; Luke 1:72; 22:20; Heb. 8:6–13). Indeed, all human-divine relationships in Scripture can be subsumed under and understood within the concept of covenant. Immediately after the fall, God made provision to save a particular people for himself by grace through the shed blood of the promised seed who would crush the head of the serpent (Gen. 3:15). Jesus Christ, the second Adam (1 Cor. 15:21–22), acting as the federal representative of this agreement, kept its obligations perfectly and took the curse for disobedience upon himself at the cross, securing blessings for all those he represented.

This brief description suggests that the concept of covenant forms the overall structural backdrop to the entire redemptive story of the Scriptures.[9] To tell the story of how God has redeemed his people is simply to tell the story of God's covenantal relationship with them. Thus, the archetypal macro story of God's redeeming work is told by way of the covenantal structure of Scripture. This structure provides the "nuts and bolts" of the redemptive message of the gospel and puts much-needed flesh on an otherwise bare biblical skeleton. We can agree with Michael Horton, who notes that the covenantal concept is "an architectonic structure, a matrix of beams and pillars that hold together the structure of biblical practice."[10]

B. The Structure of the Covenant

The connection between covenant and canon becomes clear when we examine the covenantal structure in more detail. The covenantal structure of the Old Testament is illumined by the realization that it is patterned after the treaty covenants of the ancient Near Eastern world from which it came.[11] Within these extrabiblical treaties, a suzerain king would address

---

[9]Walter Eichrodt, *Theology of the Old Testament*, vol. 1, trans. J. A. Baker (Philadelphia: Westminster, 1961), 11–17; Scott Hafemann, "The Covenant Relationship," in *Central Themes in Biblical Theology: Mapping Unity in Diversity*, ed. Scott Hafemann and Paul House (Grand Rapids: Baker Academic, 2007), 20–65.

[10]Horton, *God of Promise*, 13.

[11]Delbert R. Hillers, *Covenant: The History of a Biblical Idea* (Baltimore: Johns Hopkins University Press, 1969); George E. Mendenhall, *Law and Covenant in Israel and the Ancient Near East* (Pittsburgh: The Biblical Colloquium, 1955), 24–50; Meredith G. Kline, *The Structure of Biblical Authority*, 2nd ed. (Eugene, OR: Wipf & Stock, 1997), 27–44; D. J. McCarthy, *Treaty*

the terms of his relationship with the vassal king over whom he ruled, laying out the stipulations of their agreement, including blessings and curses. These ancient treaties—particularly Hittite ones—had a clearly defined structure.[12]

1. *Preamble.* The opening line of Hittite treaty covenants included the name of the great suzerain king who was issuing the covenant and often listed his many titles and attributes.[13]

2. *Historical prologue.* This portion of the treaty laid forth the history of the relationship between the suzerain king and the vassal. If the suzerain king had rescued the vassal king in the past, then this would provide the grounds for loyalty and love toward the suzerain. Delbert Hillers notes, "The history had a function to perform: it was meant to place the relation on a basis other than that of sheer force."[14]

3. *Stipulations.* Ancient treaty covenants set forth the terms of the covenant arrangement and the obligations that each party agreed to fulfill. Among other things, such stipulations included the loyal behavior of the vassal king and faithful protection offered by the suzerain king if any foreign armies would threaten his vassal.

4. *Sanctions (blessings and curses).* Hittite treaties also included the various punishments that either party would endure if he broke the terms of the covenant. Although the suzerain would protect his vassal from foreign armies, he would attack his vassal himself and administer discipline if he proved disloyal.

5. *Deposit of written text of the covenant.* The final component of ancient Hittite treaty covenants—and most important for our purposes here—was that a deposit of a *written* copy of the covenant documents would be given to each party to place in their holy shrines. Not only was each party to receive a written copy of the covenant terms, but there were provisions to have the covenant documents read publicly at regular intervals.

When we look at the structure of key portions of the Mosaic covenant—such as Deuteronomy and the Decalogue—we see that it is clearly patterned after the same structure of these treaty covenants from the

---

and Covenant (Rome: Biblical Institute Press, 1981); J. A Thompson, *The Ancient Near Eastern Treaties and the Old Testament* (Grand Rapids: Tyndale, 1964).

[12]Overviews of the structure of ancient treaties can be seen in G. E. Mendenhall, "Covenant Forms in Israelite Tradition," *BA* 17 (1954): 50–76; and John H. Walton, *Ancient Israelite Literature in Its Cultural Context* (Grand Rapids: Zondervan, 1989), 95–107.

[13]Hillers, *Covenant*, 29–30.

[14]Ibid., 31.

Near Eastern world.[15] The Ten Commandments given at Sinai, clearly the core of God's covenant with Israel, had a preamble (Ex. 20:2a, "I am the LORD your God"), a historical prologue (Ex. 20:2b, "who brought you out of the land of Egypt . . ."), a list of stipulations (Ex. 20:3–17), a list of blessings and curses (Ex. 20:5, 6, 7, 11, 12), and, most notably, two copies of the covenant in *written* form deposited in the holy place of worship (Ex. 31:18; Deut. 10:2).[16] As Meredith Kline notes, "The duplicate tables of the covenant at Sinai reflect the custom of preparing copies of the treaty for each covenant party."[17] Just as these ancient treaties created covenant documents as permanent witnesses to the covenant arrangement between the suzerain king and his vassal, so God supplies covenant documents to bear witness to the terms of the arrangement between him and his people.[18] Kline proceeds to argue that the entire Old Testament structure and all the books therein reflect various aspects of these ancient extrabiblical treaties.[19] In particular, he observes that ancient treaties included an "inscriptional curse," which pronounced judgment on all those who changed the wording of the covenant documents.[20] Likewise, such an inscriptional curse is evident through the biblical witness from Deuteronomy 4:2: "You shall not add to the word that I command you, nor take from it, that you may keep the commandments of the Lord your God."[21]

In light of such a historical reality, it is clear that canon is inherent to and derives its function from the concept of covenant. The canonical writings are God's documentation, as it were, of his covenantal relationship with his people, laying out the nature of their relationship, the terms and conditions, and the blessings and curses. Just as the ancient extrabiblical

---

[15]Other passages that reflect this structure include Joshua 24; see Mendenhall, *Law and Covenant*, 41ff.; Hillers, *Covenant*, 59–62; and Horton, *God of Promise*, 34, 39–40.

[16]Kline, *Treaty of the Great King*, 13–26.

[17]Kline, *The Structure of Biblical Authority*, 35.

[18]Hillers, *Covenant*, 35; Mendenhall, *Law and Covenant*, 34.

[19]Kline, *The Structure of Biblical Authority*, 45–75; see also Hillers, *Covenant*, 120–42, as he demonstrates the covenantal function of the prophetical books.

[20]Kline, *The Structure of Biblical Authority*, 29–34; Kline notes that the Hittite treaty of Tudhaliyas IV and Ulmi-Teshub states, "Whoever . . . changes but one word of this tablet . . . may the thousand gods of this tablet root that man's descendants out of the land of Hatti" (29); see also F. C. Fensham, "Common Trends in Curses of the Near Eastern Treaties and Kudurru-Inscriptions Compared with Maledictions of Amos and Isaiah," *ZAW* 75 (1963): 155–75; Stanley Gevirtz, "West-Semitic Curses and the Problem of the Origins of Hebrew Law," *VT* 11 (1961): 137–58; H. G. Güterbock, "Mursili's Accounts of Suppiluliuma's Dealings with Egypt," *RHA* 18 (1960): 59–60; Michael A. Fishbane, "Varia Deuteronomica," *ZAW* 84 (1972): 349–52; *ANET* 161.

[21]Cf. Deut. 12:32; Prov. 30:5–6. The influence of inscriptional curses is notable in other Jewish literature; e.g., *Aristeas* 310–11; *1 Enoch* 104:9–10; *1 Macc.* 8:30; Josephus, *Ag. Ap.* 1.42; 11QTemple 54:5–7; *b. Meg.* 14a. David E. Aune, *Revelation 17–22*, WBC (Nashville: Thomas Nelson, 1998), 1208–16, refers to this type of language as an "integrity formula."

treaty covenants would not have omitted a written document as witness to the relationship between the two parties, so biblical covenants would not exist without a written witness to the relationship between God and his people.[22] Canon, therefore, is the *inevitable result of covenant*. Kline concludes, "Biblical canon is covenantal canon."[23]

C. The New Covenant

Given this historical context, we now turn to the new covenant. The religious world of Judaism had already anticipated the reality of another future covenant whereby Israel would be redeemed: "'Behold the days are coming,' declares the LORD, 'when I will make *a new covenant* with the house of Israel and the house of Judah'" (Jer. 31:31). Certainly first-century Jews, when confronted with the term "covenant" (בְּרִית) in Jeremiah 31, would have understood that term within their own historical and biblical context—a context patterned after the treaty covenants of the Near Eastern world.[24] Thus, there would have been clear expectations that this new covenant, like the old covenant, would be accompanied by the appropriate *written texts* to testify to the terms of the new arrangement that God was establishing with his people. Kline shows that the New Testament documents themselves, from Gospel to epistle to Revelation, all reflect the formal covenantal structure already laid forth in the Old Testament pattern.[25] Moreover, we again see the "inscriptional curse" in Revelation 22:18–19.

> I warn everyone who hears the words of the prophecy of this book: if any-one adds to them, God will add to him the plagues described in this book, and if anyone takes away from the words of the book of this prophecy,

---

[22]Of course, this is not to say that every covenant in biblical history has a written document (e.g., the Noahic covenant did not). But, as Kline notes, "where there is a divine covenant of the *classic Old Testament kind* there is a divine covenantal document" (*The Structure of Biblical Authority*, 39, emphasis mine).

[23]Kline, *The Structure of Biblical Authority*, 75.

[24]Whether first-century Jews were still aware of ancient Near Eastern Hittite treaties is not relevant for our point here (though they may have known more than we realize). Even if they were not aware of the *background* for the Old Testament covenantal structure, they would still have been familiar with that structure through the Old Testament documents themselves (Kline, *The Structure of Biblical Authority*, 70). Moreover, we have good reasons to think that first-century Judaism (as a whole) maintained a keen interest in the concept of covenant. See E. P. Sanders, *Paul and Palestinian Judaism* (Minneapolis: Fortress, 1977), 420ff.; and N. T. Wright, *The New Testament and the People of God* (Minneapolis: Fortress, 1992), 260–79.

[25]Kline, *The Structure of Biblical Authority*, 68–74; Meredith G. Kline, "The Old Testament Origins of the Gospel Genre," *WTJ* 38 (1975): 1–27.

God will take away his share in the tree of life and in the holy city, which are described in this book.[26]

Thus, the New Testament canon, at its core, is a covenantal document. This reality is borne out by the earliest Christian writings, which recognized very early that God's redemptive acts in Jesus Christ were the beginnings of the new covenant.[27] Indeed, Paul refers to himself and the other apostles as διακόνους καινῆς διαθήκης ("ministers of a new covenant") within a *written* letter to the Corinthians (2 Cor. 3:6).[28] Such a phrase clearly harkens back to Jeremiah 31:31 and is a claim that Paul and the other apostles are authoritative messengers from God who are laying the foundations of that new covenant (2 Cor. 13:10; cf. Jer. 31:28).[29] Since the very letter Paul is writing functions as a "covenant lawsuit"[30] against the disobedience of the Corinthian church and

---

[26]Cf. Gal. 3:15. For more on the inscriptional curse in early Christianity, see M. J. Kruger, "Early Christian Attitudes Towards the Reproduction of Texts," in *The Early Text of the New Testament*, ed. C. E. Hill and M. J. Kruger (Oxford: Oxford University Press, forthcoming).

[27]E.g., Matt. 26:28; Mark 14:24; Luke 22:20; 1 Cor. 11:25; 2 Cor. 3:6, 14; Heb. 7:22; 8:6; *Barn.* 4.6–8; 13.1–6; 14.1–7; Justin Martyr, *Dial.* 11.1; 34.1; 43.1; 44.2; 51.3; 67.10; 122.5; Irenaeus, *Haer.* 1.10.3; 3.11.8; 4.9.1–3; 4.12.3.

[28]One of the most misunderstood portions of 2 Cor. 3:6 is when Paul speaks of the new covenant as "not of the letter but of the Spirit. For the letter kills, but the Spirit gives life." The contrast between letter and Spirit here, however, is not a contrast in terms of the *instrument* of revelation used by each covenant—as if the Old used written texts and the New used only oral tradition (e.g., Barr, *Holy Scripture*, 12). Instead, it is a contrast in regard to the nature of the covenants themselves. One was clearly a covenant focused on law (i.e., the "letter"), and one was focused more on the heart (i.e., the "Spirit"). This distinction is confirmed by Paul just a few verses later when he makes the same point using slightly different terminology; he calls the old covenant the "ministry of condemnation" (3:9) and contrasts it to the new covenant as a "ministry of the Spirit" (3:8). Clearly, the point of Paul's contrast in these verses is *not* that one covenant involved writing things down and the other involved keeping things oral. This understanding is confirmed by the many other biblical texts that make this same sort of contrast between the two covenants: Ezek. 36:26; John 1:17; Rom. 2:29; 7:6; 8:2; Gal. 3:17–18; 4:24–26; etc. Overall, this language in 2 Cor. 3:6 is just an application of Jer. 31:33 to the era of Christ: "I will put my law within them and I will write it on their hearts." For more, see Bernardin Schneider, "The Meaning of St. Paul's Antithesis 'The Letter and the Spirit,'" *CBQ* 15 (1953): 163–207; H. Ridderbos, *Paul: An Outline of His Theology* (Grand Rapids: Eerdmans, 1975), 218–19; Sigurd Grindheim, "The Law Kills but the Gospel Gives Life: The Letter-Spirit Dualism in 2 Cor 3:5–18," *JSNT* 84 (2001): 97–115; and Scott J. Hafemann, *Paul, Moses, and the History of Israel: The Letter/ Spirit Contrast and the Argument from Scripture in 2 Corinthians 3* (Tübingen: Mohr, 1995).

[29]P. R. Jones, "The Apostle Paul: Second Moses to the New Covenant Community. A Study in Pauline Apostolic Authority," in *God's Inerrant Word*, ed. J. W. Montgomery (Minneapolis: Bethany, 1974), 219–41. Jones makes a compelling case that Paul is directly appealing to Jer. 31:27–28 (cf. Ezek. 36:36) in the texts of 2 Cor. 3:6 and 13:10. See also Jones, "1 Corinthians 15:8: Paul the Last Apostle," *TynBul* 36 (1985): 3–34.

[30]W. L. Lane, "Covenant: The Key to Paul's Conflict with Corinth," *TynBul* 33 (1982): 3–29. Lane argues that Paul's letter takes the form of a "covenant lawsuit" in which the representative of God's covenant prosecutes God's people when they are disobedient (15–18). E.g., note 2 Cor. 5:20, "Therefore, we are ambassadors for Christ, God making his appeal through us." This same theme is evident in Kline, *The Structure of Biblical Authority*, 73; C. Roetzel, "The Judgment

is thereby an extension of his authoritative-foundational office, the connection between the new covenant and written texts cannot be missed.[31] But there is more. Paul directly connects the concept of covenant with written texts in 2 Corinthians 3:14 when he calls the written Torah the "old covenant" (τῆς παλαιᾶς διαθήκης).[32] By doing so, Paul is invoking a biblical pattern of equating the covenant with written texts themselves: for example, "the *book* of the covenant" (Ex. 24:7); "he *wrote* . . . the words of the covenant" (Ex 34:28); "the covenant *written* in this Book" (Deut. 29:21).[33] As Peter Jensen notes, "For Paul, what you did with the old covenant was read it."[34] If Paul's concept of a covenant is intimately connected to written texts, and he announces in a written text that he is the authoritative minister of a *new* covenant, it is difficult to avoid the implication that he also understands the new covenant as having written texts.[35]

The connection between canon and covenant was also recognized by early Patristic writers as they often used the term διαθήκη ("covenant") to refer to canonical writings.[36] Around AD 180, Melito of Sardis followed in

---

Form in Paul's Letters," *JBL* 88 (1969): 305–12; and J. L. White, "Introductory Formulae in the Body of the Pauline Letter," *JBL* 90 (1971): 91–97.

[31] Gamble overlooks this very point when he says, "In its origins the [New Testament] collection had nothing to do with the biblical idea of covenant" (*The New Testament Canon*, 22). Gamble bases this claim on the fact that early Christian writings do not explicitly connect the concept of covenant with written texts. Such a conclusion not only overlooks texts like 2 Cor. 3:6, but simply does not follow from the premise. The connection between covenant and written texts need not always be made *explicitly* in order for the overall covenantal backdrop of the Old Testament to affect Christian expectations about more covenantal books. Gamble also appeals to the fact that the term *new covenant* was not used to refer to New Testament canon until the second century. However, this is no more relevant than the fact that the term *Gospel* was not explicitly used for writings until the second century. Are we to think, therefore, that no one conceived of the "good news" of Jesus as something that could be in written texts prior to that point? Mark 1:1 would suggest otherwise. Terminological usage cannot be the sole determiner of historical realities for it often lags behind the realities. Campenhausen reminds us that in the earliest phases of Christianity there was no "need for a comprehensive nomenclature" to distinguish the two testaments (*The Formation of the Christian Bible*, 262).

[32] R. P. Martin, *2 Corinthians*, WBC (Waco, TX: Word, 1986), 69, argues that Paul coined this phrase. C. K. Barrett, *A Commentary on the Second Epistle to the Corinthians* (London: A&C Black, 1973), 121, argues that "old covenant" and "Old Testament" are virtually synonymous.

[33] W. Kinzig, "καινὴ Διαθήκη: The Title of the New Testament in the Second and Third Centuries," *JTS* 45 (1994): 526.

[34] Peter Jensen, *The Revelation of God* (Downers Grove, IL: InterVarsity, 2002), 81.

[35] See helpful discussion of this passage in Jean Carmignac, "II Corinthiens III. 6, 14 et le Début de la Formation du Noveau Testament," *NTS* 24 (1976): 5–14.

[36] For the theme of covenant in early Christianity, see E. Ferguson, "The Covenant Idea in the Second Century," in *Texts and Testaments: Critical Essays on the Bible and the Early Church Fathers*, ed. W. E. March (San Antonio: Trinity University Press, 1980), 135–62; W. C. van Unnik, "ἡ καινὴ Διαθήκη—A Problem in the Early History of the Canon," in *StPatr*, vol. 4, = TU 79 (Berlin, 1961), 212–27; Kinzig, "καινὴ Διαθήκη," 519–44; and J. Ligon Duncan, "The Covenant Idea in Melito of Sardis: An Introduction and Survey," *Presb* 28 (2002): 12–33.

the footsteps of Paul and referred to τῆς παλαιᾶς διαθήκης βιβλία ("the books of the Old Covenant").[37] This not only shows that he viewed a covenant as a written document, but strongly implies that there would be a corresponding set of books for the *new* covenant.[38] In the same era, an anti-Montanist writer expressly referred to the church's canonical books as τῷ τῆς τοῦ εὐαγγελίου καινῆς διαθήκης λόγῳ ("the word of the *new covenant* of the gospel"), erasing any doubts about whether the concepts of canon and covenant were closely linked in the minds of early Christians.[39] Indeed, by the time of Clement of Alexandria, the phrase *new covenant* was fully established as the official title of the church's canon.[40] Everett Ferguson observes that for Clement, "'Covenant' meant or referred to written documents."[41] Likewise, for Origen, Hans von Campenhausen argues, "*Diatheke* in the sense of 'book' was a perfectly normal usage."[42] In fact, Origen used the word ἐνδιαθήκους—an obvious derivative of διαθήκη—to refer to the books he regarded as canonical.[43]

Once the covenantal nature of the New Testament canon is understood, we can see that conceptions of canon as merely a product of the early church fundamentally miss what the canon really is. As noted above, Gamble declared, "Nothing dictated that there should be a NT at all."[44] And Barr claimed that "writing was an unworthy mode of transmission" for new covenant truth.[45] However, in light of the above discussions of canon and covenant, these statements are simply not historically or biblically accurate. In fact, we have seen that the concept of a written canon of Scripture is woven into the very covenantal fabric of *both* the Old Testament and the New. Far from being an "unworthy mode of transmission," written texts were the central manner in which God testified

---

[37]Eusebius, *Hist. eccl.* 4.26. J. N. D. Kelly, *Early Christian Doctrines* (San Francisco: HarperCollins, 1978), 56, draws a link between Melito's comments and Paul's description of the "Old Covenant" in 2 Cor. 3:14. Van Unnik, "A Problem in the Early History of the Canon," 220, disagrees and argues that Paul's theology had no influence on Patristic uses of "covenant."

[38]Duncan, "The Covenant Idea in Melito of Sardis," 25–26. Kinzig, "The Title of the New Testament," 527–28, argues that it is unclear whether Melito viewed the phrase "Old Covenant" (and implicitly "New Covenant") as a formal title. But that does not affect our point here. We are simply arguing that there was a close theological and conceptual link between canon and covenant, not that the latter was yet used as an official title.

[39]Eusebius, *Hist. eccl.* 5.16.3. Campenhausen argues that the anti-Montanist author "leaves no doubt that what he has in mind is the writing of the 'New Testament'" (*The Formation of the Christian Bible*, 265).

[40]E.g., *Strom.* 1.44.3; 3.71.3; 4.134.4; 5.85.1. See discussion in Kinzig, "The Title of the New Testament," 529–30; and Ferguson, "The Covenant Idea," 151–52.

[41]Ferguson, "The Covenant Idea," 151.

[42]Campenhausen, *The Formation of the Christian Bible*, 267.

[43]Eusebius, *Hist. eccl.* 6.25.1. Thanks to T. David Gordon for pointing out this particular reference.

[44]Gamble, *The New Testament Canon*, 12.

[45]Barr, *Holy Scripture*, 12.

to the terms of his covenant relationships within ancient Israel, and thus would be the expected means of communication in the context of the new covenant.

II. The Rationale for Canon: Redemption

It was not only early Christian beliefs about covenant that would have made the first-century environment conducive to the production of canonical books. That environment also consisted of the core rationale for why a new canon would be needed in the first place: the early Christian belief that, in Jesus of Nazareth, Israel's long-awaited eschatological redemption had finally been realized.

A. The Pattern of Redemption and Revelation

When we look to the Old Testament context once again, we recognize that God's word revelation is the distinctive result of his own redemptive activities. There is a pattern here: God acts to redeem his people, then offers word revelation to interpret, explain, and apply that redemptive activity.[46] Vos observes this biblical pattern: "Revelation does not stand by itself, but is . . . inseparably attached to another activity of God, which we call *Redemption.*"[47] Richard Gaffin writes, "It is not going too far to say that redemption is the *raison d'être* of revelation . . . revelation is either authentication or interpretation of God's redemptive action."[48] As Horton notes, to have redemptive acts without revelation "would be like watching a play without words."[49] The two go together. Before God formed his people Israel into a theocratic nation and gave them covenant documents, he first delivered them from the hand of Pharaoh in Egypt, in what is undoubtedly the archetypal redemptive event of the old covenant era.[50] When God gave the Decalogue to his people on Mount Sinai, the core of the written canon of the Old Testament, he first recounted this deliverance from Pharaoh: "I am the LORD your God, who brought you out of the land of Egypt, out of the house of slavery" (Ex. 20:2). Thus, we see here in this Old Testament pattern that canonical documents are

---

[46]Mendenhall, *Law and Covenant*, 32; Kline, *The Structure of Biblical Authority*, 76–78; C. E. Hill, "The New Testament Canon: Deconstructio Ad Absurdum?," *JETS* 52 (2009): 105–6; P. Helm, *The Divine Revelation: The Basic Issues* (London: Marshall Morgan & Scott, 1982), 35.
[47]Geerhardus Vos, *Biblical Theology* (Edinburgh: Banner of Truth, 1975), 5, emphasis his.
[48]R. B. Gaffin, *Resurrection and Redemption* (Phillipsburg, NJ: P&R, 1978), 22.
[49]M. S. Horton, *Covenant and Eschatology: The Divine Drama* (Louisville: Westminster John Knox, 2002), 233. For more on the necessity of word-act revelation, see Richard Lints, *The Fabric of Theology: A Prolegomenon to Evangelical Theology* (Grand Rapids: Eerdmans, 1993), 264.
[50]1 Sam. 8:8; 12:6; 2 Sam. 7:23; Neh. 9:9–10; Pss. 78:12–14; 135:9; Isa. 11:16; Hos. 11:1.

distinctively the *result* of God's redemptive activity in behalf of his people and function to proclaim that redemptive activity to his people (and to the nations). Canonical books, therefore, are redemptive books. They are a "divine word of triumph."[51]

When we turn our attention to the first-century context, it is evident that Jews were anticipating (and hoping) that a new deliverance from God was drawing near.[52] This coming deliverance was viewed not merely as the *next* act of redemption, but as the *consummate* act of redemption. Israel was still in "exile," so to speak, and people were looking for the Messiah (John 1:41; 4:25), who would bring the "redemption of Jerusalem" (Luke 2:38), "the consolation of Israel" (Luke 2:25), and would "restore the kingdom to Israel" (Acts 1:6).[53] This eschatological expectation that God was going to redemptively break into the world was built on a number of Old Testament texts that described this new era (e.g., Isa. 40:1–11; Jer. 31:31–40; Ezek. 36:24–28; Zeph. 3:14–20) and was also apparent within other Jewish writings available in this period.[54]

If early Christians came to believe that the actions of Jesus were the fulfillment of this long-awaited redemption of God, and if they were immersed in the Old Testament writings and the redemption-revelation pattern that it contained, then it is only natural that they would expect a new revelational deposit to accompany that redemption. Indeed, if covenant documents were given to Israel after the deliverance from Egypt by Moses, how much more would early Christians expect that new covenant documents would be given to the church after deliverance from sin by one greater than Moses, Jesus Christ (Heb. 3:1–6).[55] After all, Jesus was not just another prophet. He was the eschatological realization of all of redemptive history. He was *the* prophet (Deut. 18:18; John 7:40, 52), the

---

[51]Kline, *The Structure of Biblical Authority*, 79.

[52]Wright, *The New Testament and the People of God*, 280–338.

[53]For discussion of Israel as still in exile, see Wright, *The New Testament and the People of God*, 268–79; and C. A. Evans, "Jesus and the Continuing Exile of Israel," in *Jesus and the Restoration of Israel*, ed. C. C. Newman (Downers Grove, IL: InterVarsity, 1999), 77–100; and Stephen G. Dempster, *Dominion and Dynasty: A Biblical Theology of the Hebrew Bible* (Downers Grove, IL: InterVarsity, 2003), 224–27.

[54]E.g., *T. Mos.* 10.1–10; *Wis.* 3.7; 1QSb 5.23–29.

[55]Moses-Jesus typology is a well-established theme throughout the New Testament. In both covenants God's people are delivered by "the lamb of God" (Ex. 12:1–7; John 1:29); Jesus is portrayed as leading his own "exodus" from Egypt when in Matt. 2:15 he leaves Egypt in fulfillment of Hos. 11:1: "Out of Egypt I called my son"; in Luke's Gospel, Jesus is speaking to Moses and Elijah about his "exodus" (ἔξοδον), which "he was about to accomplish at Jerusalem" (Luke 9:31). See Vern S. Poythress, *The Shadow of Christ in the Law of Moses* (Phillipsburg, NJ: P&R, 1991), and Kline, "Old Testament Origins of the Gospel Genre," 1–27. For a broader look at images of Moses in the New Testament, see John Lierman, *The New Testament Moses* (Tübingen: Mohr Siebeck, 2004).

son of David (Matt. 12:23), one *greater* than the temple (Matt. 12:6), the Mediator of a *better* covenant (Heb. 7:22; 8:6), and the perfect and final revelation of God (Heb. 1:1–2). Charles Hill notes, "If a new written corpus should arise with the claim of embodying that new revelation in the wake of a supremely important new redemptive act of God, this can hardly be called unnatural or wholly unanticipated."[56] Thus, the New Testament canon exists because, at its core, it is an *eschatological* canon.

It is here that we recognize that the eschatological nature of early Christianity was not a hindrance to the production of new written material, but actually part of the foundation for it. A long-standing assumption of form criticism has been that early Christian eschatological expectations—that in Jesus Christ the kingdom of God had come and was coming—would have led Christians to abandon the written medium for an exclusively oral one.[57] However, this assumption faces a number of difficulties. Not only do oral and written modes of transmission often exist side by side (which we shall discuss more below), but the discovery of the Qumran literature showed that communities could be decidedly eschatological/apocalyptic and also prolific producers of texts.[58] Moreover, David Meade makes the opposite point of the form critics, namely, that apocalypticism in the early Christian communities, far from preventing literary activity, actually "provides the ideological basis for the *extension* of Scripture."[59]

B. *The Anticipation of a New Redemptive Message*

The expectation of a fresh revelational deposit in the new covenant goes beyond the redemption-revelation pattern of the Old Testament. It also is built upon express statements in the Old Testament that God would

---

[56]Hill, "The New Testament Canon," 106.

[57]E.g., H. Gamble, "Christianity: Scripture and Canon," in *The Holy Book in Comparative Perspective*, ed. Frederick M. Denny and Rodney L. Taylor (Columbia: University of South Carolina Press, 1985), 56n6, argues that the eschatological nature of Christianity "militated against the composition of Christian literature." The sharp antithesis between textuality and orality is also exemplified in W. Kelber, *The Oral and Written Gospel: The Hermeneutics of Speaking and Writing in the Synoptic Tradition, Mark, Paul, and Q* (Philadelphia: Fortress, 1983). For a critique of Kelber, see John Halverson, "Oral and Written Gospel: A Critique of Werner Kelber," *NTS* 40 (1994): 180–95.

[58]E. Earle Ellis, "New Directions in the History of Early Christianity," in *Ancient History in a Modern University: Early Christianity, Late Antiquity and Beyond*, ed. T. W. Hillard et al. (Grand Rapids: Eerdmans, 1997), 1:75–76.

[59]D. Meade, "Ancient Near Eastern Apocalypticism and the Origins of the New Testament Canon of Scripture," in *The Bible as a Human Witness: Hearing the Word of God Through Historically Dissimilar Traditions*, ed. Randall Heskett and Brian Irwin (London: T&T Clark, 2010), 308, emphasis his.

bring a new *message* with the dawning of the eschatological age.[60] In Deuteronomy 18:18, Moses cites the promise of God that another prophet like him will arise: "I will raise up for them a prophet like you from among their brothers. And I will *put my words in his mouth*, and he shall speak to them all that I command him." This new prophet will bring with him new revelation that bears the very authority of God himself. Early Christians understood the ministry of Jesus as the fulfillment of Deuteronomy 18:18 and thus would have understood the new covenant to have a distinctively new prophetic message attached to it.[61]

Jesus himself clearly understood the Old Testament to be teaching that the redemptive work of the Messiah would be accompanied by a new divine message: "It is written, that the Christ should suffer and on the third day rise from the dead, and that repentance and forgiveness of sins should be proclaimed in his name to all nations" (Luke 24:46–47). Notice here that, according to Jesus, the Old Testament anticipates both the redemptive *acts* of the Messiah (death and resurrection) and the new *revelation* about the Messiah (repentance and forgiveness). Again, the two always go together. Although it is difficult to know which specific Old Testament text(s) Jesus had in mind, it may have been something like Isaiah 2:2–3, which is a dominant passage in early Christian understanding of the new covenant.

> In the latter days
> . . . out of Zion shall go the law,
> and the word of the LORD from Jerusalem.[62]

In addition, Jesus cites Isaiah 61:1–2 and applies it to his own ministry.

> The Spirit of the Lord is upon me,
> because he has anointed me
> to proclaim good news [εὐαγγελίσασθαι] to the poor.
> He has sent me to proclaim liberty to the captives
> and recovering of sight to the blind,
> to set at liberty those who are oppressed. (Luke 4:18; cf. Matt. 11:2–6)

---

[60]Hill, "The New Testament Canon," 107–8.

[61]Peter cites this very text in Acts 3:22–23; see also John 7:40, 52; Heb. 3:5–6. In regard to John 7:52, it is noteworthy that some early Christian manuscripts (e.g., P66*) place the Greek article before the word "prophet" showing that this text was likely viewed within the context of Deut. 18:18.

[62]E.g., Justin Martyr, *Dial.* 24; *1 Apol.* 39; Irenaeus, *Haer.* 4.34.4; Tertullian, *Adv. Jud.* 3; Origen, *Cels.* 5.33; Clement of Alexandria, *Protr.* 1; See discussion in Ferguson, "The Covenant Idea," 156–57; and Hill, "The New Testament Canon," 108–9.

Again, this Old Testament text predicted that a new message of "good news" would be preached in the coming age of the Messiah. Old Testament passages like this one are the basis for the New Testament's frequent use of the verb εὐαγγελίζομαι ("to preach the good news") and the noun εὐαγγέλιον ("good news").[63] Martin Hengel even argues that Mark's Gospel understood the term εὐαγγέλιον as a reference to the "radically new eschatological message of salvation" that the prophet Isaiah predicted would come in the age of the Messiah.[64] It is no accident, then, that the canonical accounts of Jesus's life eventually were given the title *Gospel* since they were viewed as the embodiment of the divine message promised by God since Old Testament times.[65]

Thus, it is the dawning of God's long-awaited redemptive triumph in the person of Jesus, and the new divine revelation related to that triumph, that is the impetus for the formation of the canon, not Marcion's heresies, Irenaeus's influence, or fourth-century ecclesiastical politics. As D. Moody Smith declared, "The early Christian claim that the narrative and prophecies of old are fulfilled and continued in Jesus and the church prefigures, perhaps even demands, *the production of more Scripture*."[66] If so, then the next question is simply what means God would choose to deliver that scriptural deposit. To that question we now turn.

III. The Agents of Canon: Apostles

So far, it is evident that early Christians not only had a structural framework for canon (covenant), but also had a rationale for why a new revelation was needed (redemption). However, something else was needed. There needed to be a means by which God could reliably transmit and deliver that new covenant revelation to his people, especially if that message was intended to go to "all nations" (Luke 24:46–47; cf. Isa. 2:2–3). Therefore, God established the apostolic office to be the guardian, preserver, and transmitter of the message of redemption.[67] God did not simply perform

---

[63]E.g., in Paul, the noun is used sixty times, and the verb twenty-one times (G. N. Stanton, *Jesus and Gospel* [Cambridge: Cambridge University Press, 2004], 9–62).

[64]M. Hengel, *The Four Gospels and the One Gospel of Jesus Christ* (Harrisburg, PA: Trinity, 2000), 160–61. See also arguments that Mark views Jesus as the fulfillment of Isaiah passages that speak of the new messianic exodus, in Rikki Watts, *Isaiah's New Exodus in Mark* (Grand Rapids: Baker Academic, 2001).

[65]E.g., Mark 1:1; Justin Martyr, *1 Apol.* 66.3; *Dial.* 10.2; 100.1; Hengel, *The Four Gospels*, 90–106; Helmut Koester, *Ancient Christian Gospels: Their History and Development* (London: SCM, 1990), 1–31.

[66]Smith, "When Did the Gospels Become Scripture?," 12, emphasis mine.

[67]For a look at the unique authority of the apostles as bearers of authentic Christian tradition, see Oscar Cullman, "The Tradition," in *The Early Church*, ed. A. J. B. Higgins (London: SCM,

redemptive acts and then leave the announcement and promulgation of those redemptive acts to chance or to the random movements of human history. Instead, God established the authority structure of his apostolate to be the foundation of his church for generations to come. These canonical "agents" form the critical connection between the redemptive work of God and God's subsequent announcement of that redemption. They are God's eschatological "ministers of the new covenant" (2 Cor. 3:6).

A. Apostolic Tradition

It is clear from our earliest Christian documents—the New Testament itself—that the apostolic message would have borne the authority of Christ and therefore would have been seen as a divine message with the same authority as (if not more than) the Old Testament Scriptures. Jesus had commissioned his apostles "so that they might be with him and he might send them out to preach and have authority to cast out demons" (Mark 3:14–15). Thus, the apostles were his mouthpieces to the nations, his authoritative witnesses. In John 20:21, Jesus declares to the apostles, "As the Father has sent me, even so I am sending you." Peter testifies to the fact that the apostles were "chosen by God as witnesses . . . to preach to the people and to testify that [Christ] is the one appointed by God to be judge of the living and the dead" (Acts 10:41–42). The book of 2 Peter makes it clear that the words of the apostles are the words of Jesus and are on par with the authority given to the Old Testament prophets: "You should remember the predictions of the holy prophets and the commandment of the Lord and Savior through your apostles" (2 Pet. 3:2). Likewise, the author of Hebrews argues that the message of the apostles is the same message of salvation that was announced by the Lord Jesus himself and thus bears his full authority and weight—more weight even than the Old Testament message borne by angels (Heb. 2:2–3).

This apostolic message—which is really the authoritative message of Jesus Christ himself—was originally transmitted *orally*.[68] Such oral tra-

---

1956), 59–99; and C. K. Barrett, *The Signs of an Apostle* (Philadelphia: Fortress, 1972). For a survey of prior literature on the subject, see F. Agnew, "The Origin of the NT Apostle-Concept: A Review of Research," *JBL* 105 (1986): 75–96.

[68]General treatments of oral tradition include, S. Byrskog, *Story as History—History as Story: The Gospel Tradition in the Context of Ancient Oral History* (Leiden: Brill, 2002); R. Bauckham, *Jesus and the Eyewitnesses: The Gospels as Eyewitness Testimony* (Grand Rapids: Eerdmans, 2006); James D. G. Dunn, *Jesus Remembered* (Grand Rapids: Eerdmans, 2003); Henry Wansbrough, ed., *Jesus and the Oral Gospel Tradition* (Edinburgh: T&T Clark, 2004); Kelber, *The Oral and Written Gospel*; Birger Gerhardsson, *Memory and Manuscript with Tradition and Transmission in Early Christianity*, 2nd ed. (Grand Rapids: Eerdmans, 1998); K. E. Bailey, "Informal Controlled Oral Tradition and the Synoptic Gospels," *Them* 20 (1995):

dition is evident within the New Testament itself when Paul speaks to the Thessalonians about "the tradition [παράδοσιν] you have received from us" (2 Thess. 3:6).[69] In 1 Corinthians 11:23 Paul also refers to the institution of the Lord's Supper as tradition: "I received [παρέλαβον] from the Lord what I also delivered [παρέδωκα] to you."[70] By saying that this tradition is "from the Lord," Paul is not suggesting that he received it by direct revelation, but is likely referring to the fact that the Lord spoke in (and behind) the apostolic tradition and thus that tradition is really from him.[71] Similarly, in 1 Corinthians 15:3 Paul states, "For I delivered [παρέδωκα] to you as of first importance what I also received [παρέλαβον]: that Christ died for our sins in accordance with the Scriptures." The structure of this verse suggests that Paul is passing along a standardized apostolic tradition about the resurrection of Jesus.[72] Other passages speak of this same phenomenon (Luke 1:1–4; Rom. 6:17; Gal. 1:9; Phil. 4:9; Col. 2:6–8; 1 Thess. 2:13–15; 1 Tim. 6:20; 2 Tim. 1:14; 2 Pet. 2:21; Jude 1:3).[73]

Of course, the term *oral tradition* can have a variety of negative connotations. After all, Christ rebuked the Pharisees for relying on the "traditions of men," which are unreliable and often change (Mark 7:8; cf. Matt. 5:21; Col. 2:8).[74] In addition, modern versions of form criticism have continued

---

4–11; Jan M. Vansina, *Oral Tradition as History* (Madison: University of Wisconsin Press, 1985); Richard A. Horsley, Jonathan A. Draper, and John Miles Foley, eds., *Performing the Gospel: Orality, Memory, and Mark* (Minneapolis: Fortress, 2006); and, most recently, W. Kelber and S. Byrskog, eds., *Jesus in Memory: Traditions in Oral and Scribal Perspectives* (Waco, TX: Baylor University Press, 2009).

[69]Treatments of apostolic tradition include Cullmann, "The Tradition," 59–99; F. F. Bruce, *Tradition: Old and New* (Grand Rapids: Zondervan, 1970), 29–38; F. F. Bruce, "Tradition and the Canon of Scripture," in *The Authoritative Word: Essays on the Nature of Scripture*, ed. D. K. McKim (Grand Rapids: Eerdmans, 1983), 59–84; and G. W. H. Lampe, "Scripture and Tradition in the Early Church," in *Scripture and Tradition*, ed. F. W. Dillistone (London: Lutterworth, 1955), 21–52. Josephus provides a similar example of this sort of tradition when he refers to the παράδοσιν he set down in writing (*Ag. Ap.* 1.49–50; cf. *Ant.* 13.297). Josephus is referring not to anonymous community tradition but to his own firsthand testimony to what happened.

[70]This tradition language is often found in rabbinic texts; see M. Jaffee, *Torah in the Mouth: Writing and Oral Tradition in Palestinian Judaism* (Oxford: Oxford University Press, 2001), 73–80; Bruce, *Tradition*, 21–22.

[71]Cullmann, "The Tradition," 66–75; Herman N. Ridderbos, *Redemptive History and the New Testament Scripture* (Phillipsburg, NJ: P&R, 1988), 20–21.

[72]J. S. Kloppenborg, "An Analysis of the Pre-Pauline Formula in 1 Cor 15:3b–5," *CBQ* 40 (1978): 351–67; Ulrich Wilckens, *Die Missionsreden der Apostelgeschichte*, 3rd ed. (Neukirchen-Vluyn: Neukirchener Verlag, 1974), 190–223; H. Conzelmann, "On the Analysis of the Confessional Formula in 1 Cor 15:3–5," *Int* 20 (1966): 15–25.

[73]Bruce, *Tradition*, 21–22. A thorough treatment of apostolic tradition in the New Testament writings can be found in E. Earle Ellis, *The Making of the New Testament Documents* (Leiden: Brill, 2002), 49–142.

[74]This is not saying that all traditions are problematic. The tradition of the church, as represented in its historic creeds and confessions, is a very valuable part of Christian theology and hermeneutics. However, such traditions still should be distinguished from the one-time, foundational apostolic tradition. For more on the value of ecclesiastical tradition, see Daniel H. Williams, *Evangelicals*

to highlight how traditions of Jesus were orally transmitted in various early Christian communities and were subsequently modified and adapted for each new *Sitz im Leben*.[75] It is important to recognize, however, that the New Testament passages above are speaking not of human tradition or even of ecclesiastical tradition, but of *apostolic* tradition. Luke tells us that his tradition was "handed down" (παρέδοσαν) to him by "those who from the beginning were eyewitnesses and ministers of the word" (Luke 1:2),[76] a clear reference to the apostles.[77] This type of tradition was not passed down over long periods of time through anonymous communities, but was passed down by those who were eyewitnesses of Jesus's redemptive activities and were given an authoritative commission by Christ to guard and preserve these traditions by the help of the Holy Spirit (John 16:13).[78] In their role as guardians of the oral tradition, not only would the apostles have passed it along themselves in their own preaching and teaching, but, as Bauckham has argued, they would have entrusted that oral tradition to key leaders and disciples "with the skills and gifts necessary for preserving the tradition."[79] No doubt there were other streams of oral tradition about Jesus that were being promulgated

---

and Tradition: The Formative Influence of the Early Church (Grand Rapids: Baker, 2005); and Williams, *Retrieving the Tradition and Renewing Evangelicalism: A Primer for Suspicious Protestants* (Grand Rapids: Eerdmans, 1999).

[75]E.g., R. Bultmann, *The History of the Synoptic Tradition* (Oxford: Blackwell, 1968); M. Dibelius, *From Tradition to Gospel* (Cambridge: Clarke, 1971).

[76]Some central works on the prologue of Luke include, Loveday Alexander, *The Preface to Luke's Gospel* (Cambridge: Cambridge University Press, 1993); V. K. Robbins, "The Claims of the Prologues and Greco-Roman Rhetoric: The Prefaces to Luke and Acts in Light of Greco-Roman Rhetorical Strategies," in *Jesus and the Heritage of Israel*, ed. D. P. Moessner (Harrisburg, PA: Trinity, 1999), 63–83; Schuyler Brown, "The Role of the Prologues in Determining the Purpose of Luke-Acts," in *Perspectives on Luke-Acts*, ed. Charles H. Talbert (Edinburgh: T&T Clark, 1978), 99–111; and David E. Aune, "Luke 1:1–4: Historical or Scientific *Prooimion*?," in *Paul, Luke and the Graeco-Roman World*, ed. A. Christopherson et al. (Sheffield: Sheffield Academic, 2002), 138–48.

[77]Joel B. Green, *The Gospel of Luke*, NICNT (Grand Rapids: Eerdmans, 1997), 42; Allison Trites, *The New Testament Concept of Witness* (Cambridge: Cambridge University Press, 1977), 136. Luke elsewhere focuses on the eyewitness character of the apostles as those who have shared in the ministry of Jesus "during all the time" and were present "beginning from the baptism of John until the day when [Jesus] was taken up" (Acts 1:21–22). In addition, Acts 6:4 refers to the apostles as those devoted to "the ministry of the word" (τῇ διακονίᾳ τοῦ λόγου), a phrase strikingly similar to that of Luke 1:2, where they are described as "ministers of the word" (ὑπηρέται τοῦ λόγου).

[78]There have been numerous critiques of the way form criticism has overlooked the role of the apostles/eyewitnesses and portrayed oral tradition as happening only through anonymous communities. V. Taylor, *Formation of the Gospel Tradition* (London: Macmillan, 1933), commented, "If the Form-Critics are right, the disciples must have been translated to heaven immediately after the resurrection" (41). Other critiques can be found in Birger Gerhardsson, *The Reliability of Gospel Tradition* (Peabody, MA: Hendrickson, 2001), 40ff.; Hengel, *The Four Gospels*, 143; and Bauckham, *Jesus and the Eyewitnesses*, 240–63.

[79]Bauckham, *Jesus and the Eyewitnesses*, 270.

during this early time period—some of which were more reliable than others. But the apostolic stream of tradition was viewed as unique because Christ himself was speaking through it.[80]

As a result of its distinctive character, the apostolic tradition took on foundational significance for the early church. Because such tradition was invariably connected to the apostolic office itself—which was unique and unrepeatable—it was not viewed as something that would be offered perpetually throughout the church age.[81] The church's posture therefore would always be *retrospective*, looking back to the one-time deposit laid down by Christ's apostles and building upon it. Its task was not to create new apostolic tradition but to guard and preserve "the faith that was once for all delivered to the saints" (Jude 3). This distinction between the foundational role of the apostles and the ongoing role of the church is evident in the earliest Christian teachings. Paul reminds his readers that the church "is built on the foundation of the apostles and prophets, Christ Jesus himself being the cornerstone" (Eph. 2:20). Christ himself anticipated this when he declared to Peter, representing all the apostles, "On this rock I will build my church" (Matt. 16:18).[82] As a result, Oscar Cullmann notes that there is

> an essential difference, also from the point of view of tradition, between *the foundation of the Church*, which took place in the period of the apostles, and the *post-Apostolic Church*, which is no longer that of the apostles but of the bishops. There is consequently a difference between apostolic tradition and ecclesiastical tradition, the former being the foundation for the latter.[83]

---

[80]Cullmann, "The Tradition," 73. For this reason, Bauckham suggests that the term *oral tradition* is misleading. When it comes to the apostles and other eyewitnesses, he suggests that *oral history* is more appropriate (*Jesus and the Eyewitnesses*, 30–38). Although we agree with Bauckham on this point, we will continue to use the standard nomenclature throughout this study.

[81]Deference to the apostles as unique is prevalent throughout many early Christian texts; e.g., *1 Clem.* 42.1–2; 47.1–3; Ign. *Rom.* 4.4; Pol. *Phil.* 6.3; Justin Martyr, *1 Apol.* 67.3; *Dial.* 106.

[82]Unfortunately, most discussions of this passage get mired down in the question of whether Peter is, in fact, the "rock" and thereby miss the larger issues. As D. A. Carson has noted, "If it were not for Protestant reactions against extremes of Roman Catholic interpretation, it is doubtful whether many would have taken 'rock' to be anything or anyone besides Peter" (D. A. Carson, *Matthew: Chapters 13–28*, The Expositor's Bible Commentary [Grand Rapids: Zondervan, 1995], 368). Others besides Carson are also quite comfortable affirming that Jesus was referring to Peter in this passage; e.g., William Hendriksen, *Exposition of the Gospel According to Matthew* (Grand Rapids: Baker, 1973). However, while Peter is clearly the "rock," we can also agree with Gundry that Peter is the "one who represents all the disciples" (Robert H. Gundry, *Matthew: A Commentary on His Handbook for a Mixed Church under Persecution*, 2nd ed. [Grand Rapids: Eerdmans, 1994], 334).

[83]Cullmann, "The Tradition," 79, emphasis his.

If so, then that raises the following question: How could this foundational apostolic tradition have been preserved in a way that makes it always accessible to the future generations of the church? The answer is rather simple. It was written down.

B. Apostolic Tradition and Written Texts

Although this apostolic tradition was initially delivered orally as the apostles preached, taught, and visited churches (2 Thess. 2:15), it very soon began to be preserved and passed along in *written* form. Of course, this transition did not happen all at once—oral apostolic tradition and written apostolic tradition would have existed side by side for a period of time.[84] However, the transition to written texts would not have been a surprising one given the vivid "bookish" culture that Christianity inherited from Judaism.[85] Seitz notes, "In its formal and material givenness, the Law and the Prophets pattern has influenced the formal and material development of the NT as canon."[86] In addition, we do well to remember that the apostles functioned within the backdrop of Old Testament *covenantal* patterns that suggested that the inauguration of a new covenant would be accompanied by new written covenantal documents (as discussed

---

[84]Distinctions between oral and written stages of gospel traditions should not be too sharply drawn; the two are not mutually exclusive. H. Y. Gamble, *Books and Readers in the Early Church* (New Haven, CT: Yale University Press, 1995), 28–32, makes a compelling argument that written and oral aspects of a culture can exist side by side. This is particularly true of rabbinic texts; see H. L. Strack and G. Stemberger, *Introduction to the Talmud and Midrash* (Edinburgh: T&T Clark, 1991), 35–49; and M. Jaffee, "How Much Orality in 'Oral Torah'? New Perspectives on the Composition and Transmission of Early Rabbinic Tradition," *HS* 10 (1992): 53–72. Moreover, the language of "tradition" in the New Testament need not be restricted to oral communication, but could also include written communication; e.g., Luke 1:2 (Bauckham, *Jesus and the Eyewitnesses*, 37–38). Graham Stanton argues that the teachings of Jesus may have been written down in "notebooks" from the very beginning, allowing oral and written forms of Jesus's word to exist side by side (Stanton, *Jesus and Gospel*, 165–91). L. Alexander, "Memory and Tradition in the Hellenistic Schools," in Kelber and Byrskog, *Jesus in Memory*, 113–53, rightly reminds us that gospel tradition was written down so that it could be *performed* orally; the written texts functioned as *aides-mémoire* for the oral proclamation of gospel material. See also S. Talmon, "Oral Tradition and Written Transmission, or the Heard and the Seen Word in Judaism of the Second Temple Period," in Wansbrough, *Jesus and the Oral Gospel Tradition*, 121–58; and Paul J. Achtemeier, "Omne Verbum Sonat: The New Testament and the Oral Environment of Late Western Antiquity," *JBL* 109 (1990): 3–27.

[85]M. J. Kruger, "Manuscripts, Scribes, and Book Production within Early Christianity," in *Christian Origins and Classical Culture: Social and Literary Contexts for the New Testament*, ed. S. E. Porter and A. W. Pitts (Leiden: Brill, forthcoming); L. W. Hurtado, "The New Testament in the Second Century: Texts, Collections, and Canon," in *Transmission and Reception: New Testament Text-Critical and Exegetical Studies* (Piscataway, NJ: Gorgias, 2006), 25–27; and Stanton, *Jesus and Gospel*, 165–91. In regard to the literacy of early Christians, see A. Millard, *Reading and Writing in the Time of Jesus* (New York: New York University Press, 2000).

[86]Christopher Seitz, *The Goodly Fellowship of the Prophets: The Achievement of Association in Canon Formation* (Grand Rapids: Baker Academic, 2009), 103.

above). Given that they understood the redemptive work of Jesus as the inauguration of the new covenant (Luke 22:20) and viewed themselves as "ministers of a new covenant" (2 Cor. 3:6), it would have been quite natural to pass along the apostolic message through the medium of the written word.

Even more fundamentally, however, the movement toward a written text would have been driven by the very function of the apostolic office as the foundation for the ongoing ministry of the church (Eph. 2:20). As the church continued to spread throughout the world into further geographic regions, it would have become evident that the apostolic tradition could only be effectively communicated and accurately maintained in written form.[87] Obviously, the apostles were not able to provide personal attention to every church within the ever-expanding range of missionary influence. Moreover, their limited life spans made it clear that they could never bring the apostolic message to the ends of the earth in person, but would need a way to preserve it for future generations.[88] Thus, the role of the apostles as foundation layers for the church would have led them to make sure their message was preserved in a more *permanent* form, making its inscripturation a virtual inevitability.[89] One is reminded of how Isaiah is exhorted,

> And now, go, write it before them on a tablet
>   and inscribe it in a book,
> that it may be for the time to come
>   as a witness *forever*. (Isa. 30:8)[90]

The Christian transition from the oral testimony of eyewitnesses to a more permanent written testimony also finds a parallel in ancient Greco-Roman historiography.[91] Ancient historians also preferred to ascertain the truth of certain events by relying on oral eyewitness testimony—a "living

---

[87]R. Bauckham, "For Whom Were Gospels Written?," in *The Gospels for All Christians: Rethinking the Gospel Audiences*, ed. R. Bauckham (Grand Rapids: Eerdmans, 1998), 9–48.

[88]Cullmann, "Tradition," 90.

[89]In a similar manner, F. Bovon, "The Canonical Structure of Gospel and Apostle," in McDonald and Sanders, *The Canon Debate*, 516–27, has argued that a new written canon of Scripture would have been the natural result of the Gospel-apostle structure so prevalent within the theology of early Christianity. Bovon states, "The Gospel-Apostle structure, manifest from the first generation of Christians, prepares the way for the formation of a new body of Scriptures" (522). His fuller arguments can be found in F. Bovon, *L'Evangile et l'apôtre: Le Christ inséparable de ses témoins* (Aubonne: Editions du Moulin, 1993).

[90]See Hill, "The New Testament Canon," 111.

[91]F. F. Bruce, "Some Thoughts on the Beginning of the New Testament Canon," *BJRL* 65 (1983): 42–43.

voice."[92] This principle was affirmed by Polybius, Galen, Thucydides, and Tacitus, and was even applied to Christian history by Papias.[93] However, once the historical events were established by an appeal to the "living voice" of eyewitnesses, these historians pressed stylus to papyrus and recorded this oral testimony for future generations in written form. Why would they do this? Herodotus explained that he wrote down his historical accounts in order that "the memory of the past may not be blotted out from among men by time."[94] Likewise, Thucydides confessed that his *History* was written so that it would not just "be heard for the moment" but so that it would be "a possession *for all time*."[95] Byrskog comments on these ancient historians, "The writing down of an item meant that this piece of information was given a certain abiding character."[96] Thus, in such cases, we see that oral testimony is not antithetical to written testimony, but rather is the foundation for it—the former naturally leads to the latter as the eyewitnesses die out.[97] In other words, these ancient historians viewed their written documents as a way to make oral testimony *permanent*.

In sum, the New Testament documents can be understood as the written expression of the authoritative, foundational, and eyewitness tradition delivered by the apostles of Jesus Christ.[98] While some have argued that a book must have been written directly by an apostle to be considered

---

[92]For a general overview of the use of "living voice," see L. Alexander, "The Living Voice: Skepticism Toward the Written Word in Early Christian and Graeco-Roman Texts," in *The Bible in Three Dimensions* (Sheffield: JSOT, 1990), 221–47; Bauckham, *Jesus and the Eyewitnesses*, 21–29. Polybius criticizes the work of Timaeus precisely because he relies too heavily on written sources in his historical accounts (12.23–28). He then proceeds to offer three levels of historical inquiry: (1) the historian himself is an eyewitness and records what he sees; (2) the historian directly interviews an eyewitness; and (3) the historian appeals to other written sources about that event (12.25.1–2). It is noteworthy that early Christians understood the New Testament books to be written by authors in the *first two* categories: they either were direct eyewitnesses themselves (apostles), or interviewed these direct eyewitnesses (associates of the apostles). Further discussion can be found in Byrskog, *Story as History*, 59–62.

[93]Polybius, 4.2.1–2; Galen, *Temp. med.* 6 pref. (Kühn 11.796–97); Thucydides, 1.22.1–2; 5.26.5; Tacitus, *Hist.* 4.81; *Ann.* 3.16; Papias cited in Eusebius, *Hist. eccl.* 3.39.3–4. For discussion of Papias as a source, see Byrskog, *Story as History*, 272–92; Gundry, *Matthew*, 1026–45; and M. Hengel, *Studies in the Gospel of Mark* (London: SCM, 1985), 47–53.

[94]*Herodotus*, trans. A. D. Godley, Loeb Classical Library (Cambridge, MA: Harvard University Press, 1922), 1.1.

[95]*Thucydides*, trans. Charles Foster Smith, Loeb Classical Library (Cambridge, MA: Harvard University Press, 1980), 1.22.4, emphasis mine.

[96]Byrskog, *Story as History*, 122–23.

[97]Bauckham notes, "The value of oral tradition decreases with distance from the personal testimony of the eyewitnesses themselves" (*Jesus and the Eyewitnesses*, 29). In view here is *eyewitness* oral tradition, not oral tradition in general. Obviously the latter continues on well after the eyewitnesses have died, but the former is tied to the "living voice" of the eyewitness.

[98]Horton declares, "'The tradition' is not something in addition to the written word of the apostles, but is precisely that word before its inscripturization" (*Covenant and Eschatology*, 217).

"apostolic,"[99] the above discussion makes it clear that apostolicity was less about apostolic authorship and more about whether a document was considered to bear authoritative apostolic *tradition*. Obviously there are good reasons to think that a document bears such tradition if it was written directly by an apostle (as most of the New Testament documents were). But apostolic tradition did not have to be written down by an apostle to be authoritative. The apostles were quite willing to employ the help of key followers "with the skills and gifts necessary for preserving the tradition."[100] Not only was this done to aid the transmission of oral tradition (as noted above), but apparently the apostles followed this same pattern when transmitting that tradition in written form (e.g., they used Mark and Luke).

Thus, even if a document was not written directly by an apostle, there would have been good reasons to think it bore authoritative apostolic tradition if (1) it was written during the apostolic age (and thus was composed at a time when the apostles were overseeing the transmission of their tradition),[101] and (2) it was written by someone who got his information directly from an apostle.[102] This appears to be the case with the book of Hebrews, which does not claim to be written by an apostle, but comes from the apostolic time period and does claim to bear a message "attested to us by those who heard" (Heb. 2:3)—a clear indication that its message came directly from the apostles.[103] The same is true for the Gospel of Luke, which was not penned by an apostle but was written in

---

[99]R. Nicole, "The Canon of the New Testament," *JETS* 40 (1997): 199–206.

[100]Bauckham, *Jesus and the Eyewitnesses*, 270.

[101]It is clear that early Christians would receive books only if they were written while the apostles were still alive and presiding over the transmission of tradition; e.g., the *Shepherd of Hermas* was rejected by the Muratorian fragment because it was written "very recently, in our own times" (line 74); also, Eusebius records the tradition that the apostle John, before writing his own Gospel, "welcomed" (ἀποδέξασθαι) the prior three Gospels and "testified to their truth" (ἀλήθειαν αὐτοῖς ἐπιμαρτυρήσαντα), implying that he was in some sense providing apostolic oversight to the transmission of apostolic tradition into written form (*Hist. eccl.* 3.24.7). Whether or not this particular tradition recorded by Eusebius is accurate, it reflects the early Christian perception of the role of the apostles.

[102]Such considerations remind us that for a book to be "apostolic" it must have some *historical* connection to the apostles. For this reason, apostolicity cannot be determined solely by orthodoxy, as some seem to imply; e.g., R. W. Wall and E. E. Lemcio, *New Testament as Canon* (Sheffield: Sheffield Academic, 1992), 174. A book must be orthodox to be apostolic, but orthodoxy does not *make* a book apostolic. In addition, these considerations remind us that even if an author happens to *know* an apostle, that does not necessarily make his writings apostolic. For example, even though Polycarp apparently knew the apostle John, his letter to the Philippians is not to be regarded as apostolic because (1) he does not indicate that he is passing on apostolic tradition (nor is there any other reason to think his letter is an embodiment of apostolic tradition), and (2) the letter was written after the time when the apostles were presiding over the transmission of apostolic material.

[103]Hengel, *The Four Gospels*, 143.

the apostolic period and also contains tradition that was "handed down" (παρέδοσαν) to Luke by "those who from the beginning were eyewitnesses and ministers of the word" (Luke 1:2). Ridderbos sums it up when he says that the apostolicity of a book is determined by "whether its content embodies the foundational apostolic tradition, *not* whether it was written by the hand of the apostle."[104]

It seems the early church fathers understand apostolicity in this same manner.[105] Justin Martyr views the Gospels as the written embodiment of apostolic tradition, "For the apostles, in the memoirs composed by them, which are called Gospels, have thus delivered unto us what was enjoined upon them."[106] So comfortable is Justin with this definition of apostolicity, that he is willing to call the Gospels "memoirs of the apostles"[107] even though he knows two of them were not written by apostles.[108] Likewise, Irenaeus views all the New Testament Scriptures as the embodiment of apostolic teaching though he clearly knows some books were written by nonapostles: "We have learned from none others the plan of our salvation, than from those through whom the Gospel has come down to us, which they did at one time proclaim in public, and, at a later period, by the will of God, *handed down to us in the Scriptures*, to be the ground and pillar of our faith."[109] Irenaeus also refers to all four of the Gospels as "Gospels of the Apostles" and "those handed down to us from the apostles," despite the fact that two of the Gospels are not from apostles.[110] In addition, it is this same understanding of apostolicity that led Tertullian to describe Mark and Luke as "apostolic men."[111]

---

[104]Ridderbos, *Redemptive History*, 32, emphasis his.

[105]This view of apostolicity even seems to be shared (or mimicked) by heretics. Clement informs us that some of the Gnostic schools claim authority for their teachings because they received them from *disciples* of the apostles. So, Basilides claims to have received his teaching from Glaucias, who was supposedly an "interpreter" of Peter, and Valentinus claims to have received his teaching from Theodas, who was supposedly a disciple of Paul (*Strom.* 7.17). See discussion in H. E. W. Turner, *The Pattern of Christian Truth: A Study in the Relations Between Orthodoxy and Heresy in the Early Church* (London: Mowbray, 1954), 198–99. Moreover, this same principle of apostolicity seems to have been followed when the church considered potential canonical books that were eventually rejected. For example, in some circles the *Shepherd of Hermas* was deemed to be canonical no doubt because it was thought that the author was the same Hermas who was a disciple of Paul mentioned in Rom. 16:14 (Eusebius, *Hist. eccl.* 3.3.6). This might also explain Clement of Alexandria's favorable opinion of the *Epistle of Barnabas* since he seemed to think the author was the first-century companion of Paul (*Strom.* 2.20.116).

[106]*1 Apol.* 66.3.

[107]*1 Apol.* 66.3; in this passage he refers to the Gospels composed by the apostles and then proceeds to cite Luke 22:19.

[108]*Dial.* 103.

[109]*Haer.* 3.1.1, emphasis mine.

[110]*Haer.* 3.11.9.

[111]*Marc.* 4.2.

If the New Testament was the written embodiment of apostolic tradition, then it is not difficult to see why early Christians would have regarded these texts as authoritative from a very early point. Inasmuch as a text was thought to bear the apostolic message, it would have retained the authority of the apostles and thereby the authority of Christ himself. It is here that we see the vivid contrast with the historical-critical models noted above. Those approaches suggest that the writing down of these Jesus traditions took place before they were seen as authoritative (the latter happening at a much later date), whereas the historical evidence suggests that the traditions were seen as authoritative before they were written down (owing to their apostolic connections).[112] For this reason, a written New Testament was not something the church formally "decided" to have at some later date, but was instead the natural outworking of the redemptive-historical function of the apostles. As Dunn observes, "The *de facto* canon of Jesus and Paul, gospel and epistle, was already functioning with effect within the first thirty years of Christianity's existence."[113]

C. Apostolic Self-Awareness

When we examine the New Testament books more closely, their content confirms that they are to be understood as bearing apostolic tradition in written form. In other words, there seems to be a degree of self-awareness among the New Testament authors that they are producing authoritative documents that would function as a rule for the church.[114] This does not suggest that the canonical authors were able to foresee the full shape of the future twenty-seven-book New Testament when they wrote. But at the same time, we would be mistaken to think that they wrote without any sense of the authority of their message—as if they would be shocked to learn the later church used these documents for guidance and direction. It is here, then, that we come to the New Testament's own claims about itself, which is a part (though not the whole) of the Scripture's self-authentication. Of course, we only have space here to consider a few

---

[112]On this point, see J. D. G. Dunn, "How the New Testament Began," in *From Biblical Criticism to Biblical Faith*, ed. William H. Brackney and C. A. Evans (Macon, GA: Mercer University Press, 2007), 122–37.

[113]Dunn, "How the New Testament Began," 137.

[114]Peter Balla, "Evidence for an Early Christian Canon (Second and Third Century)," in McDonald and Sanders, *The Canon Debate*, 372–85. The idea that the apostles knew they were writing Scripture has been challenged; e.g., H. Hübner, *Biblische Theologie des Neuen Testaments*, vol. 1, *Prolegomena* (Göttingen: Vandenhoeck & Ruprecht, 1990), 38–43; W. Wrede, *The Origin of the New Testament*, trans. J. S. Hill (New York: Harper, 1909), 10; McDonald, *The Formation of the Christian Biblical Canon*, 142.

representative examples (well-known texts like 1 Tim. 5:18 and 2 Pet. 3:16 will be considered at a later point).

1. *Mark 1:1.* The opening phrase of Mark, "The beginning of the gospel [τοῦ εὐαγγελίου] of Jesus Christ the Son of God," is noteworthy because of the distinctive use of εὐαγγελίου. The term was not originally used among early Christians to refer to written texts, but was a reference to the authoritative message of the apostolic preaching.[115] In addition, the phrase "son of God" occurs not only in 1:1 but again at the end of Mark's Gospel in 15:39, forming a literary *inclusio*. This structure suggests that the opening line is "more than just an introduction to the Baptist's ministry," but is an implicit claim of authority designed "to characterize the work as a whole as the 'Gospel of Jesus Christ.'"[116] The apostolic nature of Mark is confirmed by the clear connections that the Gospel has with the witness of the apostle Peter himself. Aside from the fact that Mark's connection to Peter was well known among the early church fathers[117] and is attested by other parts of the New Testament (Acts 12:12–17; 1 Pet. 5:13),[118] the Gospel of Mark itself draws connections to Peter by forming another literary *inclusio* that centers on Peter himself; the first disciple mentioned in Mark is Peter (1:16) and the last disciple mentioned is Peter (16:7).[119] This Petrine *inclusio*, combined with the inordinate frequency of the name Peter in the Gospel,[120] makes it clear that Peter was to be understood as the "main eyewitness source behind Mark's gospel."[121] Hengel observes, "Simon Peter is as a disciple named first and last in the Gospel to show that it is based on his tradition and therefore his authority."[122]

---

[115]Stanton, *Jesus and Gospel*, 9–62.

[116]J. H. Roberts and A. B. du Toit, *Guide to the New Testament*, vol. 1, *Preamble to New Testament Study: The Canon of the New Testament* (Pretoria: N. G. Kerkboekhandel Transvaal, 1979), 127.

[117]E.g., Papias cited in Eusebius, *Hist. eccl.* 3.39.14–15; Justin, *Dial.* 106; and Irenaeus, *Haer.* 3.10.5. Bauckham has made a case that the term *interpreter* (ἑρμηνευτής) in Papias is better rendered "translator." See Bauckham, *Jesus and the Eyewitnesses*, 205–7.

[118]D. Trobisch, *The First Edition of the New Testament* (Oxford: Oxford University Press, 2000), 47–49.

[119]For further connections between Mark and Peter, see U. H. J. Körtner, "Markus der Mitarbeiter des Petrus," *ZNW* 71 (1980): 160–73; Hengel, *The Four Gospels*, 78–89; and C. H. Turner, "Marcan Usage: Notes Critical and Exegetical on the Second Gospel V. The Movements of Jesus and His Disciples and the Crowd," *JTS* 26 (1925): 225–40.

[120]The name Peter occurs nineteen times, and the name Simon occurs seven times, which is proportionally much more than the other three Gospels. See Hengel, *The Four Gospels*, 82.

[121]Bauckham, *Jesus and the Eyewitnesses*, 125.

[122]Hengel, *The Four Gospels*, 82.

2. John 21:24. The Gospel of John makes it clear that the "disciple whom Jesus loved" was part of the inner apostolic circle. He was present at the Last Supper (13:23), present at the crucifixion (19:26), and with Peter and Jesus at the very end of the Gospel (21:20). John 21:24a then concludes the Gospel by declaring that it is this very disciple "who is bearing witness [μαρτυρῶν] about these things, and who has written [γράψας] these things," making it clear that he is the author of John's Gospel.[123] Regardless of whether this disciple is acknowledged to be the apostle John,[124] it is clear that the Gospel is claiming to contain apostolic eyewitness testimony (μαρτυρῶν) from someone directly connected to Jesus's inner circle. Indeed, these connections with the beloved disciple led Jean Zumstein to declare that the Gospel of John "claims to have a status comparable to that which is ordinarily assigned to Scripture."[125] In addition to these considerations, it is important to see John 21:24 in light of John 20:31, which states, "These are written [γέγραπται] so that you may believe that Jesus is the Christ." Elsewhere John's Gospel uses γράφω to refer to citations from the Old Testament Scripture (2:17; 5:46; 6:31, 45; 8:17; 10:34; 15:25). Whether or not this implies that John understood he was writing new "Scripture," it clearly communicates to the reader that a new authoritative message from God was now being "written" down.[126]

3. 1 Thessalonians 2:13. Paul emphasizes that the apostolic message borne by the apostles was to be received as the authoritative word of God: "And we also thank God constantly for this, that when you received the word of God, which you heard from us, you accepted it not as the word of men but as what it really is, the word of God" (v. 13). Although this message was certainly passed along orally by the apostles, it is clear that Paul expected his written letters to bear the same weight as his words spoken in the Thessalonians' presence. Second Thessalonians 2:15 says,

---

[123]J. H. Bernard, *A Critical and Exegetical Commentary on the Gospel According to St. John* (Edinburgh: T&T Clark, 1928), and a number of other scholars depending on his work, have suggested that John 21:24 means only that John is a "source" behind the Gospel, but not the actual writer. However, Bauckham makes a compelling argument that γράψας cannot mean that John is a "source," but must mean that he has written it directly, or has dictated it to a secretary (*Jesus and the Eyewitnesses*, 358–62).

[124]Those who favor the apostle John include Leon Morris, *The Gospel According to John* (Grand Rapids: Eerdmans, 1995), 775–77; D. A. Carson, *The Gospel According to John* (Grand Rapids: Eerdmans, 1991), 682–85; and Andreas J. Köstenberger, *John*, Baker Exegetical Commentary on the New Testament (Grand Rapids: Baker, 2004), 603–6.

[125]J. Zumstein, "La naissance de la notion d'Écriture dans la littérature johannique," in *The Biblical Canons*, ed. J.-M. Auwers and H. J. de Jonge (Leuven: Leuven University Press, 2003), 377, translation mine.

[126]H. Ridderbos, *The Gospel of John* (Grand Rapids: Eerdmans, 1997), 651n67; Zumstein, "La naissance de la notion d'Écriture dans la littérature johannique," 379.

"Stand firm and hold to the traditions that you were taught by us, *either by our spoken word or by our letter.*" It is difficult to imagine that the Thessalonians would have understood Paul's letters in any other way than as the authoritative apostolic message that demanded their submission and obedience.

4. *1 Corinthians 7:12.* As Paul gives commands concerning marriage in verse 12, he offers the parenthetical terms "I, not the Lord." Although some have understood this to be Paul's making a distinction between his own lesser authority and Jesus's higher authority, a closer reading of the passage reveals the opposite.[127] Paul's statement simply means that he has no direct command from Jesus on this particular subject and therefore must speak "on his own authority."[128] This makes it clear to the Corinthians that Paul has the apostolic authority to issue binding commands and thereby to speak for Jesus on topics that have not been directly addressed by him.[129] Ridderbos declares, "Paul saw no difference between the authority of his own apostolic word and that of the words of the Lord that had been transmitted to him."[130]

5. *1 Corinthians 14:37–38.* Perhaps there is no place where Paul makes his claim to apostolic authority more plain than in 1 Corinthians 14:37–38: "If anyone thinks that he is a prophet, or spiritual, he should acknowledge that the things I am writing [γράφω] to you are a command of the Lord. If anyone does not recognize this, he is not recognized." Paul not only equates his own authority with that of Jesus Christ, but specifically applies such authority to the *written* words of his letter, employing the term γράφω, which is often used elsewhere to refer to the written Scriptures. Moreover, Paul deems his spiritual authority to be so clear that he offers a

---

[127]McDonald, *The Formation of the Christian Biblical Canon,* 9–10, makes this very mistake. Incredibly, even after acknowledging that Paul did make a "claim to be inspired by the Spirit in regard to what he said," he still goes on to insist that Paul's letters were *not* intended as Scripture because he was not "consciously aware" that he was writing Scripture (9). However, McDonald never explains how Paul could think he was speaking as an inspired agent of the Holy Spirit, and even expressly state such to his audience, and yet not think that his writings would be received with authoritative scriptural status.

[128]Gordon D. Fee, *The First Epistle to the Corinthians* (Grand Rapids: Eerdmans, 1987), 292; Wayne Grudem, "Scripture's Self-Attestation and the Problem of Formulating a Doctrine of Scripture," in *Scripture and Truth,* ed. D. A. Carson and John D. Woodbridge (Grand Rapids: Baker, 1992), 47.

[129]Balla, "Evidence for an Early Christian Canon," 375.

[130]Ridderbos, *Redemptive History,* 21. See also, Leon Morris, *The First Epistle of Paul to the Corinthians* (Grand Rapids: Eerdmans, 1975), 109. See also John Murray, "The Attestation of Scripture," in *The Infallible Word,* ed. Ned B. Stonehouse and Paul Woolley (Philadelphia: Presbyterian and Reformed, 1946), 38; and Cullmann, "The Tradition," 74.

"prophetic sentence of judgment" on all those who refuse to acknowledge it.[131] In light of a text such as this, it is difficult to imagine that McDonald is being fair with the New Testament data when he claims that Paul "was unaware of the divinely inspired status of his own advice."[132]

6. *1 John 1:1–5*. The opening verses of John's first epistle are essentially a claim to speak with apostolic authority.

> That which was from the beginning, which we have heard, which we have seen with our eyes, which we looked upon and have touched with our hands, concerning the word of life—the life was made manifest, and we have seen it, and testify [μαρτυροῦμεν] to it and proclaim [ἀπαγγέλλομεν] to you the eternal life. (1:1–2)

A number of aspects of this verse support the idea that the author is laying forth his apostolic credentials. (1) The vivid eyewitness language—hearing, seeing, even touching—confirms that the author was present to witness the ministry of Jesus and thus fits the criteria of an apostle (Luke 1:2; 24:48; Acts 1:9). Marshall affirms, "There cannot be any real doubt that the writer claims to have been an eyewitness of the earthly ministry of Jesus."[133] As an eyewitness, the author is qualified to "testify" (μαρτυροῦμεν) to what he has seen and heard. (2) In addition to testifying, the author also takes on the more authoritative task of "proclaiming" (ἀπαγγέλλομεν) the word of life. Stott notes, "In order to testify, the apostles must have seen and heard Christ for themselves; in order to proclaim they must have received a commission from him."[134] The act of proclamation confirms the apostolic office already established by the claims to be an eyewitness. (3) The author's apostolic authority to speak is established also by the use of the collective "we"—indicating that John is speaking not simply as an individual, but as part of the larger apostolic witness. After these explicit claims of apostolic authority, the text then declares, "We are writing [γράφομεν] these things so that our joy may be complete" (1 John 1:4). Thus, we have a clear example again of the apostolic message being put into written form (see John 20:31; 21:24), which would have been received by its readers as authoritative as the apostles themselves.

---

[131]Fee, *The First Epistle to the Corinthians*, 712.
[132]McDonald, *The Formation of the Christian Biblical Canon*, 9.
[133]I. Howard Marshall, *The Epistles of John* (Grand Rapids: Eerdmans, 1978), 106.
[134]John R. W. Stott, *The Letters of John* (Grand Rapids: Eerdmans, 1996), 67.

7. *Revelation 1:1–3.* The opening line of the book of Revelation directly claims that it is the inspired prophecy of Jesus Christ delivered to John by an angel. Consequently, there is a divine blessing attached to this book: "Blessed is the one who reads aloud the words of this prophecy, and blessed are those who hear, and who keep what is *written* in it, for the time is near" (1:3). Regardless of whether one takes an early or late date for the book of Revelation,[135] it is clear that by the end of the first century it was not unusual to have a written text that claimed to be inspired of God and authoritative Scripture for the church of Jesus Christ.

In the end, all of these passages (and many more could be offered) confirm that the New Testament books were written as apostolic books, thus bearing the full authority of Christ himself from the very start. Given that the apostles were "ministers of a new covenant" (2 Cor. 3:6), these apostolic books clearly functioned as *covenant documents*, demonstrating again the intimate connection between covenant and written texts. The idea of a canon, then, was not a later concept retroactively imposed upon these books, but is a concept inherent to the books themselves. N. T. Wright sums it up well.

> It used to be said that the New Testament writers "didn't think they were writing 'Scripture.'" That is hard to sustain historically today. The fact that their writings were, in various senses, "occasional" . . . is not to the point. At precisely those points of urgent need (when, for instance, writing Galatians or 2 Corinthians) Paul is most conscious that he is writing as one authorized, by the apostolic call he had received from Jesus Christ, and in the power of the Spirit, to bring life and order to the church by his words.[136]

D. Apostolicity and Pseudonymity

We have argued that the New Testament books are authoritative because they bear the apostolic message (whether written directly by an apostle or not). But what if some of the books of the New Testament are forgeries, only pretending to be from apostles? Much of critical scholarship is convinced that many of these writings are pseudonymous, including the Pastoral Epistles, Colossians, Ephesians, 2 Peter, Jude, and others.[137] As

---

[135]The two major dates suggested for the book are AD 69 and 96. For more discussion on date, see G. K. Beale, *The Book of Revelation*, NIGTC (Grand Rapids: Eerdmans, 1999), 4–27.

[136]N. T. Wright, *The Last Word: Beyond the Bible Wars to a New Understanding of the Authority of Scripture* (San Francisco: HarperSanFrancisco, 2005), 51.

[137]For general discussions of the critical positions, see Robert A. Spivey and D. Moody Smith, *Anatomy of the New Testament* (New York: Macmillan, 1989); and Bart D. Ehrman, *The*

a result, many of these books are dated much later than the time of the apostles—sometimes well into the second century[138]—and not regarded as having any credible apostolic connections. Such claims, as noted above, constitute a potential defeater for our canonical model and must therefore be addressed. The key question is this: Is it rational for Christians to continue to affirm their belief in the New Testament canon if some modern scholars claim that it contains pseudonymous books?

One possible solution is to argue that pseudonymous books in the New Testament do not really constitute a defeater in the first place because, as Bauckham has suggested, "the pseudepigraphal device is . . . not a fraudulent means of claiming apostolic authority, but embodies a claim to be a faithful mediator of the apostolic message."[139] Such a position could argue that pseudonymity was an accepted literary device in early Christianity, and that a pseudonymous author "was not consciously deceiving anybody; it is not, indeed, necessary to suppose that he did deceive anybody."[140] As attractive as such a solution might be, however, it simply does not fit with the understanding of apostolicity prevalent among the earliest Christians who consistently rejected books that were known to be forged in the name of an apostle.[141] J. A. T. Robinson declares, "If

---

New Testament: A Historical Introduction to the Early Christian Writings (New York: Oxford University Press, 1997).

[138]E.g., 2 Peter is often dated to the early or middle second century; see J. N. D. Kelly, A Commentary on the Epistles of Peter and of Jude (New York: Harper & Row, 1969), 235; J. B. Mayor, The Epistle of St. Jude and the Second Epistle of St. Peter (London: Macmillan, 1907), cxxiv; J. Neyrey, 2 Peter, Jude (New York: Doubleday, 1993), 119ff.; R. Bauckham, Jude, 2 Peter (Waco, TX: Word, 1983), 157–63.

[139]Bauckham, Jude, 2 Peter, 161–62.

[140]P. N. Harrison, The Problem of the Pastoral Epistles (London: Oxford University Press, 1921), 12; for similar views, see also D. Meade, Pseudepigrapha and Canon (Tübingen: Mohr, 1986); K. Aland, "The Problem of Anonymity and Pseudonymity in Christian Literature of the First Two Centuries," JTS 12 (1961): 39–49; A. Jülicher, An Introduction to the New Testament (London: Smith & Elder, 1904), 52; J. D. G. Dunn, "Pseudepigraphy," in Dictionary of the Later New Testament and Its Developments, ed. R. P. Martin and P. H. Davids (Downers Grove, IL: InterVarsity, 1997), 977–84; and Mark Harding, "Disputed and Undisputed Letters of Paul," in The Pauline Canon, ed. S. E. Porter (Leiden: Brill, 2004), 129–68.

[141]E.g., in 2 Thess. 2:2 Paul himself condemns forged letters in his name; Tertullian tells of how the author of The Acts of Paul and Thecla was condemned for passing off his work as Paul's even though the forgery was composed with good intentions (On Baptism, 17). Eusebius, Hist. eccl. 6.12.2, tells of Serapion condemning the Gospel of Peter along with other forged works: "We receive both Peter and the other apostles as Christ, but the writings which falsely bear their names (ψευδέπιγραφα) we reject"; the Muratorian fragment rejects Paul's so-called epistle to the Laodiceans and other apocryphal works on the grounds that they were "forgeries." Also, see numerous critiques of pseudonymity as being acceptable within early Christianity: Terry L. Wilder, Pseudonymity, the New Testament, and Deception: An Inquiry into Intention and Reception (Lanham, MD: University Press of America, 2004); Armin Daniel Baum, Pseudepigraphie und literarische Fälschung im frühen Christentum: Mit ausgewählten Quellentexten samt deutscher Übersetzung (Tübingen: Mohr Siebeck, 2001); E. Earle Ellis, "Pseudonymity and Canonicity of New Testament Documents," in Worship, Theology and Ministry in the Early Church: Essays in

we ask what is the evidence for orthodox epistles being composed in the name of the apostles within a generation or two of their lifetime, and for this being an acceptable literary convention within the church, the answer is nil."[142] Moreover, if the pseudonymous author has no credible historical ties to the apostle he is impersonating (which is often the assumption when late dates are assigned to these books), then on what basis can we suppose he is really transmitting authoritative apostolic content? On top of all of this, it is hard to avoid the issue of deception when pseudonymous authors go out of their way to convince the reader they are doing more than passing along tradition but actually *are* the apostle, such as in 2 Peter when the author claims to have seen the transfiguration himself (1:16–18). Such deception seems incompatible with a book purporting to be from God (and thus bearing divine qualities).[143] Thus, we can only conclude that pseudonymity (if true) would be incompatible with our canonical model.

If so, then we return to our original question: Are Christians rational to continue their belief in the canon in light of these claims of modern scholars? Several considerations suggest that the answer is yes.

(1) We must remember that there are many other scholars outside the critical consensus who affirm the apostolicity of these New Testament writings.[144] So much so, one wonders whether the critical consensus can really be called a "consensus" in the first place. These scholars have made an impressive historical case for the apostolic origins of the New Testament books, though the details of these arguments obviously cannot be repeated here.[145]

Honor of Ralph P. Martin, ed. M. J. Wilkins and Terence Paige (Sheffield: Sheffield Academic, 1993), 212–24; D. A. Carson, "Pseudonymity and Pseudepigraphy," in *The Dictionary of New Testament Background*, ed. Craig A. Evans and Stanley E. Porter (Downers Grove, IL: InterVarsity, 2000), 856–64; Thomas D. Lea, "Pseudonymity and the New Testament," in *New Testament Criticism and Interpretation*, ed. David Alan Black and David S. Dockery (Grand Rapids: Zondervan, 1991), 535–59; and, to some extent, Bruce M. Metzger, "Literary Forgeries and Canonical Pseudepigrapha," *JBL* 91 (1972): 3–24.

[142]J. A. T. Robinson, *Redating the New Testament* (Philadelphia: Westminster, 1976), 187.

[143]J. I. Packer, *Fundamentalism and the Word of God* (Grand Rapids: Eerdmans, 1992), 182–86.

[144]The studies are too many to mention here, but overviews can be found in the major New Testament introductions; e.g., D. A. Carson and D. J. Moo, *An Introduction to the New Testament* (Grand Rapids: Zondervan, 2005); D. Guthrie, *New Testament Introduction* (Downers Grove, IL: InterVarsity, 1990); and A. J. Köstenberger, L. Scott Kellum, and Charles L. Quarles, *The Cradle, the Cross, and the Crown: An Introduction to the New Testament* (Nashville: B&H Academic, 2009).

[145]Some representative examples of defenses of the authenticity of the Pastoral Epistles include: D. Guthrie, *The Pastoral Epistles and the Mind of Paul* (London: Tyndale, 1956); E. Earle Ellis, *Paul and His Recent Interpreters* (Grand Rapids: Eerdmans, 1961); G. W. Knight, *The Pastoral Epistles: A Commentary on the Greek Text* (Grand Rapids: Eerdmans, 1992); and especially C. Spicq, *Saint Paul: Les Épîtres Pastorales*, 4th ed. (Paris: Gabalda, 1969).

(2) Plantinga, Evans, Alston, and others have critiqued the modern historical methodologies used to reach these conclusions about pseudonymity, focusing particularly on the non-Christian and Enlightenment assumptions on which they are founded.[146] Given these non-Christian assumptions of biblical criticism, "it comes as no surprise, then, that its conclusions are at odds with traditional belief."[147] If so, are there any reasons for the Christian to think that modern biblical criticism is more likely to reach true conclusions than a method founded on biblical principles? Or, put differently, are Enlightenment assumptions superior to Christian ones? There appear to be no reasons to think this is the case.

(3) Not only is there a *lack* of reasons to accept the critical position on pseudonymity, but there are compelling reasons to think it is false. Our model has argued that apostolicity is not the only attribute of canonicity but should be viewed alongside a book's divine qualities and corporate reception by the church. By way of these other attributes (through the help of the Holy Spirit), a Christian can know a book is canonical even if he knows nothing about its apostolicity. Thus, when faced with claims of modern scholarship that a New Testament book is not apostolic (because it is a late second-century forgery) the Christian has sufficient grounds for thinking this claim is false.[148] Again, this is the benefit of a three-dimensional model of canon—each of the attributes confirms and supports the other two.[149]

(4) A final reason for rejecting this defeater is the problematic nature of the type of arguments used to demonstrate a book's pseudonymity. Evans has argued that the typical arguments from literary style, vocabulary, and the like tend to be inconclusive, subjective, and, in the end, unpersuasive.[150] It seems there are many factors that could explain such stylistic differences other than a pseudonymous author, such as the author writing at a differ-

---

[146]Alvin Plantinga, *Warranted Christian Belief* (New York: Oxford University Press, 2000), 374–421; C. Stephen Evans, *The Historical Christ and the Jesus of Faith: The Incarnational Narrative as History* (New York: Oxford University Press, 1996), 170–202; William P. Alston, "Historical Criticism of the Synoptic Gospels," in *"Behind" the Text: History and Biblical Interpretation*, ed. Craig Bartholomew (Grand Rapids: Zondervan, 2003), 151–80.

[147]Plantinga, *Warranted Christian Belief*, 418.

[148]Ibid., 410.

[149]Of course, this is not to suggest that divine qualities and corporate reception are the *only* reasons we believe in a book's apostolicity. We are arguing here that a solid historical case can be made for the apostolicity of these books apart from the other two attributes of canonicity. Nevertheless, the other two attributes constitute good grounds for rejecting the potential defeater that some of these books are forgeries.

[150]C. Stephen Evans, "Canonicity, Apostolicity, and Biblical Authority: Some Kierkegaardian Reflections," in *Canon and Biblical Interpretation*, ed. Craig Bartholomew et al. (Carlisle: Paternoster, 2006), 147–66.

ent time in his life, under different circumstances, and with different goals and different audiences, even drawing on earlier preformed traditions.[151] All of these factors would imply different vocabulary, varied themes, and a distinctive authorial tone.[152] Moreover, there is always the possibility that authors used an amanuensis at some points and not others—which could be an additional explanation of stylistic differences.[153]

Given all these considerations, we have little reason to think that claims of modern scholars regarding pseudonymity should be given precedence over the many other scholars who deny it. Therefore such claims do not constitute a genuine defeater for our canonical model.

IV. Conclusion

This chapter has explored the origins of the New Testament canon. Contra the claims of some that "the impelling force for the formation of the canon" lies in the activities and decisions of the later church, we have argued here that the historical-theological matrix of the first century made it the ideal environment out of which a new scriptural deposit could emerge. Early Christians not only had a framework for canon (covenant), and a compelling reason for a canon (redemption), but they also had agents from God as means to implement and disseminate that canon (apostles). The apostles were the mouthpieces of Christ and were given the task of delivering and preserving his redemptive message—which was originally delivered orally but eventually was embodied in a more permanent, written form. The New Testament books were considered authoritative not because the church declared them to be so, or even because they were written directly by an apostle, but because they were understood to bear

---

[151]There have been a number of recent critiques of the reliability of stylistic and statistical arguments; e.g., George K. Barr, "Two Styles in the New Testament Epistles," *LLC* 18 (2003): 235–48; A. E. Bird, "The Authorship of the Pastoral Epistles—Quantifying Literary Style," *RTR* 56 (1997): 118–37; E. Linnemann, "Echtheitsfragen und Vokabelstatistik," *JEKT* 10 (1996): 87–109; and T. A. Robinson, "Grayston and Herdan's 'C' Quantity Formula and the Authorship of the Pastoral Epistles," *NTS* 30 (1984): 282–88. In addition, Ellis, *The Making of the New Testament Documents*, has argued that the New Testament writers used an extensive amount of preformed traditions, which makes traditional forms of stylistic analysis problematic (if not obsolete).

[152]An excellent argument for how style is affected by external factors can be found in William D. Mounce, *Pastoral Epistles*, WBC (Nashville: Thomas Nelson, 2000), xcix–ci.

[153]E.g., many have suggested that Luke was Paul's amanuensis for the Pastorals: C. F. D. Moule, "The Problem of the Pastoral Epistles: A Reappraisal," *BJRL* 47 (1965): 430–52; G. D. Fee, *1 and 2 Timothy, Titus* (Peabody, MA: Hendrickson, 1988), 26; Knight, *The Pastoral Epistles*, 50–52. Michael Prior, *Paul the Letter-Writer and the Second Letter to Timothy* (Sheffield: JSOT, 1989), argues for the opposite scenario, namely, that Paul used an amanuensis for the bulk of his letters, but wrote the Pastorals himself.

this essential apostolic deposit. For this reason, Ridderbos is able to assert, "In its redemptive-historical sense, the canon is not the product of the church, rather the church is to be the product of the canon."[154]

A deeper understanding of the apostolic origins of the canon will play a critical role as we evaluate the corporate reception of the canon in the next few chapters. Under the historical-critical model, which has rejected the apostolic origins of the canon altogether, we have little reason to think that these books would have been received as authoritative from an early time period. The historical-critical assumption is that these books were not written as Scripture but only *became* authoritative over a long period of time. As a result, any early evidence for the emergence of a canon is quickly discounted as "premature" and anachronistic, the result of importing later (i.e., fourth-century) canonical ideas back into these early stages of the church. But if the concept of canon is not simply a product of the early church, but rooted in the very origins of the canonical documents themselves, then we have a new historical context in which to analyze the evidence. Instead of following the historical-critical model and discounting early references to canonical books because they had not yet become Scripture, we now have good grounds to consider the possibility that they were being read, used, and copied by early Christians because of what they *already* were—covenantal documents. If these books really did bear apostolic credentials, then we have every reason to think that this would have made an early and powerful impact on the infant church. As Cullmann reminds us, the canonical books "forced themselves on the church by their intrinsic apostolic authority."[155] With these considerations in mind, we now turn to the final chapters of the book as we evaluate how and when the early church recognized the apostolic authority of these books.

---

[154]Ridderbos, *Redemptive History*, 25.
[155]Cullmann, "The Tradition," 91.

6

THE CORPORATE RECEPTION
OF THE CANON

The Emergence of a Canonical Core

Astonishingly early, the great central core of the present New Testament was already being treated as the main authoritative source for Christians.

JOHN BARTON

Having examined the first two attributes of canonicity, divine qualities and apostolic origins, we now turn our attention to the third attribute, the corporate reception of these books by the church. In chapter 3 we argued that the internal testimony of the Holy Spirit not only was efficacious at the individual level, but would be equally (if not more) efficacious at the corporate-covenantal level, leading the church as a whole to rightly recognize these books as given by God. Such an expectation comes from Jesus himself when he says, "My sheep hear my voice, and I know them, and they follow me" (John 10:27). If so, "the fact that the church recognized the books of the New Testament as canonical is itself a powerful reason to believe that these books are indeed the revelation God intended humans to have."[1]

---

[1]C. Stephen Evans, "Canonicity, Apostolicity, and Biblical Authority: Some Kierkegaardian Reflections," in *Canon and Biblical Interpretation*, ed. Craig Bartholomew et al. (Carlisle: Paternoster, 2006), 155.

Of course, as noted above, this does not mean that the church some-how determines or creates the canon; rather it points to the authority, power, and impact of the self-authenticating Scriptures to elicit a corporate response from the church. Nor does it mean that there would never be pockets of the church in disagreement, but rather that the church, as a corporate whole, would eventually achieve predominant unity over these books—which is precisely what we find when we look at the church, both in the present and throughout the ages.

But the final consensus of the church is not the whole story. It took some time to get there. The church's recognition of the canon did not happen instantaneously but has a complex and sometimes erratic history span-ning many centuries. Indeed, it is this complex history that is the source of the most commonly suggested "defeater" for the Christian belief in the canon, particularly from adherents of the historical-critical model—what we will call the "canonical-diversity defeater." If these books are really from God, it is argued, then why did it take the church so long to recognize them? And if the Spirit was really at work in the church, then why was there so much disagreement over them? Moreover, there are segments of the church still today that have a different New Testament canon (e.g., the Syrian Orthodox Church has a twenty-two-book canon). Are we to think that these churches do not have the Spirit? The tumultuous history of the canon, then, has led critics to argue that the final consensus of the church cannot be the result of the Spirit's work, but must be the result of some theological faction imposing its preferred books on the rest of the church. It must mean that human power, not divine power, led to a canoni-cal consensus. The "winners" write the history—and choose the books.[2]

Such claims about the history of the canon have an element of truth in them. Indeed, the canon did not come together all at once, and the church did not always agree. But does this constitute a viable defeater for the self-authenticating model? Do disagreements among early Christians mean that the consensus of the church is not a reliable means of identifying canonical books? We shall argue against this purported defeater by offering two broad counterpoints (or defeater-defeaters): (1) The canonical-diversity defeater works only if the existence of disagreements over canonical books would be inconsistent with, and contradictory to, the expectations of the self-authenticating model. However, such is not the case. On the contrary,

---

[2]Roman Catholics may have a different version of this same objection. They may agree with the historical-critical model that the history of the canon was tumultuous and erratic, but then use this as an argument that the *testimonium* is not sufficient and that Christians need an infallible church and pope to declare which books are from God and which are not.

the model actually *expects* such disagreements and has explanations for them. (2) The extent of the disagreements among early Christians is not as vast as the critics claim. While the development of the canon was by no means a monolithic affair, we shall argue that its history is not nearly as problematic as is often portrayed and therefore does not constitute a viable defeater to our canonical model.

The bulk of this chapter and all of chapters 7 and 8 shall be spent on point (2), since the history of the canon's reception is the focal point of most studies on the canon. Before we proceed, however, we shall briefly address point (1).

I. The Existence of Canonical Diversity: Getting Our Expectations Straight

When the history of the canon is discussed, one question is rarely asked: What should we *expect* the development of the canon to be like? Built into the canonical-diversity defeater is the assumption that we can only believe we have the writings God intended if there are very few (if any) dissenters and there is virtually immediate and universal agreement on all twenty-seven canonical books. Put differently, if there are disagreements over books in the earliest stages of Christianity, then we have no grounds for thinking the church got it right. But where does this assumption come from? And why should we think it is true?

The degree to which this assumption pervades modern studies of the canon is evident from the relentless (if not near-obsessive) focus on early Christian diversity.[3] For many modern scholars, the validity of the church's final consensus on the canon is disproved simply by showing that at some point early Christians disagreed over its boundaries. The mere *existence* of diversity itself has become the argument. An example of this sort of appeal can be seen in Ehrman's treatment of Ptolemy's *Epistle to Flora*.[4] Despite the epistle's extensive historical problems, Ehrman presents this apocryphal letter as representing authentic Christianity as well as any other letter in the early church. Why? Because, he reminds us, the author of this letter was "earnest," "passionate," and "sincere," and that he

---

[3]E.g., J. D. G. Dunn, *Unity and Diversity in the New Testament: An Inquiry into the Character of Early Christianity* (London: SCM, 1990); J. M. Robinson and H. Koester, *Trajectories Through Early Christianity* (Philadelphia: Fortress, 1971); B. D. Ehrman, *Lost Christianities: The Battles for Scripture and the Faiths We Never Knew* (New York: Oxford University Press, 2002); Lee McDonald, *Forgotten Scriptures: The Selection and Rejection of Early Religious Writings* (Louisville: Westminster John Knox, 2009).
[4]Ehrman, *Lost Christianities*, 129–31.

"understood his views to be those of the apostles."[5] In other words, we cannot reject Ptolemy's letter because, after all, Ptolemy himself sincerely believed he held orthodox doctrines, and who are we to say otherwise. From Ehrman's perspective, once it is demonstrated that Christian groups disagreed about the extent of the canon (and who was really "apostolic"), then we are all obligated to agree that distinctions between canonical and noncanonical books are meaningless. But why is this the case? And where does Ehrman get this principle?

Helmut Koester makes a very similar "postmodern turn"[6] in his historical analysis. He argues that the canon has no "normative relevance" because all kinds of early Christian groups disagreed about who was heretical and who was not—all of them would "claim genuine apostolic origin."[7] But how does the existence of competing truth claims in early Christianity remove the "normative relevance" of the canon? Why does the existence of heretical groups mean that there can be no orthodox group? Koester attempts to answer these questions: "It is certainly untenable that the orthodox church and only this orthodox church . . . was able to preserve the apostolic heritage."[8] But Koester never explains *why* this is untenable. How does he know that the orthodox church could not preserve the apostolic heritage? The obvious principle at work in Koester's thinking is that disagreements among early Christians require us to believe that no book (and no version of Christianity) could really have gotten it right. But this principle is just assumed. He never makes an argument for it.

The reason the canonical-diversity defeater of Ehrman, Koester, and others has persuasive appeal is that they have quietly slipped a foundational assumption into the debate, namely, that the existence of diversity and disagreement is *contrary* to what we would expect if these twenty-seven books are really given by God. But that is the very issue in question. Such an assumption is directly rejected by the self-authenticating model. Indeed, several factors within the self-authenticating model would actually lead us to *expect* some disagreements: (1) The Scriptures warn of false teaching (and false teachers) in the church (2 Pet. 2:2; 1 John 2:19).[9] If so, then

---

[5]Ibid., 131.
[6]For broad overviews of this subject, see Stephen Best and Douglas Kellner, *The Postmodern Turn* (New York: Guilford, 1997); and Myron B. Penner, *Christianity and the Postmodern Turn: Six Views* (Grand Rapids: Brazos, 2005).
[7]Robinson and Koester, *Trajectories Through Early Christianity*, 115.
[8]Ibid., 115.
[9]For an overview of various false teachings battled by the New Testament books themselves, see A. J. Köstenberger and M. J. Kruger, *The Heresy of Orthodoxy: How Modern Culture's*

it is reasonable to think that the church would also face false teachings about the status of canonical and apocryphal writings. (2) We should not overlook the fact that there are spiritual forces opposing the church (Eph. 6:10–20; 1 Pet. 5:8–10; Rev. 12:13–17). Thus, we have greater reason to expect there would be controversy, opposition, and heresy in early Christianity. (3) People often resist the Spirit by their sin and disobedience (Acts 7:51; Eph. 4:30; 5:18; 1 Thess. 5:19). For this reason, the *testimonium* was never understood by the Reformers as something that would lead to an absolute unity over the canonical books. (4) Not all groups who claim to be the "church" are really part of it.[10] Some claim the name of Christ who are not really his followers (Matt. 7:21–23; John 2:23–25; Phil. 1:15–16; 1 John 2:19). Thus, the canons of these so-called Christian groups (Valentinians?) might differ significantly from those of true Christians. This can give the impression that there was more canonical diversity among early Christians than there actually was.

In addition to all these factors, the most critical issue is that God chose to deliver his canonical books to his church through the normal historical channels. Given that the twenty-seven canonical books were not lowered down from heaven in final form, but written by a variety of different authors, in a variety of different time periods, and in a variety of different geographical locations, we can expect that there would be an inevitable delay between the time a book was known and accepted in one portion of the empire as opposed to another. Such a delay would have eventually led to some disagreements and discussion over various books. If God chose to deliver his books in real time and history, then such a scenario would be inevitable and natural. Moreover, the earliest Christians lacked what we often take for granted: the historical witness of generations of saints who have heard the voice of God in these books. Since they were at the beginning of the entire process, there was not the same degree of a "communion of consciousness" (as Kuyper put it) that could inform their canonical thinking. It takes time for this to fully develop, which is

---

Fascination with Diversity Has Reshaped Our Understanding of Early Christianity (Wheaton, IL: Crossway, 2010), 89–101.

[10] As noted above, we have good biblical grounds for thinking that Christians can rightly identify the true church (at least in a manner that is sufficient for our purposes here). At its core, the church is marked by the true preaching of the gospel (John 8:31–47; 14:23; 1 John 4:1–3; 2 John 9) and the right administration of the sacraments Christ gave his church (Matt. 28:19; Acts 2:42; 1 Cor. 11:23–30). Added to this can be a variety of other things, including Jesus's teachings that true Christians are identified by their love for one another (John 13:35; cf. 1 John 4:7–8; 5:1). For more on the marks of the church see John Calvin, *Institutes of the Christian Religion*, ed. John T. McNeill, trans. Ford Lewis Battles (Philadelphia: Westminster, 1960), 4.2.1–3; and Edmund P. Clowney, *The Church* (Downers Grove, IL: InterVarsity, 1995), 99–115.

no doubt part of the reason why the reception of the canon itself took some time to complete.

These considerations indicate that the Scriptures themselves give us good reasons for expecting some level of disagreement over the canon in the earliest stages (and even some level of ongoing disagreement). Therefore, such disagreements do not invalidate our biblical warrant for also believing that the church's eventual consensus around these twenty-seven books is a reliable indicator of their canonicity. The Scriptures see no conflict between these two realities. Now, this does not mean that there could not be, in principle, a situation where the Spirit's testimony was so obscured by the church's sin and rebellion that the church reached consensus on books that are *not* canonical. But there would have to be good reasons to think this happened. Without such reasons, we have no cause for rejecting the church's consensus as a reliable indicator of canonicity. Consider again our sense perception as a helpful example. I don't reject the reliability of my eyesight just because it is *possible* that I might be hallucinating (or because others have, on occasion, hallucinated). Unless I have good reasons to think I am hallucinating when I see a phone on my desk, then I am justified in believing that there is a phone on my desk. I don't have to *prove* that I am not hallucinating in order for my belief to be justified. At this point one could object that Christians therefore do not have infallible certainty about the canon. But, as we noted above, our model does not purport to provide some sort of infallible, incontrovertible certainty about the canon (in a Cartesian sense). Rather our model is arguing that Christians have sufficient epistemic grounds for thinking that the books of the New Testament can be *known*. One does not need infallibility to have knowledge.[11]

---

[11]The principles in this paragraph may help address a potential objection to the self-authenticating model. If the *testimonium* leads to the church's corporate reception of the canonical books, then how do we understand the fact that Roman Catholics and Protestants have differed over the extent of the *Old* Testament canon (with the Catholic Church eventually accepting the Apocrypha)? Does this not prove that the church's consensus is an unreliable indicator of canonicity? Although the story of the Apocrypha is too complex to fully address here, there is no indication that it contradicts our model. Several considerations: (1) It should be kept in mind that the books of the Old Testament canon *were*, in fact, widely recognized by the Old Testament "church." There are good reasons to think that the Hebrew canon was established within Judaism prior to the first century. This is confirmed by the writings of the New Testament themselves, which are some of our best first-century sources and regularly cite the Old Testament as Scripture, but give no similar treatment to the books of the Apocrypha. God had entrusted the Old Testament books to the Jews, and they received them by a wide consensus (Rom. 3:2). Thus, the full reception of the Old Testament by the people of God in Israel is a sufficient justification for our belief in them as canonical. (2) It was the church's duty to receive what had been handed down to the people of God before her. In the first few centuries of the church we have good evidence that the dominant position (though not the

Positively speaking, we should also remember that disagreements and debates among early Christians were not necessarily detrimental to the church or its ability to recognize the canonical books. Indeed, such debates would have encouraged critical thinking about these texts, deeper reflection on their content, and more vigorous historical investigation into their origins. Robert Grant argues that a number of early church fathers—Papias, Justin, Irenaeus, Clement of Alexandria, and others—were astute "literary critics" who carefully analyzed the literary merits and historical origins of canonical and noncanonical books.[12] As a result, they took the task of distinguishing between canonical and apocryphal books very seriously, giving us reason for greater confidence in their final conclusions. Ironically, much of modern critical scholarship would affirm that open debate and disagreement often lead to a clearer and more certain understanding of the truth—such is the nature of the academic enterprise, we

---

only position) was an acceptance of the Jewish Old Testament canon and not the Apocrypha. This would include church fathers like Melito of Sardis, Origen, Eusebius, Athanasius, Cyril of Jerusalem, Epiphanius, Hilary of Poitiers, Gregory of Nazianzus, Rufinus, and Jerome. Thus, it appears that both the Jewish "church" and the first centuries of the Christian church widely adopted the Old Testament books and not the Apocrypha (of course there were minority opinions, but this does not contradict the model). (3) If so, then we must explain how the church in the Middle Ages, and ultimately at the Council of Trent, could divert from this clear foundation and affirm additional books that were not canonical. We noted above that there can be, in principle, "a situation where the Spirit's testimony was so obscured by the church's sin and rebellion that the church reached consensus on books that are *not* canonical." No doubt we have good reasons to think that the extensive moral and doctrinal corruption of the church in the Middle Ages—which stood in opposition to the consensus of the Jewish believers, as well as the teachings of Jesus and the New Testament—would constitute just such a situation. The apocryphal books would have been attractive to the church during this time since they were used to justify doctrines, like purgatory and prayers for the dead, that were at the heart of the ecclesiastical abuse of power. Indeed, so substantial was this corruption, especially in regard to the gospel message, that legitimate questions can be raised about whether the Roman Catholic Church continued to be the true church of Jesus Christ—and therefore a place where the Spirit was actively working (and if, lacking the Spirit, it is not the true church, then its affirmation of the apocryphal books is not relevant). But even if one accepts Roman Catholicism as a true church, the fact remains that we have good grounds for believing that, in this instance, the Spirit's witness was widely obscured by the church's sin and rebellion. Of course, at this point one might raise the following objection: If the church was mistaken about the Old Testament books, how can we be sure that it was not mistaken about the New Testament books? But it is here that we must remember our model: we have warrant for thinking that the church's consensus is a reliable indicator of canonicity, *unless we have good reasons to think the contrary.* In regard to the very specific situation of the Roman Catholic Church's acceptance of the Apocrypha at the Council of Trent, we *do* have good reasons to think the contrary. But in regard to the New Testament canon, we have no reasons to think that the church was mistaken in this regard. We do not have to *prove* that the church is not mistaken in order to be rational in our belief that the church is not mistaken. Again, consider the eyesight analogy above. Even if my eyesight were unreliable at some point (perhaps I had a bad reaction to medication and hallucinated), that wouldn't mean that I must reject the reliability of my eyesight at *all other* times (like after I stopped taking my medication).

[12]Robert M. Grant, "Literary Criticism and the New Testament Canon," *JSNT* 16 (1982): 24–44.

are told. Indeed, few would challenge the validity of the established views of an academic discipline merely on the grounds that they were born out of vigorous debate and disagreements among scholars. One would hope, therefore, that this same principle would be applied to the deliberations of the ancient church.

In the end, contrary to claims of the critics, the key issue in the history of the canon is not the existence of diversity and disagreement—some of that is to be expected. Rather, the critical issue is whether we have good reasons to think that the early church, as a whole, would have rightly identified the canonical books even in the midst of some of these disagreements. As we argued in prior chapters, the compelling and powerful nature of the divine qualities and apostolic origins of these books, coupled with the internal testimony of the Holy Spirit, provides very good reasons to think that the church would eventually recognize and receive them. They imposed themselves on the church and it could not, in the end, resist them. But this could not be completed overnight. It took some time. And all these factors above would have no doubt increased the amount of time it took. This reminds us that the recognition of the canon is a *process* and therefore cannot be subjected to our own arbitrary requirements about how long it should have taken or how much disagreement was allowed.

II. The Extent of Canonical Diversity: The Emergence of a Canonical Core

We now turn our attention to the second "defeater-defeater," which will argue that the extent of disagreement in the reception of the New Testament canon is less than the critics claim. Indeed, there are many positive indications of an early and widespread consensus around a canonical core. We shall explore the historical evidence for the reception of the canon for the remainder of this chapter and also chapters 7 and 8. As we explore this evidence, we must be reminded what it is (and is not) intended to accomplish. The evidence is not being used to somehow "prove" the canonicity of these books to the critic—that was never the goal of the volume and is certainly not the goal here.[13] Nor is the historical evidence surveyed here necessary to establish that the church has (and has had) a consensus on

---

[13] John M. Frame, *The Doctrine of the Word of God* (Phillipsburg, NJ: P&R, 2010), provides the helpful reminder that "studies of the historical process by which the church came to identify the canon certainly do reveal interesting facts. . . . But inductive study alone is unlikely to show us with certainty which books God has given to rule the church" (134).

these twenty-seven books. It may tell us *how* that consensus happened, but not all of these details are needed for us to know *that* it happened.[14] Instead, the historical evidence surveyed in these next three chapters is being used specifically to challenge the canonical-diversity defeater that claims the canon's history is too erratic for God to have been at work in the reception of these books.[15]

In this current chapter, we will begin our historical investigations by exploring *when* these books were received as canonical by the early church. How early was it? How far back can we see evidence for a New Testament? Critics of the New Testament have argued that it took a while before Christians began to view these books as Scripture. McDonald argues that "these documents were not generally recognized as Scripture until the end of the second century C.E."[16] Elaine Pagels also suggests that the canon did not emerge until the end of the second century, primarily through the efforts of Irenaeus.[17] Contrary to these claims, however, we shall argue that there is evidence for the emergence of the canon that precedes the end of the second century. Of course, we are not speaking here of the "exclusive" definition of canon—as if there were a closed and rigidly defined canon by c. 200. Rather we are speaking of the "functional" definition of canon, namely, that canonical books were *being used* as Scripture by this time.[18] In other words, we will be arguing that a "core" collection of New Testament books was already well received before the end of the second century, even though the boundaries of the canon were still a little fuzzy.

---

[14]One could know that there has been a strong consensus around these books since the fourth century without knowing all the historical details of exactly how that consensus was reached.
[15]In many ways, much of the evidence adduced in the next three chapters would also serve to argue for the apostolicity of these books. Indeed, part of the evidence for apostolicity is the opinion of some early church fathers about these books. So this same historical evidence could serve two purposes: (1) challenge the viability of a defeater; and (2) help establish the apostolicity of some New Testament books (though it is not the *only* evidence for apostolicity).
[16]L. M. McDonald, *The Biblical Canon: Its Origin, Transmission, and Authority* (Peabody, MA: Hendrickson, 2007), 359.
[17]Elaine Pagels, *Beyond Belief: The Secret Gospel of Thomas* (New York: Random House, 2003), 114–42; see also Helmut Koester, *Introduction to the New Testament*, vol. 2, *History and Literature of Early Christianity* (Philadelphia: Fortress, 1982), 10.
[18]Craig D. Allert, *A High View of Scripture? The Authority of the Bible and the Formation of the New Testament Canon* (Grand Rapids: Baker Academic, 2007), 44–47, suggests that one cannot discuss the emergence of the canon prior to the fourth century lest one falls into "anachronism." However, this objection already presupposes that Sundberg's exclusive definition of canon is the only valid definition. If there is not the sharp divide between Scripture and canon that Allert supposes (as I have argued in prior chapters), then one indeed *can* discuss when Christians began to receive books as canonical even in the second century.

A. The New Testament Writings

When we begin to look for evidence of an emerging canon within early Christianity, some of our best (and earliest) evidence comes from the New Testament itself. As we shall see, however, such evidence is often too quickly dismissed by those committed to a late date for the emergence of the canon. Let us consider several examples here.

1. Early References to Canonical Books

One of the earliest examples comes from the well-known phrase in 2 Peter 3:16, where Paul's letters are regarded as on par with the τάς λοιπάς γραφάς ("the other Scriptures") of the Old Testament. Most notably, this passage does not refer to just one letter of Paul, but to a *collection* of Paul's letters (how many is unclear) that already began to circulate throughout the churches—so much so that the author could refer to "all his [Paul's] letters" and expect his audience would understand the corpus to which he was referring.[19] Indeed, the author presents Paul's letters as Scripture with no indication that this is an innovation or that his audience may not agree; he mentions it quite casually, offering no introduction, defense, or explanation of this idea. This suggests that the scriptural status of at least some of Paul's letters was reasonably widespread by this time. Moreover, if Paul's letters are regarded as Scripture, it is difficult to avoid the implication that *other* apostolic letters would be regarded as Scripture as well. Given that 2 Peter begins with a very clear claim to apostolic authority (1:1), there is little reason to think that its readers would have seen it as any less authoritative than Paul's letters (particularly given Peter's status in early Christianity). Indeed, this is confirmed by Peter's description of Paul as "*our* [ἡμῶν] beloved brother" in 3:15, which is likely a reference to the college of apostles in which he would certainly include himself.[20] On the basis of this text, Meade concludes that 2 Peter "clearly articulates a doctrine of . . . Christian Scripture, which represents a significant milestone in Christian thought."[21]

---

[19]Regarding Pauline letter collections, see David Trobisch, *Die Entstehung der Paulusbriefsammlung: Studien zu den Anfängen christlicher Publizistik*, Novum testamentum et orbis antiquus (Göttingen: Vandenhoeck & Ruprecht, 1989); S. E. Porter, "When and How Was the Pauline Canon Compiled? An Assessment of Theories," in *The Pauline Canon*, ed. S. E. Porter (Leiden: Brill, 2004), 95–127; H. Gamble, "The Redaction of the Pauline Letters and the Formation of the Pauline Corpus," *JBL* 94 (1975): 403–18; K. L. Carroll, "The Expansion of the Pauline Corpus," *JBL* 72 (1953): 230–37; and C. Buck, "The Early Order of the Pauline Corpus," *JBL* 68 (1949): 351–57.

[20]D. Meade, "Ancient Near Eastern Apocalypticism and the Origins of the New Testament Canon of Scripture," in *The Bible as a Human Witness: Hearing the Word of God Through Historically Dissimilar Traditions*, ed. Randall Heskett and Brian Irwin (London: T&T Clark, 2010), 318.

[21]Ibid.

Although those scholars who hold to the pseudonymity of 2 Peter gen-erally date the letter to the end of the first century (AD 80–90),[22] or the beginning of the second (c. 100–125),[23] the pseudonymous status of 2 Peter has not gone unchallenged.[24] Numerous historical considerations—which we cannot delve into here—suggest that the author was likely the apostle Peter himself. Either way, it is clear that a number of Paul's letters were considered Scripture by the turn of the century, and possibly even earlier.

Another noteworthy witness is 1 Timothy 5:18: "For the Scripture [ἡ γραφή] says, 'You shall not muzzle an ox when it treads out the grain,' and, 'The laborer deserves his wages.'" The first citation is clearly derived from Deuteronomy 25:4, and the second is identical in wording to Luke 10:7, where it is found on the lips of Jesus. Although it could be natu-ral to conclude that 1 Timothy is citing Luke's Gospel as Scripture, this understanding of the passage has been resisted by some. However, there are a number of good reasons to take the text at face value.

(1) Suggestions that this text is merely alluding to oral tradition of Jesus do not fit with its placement alongside an Old Testament citation likewise referred to as ἡ γραφή.[25] Marshall notes, "A *written* source is surely required, and one that would have been authoritative."[26] Thus, regardless of which book 1 Timothy is citing, it is clear that the passage treats *some* book as Scripture alongside the Old Testament. That fact

---

[22]E.g., R. Bauckham, *Jude, 2 Peter* (Waco, TX: Word, 1983), 158; and B. Reicke, *The Epistles of James, Peter, and Jude* (New York: Doubleday, 1964).

[23]J. N. D. Kelly, *A Commentary on the Epistles of Peter and of Jude* (New York: Harper & Row, 1969), 237; C. E. B. Cranfield, *I & II Peter and Jude: Introduction and Commentary* (London: SCM, 1960), 149; J. B. Mayor, *The Epistle of St. Jude and the Second Epistle of St. Peter* (London: Macmillan, 1907), cxxvii; D. J. Harrington, *Jude and 2 Peter* (Collegeville, MN: Liturgical Press, 2003), 237. Some have tried to push the epistle's date as late as the middle of the second century (e.g., McDonald, *The Biblical Canon*, 277), but this position is decidedly in the minority, and there seems to be little evidence to justify it. Of course, even if such a date were correct, we still have a collection of New Testament books that was viewed as Scripture by c. 150.

[24]Michael J. Kruger, "The Authenticity of 2 Peter," *JETS* 42 (1999): 645–71; E. M. B. Green, *2 Peter Reconsidered* (London: Tyndale, 1960); Donald Guthrie, *New Testament Introduction* (Downers Grove, IL: InterVarsity, 1990), 805–42.

[25]That Paul is using oral tradition here is suggested by Lorenz Oberlinner, *Kommentar zum ersten Timotheusbrief* (Freiburg im Breisgau: Herder, 1994), 254. Some have argued that the introductory phrase λέγει γὰρ ἡ γραφή refers only to the first citation and not the second; e.g., J. N. D. Kelly, *A Commentary on the Pastoral Epistles* (Peabody, MA: Hendrickson, 1960), 126; Martin Dibelius and Hans Conzelmann, *The Pastoral Epistles* (Philadelphia: Fortress, 1972), 79. However, the manner in which the citations follow right after one another and are joined with the simple καί suggests that "Scripture" applies to both. Indeed, other New Testament examples of double citations—Matt. 15:4; Mark 7:10; Acts 1:20; 1 Pet. 2:6; 2 Pet. 2:22—have both citations included in the introductory formula (George W. Knight, *The Pastoral Epistles: A Commentary on the Greek Text*, NIGTC [Grand Rapids: Eerdmans, 1992], 234). Thus, I. Howard Marshall declares, "Both quotations are envisaged as coming from 'Scripture'" (*A Critical and Exegetical Commentary on the Pastoral Epistles*, ICC [Edinburgh: T&T Clark, 1999], 615).

[26]Marshall, *Pastoral Epistles*, 616, emphasis mine.

alone should reshape our understanding of when Christians began to consider their own books "Scripture." Indeed, Meade sees evidence here of an early "canon consciousness."[27]

(2) That 1 Timothy is using some other written source besides Luke (such as Q[28] or an apocryphal gospel[29]) is certainly possible, but seems unnecessary when Luke 10:7 provides such a clear and obvious source for this citation. Not only is the Greek identical in these two texts, but it is *only* in these two texts that this passage occurs in this form.[30] Although it is true that we can never be certain about the use of Luke, it seems reasonable to prefer known historical sources over hypothetical and conjectural ones.[31]

(3) The idea that a Pauline book would cite Luke is also more plausible when one considers the way other historical sources link the two together. Not only is Luke presented as a frequent traveling companion of Paul's throughout the book of Acts, but his name is mentioned a number of times in other Pauline letters (Col. 4:14; 2 Tim. 4:11; Philem. 1:24). Moreover, there is a regular connection between Paul and Luke's Gospel in the writings of the early church fathers.[32] Eusebius even mentions an early tradition that "Paul was actually accustomed to quote from Luke's gospel."[33] And some have suggested that Luke was Paul's amanuensis for 1 Timothy.[34] Such a strong historical connection between these two individuals makes it more plausible that a Pauline letter would cite from Luke's Gospel.

---

[27]Meade, "Ancient Near Eastern Apocalypticism," 318.

[28]A. T. Hanson, *The Pastoral Epistles* (Grand Rapids: Eerdmans, 1982), 102.

[29]Kelly, *Pastoral Epistles*, 126; Dibelius and Conzelmann, *The Pastoral Epistles*, 79.

[30]The similar phrase in Matt. 10:10 is still different from Luke 10:7 and 1 Tim. 5:18. Echoes of this phrase also occur in 1 Cor. 9:14 and *Didache* 13.2. For more, see A. E. Harvey, "'The Workman Is Worthy of His Hire': Fortunes of a Proverb in the Early Church," *NovT* 24 (1982): 209–21.

[31]W. L. Petersen, "Textual Traditions Examined: What the Text of the Apostolic Fathers Tells Us About the Text of the New Testament in the Second Century," in *The Reception of the New Testament in the Apostolic Fathers*, ed. Andrew Gregory and Christopher Tuckett (Oxford: Oxford University Press, 2005), 29–46, argues that even if we have an *exact* match between the apostolic fathers and a New Testament writing, we still cannot be sure that the New Testament writing is really being cited because the text of these books was in flux. How do we know that Luke in the second century was the "Luke" we have now in our NA27 text? Petersen's point is a fair one; he is right that we cannot be absolutely sure. However, historical study is never about what is absolutely certain, but about what is most probable or reasonable. In this short volume we cannot delve deeper into the methodology of how to identify a citation/allusion from a book, but more discussion can be found in Andrew Gregory, *The Reception of Luke and Acts in the Period Before Irenaeus* (Tübingen: Mohr Siebeck, 2003), 5–20.

[32]E.g., Irenaeus (Eusebius, *Hist. eccl.* 5.8.3); Origen (*Hist. eccl.* 6.25.6); and the Muratorian fragment.

[33]*Hist. eccl.* 3.4.7. C. E. Hill, "What Papias Said About John (and Luke): A New Papias Fragment," *JTS* 49 (1998): 582–629, argues that this tradition goes back to Papias.

[34]C. F. Moule, "The Problem of the Pastoral Epistles: A Reappraisal," *BJRL* 47 (1965): 430–52.

Although those who hold to the pseudonymity of 1 Timothy typically date it to the end of the first century (AD 90–100),[35] an impressive case has been made over the years for the authenticity of this epistle.[36] Regardless, it is clear that Luke's Gospel was received as authoritative Scripture alongside the Old Testament at least by the turn of the century—remarkably early, on anyone's reckoning. In the end, we can agree with John Meier when he declares, "The only interpretation that avoids contorted intellectual acrobatics or special pleading is the plain, obvious one. [First Timothy] is citing Luke's Gospel alongside Deuteronomy as normative Scripture for the ordering of the church's ministry."[37]

2. Allusions to a Bi-covenantal Canon

A key indication of an emerging canon within early Christianity is that Christians began to conceive of something like a New Testament alongside, and parallel to, the Old. Although such references are rare in the earliest stages of the church, the New Testament evidence itself cannot be overlooked. There may be just such an allusion in 2 Peter 3:2 when the reader is asked to submit to "the predictions of the holy prophets and the commandment of the Lord and Savior through your apostles." Most noteworthy here is the juxtaposition of "prophets" of the old covenant and the "apostles" of the new covenant as two equal sources of divine authority. This suggests that 2 Peter views divine revelation in two distinct phases or epochs—perhaps an allusion to the beginnings of a bi-covenantal canon. The mention of plural "apostles" would also indicate that any emerging New Testament would be composed of more than just one apostle's teaching (thus making it clear that Paul is not the only author in view).

---

[35]Hanson, *The Pastoral Epistles*, 13; W. G. Kümmel, *Introduction to the New Testament* (Nashville: Abingdon, 1973), 387; Marshall, *Pastoral Epistles*, 58; J. P. Meier, "The Inspiration of Scripture: But What Counts as Scripture?," *Mid-Stream* 38 (1999): 78. Campenhausen's well-known claim that the Pastoral Epistles derive from the time of Polycarp has not been widely accepted and places the letters too late to be so readily received by Irenaeus and the Muratorian fragment just a short time later (H. von Campenhausen, *The Formation of the Christian Bible* [London: A&C Black, 1972], 181). See critiques of Campenhausen in L. T. Johnson, *The First and Second Letters to Timothy* (New York: Doubleday, 2001), 85; and Kümmel, *Introduction to the New Testament*, 386–87.

[36]See discussion in Guthrie, *New Testament Introduction*, 607–49. Given the dating of Acts on the eve of Paul's death (e.g., John Wenham, *Redating Matthew, Mark, and Luke: A Fresh Assault on the Synoptic Problem* [Downers Grove, IL: InterVarsity, 1992], 223–230), many have suggested that Luke may have been written in the early 60s, and thus could have been known by Paul. For more on the dating of Luke, see D. A. Carson and Douglas J. Moo, *An Introduction to the New Testament* (Grand Rapids: Zondervan, 2005), 207–8; Leon Morris, *The Gospel According to St. Luke: An Introduction and Commentary*, TNTC (Grand Rapids: Eerdmans, 1974), 22–26; and I. Howard Marshall, *The Gospel of Luke* (Grand Rapids: Eerdmans, 1978), 33.

[37]Meier, "The Inspiration of Scripture," 77.

Moreover, the fact that "holy prophets" is clearly a reference to written texts[38] suggests the possibility that the "commandment of the Lord [ἐντολῆς τοῦ κυρίου] . . . through your apostles" may also refer, at least in part, to written texts.[39] This possibility finds support in the immediate context, which expressly mentions written apostolic texts (2 Pet. 3:1, 16). In addition, the phrase ἐντολῆς τοῦ κυρίου not only is used regularly to refer to written Old Testament commands, but also finds a notable parallel in Paul: "If anyone thinks that he is a prophet, or spiritual, he should acknowledge that the *things I am writing to you are a command of the Lord* [κυρίου ἐντολή]" (1 Cor. 14:37). This passage is at least one instance where a "command of the Lord" from an apostle appears in a written text.

However, even if one does not take 2 Peter 3:2 as an allusion to written apostolic texts, this verse clearly lays a critical foundation for the *future* emergence of the New Testament collection alongside the Old. It reveals that early Christians had a theological conviction that apostolic teaching (and writings, cf. 3:16) were the next phase of God's covenantal revelation. For this reason, Denis Farkasfalvy argues that this text "appears to sketch a theology of the Canon, or, as I prefer to call it, a theology of the 'pre-Canon' or 'proto-Canon.'"[40] In addition, he observes that this prophet-apostle structure is also well attested throughout other early Christian texts, such as the apostolic fathers, Justin Martyr, Irenaeus, Tertullian, and others.[41]

Allusions to a bi-covenantal structure for God's revelation also occur in a number of other New Testament texts, though we can only mention a couple here. As noted above, it is significant that in 2 Corinthians 3:6 Paul refers to himself and the other apostles as διακόνους καινῆς διαθήκης ("ministers of a new covenant") within a *written* letter to the Corinthians and then in 3:14 contrasts this to another written document, namely, the "old covenant" (τῆς παλαιᾶς διαθήκης).[42] The implications of this pas-

---

[38]Attempts to make "prophets" here refer to New Testament prophets has been roundly rejected; see Bauckham, *Jude, 2 Peter*, 287.

[39]The reference in 2 Pet. 3:2 to the singular "command" of the apostles has confused some. Daniel J. Harrington, *Jude and 2 Peter*, sums it up well when he says, "[The command] refers not so much to one commandment (e.g., the love command) but rather to the substance of the Christian faith proclaimed by the apostles" (281–82).

[40]D. Farkasfalvy, "'Prophets and Apostles': The Conjunction of the Two Terms before Irenaeus," in *Texts and Testaments: Critical Essays on the Bible and the Early Church Fathers*, ed. W. E. March (San Antonio: Trinity University Press, 1980), 120.

[41]E.g., in the apostolic fathers it occurs in *2 Clem.* 14.2; Ign. *Phld.* 5.1–2 (cf. 9.1); Pol. *Phil.* 6.3. See Farkasfalvy, "Prophets and Apostles," 109–34.

[42]R. P. Martin, *2 Corinthians*, WBC (Waco, TX: Word, 1986), 69, argues that Paul coined this phrase. C. K. Barrett, *A Commentary on the Second Epistle to the Corinthians* (London: A&C

sage for a bi-covenantal canon are difficult to miss. Likewise, Hebrews
2:2–3 juxtaposes the "message declared by angels" (a clear reference to
the Old Testament) with the message "declared at first by the Lord, and
. . . attested to us *by those who heard*" (a clear reference to the apostles).
Although not an obvious reference to written texts by apostles, this passage continues to lay the foundation for a future bi-covenantal canonical
structure.[43]

3. Public Reading of Canonical Books

A number of Paul's epistles include commands that they be read publicly at the gathering of the church. Colossians 4:16 declares, "And when
this letter has been read among you, have it also read in the church of
the Laodiceans." Also, in 1 Thessalonians 5:27 Paul strongly exhorts his
audience, "I put you under oath before the Lord to have this letter read to
all the brothers." In 2 Corinthians 10:9, in the context of Paul's defending his apostolic authority, he mentions the public reading of his letters
and expresses concern over their impact: "I do not want to appear to be
frightening you with my letters." The book of Revelation also anticipates
that it will be read publicly when it pronounces a blessing on "the one
who reads aloud the words of this prophecy, and . . . those who hear"
(1:3).[44] This practice of reading Scripture in worship can be traced back
to the Jewish synagogue, where portions from the Old Testament were
routinely read aloud to the congregation (Luke 4:17–20; Acts 13:15;
15:21).[45] Others have suggested that the Gospels of Matthew and Mark
were written with a liturgical structure that implied they were used for
year-round public reading in worship.[46]

Paul's insistence that his letters be publicly read, his overt claims to
apostolic authority, and his readers' understanding of what public reading
would mean within a synagogue context provide good reasons to think
that his letters would have been viewed as being in the same category
as other "Scripture" read during times of public worship. Indeed, Paul

---

Black, 1973), 121, argues that "old covenant" and "Old Testament" are virtually synonymous.
[43]The juxtaposition of "prophets" and "apostles" continues among the second-century church
fathers; e.g., Justin, *1 Apol.* 67.3 (see discussion below); *Dial.* 119.6; *2 Clement* 14.2; Irenaeus,
Haer. 1.3.6; 2.27.2; see also discussion below regarding Ignatius.
[44]Harry Y. Gamble, *Books and Readers in the Early Church* (New Haven, CT: Yale University
Press, 1995), 206.
[45]Ibid., 209–11.
[46]G. D. Kilpatrick, *The Origins of the Gospel according to St. Matthew* (Oxford: Clarendon,
1950), 72–100; Michael D. Goulder, *Midrash and Lection in Matthew* (London: SPCK, 1974),
182–83; Phillip Carrington, *The Primitive Christian Calendar: A Study in the Making of the
Marcan Gospel* (Cambridge: Cambridge University Press, 1952).

himself makes this connection clear when he exhorts Timothy, "Devote yourself to the public reading of *Scripture*" (1 Tim. 4:13).

The practice of reading canonical books in worship—though visible only in seed form in the books of the New Testament—is more explicitly affirmed as commonplace by the time of Justin Martyr in the middle of the second century.

> And on the day called Sunday, all who live in cities or in the country gather together to one place, and the memoirs of the apostles or the writings of the prophets are read, as long as time permits; then, when the reader has ceased, the president verbally instructs, and exhorts to the imitation of these good things.[47]

Not only does Justin put the "memoirs of the apostles" (more on this below) on par with the Old Testament prophets, but he mentions them first, showing that by this time the reading of New Testament Scriptures had in some ways superseded the reading from the Torah.[48] Remarkably, this passage reveals that Justin's twofold source of scriptural revelation—the prophets and the apostles—is precisely the twofold source affirmed by 2 Peter 3:2 as discussed above. Again, it seems that the emerging structure of the New Testament canon was already present during the time of Peter and Paul, though more fully realized during the time of Justin.[49]

B. The Apostolic Fathers

We have seen that by the end of the first century there is already important evidence for an emerging New Testament canon composed of written apostolic texts—of both epistles and Gospels—and considered authoritative alongside the Old Testament. As we move out of the New Testament period and into the early second century, we will explore whether this trend is substantiated by the writings of the apostolic fathers. Needless

---

[47]*1 Apol.* 67.3.

[48]Martin Hengel, "The Titles of the Gospels and the Gospel of Mark," in *Studies in the Gospel of Mark* (London: SCM, 1985), 76.

[49]It is well known that noncanonical books were occasionally read in churches; e.g., the so-called *Gospel of Peter* (Eusebius, *Hist. eccl.* 6.12.2). However, this does not alter the point being made here. Public reading of books in worship was critical for a book's acceptance, even if there was disagreement in certain areas of the church regarding what should be read (Gamble, *Books and Readers*, 216). In addition, it is not at all clear that the *Gospel of Peter* was read publicly alongside the Old Testament in the same manner Justin says was true of the "memoirs of the apostles."

to say, this is an enormous field of study, and we must restrict ourselves to the mention of only a few selected texts here.[50]

1. 1 Clement

The epistle of *1 Clement* (c. AD 95) offers the following statement: "Take up the epistle of that blessed apostle, Paul. . . . To be sure, he sent you a letter in the Spirit [πνευματικῶς] concerning himself and Cephas and Apollos."[51] This citation has a number of notable features that are consistent with what was observed in the New Testament evidence above. (1) It is immediately apparent that the author (likely a Christian leader in Rome) acknowledges the unique apostolic authority of Paul and refers to him as "blessed apostle." Indeed, *1 Clement* notes elsewhere, "The Apostles received the Gospel for us from the Lord Jesus Christ, Jesus the Christ was sent from God. The Christ therefore is from God and the Apostles from the Christ."[52] In addition he refers to the apostles as "the greatest and most righteous pillars of the Church."[53] (2) In this statement the author makes a clear reference to 1 Corinthians and assumes his audience is familiar with it, showing again that at least some of Paul's letters seem to be broadly known by this time.[54] *First Clement* also makes likely allusions to other epistles of Paul, including Romans, Galatians, Philippians, Ephesians, and Hebrews (depending on whether one considers it Pauline)—though we cannot explore this topic further here.[55] (3) Although *1 Clement* does not explicitly refer to 1 Corinthians as γραφή ("Scripture"), it

---

[50]For more on this enormous subject, see Gregory and Tuckett, *The Reception of the New Testament in the Apostolic Fathers*; Andrew Gregory and Christopher Tuckett, eds., *Trajectories through the New Testament and the Apostolic Fathers* (Oxford: Oxford University Press, 2005); D. A. Hagner, "The Sayings of Jesus in the Apostolic Fathers and Justin Martyr," in *Gospel Perspectives: The Jesus Tradition Outside the Gospels*, ed. D. Wenham (Sheffield: JSOT, 1985), 233–68; A Committee of the Oxford Society of Historical Theology, *The New Testament in the Apostolic Fathers* (Oxford: Clarendon, 1905); and, most recently, Paul Foster, "The Text of the New Testament in the Apostolic Fathers," in *The Early Text of the New Testament*, ed. C. E. Hill and M. J. Kruger (Oxford: Oxford University Press, forthcoming).

[51]*1 Clem.* 47.1–3.

[52]*1 Clem.* 42.1–2.

[53]*1 Clem.* 5.2.

[54]Those arguing for a clear reference to 1 Corinthians include, Andreas Lindemann, *Paulus im ältesten Christentum: Das Bild des Apostels und die Rezeption der paulinischen Theologie in der frühchristlichen Literatur bis Marcion* (Tübingen: Mohr Siebeck, 1979), 190–91; Andrew F. Gregory, "1 Clement and the Writings That Later Formed the New Testament," in Gregory and Tuckett, *The Reception of the New Testament in the Apostolic Fathers*, 129–57; and D. A. Hagner, *The Use of the Old and New Testaments in Clement of Rome* (Leiden: Brill, 1973), 196–97.

[55]See A. J. Carlyle, "1 Clement," in *The New Testament in the Apostolic Fathers*, 37–62; Gregory, "1 Clement and the Writings That Later Formed the New Testament," 143; and Bruce M. Metzger, *The Canon of the New Testament: Its Origin, Development, and Significance* (Oxford: Clarendon, 1987), 42.

does seem to give it considerable weight, noting that it was written "in the Spirit" (πνευματικῶς).[56] This type of language is not always easy to interpret in the apostolic fathers. Sometimes it seems to be used to refer to *ecclesiastical* authority—Christian leaders who speak for Christ[57] and through the Holy Spirit[58]—but other times it seems to be used more clearly for the inspiration of Scripture.[59] However, given that the author of *1 Clement* elsewhere makes a sharp distinction between his own authority and that of the apostles, it seems that the latter use is in view here.[60] Either way, it is clear that *1 Clement* knows and values Paul's letters (though we do not know how many).

2. The Didache

The *Didache* is an early Christian manual of church practice probably from around the turn of the century (c. AD 100). At one point the manual declares, "Nor should you pray like the hypocrites, but as the *Lord commanded in his gospel*, you should pray as follows, 'Our Father in heaven. . . .'"[61] Here we have a reference to what Jesus "commanded" and are told it is contained in a "gospel," and then this text proceeds to cite the Lord's Prayer in a manner very close to Matthew 6:9–13. Although we cannot know for certain that it is a citation from Matthew's Gospel,[62] Christopher Tuckett comments, "It seems hard to resist the notion that

---

[56]Although Ehrman translates πνευματικῶς as "in the Spirit," the phrase has been translated in different ways. E.g., Kirsopp Lake, trans., *The Apostolic Fathers*, 2 vols. (London: William Hienemann, 1919), says that Paul wrote with "true inspiration"; and A. Roberts and J. Donaldson, eds., *The Ante-Nicene Fathers*, vol. 1 (1885; repr., Peabody, MA: Hendrickson, 1994), say that Paul wrote "under the inspiration of the Spirit."

[57]E.g., Ign. *Trall.* 2.1; *1 Clem.* 59.1.

[58]*1 Clem.* 63.2. In this passage it is ambiguous whether the phrase διὰ τοῦ ἁγίου πνεύματος ("through the Holy Spirit") modifies the things written or describes the means by which the "wanton anger" in a person is rooted out.

[59]E.g., *Barn.* 14.2; see similar language in Ezek. 37:1; Matt. 22:43; Rev. 1:10.

[60]Allert, *A High View of Scripture?*, 60–65, observes the same ambiguity in this "in the Spirit" language, but seems content to conclude that the apostolic fathers therefore saw no difference between ecclesiastical authority and apostolic authority. However, the fact that the apostolic fathers often make a sharp distinction between these two kinds of authority suggests otherwise; see Frank Thielman, "The New Testament Canon: Its Basis for Authority," *WTJ* 45 (1983): 400–410. There are also numerous examples of apostolic fathers acknowledging the distinctive authority of the apostles. For an example of such references in Ignatius, see Charles E. Hill, "Ignatius and the Apostolate," in *StPatr*, vol. 36, ed. M. F. Wiles and E. J. Yarnold (Leuven: Peeters, 2001), 226–48.

[61]*Didache* 8.2, emphasis mine.

[62]For a helpful treatment of the methodology of identifying citations (a topic we do not have space to address here), see Andrew Gregory and Christopher Tuckett, "Reflections on Method: What Constitutes the Use of the Writings That Later Formed the New Testament in the Apostolic Fathers?," in Gregory and Tuckett, *The Reception of the New Testament in the Apostolic Fathers*, 61–82.

there is some relationship between the *Didache* and Matthew here."[63]
Likewise, Udo Schnelle argues that "the Didache means by 'the gospel'
[*Did.* 8.2; 11.3; 15.3, 4] the Gospel of Matthew."[64] If so, we are continuing
to see evidence of an emerging written canon by the turn of the century
as the apostolic fathers look to Gospel texts like Matthew as authoritative sources for the life of Jesus. By this time it is clear not only that "the
Lord" offers his commands through the Old Testament writings, but that
now his commands are also offered through a new set of writings, one of
which the *Didache* calls a "gospel."

In addition, the manual states, "Do not abandon the commandments of
the Lord [ἐντολὰς κυρίου], but guard [φυλάξεις] what you have received,
neither adding to them [προστιθεὶς] or taking away [ἀφαιρῶν]."[65] It is
obvious that the author is drawing an express parallel to Deuteronomy
4:2 (LXX): "You shall not add [προσθήσετε] to the word that I command
you, nor take from it [ἀφελεῖτε], that you may keep [φυλάσσεσθε] the
commandments of the LORD [ἐντολὰς κυρίου]." Most noteworthy, the
"commandments of the Lord" in this passage of the *Didache* no longer
refer to the Old Testament commandments as in Deuteronomy 4:2, but
now refer to the teachings of Jesus. Therefore, the teachings of Jesus, wher-
ever those may be found, not only bear equal (if not superior) authority to
the Old Testament, but now have a new "inscriptional curse" attached to
them—the people must be careful that they are "neither adding to them
or taking away." Although such an inscriptional curse could be adapted
to preserve oral tradition (as is possibly done by Polycarp and the *Epistle
of Barnabas*),[66] its historical usage from Deuteronomy to Josephus, as

---

[63]Christopher Tuckett, "The *Didache* and the Writings That Later Formed the New Testament,"
in Gregory and Tuckett, *The Reception of the New Testament in the Apostolic Fathers*, 106. In
agreement are F. E. Vokes, "The Didache and the Canon of the New Testament," *SE* 3 (1964):
427–36; and Metzger, *The Canon of the New Testament*, 51 (who is even more confident than
Tuckett). Other scholars disagree, and some have argued either that Matthew is dependent upon
the *Didache* or that they are both dependent upon a common source; see H. Koester, *Synoptische
Überlieferung bei den apostlischen Vätern* (Berlin: Akademie-Verlag, 1957); R. Glover, "The
Didache's Quotations and the Synoptic Gospels" *NTS* 5 (1958): 12–29; J. S. Kloppenborg, "The
Use of the Synoptics or Q in Did. 1.3b–2.1," in *The Didache and Matthew: Two Documents from
the Same Jewish-Christian Milieu?*, ed. H. van de Sandt (Minneapolis: Fortress, 2005), 105–29;
A. Milavec, "Synoptic Tradition in the Didache Revisited," *JECS* 11 (2003): 443–80; and A. J. P.
Garrow, *The Gospel of Matthew's Dependence on the Didache* (London: T&T Clark, 2004).
[64]Udo Schnelle, *The History and Theology of the New Testament Writings* (Minneapolis: Fortress,
1998), 355. In agreement with Schnelle are J. A. Kelhoffer, "'How Soon a Book' Revisited:
ΕΥΑΓΓΕΛΙΟΝ as a Reference to 'Gospel' Materials in the First Half of the Second Century,"
ZNW 95 (2004): 1–34; and C. N. Jefford, *The Sayings of Jesus in the Teaching of the Twelve
Apostles* (Leiden: Brill, 1989), 143.
[65]*Didache* 4.13.
[66]Pol. *Phil.* 7.1; *Barn.* 19.11.

noted in chapter 4 above, implies a *written* text.[67] Given that the *Didache* likely cites from the written text of Matthew, such language is at least suggestive that the manual may have viewed Matthew as an authoritative writing worthy of its own inscriptional curse.

3. Ignatius

Ignatius was the bishop of Antioch at the turn of the century and wrote a number of epistles en route to his martyrdom in Rome in about AD 110.[68] Although there is much in Ignatius worthy of our attention,[69] we will limit our discussion to only a few passages, beginning with his letter to the Ephesians: "Paul, who was sanctified, who gained a good report, who was right blessed, in whose footsteps may I be found when I shall attain to God, who in *every epistle* makes mention of you in Christ Jesus."[70] Most noteworthy here is that Ignatius, writing to the Ephesians, makes reference to multiple letters of Paul. It is not clear exactly which of Paul's letters he is referring to—Paul explicitly mentions the Ephesians in numerous New Testament epistles,[71] or Ignatius may be referring to the way Paul generally addresses the saints in his letters—but it is clear that Ignatius knows, and assumes his readers already know, about some collection of Paul's letters. Although this collection would certainly have included 1 Corinthians, Ephesians, and 1 and 2 Timothy,[72] the fact that Ignatius also appears to know Romans,

---

[67] The influence of inscriptional curses is notable in other Jewish literature; e.g., *Aristeas* 310–11; *1 Enoch* 104:9–10; *1 Macc.* 8:30; Josephus, *Ag. Ap.* 1.42; 11QTemple 54:5–7; *b. Meg.* 14a. David E. Aune, *Revelation 17–22*, WBC (Nashville: Thomas Nelson, 1998), 1208–16, refers to this type of language as an "integrity formula." This formula also occurs regularly among Greco-Roman writers, who use it to bolster confidence in the accuracy of their accounts; e.g., Artemidorus (*Onir.* 2.70), Aristides (*Or.* 30.20), Chariton (*Chaereas and Callirhoe* 3.1.5), Cicero (*De oratore* 3.8.29), Dionysius of Halicarnassus (*Ant. rom.* 5.8), and Lucian (*Hist.* 47). For more, see M. J. Kruger, "Early Christian Attitudes Towards the Reproduction of Texts," in Hill and Kruger, *The Early Text of the New Testament*.

[68] For a helpful introduction to Ignatius and his writings, see Paul Foster, *The Writings of the Apostolic Fathers* (London: T&T Clark, 2007), 81–107 (though he takes a later date for the letters, c. 125–150); and W. R. Schoedel, *Ignatius of Antioch* (Philadelphia: Fortress, 1985).

[69] For the many other possible New Testament connections, see Paul Foster, "The Epistles of Ignatius of Antioch and the Writings That Later Formed the New Testament," in Gregory and Tuckett, *The Reception of the New Testament in the Apostolic Fathers*, 159–86; and W. Inge, "Ignatius," in *The New Testament and the Apostolic Fathers*, 61–83.

[70] Ign. *Eph.* 12.2, emphasis mine.

[71] 1 Cor. 15:32; 16:8; Eph. 1:1 (though ἐν Ἐφέσῳ is omitted in P46, ℵ* and B); 1 Tim. 1:3; 2 Tim. 1:18; 4:12; and possibly Rom. 16:5 (see discussion in J. Lightfoot, *The Apostolic Fathers*, 2 vols. [London: Macmillan, 1889], 2:65–66). For more on the critical and central role of Ephesus in early Christianity, see Paul R. Trebilco, *The Early Christians in Ephesus from Paul to Ignatius* (Tübingen: Mohr Siebeck, 2004); and E. E. Lemcio, "Ephesus and the New Testament Canon," *BJRL* 69 (1986): 210–34.

[72] Foster, "The Epistles of Ignatius of Antioch," 172, suggests that Ignatius only knew the four letters of Paul that expressly mention the Ephesians.

Philippians, and Galatians suggests that his Pauline letter collection might have been quite extensive.[73]

Ignatius also gives indications that he knows of other apostolic writings besides those from Paul. He refers numerous times to the "decrees" (δόγμασιν) and "ordinances" (διαταγμάτων) of the apostles,[74] terms that were often used of *written* texts such as the Old Testament.[75] His use of the plural "apostles" suggests that he is thinking of a larger corpus of writings beyond Paul, perhaps including Peter, John, and others. This finds confirmation in that there are allusions in Ignatius to some of the canonical Gospels, particularly Matthew, Luke, and John.[76] Michael Goulder and Charles Hill argue that Ignatius often uses the term *gospel* not to refer to oral preaching as is so often claimed,[77] but as a reference to the written Gospels.[78] For instance, in *To the Philadelphians* 8.2 Ignatius observes that the Judaizing opposition will not believe a truth found ἐν τῷ εὐαγγελίῳ ("in the gospel") unless they can also find it ἐν τοῖς ἀρχείοις ("in the archives"), the latter being a clear reference to the Old Testament. The parallel structure of this passage, highlighted by the fact that both "gospel" and "archives" are introduced with dative constructions, suggests the possibility that *both* are written sources.[79] If so, then when Ignatius responds to these Judaizers in the very next sentence with the simple, "it is written" (γέγραπται), he would be using this term to refer to the Gospel books, not the Old Testament. Thus, argues Goulder, Ignatius's complaint about the Judaizers is simple: they "refuse to regard the Gospel as Scripture (γέγραπται)" as he does.[80]

---

[73]Others scholars have suggested that Ignatius knew more letters of Paul, but was simply using hyperbole in this particular passage; e.g., Lightfoot, *The Apostolic Fathers*, 2:65–66; Schoedel, *Ignatius of Antioch*, 73. Metzger, *The Canon of the New Testament*, 49, suggests that Ignatius also knew Romans, Philippians, and Galatians.

[74]E.g., Ign. *Magn.* 13.1; Ign. *Trall.* 7.1.

[75]Hill, "Ignatius and the Apostolate," 235–39.

[76]E.g., *Smyrn.* 6.1 (Matt. 19:12); *Smyrn.* 1.1 (Matt. 3:15); *Magn.* 8.2 (John 1:14; 17:16); *Phld.* 7.1 (John 3:8); *Smyrn.* 3.2 (Luke 24:39). For more, see Inge, "Ignatius," 63–83; C. E. Hill, "Ignatius, 'The Gospel,' and the Gospels," in Gregory and Tuckett, *Trajectories Through the New Testament and the Apostolic Fathers*, 267–85; Metzger, *The Canon of the New Testament*, 44–49.

[77]Helmut Koester, *Ancient Christian Gospels: Their History and Development* (London: SCM, 1990), 7–8.

[78]M. D. Goulder, "Ignatius' 'Docetists,'" *VC* 53 (1999): 16–30; Hill, "Ignatius," 271–74.

[79]In addition to this passage, the "gospel" is compared/contrasted or set alongside the Old Testament (or the "prophets") in a number of other passages in Ignatius; e.g., *Smyrn.* 5.1; 7.2; *Phld.* 5.1–2; 9.1–2.

[80]Goulder, "Ignatius," 16; Hill, "Ignatius," 271–74. This text in Ignatius is understood in the same manner by R. Heard, "Papias' Quotations from the New Testament," *NTS* 1 (1954): 133; and F. F. Bruce, "Some Thoughts on the Beginning of the New Testament Canon," *BJRL* 65 (1983): 41. Allert, *A High View of Scripture?*, 111, interacts with none of these works (or the arguments they contain) when he asserts, "Ignatius places authority in the Hebrew Scriptures [but] he fails to locate the same authority in . . . the canonical gospels."

But aside from such passages, there are other ways to ascertain the type of authority Ignatius would attach to apostolic books. Throughout his writings, Ignatius offers repeated and overt references to the absolute and unparalleled authority of the apostles.[81] Hill draws the natural implications from such a fact when he notes that any apostolic texts known by Ignatius would have "held an extremely if not supremely high standing with him."[82] Thus, there is no need for Ignatius explicitly to use the term *Scripture* in reference to Paul's letters or other apostolic writings—his opinion of such texts would already have been clear to the reader.

4. Polycarp

Polycarp, bishop of Smyrna, wrote his epistle to the church at Philippi around AD 110. In this letter he declares, "As it is written in these Scriptures, 'Be angry and do not sin and do not let the sun go down on your anger.'"[83] The first part of this quote could come from Psalm 4:5, but the two parts together appear to come from Ephesians 4:26. While Bruce Metzger suggests that "[Polycarp] calls Ephesians 'Scripture,'"[84] others have offered alternative explanations.[85] In particular, Koester suggests that Polycarp simply made a mistake here and thought (erroneously) that the entire phrase in Ephesians 4:26 came from Psalm 4:4.[86] Thus, argues Koester, Polycarp only meant to use the term *Scripture* to refer to the Old Testament portion. Although this is possible, there is no evidence within the text that Polycarp made such a mistake. On the contrary, Polycarp's knowledge of Paul's writing is well established, and he demonstrated a "very good memory" regarding Pauline citations.[87] Consequently, Boudewijn Dehandschutter considers such a mistake by Polycarp to be "very unlikely" and argues that "the real reason for Köster's reservation seems to be the implications for the history of the Canon."[88] Even McDonald agrees that Polycarp calls both Psalms and Ephesians

---

[81] Hill, "Ignatius and the Apostolate," 226–48.
[82] Ibid., 234.
[83] Pol. *Phil.* 12.1. Latin text: *Modo, ut his scripturis dictum est, irascimini et nolite peccare, et sol non occidat super iracundiam vestram.*
[84] Metzger, *The Canon of the New Testament*, 62.
[85] For a survey of the different options, see Kenneth Berding, *Polycarp and Paul: An Analysis of Their Literary and Theological Relationship in Light of Polycarp's Use of Biblical and Extra-Biblical Literature* (Leiden: Brill, 2002), 204ff.; and Paul Hartog, "Polycarp, Ephesians, and 'Scripture,'" *WTJ* 70 (2008): 255–75.
[86] Koester, *Synoptische Überlieferung*, 113.
[87] Berding, *Polycarp and Paul*, 118.
[88] Boudewijn Dehandschutter, "Polycarp's Epistle to the Philippians: An Early Example of 'Reception,'" in *The New Testament in Early Christianity*, ed. J.-M. Sevrin (Leuven: Leuven University Press, 1989), 282.

"Scripture."[89] Polycarp also alludes to other epistles of Paul, including Romans, 1 Corinthians, Galatians, Philippians, 2 Thessalonians, and 1 and 2 Timothy.[90] There is no reason to think Polycarp would not have acknowledged that these other letters of Paul bear the same authority as Ephesians.[91] Indeed, C. M. Nielsen argues that Polycarp's letter is a strong indication that by the early second century "a sacred Christian Scripture was emerging with the Pauline corpus as its foundation."[92]

In addition to Paul's epistles, Polycarp appears to quote from some of the Synoptic Gospels.[93] However, such possible references to the Gospels prove to be unpersuasive to some scholars, because sometimes Polycarp cites the Gospels more loosely and even combines Gospel citations together.[94] The loose and harmonized wording in these references has led some to argue that they derive from an earlier written or oral source and not from the canonical Gospels themselves.[95] While the possibility of earlier sources must seriously be considered—especially since we know they existed (Luke 1:1)—we should be hesitant to invoke them too quickly. After all, if the wording of a particular citation can be adequately explained on the basis of a *known* text, this is a methodologically preferable option to making conjectures about oral tradition or an *unknown* (and hypothetical) written source. Metzger concurs: "It is generally preferable, in estimating doubtful cases, to regard variation from a canonical text as a free quotation from a document known to us than to suppose it to be a quotation from a hitherto unknown document, or the persistence of primitive tradition."[96]

---

[89]McDonald, *The Biblical Canon*, 276. See also C. M. Nielsen, "Polycarp, Paul, and the Scriptures," *AThR* 47 (1965): 199–216.

[90]Paul Hartog, *Polycarp and the New Testament: The Occasion, Rhetoric, Theme, and Unity of the Epistle to the Philippians and Its Allusions to New Testament Literature* (Tübingen: Mohr Siebeck, 2001), 195; Berding, *Polycarp and Paul*, 187. For further discussion, see M. W. Holmes, "Polycarp's *Letter to the Philippians* and the Writings That Later Formed the New Testament," in Gregory and Tuckett, *The Reception of the New Testament in the Apostolic Fathers*, 187–227.

[91]Polycarp's view of the apostles' authority is clear in *Phil.* 6.3.

[92]Nielsen, "Polycarp, Paul, and the Scriptures," 216.

[93]E.g., *Phil.* 2.3; 7.2. Although Polycarp does not cite John's Gospel directly, C. E. Hill, *The Johannine Corpus in the Early Church* (Oxford: Oxford University Press, 2004), 418–20, makes a compelling case that he knew it. Also, Irenaeus sat under the teaching of Polycarp and indicates that Polycarp knew John personally, making it even more likely that Polycarp would have known about any Gospel that John would have written (Eusebius, *Hist. eccl.* 5.20.4–6).

[94]At the end of *Phil.* 2.3 he combines Luke 6:20 and Matt 5:10.

[95]E.g., Helmut Koester, "Written Gospels or Oral Tradition?" *JBL* 113 (1994): 293–97; Koester, "The Text of the Synoptic Gospels in the Second Century," in *Gospel Traditions in the Second Century: Origins, Recensions, Text, and Transmission*, ed. W. L. Petersen (Notre Dame: University of Notre Dame Press, 1989), 19–37; and W. L. Petersen, "The Genesis of the Gospel," in *New Testament Textual Criticism and Exegesis, Festschrift J. Delobel*, ed. A. Denaux (Leuven: Leuven University Press, 2002), 33–65.

[96]Metzger, *The Canon of the New Testament*, 73n47.

Moreover, it must be remembered that even in situations where a written text was known and highly regarded, it was encountered by most people in the ancient world primarily in *oral* forms (public readings, recitations and retelling of stories, etc.) inasmuch as society was largely nonliterate.[97] Thus, as people would make oral *use* of the Gospel texts, drawing from memory, loose and conflated citations would be a natural occurrence.[98] Such a practice does not suggest that there is no written text behind this activity. Barton comments:

> The often inaccurate quotations in the Fathers, it is argued, show that they were drawing on "synoptic tradition" but not actually on the Synoptic Gospels. Such a theory cannot be ruled out absolutely, but it is not the only or, probably, the best explanation for loose quotation. . . . The explanation is to be found not in oral transmission in the strict sense, but in the oral *use* of texts which were already available in written form.[99]

Irenaeus, who knew the fourfold Gospel intimately, is a good example of such a practice, as he often makes general statements like, "the Lord said," or "the Lord declared," when introducing a Gospel quote, and often conflates and abbreviates citations.[100] Graham Stanton suggests that the pattern in Irenaeus is a "warning sign" to any who might think that a loose citation implies an author is unfamiliar with a given text.[101] Such loose citations were also common in Greco-Roman literature.[102] E. G. Turner notes that the need for exact citations "is a presupposition of scholarship we take for granted, but it was not part of the tradition of classical Greece. Used to the cut and thrust of oral dialectic, the Greeks tended to be careless of exact quotation or copying and of precise chronology, undisturbed by anachronisms."[103]

---

[97]The standard work on literacy in the ancient world is William V. Harris, *Ancient Literacy* (Cambridge, MA: Harvard University Press, 1989). Although Harris is generally accepted among scholars, a helpful supplement can be found in Alan Millard, *Reading and Writing in the Time of Jesus* (New York: New York University Press, 2000).

[98]C. D. Stanley, *Paul and the Language of Scripture: Citation Technique in the Pauline Epistles and Contemporary Literature* (Cambridge: Cambridge University Press, 1992); and C. E. Hill, "'In These Very Words': Methods and Standards of Literary Borrowing in the Second Century," in Hill and Kruger, *The Early Text of the New Testament*.

[99]J. Barton, *The Spirit and the Letter: Studies in the Biblical Canon* (London: SPCK, 1997), 92, emphasis his.

[100]E.g., *Haer.* 3.10.2–3.

[101]Graham Stanton, "The Fourfold Gospel," *NTS* 43 (1997): 321–22.

[102]E.g, John Whittaker, "The Value of Indirect Tradition in the Establishment of Greek Philosophical Texts or the Art of Misquotation," in *Editing Greek and Latin Texts: Papers Given at the Twenty-Third Annual Conference on Editorial Problems, University of Toronto 6–7 November 1987*, ed. John Grant (New York: AMS, 1989), 63–95.

[103]E. G. Turner, *Greek Papyri: An Introduction* (Oxford: Clarendon, 1968), 106–7.

With these considerations in mind, Polycarp provides a noteworthy confirmation of the trend we have been observing all along. By an early point—in this case around AD 110—New Testament books were not only called but were also functioning as authoritative Scripture. Given Polycarp's connections to the apostle John, his friendship with Papias, and his instruction of Irenaeus, it is reasonable to think that his beliefs concerning the canon of Scripture would be fairly widespread by this time.

5. The Epistle of Barnabas

The *Epistle of Barnabas*, a theological treatise written in the early second century (c. AD 130), proved to be quite popular with early Christians.[104] At one point it states, ὡς γέγραπται πολλοὶ κλητοί ὀλίγοι δὲ ἐκλεκτοὶ εὑρεθῶμεν ("As it is written, 'Many are called, but few are chosen.'")[105] This citation finds its only parallel in Matthew 22:14, in nearly identical Greek, leading Wolf-Dietrich Köhler and Carleton Paget to suggest that Matthew is the most likely source.[106] Although some have suggested that *Barnabas* is pulling from oral tradition, this option does not fully account for the word γέγραπται ("it is written"). While the possibility that Barnabas is drawing upon another written Gospel source certainly cannot be ruled out, there is again no need, methodologically speaking, to insist on hypothetical sources when a known source can adequately account for the data. Carleton Paget comments:

> But in spite of all these arguments, it still remains the case that the closest existing text to *Barn* 4.14 in all known literature is Matt 22.14, and one senses that attempts to argue for independence from Matthew are partly motivated by a desire to avoid the implications of the *formula citandi* ["it is written"] which introduces the relevant words: namely, that the author of *Barnabas* regarded Matthew as scriptural.[107]

If *Barnabas* is citing from the Gospel of Matthew with the phrase "it is written" (γέγραπται)—which was normally reserved for Old Testament passages—it is clear that Barnabas was not, in principle, opposed to or

---

[104]For a broad overview, see J. Carleton Paget, *The Epistle of Barnabas: Outlook and Background* (Tübingen: Mohr Siebeck, 1994).

[105]*Barn.* 4.14, trans. Roberts and Donaldson, *The Ante-Nicene Fathers*, vol. 1.

[106]W.-D. Köhler, *Die Rezeption des Matthäusevangeliums in der Zeit vor Irenäus* (Tübingen: Mohr, 1987), 113; James Carleton Paget, "The *Epistle of Barnabas* and the Writings That Later Formed the New Testament," in Gregory and Tuckett, *The Reception of the New Testament in the Apostolic Fathers*, 229–49.

[107]Carleton Paget, "The *Epistle of Barnabas*," 233.

unfamiliar with the idea that a written New Testament text could be considered Scripture on par with the Old.[108]

6. Papias

One of the most intriguing figures during the time of the apostolic fathers is Papias, bishop of Hierapolis, who, according to Irenaeus, was known to have been a friend of Polycarp and who had heard the apostle John preach.[109] Most noteworthy for our purposes here is the information Papias provides about the Gospels: "The Elder used to say: Mark became Peter's interpreter and wrote accurately all that he remembered. . . . Matthew collected the oracles [τὰ λόγια] in the Hebrew language ['Εβραΐδι διαλέκτῳ], and each interpreted them as best he could."[110] Although Papias is writing around AD 125 (which is quite early),[111] the time period to which he is referring is actually *earlier*, namely, AD 90–100, when "the Elder" would have shared these traditions with him.[112] There is little doubt that the "Elder" whom Papias has in mind is the "John the Elder" he discusses elsewhere, who was a disciple and eyewitness of Jesus himself.[113] Of course, the identity of this particular John is much-disputed in modern scholarship with some scholars suggesting that it was not the apostle John, the son of

---

[108]The fact that *Barnabas* cites other literature outside the Old and New Testaments as "Scripture" (e.g., 16.5 cites *1 Enoch* 89 with "For Scripture says") is beside the point being made here for two reasons: (1) The question is not whether there was agreement among early Christians on the extent of "Scripture," but simply whether early Christians understood that new scriptural books had been given under the administration of the new covenant. Disagreements over which books does not change this fact, contra Allert, *A High View of Scripture?*, 88. He is confusing the *existence* of canon, with the *extent* of canon (owing to his commitment to Sundberg's exclusive definition). (2) Although early Patristic writers do occasionally cite sources outside our current canon, it must be acknowledged that the vast majority of books they regard as "Scripture" are ones that are inside our current canon. Thus, one must be careful not to overplay the citations from noncanonical books as if they are the norm or majority. There still seems to be an agreed-upon core, though there is disagreement about the borders in various places. It is misleading to use the occasional citation of noncanonical books as grounds for denying that there is any canonical consciousness at all.

[109]Irenaeus, *Haer.* 5.33.4. For discussion of Papias as a source, see S. Byrskog, *Story as History—History as Story: The Gospel Tradition in the Context of Ancient Oral History* (Leiden: Brill, 2002), 272–92; R. H. Gundry, *Matthew: A Commentary on His Handbook for a Mixed Church under Persecution*, 2nd ed. (Grand Rapids: Eerdmans, 1994), 609–22; T. K. Heckel, *Vom Evangelium des Markus zum viergestaltigen Evangelium* (Tübingen: Mohr, 1999), 219–22; W. D. Davies and D. C. Allison, *The Gospel According to Saint Matthew*, ICC (Edinburgh: T&T Clark, 1997), 7–17; and M. Hengel, *Studies in the Gospel of Mark* (London: SCM, 1985), 47–53.

[110]Eusebius, *Hist. eccl.* 3.39.15–16.

[111]Some have argued for an even earlier date, around 110; see V. Bartlet, "Papias's 'Exposition': Its Date and Contents," in *Amicitiae Corolla* (London: University of London Press, 1933), 16–22; R. W. Yarbrough, "The Date of Papias: A Reassessment," *JETS* 26 (1983): 181–91.

[112]R. Bauckham, *Jesus and the Eyewitnesses: The Gospels as Eyewitness Testimony* (Grand Rapids: Eerdmans, 2006), 202–39.

[113]Eusebius, *Hist. eccl.* 3.39.3–4.

Zebedee, but a different John, who was also a disciple of Jesus (and the author of the Johannine Epistles and the Gospel of John).[114] Others have suggested that when Papias mentions "John the Elder," he is simply referring to the apostle because he explicitly lists the apostle John as one of the "elders" within the same passage.[115] This option finds support in Irenaeus's acknowledgment that Papias heard from the apostle John in person.[116] Regardless of which option one takes, it is clear that Papias received his information about the Gospels from a very reliable eyewitness source. Thus, the testimony of Papias allows us to go back to one of the most crucial junctures in the history of the canon, the end of the first century.

This early testimony from Papias indicates that Mark's Gospel was received as authoritative on the basis of its connections with the apostle Peter—a very old tradition that is widespread throughout early Christianity.[117] This fits well with the observation made in the prior chapter that Mark's Gospel forms an impressive literary *inclusio* centered on the person of Peter. If Papias receives Mark's Gospel on the basis of its apostolic (and eyewitness) connections, no doubt this is the reason he also receives the Gospel of Matthew.[118] The statement that Matthew originally wrote in the Hebrew language is a baffling one, given that the

---

[114]M. Hengel, *The Four Gospels and the One Gospel of Jesus Christ* (Harrisburg, PA: Trinity, 2000), 67–68; Hengel, *Die johanneische Frage: Ein Lösungsversuch* (Tübingen: Mohr, 1993), esp. 210–19; and Bauckham, *Jesus and the Eyewitnesses*, 412–37. Of course, it is possible to believe Papias's "Elder" is not the apostle John while still affirming that the apostle John wrote the Gospel, the epistles, and the book of Revelation.

[115]Eusebius, *Hist. eccl.* 3.39.3–4; cf. 1 Pet. 5:1; Gundry, *Matthew*, 611–12; D. A. Carson, *The Gospel According to John* (Grand Rapids: Eerdmans, 1991), 69–70; C. S. Keener, *The Gospel of John* (Peabody, MA: Hendrickson, 2003), 95–98; and, more extensively, John Chapman, *John the Presbyter and the Fourth Gospel* (Oxford: Clarendon, 1911). Bauckham avoids this problem by suggesting a unique translation of Papias's statement where Papias does not refer to the apostles as "elders" (*Jesus and the Eyewitnesses*, 16). For a critique of this translational option, see Gundry, *Matthew*, 611–12.

[116]Irenaeus, *Haer.* 5.33.4. Irenaeus also confirms that Polycarp, a friend of Papias, heard the apostle John (as recorded in Eusebius, *Hist. eccl.* 5.20.6), and Polycarp himself spoke of "the apostles who proclaimed the gospel to us" (*Phil.* 6.3). Thus, it is not difficult to see how Papias, a companion of Polycarp, would have heard directly from the apostle John. Although Eusebius also acknowledges that Papias heard from "John," he takes this as a reference to John the disciple and not the apostle (*Hist. eccl.* 3.39.5–6). Gundry argues that Eusebius makes a mistake here as a result of his dislike of the book of Revelation and his desire to assign it to a John other than the apostle (*Matthew*, 612–14).

[117]E.g., Justin, *Dial.* 106; and Irenaeus, *Haer.* 3.10.5; Tertullian, *Marc.* 4.5; Eusebius, *Hist. eccl.* 2.15; 6.14.6 (attributed to Clement of Alexandria); for more on this point, see E. Kalin, "Early Traditions About Mark's Gospel: Canonical Status Emerges as the Story Grows," *CurTM* 2 (1975): 332–41.

[118]Papias's preference for eyewitness testimony (including Matthew's) is evident elsewhere (Eusebius, *Hist. eccl.* 3.39.4).

Greek Matthew we possess gives no indication that it was translated from Hebrew (or Aramaic).[119] However, whether one takes the statement to indicate that Matthew just wrote in a Hebraic *style*[120] or that Papias was simply confused on this particular point,[121] there is little reason to think that Papias is referring to something entirely different from the Gospel of Matthew known widely in the early church—especially given the reliability of his source.[122] As for the Gospel of John, the fact that Papias sat under John's preaching and knew both 1 John and Revelation makes it probable that he knew and used the Gospel.[123] This probability is increased to near certainty when we recognize that the list of disciples given by Papias matches the order in which they appear in John's Gospel.[124] Thus, Bauckham declares, "There should be no doubt that Papias knew John's gospel."[125] There are also good reasons to think that Papias knew Luke since Andrew of Caesarea, in his commentary on Revelation, tells

[119]Josef Kürzinger, *Papias von Hierapolis und die Evangelien des Neuen Testaments* (Regensburg: Pustet, 1983), 9–32; A. F. J. Klijn, *Jewish-Christian Gospel Tradition* (Leiden: Brill, 1992), 11. However, some have proposed the theory that there was an early form of Matthew in Hebrew (a proto-Matthew) that was later expanded into our current Greek Matthew; see Malcolm Lowe and David Flusser, "Evidence Corroborating a Modified Proto-Matthean Synoptic Theory," *NTS* 29 (1983): 25–47.

[120]Kürzinger, *Papias von Hierapolis*; Gundry, *Matthew*, 619–20.

[121]Given that it was well known that Matthew was the most Jewish Gospel, and given that there was an early tradition of Aramaic/Hebrew gospels somehow connected to Matthew (e.g., the *Gospel of the Hebrews*), it is not difficult to imagine Papias getting confused on this specific point. Confusion on this point, however, would not necessitate that Papias is confused at other points; see R. T. France, *Matthew: Evangelist and Teacher* (Grand Rapids: Zondervan, 1989), 64–66. For an introduction to the history and complexities of the Jewish-Christian gospels, see Klijn, *Jewish-Christian Gospel Tradition*, 3–43; and P. Vielhauer and G. Strecker, "Jewish-Christian Gospels," in *New Testament Apocrypha*, ed. W. Schneemelcher, trans. R. McL. Wilson, 2 vols. (Louisville: Westminster John Knox, 1991), 1:134–78.

[122]For the widespread popularity of Matthew in early Christianity see É. Massaux, *Influence de L'Évangile de Saint Matthieu sur la littérature chrétienne avant Saint Irénée* (Leuven: Leuven University Press, 1986); and Köhler, *Die Rezeption des Matthäusevangeliums in der Zeit vor Irenäus*. Some have suggested τὰ λόγια is a reference to an Aramaic sayings source like Q; e.g., J. Nolland, *The Gospel of Matthew: A Commentary on the Greek Text*, NIGTC (Grand Rapids: Eerdmans, 2005), 3; T. W. Manson, "The Gospel of St. Matthew," in *Studies in the Gospels and Epistles*, ed. M. Black (Edinburgh: T&T Clark, 1962), 68–104; and Matthew Black, "The Use of Rhetorical Terminology in Papias on Mark and Matthew," *JSNT* 37 (1989): 31–41. However, the same root word is used by Papias to describe Mark's Gospel (λογίων), and we have no reason to think that it was anything other than canonical Mark (it is clearly not just a sayings source because it included "things said or done by the Lord"; Eusebius, *Hist. eccl.* 3.39.15). For more on this point, see France, *Matthew*, 58–60.

[123]Eusebius, *Hist. eccl.* 3.39.17; Andrew of Caesarea, *On the Apocalypse* 34.12; Hill, *The Johannine Corpus*, 385–96.

[124]Eusebius, *Hist. eccl.* 3.39.3–4. The so-called anti-Marcionite prologues describe Papias as a disciple of John and even the amanuensis of John's Gospel. While these connections are consistent with the other evidence we have seen, the date and reliability of these prologues are too uncertain to put much weight on them.

[125]Bauckham, *Jesus and the Eyewitnesses*, 225.

us that Papias declared, "I saw Satan fallen from heaven"—a saying of Jesus found only in Luke 10:18.[126] If so, then the evidence from Papias is suggestive of a fourfold Gospel in the first half of the second century (maybe as early as c. AD 125).[127]

Some have argued, however, that Papias still preferred oral tradition over written texts, thus showing he did not consider Matthew, Mark, or the other Gospels to bear any real authority. This argument is based on Papias's statement, "I did not suppose that information from books would help me so much as the word of the living and surviving voice."[128] However, not only would such an interpretation be out of sync with the trends in the early second century that we have already observed in this chapter, but, as Bauckham has shown, it misses what Papias is really trying to say. Papias is not addressing *oral tradition* at all but is simply noting a truth that was commonplace in the ancient world at this time: historical investigations are best done when one has access to an actual eyewitness (i.e., a *living* voice). Bauckham explains, "Against a historiographic background, what Papias thinks preferable to books is not oral tradition but access, while they are still alive, to those who were direct participants in the historical events—in this case 'disciples of the Lord.'"[129]

As the evidence of Papias is assessed, it must be remembered that he was an influential bishop who can be connected directly to Polycarp, appears to have known the apostle John, and was a noteworthy influence in the writings of Irenaeus, Eusebius, and many others. It is reasonable to

---

[126]Translation from C. E. Hill, *Who Chose the Gospels? Probing the Great Gospel Conspiracy* (Oxford: Oxford University Press, 2010), 214. For more on Papias's knowledge of Luke, see Hill, "What Papias Said about John (and Luke)," 625–29. D. Farkasfalvy, "The Papias Fragments on Mark and Matthew and Their Relationship to Luke's Prologue: An Essay on the Pre-History of the Synoptic Problem," in *The Early Church in Its Context: Essays in Honor of Everett Ferguson*, ed. A. J. Malherbe, F. W. Norris, and J. W. Thompson (Leiden: Brill, 1998), 92–106, argues that Papias's source, the Elder, knew Luke's prologue and thus Luke's Gospel. This suggests that Papias too would likely have known the Gospel of Luke.

[127]A date for the fourfold Gospel in the first half of the second century is also affirmed by C. B. Amphoux, "La finale longue de Marc: Un épilogue des quatre évangiles," in *The Synoptic Gospels: Source Criticism and the New Literary Criticism*, ed. Camille Focant (Leuven: Leuven University Press, 1993), 548–55 (early second century); T. C. Skeat, "The Origin of the Christian Codex," *ZPE* 102 (1994): 263–68 (early second century); Stanton, "The Fourfold Gospel," 317–46 (c. AD 150); and James A. Kelhoffer, *Miracle and Mission: The Authentication of Missionaries and Their Message in the Longer Ending of Mark* (Tübingen: Mohr Siebeck, 2000). Older works include Theodor Zahn, *Geschichte des neutestamentlichen Kanons* (Erlangen: Deichert, 1888–1892); Adolf von Harnack, *Origin of the New Testament and the Most Important Consequences of a New Creation* (London: Williams and Northgate, 1925), 68–83; and Edgar J. Goodspeed, *The Formation of the New Testament* (Chicago: University of Chicago Press, 1926), 33–41.

[128]Eusebius, *Hist. eccl.* 3.39.4.

[129]Bauckham, *Jesus and the Eyewitnesses*, 24.

think, therefore, that his reception of Mark and Matthew (not to mention Revelation, 1 John, 1 Peter,[130] and possibly John, Luke, and some Pauline epistles[131]) would not have been an isolated event but part of a larger trend within early Christianity—such a trend that has been borne out by all the evidence we have seen thus far.

7. The Use of New Testament Writings

This brief tour through the writings of the apostolic fathers has focused primarily upon instances where New Testament writings are explicitly cited as "Scripture" or regarded as substantially authoritative by early Christians. However, explicit Patristic statements regarding a book's authority do not tell the whole story. In John Barton's recent study on the canon, he appeals to the work of the Austrian statistician Franz Stuhlhofer, who argues that the degree to which books were *used*, and not just how they were cited, reveals even more about their standing in early Christian communities.[132] When it comes to *how often* books were cited, proportional to their size, it quickly becomes clear that the "core" books of the New Testament, mainly the four Gospels and Paul's epistles, stood out from all the others and were the authoritative source for Christians "astonishingly early."[133] Indeed, the apostolic fathers employed the New Testament writings with much greater frequency than the Old Testament writings—from five to fifty times more often.[134] Thus, functionally speaking, the New Testament was certainly as authoritative as the Old Testament, if not more so. On this basis, Barton concludes that it would be "mistaken to say that [by the early second century] 'there was no Christian Scripture other than the Old Testament' for much of the core already had as high a status as it would ever have."[135]

The unique status of these New Testament books becomes more apparent when they are contrasted to apocryphal and noncanonical writings. Barton observes, "Citations of apocryphal gospels and of other books that were later excluded from the canon *do not begin to compete* with the frequency of citation of the basic core."[136] Although the other New

---

[130]Eusebius, *Hist. eccl.* 3.39.17
[131]Heard, "Papias' Quotations from the New Testament," 130–34, argues that Papias likely used a number of Paul's epistles (particularly 1 and 2 Corinthians).
[132]Barton, *The Spirit and the Letter*, 14–24; Franz Stuhlhofer, *Der Gebrauch der Bibel von Jesus bis Euseb: Eine statistische Untersuchung zur Kanonsgeschichte* (Wuppertal: Brockhaus, 1988).
[133]Barton, *The Spirit and the Letter*, 18.
[134]Ibid. The statistical variance depends on the particular author and the inevitable disagreements about what "counts" as a New Testament citation.
[135]Barton, *The Spirit and the Letter*, 19.
[136]Ibid., emphasis mine.

Testament books (e.g., some of the General Epistles, Revelation) were not cited as often as the core books, they still were used quite often when compared to the apocryphal or noncanonical books, which were "scarcely cited at all."[137] Thus, there appears to be three categories of books in the earliest stages: (1) core New Testament books (cited very frequently), (2) peripheral New Testament books (cited less frequently), and (3) apocryphal/noncanonical books (cited hardly at all).

C. Other Second-Century Sources

Up to this point in our discussion, the historical sources have indicated that by the early second-century Christians already had a conception of a bi-covenantal canon—that apostolic documents stand alongside the Old Testament books as the next stage of God's revelation. Some of these books were even being read publicly in worship. Moreover, by this time, a substantial collection of Paul's letters (exactly how many is unclear), the four canonical Gospels, and a number of other books (Hebrews, 1 John, Revelation, etc.) were functioning as authoritative documents for early Christian communities. As we now move out of the apostolic fathers and further into the second century, we encounter a number of other important sources for tracing the emergence of the New Testament canon.

1. Justin Martyr

As one of the great early Christian apologists, Justin Martyr wrote various works—primarily c. 150–160—offering a vigorous defense of the Christian faith.[138] He regularly refers to the canonical Gospels as the "memoirs of the apostles" (ἀπομνημονεύματα τῶν ἀποστόλων).[139] Although he does not mention them by name, he does call them "gospels"[140] and at one point he describes the memoirs as "drawn up by His apostles and

---

[137]Ibid., 17.

[138]For a helpful overview of Justin, see Sara Parvis and Paul Foster, eds., *Justin Martyr and His Worlds* (Minneapolis: Fortress, 2007).

[139]H. Koester, "From the Kerygma Gospel to the Written Gospels," *NTS* 35 (1989): 361–81. The term ἀπομνημονεύματα ("memoirs") was used in classical literature, such as Xenophon's *Memorabilia* concerning Socrates. Dibelius understood the use of this word as an apologetic by Justin to ensure that the Gospels "would be classified as literature proper" (M. Dibelius, *From Tradition to Gospel* [Cambridge: Clarke, 1971], 40). It is also likely that Justin is drawing upon a similar tradition in Papias (Eusebius, *Hist. eccl.* 3.39.15) where he refers to Mark writing down what he "remembered" (ἐμνημόνευσεν). For more on this point, see R. Heard, "The ΑΠΟΜΝΗΜΟΝΕΥΜΑΤΑ in Papias, Justin, and Irenaeus," *NTS* 1 (1954): 122–33.

[140]*1 Apol.* 66.3. The fact that Justin does not explicitly name the Gospels is likely due to the apologetic context in which he writes. Unbelieving Jews and Gentiles would not have had an interest in such names. For more, see J. B. Lightfoot, *Essays on the Work Entitled Supernatural Religion* (London: Macmillan, 1889), 33.

those who followed them,"[141] suggesting that he is referring to the four
canonical Gospels, two penned directly by apostles and two by apostolic
companions.[142] This finds confirmation in the fact that he cites from all
three Synoptic Gospels[143] and even refers to Mark's Gospel as "[Peter's]
Memoirs,"[144] showing that he was familiar with the tradition linking Peter
and Mark.[145] There are good reasons to think that Justin knew the Gospel
of John, given that he knew more than one Gospel penned by an apostle,
knew the book of Revelation and regarded it as written by the apostle
John,[146] lived in John's former residence of Ephesus during his dialogue with
Trypho,[147] appears to be quite familiar with Johannine terminology like
"logos,"[148] and even seems to cite the Gospel of John directly: "For Christ
also said, 'Except ye be born again, ye shall not enter into the kingdom of
heaven.'"[149] Consequently, Stanton suggests that Justin "may well have
possessed a four-gospel codex in the library of his catechetical school."[150]

Some have disputed Justin's knowledge (or use) of the canonical Gospels
because Justin's Gospel citations often differ from the Synoptics' and look
like a harmonized version of Matthew and Luke.[151] William Petersen argues
that the nature of these citations suggests that Justin was not drawing
upon our canonical Gospels at all but rather a harmonized gospel he had

---

[141]*Dial.* 103.

[142]Stanton, "The Fourfold Gospel," 317–46.

[143]E.g., *Dial.* 100.1; 103.8; 106.3–4. Koester, *Ancient Christian Gospels*, 38, declares that
the citations in Justin "derive from written gospels, usually from Matthew and Luke, in one
instance from Mark."

[144]*Dial.* 106.

[145]Eusebius, *Hist. eccl.* 3.39.15–16.

[146]*Dial.* 81.4.

[147]Eusebius, *Hist. eccl.* 4.18.6.

[148]*1 Apol.* 46.2; cf. *Dial.* 88.7.

[149]*1 Apol.* 61.4; further argument for Papias's reception of John can be found in C. E. Hill, "Was
John's Gospel among Justin's Apostolic Memoirs?," in Parvis and Foster, *Justin Martyr and His
Worlds*, 88–94. Others argued that Papias knew John but did not regard it as authoritative; e.g.,
J. W. Pryor, "Justin Martyr and the Fourth Gospel," *SecCent* 9 (1992): 153–67; and L. W. Barnard,
Justin Martyr (Cambridge: Cambridge University Press, 1967). Koester, *Ancient Christian
Gospels*, 246, argues that Justin had no knowledge of John at all.

[150]Stanton, "The Fourfold Gospel," 332.

[151]E.g., Wilhelm Bousset, *Die Evangeliencitate Justins des Märtyrers in ihrem wert für die
Evangelienkritik* (Göttingen: Vandenhoeck & Ruprecht, 1891), 114–16, argued that Justin
was using traditions earlier than the Synoptics; A. Hilgenfeld, *Kritische Untersuchungen über
die Evangelien Justin's, der clementinischen Homilien und Marcion's* (Halle: Schwetschke, 1850),
101–304, argues that Justin is dependent on an apocryphal gospel; D. A. Hagner, "The Sayings
of Jesus in the Apostolic Fathers and Justin Martyr," in Wenham, *Gospel Perspectives*, 233–68,
argues that Justin is more dependent on oral tradition. For an argument that Justin was using
Matthew, see É. Massaux, "Le texte du Sermon sur la Montagne de Matthieu utilisé par Saint
Justin," *ETL* 28 (1952): 411–48.

created, which was a later influence on his student Tatian.[152] Koester even
argues that this harmonization was a "new" gospel created by Justin
and was designed to replace all the other Gospels that had been created
up to that point.[153] Often overlooked in these arguments, however, is the
way ancient authors made frequent use of "extracts" or testimony books
that contained excerpts from a particular writing.[154] These testimony
books would often be used for catechetical instruction and would help
overcome the impracticality of an author having always to check his
source. As these testimony books were constructed, the author would
inevitably interact with, reshape, and harmonize the various portions of
the text he was copying.[155] Stanton suggests that many of Justin's Gospel
citations were drawn from such a testimony book that already contained
conflated quotes from the Gospel accounts.[156] If so, there is no reason to
think that Justin was unaware of the canonical Gospels or knew them in
a substantially different textual form.[157]

Most noteworthy for our purposes here is the degree of authority
Justin attributed to these "memoirs." As noted above, these memoirs
were read alongside the Old Testament prophets in Sunday worship, a

---

[152]W. L. Petersen, "Textual Evidence of Tatian's Dependence upon Justin's ΑΠΟΜΝΗΜΟΝΕΥΜΑΤΑ,"
NTS 36 (1990): 512–34. For more on Petersen's approach to Justin's text, see Petersen, "What
Text Can New Testament Textual Criticism Ultimately Reach?," in New Testament Textual
Criticism, Exegesis, and Early Church History: A Discussion of Methods, ed. B. Aland and
J. Delobel (Kampen: Kok Pharos, 1994), 136–52; in response to Petersen is J. Verheyden,
"Assessing Gospel Quotations in Justin Martyr," in Denaux, New Testament Textual Criticism
and Exegesis, Festschrift J. Delobel, 361–78.

[153]Koester, "The Text of the Synoptic Gospels in the Second Century," 28–33.

[154]E.g., Pliny the Younger, Ep. 3.5; Eusebius, Hist. eccl. 4.26.12; Clement of Alexandria, Exc. The
most thorough analysis of Justin's extracts from the Gospels is A. J. Bellinzoni, The Sayings of
Jesus in the Writings of Justin Martyr (Leiden: Brill, 1967). See also Leslie L. Kline, "Harmonized
Sayings of Jesus in the Pseudo-Clementine Homilies and Justin Martyr," ZNW 66 (1975):
223–41. For more on how such testimonia books were used for collecting excerpts from the
Old Testament, see J. R. Harris, Testimonies (Cambridge: Cambridge University Press, 1916);
J. A. Fitzmyer, "'4Q Testimonia' and the New Testament," TS 18 (1957): 513–37; and, more
recently, Martin C. Albl, And Scripture Cannot Be Broken: The Form and Function of the Early
Christian Testimonia Collections (Leiden: Brill, 1999).

[155]Whittaker, "The Value of Indirect Tradition," 86–90; B. M. Metzger, "Patristic Evidence
and the Textual Criticism of the New Testament," in New Testament Studies: Philological,
Versional, and Patristic (Leiden: Brill, 1980), 167–88, esp. 186. As an example, see Clement of
Alexandria's Excerpts from Theodotus.

[156]G. N. Stanton, "Jesus Traditions and Gospels in Justin Martyr and Irenaeus," in The Biblical
Canons, ed. J.-M. Auwers and H. J. de Jonge (Leuven: Leuven University Press, 2003), 364–65;
a similar position is held by O. Skarsaune, "Justin and His Bible," in Parvis and Foster, Justin
Martyr and His Worlds, 66–67.

[157]Even though many of Justin's Gospel citations are in a harmonized form, these most often
occur in the Apology. By contrast, there are numerous Gospel citations in the Dialogue that
seem to be drawn directly from the canonical Gospels (esp. 97–107).

practice that showed their full scriptural authority.[158] Just as the Spirit of God spoke through Moses and the prophets,[159] so Justin believes that Christ speaks authoritatively through his apostles.[160] Moreover, when drawing upon the Gospels, Justin sometimes uses "it is written," the *formula citandi* for introducing scriptural books.[161] As for other New Testament books, Justin must have known of Paul's letters (given his interactions with Marcion), though he uses them little;[162] he also shows knowledge of Acts, 1 Peter, Hebrews, and the book of Revelation.[163] As for Revelation, he affirms its apostolic character[164] and even refers to it as one of "our writings."[165] Justin, then, continues the trend we have already witnessed in the discussion above, namely, that a number of New Testament books were received as authoritative relatively early, and this was often due to their apostolic connections.

2. Irenaeus

One of the most influential voices in the early church was Irenaeus, bishop of Lyons and disciple of Polycarp.[166] Writing soon after Justin Martyr (c. 170–180), Irenaeus quotes New Testament books extensively, even more than the Old Testament, and clearly regards them as "Scripture."[167] These include the four Gospels, Acts, the entire Pauline corpus (minus Philemon), Hebrews, James, 1 Peter, 1 and 2 John, and Revelation—over one thousand New Testament passages in total.[168] There is no indication that he rejects the unmentioned New Testament books

---

[158]*1 Apol.* 67.3. Of course, we have early records of other writings being read publicly; e.g., Dionysius of Corinth tells of *1 Clement* and letters from Bishop Soter being read (Eusebius, *Hist. eccl.* 4.23.11). But these are clearly instances of correspondence between churches, and there is no indication from Dionysius that they were read *alongside* the Old Testament or were the basis of the preacher's exhortations—as was the case with the memoirs to which Justin refers.

[159]*1 Apol.* 31.1.

[160]*1 Apol.* 42.4; *Dial.* 114.4; 119.6.

[161]E.g., *Dial.* 100.1.

[162]Skarsaune, "Justin and His Bible," 74, 187n95, argues that Justin shows "extensive" use of Romans and Galatians, as well as Ephesians; see also Lindemann, *Paulus im ältesten Christentum*, 353–67. For more on why Justin did not use Paul more often, see C. E. Hill, "Justin and the New Testament Writings," in *StPatr*, vol. 30, ed. E. A. Livingstone (Leuven: Peeters, 1997), 42–48.

[163]Eric Francis Osborn, *Justin Martyr* (Tübingen: Mohr Siebeck, 1973), 135.

[164]*Dial.* 81.4.

[165]*1 Apol.* 28.1.

[166]*Haer.* 3.3.4; 3.4.4; Eusebius, *Hist. eccl.* 5.20.4–8. It is clear that Irenaeus had more than a mere acquaintance with Polycarp, but regularly sat under his teaching; see discussion in Hill, *The Johannine Corpus*, 351–59. A general introduction to Irenaeus can be found in Robert M. Grant, *Irenaeus of Lyons* (London: Routledge, 1997).

[167]E.g., *Haer.* 1.3.6; 2.27.2; 3.11.8; 3.12.12; 3.12.9; 5.5.2. See discussion in Graham Stanton, *Jesus and Gospel* (Cambridge: Cambridge University Press, 2004), 105–6; and Metzger, *The Canon of the New Testament*, 154–55.

[168]Irenaeus may also have considered the *Shepherd of Hermas* to be Scripture (*Haer.* 4.20.2), but apocryphal books will be discussed in chap. 8, below.

(2 Peter, 3 John, and Jude); the extant writings of Irenaeus simply do not
refer to them. By the time of Irenaeus, the four Gospels have become so
certain that he can declare them built into the very structure of creation:
"It is not possible that the gospels can be either more or fewer than the
number they are. For, since there are four zones of the world in which
we live and four principle winds."[169]

Irenaeus's very clear affirmation of these New Testament books, particularly the four Gospels, has led a number of scholars to suggest that
his position was an innovation designed to bolster the church's defenses
against Marcion (and other heretics).[170] However, Irenaeus's defense of
the fourfold Gospel—though all may not be persuaded by its theological
rationale—appears to draw upon tradition that has been entrenched
within the church for quite some time.[171] Indeed, T. C. Skeat argues that
Irenaeus's material (in *Haer.* 3.11.8) was "taken by him from an earlier source."[172] Likewise, Stanton suggests that Irenaeus "is not making
a case for a recent innovation, but underpinning what he and others
had long accepted, i.e., that the church had been given one Gospel in
fourfold form—four authoritative writings, no more, no less."[173] Given
that Irenaeus appears to have known Justin's works (and maybe Justin
himself),[174] and certainly knew Polycarp, it is possible that he received
this tradition from them.[175] That the fourfold Gospel collection predates
Irenaeus finds confirmation in a number of recent studies—by Hengel,
Heckel, Kelhoffer, and others—that have argued that the fourfold Gospel
was established by the early or middle second century.[176]

---

[169] *Haer.* 3.11.8.

[170] McDonald, *The Biblical Canon*, 290–91. Similar ideas can be found in Koester, *History and Literature of Early Christianity*, 10; Campenhausen, *The Formation of the Christian Bible*, 182–86, 199; H. Y. Gamble, *The New Testament Canon: Its Making and Meaning* (Philadelphia: Fortress, 1985), 31–32; G. M. Hahneman, *The Muratorian Fragment and the Development of the Canon* (Oxford: Clarendon, 1992), 101; and Pagels, *Beyond Belief*, 111–12.

[171] Claus-Jürgen Thornton, *Der Zeuge des Zeugen: Lukas als Historiker der Paulusreisen* (Tübingen: Mohr Siebeck, 1991), 10–54; Hill, *Who Chose the Gospels?*, 34–51; and Hengel, *The Four Gospels*, 34–38.

[172] T. C. Skeat, "Irenaeus and the Four-Gospel Canon," *NovT* 34 (1992): 198.

[173] Stanton, "Jesus Traditions and Gospels in Justin Martyr and Irenaeus," 105. See also the discussion of Irenaeus's fourfold Gospel in Ronald A. Piper, "The One, the Four, and the Many," in *The Written Gospel*, ed. Markus Bockmuehl and Donald A. Hagner (Cambridge: Cambridge University Press, 2005), 254–73.

[174] E.g., D. Jeffrey Bingham, *Irenaeus' Use of Matthew's Gospel in Adversus Haereses* (Leuven: Peeters, 1998), 27–32.

[175] Irenaeus also affirms that Polycarp knew Papias (*Haer.* 5.33.4), which suggests that he may also be a source of this fourfold Gospel tradition. The possibility of such connections is increased by the fact that Irenaeus reaffirms the same tradition affirmed by Papias and Justin, namely, that Mark's Gospel came from the teachings of Peter (*Haer.* 3.1.1).

[176] See n. 121 above. Of course, some have objected to the establishment of the fourfold Gospel during this time on the grounds that the church fathers continued to cite oral tradition or

3. Muratorian Fragment

Our earliest canonical list comes from the Muratorian fragment toward the end of the second century (c. 180).[177] The list affirms the scriptural status of twenty-two of the twenty-seven New Testament books, including all four Gospels, Acts, the thirteen epistles of Paul, 1 and 2 John (and possibly 3 John),[178] Jude, and Revelation. Hebrews, James, and 1 and 2 Peter are not mentioned, though it is unclear why.[179] In addition, the list continues the trend we have seen thus far by acknowledging the clear apostolic status of these books as written by either apostles or their immediate followers. Indeed, this is the reason the fragment rejects the *Shepherd of Hermas*, which was written "quite recently, in our own times" and not during the period of the apostles who ministered "at the end of the times."[180] In a similar manner, the fragment rejects the pseudonymous epistle to the Laodiceans because it was "forged" in Paul's name[181]—a clear affirmation, once again, of the preeminence the early church placed upon apostolicity.

It should also be noted that toward the end of the fragment, before the discussion of heretical books, the list appears to include two apocryphal books, namely, the *Apocalypse of Peter* and the Wisdom of Solomon. However, the status of these books is unclear. Although the *Apocalypse of Peter* is mentioned, its disputed status is quickly acknowledged: "though

---

apocryphal material; e.g., Allert, *A High View of Scripture?*, 121–26; and Hahneman, *The Muratorian Fragment*, 93–110. But this issue will be addressed in chap. 8.

[177]The date of the Muratorian fragment has been disputed by A. C. Sundberg, "Canon Muratori: A Fourth-Century List," *HTR* 66 (1973): 1–41; Sundberg, "Towards a Revised History of the New Testament Canon" *SE* 4 (1968): 452–61; and more recently by Hahneman, *The Muratorian Fragment*; and McDonald, *The Biblical Canon*, 369–78. See responses from Charles E. Hill, "The Debate over the Muratorian Fragment and the Development of the Canon," *WTJ* 57 (1995): 437–52; Everett Ferguson, "Review of Geoffrey Mark Hahneman, *The Muratorian Fragment and the Development of the Canon*," *JTS* 44 (1993): 691–97; Heckel, *Vom Evangelium des Markus zum viergestaltigen Evangelium*, 339–54; P. Henne, "La datation du *canon de Muratori*," *RB* 100 (1993): 54–75; and J. Verheyden, "The Canon Muratori: A Matter of Dispute," in Auwers and de Jonge, *The Biblical Canons*, 487–556. The debate centers on the author's claim that the *Shepherd* was written *nupperime temporibus nostris* ("recently, in our own times"). While Sundberg and Hahneman wish to make the phrase mean simply "post-apostolic" times, Verheyden rightly points out that the distinction between apostolic and postapostolic times "makes less sense" by the time of the fourth century ("The Canon Muratori," 504).

[178]Since the fragment cites from 1 John at an earlier point (lines 29–31), it is reasonable to think that the other two epistles mentioned in lines 68–69 are 2 and 3 John. For more on this possibility, see the arguments of P. Katz, "The Johannine Epistles in the Muratorian Canon," *JTS* 8 (1957): 273–74.

[179]The poor quality and fragmentary nature of the Muratorian fragment have led Zahn and others to suggest that the omission of books like 1 Peter may have been a scribal error; see T. Zahn, *Geschichte des neutestamentlichen Kanons*, 2:143.

[180]Lines 74, 80.

[181]Line 67.

some of us are not willing for the latter to be read in church."[182] The mention of the Wisdom of Solomon is particularly perplexing because it would be more fitting under an *Old* Testament list. One possible explanation has been suggested by William Horbury, namely, that there was a widespread practice in the church of first listing the received books of both the Old and New Testaments and then, at the end, mentioning the "disputed" books from both Testaments that were useful for the church but not necessarily regarded as canonical.[183] This pattern is visible in Athanasius's Festal Letter, which lists both Old and New Testament books and then, at the end, lists the combined "disputed" books, which include Wisdom and the *Shepherd* among others. A similar pattern is visible in the early biblical codices like Sinaiticus (which ends with the *Shepherd* and the *Epistle of Barnabas*) and Alexandrinus (which included *1 and 2 Clement* at the end). Likewise, Eusebius,[184] Codex Claromontanus, and Epiphanius[185] exhibit a similar structure in their canonical "lists."[186] If Horbury is correct, then the books listed toward the end of the Muratorian fragment are placed there because they are understood to be "disputed" books from both Testaments that are acceptable for general use, but not necessarily canonical. These disputed books would include Revelation, the *Apocalypse of Peter*, the Wisdom of Solomon, and (to a lesser extent) the *Shepherd of Hermas*.

III. Conclusion

By no means has the above survey been exhaustive. Our limited space has required us to leave out a number of important second-century sources— such as Tatian, Theophilus of Antioch, Melito of Sardis, Dionysius of Corinth—and to examine others on only a cursory level. However, the evidence we have examined is sufficient to make our overall point: a number of New Testament writings, largely by virtue of their apostolic connections, were recognized and received as authoritative from a very early time, so that by the middle of the second century there appears to be a "core" New Testament canon widely recognized by early Christians. This core consisted of the four Gospels, Paul's epistles, Acts, 1 Peter, 1 John, and perhaps a few others. As Barton notes, "Astonishingly early, the great central core of the present New Testament was already being

---

[182]Line 72.
[183]W. Horbury, "The Wisdom of Solomon in the Muratorian Fragment," *JTS* 45 (1994): 149–59.
[184]*Hist. eccl.* 5.8.8, also joins the Wisdom of Solomon and the *Shepherd* together.
[185]*Pan.* 76.5.
[186]Horbury, "The Wisdom of Solomon," 152–56.

treated as the main authoritative source for Christians."[187] This is not to say, of course, that by this point the *boundaries* of the emerging canon had solidified. Even though there was an established core, the edges of the canon were still "fuzzy," and there were ongoing discussions over a handful of books like 2 Peter, 2 and 3 John, and Revelation. And, as we shall observe below, apocryphal books still played an active role in certain portions of the early church. Nevertheless, the discussions of these disputed books would take place within a context where the main canonical foundation had *already* been laid. Thus, whatever their outcome, by the middle of the second century the overall canonical direction of early Christianity had been determined. Therefore, dramatic claims that the canon was not finalized until the fourth century may be true on a technical level, but often miss the larger and more important point, namely, that the core of the canon had already been in place (and exhibiting scriptural authority) for centuries.

---

[187]Barton, *The Spirit and the Letter*, 18.

7

THE CORPORATE RECEPTION
OF THE CANON

Manuscripts and Christian Book Production

> When you come, bring . . . the books, and above all the
> parchments.
>
> THE APOSTLE PAUL (2 TIM. 4:13)

Thus far in our study of the reception and recognition of the New Testament canon, we have focused almost entirely on evidence available to us in the statements of the church fathers—that is, how they discuss, use, and cite New Testament writings. While this is certainly an invaluable area of study and the one most frequently explored in prior canonical research, there are other lines of potentially fruitful inquiry. One area of study that has been regularly (and unfortunately) overlooked by canonical scholars, at least until recent years, is the study of the New Testament manuscripts themselves.[1] While the *content* of early Christian texts has been care-

---

[1]Recent works on early Christian manuscripts include Harry Gamble, *Books and Readers in the Early Church* (New Haven, CT: Yale, 1995); David Trobisch, *The First Edition of the New Testament* (Oxford: Oxford University Press, 2000); Kim Haines-Eitzen, *Guardians of Letters: Literacy, Power, and the Transmitters of Early Christian Literature* (Oxford: Oxford University Press, 2000); Larry W. Hurtado, *The Earliest Christian Artifacts: Manuscripts and Christian Origins* (Grand Rapids: Eerdmans, 2006); Thomas J. Kraus and Tobias Nicklas, eds., *New Testament Manuscripts: Their Texts and Their World* (Leiden: Brill, 2006); and M. J. Kruger,

fully studied,[2] the actual physical *vehicle* of these early Christian texts has generally been ignored as if it were a disposable husk that could be separated from its content and discarded.

This chapter will argue that the "husks" in question hold tremendous potential in helping us understand the origins and development of the New Testament canon. For one, we have collections of New Testament books within a single manuscript that date to the second and third centuries, earlier than the time of many of our canonical "lists." Moreover, the physical and visual features of these manuscripts—the codex form, scribal hand, and other inscriptional features—together provide a fresh window into the literary culture of early Christianity and how Christians would have viewed and used these texts.

I. The Quantity of Early Manuscripts

We begin our discussion by asking a rather simple question: Which books or writings did early Christians prefer to use? That question can be answered, in part, by exploring the way the early church fathers cited and used books. And that is basically what we did in the prior chapter. But the question can also be answered by examining the physical remains of early Christian writings themselves. The manuscripts left behind can tell us what texts Christians were busy reading, using, and, of course, copying. When we examine the physical remains of Christian texts from the earliest centuries (second and third), we quickly discover that the New Testament writings were, far and away, the most popular. Currently we have over sixty extant manuscripts (in whole or in part) of the New Testament from this period, with most of our copies coming from Matthew, Luke, John, Acts, Romans, Hebrews, and Revelation.[3] The Gospel of John proves to

---

"Manuscripts, Scribes, and Book Production within Early Christianity," in *Christian Origins and Classical Culture: Social and Literary Contexts for the New Testament*, ed. S. E. Porter and A. W. Pitts (Leiden: Brill, forthcoming).

[2] In regard to the content of these manuscripts, there has been much discussion in recent years about restoring the "original" text of the New Testament. Some examples include, W. L. Petersen, ed., *The Gospel Traditions of the Second Century: Origins, Recensions, Text, and Transmission* (South Bend, IN: University of Notre Dame Press, 1989); C. B. Amphoux and J. K. Elliott, eds., *The New Testament Text in Early Christianity* (Lausanne: Éditions du Zèbre, 2003); B. D. Ehrman and M. W. Holmes, *The Text of the New Testament in Contemporary Research: Essays on the Status Quaestionis* (Grand Rapids: Eerdmans, 1995); E. J. Epp and G. D. Fee, *Studies in the Theory and Method of New Testament Textual Criticism* (Grand Rapids: Eerdmans, 1993); and C. E. Hill and M. J. Kruger, eds., *The Early Text of the New Testament* (Oxford: Oxford University Press, forthcoming).

[3] Hurtado, *The Earliest Christian Artifacts*, 20–21, 217–24. For the sake of this discussion, we will generally follow the dates indicated by Hurtado. Other listings of New Testament manuscripts can be found primarily in K. Aland, *Repertorium der griechischen christlichen Papyri, I, Biblische*

be the most popular of all, with eighteen manuscripts, a number of which derive from the second century (e.g., P52,[4] P90,[5] P66,[6] P75[7]).[8] Matthew is not far behind, with twelve manuscripts; and some of these also have been dated to the second century (e.g., P64–67,[9] P77,[10] P103,[11] P104[12]).[13] Compared with other documents of antiquity, the sheer quantity of these New Testament texts is impressive.[14] This is particularly noteworthy in that, generally speaking, ancient manuscripts of any writing are hard to come by. Most have perished over the ages for a variety of reasons—they were burned in garbage dumps, were destroyed by foreign armies, rotted

---

Papyri (Berlin: de Gruyter, 1976); and J. van Haelst, *Catalogue des papyrus littéraires juifs et chrétiens* (Paris: Publications de la Sorbonne, 1976). Of course, some manuscripts, like P46 (Paul's epistles), P45 (four Gospels plus Acts), and P75 (Luke and John), all contain multiple books. Recently, R. S. Bagnall, *Early Christian Books in Egypt* (Princeton, NJ: Princeton University Press, 2009), has challenged the early dating of some of these papyri. While such challenges are welcome, in a brief volume such as this we can only go with the general consensus of scholars up to this point.

[4]C. H. Roberts, "An Unpublished Fragment of the Fourth Gospel in the John Rylands Library," *BJRL* 20 (1936): 45–55; for an even earlier date of c. AD 100, see K. Aland, "Neue neutestamentliche Papyri II," *NTS* 9 (1962–1963): 303–16.

[5]An updated analysis of P90 can be found in Peter Rodgers, "The Text of the New Testament and Its Witnesses Before 200 A.D.: Observations on P90 (P.Oxy. 3523)," in *The New Testament Text in Early Christianity: Proceedings of the Lille Colloquium, July 2000* (Lausanne: Éditions du Zèbre, 2003), 83–91.

[6]Although P66 is typically dated at the end of the second century, a date in the first half of the second century has been suggested by Herbert Hunger, "Zur Datierung des Papyrus Bodmer II (P66)," *Anzeiger der Österreichischen Akademie der Wissenschaften* 4 (1960): 12–33.

[7]The original editors of P75 proposed a date between 175 and 225, making this a possible second-century text; see V. Martin and R. Kasser, *Papyrus Bodmer XIV–XV*, 2 vols. (Geneva: Bibliotheca Bodmeriana, 1961), 1:13.

[8]Hurtado, *The Earliest Christian Artifacts*, 20, notes sixteen manuscripts of John, but two more from the third century have been discovered since then: P119 (P.Oxy. 4803) and P121 (P.Oxy. 4805). For an updated analysis of John's manuscripts (and text), see Juan Chapa, "The Early Text of the Gospel of John," in Hill and Kruger, *The Early Text of the New Testament*.

[9]C. H. Roberts, "An Early Papyrus of the First Gospel," *HTR* 46 (1953): 233–37. P64–67, and possibly P4 (see more on this below), are commonly dated c. 200. Some have attempted an earlier date for these manuscripts; e.g., C. P. Thiede, "Papyrus Magdalen Greek 17 (Gregory-Aland P64): A Reappraisal," *ZPE* 105 (1995): 13–20. But this has been rightly rejected in favor of Roberts's original dating; see Klaus Wachtel, "P64/67: Fragmente des Matthäusevangeliums aus dem 1. Jahrhundert?," *ZPE* 107 (1995): 73–80.

[10]It is possible that P77 (P.Oxy 2683 + P.Oxy. 4405) is part of the same codex as P103 (P.Oxy. 4403).

[11]E. W. Handley and et al., eds., *The Oxyrhynchus Papyri* (London: Egypt Exploration Society, 1997), 64:5–7; discussion also in P. M. Head, "Some Recently Published NT Papyri From Oxyrhynchus: An Overview and Preliminary Assessment," *TynBul* 51 (2000): 1–16, esp. 8.

[12]P104 (P.Oxy. 4404) is one of the earliest New Testament manuscripts we possess, dating to the middle or late second century.

[13]For more on Matthew's reception in early Christianity, see W.-D. Köhler, *Die Rezeption des Matthäusevangeliums in der Zeit vor Irenäus* (Tübingen: Mohr, 1987); and É. Massaux, *Influence de L'Évangile de Saint Matthieu sur la littérature chrétienne avant Saint Irénée* (Leuven: Leuven University Press, 1986).

[14]Eldon Jay Epp, "Textual Criticism," in *The New Testament and Its Modern Interpreters*, ed. Eldon Jay Epp and George W. MacRae (Atlanta: Scholars Press, 1989), 91.

or decayed, or were damaged by insects.[15] Historians never have as many as they would like. Thus, the fact that we possess so many New Testament manuscripts provides a critical clue to how central these books were to the religious life of the burgeoning Christian communities.

The critical role played by New Testament writings is put into sharper relief when we examine the textual remains of the Christian "Apocrypha." These are writings that have a similar genre and subject matter as the writings of the New Testament, are often attributed to apostles, but never made it into the canon (though they were occasionally treated as Scripture by some early Christian groups).[16] During the same time period, the second and third centuries, we possess approximately seventeen manuscripts of apocryphal writings such as the *Gospel of Thomas*, the *Gospel of Mary*, the *Gospel of Peter*,[17] the *Protevangelium of James*, and more.[18] The *Gospel of Thomas* has the most manuscripts of all, with just three.[19]

Since most of these writings (canonical and apocryphal) were discovered in Egypt, particularly the ancient city of Oxyrhynchus,[20] this raises the question of whether we can expect that this distribution of texts accurately reflects their broad Christian use, or whether it just reflects the fortuitous (and random) preservation of texts in Egypt. Although we can never be absolutely certain about whether manuscript discoveries in one locale are representative of broader trends, Eldon Epp has observed that

---

[15] Alan Millard, *Reading and Writing in the Time of Jesus* (New York: New York University Press, 2000), 33–41.

[16] Our formal understanding of New Testament Apocrypha includes the types of books found in W. Schneemelcher, ed., *New Testament Apocrypha*, trans. R. McL. Wilson, 2 vols. (Louisville: Westminster John Knox, 1991); and J. K. Elliott, *The Apocryphal New Testament* (Oxford: Clarendon, 1993). Thus, it would include books like the *Gospel of Peter*, but not books like *1 Clement* (which is not typically regarded as apocryphal in the narrow sense).

[17] Whether the *Gospel of Peter* has two early fragments depends on whether one accepts the arguments of D. Lührmann, "P.Oxy. 4009: Ein neues Fragment des Petrusevangeliums?," *NovT* 35 (1993): 390–410; and Lührmann, "P.Oxy. 2949: EvPet 3–5 in einer Handschrift des 2/3 Jahrhunderts," *ZNW* 72 (1981): 216–26. For a contrary position, see P. Foster, "Are There Any Early Fragments of the So-Called Gospel of Peter?," *NTS* 52 (2006): 1–28.

[18] Hurtado, *The Earliest Christian Artifacts*, 21–22. The *Gospel of Peter* and *Thomas* will be discussed in more detail in chap. 8.

[19] P.Oxy. 1, P.Oxy. 654, and P.Oxy. 655. For a general introduction to the Nag Hammadi material, see Christopher Tuckett, *Nag Hammadi and the Gospel Tradition* (Edinburgh: T&T Clark, 1986). For more on these papyri, see J. A. Fitzmyer, "The Oxyrhynchus Logoi of Jesus and the Coptic Gospel According to Thomas," *TS* 20 (1959): 505–60.

[20] Eldon J. Epp, "The New Testament Papyri at Oxyrhynchus in Their Social and Intellectual Context," in *Sayings of Jesus: Canonical and Non-Canonical*, ed. William L. Petersen (Leiden: Brill, 1997), 47–68; Epp, "The Oxyrhynchus New Testament Papyri: 'Not Without Honor Except in Their Hometown'?," *JBL* 123 (2004): 5–55. For more on the site of Oxyrhynchus as a whole, see AnneMarie Luijendijk, *Greetings in the Lord: Early Christians in the Oxyrhynchus Papyri* (Cambridge, MA: Harvard University Press, 2008); P. J. Parsons et al., ed., *Oxyrhynchus: A City and Its Texts* (London: Egypt Exploration Society, 2007); E. G. Turner, "Roman Oxyrhynchus," *JEA* 38 (1952): 78–93.

the circulation of literature in this era was quite rapid and remarkably efficient, which suggests that the distribution of texts in Egypt is generally indicative of attitudes and practices within Christianity as a whole.[21] For instance, P.Oxy. 405, a copy of *Against Heresies* by Irenaeus dated to the late second century, was discovered in Egypt only about twenty years after its initial composition in Gaul in c. 180, "not long after the ink was dry on the author's manuscript."[22] Likewise, the *Shepherd of Hermas*, which was composed in Rome in the mid-second century, was discovered in Egypt in a late-second-century manuscript (P.Mich. 130).[23] Also, the famous P52, a copy of John dated at the beginning of the second century (c. 125), was discovered in Egypt only a few years after the original composition of John in the late first century.[24] This extensive sort of literary interchange suggests that we have little reason to think that Christian textual preferences in Egypt—as indicated by the extant manuscripts discussed above—would be substantially different from preferences in other Christian communities in the Mediterranean world.[25]

If so, then the above numbers provide important insights into the literary culture of earliest Christianity. First, the sheer volume of extant Christian texts from this period (canonical and noncanonical) reminds us again that early Christianity was a very "bookish" religion that found its identity within literary texts. Christianity was distinguished from the surrounding religions in the Greco-Roman world precisely by its prolific production of literature and its commitment to an authoritative body of Scripture as its foundation.[26] So prominent were these scriptural books for Christians that even their pagan critics noted the Christian predilection for writing (and using) books and thus were forced to reckon with these books in their anti-Christian attacks.[27] All of these factors indicate

---

[21]Eldon Jay Epp, "New Testament Papyrus Manuscripts and Letter Carrying in Greco-Roman Times," in *The Future of Early Christianity: Essays in Honor of Helmut Koester*, ed. B. A. Pearson et al. (Minneapolis: Fortress, 1991), 35–56; see also L. Alexander, "Ancient Book Production and the Circulation of the Gospels," in *The Gospels for All Christians: Rethinking the Gospel Audiences*, ed. R. Bauckham (Grand Rapids: Eerdmans, 1998), 71–111.

[22]C. H. Roberts, *Manuscript, Society and Belief in Early Christian Egypt* (London: Oxford University Press, 1979), 53.

[23]Campbell Bonner, "A New Fragment of the Shepherd of Hermas, Michigan Papyrus 44," *HTR* 20 (1927): 105–16.

[24]Roberts, "An Unpublished Fragment of the Fourth Gospel," 45–55.

[25]Hurtado, *The Earliest Christian Artifacts*, 26–27.

[26]William V. Harris, *Ancient Literacy* (Cambridge, MA: Harvard University Press, 1989); A. K. Bowman and G. Wolf, eds., *Literacy and Power in the Ancient World* (Cambridge: Cambridge University Press, 1994).

[27]Lucian, *Peregr.* 11–12; Origen, *Cels.* 1.34–40; A. Meredith, "Porphyry and Julian Against the Christians," in *ANRW* 2.23.2 (1980): 1119–49. For more on pagan critiques of Christianity, see the helpful overview in Wayne C. Kannaday, *Apologetic Discourse and the Scribal Tradition:*

that the emerging Christian movement, like its Jewish counterpart, would be defined and shaped for generations to come by the same means: the production and use of books. Loveday Alexander notes:

> It is clear that we are dealing with a group [early Christians] that used books intensively and professionally from very early on in its existence. The evidence of the papyri from the second century onwards suggests . . . the early development of a technically sophisticated and distinctive book technology.[28]

Second, we should observe the disparity between the popularity of the New Testament books (particularly the Gospels) and that of the "apocryphal" books. Not only do canonical manuscripts outnumber apocryphal ones almost four to one, but there are more manuscripts of the Gospel of John than there are of all the "apocryphal" books combined.[29] The fact that early Christians vastly preferred the canonical texts is consistent with what we discovered in the prior chapter, namely, that the core New Testament books functioned as the foundational documents of Christianity from a very early time. Larry Hurtado argues that the low numbers of apocryphal manuscripts "do not justify any notion that these writings were particularly favored," and he adds that whatever circles used these writings "were likely a clear minority among Christians of the second and third centuries."[30] Similarly, C. H. Roberts observes, "Once the evidence of the papyri is available, indisputably Gnostic texts are conspicuous by their rarity."[31] Such a scenario presents substantial challenges to the Bauer thesis and its portrayal of early Christianity as dominated by heterodox groups and their apocryphal literature. Scott Charlesworth notes, "If the 'heterodox' were in the majority for so long, the noncanonical gospels should have been preserved in greater numbers in Egypt."[32]

Evidence of the Influence of Apologetic Interests on the Text of the Canonical Gospels (Atlanta: Society of Biblical Literature, 2004), 24–57; Stephen Benko, "Pagan Criticism of Christianity During the First Two Centuries A.D.," in *ANRW* 2.23.2 (1980): 1055–118; Robert L. Wilken, *The Christians as the Romans Saw Them* (New Haven, CT: Yale University Press, 1984); and Wilken, "Pagan Criticism of Christianity: Greek Religions and Christian Faith," in *Early Christian Literature and the Classical Intellectual Tradition: In Honorem Robert M. Grant*, ed. William R. Schoedel and Robert L. Wilken (Paris: Editions Beauchesne, 1979), 117–34.
[28] Alexander, "Ancient Book Production and the Circulation of the Gospels," 71–111.
[29] Hurtado, *The Earliest Christian Artifacts*, 22–23.
[30] Ibid., 21–22.
[31] Roberts, *Manuscript, Society and Belief*, 52.
[32] Scott Charlesworth, "Indicators of 'Catholicity' in Early Gospel Manuscripts," in Hill and Kruger, *The Early Text of the New Testament*.

Of course, it is important to remember that the relative popularity of books (on the basis of extant manuscripts) is not the whole story. The above evidence is offered only as a general *confirmation* of the trend we have seen in the prior chapter, not as definitive in and of itself. After all, some books were clearly canonical but, for whatever reasons, remained relatively unpopular in terms of usage. The Gospel of Mark is a good example. We have little reason to doubt its canonicity in the second and third centuries, but we have only one extant manuscript from this time period (P45).[33] Likewise, the *Shepherd of Hermas*, though clearly rejected by the Muratorian fragment (and others), was very popular within early Christianity and has left eleven extant copies.[34] These instances aside, the overall trend of early Christian papyri is still clear: early Christians were prolific users of books, especially those books that were to become part of the New Testament canon.

II. Early Manuscript Collections

In addition to observing the overall quantity of manuscripts within early Christianity, we must also note the practice of combining multiple New Testament books within a single manuscript. Such combinations can tell us much about the early development of the canon because they indicate how early Christians associated some texts with others and often joined them together into larger groups. Obviously such combinations were intentional and thus reflect early Christian literary preferences and per-ceived relationships between documents. Of course, as we examine the earliest manuscripts (second and third centuries), we should remember that our evidence from this early period is still quite fragmentary. Our earliest codices of a complete New Testament are not found until the fourth century, prior to which books often circulated independent of one another. Nevertheless, some connections between manuscripts are still visible in this earliest period and anticipate what would eventually become the four New Testament collection units: the four Gospels, the Pauline Epistles, Acts/General Epistles, and Revelation.

---

[33]No doubt, the relative lack of use of Mark is because much of the same material is repeated in Matthew and Luke. As the popularity of the latter two rose, it would be natural that the popularity of the former would decline. For more on Mark's reception, see B. D. Schildgen, *Power and Prejudice: The Reception of the Gospel of Mark* (Detroit: Wayne State University Press, 1999).
[34]Although some early Christians appeared to give the *Shepherd* scriptural status, it was not considered in the list of apocryphal New Testament books above because it is technically part of the apostolic fathers. This same distinction is made by Hurtado, *The Earliest Christian Artifacts*, 23. For more on the *Shepherd*, see Carolyn Osiek, *The Shepherd of Hermas* (Minneapolis: Fortress, 1999).

A. The Gospels

As for the Gospels, we begin with P75, which dates to the end of the second or early third century and contains portions of both Luke and John in the same volume.[35] T. C. Skeat has argued that it would have likely contained Matthew and Mark as well, making it a four-Gospel codex.[36] Stanton agrees: "Why would Luke and John be bound together without Matthew and Mark?"[37] In addition, Skeat has made a compelling case that P4 (Luke) and P64+67 (Matthew) come from the same codex, and he dates it to the late second century.[38] He argues that Mark and John were also included in this same codex—which would make it the earliest four-Gospel codex—but this has been disputed.[39] Whether or not either of these manuscripts was a four-Gospel codex, they at least show early connections between the canonical Gospels. And each of them would have had predecessors. The relationship between the canonical Gospels is confirmed in the Chester Beatty codex P45, dated c. 250, which contains all four canonical Gospels (Matthew, Mark, Luke, and John), which are followed by the book of Acts.[40] Noteworthy here is the position of Acts, which has been separated from Luke though they were clearly written as a two-volume work. This suggests a conscious and intentional linking of Luke with the other three Gospels as a distinctive corpus, requiring a separation from Acts.[41] In addition, Trobisch argues that P45 may have also

---

[35] A detailed analysis of the manuscript can be found in S. A. Edwards, "P75 Under the Magnifying Glass," *NovT* 18 (1976): 190–212; and C. L. Porter, "Papyrus Bodmer XV (P75) and the Text of Codex Vaticanus," *JBL* 81 (1962): 363–76.

[36] T. C. Skeat, "The Origin of the Christian Codex," *ZPE* 102 (1994): 263–68. Although P75 is a single-quire codex, it may have originally consisted of two single quires, one that held Matthew and Mark (now lost), and one that held Luke and John.

[37] Graham Stanton, *Jesus and Gospel* (Cambridge: Cambridge University Press, 2004), 72.

[38] T. C. Skeat, "The Oldest Manuscripts of the Four Gospels?," *NTS* 43 (1997): 1–34; for similar opinions, see also K. Aland, "Neue neutestamentliche Papyri II," 193–95; van Haelst, *Catalogue des papyrus littéraires juifs et chrétiens*, no. 403; and Roberts, *Manuscript, Society and Belief*, 13.

[39] P. M. Head, "Is P4, P64, and P67 the Oldest Manuscript of the Four Gospels? A Response to T. C. Skeat," *NTS* 51 (2005): 450–57; Scott Charlesworth, "T. C. Skeat, P64+67 and P4, and the Problem of Fibre Orientation in Codicological Reconstruction," *NTS* 53 (2007): 582–604. While conceding that these three manuscripts all come from the same scribe and are "virtually indistinguishable" (451), Head disputes whether they were in the same codex. Recently, Hill has argued that Skeat's original thesis was more plausible than Head and Charlesworth have allowed because P4+64+67 may have been a part of a *multiple*-quire codex, thus reopening the possibility that it contained all four Gospels. See C. E. Hill, "Skeat's Thesis, Not Dead Yet? On the Making of P4, P64, and P67," paper presented at the 2010 meeting of the Society of Biblical Literature, Atlanta, GA.

[40] For a recent treatment, see T. C. Skeat, "A Codicological Analysis of the Chester Beatty Papyrus Codex of the Gospels and Acts (P45)," *Hermathena* 155 (1993): 27–43.

[41] C. Kavin Rowe, "History, Hermeneutics and the Unity of Luke-Acts," *JSNT* 28 (2005): 131–57, has argued the reverse, namely, that Luke and Acts did not originally circulate together, and that Luke was attached to the other Gospels *prior* to being linked with Acts. Rowe suggests

contained the General Epistles after the book of Acts, though we cannot be sure.[42] Similarly, P53 is a third-century codex containing the remains of Matthew and Acts, and likely would have originally contained all four Gospels and Acts, like P45.[43] Manuscript 0171 (P.Berl.inv. 11863+PSI 1.2, 2.124) has been dated to c. 300 and contains portions of Matthew and Luke and may also have contained all four Gospels.[44]

Although some of our earliest extant manuscripts contain only a single Gospel, this does not necessarily mean that they were produced with no awareness of, and no connection to, other Gospels. Take, for example, P66, which dates from the late second century.[45] Although this manuscript contains only John's Gospel, what is noteworthy is that it bears the title εὐαγγέλιον κατὰ Ἰωάννην ("the Gospel according to John"). Martin Hengel has argued that not only were the titles of the canonical Gospels extremely early (likely by the beginning of the second century), but also their structure was quite distinctive.[46] While most ancient titles typically used a genitive construction—e.g., "of Plutarch"—the canonical Gospels employ the unusual κατά ("according to").[47] The title of John is not "the Gospel *of* John" but, in essence, "the (one and only) Gospel *according to* John's account." Thus, the very structure of the titles not only presupposes multiple Gospel accounts, but multiple Gospel accounts that are somehow connected to one another because each of them testifies to the one true gospel story.[48] Bauckham observes, "A Christian community that knew only one gospel writing would not have needed to entitle it

---

that this would actually be evidence for "an early fourfold gospel" (142n36). Responses to Rowe's historical reconstruction include Markus Bockmuehl, "Why Not Let Acts Be Acts? In Conversation with C. Kavin Rowe," *JSNT* 28 (2005): 163–66; and Andrew Gregory, "The Reception of Luke and Acts and the Unity of Luke-Acts," *JSNT* 29 (2007): 459–72.

[42] Trobisch, *The First Edition of the New Testament*, 33.

[43] H. A. Sanders, "A Third-Century Papyrus of Matthew and Acts," in *Quantulacumque: Studies Presented to Kirsopp Lake*, ed. R. P. Casey, S. Lake, and A. K. Lake (London: Christophers, 1937), 151–61.

[44] K. Treu, "Neue neutestamentliche Fragmente der Berliner Papyrussammlung," *APF* 18 (1966): 25–28; J. Neville Birdsall, "A Fresh Examination of the Fragments of the Gospel of St. Luke in ms. 0171 and an Attempted Reconstruction with Special Reference to the Recto," in *Philologia sacra*, ed. Roger Gryson (Freiburg: Herder, 1993), 212–27.

[45] An overview of this manuscript can be found in G. D. Fee, *Papyrus Bodmer II (p66): Its Textual Relationships and Scribal Characteristics* (Salt Lake City: University of Utah Press, 1968).

[46] M. Hengel, *Studies in the Gospel of Mark* (London: SCM, 1985), 64–84; see also Hengel, *Die Evangelienüberschriften* (Heidelberg: Winter, 1984). Trobisch also argues for an early date by suggesting that these titles derive from the original "canonical edition" that was published in the early second century (*The First Edition of the New Testament*, 38).

[47] Hengel, *Die Evangelienüberschriften*, 9.

[48] The fact that apocryphal gospels used this same title structure does not affect the point being made here because the apocryphal gospels patterned themselves after the titles of the canonical Gospels (Hengel, *Studies in the Gospel of Mark*, 70).

in this way."[49] These titles are evidence that Christians, at a very early point, were conceptually linking Gospels with one another, even when they occurred within single-Gospel manuscripts.

The manner in which early Christian manuscripts regularly connect the four canonical Gospels is borne out by the telling fact that we possess no instance where an *apocryphal* gospel is joined with canonical Gospels within a single manuscript. J. K. Elliott comments, "There are no manuscripts that contain say Matthew, Luke, and Peter, or John, Mark, and Thomas. Only the Gospels of Matthew, Mark, Luke, and John were considered as scriptural and then as canonical."[50] Apparently early Christians were willing to link some Gospels together in a single manuscript and not others. Even though early Christians read and used apocryphal gospels (as we shall see in the next chapter), their uniform exclusion from manuscripts containing canonical Gospels suggests that they were not seen as sufficiently compatible with, or on the same level as, the canonical Gospels.

B. The Pauline Epistles

We also have early evidence that Paul's letters were grouped together within a single manuscript.[51] P46, dated c. 200, contains Romans, Hebrews, 1 Corinthians, 2 Corinthians, Ephesians, Galatians, Philippians, Colossians, and 1 Thessalonians.[52] Because the outer leaves of the codex are missing, we cannot be sure of what final Pauline epistles were included. Since there would not have been space for the Pastoral Epistles in the remaining pages, some have argued that P46 is an early witness for a ten-letter version of Paul's letters, implying that the Pastorals were not yet canonical.[53] However, this interpretation of the evidence is not the only option. Even if the Pastorals were not included in P46, there is no reason to think this implies their noncanonical status, given that all thirteen epistles of Paul were received as canonical prior to this time by significant Patristic witnesses like Irenaeus and the Muratorian fragment

---

[49]Bauckham, *Jesus and the Eyewitnesses*, 302.

[50]J. K. Elliott, "Manuscripts, the Codex, and the Canon," *JSNT* 63 (1996): 107.

[51]A helpful overview of the textual evidence for Paul's letters can be found in D. C. Parker, *New Testament Manuscripts and Their Texts* (Cambridge: Cambridge University Press, 2008), 246–82.

[52]H. A. Sanders, *A Third-Century Papyrus Codex of the Epistles of Paul* (Ann Arbor: University of Michigan Press, 1935); Y. K. Kim, "Palaeographical Dating of P46 to the Later First Century," *Biblica* 69 (1988): 248–61, dates the fragment to the first century, though this has not been widely accepted.

[53]B. M. Metzger and B. D. Ehrman, *The Text of the New Testament: Its Transmission, Corruption, and Restoration*, 4th ed. (Oxford: Oxford University Press, 2005), 54; Gamble, *Books and Readers*, 59n74.

(as discussed above). It seems possible, then, that P46 may have been just a collection of Paul's letters with a *general* address (e.g., Romans), rather than a *personal* address (e.g., Timothy, Titus). Such a distinction between Paul's general and personal letters is evident in other early sources, such as the Muratorian fragment[54] and Tertullian.[55] But there is another possible explanation for the ending of P46. Jeremy Duff has argued that the scribe of P46 originally included the Pastorals by adding a small, four-page quire on the end of the codex to extend its length.[56] Duff points out that in the second half of P46, the scribe continues to increase the words per page, which suggests a substantial concern about whether the codex would have enough room for the material he intended to include.[57] Such a concern would not have been necessary if the scribe only intended to add 2 Thessalonians and Philemon, because that would have still left almost ten blank pages at the end of the codex. Thus, argues Duff, it is more reasonable to assume the scribe was also intending to include the Pastorals and probably had to add some extra pages to the codex to accomplish his task.[58] Regardless of which option one takes, P46 stands as an impressively early witness that Paul's letters were grouped together as a unit by early Christians.

In addition to P46, there are a number of other early manuscripts that combine epistles of Paul. P30 is a third-century manuscript preserving portions of 1 and 2 Thessalonians, but the high page numbers suggest that it was originally a more extensive Pauline corpus. The third-century P49 (Ephesians) and the third-century P65 (1 Thessalonians) likely come from the same codex (considering their nearly identical scribal hands)[59] and would, therefore, be another example of a Pauline letter collection (given the unlikelihood a codex would include *just* Ephesians and

---

[54]Parker, *New Testament Manuscripts and Their Texts*, 252.

[55]*Marc.* 5.21; Jerome D. Quinn, "P46—The Pauline Canon?," *CBQ* 36 (1974): 379–85.

[56]Jeremy Duff, "P46 and the Pastorals: A Misleading Consensus?," *NTS* 44 (1998): 578–90. Duff's arguments have been critiqued by Eldon Jay Epp, "Issues in the Interrelation of New Testament Textual Criticism and Canon," in *The Canon Debate*, ed. Lee Martin McDonald and James A. Sanders (Peabody, MA: Hendrickson, 2002), 495–502, who points out that the extra quire would have needed to be nine pages, not four (498).

[57]Duff, "P46 and the Pastorals," 578–90. However, Epp, "Issues," 499, rightly argues that the scribe did not increase the letters as much as Duff contends because the middle pages of the codex are smaller (in that they are trimmed when the papyrus leaves are folded over) and thus could hold fewer letters.

[58]Duff appeals to the Toura papyrus of Origen as an analogy because the scribe ran out of space and added a short quire of just four pages (one sheet); see Duff, "P46 and the Pastorals," 578–90. However, it is doubtful whether this analogy is fitting because the Toura manuscript is sixth century, when book technology would have been much better developed.

[59]J. F. Oates, A. E. Samuel, and C. B. Welles, *Yale Papyri in the Beinecke Rare Book and Manuscript Library* (New Haven, CT: American Society of Papyrologists, 1967), 9–13.

1 Thessalonians).[60] Similarly, P92 (c. 300) contains portions of Ephesians and 2 Thessalonians, which suggests yet another collection of Paul's epistles.[61] Grenfell and Hunt raised the possibility that P15 (portions of 1 Corinthians) and P16 (portions of Philippians) may come from the same late third-century codex.[62] Again, since the odds of a manuscript containing only 1 Corinthians and Philippians are quite low, we are likely dealing with the remains of another larger Pauline collection. P32 is a fragmentary copy of Titus from c. 200 that likely contained more letters than just this one.[63] Since the remaining text begins with Titus 1:11 on the recto, the epistle must have begun on the verso of the prior page.[64] Since it is unlikely that a codex containing a single text would begin on the verso, we have good reasons to think other books preceded Titus (perhaps 1 and 2 Timothy).[65]

Of course, we have a number of manuscripts where only a single letter of Paul has been preserved—for example, P87 (Philemon), P113 (Romans), 0220 (Romans). It is possible that some, if not all, of these manuscripts would have originally contained a larger collection of Paul's letters, but it is difficult to know.[66] But even if these manuscripts each originally contained only a single letter of Paul, this does not necessarily

---

[60]Hurtado, *The Earliest Christian Artifacts*, 38. The fact that P65 (1 Thessalonians) has more letters per line than P49 (Ephesians) fits with the suggestion that these books were part of a larger Pauline corpus; the scribe may have included more letters in later books to make sure the corpus fit into the codex. See discussion in P. W. Comfort, "New Reconstructions and Identifications of New Testament Papyri," *NovT* 41 (1999): 216.

[61]Epp, "Issues,"495–96, rightly reminds us that we can never know for sure what other books were in a given manuscript. At the same time, however, he argues that a manuscript that contained 2 Thessalonians would have likely contained at least 1 Thessalonians.

[62]B. P. Grenfell and A. S. Hunt, *The Oxyrhynchus Papyri*, vol. 7 (London: Egypt Exploration Society, 1910), 4–8.

[63]For discussion of date, see A. S. Hunt, *Catalogue of the Greek Papyri in the John Rylands Library*, vol. 1 (Manchester: Manchester University Press, 1911), 10–11; and H. I. Bell and T. C. Skeat, *Fragments of an Unknown Gospel and Other Early Christian Papyri* (London: Trustees of the British Museum, 1935), 6.

[64]In a strict sense, the term *recto* simply refers to the front of a folio, and *verso*, to the back (Gamble, *Books and Readers*, 265n9). As these terms were applied to papyrus and parchment manuscripts, however, the *recto* became associated with the side of the manuscript with the better writing surface (which was normally used as the front of the page). Thus, *recto* became associated with the side with horizontal fibers on papyrus manuscripts and with the flesh side of parchment manuscripts. Likewise, *verso* was often (though not exclusively) used to refer to the side with vertical fibers on a papyrus manuscript and to the hair side of a parchment manuscript. For more, see E. G. Turner, "Recto and Verso," *JEA* 40 (1954): 102–6.

[65]Quinn, "P46—The Pauline Canon?," 380, suggests that P32 may have been a codex of just the personal letters of Paul (1 and 2 Timothy, Titus, Philemon) and functioned as a companion codex to P46, which just contained Paul's general letters.

[66]D. Trobisch, *Paul's Letter Collection: Tracing the Origins* (Minneapolis: Fortress, 1994), is more certain when he states, "There is no manuscript evidence to prove that the letters of Paul ever existed in an edition containing only some of the thirteen letters" (22).

mean that they were produced with no awareness of, and no connection to, other letters of Paul. Again, the structure of the titles would have provided a link to the larger Pauline corpus. Trobisch points out two features of the titles that imply the existence of other Pauline books: (1) The titles were based on the addressee and not on authorship. If one possessed only a single letter of Paul and perhaps was unaware of his other letters, it might be natural to name the letter after its author (similar to the titles of Jude and James). But one would be more likely to name a letter after its addressee if it were understood to be part of a larger corpus of letters from that same author and there was a need to distinguish between them.[67] Trobisch observes that "to name a letter by its addressee makes sense if the letter is part of a collection of letters written by one author."[68] (2) The titles of Pauline books (and even non-Pauline books) were sometimes numbered (1 and 2 Corinthians, 1 and 2 Thessalonians, 1 and 2 Timothy). Such numbering is required only if multiple letters to the same addressee are published (or at least conceptually linked) together in the same collection; that is, you would not have a First Thessalonians if there were not also a Second.[69]

Trobisch argues that the remarkable uniformity among the titles of Paul's letters suggests that they must have been established quite early, perhaps by the beginning of the second century.[70] If these titles were established by this point, then that means that the Pauline books (or at least some of them) were already conceptually linked together as a corpus by this point. Although it is possible that by the turn of the century this corpus was contained within a single manuscript (more on this below), that would not have been necessary for there to have been a conceptual unity among the letters—the titles themselves (among other things) would have helped communicate that unity.[71] Thus, even if a given Christian community possessed a manuscript with only a single Pauline letter, say, 1 Corinthians, readers still would have known that it was connected to, and a part of, the other Pauline letters.

---

[67]Obviously, we have multiple letters of Peter named after their author (1 and 2 Peter). However, these were part of the collection of general letters that included multiple authors (Peter, John, James, Jude), whereas the Pauline collection consisted of a single author. Thus, one could not simply name 1 Peter after its recipients because that letter had to be distinguished from other letters in the corpus written by different authors.

[68]Trobisch, *Paul's Letter Collection*, 26.

[69]Trobisch, *The First Edition of the New Testament*, 39–40.

[70]Ibid., 40.

[71]G. Zuntz, *The Text of the Epistles: A Disquisition upon the Corpus Paulinum* (London: British Academy, 1953), argues that there was an established Pauline corpus by c. 100.

C. *Other New Testament Books*

As noted above, the other two early collection units were the General Epistles (and Acts) and the book of Revelation. The manuscript evidence for Revelation is well established by this time as we have five extant manuscripts of Revelation from this period: P18, P47, P98, P115, and 0308.[72] Not surprisingly, we have much less evidence for the smaller books that make up the General Epistles. We do have a number of early manuscripts that preserve single books from this corpus—for example, James (P20, P23, P100), 1 Peter (P125), 1 John (P9), and Jude (P78). Although it is likely some of these manuscripts would have also contained additional books from the General Epistles, the fragmentary nature of the evidence does not allow us to be certain.[73]

As for books from the General Epistles explicitly grouped together, we do have 1 and 2 Peter and Jude preserved in the same third-century manuscript, P72.[74] However, this manuscript seems to be an oddity in that it also includes a number of noncanonical works, such as the Nativity of Mary, 3 Corinthians, and others. As we have observed thus far, such a mix of canonical and noncanonical books in the same manuscript is quite rare. Thus, P72 appears to be the exception that proves the rule. The fact that this manuscript was clearly not produced by a professional scribe or scribes and was a combination of multiple codices woven together (as indicated by disparate page numbers and different scribal hands), suggests that it was made for private use and not to be taken as typical of early Christian manuscripts.[75] Nevertheless, it does reveal an early textual linkage between the two epistles of Peter. It is interesting to note that these two epistles, according to Turner, are copied by a different scribe than the rest of the codex[76] and share pagination that is distinct from the rest of the codex.[77] This suggests that 1 and 2 Peter originally circulated separately as a unit—as a type of Petrine corpus—before they were taken and woven into this new codex.

---

[72]For an overview of the early manuscripts of Revelation, see Parker, *New Testament Manuscripts and Their Texts*, 232–36.

[73]Some of these manuscripts obviously did not have other books in them; e.g., P78 (Jude) was most likely an amulet. For more on amulets and miniature codices, see M. J. Kruger, "P.Oxy. 840: Amulet or Miniature Codex?," *JTS* 53 (2002): 81–94.

[74]For more on P72, see Tommy Wasserman, *The Epistle of Jude: Its Text and Transmission* (Stockholm: Almqvist & Wiksell, 2006).

[75]Haines-Eitzen, *Guardians of Letters*, 96–104.

[76]E. G. Turner, *The Typology of the Early Codex* (Philadelphia: University of Pennsylvania Press, 1977), 79–80.

[77]Haines-Eitzen, *Guardians of Letters*, 97. There are other opinions about the scribes of P72; for more, see Wasserman, *The Epistle of Jude*, 30–50.

In addition, we possess a late third-century fragment of 2 John (0232) with high page numbers (164 and 165) at the top of the page.[78] This suggests that the manuscript originally contained a number of other books, though we cannot be sure which ones. Roberts originally suggested that this manuscript may be a Johannine corpus filled with the Gospel of John, Revelation, and the Johannine epistles.[79] However, I have argued elsewhere that there is not space for all of these books. Instead, this manuscript likely contained the book of Hebrews and the full collection of Catholic Epistles.[80]

In summary, the manuscript evidence shows that even in the earliest stages of the canon's development (second and third centuries), New Testament books were already being grouped together and linked with one another. This confirms our conclusions in the prior chapter that there was a core of New Testament books (mainly the four Gospels and Paul's epistles) in place from an early time period. Although the four collection units are only partially visible during the second and third centuries (due to the limited number of surviving manuscripts from this period), we see their full shape by the time we reach the fourth century. The major biblical codices—Sinaiticus, Vaticanus, and Alexandrinus—each contain all twenty-seven books of our New Testament (although the end of Vaticanus is missing), divided into four clear collections: the four Gospels, the Pauline Epistles (including Hebrews), Acts and the General Epistles, and Revelation.[81]

III. The Early Christian Use of the Codex

The most notable feature of early Christian manuscripts was that they were almost always in the form of a codex.[82] The primary form of a book

---

[78]C. H. Roberts suggests a date in the middle of the third century; see Colin H. Roberts, John W. B. Barns, and Henrik Zilliacus, *The Antinoopolis Papyri* (London: Egypt Exploration Society, 1950), 24–26.

[79]Ibid., 24–25.

[80]Michael J. Kruger, "The Date and Content of P. Antinoopolis 12 (0232)," *NTS* (forthcoming).

[81]Trobisch, *The First Edition of the New Testament*, 24–25. The inclusion of the *Shepherd* and *Barnabas* at the end of Sinaiticus, and *1 and 2 Clement* at the end of Alexandrinus has been addressed above.

[82]Relevant works on the codex include A. Blanchard, ed., *Les débuts du codex* (Turnhout: Brepols, 1989); C. H. Roberts and T. C. Skeat, *The Birth of the Codex* (London: Oxford University Press, 1987); Turner, *The Typology of the Early Codex*; Skeat, "The Origin of the Christian Codex," 263–68; H. A. Sanders, "The Beginnings of the Modern Book," *University of Michigan Quarterly Review* 44, no. 15 (1938): 95–111; C. C. McCown, "Codex and Roll in the New Testament," *HTR* 34 (1941): 219–50; L. W. Hurtado, "The Earliest Evidence of an Emerging Christian Material and Visual Culture: The Codex, the Nomina Sacra, and the Staurogram," in *Text and Artifact in the Religions of Mediterranean Antiquity: Essays in Honour of Peter*

in the broader Greco-Roman world was the scroll (or roll), which was made from sheets of papyrus or parchment pasted together (end to end) in a long strip and rolled up.[83] Writing was done only on the inside of the scroll so that when it was rolled up the words were protected.[84] The codex, in contrast, was created by taking a stack of papyrus or parchment leaves, folding them in half, and binding them at the spine. This format allowed for the traditional leaf book with writing on both sides of each page.[85] It is now well established among modern scholars that early Christians not only preferred the codex over the roll, but they did so at a remarkably early point. Various manuscript discoveries indicate that the codex was the widely established Christian practice by the early second century, if not late in the first.[86]

Richardson, ed. Stephen G. Wilson and Michael Desjardins (Waterloo, ON: Wilfrid Laurier University Press, 2000), 271–88; S. R. Llewelyn, "The Development of the Codex," in *New Documents Illustrating Early Christianity*, vol. 7, *A Review of the Greek Inscriptions and Papyri Published in 1982–83*, ed. S. R. Llewelyn and R. A. Kearsley (North Ryde, NSW: Macquarie University Ancient History Documentary Research Center, 1994), 249–56; Graham N. Stanton, "Why Were Early Christians Addicted to the Codex?," in *Jesus and Gospel*, 165–91; and Eldon J. Epp, "The Codex and Literacy in Early Christianity at Oxyrhynchus: Issues Raised by Harry Y. Gamble's *Books and Readers in the Early Church*," in *Critical Review of Books in Religion 1997*, ed. Charles Prebish (Atlanta: American Academy of Religion and Society of Biblical Literature, 1997), 15–37.

[83] A helpful discussion of scrolls is found in Gamble, *Books and Readers*, 43–48, and more recently in William A. Johnson, *Bookrolls and Scribes in Oxyrhynchus: Studies in Book and Print Culture* (Toronto: University of Toronto Press, 2004).

[84] Occasionally, scrolls were reused, and writing was done also on the backside (or outside) of the parchment or papyrus. Such a scroll, known as an opisthograph, is likely referred to by Pliny the Younger (*Ep.* 3.5.17).

[85] A single-quire codex could hold a maximum of about 250 pages (approximately 125 leaves) before the binding at the spine became overtaxed and the central pages of the codex would protrude too far when the book was closed. Many of our earliest papyrus codices—such as P46 (Paul), P47 (Revelation), and P75 (John and Luke)—were single-quire in their construction. Larger volumes, like P45 (four Gospels and Acts), often used a multiple-quire codex made up of numerous single-quire units (often four to twelve pages each) all bound together at the spine. However, sometimes a multiple-quire codex was also used for smaller works like P66, a late second-century codex containing only the Gospel of John. This suggests that the multiple-quire format might go back well into the second century. For more on the capacity of early codices, see Roberts and Skeat, *The Birth of the Codex*, 65–66; Turner, *The Typology of the Early Codex*, 55–60.

[86] Roberts and Skeat confirmed the early dominance of the codex by showing how it was the format of choice for Christians from the very beginning of Christian book production (*The Birth of the Codex*, 38–44). This early date has been challenged by J. van Haelst, "Les origines du codex," in Blanchard, *Les débuts du codex*, 13–36, where he argues for a later date for some of these manuscripts. E. G. Turner, *Greek Papyri: An Introduction* (Oxford: Clarendon, 1968), 10, also cautions against excessively early dates. However, T. C. Skeat, "Early Christian Book-Production," in *The Cambridge History of the Bible*, ed. G. W. H. Lampe (Cambridge: Cambridge University Press, 1969), 54–79, and C. H. Roberts, "P Yale 1 and the Early Christian Book," *American Studies in Papyrology* 1 (1966): 25–28, maintain an early date by appealing to the discovery of P.Yale 1, the papyrus codex that contains Genesis and dates from AD 80–100. Moreover, recent manuscript discoveries continue to confirm the dominance of the codex. Between 1997 and 1999, a number of early manuscripts from Oxyrhynchus were discovered,

A. Why Did Christians Prefer the Codex?

What is remarkable about the early Christian preference for the codex is that it stood in sharp contrast to the surrounding culture. While Christians overwhelmingly used the codex, both Judaism and the broader Greco-Roman world continued to prefer the roll for centuries to come.[87] Indeed, it was not until the fourth century and beyond that the rest of the ancient world began to prefer the codex to the roll, something Christians had done centuries earlier.[88] Such a dramatic preference for the codex requires some explanation. Why was the Christian form of book production so decidedly different from both its heritage (Judaism) and its immediate context (the surrounding Greek culture)? As one can imagine, this question has been widely debated. Suggestions that the codex was chosen for practical advantages (convenience, size, cost) or for socioeconomic reasons (the lack of education among Christians made the informal codex more palatable) have been largely considered inadequate.[89] Although such factors may have played some role, they would only have allowed an incremental and gradual transition to the codex over many years and thus cannot account for the fact that the transition to the codex was rather abrupt, early, and widespread.[90] A more foundational and influential cause is needed to explain the transition.

The most plausible suggestions link the codex with the early development of the New Testament canon. It is evident that the Christians began to prefer the codex about the same time that the New Testament canon was beginning to take shape. Skeat has suggested that the codex was chosen because it was able to do something a roll could never do: hold all four Gospels in one volume.[91] In a similar vein, Gamble has suggested

---

all on codices: P.Oxy. 4403–4404 (Matthew); P.Oxy 4445–4448 (John); and P.Oxy. 4494–4500 (fragments of Matthew, Luke, Acts, Romans, Hebrews, and Revelation).

[87]See statistics offered by Hurtado, *The Earliest Christian Artifacts*, 44–53.

[88]Roberts and Skeat, *The Birth of the Codex*, 35–37.

[89]Ibid., 45–53; Hurtado, *The Earliest Christian Artifacts*, 63–69; T. C. Skeat, "The Length of the Standard Papyrus Roll and the Cost Advantage of the Codex," *ZPE* 45 (1982): 169–75.

[90]Other theories about the origin of the codex suffer from some of the same problems. For example, Epp, "The Codex and Literacy," 15–37, and Michael McCormick, "The Birth of the Codex and the Apostolic Life-Style," *Scriptorium* 39 (1985): 150–58, suggest that the codex was established by its use in the travels of itinerant missionaries; and Stanton, "Why Were Early Christians Addicted to the Codex?," 181–91, suggests that it was early Christian uses of primitive "notebooks" (e.g., wax, wooden, and parchment tablets) for recording sayings of Jesus or Old Testament proof texts that led to the wholesale adoption of the codex.

[91]Skeat, "The Origin of the Christian Codex," 263–68. One is also reminded of the comment of Frederick Kenyon: "When, therefore, Irenaeus at the end of the second century writes of the four Gospels as the divinely provided evidence of Christianity, and the number four as almost axiomatic, it is now possible to believe that he may have been accustomed to the sight of volumes in which all four [Gospels] were contained" (F. G. Kenyon, *The Chester Beatty Biblical Papyri:*

that the codex was chosen because it could hold all of Paul's epistles in one volume and allow easy access to individual letters.[92] Regardless of which of these theories proves to be more plausible—and each has strengths and weaknesses—they agree that the significance of the codex lies in its role in the development of the corpus of New Testament books. In this regard, the codex performed two critical functions: (1) positively, it allowed certain books to be physically grouped together by placing them in the same volume; and (2) negatively, it provided a natural way to limit the number of books to those contained within the codex; that is, it functioned as a safeguard. As Elliott has noted, "Canon and codex go hand in hand in the sense that the adoption of a fixed canon could be more easily controlled and promulgated when the codex was the means of gathering together originally separate compositions."[93]

If Elliott, Skeat, Gamble, and others are correct, then it seems that the dramatic adoption of the codex by early Christians could rightly be regarded as a *symptom* of the canon's development. It is a sign that Christians were already linking some books together and excluding others. Thus, the widespread Christian use of the codex proves to be a substantial piece of historical evidence that the establishment of the New Testament canon was well under way by the turn of the century—long before Marcion, and long before most critical scholars have allowed.

B. The Content of Christian Codices

As we have seen, early Christians vastly preferred the codex. On some occasions, however, they would still use rolls.[94] This raises the question of whether there was any correlation between the *form* of a book and the *content* of a book in early Christianity. What sort of writings did Christians like to put into the codex form? And what sort of writings did Christians put on rolls (on the occasions that they used them)?

When it comes to just scriptural books, the Christian preference for the codex is so overwhelming that one is hard-pressed to find copies that are not on codices.[95] Indeed, in the entire second and third centuries, we do

---

Descriptions and Texts of Twelve Manuscripts on Papyrus of the Greek Bible, vol. 1 [London: Emery Walker, 1933–1937], 13).

[92]Gamble, *Books and Readers*, 58–66; Hurtado, *The Earliest Christian Artifacts*, 69–83.

[93]Elliott, "Manuscripts, the Codex, and the Canon," 111.

[94]Hurtado, *The Earliest Christian Artifacts*, 80, notes that about a third of Christian manuscripts in the second and third centuries were still placed on rolls.

[95]E.g., during the second century we have only the following Christian scriptural books not on codices: P.IFAO (Revelation); P.Oxy. 4443 (Esther); P.Barc.inv. 2 (Psalms). It should be noted, however, that the manuscript of Revelation is simply a reused roll (opisthograph) and therefore does not represent a conscious decision to use a roll. Moreover, it is uncertain whether the

not have a single example of a New Testament document copied onto an unused roll.[96] At the same time, Christians still employed the roll format on occasion for other kinds of books: for example, P.Oxy. 405 (Irenaeus, *Against Heresies*); P.Mich. 130 (*Shepherd of Hermas*); P.Vindob.G. 2325 (The Fayûm Gospel fragment); P.Oxy. 655 (*Gospel of Thomas*). In fact, about one third of all nonscriptural Christian books were written on rolls. Of course, this pattern does not suggest that any book copied onto a codex was considered scriptural by early Christians—we have numerous extrabiblical books on codices.[97] However, it does suggest that Christians (in certain instances) may have reserved the roll format for books that they did *not* consider scriptural. Put differently, Christians not only had a general preference for the codex, but, as Hurtado has stated, "Christians favored the codex *particularly* for the writings they treated as Scripture."[98]

If so, then this textual evidence provides additional confirmation of our findings in the prior chapter. The fact that no New Testament books are found on an unused roll during this time period, while apocryphal books like the *Gospel of Thomas* and the Fayûm Gospel were, suggests that some Christians *were* making distinctions about the canonical status of books from an early time period. Moreover, those distinctions appear to be remarkably consistent with what would eventually be the final shape of the New Testament canon.

C. *"And above All the Parchments"*

Understanding the early Christian preference for the codex may also provide some illumination about an interesting passage from 2 Timothy where Paul says to Timothy, "When you come, bring the cloak that I left with Carpus at Troas, also the books, and above all the parchments" (4:13). Paul makes a curious distinction here between "the books" (τὰ βιβλία) and "the parchments" (τὰς μεμβράνας), suggesting that they are two different kinds of writings.[99] Scholars widely regard τὰ βιβλία as a

---

manuscripts of Esther and Psalms derive from a Christian or Jewish provenance. For more discussion, see Hurtado, *The Earliest Christian Artifacts*, 54–56.

[96] We do have some New Testament texts copied onto the back of used rolls; e.g., P13, P18, P22. But such a practice is usually driven by the desire to reuse material and is typically for personal or private use.

[97] E.g., P.Iand. 1.4 (*Shepherd of Hermas*); P.Lond.Christ.1 (P.Egerton 2); and P.Ryl. 463 (*Gospel of Mary*).

[98] Hurtado, *The Earliest Christian Artifacts*, 59, emphasis mine.

[99] T. C. Skeat, "'Especially the Parchments': A Note on 2 Timothy iv.13," *JTS* 30 (1979): 173–77, has argued that these two kinds of writings are one and the same. He understands Paul to be saying, "Bring the books, that is (μάλιστα) the parchments." However, this suggestion has gained only limited support. See discussion in Stanton, "Why Were Early Christians Addicted to the Codex?," 177–78.

reference to books of the Old Testament, most likely on scrolls.[100] We do not know how many of these Old Testament books Paul had in mind, but it must have been limited to a reasonable number that Timothy could have borne during his travels.

But what is Paul referring to when he mentions "the parchments"? The term μεμβράνας is significant because it is not a Greek word, but a loan word transliterated from the Latin *membrana*. The history of this term in the first century makes it clear that it is a reference to a parchment codex. Not only does Quintilian use the term to refer to parchment notebooks,[101] but the Roman poet Martial (writing c. 84–86) refers to a small codex called *membrana* that can be easily carried on journeys and held in one hand.[102] Martial emphasizes that these *membranae* are more convenient than rolls, and he even mentions other popular authors (e.g., Homer, Virgil, Cicero) whose works were available in this format. Although the codex format would not gain widespread favor in the Greco-Roman world for centuries to come, these historical references make it clear that it was used on occasion even in the first century. There is little doubt, then, that Paul uses the term τὰς μεμβράνας to refer to parchment codices. If parchment rolls were meant, then the term διφθέραι would surely have been used.[103]

As for the content of these codices (or notebooks), a number of suggestions have been made over the years.[104] Given that Paul distinguishes these codices from the Old Testament writings, many scholars have argued that they likely contained some sort of Christian writings. This may have included a variety of things, such as excerpts of Jesus's teachings[105] or early Christian *testimonia* (Old Testament proof texts supporting Messianic

---

[100]G. Schrenk, "βίβλος, βιβλίον," in *TDNT* 1:615–20; Luke 4:20; Gal. 3:10; Heb. 9:19; Josephus, *Ant.* 3.74; *2 Clem.* 14.2; Stanton, "Why Were Early Christians Addicted to the Codex?," 177.

[101]*Inst. Or.* 10.3.31–32. Quintilian states, "Scribi optime ceris, in quibus facillima est ratio delendi, nisi forte visus infirmior membranarum potius usum exiget." The reference to the wax tablet (*ceris*) here makes it evident that the codex form is in question. Thus, the advice to use *membranarum* can mean nothing other than a vellum codex. See Roberts and Skeat, *Birth of the Codex*, 21, and Gamble, *Books and Readers*, 50.

[102]*Epigr.* 1.2: "quos arat brevibus membrana tabellis." See full discussion in Roberts and Skeat, *Birth of the Codex*, 24–29.

[103]Gamble, *Books and Readers*, 50.

[104]For various views, see I. H. Marshall, *A Critical and Exegetical Commentary on the Pastoral Epistles* (Edinburgh: T&T Clark, 1999), 818–21.

[105]That such notebooks were used to record Jesus traditions has been argued by Roberts and Skeat, *The Birth of the Codex*, 59; S. Lieberman, *Hellenism in Jewish Palestine*, 2nd ed. (New York: Jewish Theological Seminary, 1962), 203; and Birger Gerhardsson, *Memory and Manuscript with Tradition and Transmission in Early Christianity*, 2nd ed. (Grand Rapids: Eerdmans, 1998), 157–63. Given Paul's possible knowledge of canonical Gospels (1 Tim. 5:18, discussed above), one must at least consider the possibility that Gospel accounts may have been contained within these codices.

claims about Jesus).[106] However, one of the most compelling possibilities is that these notebooks contained (among other things) *copies of Paul's own letters.*[107] It was not at all unusual in the Greco-Roman world to keep copies of (and even publish) one's own letters. Cicero exemplifies this practice as his personal secretary, Tiro, kept extensive copies of his letters.[108] Cicero would occasionally receive a complaint from friends that one of their letters (from Cicero) was lost or damaged; on such occasions Cicero would quickly dispatch a replacement copy from his own collection.[109] And where did Cicero make and keep copies of his letters? He tells us: "I am jotting down a copy of this letter into my notebook."[110] In other words, Cicero kept copies of his letters in a *codex.*

If these "parchments" in 2 Timothy 4:13 contained copies of Paul's letters in a codex, then this opens up fresh insights into the development of the New Testament canon. Such a scenario lends substantial support to Gamble's thesis that the codex was widely adopted because it could hold all of Paul's epistles (something a single roll could not do). Since Paul had already begun to use the codex to contain his letters, it is not difficult to imagine that early Christians would have retained that format when it became desirable to circulate a defined Pauline letter collection more broadly to the churches.[111] Moreover, this scenario provides a compelling explanation for why some letters of Paul were preserved for the church and some letters were ultimately lost (1 Cor. 5:9). The answer appears to be that some letters were lost because Paul, for whatever reasons, did not make a personal copy of them before sending them out.[112] Thus, they were not available when Paul's completed letter collection was circulating more broadly to the churches.

---

[106]Martin C. Albl, *And Scripture Cannot Be Broken: The Form and Function of the Early Christian Testimonia Collections* (Leiden: Brill, 1999). For further discussion, see Stanton, "Why Were Early Christians Addicted to the Codex?," 182–85.

[107]E. Randolph Richards, "The Codex and the Early Collection of Paul's Letters," *BBR* 8 (1998): 151–66; Trobisch, *Paul's Letter Collection*; Gamble, *Books and Readers*, 100–101.

[108]*Att.* 16.5.5. There are also other examples. As Plutarch records, after Alexander set fire to his secretary's tent, he regretted that all the copies of his letters were destroyed—so much so that he sent new letters to various people asking for copies of the letters he had originally sent (*Eum.* 2.2–3).

[109]*Fam.* 7.25.1.

[110]*Fam.* 9.26.1.

[111]Richards, "The Codex and the Early Collection of Paul's Letters," 154–55, argues that Paul's early use of the codex to retain copies of his letters is evidence against Gamble's thesis, and he suggests that the codex was adopted only gradually and unintentionally. However, Gamble's idea that the codex was widely adopted because it could hold all of Paul's letters does not seem to exclude the idea that Paul himself may have personally used the codex earlier. Indeed, one seems naturally to lead to the other. See Gamble, *Books and Readers*, 65.

[112]E. R. Richards, *Paul and First-Century Letter Writing: Secretaries, Composition, and Collection* (Downers Grove, IL: InterVarsity, 2004), 220–21.

Most importantly, 2 Timothy 4:13 provides additional support to the idea that, at a very early stage, Christians conceived of their religious writings in two parts: the Old Testament writings (τὰ βιβλία) and their Christian writings (τὰς μεμβράνας). In Paul's day the latter would have still been fairly undefined, including not only copies of his own letters, but possibly excerpts of Jesus tradition, Christian *testimonia*, and the like. However, even though the content was undefined, there are hints here of a "proto-canon" of sorts, where valuable Christian texts are gathered into one place, in the form of a codex, with some even written by apostles. Once the codex form was widely adopted for Christian writings, it also became the preferred format for Old Testament books as well.

IV. Public and Private Manuscripts

Thus far in our study of New Testament manuscripts we have focused almost exclusively on their broad features: quantity, content, and codex form. We now turn our attention to some visual and inscriptional features of early Christian manuscripts. These visual features should not be overlooked for they can provide critical clues about the purpose for which a manuscript may have been produced. In general, it seems that New Testament manuscripts were produced with two broad categories of usage in mind: public use (reading in corporate worship) and private use (reading by individuals).[113] Of course, it is not always easy to determine whether a manuscript is designed for public or private use—these are not absolute categories that can be entirely separated from one another.[114] Nevertheless, the following features are at least suggestive that a document is designed for public use.

1. *Reading aids*. Generally speaking, manuscripts in the ancient world were not easy to read. They were often produced with no spaces between words (*scriptio continua*) and often no punctuation or reader's aids.[115] Colin Roberts observed, "As a rule Greek manuscripts make very few concessions to the reader."[116] Johnson also notes that the typical Greek

---

[113]Scott Charlesworth, "Public and Private—Second- and Third-Century Gospel Manuscripts," in *Jewish and Christian Scripture as Artifact and Canon*, ed. C. A. Evans and H. Daniel Zacharias (London: T&T Clark, 2009), 148–75.

[114]A manuscript may have been designed for public use but still acquired by an individual who used it privately; or it may have been written for private use and then used publicly.

[115]W. A. Johnson, "Towards a Sociology of Reading in Classical Antiquity," *AJP* 121 (2000): 593–627; Johnson, *Bookrolls and Scribes in Oxyrhynchus*.

[116]C. H. Roberts, "Two Biblical Papyri in the John Rylands Library, Manchester," *BJRL* 20 (1936): 227.

manuscript was "spectacularly, even bewilderingly, impractical and inefficient as a reading tool."[117] Thus, manuscripts that *do* contain reading aids are particularly noteworthy. The fact that some New Testament manuscripts contain such reading aids, argues Stanton, would "strongly suggest that they were used for liturgical reading in public rather than for private reading."[118] Examples of these reading aids include sense breaks,[119] diairesis,[120] rough breathing marks,[121] punctuation points,[122] and accents.[123] All of these features helped divide up the text in a manner that would be particularly suitable for public reading.

2. *Lines per page.* Critical to making reading an easier task was the spacing of the lines, which in turn affected both the size and spacing of individual letters. Turner notes that while classical literary texts can have upwards of 50 lines per page, some Christian texts of the same size average far fewer lines (and letters per line).[124] A noteworthy example of this trend is P46, which is estimated to have about 25–28 lines per page (at least in the earliest portions), whereas P.Oxy. 2537 (Lysias), a classical text approximately the same size, averages 45 or more lines per page.[125] Such spacing was clearly designed "to ease the task of [public] reading aloud."[126]

---

[117]Johnson, "Towards a Sociology of Reading in Classical Antiquity," 609.

[118]G. N. Stanton, "What Are the Gospels? New Evidence from Papyri," in *Jesus and Gospel*, 204.

[119]These are small spaces placed by the scribe in the text. Examples of such spacing in Christian manuscripts include P.Egerton 2 (second century); P46 (second/third century); P.Dura inv. 24 (third century); P75 (third century); P100 (third/fourth century); P115 (third/fourth century); P.Oxy. 1080 (fourth century); the Chester Beatty Melito (fourth century); Codex Sinaiticus (fourth century); and Codex Alexandrinus (fifth century). E. J. Revell, "The Oldest Evidence for the Hebrew Accent System," *BJRL* 54 (1971): 214–22, esp. 214–15, notes that a number of Hebrew texts from Qumran exhibit such spacing in order to mark various divisions in the text. See also E. Tov, *Textual Criticism of the Hebrew Bible* (Minneapolis: Fortress, 1992), 210–11, 299–315, who argues that spacing was used in both Hebrew and Greek Old Testament texts.

[120]Diairesis consists of two dots (like an umlaut) that occur over certain vowels so that the reader does not confuse that vowel with the vowel that goes with the prior word. E. G. Turner, *Greek Manuscripts of the Ancient World* (London: Institute of Classical Studies, 1987), 10.

[121]Breathings are found occasionally in the oldest Christian manuscripts, and when they do appear, they are normally rough breathings. Examples include P5, P37, P45, P46, P75, P113, P.Oxy. 1779, and the Chester Beatty Genesis. Rough breathing marks were found in the recently discovered P104 (P.Oxy. 4404), which was dated to the late second century.

[122]Turner, *Greek Manuscripts of the Ancient World*, 8–12.

[123]Accents were relatively rare in early Christian writings, but they do appear on occasion; e.g., P46 (third century) has an example of an acute accent, P.Yale 1 (third century) may have an accent, but it is uncertain, and P.Mich. 130 (third century) and P.Ryl. 1.1 (third/fourth century) contain a surprising number of accents and other lectional aids. See Roberts, *Manuscript, Society and Belief*, 10.

[124]Turner, *The Typology of the Early Codex*, 85–87.

[125]Hurtado, *The Earliest Christian Artifacts*, 174.

[126]Turner, *The Typology of the Early Codex*, 85.

3. *Size of the codex.* Early Christian codices were produced in a number of different sizes—with heights ranging from 41 to 2.9 cm—and such sizes can reveal much about their intended use.[127] Miniature codices (defined by Turner as less than 10 cm wide) were quite popular among early Christians[128] and most likely indicated that a book was designed for private (and portable) use.[129] In contrast, larger codices would have aided the task of reading aloud and thus suggest that a document was created for use in the public worship of the church.[130] When we examine the earliest codices of New Testament writings, most are not in the miniature format but have an average height that regularly exceeds 20 cm, and some even exceed 30 cm.[131] This range is borne out in some of our most significant New Testament manuscripts: P45 (20.4 × 25.4 cm),[132] P47 (14 × 24.2 cm), P52 (18 × 21.3 cm),[133] and P75 (13 × 26 cm). It is interesting to note that apocryphal writings in early Christianity often appeared in the miniature (and thus private) formats, which suggests that they (or at least these copies) were not intended for public reading in the church.[134]

4. *Scribal hand.* It is well known that most early Christian papyri (second and third centuries) were not characterized by the formal bookhand

---

[127]For more on the size of codices, see ibid., 13–34; and Hurtado, *The Earliest Christian Artifacts*, 155–69.

[128]The fact that miniature codices are dominated by Christian texts has spurred speculation that the miniature codex was a distinctively Christian invention. Roberts says, "On present evidence the miniature codex would seem to be a Christian invention" (*Manuscript, Society and Belief*, 12). Gamble takes a more moderate approach: "The miniature format was, if not a uniquely Christian phenomenon, one heavily favored by Christians" (*Books and Readers*, 236).

[129]Roberts, *Manuscript, Society and Belief*, 10–11. For more on miniature codices, see Kruger, "P.Oxy. 840: Amulet or Miniature Codex?," 81–94; and T. J. Kraus, "P.Oxy. V 840—Amulett oder Miniaturkodex? Grundsätzliche unde ergänzende Anmerkungen zu zwei Termini," *ZAC* 8 (2004): 485–97; and Kraus, "Die Welt der Miniaturbücher in der Antike und Spätantike. Prolegomena und erste methodische Annäherungen für eine Datensammlung," *SNTSU* 35 (2010): 79–110. We have numerous examples of New Testament writings (and Old Testament) in miniature formats (e.g., Revelation in P.Oxy. 1080, and 2 John in 0232).

[130]Hill, *Who Chose the Gospels?*, 30.

[131]Turner, *The Typology of the Early Codex*, 14–22; Hurtado, *The Earliest Christian Artifacts*, 162–63.

[132]These dimensions list breadth first and then height, in accordance with Turner's methodology.

[133]Although P52 is a tiny fragment, its overall dimensions can be estimated with a fair degree of accuracy.

[134]Of course, some may have considered these books Scripture even though they were not read publicly in worship. Examples of apocryphal material in miniature codices include *Shepherd of Hermas* (P.Oxy. 1783); *Acts of Peter* (P.Oxy. 849); *Acts of Paul and Thecla* (P.Ant. 1.13 and P.Ant 1.6); *Protevangelium of James* (P.Grenf. 1.8); *Didache* (P.Oxy. 1782; see also R. H. Connolly, "New Fragments of the Didache," *JTS* 25 [1924]: 151–53); *Life of Mani* (P.Colon. inv. 4780); *Bel and the Dragon* (Bodl. gr. bib. d2); *Gospel of Mary* (P.Ryl. 3.463); 4 Ezra (P.Oxy. 1010); Tobit (P.Oxy. 1594); and an apocryphal gospel (P.Oxy. 840). For more on this last fragment, see M. J. Kruger, *The Gospel of the Savior: An Analysis of P.Oxy. 840 and Its Place in the Gospel Traditions of Early Christianity* (Leiden: Brill, 2005).

that was common among Jewish scriptural books or Greco-Roman literary texts, but were often marked by a more plain hand that could be called "informal uncial" or even "reformed documentary."[135] Although this style did not share the elegance and artistry of the typical literary script, it was not as rough and rapidly written as most documentary papyri. Roberts is quick to point out that "a degree of regularity and clarity is aimed at and achieved."[136] And, while early Christian papyri certainly exhibit a mix of literary and documentary features, Hanes-Eitzen acknowledges that early Christian papyri "appear toward the literary end of the spectrum."[137] While the presence of a literary or semi-literary scribal hand does not guarantee that a document was designed for public use, a substantial lack of quality in the scribal hand strongly suggests that a document was written for private use (and likely within the context of an informal and uncontrolled scribal environment).[138] For instance, P37 (P.Mich. 3.137), a fragmentary codex of Matthew, has a scribal hand that is near the documentary end of the scale, and this suggests that it was produced as a private manuscript (it also lacks the other reader's aids that are typical of manuscripts designed for public use).[139]

Though the categories of public and private are not always easy to distinguish (and some manuscripts contained a mix of characteristics), the presence of the above characteristics in a single manuscript would imply that it was designed to be read in public worship. Charlesworth offers P75 as a standard example of such a manuscript.[140] The scribal hand is of high quality, the letters are written larger than normal size, the codex is large enough to suggest public reading (13 × 26 cm), and it contains a number

---

[135]Roberts, *Manuscript, Society and Belief*, 14. It is important to note that some *literary* papyri of classical works were also written in a rather plain, unadorned, and non-calligraphic hand (e.g., P.Oxy. 1809, 2076, 2288). However, E. G. Turner does not necessarily consider this as an indication of low scribal quality; indeed, he declares that "'calligraphic' hands are suspect. . . . It is not uncommon for the finest looking hands to be marred by gross carelessness in transcription" ("Scribes and Scholars," in *Oxyrhynchus: A City and Its Texts*, ed. A. K. Bowman et al. [London: Egypt Exploration Society, 2007], 258–59).

[136]Roberts, *Manuscript, Society and Belief*, 14. In addition, Stanton points out that recently discovered New Testament manuscripts contain a scribal hand more on the literary end of the perspective; see Stanton, "What Are the Gospels?," 192–206.

[137]Hanes-Eitzen, *Guardians of Letters*, 65. The general distinction between "literary" and "documentary" papyri has come under criticism as some scholars have challenged the sharp dichotomy that is often drawn between the two. For more on this point, see Turner, *Greek Papyri*, vi–vii; Roger A. Pack, *The Greek and Latin Literary Texts from Greco-Roman Egypt*, 2nd ed. (Ann Arbor: University of Michigan Press, 1967), 1; and Epp, "New Testament Papyrus Manuscripts and Letter Carrying," 39–40.

[138]Charlesworth, "Public and Private," 168.

[139]Turner, *Greek Papyri*, 88–96; Charlesworth, "Public and Private," 161.

[140]Charlesworth, "Public and Private," 159–61.

of lectional aids (diairesis, rough breathings, and punctuation points).[141] Charlesworth argues that manuscripts designed for public use, like P75, were likely created in more controlled Christian copy "centers" (though not formally scriptoria) associated with a larger Christian congregation and were likely based on the master copy that was normally used by that congregation in public worship.[142] We have good reasons to think that such copy "centers" would have existed in major Christian locales such as Rome, Jerusalem, Alexandria, and Caesarea.[143] The extensive amount of Christian papyri recovered at Oxyrhynchus[144] suggests that it also may have contained a copying center of sorts.[145]

When we look at the spectrum of New Testament manuscripts in the second century (which are mainly Gospel texts), a significant fact stands out: most of them appear to be produced for the purpose of public reading. Examples include P4+P64+P67 (Matthew and Luke), P103 (Matthew), P77 (Matthew), P90 (John), P104 (Matthew), and P66 (John).[146] Charlesworth observes, "The majority of *second-century* gospel manuscripts (MSS) can be designated 'public,' in the sense that they were intentionally produced to be read aloud by lectors in Christian meetings."[147] The implications of this on the development of the canon are immediately evident. It tells us that New Testament manuscripts, in their earliest phase, were often produced within, and used within, the context of public worship—they were at the core of the devotional life of early Christians. This scenario fits precisely with the testimony of Justin Martyr (as we observed above) that "on the day called Sunday, all who live in cities or in the country gather together to one place, and the memoirs of the apostles or the writings of the prophets are read."[148]

---

[141]For more on this fragment, see Martin and Kasser, *Papyrus Bodmer XIV–XV*; and Porter, "Papyrus Bodmer XV (P75) and the Text of Codex Vaticanus," 363–76.

[142]Charlesworth, "Public and Private," 171–72.

[143]The fact that these major Christian centers contained established Christian libraries makes publication and copying resources all the more likely. E.g., the library at Caesarea was established by the early third century (Jerome, *Vir. ill.* 112; Eusebius, *Hist. eccl.* 7.32.25) and contained extensive resources for copying, editing, and publishing biblical manuscripts (some colophons in biblical manuscripts, like Sinaiticus, indicate that manuscripts were collated and corrected there even by Pamphilus and Eusebius themselves). Jerusalem also contained a library by the early third century (*Hist. eccl.* 6.20.1), and most likely Alexandria as well (as can be seen by the extensive literary work and possible "catechetical schools" in Alexandria under Pantaenus, Clement, and Origen; *Hist. eccl.* 5.10; 6.3.3). For more discussion, see Gamble, *Books and Readers*, 155–59.

[144]For a detailed catalogue of Oxyrhynchus papyri, see Julian Krüger, *Oxyrhynchos in der Kaiserzeit: Studien zur Topographie und Literaturrezeption* (Frankfurt: Peter Lang, 1990).

[145]For more on the site of Oxyrhynchus as a whole, see Luijendijk, *Greetings in the Lord*, 1–21; Parsons et al., *Oxyrhynchus*; Turner, "Roman Oxyrhynchus," 78–93.

[146]Charlesworth, "Public and Private," 155.

[147]Ibid., 148, emphasis his.

[148]*1 Apol.* 67.3.

V. Conclusion

In this chapter, we have journeyed (albeit briefly) into the world of ancient manuscripts. The formation of the New Testament canon is a story told not only by the early church fathers who used and cited these books, but also by the earliest physical remnants of Christianity, the manuscripts themselves. When these manuscripts are seen as more than mere "husks" that bear the New Testament text (and thus are not easily discarded), they can provide intriguing clues about the way early Christians viewed these texts. First, the sheer quantity of New Testament manuscripts reveals that these books were by far the most popular books among early Christians, far outpacing the apocryphal writings. Second, we have seen that from a very early time certain books were textually linked to other books within the same manuscript. This demonstrates that early Christians viewed these writings as somehow connected and belonging with one another (and not with other books). Third, early Christians, in stark contrast to the surrounding literary culture, vastly preferred the codex book form over the roll. No doubt the adoption of the codex is closely linked to the origins of the New Testament canon and the desire to place multiple books inside the confines of a single manuscript. Fourth, the visual features of our earliest manuscripts (scribal hand, reader's aids, line spacing), and the size of the codices themselves, strongly suggest that they were created to be read as Scripture in corporate worship.

All these factors provide remarkable confirmation of the Patristic evidence surveyed in the prior chapter. They confirm, once again, that early Christians had a canon consciousness from a very early point as they read, copied, collected, and distributed those documents they viewed as central to their religious life and worship. They busied themselves not just with oral proclamation but also, and perhaps primarily, with the *written text*. At their core, they were people of the book.

8

THE CORPORATE RECEPTION
OF THE CANON

Problem Books and Canonical Boundaries

The net of the law and prophets had to be completed. . . .
And the texture of the net has been completed in the Gospels,
and in the words of Christ through the Apostles.

ORIGEN

These final chapters have been concerned with answering a potential "defeater" to the self-authenticating model, namely, that the erratic and tumultuous history of the canon's reception makes it irrational to believe that books finally received by the church are the ones God intended. Our answer has been a simple one: the history of the canon is not nearly as erratic as the critics claim. In the prior two chapters we argued that the New Testament writings made such an impact on the earliest Christian communities that there was a "core" canon of books firmly in place by the middle second century. While this no doubt deals a substantial blow to the integrity of this defeater, there is more work to be done. While the core of a New Testament canon was already established by this time, the boundaries of the canon were not yet solidified in their entirety. Inevitably, there were some differences among various early Christian groups concerning which books they considered authoritative Scripture and which books they did not. Some of these differences concerned "disputed" New Testament books, which fell outside the core (e.g., 2 Peter, Revelation), and others concerned books that never made it into the final form of the New Testament (e.g., the *Gospel of Peter*, the *Shepherd of Hermas*). And it is the existence of these differences and disagreements about the final boundaries of the canon that constitutes the essence of the canonical-diversity defeater.

It is the purpose of this chapter to probe more deeply into the extent of disagreement in early Christianity over the boundaries of the canon. First, we will examine particular types of arguments that have been used to bolster the claim that the canon was wildly diverse until well into the fourth century. Second, we will examine some specific books—disputed books and apocryphal books—to learn the details about their canonical journeys and historical merits. Were disagreements over these books really as extensive as the critics claim? Is it true that apocryphal books have just as much claim to the canon as those that made it in? And third, we will look at some indicators of canonical consensus among early Christians. When do we begin to see broad-based agreement about the boundaries of the New Testament?

I. Arguments for Canonical Diversity

In order to assess the viability of the canonical-diversity defeater, we need to examine more closely the kinds of arguments that are used to show that there was little agreement over canonical books prior to the fourth century. Are these arguments a sufficient basis for considering the pre-fourth-century canon to be the loose, unbounded affair it is often made out to be? We shall examine two of these arguments here.

A. Use of Apocryphal Books

One of the most common methods used to show the diversity of the canon (and thus to push back its final date) is to appeal to the way early Christians used apocryphal literature. Geoffrey Hahneman is a typical example in this regard.[1] Hahneman rightly observes that "Christian writers of the second century refer to many other gospels beside the canonical four."[2] This is particularly true if one includes Patristic citations of noncanonical Jesus

---

[1]G. M. Hahneman, *The Muratorian Fragment and the Development of the Canon* (Oxford: Clarendon, 1992), 94.
[2]Ibid.

sayings (*agrapha*) where their source is unknown.[3] However, Hahneman then draws an unexpected conclusion from this fact: "This would seem unlikely if the Fourfold Gospel canon had already been established."[4] But how does this follow? Hahneman never explains how the mere *use* of noncanonical Jesus tradition is evidence that the fourfold Gospel was not established. Why are the two mutually exclusive? Apparently Hahneman is operating under the assumption that the adoption of certain books as canonical (say the four Gospels) somehow means that you can never again use material that falls outside these books. But it is unclear where this assumption comes from, and Hahneman never offers an argument for it. Indeed, the historical situation of early Christianity suggests that we should expect the contrary. We know that oral traditions of Jesus continued well into the second century (and beyond) and were often found to be beneficial and useful.[5] Likewise, Patristic writers would occasionally draw on apocryphal gospels as helpful sources for the life of Jesus.[6] But this did not necessarily mean that they considered these sources equal in authority to the canonical books. Patristic writers were quite capable of distinguishing between material that was Scripture and material that, though not Scripture, was nevertheless useful.[7]

The fact that Hahneman fails to make this distinction is particularly stunning given that, one paragraph earlier, he chides other scholars for confusing "acquaintance with the four gospels and the Fourfold Gospel canon."[8] In other words, mere use does not imply authoritative status. How then is Hahneman able to turn around and claim that mere use of apocryphal material shows it had an authoritative status—the type of status that would have threatened the existence of the canonical four? This same type of confusion also seems to exist in other writers. For instance, Gamble appeals to the well-known story of the *Gospel of Peter* being used by the church of Rhossus (which was under the

---

[3]For more on this topic, see H. Koester, "The Extracanonical Sayings of the Lord as Products of the Christian Community," *Semeia* 44 (1988): 57–78; and J. H. Charlesworth and C. A. Evans, "Jesus in the Agrapha and Apocryphal Gospels," in *Studying the Historical Jesus: Evaluations of the State of Current Research*, ed. B. Chilton and C. A. Evans (Leiden: Brill, 1994), 478–533.
[4]Hahneman, *The Muratorian Fragment*, 94. Craig D. Allert, *A High View of Scripture? The Authority of the Bible and the Formation of the New Testament Canon* (Grand Rapids: Baker Academic, 2007), 121, makes the same sort of argument when he observes that Irenaeus occasionally appeals to apocryphal material; likewise R. P. C. Hanson, *Origen's Doctrine of Tradition* (London: SPCK, 1954), 137.
[5]See discussion in chap. 5 on oral tradition.
[6]E.g., Clement of Alexandria and Origen often used apocryphal material (more on this below).
[7]For an overview of this practice among Patristic writers, see C. E. Hill, *Who Chose the Gospels? Probing the Great Gospel Conspiracy* (Oxford: Oxford University Press, 2010), 69–92.
[8]Hahneman, *The Muratorian Fragment*, 94.

bishop Serapion) as evidence that "the four-Gospel collection had not yet become normative."[9] Similarly, McDonald refers to the same story as evidence that there was no "notion of a closed four-gospel canon."[10] However, there is no indication in Serapion's own description of the event that the *Gospel of Peter* was regarded as Scripture by that church or read as Scripture in the context of public worship.[11] On the contrary, we would hardly expect a bishop like Serapion to have allowed a congregation to use a gospel as Scripture that he had not even read![12] Moreover, Serapion expressly states that he is aware of the scriptural books "handed down to us" and that the *Gospel of Peter* is not one of them.[13] Thus, there seems to be confusion in these authors between the use of apocryphal materials as beneficial and helpful, and the acceptance of them as Scripture.

The ability of Patristic writers to distinguish between scriptural books and merely useful books is particularly evident in the writings of Clement of Alexandria and Origen. Both of these men were intellectual giants, widely read and familiar with vast amounts of literature beyond the Scriptures—which they often put to use in their various theological treatises. Hengel observes that Clement liked to "show off his learning" by citing a variety of sources (canonical and apocryphal), often mixed together, and often without giving the title or author.[14] Clement quotes from the *Preaching of Peter*,[15] the *Gospel of the Egyptians*,[16] the *Gospel of the Hebrews*,[17] and other noncanonical writings. At the same time, however, he expressly affirms that there are four, and only four, "traditional" Gospels that the church receives: Matthew, Mark, Luke, and John.[18] At one point, while using a saying from the *Gospel of the Egyptians*, he intentionally downplays its authority by noting that the saying does not occur in our canonical four.[19] Hengel reminds us:

---

[9]H. Y. Gamble, *The New Testament Canon: Its Making and Meaning* (Philadelphia: Fortress, 1985), 34.

[10]L. M. McDonald, *The Formation of the Christian Biblical Canon* (Peabody, MA: Hendrickson, 1995), 291–92.

[11]Eusebius, *Hist. eccl.* 6.12.3–6.

[12]Eusebius, *Hist. eccl.* 6.12.4.

[13]Eusebius, *Hist. eccl.* 6.12.3.

[14]M. Hengel, *The Four Gospels and the One Gospel of Jesus Christ* (Harrisburg, PA: Trinity, 2000), 17.

[15]*Strom.* 1.29; 6.5–7.

[16]*Strom.* 3.6–13.

[17]*Strom.* 2.9; 5.14.

[18]Eusebius, *Hist. eccl.* 6.14.5–7.

[19]*Strom.* 3.13.

Clement's relative generosity towards "apocryphal" texts and traditions, which is connected with the unique spiritual milieu in Alexandria and his constant controversies with many kinds of discussion partners . . . should not obscure the fact that even for him the apostolic origin and special church authority of the four gospels was already unassailable.[20]

Likewise, Origen uses a variety of noncanonical writings for the same reasons, including the *Gospel of Peter*[21] and the *Gospel of the Hebrews*.[22] Origen was able to glean useful material from these writings without endorsing them as a whole because he realized that such works often contained a "mixture" of authentic and inauthentic content.[23] At the same time, however, Origen goes out of his way to make it clear that he receives four, and only four, Gospels as Scripture,[24] and he often downplays the authority of the *Gospel of the Hebrews*.[25] At one point he declares that the four canonical Gospels "alone are unquestionable in the Church of God under heaven,"[26] and in another place he says, "We approve nothing else but that which the Church approves, that is, four Gospels only as proper to be received."[27]

Incredibly, even with these clarifications by Clement and Origen, Hahneman appeals to both as evidence that the fourfold Gospel is *not* established. He declares, "If the principle [of the fourfold Gospel] was one of long standing, then their use of other gospels would be particularly troublesome."[28] But, again, Hahneman never explains why the two are mutually exclusive. Clement and Origen clearly did not see things this way. For this reason, they are evidence for the *opposite* of Hahneman's point. They show that Patristic writers often saw no contradiction between affirming some Gospels as exclusively canonical, while still benefitting from other Jesus tradition outside these Gospels. Thus, we should be cautious about drawing too many implications from just their use of apocryphal works.

---

[20]Hengel, *The Four Gospels*, 18–19. J. A. Brooks, "Clement of Alexandria as a Witness to the Development of the New Testament Canon," *SecCent* 9 (1992): 41–55, confirms Clement's preference for canonical literature by showing that "Clement quoted books now in the New Testament about sixteen times more often than apocryphal and patristic writings" (48).
[21]*Comm. Matt.* 10.17.
[22]*Hom. Jer.* 15.4; *Comm. Matt.* 15.4.
[23]*Comm. Jo.* 13.17 (here Origen refers to the *Preaching of Peter*).
[24]*Hom. Jos.* 7.1. This passage will be discussed further below.
[25]*Hom. Jer.* 15.4; *Comm. Matt.* 15.4.
[26]Eusebius, *Hist. eccl.* 6.25.3.
[27]*Hom. Luc.* 1.
[28]Hahneman, *The Muratorian Fragment*, 105.

B. Disagreements over Canonical Books

A second kind of argument used by Hahneman (and other scholars) is to appeal to particular instances of canonical dissent or disagreement and use those instances as evidence that there is no broader unity about the canon. Indeed, one gets the impression that it would require an extremely high (if not unanimous) amount of agreement about a book before Hahneman would regard its canonical status as decided. For instance, he again rejects the existence of the fourfold Gospel canon by appealing to the third-century orthodox theologian Gaius of Rome, who supposedly rejected the Gospel of John as a work of Cerinthus.[29] Aside from the fact that Charles Hill has argued that it is unclear whether Gaius actually did reject John, it is difficult to see how it proves Hahneman's point even if he did.[30] Does the broad acknowledgment of a fourfold Gospel require zero disagreement? Does the existence of some objections to John's Gospel override the evidence we have already seen in other chapters for its wide acceptance? With this sort of standard in place, we would *never* be able to say that we have a canon, even in the modern day. We would have to argue that there was no canon in the sixteenth century because Luther objected to the epistle of James, and there is not even a canon in the twenty-first century because the Syrian church continues to have a different list. Again, it seems that Hahneman has applied an unreasonably strict standard for the level of agreement required for a book to count as canon.

This overplaying of disagreements over canonical books also happens in other areas. Throughout early Patristic testimony about the canon, the church fathers occasionally acknowledge that a particular book is "disputed" by some.[31] A well-known example is Origen's comments on 2 and 3 John in which he acknowledges that "not all say that these are genuine."[32] Although Hahneman uses this comment to point out that universal agreement on these epistles has not yet been achieved, he entirely overlooks the implications of Origen's comments in the other direction, namely, that apparently most Christians *do* consider them genuine—including Origen himself. The phrase "not all say" indicates that Origen is simply noting exceptions to a more broadly established trend. Thus, it is misleading to use this passage as evidence that John's letters were not

---

[29]Eusebius, *Hist. eccl.* 2.25.6.
[30]C. E. Hill, *The Johannine Corpus in the Early Church* (Oxford: Oxford University Press, 2004), 172–204.
[31]E.g., Eusebius, *Hist. eccl.* 3.25.3; 2.23.25; 6.25.8.
[32]Eusebius, *Hist. eccl.* 6.25.10.

regarded as canonical. That is more than this language can bear. At most, it reveals that in certain quarters of the church some disagreements over these books continued to occur (which is hardly surprising).

II. Disputed Books and Apocryphal Books

In addition to addressing the argument from canonical diversity in general terms, it is important that we also consider the specific books over which Christians disagreed. What are the historical merits of these books? How significant were the disagreements over them? Given the vastness of early Christian literature, it is helpful to divide these writings into various categories. In order to do so, we shall take a cue from the structure provided for us by Eusebius's well-known listing of books in the early fourth century.[33] Eusebius functions as a key witness to the state of the canon during this period and to the many different kinds of Christian literature that were under consideration. Although Eusebius's list can be a bit confusing (and even inconsistent) at various points,[34] he appears to divide Christian writings into four categories:[35]

(1) The "recognized books" (ὁμολογούμενα) are the books universally received as canonical and include: the four Gospels, Acts, the epistles of Paul (including Hebrews),[36] 1 John, 1 Peter, and Revelation. Oddly, Eusebius qualifies the inclusion of Revelation by saying "if it seems desire-

---

[33]*Hist. eccl.* 3.25.1–7.

[34]For more discussion on the nuances of this passage, see B. M. Metzger, *The Canon of the New Testament: Its Origin, Development, and Significance* (Oxford: Clarendon, 1987), 201–7; David R. Nienhuis, *Not by Paul Alone: The Formation of the Catholic Epistle Collection and the Christian Canon* (Waco, TX: Baylor University Press, 2007), 63–68; A. D. Baum, "Der neutestamentliche Kanon bei Eusebius (Historia ecclesiastica 3.25.1–7) im Kontext seiner literaturgeschichtlichen Arbeit," *ETL* 73 (1997): 307–48; G. A. Robbins, "Eusebius' Lexicon of Canonicity," in *StPatr*, vol. 25, ed. E. A. Livingstone (Leuven: Peeters, 1993), 134–41; and E. Kalin, "The New Testament Canon of Eusebius," in *The Canon Debate*, ed. Lee Martin McDonald and James A. Sanders (Peabody, MA: Hendrickson, 2002), 386–404.

[35]Kalin, "The New Testament Canon of Eusebius," 391, argues that the "disputed" books and the "rejected" books are one and the same, thus giving us only three categories instead of four. This same position is followed by Allert, *A High View of Scripture?*, 132–39. On this basis, Kalin argues that Eusebius had only a twenty-one-book canon. However, this is rightly rejected by Nienhuis, *Not by Paul Alone*, 63–68; Metzger, *The Canon of the New Testament*, 201–7; L. M. McDonald, *The Biblical Canon: Its Origin, Transmission, and Authority* (Peabody, MA: Hendrickson, 2007), 308–9; and F. F. Bruce, *The Canon of Scripture* (Downers Grove, IL: InterVarsity, 1988), 197–205. Even B. D. Ehrman, *Lost Christianities: The Battles for Scripture and the Faiths We Never Knew* (New York: Oxford University Press, 2002), 244, acknowledges that Eusebius has four categories.

[36]Although Eusebius does not expressly mention Hebrews in this particular passage, he includes it among Paul's letters elsewhere when he affirms, "The fourteen letters of Paul are obvious and plain" (*Hist. eccl.* 3.3.4).

able," showing that he may have doubted it personally while still acknowledging it was widely received by others.[37]

(2) The "disputed books" (ἀντιλεγόμενα) are ones that have been the
subject of some ecclesiastical disagreement but are still regarded as canonical because they "are nevertheless known to most."[38] These include, not
surprisingly, James, Jude, 2 Peter, and 2 and 3 John.

(3) The "rejected books" (νόθα)[39] are books acknowledged to be generally "orthodox" in their theology (and thus presumably allowed to be
used in the churches), but rejected as it pertains to their canonical status.[40] These writings include the *Acts of Paul*, the *Shepherd of Hermas*,
the *Apocalypse of Peter*, the *Epistle of Barnabas*, the *Didache*, and the
Gospel of the Hebrews.

(4) The "heretical books" are those that are roundly rejected as unorthodox "forgeries" and "altogether wicked and impious."[41] These include
the *Gospel of Peter*, the *Gospel of Thomas*, the *Gospel of Matthias*, the
Acts of Andrew, and the *Acts of John*.

In sum, Eusebius views early Christian writings in four categories:
two kinds of canonical books (recognized and disputed) and two kinds
of apocryphal books (rejected but useful, and heretical).[42] Such divisions
confirm the discussions in prior chapters where we argued that there
was a canonical "core" from a very early time (similar to Eusebius's recognized books) and also a peripheral set of canonical books that most

---

[37]*Hist. eccl.* 3.25.2; Metzger, *The Canon of the New Testament*, 205. Eusebius's hesitancy with
Revelation is evidenced by his including it in the list of "rejected" books. This may indicate
that he believes another John besides the apostle wrote it (*Hist. eccl.* 7.25.15). The book of
Revelation will be discussed more below.

[38]*Hist. eccl.* 3.25.3.

[39]The Greek term here is νόθα, which can be translated "spurious" (as it pertains to canonical
status) or, more accurately, "illegitimate" or just "uncanonical." See discussion in Nienhuis,
Not by Paul Alone, 65.

[40]Eusebius's repeated use of the term *disputed* (ἀντιλεγόμενα) at the end of his discussion of
the "rejected" (νόθα) books (3.25.6) has led Kalin and Allert to argue that the two are simply
synonymous. Two considerations should be kept in mind, however: (1) Eusebius is quite flexible
with his terminology and often interchanges terms without suggesting that they are synonymous;
e.g., in 3.31.6 he uses νόθα to refer not to the rejected books, as he does in 3.25.4, but to the
heretical, fictitious books. (Kalin, "The New Testament Canon of Eusebius," 396, does not probe
further into this vocabulary shift but just notes that Eusebius uses this term "paradoxically.")
(b) It is possible to understand ἀντιλεγόμενα and νόθα as part of one larger category of disputed
books, within which there are two subcategories: disputed but accepted by most (and therefore
canonical), and disputed but rejected by most (and therefore not canonical). This is the view of
Robert M. Grant, *Eusebius as Church Historian* (Eugene, OR: Wipf and Stock, 1980), 133. If so,
then one could understand how, in some sense, Eusebius could lump both of these subcategories
together under the heading of "disputed" books. Regardless, there is little reason to think these
terms are identical.

[41]*Hist. eccl.* 3.25.7.

[42]Metzger, *The Canon of the New Testament*, 205.

received, yet some doubted (similar to Eusebius's disputed books). It is noteworthy that these first two categories of Eusebius make up exactly our twenty-seven New Testament books. In addition, it should be noted that Eusebius has three categories of "orthodox" books (recognized, disputed, and rejected). The existence of this third category—books that were not canonical but still orthodox—confirms our discussion above about how church fathers were able to regard a book as useful and beneficial, yet not canonical. Thus, contra Hahneman, Gamble, and others, a church father could use an apocryphal book without implying that the boundaries of the canon were loose and undefined.[43] These four categories can be seen visually in figure 2.

Figure 2. Categories of early Christian literature

indicates canonical books.   indicates orthodox books.

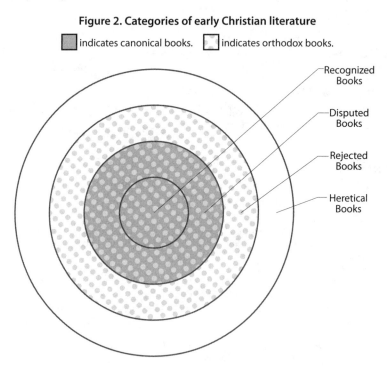

Recognized Books

Disputed Books

Rejected Books

Heretical Books

With these books in mind, we now turn our attention to analyzing some of them in more detail. Of course, we have already addressed the reception of the "recognized" books in prior chapters, so we will focus our attention primarily on the other three categories.

---

[43]That some Patristic writers may have disagreed about which particular apocryphal books were "rejected" and which were "heretical" is beside the point (e.g., Clement of Alexandria and Origen use the *Gospel of Peter* even though Eusebius places it in the heretical camp). Even if there were disagreements about which books fell into these categories, the important fact is that early church fathers *had* these categories.

A. Disputed Books

1. *James*. The book of James has been assigned various dates over the years, some as late as the second century (though this position has been largely abandoned).[44] Traditionally the epistle has been given a first-century date (ranging from AD 40 to 62) and attributed to James the Lord's brother, who was intimately involved with the apostolic circle and retained authority over the Jerusalem church (Acts 15; 1 Cor. 15:7).[45] If this is correct, then there are good grounds for thinking it would have possessed reliable apostolic teaching. James clearly did not enjoy the same popularity in the early church as the core New Testament books (like Paul's epistles), as is evidenced by the paucity of explicit Patristic citations of the book. However, its impact can be seen more indirectly as it appears to have influenced a number of other early Christian writings, such as *1 Clement* and the *Shepherd of Hermas*.[46] In addition, James is cited by Irenaeus,[47] Clement of Alexandria wrote a commentary on it which is now lost,[48] and it was recognized as canonical Scripture by Origen, who cites it frequently and refers to it as from "James, the brother of

---

[44]This position was largely held by the Tübingen School, and by scholars like Harnack and Jülicher; see discussion in Joseph B. Mayor, *The Epistle of St. James* (London: Macmillan, 1892), cxxi–clxxviii. This position has been revived in the present day by Nienhuis, *Not by Paul Alone*, 100ff.

[45]Helpful discussions of date and authorship can be found in P. H. Davids, *The Epistle of James*, NIGTC (Grand Rapids: Eerdmans, 1982), 2–22; James B. Adamson, *The Epistle of James*, NICNT (Grand Rapids: Eerdmans, 1976), 18–40.

[46]Mayor, *The Epistle of St. James*, lxix–lxxxiv; Davids, *The Epistle of James*, 7–9; L. T. Johnson, *The Letter of James*, Anchor Bible Commentary (New York: Doubleday, 1995), 66–80, 124–40. Regarding the *Shepherd* note *Sim.* 8.6; *Mand.* 12.5; 12.6. Nienhuis is quite dismissive of these textual connections because he claims that no one has offered a compelling explanation for why James was cited sparingly if in fact it was known during this time (*Not by Paul Alone*, 102–6). But why does one have to know the *reason* James was overlooked in order to search for historical evidence of its influence? The reasons a book was infrequently cited can be quite complex and are not always historically accessible to us. Nienhuis seems unwilling to consider that these textual connections might point to James unless this requirement is first met. The book should not be guilty until proven innocent. There is certainly no reason that James *must* be pseudonymous simply because we do not know why it was rarely employed by early Christians.

[47]*Haer.* 4.16.2. Bruce, *The Canon of Scripture* , 176, calls this a "fairly clear quotation of James." Likewise, Metzger includes James in the books that Irenaeus knew (*The Canon of the New Testament*, 154). In disagreement is Nienhuis, *Not by Paul Alone*, 36.

[48]Eusebius tells us that Clement, in his *Hypotyposeis*, wrote a commentary on "all the Canonical Scriptures, not passing over the disputed writings, I mean the epistle of Jude, and the remaining Catholic Epistles" (*Hist. eccl.* 6.14.1). Elsewhere, Eusebius very clearly includes James in these "disputed writings" (*Hist. eccl.* 3.25.3) and also clearly numbers James among the "catholic epistles" (*Hist. eccl.* 2.23.25). See B. F. Wescott, *A General Survey of the History of the Canon of the New Testament* (London: Macmillan, 1870), 357–58. Again, Nienhuis is not persuaded by this because he says Eusebius's statements are "casually worded" (*Not by Paul Alone*, 49). But this hardly seems substantial enough to override what he admits is the meaning of Eusebius's statements "taken at face value" (*Not by Paul Alone*, 49).

the Lord."[49] Eusebius acknowledges that some had doubts about it, but counts it among the canonical books "known to most,"[50] and the letter is fully received by Jerome, Augustine, and the councils of Hippo and Carthage.[51] Moreover, as noted above, we possess several early manuscripts of James: P20, P23, P100 are all third century and suggest that the book was known and used by early Christians. While James's canonical path was not as smooth as that of other books, these factors give no reason to doubt its place in the canon.

   2. *Jude.* Although some scholars have argued that Jude is pseudonymous and produced at the turn of the century,[52] others have made good arguments that Jude was likely written by the brother of James (and Jesus) as the opening verse claims.[53] Bauckham has made a compelling case for a date in the 50s, but it may also have been produced as late as the 80s (depending on its relationship with 2 Peter).[54] Either way, we have good reason to think that this letter stems from apostolic circles and would therefore contain apostolic teaching. Like the book of James, Jude was also largely overlooked by many Patristic authors. Of course, as with many of these "disputed" books, the small size of the writing becomes a significant factor in why these books have received less attention. Jude is particularly small—containing only 602 words—which makes the lack of extant evidence for the book less surprising. Also, according to Jerome, Jude's use of Enoch may explain why some had doubts about it.[55] Nevertheless, Jude's reception is remarkably positive: it was included in our earliest canonical list (the Muratorian canon), Tertullian acknowledged it as apostolic Scripture,[56] Clement of Alexandria clearly cited it and wrote a commentary on it,[57] Origen received it as fully canonical,[58] and Eusebius placed it firmly in the canonical Catholic Epistles as a book "used publicly with the rest in most churches."[59]

---

[49]*Comm. Rom.* 4.8; *Comm. Jo.* 19.23.152; *Hom. Jos.* 7.1. Origen offers only faint indications that others in his day had doubts about the letter (*Comm. Jo.* 20.10.66). For discussion of whether Rufinus altered the text of Origen, see discussion below.

[50]*Hist. eccl.* 3.25.3.

[51]Davids, *The Epistle of James,* 7.

[52]J. N. D. Kelly, *A Commentary on the Epistles of Peter and of Jude* (New York: Harper & Row, 1969), 232–34; A. Leaney, *The Letters of Peter and Jude* (Cambridge: Cambridge University Press, 1967), 82; W. G. Kümmel, *Introduction to the New Testament* (Nashville: Abingdon, 1973), 428.

[53]R. Bauckham, *Jude, 2 Peter* (Waco, TX: Word, 1983), 13–16; D. Guthrie, *New Testament Introduction* (Downers Grove, IL: InterVarsity, 1990), 902–9.

[54]Bauckham, *Jude, 2 Peter,* 13–14.

[55]*Vir. ill.* 4.

[56]*Cult. fem.* 1.3.1–3.

[57]*Strom.* 3.2.11; Eusebius, *Hist. eccl.* 6.14.1.

[58]*Hom. Jos.* 7.1; *Hom. Gen.* 6.115–16.

[59]*Hist. eccl.* 2.23.25; cf. 3.25.3.

3. *2 Peter*. Perhaps no book has had a more difficult journey into the canon than 2 Peter. It is widely regarded as pseudonymous by modern scholars and often dated to the early second century.[60] However, a substantial case has been made for the traditional authorship of the book, which would suggest a date in the mid-60s.[61] This date finds confirmation in a number of early sources that may have known and used 2 Peter, such as *1 Clement* (c. 96), which has several places of overlap (e.g., 23.3 [2 Pet. 3:4]; 9.2 [2 Pet. 1:17]; 35.5 [2 Pet. 2:2]),[62] and the *Apocalypse of Peter* (c. 110), which also seems to have known the letter.[63] Bauckham considers the connections to the *Apocalypse of Peter* to be "very good" and "sufficient to rule out a late date for 2 Peter."[64] In addition, Justin Martyr makes a striking allusion to 2 Peter 2:1 in his *Dialogue with Trypho*,[65] Irenaeus appears to cite it,[66] and Hippolytus also seems to show knowledge of it.[67] Clement of Alexandria wrote a now-lost commentary on 2 Peter,[68] Origen cited it six times and clearly received it as canonical Scripture,[69] and Eusebius considered it to be part of the "disputed" books in the canon that were nevertheless known to most of the church.[70] Despite some initial hesitancy toward 2 Peter from some quarters of the church, in the end it was widely received by such figures as Jerome, Athanasius, Gregory of Nazianzus, and Augustine.[71] Thus, even with its slow start,

---

[60]Kelly, *A Commentary on the Epistles of Peter and of Jude*, 235; J. B. Mayor, *The Epistle of St. Jude and the Second Epistle of St. Peter* (London: Macmillan, 1907), cxxiv.; J. Neyrey, *2 Peter, Jude* (New York: Doubleday, 1993), 119ff.; Bauckham, *Jude, 2 Peter*, 157–63 (dates it to the 80s).

[61]E. M. B. Green, *2 Peter Reconsidered* (London: Tyndale, 1960); Guthrie, *New Testament Introduction*, 805–42; B. B. Warfield, "The Canonicity of 2 Peter," in *Selected Shorter Writings of Benjamin B. Warfield*, ed. John E. Meeter, vol. 2 (Nutley, NJ: Presbyterian and Reformed, 1973), 49–79; Michael J. Gilmour, "Reflections on the Authorship of 2 Peter," *EvQ* 73 (2001): 291–309; and M. J. Kruger, "The Authenticity of 2 Peter," *JETS* 42 (1999): 645–71.

[62]Robert E. Picirilli, "Allusions to 2 Peter in the Apostolic Fathers," *JSNT* 33 (1988): 59; H. C. C. Cavallin, "The False Teachers of 2 Peter as Pseudoprophets," *NovT* 21 (1979): 268; Kruger, "The Authenticity of 2 Peter," 654–55.

[63]Mayor, *The Epistle of St. Jude and the Second Epistle of St. Peter*, cxxx–cxxxiv.

[64]Bauckham, *Jude, 2 Peter*, 162. See also T. V. Smith, *Petrine Controversies in Early Christianity* (Tübingen: Mohr, 1985), 53; and J. A. T. Robinson, *Redating the New Testament* (Philadelphia: Westminster, 1976), 178.

[65]*Dial.* 82.1; the rare word ψευδοδιδάσκαλοι is found in only these two passages up to the time of Justin; see Bauckham, *Jude, 2 Peter*, 237.

[66]See *Haer.* 5.23.2, which is virtually identical with 2 Pet. 3:8 (and differs substantially from the LXX of Ps. 90:4). Further discussion can be found in Kruger, "The Authenticity of 2 Peter," 653.

[67]Hippolytus, *Haer.* 9.7.3 (2 Pet. 2:22). Gamble agrees that Hippolytus knew 2 Peter (*New Testament Canon*, 51).

[68]Again, Eusebius tells us that Clement, in his *Hypotyposeis*, wrote a commentary even on the "disputed writings" (*Hist. eccl.* 6.14.1), which clearly included 2 Peter (*Hist. eccl.* 3.25.3).

[69]*Hom. Num.* 2.676; *Hom. Jos.* 7.1. Origen acknowledged that others had doubts about 2 Peter (Eusebius, *Hist. eccl.* 6.25.11), but they did not seem to affect his reception of the book.

[70]*Hist. eccl.* 3.25.3.

[71]Green, *2 Peter Reconsidered*, 6.

it is important to remember that 2 Peter still has significantly more support for its inclusion in the canon than the best of those books that have been rejected.

4. *2 and 3 John*. Most scholars agree that a single author penned all three of the Johannine epistles, though there is debate about who that author might be.[72] Given that Irenaeus (*Haer.* 3.16.18) and Clement of Alexandria (*Strom.* 2.15.66) attribute at least 1 John to John the son of Zebedee, there is solid external support for the traditional view that the apostle is the author of all three letters. As would be expected, 2 and 3 John are cited less frequently than 1 John, no doubt owing (in part) to their very small size. However, these two little letters have still left their mark on the historical record. Polycarp appears to know both 1 and 2 John,[73] and there are also reasons to think that Ignatius knew 2 John.[74] By the end of the second century, our first canonical list, the Muratorian fragment, mentions at least two of the epistles of John (and possibly all three).[75] Irenaeus received at least the first and second epistle,[76] and Clement of Alexandria cited from 2 John and wrote commentaries on 2 and 3 John that are now lost.[77] Hippolytus accepted at least 1 and 2 John (but is silent about 3 John),[78] Cyprian was familiar with 2 John,[79] and Dionysius of Alexandria mentions 2 and 3 John quite confidently as canonical Scripture.[80] Although Origen recognized that some had doubts about 2 and 3 John, it appears most in his day regarded the two letters as genuine—including Origen himself.[81] By the time we reach Eusebius in the fourth century, as noted above, 2 and 3 John have found a firm home as part of the seven "Catholic Epistles."[82] Hill has made the case that the reception of two tiny epistles like 2 and 3 John by the third cen-

---

[72]I. H. Marshall, *The Epistles of John* (Grand Rapids: Eerdmans, 1978), 31.

[73]Compare *Phil.* 7.1 with 2 John 7 (Hill, *The Johannine Corpus*, 418–19).

[74]Ign. *Eph.* 6.2; 9.1; 11.2 (cf. 2 John 4, 10). For more discussion on these texts, see Hill, *The Johannine Corpus*, 441.

[75]The book of 1 John is alluded to at an earlier point in the epistle (line 28), thus the later mention of "two" epistles of John may refer to 2 and 3 John. For the view that all three Johannine epistles are included, see P. Katz, "The Johannine Epistles in the Muratorian Canon," *JTS* 8 (1957): 273–74; Hill, *The Johannine Corpus*, 135–36; and Metzger, *The Canon of the New Testament*, 197.

[76]*Haer.* 1.16.3; 3.16.8; 3 John 9 may be referenced in *Haer.* 4.26.3.

[77]Clement's *Hypotyposeis*, a commentary on even the "disputed writings," clearly included 2 and 3 John, according to Eusebius (*Hist. eccl.* 3.25.3).

[78]Nienhuis, *Not by Paul Alone*, 45.

[79]*Sent.* 81.

[80]Eusebius, *Hist. eccl.* 7.25.11.

[81]Eusebius, *Hist. eccl.* 6.25.10.

[82]Eusebius, *Hist. eccl.* 2.23.25; 3.25.3.

tury, though they were not used as much as other books, suggests that they were likely bound together with 1 John (and maybe other Johannine works) at a much earlier point.[83] In other words, we are hard-pressed to think that these two letters would have made it into the Catholic Epistles if they had been circulating independently and were latecomers to the canonical scene. Their historical and textual association with the other Johannine works—even though they were not cited as frequently—is the best explanation for their preservation and eventual reception. This scenario finds confirmation in the third-century codex of 2 John, P.Ant. 12 (0232), which was discussed above. The fragment has a high page number, suggesting that 2 John originally circulated with the other Johannine letters, along with other books.

5. *Revelation.* Although the authorship of Revelation, like any book, continues to be debated, the testimony of early church writers was remarkably uniform that it was John the son of Zebedee.[84] While some early Christians, like Dionysius of Alexandria, argued that another John wrote the book of Revelation[85]—apparently increasing doubts among some, including Eusebius[86]—the arguments do not prove to be compelling enough to overturn the dominant tradition of the early church.[87] In the early second century, we know that Papias used the book of Revelation because Andrew of Caesarea refers to Papias's exegesis of Revelation 12:9[88] and even indicates that Papias "bore witness to its trustworthiness"[89]—likely evidence that Papias attributed the book to John the apostle. In addition, Eusebius mentions Papias's belief in a millennial reign of Christ and argues that Papias misunderstood the things

---

[83]Hill, *The Johannine Corpus*, 135–36; and Metzger, *The Canon of the New Testament*, 459–60.

[84]Such testimony is widespread and comes from Justin Martyr, Melito of Sardis, the Muratorian canon, Irenaeus, Clement of Alexandria, Tertullian, Hippolytus, Origen, and others. See Guthrie, *New Testament Introduction*, 929–32.

[85]Eusebius, *Hist. eccl.* 7.25.7–27. Gaius of Rome also rejected Revelation (Eusebius, *Hist. eccl.* 3.27.1–2), likely due to the manner in which it was abused by the Montanists. But these arguments seemed to have little effect on the reception of Revelation in the West. Moreover, Hill has raised doubts about whether Gaius really did oppose the Johannine literature (*The Johannine Corpus*, 172–204).

[86]Eusebius, *Hist. eccl.* 3.25.1–4.

[87]Those who have argued for the traditional authorship of Revelation include G. K. Beale, *The Book of Revelation*, NIGNTC (Grand Rapids: Eerdmans, 1999), 34–36; Guthrie, *New Testament Introduction*, 929–32; Robert H. Mounce, *The Book of Revelation*, NICNT (Grand Rapids: Eerdmans, 1998), 8–15; S. S. Smalley, "John's Revelation and John's Community," *BJRL* 69 (1987): 549–71; and V. S. Poythress, "Johannine Authorship and the Use of Intersentence Conjunctions in the Book of Revelation," *WTJ* 47 (1985): 329–36. See also N. B. Stonehouse, *The Apocalypse in the Ancient Church* (Goes: Oosterbaan & Le Cointre, 1929).

[88]*On the Apocalypse* 34.12.

[89]Preface to *On the Apocalypse*.

"spoken mystically and symbolically" that come from the "apostolic accounts," which was no doubt a reference to the symbolism of the book of Revelation.[90] Soon thereafter, Justin Martyr also received the book of Revelation as apostolic,[91] Melito of Sardis wrote a commentary on it,[92] Irenaeus affirmed it as fully canonical and apostolic,[93] and it was included in the Muratorian canon.[94] This strong trend continued as the book's canonical status was also affirmed by Hippolytus,[95] Tertullian,[96] Clement of Alexandria,[97] and Origen.[98]

The impressive early attestation for Revelation led B. W. Bacon to say, "There is no book in the entire New Testament whose external attestation can compare with that of Revelation, in nearness, clearness, definiteness, and positiveness of statement."[99] This is confirmed by the relatively high number of extant manuscripts of Revelation from the second and third centuries: P18, P47, P98, P115, and 0308. This demonstrates that the doubts about Revelation primarily developed at a *later* point in the history of the canon, mainly in the East, possibly sparked by the criticisms of Dionysius. However, it is evident that Dionysius's criticism was driven primarily by his dislike of chiliastic teaching and was not based on any historical arguments from the tradition of the church.[100] Although this theological controversy led to some doubts in the East for a period of time—e.g., Gregory Nazianzus, Cyril of Jerusalem, Synod of Laodicea—the book of Revelation was still widely affirmed by others such as the list of Codex Claromontanus (c. 300), Athanasius's Festal Letter (c. 367), Epiphanius (c. 374), the council of Carthage (c. 397), Jerome (c. 414), and Augustine (c. 426). With such broad support for Revelation, along with its very early attestation and reception, the confusion in the East eventually dissipated, and the book was once again universally acknowledged.

---

[90]Eusebius, *Hist. eccl.* 3.39.12; Hill, *The Johannine Corpus*, 394–95.

[91]*Dial.* 81.15; cf. Eusebius, *Hist. eccl.* 4.18.

[92]Eusebius, *Hist. eccl.* 4.26.2.

[93]*Haer.* 4.14.1; 5.26.1.

[94]As noted above, the book of Revelation was included in the Muratorian canon but was placed along with other "disputed" books at the end. However, the writer of the fragment expresses specific reservations about the other apocalyptic writings (*Apocalypse of Peter, Shepherd of Hermas*), but mentions none about the book of Revelation.

[95]*Antichr.* 36, 50.

[96]*Marc.* 3.14, 24.

[97]*Strom.* 6.106–7.

[98]*Comm. Jo.* 2.2; Eusebius, *Hist. eccl.* 6.25.10.

[99]B. W. Bacon, *The Making of the New Testament* (Folcroft, PA: Folcroft Library Editions, 1900), 190–91.

[100]Gerhard Maier, *Die Johannesoffenbarung und die Kirche* (Tübingen: Mohr, 1981), 96–107; and Mounce, *The Book of Revelation*, 13.

B. Rejected Books

For space reasons we cannot treat all the rejected books listed by Eusebius. Thus, we will focus on two of the most important, the *Shepherd of Hermas* and the *Epistle of Barnabas*.

1. *Shepherd of Hermas*. Of all the books outside the New Testament, the *Shepherd* may have been the most well known by early Christians. It is an "apocalypse" of sorts that details a series of visions and revelations given by an angelic messenger (sometimes dressed as a shepherd) to a second-century Christian from Rome named Hermas.[101] The book was probably written around the middle of the second century and has no claim to apostolic authorship or to apostolic tradition.[102] It was expressly rejected by the Muratorian canon as something written "very recently, in our times" and not during the time of the apostles. Irenaeus seems to refer to it as γραφή ("Scripture") on one occasion, but pays no further attention to it, never citing it again.[103] This has led Grant, Campenhausen, and others to suggest that Irenaeus may simply have used γραφή to refer to the *Shepherd* as a "writing," but we cannot be sure.[104] Although Clement of Alexandria uses the *Shepherd* more often—as he does with many non-canonical books—he never affirms its canonical status.[105] Origen clearly values the *Shepherd*, sometimes citing it alongside scriptural books (which

---

[101]For overviews of the *Shepherd*, see J. Verheyden, "The Shepherd of Hermas," in *The Writings of the Apostolic Fathers*, ed. Paul Foster (London: T&T Clark, 2007), 63–71; B. D. Ehrman, *The Apostolic Fathers*, 2 vols. (Cambridge, MA: Harvard University Press, 2003), 2:162–73; G. F. Snyder, "Hermas' The Shepherd," *ABD* 3:148; and Carolyn Osiek, *The Shepherd of Hermas* (Minneapolis: Fortress, 1999).

[102]The Muratorian fragment tells us that it was written by the brother of Pius, the bishop of Rome (c. 140–54), but we cannot be sure. Origen erroneously connects the author of the *Shepherd* to the Hermas mentioned in Rom. 16:14 (*Comm. Rom.* 10.31), and the tradition is repeated by Eusebius (*Hist. eccl.* 3.3.6) and Jerome (*Vir. ill.* 10).

[103]Irenaeus, *Haer.* 4.20.2. It is no doubt this passage to which Eusebius refers when he says that Irenaeus received the *Shepherd* as "Scripture" (*Hist. eccl.* 5.8.7).

[104]Robert M. Grant, *Irenaeus of Lyons* (London: Routledge, 1997), 38; H. von Campenhausen, *The Formation of the Christian Bible* (London: A&C Black, 1972), 219n52; Adelin Rousseau et al., eds., *Irénée de Lyon: Contre les hérésies, Livre 4*, vol. 2: Texte et traduction, Sources chrétiennes 100 (Paris: Cerf, 1965), 248–50. In disagreement is M. C. Steenberg, "Irenaeus on Scripture, Graphe, and the Status of Hermas," *St Vladimir's Theological Quarterly* 53 (2009): 29–66.

[105]E.g., *Strom.* 2.1; 2.9; 2.12; 4.9; 6.15. Although the last text is sometimes used to argue that Clement saw the *Shepherd* as canonical, the context suggests otherwise. In this passage, Clement is arguing about how the meaning of the Scriptures can be veiled, and in typical Clement fashion he appeals to all sources at his disposal that support his point, including the *Preaching of Peter* and the *Shepherd*. We know that he did not receive the former as canonical (see above), and we have little reason to think that the latter is in a different category. While Clement appears to affirm the inspiration of the *Shepherd* at one point (*Strom.* 1.29), we must remember that Clement used inspiration language quite broadly, even affirming the "inspiration" of Plato on one occasion (*Strom.* 1.8).

he is apt to do with other noncanonical literature),[106] but explicitly leaves it out of his own canonical lists.[107] Tertullian not only rejects the book outright as false, but even indicates that "every council of Churches" has judged it to be apocryphal.[108] Eusebius does not even regard it as "disputed," but considers it "spurious" (νόθα),[109] and Athanasius denies its canonical status but affirms its usefulness for catechetical instruction. Most notably, the book does not appear in any of the fourth-century canonical lists.[110] Although the *Shepherd* is included at the end of Codex Sinaiticus (along with *Barnabas*), we should remember our discussion above that it was a common practice to place either disputed books or books found generally useful (though not canonical) at the back of such lists.[111] In the end, there is little here to suggest that the *Shepherd* ought to have a place among the canonical Scriptures.

2. *Epistle of Barnabas.* The *Epistle of Barnabas* was a theological treatise written as a letter in the second century (c. 130) that proved to be quite popular within some early Christian circles.[112] Much of the epistle is concerned with how the Jews have misunderstood their own books and how Christ fulfills the sacrificial portions of the Old Testament. Although the letter is attributed to the Barnabas who was a companion of Paul, it was written by a second-century author whose identity remains unknown. Clement of Alexandria comes closest to regarding *Barnabas* as canonical—Eusebius tells us he wrote a commentary on the book[113]—though Clement never calls it Scripture and in other places is quite willing to critique the epistle.[114] Although at one point Origen refers to *Barnabas*

---

[106]E.g., *Princ.* 2.1.5.

[107]*Hom. Jos.* 7.1; *Hom. Gen.* 13. The *Shepherd* is also absent from Eusebius's list of Origen's books (*Hist. eccl.* 6.25.3–14).

[108]*Pud.* 10. See also J. F. Jansen, "Tertullian and the New Testament," *SecCent* 2 (1982): 191–207.

[109]Eusebius, *Hist. eccl.* 3.25.4.

[110]Although it is mentioned in the list of Codex Claromontanus, the scribe has placed a dash next to it and *Barnabas* in an effort to distinguish them from the canonical books.

[111]See again W. Horbury, "The Wisdom of Solomon in the Muratorian Fragment," *JTS* 45 (1994): 149–59.

[112]For more on *Barnabas*, see James Carleton Paget, *The Epistle of Barnabas: Outlook and Background* (Tübingen: Mohr Siebeck, 1994); L. W. Barnard, "The Epistle of Barnabas and Its Contemporary Setting," in *ANRW* 11.27.1 (1993): 159–207; and Jay Curry Treat, "Epistle of Barnabas," *ABD* 1:611–14.

[113]Eusebius, *Hist. eccl.* 6.14.1; *Strom.* 2.6.31; 2.7.35; 2.20.116; 5.10.63. Clement's high opinion of *Barnabas* was no doubt driven by his apparent belief that the author was the first-century companion of Paul (*Strom.* 2.20.116).

[114]*Paed.* 2.10.3; *Strom.* 2.15.67. See discussion in J. Lightfoot, *The Apostolic Fathers*, 2 vols. (London: Macmillan, 1889), 2:504.

with the phrase "it is written,"[115] he explicitly leaves *Barnabas* out of his list of canonical books,[116] and he writes no commentary or homily on it. The book is absent from the Muratorian canon, and Eusebius even classifies the epistle into the category of "rejected" books.[117] Although Irenaeus and Tertullian comment extensively on canonical books, they show little interest in *Barnabas*.[118] It also lacks a place in most of our fourth-century canonical lists, including Claromontanus, Cyril of Jerusalem, Laodicea, Athanasius, Gregory Nazianzus, and the councils of Hippo and Carthage.[119] Since *Barnabas* lacks the historical credentials of the other New Testament letters, being a second-century production written well after the time of the apostles, it is difficult to take it seriously as a contender for a place in the canon.

C. Heretical Books

Eusebius mentions a number of "heretical" books that we will not be able to cover here. However, we will briefly address two of the most well known, namely, the *Gospel of Thomas* and the *Gospel of Peter*.

1. *Gospel of Thomas.* Doubtless *Thomas* is the best-known apocryphal gospel to modern readers, and the modern scholarly works on the subject are too numerous to mention.[120] Part of the now well-known cache of documents discovered at Nag Hammadi in 1945, *Thomas* contains 114 sayings of Jesus, many of which are rather cryptic and esoteric, and others of which bear a closer affinity to the canonical Jesus.[121] Most infamous

---

[115]*Cels.* 1.63. In *Princ.* 3.2.4 Origen quotes *Barnabas* alongside New Testament books but lists it at the end, after the *Shepherd of Hermas.* Thus, Carleton Paget considers the evidence "not conclusive" about whether Origen considers it Scripture (*The Epistle of Barnabas*, 251).

[116]*Hom. Jos.* 7.1 (for discussion of the reliability of this list, see below); *Hom. Gen.* 13. *Barnabas* is also absent from Eusebius's list of Origen's books (*Hist. eccl.* 6.25.3–14).

[117]*Hist. eccl.* 3.25.4.

[118]Tertullian mentions the *Epistle of Barnabas* in *Pud.* 1.20, but clearly subordinates it to the canonical works and mentions only that it is more well known in the churches than the *Shepherd.*

[119]Carleton Paget, *The Epistle of Barnabas*, 255–56. Again, although *Barnabas* was included in Claromontanus, the scribe placed a dash next to the book to distinguish it from the canonical books.

[120]A broad survey of the scholarly literature can be found in Francis T. Fallon and Ron Cameron, "The *Gospel of Thomas*: A *Forschungsbericht* and Analysis," in *ANRW* 2.25.6 (1988): 4195–251. A helpful overview of some of the key modern works is provided in Nicholas Perrin, *Thomas: The Other Gospel* (Louisville: Westminster John Knox, 2007). See also the bibliography in J. K. Elliott, *The Apocryphal New Testament* (Oxford: Clarendon, 1993), 126–27.

[121]For a general introduction to the Nag Hammadi material see Christopher Tuckett, *Nag Hammadi and the Gospel Tradition* (Edinburgh: T&T Clark, 1986). A fragmentary version of Thomas was known through the earlier discoveries of P.Oxy. 1, P.Oxy. 654, and P.Oxy. 655. For more on these papyri, see Joseph A. Fitzmyer, "The Oxyrhynchus Logoi of Jesus and the Coptic Gospel According to Thomas," *TS* 20 (1959): 505–60.

is its final line: "Jesus said . . . 'For every woman who makes herself male will enter the kingdom of heaven.'" In addition, *Thomas* lacks the narrative structure so common to the canonical Gospels, leaving out any account of the birth, death, and resurrection of Jesus. Despite the efforts of more radical scholars,[122] the broad consensus is that *Thomas* was written in the middle of the second century by an unknown author (certainly not the apostle Thomas).[123] Not only is this substantially later than our canonical Gospels (which are all first century), but *Thomas* also appears to be derivative from and dependent upon the canonical material.[124] In addition, the book has a strong Gnostic flavor throughout, advocating a Jesus less concerned with showing that he is divine and more concerned with teaching us to find the divine spark within ourselves.[125] As John Meier notes, this Gnostic tendency also indicates a second-century date for *Thomas*.

> Since a gnostic world view of this sort [in *Thomas*] was not employed to reinterpret Christianity in such a thoroughgoing way before sometime in the second century AD, there can be no question of the *Gospel of Thomas* . . . being a reliable reflection of the historical Jesus or of the earliest sources of 1st-century Christianity.[126]

It is not surprising, then, that *Thomas* is never mentioned in any early canonical list, is not found in any of our New Testament manuscript collections, never figured prominently in canonical discussions, and often was condemned outright by a variety of church fathers.[127] Thus, if *Thomas* does represent authentic, original Christianity, then it has left very little historical evidence of that fact.

---

[122]Stephen J. Patterson, *The Gospel of Thomas and Jesus* (Sonoma: Polebridge, 1993); E. Pagels, *Beyond Belief: The Secret Gospel of Thomas* (New York: Random House, 2003); J. D. Crossan, *Four Other Gospels: Shadows on the Contours of Canon* (New York: Seabury, 1985).

[123]Elliott, *The Apocryphal New Testament*, 124.

[124]E.g., John P. Meier, *A Marginal Jew: Rethinking the Historical Jesus*, vol. 1 (New York: Doubleday, 1991), 123–39; Christopher M. Tuckett, "Thomas and the Synoptics," *NovT* 30 (1988): 132–57; Hurtado, *Lord Jesus Christ*, 473–74; Klyne R. Snodgrass, "The Gospel of Thomas: A Secondary Gospel," *SecCent* 7 (1989–1990): 19–38; and Raymond E. Brown, "The Gospel of Thomas and St. John's Gospel," *NTS* 9 (1962–1963): 155–77. More recently, Perrin, *Thomas: The Other Gospel*, has suggested that *Thomas* is dependent on Tatian's *Diatessaron*.

[125]*Gospel of Thomas* 70; Pagels, *Beyond Belief*, 30–73. On the Gnostic or non-Gnostic nature of this gospel, see Robert M. Grant, *The Secret Sayings of Jesus* (Garden City, NY: Doubleday, 1960), 186; A. J. B. Higgins, "The Non-Gnostic Sayings in the Gospel of Thomas," *NovT* 4 (1960): 30–47; William K. Grobel, "How Gnostic Is the Gospel of Thomas?," *NTS* 8 (1962): 367–73. For a theory of two versions of *Thomas*, see Gilles Quispel, *Makarius, das Thomasevangelium und das Lied von der Perle* (Leiden: Brill, 1967).

[126]Meier, *Marginal Jew*, 127.

[127]E.g., Hippolytus, *Haer.* 5.7.20; Origen, *Hom. Luc.* 1; Eusebius, *Hist. eccl.* 3.25.6.

2. *Gospel of Peter*. The *Gospel of Peter* is certainly one of the best-known apocryphal gospels that we possess and is primarily preserved in the eighth/ninth-century "Akhmîm Fragment."[128] Although we have fragmentary remains dating from c. 200 (P.Oxy. 2949), they are so incomplete that they offer little to our extant text.[129] The *Gospel of Peter* is a narrative-style gospel account, mainly focused upon the crucifixion and resurrection of Jesus (but may have contained more than that). Its composition dates from the middle of the second century, most likely in Syria.[130] Although the relation of the *Gospel of Peter* to the canonical texts is an ongoing debate, it seems a majority of scholars recognize its dependence on the canonical material.[131] This is confirmed by its obvious embellishments of the canonical story, including a "giant" Jesus who exits the tomb with his head reaching beyond the heavens and a cross that follows Jesus out of the tomb and begins to speak (!). Thus, there is little reason to think that this writing is historically authentic or contains genuine apostolic reports. In addition, some have seen Gnostic (specifically docetic) tendencies in the *Gospel of Peter* as Jesus hangs on the cross while feeling no pain and cries, "My Power, my Power, why have you forsaken me?"—the very basis for Serapion's objection to the writing.[132] Although it was used on occasion by some of the church fathers,[133] it never factored into canonical

---

[128]M. G. Mara, *Évangile de Pierre: Introduction, text critique, traduction, commentaire, et index* (Paris: Éditions du Cerf, 1973); H. B. Swete, *The Akhmîm Fragment of the Apocryphal Gospel of St. Peter* (London: Macmillan, 1893); Thomas J. Kraus and Tobias Nicklas, *Das Petrusevangelium und die Petrusapokalypse* (Berlin: de Gruyter, 2004); and, most recently, Paul Foster, *The Gospel of Peter: Introduction, Critical Edition and Commentary* (Leiden: Brill, 2010).

[129]For a discussion of this fragment, see R. A. Coles, "Apocryphal Gospel (?)," in *The Oxyrhynchus Papyri*, vol. 41, ed. G. M. Browne et al. (London: Egypt Exploration Society, 1972), 15–16; and Dieter Lührmann, "P.Oxy. 2949: EvPet 3–5 in einer Handschrift des 2/3 Jahrhunderts," *ZNW* 72 (1981): 216–26. In a more recent study, Lührmann proposed a new fragment of the *Gospel of Peter*, "P.Oxy. 4009: Ein neues Fragment des Petrusevangeliums?," *NovT* 35 (1993): 390–410, but this has been challenged by P. Foster, "Are There Any Early Fragments of the So-Called Gospel of Peter?," *NTS* 52 (2006): 1–28.

[130]See the analysis by Maurer and Schneemelcher in *New Testament Apocrypha*, ed. W. Schneemelcher, trans. R. McL. Wilson, 2 vols. (Louisville: Westminster John Knox, 1991), 1:216–22.

[131]David F. Wright, "Apocryphal Gospels: The 'Unknown Gospel' (Pap. Egerton 2) and the *Gospel of Peter*," in *Gospel Perspectives: The Jesus Tradition Outside the Gospels*, ed. David Wenham (Sheffield: JSOT, 1985), 207–32; Raymond E. Brown, "The Gospel of Peter and Canonical Authority," *NTS* 33 (1987): 321–43; and L. Vaganay, *L'Évangile de Pierre* (Paris: Librairie LeCoffre, 1930). Others have argued for its independence: Jürgen Denker, *Die theologiegeschichtliche Stellung des Petrusevangeliums: Ein Beitrag zur Frühgeschichte des Doketismus* (Bern and Frankfurt: Lang, 1975); and Helmut Koester, *Ancient Christian Gospels: Their History and Development* (London: SCM, 1990), 216–30.

[132]Eusebius, *Hist. eccl.* 6.12.2. The Gnostic nature of the *Gospel of Peter* has been challenged in recent years: J. W. McCant, "The Gospel of Peter: Docetism Reconsidered," *NTS* 30 (1984): 258–73; and P. M. Head, "On the Christology of the *Gospel of Peter*," *VC* 46 (1992): 209–24.

[133]E.g., Origen, *Comm. Matt.* 10.17.

discussions, never made a canonical list, and was condemned outright by Eusebius and others as "altogether wicked and impious."[134]

III. The "Closing" of the Canon

There is little doubt that most scholars would agree that the canon was "closed" sometime in the fourth century. Despite this general agreement, however, there seems to be a fair amount of confusion about what is meant by the term *closed*. As noted in prior chapters, many in modern canonical studies (particularly those in the historical-critical camp) tend to view canon solely in terms of the actions of the fourth-century church. Hahneman is typical in this regard: "Not until the fourth century did the church appear to define and restrict that New Testament collection."[135] As a result, the closing of the canon is inevitably seen as a human affair; it is something the church does. While this is true from one perspective, entirely absent in this approach is any recognition that the canonical books may be the result of the redemptive-historical deposit that God gave through his apostles. If the canon did originate with the foundational activities of the apostles (as argued in prior chapters), then we may need to rethink our view of the closing of the canon. From this perspective, the canon would be closed not in the fourth century (as is so commonly stated) but as soon as the final apostolic book was written.[136] Of course, there would still be the long process of the church recognizing books as apostolic, but that process is not really something that officially closes the canon as much as it acknowledges what is already there.[137] As Gamble has rightly noted, "This canon was never authorized and mandated by any ecumenical (general) council of the ancient church," but instead rests upon "the early and largely informal consensus of the ancient church."[138] In short, the church cannot close the canon because it never started it to begin with. It was inherited from the apostles.

---

[134]*Hist. eccl.* 3.25.7.

[135]Hahneman, *The Muratorian Fragment*, 129.

[136]Karel van der Toorn, *Scribal Culture and the Making of the Hebrew Bible* (Cambridge, MA: Harvard University Press, 2007), makes a very similar argument for the closing of the Old Testament canon. Van der Toorn observes, "The early Hellenistic scribes did not close the canon but declared the era of revelation to be closed" (260).

[137]Instead of saying the canon is "closed," perhaps we would do better to say that the canon is "settled." This term more accurately captures the role of the church in the process.

[138]H. Gamble, "Christianity: Scripture and Canon," in *The Holy Book in Comparative Perspective*, ed. Frederick M. Denny and Rodney L. Taylor (Columbia: University of South Carolina Press, 1985), 44–45.

This perspective on a closed canon appears to be shared by early Christians.[139] As noted above, the very popular *Shepherd of Hermas* was rejected by the Muratorian fragment on the grounds that it was written "very recently, in our own times."[140] In other words, the author of the fragment reflects the conviction that early Christians were not willing to accept books written in the second century or later, but restricted themselves to books from the redemptive-historical time period, that is, books that were apostolic.[141] In this regard, the canon was not "open." Ridderbos comments:

> When understood in terms of the history of redemption, the canon cannot be open; in principle it must be *closed*. That follows directly from the unique and exclusive nature of the power the apostles received from Christ and from the commission he gave them to be witnesses to what they had seen and heard of the salvation he had brought. The result of this power and commission is the foundation of the church and the creation of the canon, and therefore these are naturally unrepeatable and exclusive in character.[142]

This understanding of a closed canon is an essential corrective to much of canonical studies today. Images of early Christianity as a wide-open literary contest between books of every kind and from every place—a primitive writing competition of sorts—simply do not square with the convictions of early believers. In their understanding, there was something inherently closed about the canon from the very beginning, even in the midst of ongoing discussions about its boundaries. And this fact reveals that long before the fourth century there was a fundamental trend toward limitation and restriction, not invitation and expansion.

A. Attitudes toward Limiting the Canon

If we are correct that Christians had such a theological category for a closed canon prior to fourth-century ecclesiastical declarations, then, contrary to Hahneman's statement above, we should see further evidence, beyond the Muratorian fragment, that Christians sought to limit and restrict the

---

[139]This is not to suggest that later Christians never *used* the term *closed* to speak of the canon being settled or decided. One can use that term and, at the same time, recognize the theological truth that the canon has always been closed in principle from the very start.

[140]Muratorian canon, 74. The meaning of this phrase has recently been disputed by Hahneman, *The Muratorian Fragment*, 34–72. See response from Charles E. Hill, "The Debate over the Muratorian Fragment and the Development of the Canon," *WTJ* 57 (1995): 437–52.

[141]Bruce, *The Canon of Scripture*, 166. It is noteworthy that Tertullian also rejects the *Shepherd of Hermas* on very similar grounds, calling it "apocryphal and false" (*Pud.* 10).

[142]H. N. Ridderbos, *Redemptive History and the New Testament Scripture* (Phillipsburg, NJ: P&R, 1988), 25, emphasis his.

canon in various ways prior to that time. In fact, we do see evidence for such a trend, although we can only mention a sampling of it here.

1. *Dionysius of Corinth* (c. 170). Around the middle of the second century, Dionysius, the well-known bishop of Corinth, goes to great lengths to distinguish his letters from the "Scriptures of the Lord" lest anyone think he was writing new canonical books.[143] He specifically mentions that he only wrote "when Christians asked me" and even refers to his own letters as "inferior."[144] Such a distinction makes it clear that, at least in the eyes of this bishop, the Scriptures were a closed entity, and no new letters would be eligible for addition—even those written by a bishop. Moreover, the phrase "Scriptures of the Lord" is noteworthy here, suggesting a distinguishable body of writings about the Lord Jesus Christ, separate from the Old Testament books.[145] Although Dionysius does not enumerate which books he includes in the "Scriptures of the Lord," he uses the phrase in a manner that assumes his readers will readily know about the books to which he is referring.

2. *Irenaeus* (c. 180). As noted in chapter 6, Irenaeus in the late second century did not have an "open" canon, void of concern to draw limits or boundaries. At least as it pertains to the four Gospels, he was keen to draw very firm lines: "It is not possible that the gospels can be either more or fewer than the number they are."[146] For Irenaeus, the Gospel canon was certainly closed.

3. *Anonymous critic of Montanism* (c. 196). Eusebius relays the comments of an anti-Montanist writer who is hesitant to produce a document against the Montanists,

> not from the lack of any ability to refute the lie . . . but from timidity and scruples lest I might seem to some to be adding to the writings or injunctions of the word of the new covenant of the gospel [τῷ τῆς τοῦ εὐαγγελίου

---

[143]Eusebius, *Hist. eccl.* 4.23.12.

[144]Eusebius, *Hist. eccl.* 4.23.12. Eusebius compares the letters of Dionysius to other letters of ecclesiological correspondence, such as Dionysius's letter to Soter and *1 Clement* (all of which can be distinguished from the "Scriptures of the Lord").

[145]Hill, "The Debate over the Muratorian Fragment and the Development of the Canon," 450. Bart D. Ehrman, *The Orthodox Corruption of Scripture* (New York: Oxford University Press, 1993), uses this reference to Dionysius to argue that scribes (whether heretical or orthodox) were changing the text of the New Testament, showing that Dionysius, at least, views "Scriptures of the Lord" as referring to New Testament writings (26).

[146]*Haer.* 3.11.8.

καινῆς διαθήκης λόγῳ] to which no one . . . can add and from which he cannot take away.[147]

The writer explicitly applies the Deuteronomy 4:2 principle ("neither add nor take away") to the canon as a whole, showing that he does not see it as appropriate to either add or take away *books*.[148] He even refers to the Christian canon as the writings "of the new covenant," suggesting that it was seen as parallel to the "old covenant" (2 Cor. 3:6, 14). It is difficult to deny that at least this writer viewed the New Testament collection as "closed" in a way that no one could add to or take away from it.

4. *Gaius* (c. 200). Eusebius records a debate that occurred at the beginning of the third century between a certain Gaius from Rome and Montanist heretics.[149] The debate with the Montanists had very much to do with the development of the canon since their claim to receive ongoing "revelations" from God implied the possibility of new canonical books. Eusebius mentions that Gaius affirmed a thirteen-letter collection of Paul—the same number affirmed by the Muratorian canon—and that Gaius chided his Montanist opponents for their "recklessness and audacity . . . in composing new Scriptures."[150] Not only is it noteworthy here that Gaius drew up a closed list of Pauline letters, but then he went on to mention his opposition to anyone producing *new* scriptural books. But if the canon was wide open at this juncture, why would Gaius be so upset at the production of more books? It seems that Gaius did not have an open canon at all, but is yet another example of how early Christians viewed the canon as, in principle, closed.

5. *Origen* (c. 250). Despite the claims that canonical lists occur only in the fourth century, Origen, in the middle of the third century, lists the New Testament books in one of his homilies on Joshua and seems to include

---

[147]*Hist. eccl.* 5.16.3.

[148]For more on the Deut. 4:2 formula, see M. J. Kruger, "Early Christian Attitudes Towards the Reproduction of Texts," in *The Early Text of the New Testament*, ed. C. E. Hill and M. J. Kruger (Oxford: Oxford University Press, forthcoming).

[149]*Hist. eccl.* 6.20.3. For further discussion on Gaius, the Montanists, and John's writings, see Hill, *The Johannine Corpus*, 172–204.

[150]*Hist. eccl.* 6.20.3. Gaius is well known for his rejection of John's Gospel, though doubts have been raised about whether in fact he did reject it (Hill, *The Johannine Corpus*, 172–204). Nevertheless, even if Gaius rejected John's Gospel, that would not change the point being made here. Whether Gaius was correct in *how* he limited the canon does not change the fact that he understood there to *be* limitations to the canon, and at quite an early date.

all twenty-seven of them.[151] Such a list indicates that a concept of a closed canon was prevalent over a century before Athanasius's famous Festal Letter. This is confirmed elsewhere in Origen when, after comparing the Scriptures to a net, he declares that "before our Savior Jesus Christ this net was not wholly filled; for the net of the law and prophets had to be completed. . . . And the texture of the net *has been completed* [πεπλήρωται] in the Gospels, and in the words of Christ through the Apostles."[152] Some have challenged the reliability of this list of books in the homilies on Joshua because it comes from a Latin translation of Origen made by Rufinus, who has been accused of changing his sources.[153] However, it is not clear that this list can so quickly be dismissed on these grounds. While it is true that in Rufinus's translation of Origen's *De principiis* he edits out perceived discrepancies in Origen's text,[154] R. J. Rombs points out that more recent scholars like Henri Crouzel[155] and John Rist[156] have shown "the complete distrust of Rufinus's text to be excessive."[157] Although Rufinus sometimes paraphrases or condenses, "he never deliberately does violence to Origen's meaning" and "remains in the main true to Origen's sense."[158] Nevertheless, Everett Kalin remains skeptical of Rufinus on the grounds that Rufinus changed Eusebius's list of Origen's books (*Hist. eccl.* 6.25.3–14) when he translated it from Greek to Latin.[159] However, the specific changes that Kalin catalogs are not persuasive as an argument against Rufinus's reliability. The changes are precisely the type of paraphrases or rewordings that we might expect from Rufinus and are not inconsistent with what we know of Origen's positions.[160]

---

[151]*Hom. Jos.* 7.1. There is a text-critical issue with Revelation, as some manuscripts leave it out. If it is not original, this would then be a twenty-six-book list, still remarkably early.

[152]*Comm. Matt.* 10.12, emphasis mine.

[153]Most recently it has been challenged by E. Kalin, "Re-examining New Testament Canon History: 1. The Canon of Origen," *CurTM* 17 (1990): 274–82. However, its authenticity is accepted by A. von Harnack, *Der kirchengeschichtliche Ertrag der exegetischen Arbeiten des Origenes*, vol. 1 (Leipzig: Hinrichs, 1918), 12; Otto Bardenhewer, *Geschichte der alterkirchlichen Literatur*, vol. 2 (Freiburg im Bresgau: Herder, 1912), 152–56; and Metzger, *The New Testament Canon*, 138–40.

[154]Hanson, *Origen's Doctrine of Tradition*, 40–47. Hanson is largely critical of Rufinus but is dependent on older works like, Origen, *On First Principles*, trans. G. W. Butterworth (Gloucester, MA: P. Smith, 1973).

[155]Henri Crouzel, "Comparisons précises entre les fragments du Peri Archôn selon la Philocalie et la traduction de Rufin," in *Origeniana: premier colloque international des études origéniennes, Montserrat, 18–21 septembre 1975* (Bari: Università di Bari, 1975), 121.

[156]John Rist, "The Greek and Latin Texts of the Discussion on Free Will in De Principiis, Book III," in *Origeniana*, 111.

[157]R. J. Rombs, "A Note on the Status of Origen's *De Principiis* in English," *VC* 61 (2007): 23.

[158]Ibid.

[159]Kalin, "Re-examining New Testament Canon History," 280–81.

[160]Kalin mentions several changes that Rufinus made to Eusebius's list of Origen's books: (1) Rufinus uses "New Testament canon" instead of "ecclesiastical canon." However, this

As for Origen's list of books in his homilies on Joshua, Kalin's arguments are no more convincing. Kalin claims that Rufinus must have altered this list because Origen is presented as receiving 2 Peter and 2 and 3 John as canonical.[161] This cannot be true, argues Kalin, because elsewhere Origen acknowledges that some had doubts about these books.[162] However, it is unclear how these two facts are incompatible. Why cannot Origen accept a book as genuine and, at the same time, acknowledge that others had doubts about it? Kalin seems to think that if Origen admits that some have doubts about a book, then that must mean Origen himself rejects it—but this simply does not follow. The fact that Origen does not repeat the doubts of others in this particular passage is likely because it is a homily. The people in the pew would not have required critical reflections on each of these books.

Beyond these objections from Kalin, there are positive reasons to accept this list as genuine: (1) Harnack has pointed out that the position of Acts in the list does not reflect a fourth/fifth-century opinion, as would be the case if Rufinus altered it.[163] Moreover, the position of Acts does not reflect Rufinus's own list elsewhere.[164] (2) Metzger acknowledges that the list contains "characteristic Alexandrian oratory," which is consistent with it being originally from Origen.[165] (3) The list lacks the canonical embellishments we might expect if Rufinus were altering it. For instance, why does Rufinus not have Origen explicitly tell us that there were *three* Johannine epistles (particularly since Rufinus explicitly affirms these three elsewhere)?[166]

---

change rightly captures the sense of the text and does no violence to Eusebius's original account. (2) Rufinus clarifies that Origen accepted fourteen epistles of Paul (including Hebrews), while the original text of Eusebius doesn't give a number. However, this sort of clarification is consistent with the types of changes Rufinus makes elsewhere and likely stems from his knowledge of which books Origen actually accepted. The inclusion of Hebrews in the list of Pauline books is not inconsistent with Origen's doubts about its authorship (Eusebius, *Hist. eccl.* 6.25.14). Origen agrees that "the thoughts are the apostle's" and says, "For not without reason have the men of old handed it down as Paul's" (6.25.13). Moreover, Metzger reminds us that "in the vast majority" of Origen's references to Hebrews "he is content to attribute it to Paul as its author" (*The Canon of the New Testament*, 138). (3) Kalin argues that Rufinus portrays Origen as having no personal doubt about 2 Peter and 2 and 3 John. However, Eusebius's original Greek edition does not portray Origen has having personal doubts about these books, but observes only that they are disputed by some. It is difficult to see any meaningful difference between these two accounts. In the end, Kalin does not demonstrate that Rufinus has misrepresented Origen's views in this passage.

[161]Kalin, "Re-examining New Testament Canon History," 281.
[162]E.g., Eusebius, *Hist. eccl.* 6.25.10.
[163]Harnack, *Der kirchengeschichtliche*, 12. The only list that also has Acts following Revelation is the one found in the Eastern Codex Claromontanus (sixth century). The list itself likely has a Greek original that dates to c. 300, just after the time of Origen. Given that Rufinus represents a Western influence, we see again that the order of the books suggests that Origen is the source.
[164]*Commentary on the Apostles' Creed*, 37.
[165]Metzger, *The Canon of the New Testament*, 139.
[166]*Commentary on the Apostles' Creed*, 37.

Instead, Origen simply refers to the plural "[John's] Epistles." The vague-ness of this description favors its authenticity. (4) Barbara Bruce, in her introduction to the *Homilies on Joshua*, appeals to the work of Origen scholar Annie Jaubert and concludes that the evidence is "very commend-able in favor of Rufinus's faithfulness."[167] (5) Elsewhere, Origen affirms the same canonical authors that appear in this list. In his classic allegorizing fashion, Origen declares, "Isaac, therefore, digs also new wells, nay rather Isaac's servants dig them. Isaac's servants are Matthew, Mark, Luke, John; his servants are Peter, James, Jude; the apostle Paul is his servant. These all dig the wells of the New Testament."[168] No doubt Origen is here referring to all the authors of the New Testament canon, which fits quite well with the twenty-seven-book canon we have.

In the end, there are few reasons to distrust Origen's list of New Testament books. Regardless of whether Origen was overconfident in his assessment of the canon's boundaries, he reveals a profound degree of comfort with such boundaries at quite an early stage.

B. The Consensus of the Church

The above examples are merely a sampling of pre-fourth-century attitudes toward the extent of the canon. They reveal that the early stages of the canon were not a wide-open affair where newly produced apocryphal literature could have easily found a welcome home, but were marked by concern to affirm only books from the apostolic time period. In this sense, the canon was closed when the last apostolic book was written. Nevertheless, it took a while for the church to reach a consensus about all of these books. When we look at the canon from the perspective of when consensus was achieved, we can affirm that it was not closed (in this sense) until the fourth century.

We are reminded that there was no formal, official declaration of the church that closed the canon. We can agree with Ehrman that "the canon of the New Testament was ratified by widespread consensus rather than by official proclamation."[169] There are numerous examples of this consensus, most notably the Festal Letter of Athanasius in 367, where he affirms the

---

[167]Barbara J. Bruce, trans., *Origen: Homilies on Joshua* (Washington, DC: Catholic University Press, 2002), 18; see also Annie Jaubert, *Homélies sur Josué* (Paris: Éditions du Cerf, 1960), 75–82.
[168]*Hom. Gen.* 13.2, in *Origen: Homilies on Genesis and Exodus*, trans. Ronald E. Heine (Washington, DC: Catholic University Press, 1982). Of course, these homilies were also translated by Rufinus. But Heine gives an extended defense of Rufinus and concludes, "On the whole, the substance [of Rufinus's translation] can be regarded as representing Origen's thought" (38). The fact that the list in *Homilies on Joshua* and the list in *Homilies on Genesis* give the canonical authors in the same order is suggestive that they both come from Origen—otherwise one would have to suppose that Rufinus altered both lists in precisely the same manner.
[169]Ehrman, *Lost Christianities*, 231.

precise twenty-seven books of our current New Testament. In agreement are also Eusebius,[170] Codex Claromontanus,[171] Rufinus, Jerome, Augustine, the African Canons, and the Synods of Hippo and Carthage. Although there was not absolute uniformity (which is true still today), after this period the church coalesced around these twenty-seven books with remarkable unity.

IV. Conclusion

The development of the canon was not a simple affair, but a complex and often confusing process. Although there was a "core" New Testament canon by the end of the second century, there was ongoing debate and disagreement over the remaining books for centuries. Even so, such "canonical diversity" must not be overplayed. We should expect that there would have been some level of disagreement throughout the recognition process—that is inevitable if God delivered his books in the real world of history. Such disagreements do not require that we declare all books inherently "equal," nor do they prevent us from knowing which books are from God. Indeed, when the individual merits of each book are examined, it quickly becomes clear that the early church had reasons (and quite good ones) for rejecting some and accepting others.

Although the story of the development of the New Testament canon, with all its extensive and complicated historical details, is important to understand, it should not distract us from appreciating the final outcome. The length of the journey should not overshadow the significance of the destination. When all the dust had settled, the church had reached an impressive degree of unity about which books it recognized as speaking with the voice of its Master. It is remarkable that such unity is entirely overlooked and dismissed by some models of the canon as merely an accident of history. Apparently, *disagreements* among early Christians are historically significant and should be weighed heavily, whereas *unity* among early Christians is historically arbitrary and should be ignored. Why is that? The fact that the church was able to reach such unity in the midst of such diversity would indicate that more was in play than just the random flow of history. Indeed, such a scenario gives us good reason to think that the church reached unity on these books precisely because Christ himself was speaking in them.

---

[170]See discussion above about his canon consisting of "accepted" and "disputed" books, totaling twenty-seven.

[171]The absence of Philippians, 1 and 2 Thessalonians, and Hebrews is likely the result of a scribal error; see discussion in Metzger, *The Canon of the New Testament*, 230.

Conclusion

The canon is a theological issue.

FLOYD FILSON

As we near the end of our journey into the world of canon, it is important that we remember the particular goal of this volume. Our purpose here, simply put, has been to answer the question about whether the Christian belief in the canon is intellectually acceptable. Is it rational for Christians to believe that we have the right twenty-seven books in our New Testament? Historically speaking, there have been two kinds of objections to this belief. Some have offered *de facto* objections, arguing that such a belief about the canon is intellectually unacceptable on the grounds that it is false. Christians shouldn't believe these books are from God, it is argued, because it simply isn't true; instead they are products of church politics, or are forgeries, or what have you. As noted in the introduction, it has not been the goal of this volume to answer the *de facto* question; we have not tried to "prove" the truth of the canon to the critic or the skeptic (if that is even possible). Instead, our concern here has been with the second kind of objection, those of the *de jure* variety. The *de jure* objection against the Christian belief in the canon is not that it is false, but that it is intellectually unjustifiable (even if it happens to be true). Given the tumultuous history of the canon, the disagreements among early Christians, and the limited access we have to ancient history, how could a Christian ever really know such a thing in the first place? In other words, the problem with the Christian belief in the canon is something other than its truth or falsehood—the problem is that it lacks sufficient *grounds*. Sure, Christians can continue to believe in the canon if they wish, but they have no basis for doing so. It must be taken on "blind faith."

Is it true that Christians lack an intellectually sufficient basis for their belief in the New Testament canon? The answer of this volume, of course, has been no. On the contrary, we have argued here that Christians have more than adequate grounds for their belief in the truth of the canon. Let us briefly review our argument.

I. Summary of the Self-Authenticating Model

In the first part of this volume, "Determining the Canonical Model," we surveyed a variety of different attempts to answer the question of how we know which books belong in the New Testament canon. Community-determined models argue that we can know which books are properly canonical by turning to the decisions of the church itself (or individuals within it). In some sense, canon is constituted by the response of the Christian community. Historically determined models were quite the opposite. Rather than appealing to the reception of the New Testament books, these models appeal to the historical origins of the books themselves. If these books, according to the accepted canons of historical research, are deemed to contain authentic or apostolic material, then they are considered canonical. While both of these categories of canonical models have many positives—the canon is intimately connected to the church and does have authentic content—we have argued that these models do not provide a sufficient answer to the *de jure* objection. The reason is that all these models, despite their many differences, share one thing in common: they authenticate the canon on the basis of something external to it. To insist that the canon must measure up to some independent standard that we have erected is to inevitably produce a canon of our own making.

In order for us to have knowledge about which books belong in the canon and, at the same time, not subordinate the canon to outside authorities, that knowledge must be determined by the canon itself. The canon must be *self-authenticating*. This, of course, does not mean that the twenty-seven books of the canon are listed for us within the covers of our New Testaments. But it does mean that the canon guides, controls, and determines how it is authenticated. Again, we must remember the specific question we are asking. We are not asking how a person comes to believe in the canon (for the first time). Nor are we trying to prove the truth of the canon. We are asking whether the Christian religion can give an adequate *account* for the knowledge it claims to have. But such a question can be answered only on the basis of the Christian faith itself—that is, on the basis of the Christian conception of God, his purpose and plan, the nature of human knowledge, and so forth. And where else would we turn to acquire this information but to the very scriptural books in question?

In chapter 3 we looked to the Scriptures to guide our authentication of canon and argued that God has created the proper epistemic environment in which belief in the canon could be reliably formed. The environment involved the following components:

- *Providential exposure.* We trust in the providence of God to expose the church to the books it is to receive as canonical. How can the church recognize books it does not have? Thus, our model, by definition, does not address "lost" apostolic books.
- *Attributes of canonicity.* The Scriptures indicate that there are three attributes that all canonical books have: (1) divine qualities (canonical books bear the "marks" of divinity), (2) corporate reception (canonical books are recognized by the church as a whole), and (3) apostolic origins (canonical books are the result of the redemptive-historical activity of the apostles).
- *Internal testimony of the Holy Spirit.* Because of the noetic effects of sin, the natural man cannot reliably recognize these attributes of canonicity. Thus, we need the internal testimony of the Holy Spirit. The internal testimony is not private revelation that tells us which books belong in the canon, but it is the Spirit opening our eyes to the truth of these attributes and producing belief that these books are from God.

What is noteworthy about the three attributes of canonicity is that they are mutually reinforcing—they imply one another and involve one another. Any book with apostolic origins is a book constituted by the Holy Spirit and therefore will possess divine qualities. And if a book has divine qualities, then its content must derive from someone who speaks with the authority of God, namely, an apostolic source. And any book with divine qualities and apostolic origins will, through the internal testimony of the Holy Spirit, impose itself on the church. And any book received by the corporate church must have the divine qualities and apostolic origins that would allow the church to recognize the voice of Christ in it (again through the testimony of the Holy Spirit). This three-dimensional model, then, is self-supporting and self-correcting. If one attribute is misconstrued, it can be corrected by the other two.

On the basis of this model, we concluded that the Christian has intellectually sufficient ground for affirming that these twenty-seven books, and only these twenty-seven books, belong in the New Testament. Of course, this didn't entirely settle the issue of whether our belief in canon is justified (or warranted). At best, it only demonstrated that it is justified *absent "defeaters."* But there are potential defeaters that can be offered against the Christian belief in the canon—particularly against the viability of the attributes of canonicity. Therefore, in the second half of the volume, "Exploring and Defending the Canonical Model," we delved further into these attributes of canonicity and addressed the major defeaters leveled against them. In chapter 4, we further explored the Christian claim that the New Testament books contain divine qualities. Defeaters against this claim were offered by Walter Bauer and F. C. Baur. The former argued that concepts like "orthodoxy" could never have guided the early church's reception of books because there was no basis for orthodoxy until after the canon had been established. In refutation of Bauer, however, we argued that the church did have the Old Testament, core New Testament books, and the "rule of faith" to guide it. F. C. Baur argued that the books of the New Testament represent divergent and contradictory theologies and thus could not bear divine qualities. However, not only have many of these specific charges of inconsistency been sufficiently addressed (e.g., Paul vs. James), but we have no reason to think that those without the Spirit are in a position to reliably determine such things (1 Cor. 2:14).

In chapter 5, we explored the concept of apostolicity. We argued that all canonical books are apostolic, meaning that they bear authoritative apostolic tradition. Since the apostles used the help of key leaders and disciples to transmit the tradition orally, we are not surprised that they used such help to transmit the tradition in written form. Thus, a book did not need to be written directly by an apostle to be regarded as apostolic. The primary defeater offered against the apostolicity of New Testament books is that modern scholars have concluded that many of these books were pseudonymous and written neither by apostles nor during the apostolic age. Again, however, this defeater did not prove viable. For one thing, a significant number of scholars outside the critical consensus have made a credible defense of the authenticity of these books. So, the "consensus" itself is in question. In addition, the sort of stylistic arguments typically used to "prove" pseudonymity are less than compelling and open to all sorts of competing interpretations. But even more fundamentally, the methodologies of much of modern critical scholarship, as Plantinga, Alston, and others have shown, are founded upon Enlightenment assumptions that are already hostile to historic Christianity. Why should we think Enlightenment-based methodologies are more likely to produce true conclusions than Christian ones? There seems little reason to think so.

In chapters 6–8, we examined the reception of the canon by the corporate church. While it is clear that the church eventually achieved a remarkable degree of unanimity over these twenty-seven books, it was not always so in the early stages. The development of the canon was erratic at points, and there were periods of disagreement and dissent over a variety of books. Indeed, this dissent and disagreement is the basis for the most commonly suggested defeater to the New Testament canon. If these books are really from God, then why did the church disagree over them? Why did it take so long to recognize them? Therefore, it is argued, the final consensus of the church is not a reliable indicator of canonicity but simply the result of one theological party achieving victory over another. While this sort of argument has been repeated so often it has nearly attained the status of a universal truth, it does not prove to be a compelling argument against our canonical model. We offered two arguments against it.

First, this defeater only works if some level of disagreement over canonical books would be *inconsistent* with the predictions of the self-authenticating model. But this is simply not the case. Our model does not require immediate and absolute agreement. Indeed, given the effects of sin and the spiritual forces attacking the church, not to mention the practical realities of God delivering canonical books through normal historical channels, we should expect some level of disagreement and dissent before (and even after) a final consensus is reached.

Second, we argued against this defeater on the grounds that it overplays the level of disagreement and dissent. While the canonical path was not always a smooth one (as we have already noted), it was much less erratic than is often claimed. The historical evidence reviewed in chapters 6–8 was intended to demonstrate precisely this point. Not only was there a "core" canon of New Testament books that were well established from a very early time, but disagreements over peripheral canonical books were less problematic than is often portrayed.

II. Implications of the Self-Authenticating Model

With this brief summary fresh in our minds, we can now conclude this volume by considering some implications of this model for the field of canonical studies.

1. *There is more common ground between competing canonical models than is often realized.* In the first section of this book, we learned that the question of canon has been at the nexus of theological and historical

battles for many generations. And we have, to some extent, joined in these battles by offering our own assessment and critique of the various canonical models in existence today. However, our purpose has not been entirely negative. While the self-authenticating model should be clearly distinguished from these other canonical models, it has also served to unite them by combining their greatest strengths into one system. The community-determined models are correct that the church plays a key role that should not be unduly diminished (but not the decisive and only role). The historically determined models are right that canonical books are those that contain authentic apostolic content (but there is no such thing as a neutral historical methodology). The Reformers are correct that the canonical books contain the marks of divinity within them (but that doesn't mean that the role of the church and the origins of these books should be ignored). We are not forced to pick just one of these three perspectives. Each of them brings something important to the table.

Here then is one of the key implications of the self-authenticating model. It helps us recognize that canon is a complex and multidimensional concept that cannot be artificially flattened out. Canon has an ecclesiological dimension, a historical dimension, and an aesthetic/internal dimension. It is when a single aspect of canon is absolutized at the expense of the others that distortions inevitably arise. When these three aspects are kept in their proper biblical balance, we can begin to see the controversial issues more clearly. Take, for instance, the never-ending debates over the "date" of the canon. While some models want to stake their claim on a particular moment in time, the three-dimensional nature of the self-authenticating model reminds us that it is more appropriate to think of the date of canon in "stages" rather than in a single airtight category. There is a sense in which we already have a canon in the first century (owing to its apostolic origins). There is another sense in which we have a canon in the second (as its scriptural quality was increasingly recognized). And there is another sense in which the date of the canon is legitimately in the fourth century (when a widespread consensus in the church was achieved). If so, then perhaps there is room for more agreement between conflicting canonical camps than is typically recognized.

2. *The decisive issue in canonical studies is one's ontology of canon.* Even with the common ground noted above, there are still real places of disagreement between these models. While the self-authenticating model shares a lot in common with these other models, this study has also strived to demonstrate what makes it distinctive. Putting our finger on the nub of

the disagreement can help to advance the discussion and generate further reflection. In essence, we have seen that the self-authenticating model is set apart by its *ontology* of canon. What is the canon in and of itself? For many community-determined models the answer is that there is no ontology of canon. Since the canon is merely the product of the community of faith, it is nothing in and of itself. It only *becomes* something once the community has acted. For this reason, these community-determined models have no choice but to absolutize the ecclesiological dimension of canon. For some of the historically determined models, the canon does contain authentic and even inspired content apart from its reception by the church. However, the canon is still not the kind of book that can demonstrate its own divinity. That is something it simply cannot do. Thus, these models are forced to absolutize the historical dimension as the only way the canon can be known. What sets the self-authenticating model apart is that it recognizes not only that the books of the canon have divine authority apart from their reception by the community of faith, but also that this authority can be known *through the books themselves* as the power of the Spirit works within them. Thus, it is a distinctive view about what *kind* of books are in the canon that makes the self-authenticating model unique. Once this critical component is in place, we are no longer forced to absolutize one aspect of canon over the others. All three aspects of canon—divine qualities, apostolic origins, and corporate reception—are able to work in tandem to provide a solid foundation for our knowledge of the canon.

Of course, the self-authenticating model's commitment to a particular ontology of canon is unlikely to be welcomed by the broader world of critical scholarship. No doubt, such an approach will be criticized as question begging or irrelevant theologizing. However, throughout this study we have seen that the canon is, at its core, a theological issue. To be sure, there are historical and ecclesiastical components as well, but these too are driven by theological concerns. The manner in which one authenticates canon is integrally connected to one's view about the kind of books being authenticated. Even the historical-critical model has a theology of canon—despite critics' claims to be theologically neutral. They consider the canon to be a collection of human writings that are merely the product of random historical circumstances. This is not something proved by the historical-critical model, but is more the starting place of that model. Thus, one of the key implications of our study is that everyone brings a canonical theology to the table whether they recognize it or not.

3. *Christians have intellectually sufficient grounds for claiming that they know which books belong in the New Testament.* Perhaps the most significant implication of this study has to do with the intellectual acceptability of the Christian belief in the canon. While the *de facto* objection may appear, at first glance, to be the more problematic one, it is the *de jure* objection that has created the deeper epistemological crisis for Christians today. The culture of postmodernity in our Western world already gives us reason to doubt the basis for virtually every belief we hold—particularly religious ones. Any claim to actually *know* that one's religious beliefs are true is regarded as a violation of the rules of intellectual inquiry. Such things simply cannot be known, we are told, regardless of whether they are true. As human beings we do not have access to knowledge outside our own self-constructed realities. In the categories of Kant, we can know the world of the phenomenal, but not the world of the noumenal. Thus, to claim such knowledge is to be uninformed or arrogant or both. It is within this context that the *de jure* objection finds traction. It aims not so much at whether the Christian claims about canon are true, but at whether it is even rational or reasonable to make such claims from the outset. And this strategy is an effective one. Religious claims do not need to be refuted if they are disallowed in the first place.

But if our canonical model proves to be valid, then the power of this objection is dissolved. Whatever other objections the critic may have, it can no longer be this one. Contrary to the claims of modern critics, Christians do have intellectually sufficient grounds for knowing which books belong in the canon. Of course, this should not really come as a surprise. For the last two millennia, the church has shown remarkable unity around these twenty-seven books, even if it has not always articulated the grounds for that unity. Apparently, Christians *did* have a way of knowing which books God had given them. Thus, the quote of Ernest Best at the beginning of this volume proves rather ironic: "No one has come up with a satisfactory solution as to how we determine which books should be in the canon."[1] Christians throughout the ages would disagree. Although this volume has attempted to offer a detailed answer to Best's concern, it has not done so by coming up with something new. Indeed, it has done so by turning to something very old. It turns out that the solution to the problem of canon has not been lacking—it has actually been there the whole time. Jesus himself declared it: "My sheep hear my voice, and I know them, and they follow me" (John 10:27).

---

[1] E. Best, "Scripture, Tradition, and the Canon of the New Testament," *BJRL* 61 (1979): 282.

BIBLIOGRAPHY

Abbott, Walter M., ed. *The Documents of Vatican II.* New York: America Press, 1966.

Abraham, William J. *Canon and Criterion in Christian Theology: From the Fathers to Feminism.* New York: Oxford University Press, 2002.

Abraham, William J., Jason E. Vickers, and Natalie B. Van Kirk, eds. *Canonical Theism: A Proposal for Theology and the Church.* Grand Rapids: Eerdmans, 2008.

Achtemeier, Paul J. *Inspiration and Authority: Nature and Function of Christian Scripture.* Peabody, MA: Hendrickson, 1999.

———. "Omne Verbum Sonat: The New Testament and the Oral Environment of Late Western Antiquity." *Journal of Biblical Literature* 109 (1990): 3–27.

Ackroyd, Peter R. *Continuity: A Contribution to the Study of Old Testament Religious Tradition.* Oxford: Blackwell, 1962.

Adamson, James B. *The Epistle of James.* New International Commentary on the New Testament. Grand Rapids: Eerdmans, 1976.

Adriaanse, H. J. "Canonicity and the Problem of the Golden Mean." In *Canonization and Decanonization*, edited by Arie van der Kooij and K. van der Toorn, 313–30. Leiden: Brill, 1998.

Agnew, Francis. "The Origin of the NT Apostle-Concept: A Review of Research." *Journal of Biblical Literature* 105 (1986): 75–96.

Aichele, George. "Canon, Ideology, and the Emergence of an Imperial Church." In *Canon and Canonicity: The Formation and Use of Scripture*, edited by Einar Thomassen, 45–65. Copenhagen: Museum Tusculanum Press, 2010.

———. *The Control of Biblical Meaning: Canon as Semiotic Mechanism.* Harrisburg, PA: Trinity, 2001.

Aland, Kurt. "Neue neutestamentliche Papyri II." *New Testament Studies* 9 (1962–1963): 303–16.

———. "The Problem of Anonymity and Pseudonymity in Christian Literature of the First Two Centuries." *Journal of Theological Studies* 12 (1961): 39–49.

———. *The Problem of the New Testament Canon.* London: Mowbray, 1962.

———. *Repertorium der griechischen christlichen Papyri, I, Biblische Papyri.* Berlin: de Gruyter, 1976.

Albl, Martin C. *And Scripture Cannot Be Broken: The Form and Function of the Early Christian Testimonia Collections.* Leiden: Brill, 1999.

Alexander, Loveday. "Ancient Book Production and the Circulation of the Gospels." In *The Gospels for All Christians: Rethinking the Gospel Audiences,* edited by Richard Bauckham, 71–111. Grand Rapids: Eerdmans, 1998.

———. "Canon and Exegesis in the Medical Schools of Antiquity." In *The Canon of Scripture in Jewish and Christian Tradition,* edited by P. S. Alexander and K. Jean-Daniel, 115–53. Lausanne: Éditions du Zèbre, 2007.

———. "The Living Voice: Skepticism Towards the Written Word in Early Christian and in Greco-Roman Texts." In *The Bible in Three Dimensions,* edited by D. J. A. Clines, S. E. Fowl, and S. E. Porter, 221–47. Sheffield: Sheffield Academic, 1990.

———. "Memory and Tradition in the Hellenistic Schools." In *Jesus in Memory: Traditions in Oral and Scribal Perspectives,* edited by W. Kelber and S. Byrskog, 113–53. Waco, TX: Baylor University Press, 2009.

———. *The Preface to Luke's Gospel.* Cambridge: Cambridge University Press, 1993.

Allert, Craig D. *A High View of Scripture? The Authority of the Bible and the Formation of the New Testament Canon.* Grand Rapids: Baker Academic, 2007.

Alston, William P. *Epistemic Justification: Essays in the Theory of Knowledge.* Ithaca, NY: Cornell University Press, 1989.

———. "Historical Criticism of the Synoptic Gospels." In *"Behind" the Text: History and Biblical Interpretation,* edited by Craig Bartholomew, C. Stephen Evans, Mary Healy, and Murray Rae, 151–80. Grand Rapids: Zondervan, 2003.

———. *Illocutionary Acts and Sentence Meaning.* Ithaca, NY: Cornell University Press, 2000.

———. "Knowledge of God." In *Faith, Reason, and Skepticism,* edited by Marcus Hester, 6–49. Philadelphia: Temple University Press, 1992.

Amphoux, Christian B. "La finale longue de Marc: Un épilogue des quatre évangiles." In *The Synoptic Gospels: Source Criticism and the New Literary Criticism,* edited by Camille Focant, 548–55. Leuven: Leuven University Press, 1993.

Amphoux, Christian B., and J. K. Elliott, eds. *The New Testament Text in Early Christianity.* Lausanne: Éditions du Zèbre, 2003.

Anderson, Paul. *The Fourth Gospel and the Quest for Jesus: Modern Foundations Reconsidered.* London: T&T Clark, 2006.

Appel, Nicolaus. *Kanon und Kirche: Die Kanonkrise im heutigen Protestantismus als kontroverstheologisches Problem.* Paderborn: Bonifacius-Druckerei, 1964.

Armstrong, John H. *A View of Rome: A Guide to Understanding the Beliefs and Practices of Roman Catholics.* Chicago: Moody Press, 1995.

Ashcraft, Morris. *Rudolf Bultmann.* Waco, TX: Word, 1972.

Assmann, Aleida, and Jan Assmann, eds. *Kanon und Zensur, Archäologie der literarischen Kommunikation II.* Munich: Wilhelm Fink Verlag, 1987.

Aune, David E. "Luke 1:1–4: Historical or Scientific *Prooimion?*" In *Paul, Luke and the Graeco-Roman World*, edited by Alf Christopherson, Bruce Longenecker, Jýrg Frey, and Carten Claussen, 138–48. Sheffield: Sheffield Academic, 2002.

———. *Revelation 17–22*. Word Biblical Commentary. Nashville: Thomas Nelson, 1998.

Austin, John L. *How to Do Things with Words*. Oxford: Oxford Paperbacks, 1976.

Bacon, Benjamin W. *The Making of the New Testament*. Folcroft, PA: Folcroft Library Editions, 1900.

Bagnall, Roger S. *Early Christian Books in Egypt*. Princeton, NJ: Princeton University Press, 2009.

Bailey, Kenneth E. "Informal Controlled Oral Tradition and the Synoptic Gospels." *Themelios* 20 (1995): 4–11.

Balás, David L. "Marcion Revisited: A 'Post-Harnack' Perspective." In *Texts and Testaments: Critical Essays on the Bible and the Early Church Fathers*, edited by W. E. March, 95–107. San Antonio: Trinity University Press, 1980.

Balla, Peter. *Challenges to New Testament Theology: An Attempt to Justify the Enterprise*. Peabody, MA: Hendrickson, 1998.

———. "Evidence for an Early Christian Canon (Second and Third Century)." In *The Canon Debate*, edited by Lee Martin McDonald and James A. Sanders, 372–85. Peabody, MA: Hendrickson, 2002.

Bardenhewer, Otto. *Geschichte der alterkirchlichen Literatur*, vol. 2. Freiburg im Bresgau: Herder, 1912.

Barnard, Leslie W. "The Epistle of Barnabas and Its Contemporary Setting." In *Aufstieg und Niedergang der römischen Welt: Geschichte und Kultur Roms im Spiegel der neueren Forschung*, edited by H. Temporini and W. Haase, 2:159–207. Berlin: de Gruyter, 1993.

———. *Justin Martyr*. Cambridge: Cambridge University Press, 1967.

Barr, George K. "Two Styles in the New Testament Epistles." *Literary and Linguistic Computing* 18 (2003): 235–48.

Barr, James. *Beyond Fundamentalism*. Philadelphia: Westminster, 1984.

———. *The Bible in the Modern World*. New York: Harper & Row, 1973.

———. *Holy Scripture: Canon, Authority and Criticism*. Philadelphia: Westminster, 1983.

———. *The Scope and Authority of the Bible*. Philadelphia: Westminster, 1980.

Barrera, Julio C. Trebolle. "Origins of a Tripartite Old Testament Canon." In *The Canon Debate*, edited by Lee Martin McDonald and James A. Sanders, 128–45. Peabody, MA: Hendrickson, 2002.

Barrett, Charles K. *A Commentary on the Second Epistle to the Corinthians*. London: A&C Black, 1973.

———. *The Signs of an Apostle*. Philadelphia: Fortress, 1972.

Barth, Karl. *Church Dogmatics*. 2nd ed. Translated by G. W. Bromiley and T. F. Torrance. Edinburgh: T&T Clark, 1956–1975.

————. *The Holy Ghost and the Christian Life.* London: Muller, 1938.

————. "Rudolf Bultmann: An Attempt to Understand Him." In *Kerygma and Myth*, edited by Hans-Werner Bartsch, 83–132. London: SPCK, 1962.

Bartholomew, Craig, et al., eds., *Canon and Biblical Interpretation.* Carlisle: Paternoster, 2006.

Bartlet, Vernon. "Papias's 'Exposition': Its Date and Contents." In *Amicitiae Corolla*, edited by H. G. Wood, 16–22. London: University of London Press, 1933.

Barton, John. "Canonical Approaches Ancient and Modern." In *The Biblical Canons*, edited by Jean-Marie Auwers and Henk Jan de Jonge, 199–209. Leuven: Leuven University Press, 2003.

————. "Marcion Revisited." In *The Canon Debate*, edited by Lee Martin McDonald and James A. Sanders, 341–54. Peabody, MA: Hendrickson, 2002.

————. *Oracles of God: Perceptions of Ancient Prophecy in Israel After the Exile.* London: Darton, Longman, and Todd, 1985.

————. *Reading the Old Testament: Method in Biblical Study.* London: Darton, Longman, and Todd, 1996.

————. *The Spirit and the Letter: Studies in the Biblical Canon.* London: SPCK, 1997.

Bauckham, Richard. "For Whom Were Gospels Written?," In *The Gospels for All Christians: Rethinking the Gospel Audiences*, edited by Richard Bauckham, 9–48. Grand Rapids: Eerdmans, 1998.

————. *Jesus and the Eyewitnesses: The Gospels as Eyewitness Testimony.* Grand Rapids: Eerdmans, 2006.

————. *Jude, 2 Peter.* Waco, TX: Word, 1983.

Bauer, Walter. *Orthodoxy and Heresy in Earliest Christianity.* Edited by Robert Kraft and Gerhard Krodel. Translated by Paul J. Achtemeier. Philadelphia: Fortress, 1971.

Baum, Armin Daniel. "Der neutestamentliche Kanon bei Eusebius (Historia ecclesiastica 3.25.1–7) im Kontext seiner literaturgeschichtlichen Arbeit." *Ephemerides theologicae lovanienses* 73 (1997): 307–48.

————. *Pseudepigraphie und literarische Fälschung im frühen Christentum: Mit ausgewählten Quellentexten samt deutscher Übersetzung.* Tübingen: Mohr Siebeck, 2001.

Baur, Ferdinand Christian. *Paul, the Apostle of Jesus Christ, His Life and Work, His Epistles and Teachings.* London: Williams and Norgate, 1873.

Bavinck, Herman. *Reformed Dogmatics.* Vol. 1, *Prolegomena.* Edited by John Bolt. Translated by John Vriend. Grand Rapids: Baker, 2003.

Beale, G. K. *The Book of Revelation.* New International Greek Testament Commentary. Grand Rapids: Eerdmans, 1999.

Beckwith, R. T. *The Old Testament Canon of the New Testament Church, and Its Background in Early Judaism.* Grand Rapids: Eerdmans, 1986.

Behr, John. *Formation of Christian Theology.* Vol. 1, *The Way to Nicaea.* Crestwood, NY: St Vladimir's Seminary Press, 2001.

Bell, H. Idris, and T. C. Skeat, *Fragments of an Unknown Gospel and Other Early Christian Papyri*. London: Trustees of the British Museum, 1935.

Bellinzoni, Arthur J. *The Sayings of Jesus in the Writings of Justin Martyr*. Leiden: Brill, 1967.

Bender, Kimlyn J. "Scripture and Canon in Karl Barth's Early Theology." In *From Biblical Criticism to Biblical Faith*, edited William H. Brackney and Craig A. Evans, 164–98. Macon, GA: Mercer University Press, 2007.

Benko, Stephen. "Pagan Criticism of Christianity During the First Two Centuries A.D." In *Aufstieg und Niedergang der römischen Welt: Geschichte und Kultur Roms im Spiegel der neueren Forschung*, edited by H. Temporini and W. Haase, 2:1055–118. Berlin: de Gruyter, 1980.

Berding, Kenneth. *Polycarp and Paul: An Analysis of Their Literary and Theological Relationship in Light of Polycarp's Use of Biblical and Extra-Biblical Literature*. Leiden: Brill, 2002.

Berkhof, Louis. *Systematic Theology*. Grand Rapids: Eerdmans, 1941.

Berkouwer, G. C. *The Second Vatican Council and the New Catholicism*. Grand Rapids: Eerdmans, 1965.

———. *Studies in Dogmatics: Holy Scripture*. Translated by Jack Rogers. Grand Rapids: Eerdmans, 1975.

———. "The Testimony of the Spirit." In *The Authoritative Word*, edited by Donald K. McKim, 155–81. Grand Rapids: Eerdmans, 1983.

Bernard, John Henry. *A Critical and Exegetical Commentary on the Gospel According to St. John*. Edinburgh: T&T Clark, 1928.

Best, Ernest. *A Critical and Exegetical Commentary on Ephesians*. International Critical Commentary. Edinburgh: T&T Clark, 1998.

———. "Scripture, Tradition, and the Canon of the New Testament." *Bulletin of the John Rylands University Library of Manchester* 61, 1979.

Best, Stephen, and Douglas Kellner. *The Postmodern Turn*. New York: Guilford, 1997.

Bingham, D. Jeffrey. *Irenaeus' Use of Matthew's Gospel in Adversus Haereses*. Leuven: Peeters, 1998.

Bird, Anthony E. "The Authorship of the Pastoral Epistles—Quantifying Literary Style." *Reformed Theological Review* 56 (1997): 118–37.

Birdsall, J. Neville. "A Fresh Examination of the Fragments of the Gospel of St. Luke in ms. 0171 and an Attempted Reconstruction with Special Reference to the Recto." In *Philologia sacra*, edited by Roger Gryson, 212–27. Freiburg: Herder, 1993.

Black, Matthew. "The Use of Rhetorical Terminology in Papias on Mark and Matthew." *Journal for the Study of the New Testament* 37 (1989): 31–41.

Blanchard, Alain, ed. *Les débuts du codex*. Turnhout: Brepols, 1989.

Blenkinsopp, Joseph. *Prophecy and Canon: A Contribution to the Study of Jewish Origins*. Notre Dame: University of Notre Dame Press, 1986.

Bloesch, Donald G. *Holy Scripture: Revelation, Inspiration, and Interpretation*. Downers Grove, IL: InterVarsity, 1994.

Blomberg, Craig. *The Historical Reliability of the Gospels*. 2nd ed. Downers Grove, IL: InterVarsity, 2007.

———. "The Legitimacy and Limits of Harmonization." In *Hermeneutics, Authority, and Canon*, edited by D. A. Carson and John D. Woodbridge, 135–74. Grand Rapids: Zondervan, 1986.

Blowers, Paul M. "The *Regula Fidei* and the Narrative Character of Early Christian Faith." *Pro ecclesia* 6 (1997): 199–228.

Boa, Kenneth D., and Robert W. Bowman Jr. *Faith Has Its Reasons: An Integrative Approach to Defending Christianity*. Colorado Springs: NavPress, 2001.

Bock, Darrell L. "The Words of Jesus in the Gospels: Live, Jive, or Memorex?" In *Jesus Under Fire*, edited by Michael J. Wilkins and J. P. Moreland, 74–99. Grand Rapids: Zondervan, 1995.

Bockmuehl, Markus. "Why Not Let Acts Be Acts? In Conversation with C. Kavin Rowe." *Journal for the Study of the New Testament* 28 (2005): 163–66.

Boettner, Loraine. *Roman Catholicism*. Philadelphia: Presbyterian and Reformed, 1962.

Bonner, Campbell. "A New Fragment of the Shepherd of Hermas, Michigan Papyrus 44." *Harvard Theological Review* 20 (1927): 105–16.

Bornkamm, Günther. "The Stilling of the Storm in Matthew." In *Tradition and Interpretation in Matthew*, edited by G. Bornkamm, G. Barth, and H. J. Held, 52–57. Philadelphia: Westminster, 1963.

Bousset, Wilhelm. *Die Evangeliencitate Justins des Märtyrers in ihrem wert für die Evangelienkritik*. Göttingen: Vandenhoeck & Ruprecht, 1891.

Bovon, François. "The Canonical Structure of Gospel and Apostle." In *The Canon Debate*, edited by Lee Martin McDonald and James A. Sanders, 516–27. Peabody, MA: Hendrickson, 2002.

———. *L'Évangile et l'apôtre: Le Christ inséparable de ses témoins*. Aubonne: Editions du Moulin, 1993.

Bowman, Alan K., and Greg Wolf, eds. *Literacy and Power in the Ancient World*. Cambridge: Cambridge University Press, 1994.

Bowman, Robert M. *Orthodoxy and Heresy*. Grand Rapids: Baker, 1992.

Brakke, David. "Canon Formation and Social Conflict in Fourth Century Egypt: Athanasius of Alexandria's Thirty-Ninth Festal Letter." *Harvard Theological Review* 87 (1994): 395–419.

Brawley, Robert L. "Canonical Coherence in Reading Israel's Scriptures with a Sequel." In *The Biblical Canons*, edited by Jean-Marie Auwers and Henk Jan de Jonge, 627–34. Leuven: Leuven University Press, 2003.

Brenneman, James E. *Canons in Conflict: Negotiating Texts in True and False Prophecy*. New York: Oxford University Press, 1997.

Brett, Mark G. "Against the Grain: Brevard Childs' Biblical Theology of the Old and New Testaments: Theological Reflections on the Christian Bible." *Modern Theology* 10 (1994): 281–87.

———. "Canonical Criticism and Old Testament Theology." In *Text in Context: Essays by Members of the Society for Old Testament Study*, edited by A. D. H. Mayes, 63–85. Oxford: Oxford University Press, 2000.

Briggs, Charles A. *Church Unity: Studies of Its Most Important Problems*. New York: Scribner, 1909.

———. *General Introduction to the Study of Holy Scripture*. New York: Scribner, 1899.

Bromiley, Geoffrey W. "The Authority of Scripture in Karl Barth." In *Hermeneutics, Authority, and Canon*, edited by D. A. Carson and John D. Woodbridge, 271–94. Grand Rapids: Zondervan, 1986.

Brooks, James. "Clement of Alexandria as a Witness to the Development of the New Testament Canon." *Second Century* 9 (1992): 41–55.

Brown, Harold O. J. *Heresies: Heresy and Orthodoxy in the History of the Church*. Peabody, MA: Hendrickson, 1988.

Brown, Raymond E. "The Gospel of Peter and Canonical Authority." *New Testament Studies* 33 (1987): 321–43.

———. "The Gospel of Thomas and St. John's Gospel," *New Testament Studies* 9 (1962–1963): 155–77.

Brown, Schuyler. "The Role of the Prologues in Determining the Purpose of Luke-Acts." In *Perspectives on Luke-Acts*, edited by Charles H. Talbert, 99–111. Edinburgh: T&T Clark, 1978.

Bruce, F. F. *The Canon of Scripture*. Downers Grove, IL: InterVarsity, 1988.

———. *The Epistle to the Galatians: A Commentary on the Greek Text*. Grand Rapids: Eerdmans, 1982.

———. *The Epistle to the Hebrews*. Grand Rapids: Eerdmans, 1990.

———. "Some Thoughts on the Beginning of the New Testament Canon." *Bulletin of the John Rylands University Library of Manchester* 65 (1983): 42–43.

———. "Tradition and the Canon of Scripture." In *The Authoritative Word: Essays on the Nature of Scripture*, edited by D. K. McKim, 59–84. Grand Rapids: Eerdmans, 1983.

———. *Tradition: Old and New*. Grand Rapids: Zondervan, 1970.

Brueggemann, Walter. *Creative Word*. Philadelphia: Fortress, 1982.

Brunner, Emil. *The Divine-Human Encounter*. Translated by W. Amandus Loos. Westport, CT: Greenwood, 1980.

———. *Dogmatics*. Vol. 1, *The Christian Doctrine of God*. Translated by O. Wyon. Philadelphia: Westminster, 1950.

———. *Our Faith*. New York: Scribner, 1926.

———. *Revelation and Reason*. Philadelphia: Westminster, 1946.

———. *Truth as Encounter*. Philadelphia: Westminster, 1943.

Bruns, Gerald L. "Canon and Power in the Hebrew Scriptures." *Critical Inquiry* 10 (1984): 462–80.

Buck, Charles H. "The Early Order of the Pauline Corpus." *Journal of Biblical Literature* 68 (1949): 351–57.

Bultmann, Rudolph. *The History of the Synoptic Tradition*. Oxford: Blackwell, 1968.

———, ed. *Kerygma and Myth: A Theological Debate*. New York: Harper & Brothers, 1961.

———. *New Testament and Mythology and Other Basic Writings*. Translated by Schubert Ogden. Philadelphia: Fortress, 1984.

Burton, Ernest De Witt. *The Epistle to the Galatians*. Edinburgh: T&T Clark, 1952.

Byrskog, Samuel. *Story as History—History as Story: The Gospel Tradition in the Context of Ancient Oral History*. Leiden: Brill, 2002.

Calvin, John. *Commentaries on the Epistles of Paul to the Galatians and Ephesians*. Grand Rapids: Baker, 1993.

———. *Institutes of the Christian Religion*. Edited by John T. McNeill. Translated by Ford Lewis Battles. 2 vols. Philadelphia: Westminster, 1960.

———. *Tracts and Treatises*. Edited by Thomas F. Torrance. Translated by Henry Beveridge. Grand Rapids: Eerdmans, 1958.

Campenhausen, Hans von. *The Formation of the Christian Bible*. Translated by J. A. Baker. London: A&C Black, 1972. Translation of *Die Entstehung der christlichen Bibel*. Tübingen: Mohr, 1968.

Carleton Paget, James. *The Epistle of Barnabas: Outlook and Background*. Tübingen: Mohr Siebeck, 1994.

———. "The *Epistle of Barnabas* and the Writings That Later Formed the New Testament." In *The Reception of the New Testament in the Apostolic Fathers*, edited by Andrew Gregory and Christopher Tuckett, 229–49. Oxford: Oxford University Press, 2005.

Carlson, Stephen C. *The Gospel Hoax: Morton Smith's Invention of Secret Mark*. Waco, TX: Baylor University Press, 2005.

Carlyle, A. J. "1 Clement." In *The New Testament in the Apostolic Fathers* edited by a Committee of the Oxford Society of Historical Theology, 37–62. Oxford: Clarendon, 1905.

Carmignac, Jean. "II Corinthiens III. 6, 14 et le Début de la Formation du Noveau Testament." *New Testament Studies* 24 (1976): 5–14.

Carrington, Phillip. *The Primitive Christian Calendar: A Study in the Making of the Marcan Gospel*. Cambridge: Cambridge University Press, 1952.

Carson, D. A. *The Gagging of God: Christianity Confronts Pluralism*. Grand Rapids: Zondervan, 1996.

———. *The Gospel According to John*. Grand Rapids: Eerdmans, 1991.

———. *Matthew: Chapters 13–28*. The Expositor's Bible Commentary. Grand Rapids: Zondervan, 1995.

———. "Pseudonymity and Pseudepigraphy." In *The Dictionary of New Testament Background*, edited by Craig A. Evans and Stanley E. Porter, 856–64. Downers Grove, IL: InterVarsity, 2000.

———. "Unity and Diversity in the New Testament: The Possibility of Systematic Theology." In *Scripture and Truth*, edited by D. A. Carson and John D. Woodbridge, 65–95. Grand Rapids: Baker, 1992.

Carson, D. A., and Douglas J. Moo. *An Introduction to the New Testament*. Grand Rapids: Zondervan, 2005.

Carroll, Kenneth L. "The Expansion of the Pauline Corpus." *Journal of Biblical Literature* 72 (1953): 230–37.

———. "Tatian's Influence on the Developing New Testament." In *Studies in the History and Text of the New Testament in Honor of Kenneth Willis Clark*, edited by B. L. Daniels and M. J. Suggs, 59–70. Salt Lake City: University of Utah Press, 1967.

Casey, Maurice. *From Jewish Prophet to Gentile God*. Cambridge: Clarke, 1991.

Catchpole, David R. "Paul, James, and the Apostolic Decree." *New Testament Studies* 23 (1976–1977): 428–44.

Catechism of the Catholic Church. San Francisco: Ignatius, 1994.

Cavallin, Hans C. C. "The False Teachers of 2 Peter as Pseudoprophets." *Novum Testamentum* 21 (1979): 263–70.

Chapa, Juan. "The Early Text of the Gospel of John." In *The Early Text of the New Testament*, edited by Charles E. Hill and Michael J. Kruger. Oxford: Oxford University Press, forthcoming.

Chapman, John. *John the Presbyter and the Fourth Gospel*. Oxford: Clarendon, 1911.

Chapman, Stephen B. "The Canon Debate: What It Is and Why It Matters." Presented at the Society of Biblical Literature, San Diego, 2007.

———. "How the Biblical Canon Began: Working Models and Open Questions." In *Homer, the Bible, and Beyond: Literary and Religious Canons in the Ancient World*, edited by Margalit Finkelberg and Guy G. Strousma, 29–51. Leiden: Brill, 2003.

———. *The Law and the Prophets: A Study in Old Testament Canon Formation*. Tübingen: Mohr Siebeck, 2000.

———. "The Old Testament Canon and Its Authority for the Christian Church." *Ex auditu* 19 (2003): 125–48.

———. "Reclaiming Inspiration for the Bible." In *Canon and Biblical Interpretation*, edited by Craig Bartholomew, Robin Parry, and Scott Hahn, 167–206. Carlisle: Paternoster, 2006.

Charlesworth, James A., and Craig A. Evans. "Jesus in the Agrapha and Apocryphal Gospels." In *Studying the Historical Jesus: Evaluations of the State of Current Research*, edited by B. Chilton and C. A. Evans, 478–533. Leiden: Brill, 1994.

Charlesworth, Scott. "Indicators of 'Catholicity' in Early Gospel Manuscripts." In *The Early Text of the New Testament*, edited by Charles E. Hill and Michael J. Kruger. Oxford: Oxford University Press, forthcoming.

————. "Public and Private—Second- and Third-Century Gospel Manuscripts." In *Jewish and Christian Scripture as Artifact and Canon*, edited by Craig A. Evans and H. Daniel Zacharias, 148–75. London: T&T Clark, 2009.

————. "T. C. Skeat, P64+67 and P4, and the Problem of Fibre Orientation in Codicological Reconstruction." *New Testament Studies* 53 (2007): 582–604.

Childs, Brevard S. *Biblical Theology in Crisis*. Philadelphia: Westminster, 1970.

————. *Biblical Theology of the Old and New Testaments: Theological Reflection on the Christian Bible*. Philadelphia: Augsburg Fortress, 1993.

————. "Interpretation in Faith: The Theological Responsibility of the Old Testament Commentary." *Interpretation* 18 (1964): 432–49.

————. *Introduction to the Old Testament as Scripture*. Philadelphia: Fortress, 1979.

————. *The New Testament as Canon: An Introduction*. London: SCM, 1984.

————. "The One Gospel in Four Witnesses." In *The Rule of Faith: Scripture, Canon, and Creed in a Critical Age*, edited by Ephraim Radner and George Sumner, 51–62. Harrisburg, PA: Morehouse, 1998.

————. "On Reclaiming the Bible for Christian Theology." In *Reclaiming the Bible for the Church*, edited by C. E. Braaten and R. W. Jenson, 1–17. Grand Rapids: Eerdmans, 1995.

————. "A Response." *Horizons in Biblical Theology* 2 (1980): 199–211.

Clements, Ronald E. *Prophecy and Tradition*. Atlanta: John Knox, 1975.

Clifford, William K. "The Ethics of Belief." In *Classics of Philosophy*. Vol. 2, *Modern and Contemporary*, edited by Louis J. Pojman, 1047–51. Oxford: Oxford University Press, 1998.

Clouser, Roy A. *The Myth of Religious Neutrality: An Essay on the Hidden Role of Religious Belief in Theories*. Notre Dame: University of Notre Dame Press, 2005.

Clowney, Edmund P. *The Church*. Downers Grove, IL: InterVarsity, 1995.

Coles, Revel A. "Fragments of an Apocryphal Gospel (?)." In *The Oxyrhynchus Papyri*, edited by Gerald M. Browne and Arthur S. Hunt, 41:15–16. London: Egypt Exploration Society, 1972.

Collins, Adela Y. "Numerical Symbolism in Jewish and Early Christian Apocalyptic Literature." In *Aufstieg und Niedergang der römischen Welt: Geschichte und Kultur Roms im Spiegel der neueren Forschung*, edited by H. Temporini and W. Haase, 2:1221–87. Berlin: de Gruyter, 1984.

Collins, John. "Is a Critical Biblical Theology Possible?" In *The Hebrew Bible and Its Interpreters*, edited by W. Propp, 1–17. Winona Lake: Eisenbrauns, 1990.

Comfort, Philip W. "New Reconstructions and Identifications of New Testament Papyri." *Novum Testamentum* 41 (1999): 216.

Committee of the Oxford Society of Historical Theology. *The New Testament in the Apostolic Fathers*. Oxford: Clarendon, 1905.

Congdon, David. "The Word as Event: Barth and Bultmann on Scripture." In *The Sacred Text*, edited by Michael Bird and Michael Pahl, 241–65. Piscataway, NJ: Gorgias, 2010.

Connolly, Richard H. "New Fragments of the Didache." *Journal of Theological Studies* 25 (1924): 151–53.

Conzelmann, Hans. "On the Analysis of the Confessional Formula in 1 Cor 15:3–5." *Interpretation* 20 (1966): 15–25.

———. *Theology of St. Luke.* New York: Harper & Row, 1960.

Coote, Robert P., and Mary P. Coote. *Power, Politics, and the Making of the Bible.* Minneapolis: Fortress, 1990.

Countryman, L. William. "Tertullian and the *Regula Fidei.*" *Second Century* 2 (1982): 208–27.

Cover, Jan A. "Miracles and Christian Theism." In *Reason for the Hope Within,* edited by Michael J. Murray, 345–74. Grand Rapids: Eerdmans, 1999.

Craig, William Lane. "Classical Apologetics." In *Five Views on Apologetics,* edited by S. B. Cowan, 35–38. Grand Rapids: Zondervan, 2000.

Cranfield, C. E. B. *I & II Peter and Jude: Introduction and Commentary.* London: SCM, 1960.

Crossan, John Dominic. *Four Other Gospels: Shadows on the Contours of Canon.* New York: Seabury, 1985.

———. *The Historical Jesus: The Life of a Mediterranean Jewish Peasant.* San Francisco: HarperCollins, 1991.

Crouzel, Henri. "Comparisons précises entre les fragments du Peri Archôn selon la Philocalie et la traduction de Rufin." In *Origeniana: premier colloque internatio-nal des études origéniennes, Montserrat, 18–21 septembre 1975,* 113–21. Bari: Università di Bari, 1975.

Cullmann, Oscar. "The Tradition." In *The Early Church,* edited by A. J. B. Higgins, 59–99. London: SCM, 1956.

Cunningham, Mary Kathleen. "Karl Barth." In *Christian Theologies of Scripture,* edited by Justin S. Holcomb, 183–201. New York: New York University Press, 2006.

Currie, David. *Born Fundamentalist, Born Again Catholic.* San Francisco: Ignatius, 1996.

Daniels, Jon B. "The Egerton Gospel: Its Place in Early Christianity." PhD diss., Claremont Graduate School, 1990.

Dassmann, Ernst. *Reallexikon für Antike und Christentum: Sachwörterbuch zur Auseinandersetzung des Christentums mit der antiken Welt.* Edited by Theodor Kluster. Stuttgart: Anton Hiersemann, 1986.

Davids, Peter H. *The Epistle of James.* New International Greek Testament Commentary. Grand Rapids: Eerdmans, 1982.

Davies, Paul. *Whose Bible Is It Anyway?* Sheffield: Sheffield Academic, 1995.

Davies, W. D., and Dale C. Allison. *The Gospel According to Saint Matthew.* International Critical Commentary. Edinburgh: T&T Clark, 1997.

Dehandschutter, Boudewijn. "Polycarp's Epistle to the Philippians: An Early Example of 'Reception.'" In *The New Testament in Early Christianity*, edited by J.-M. Sevrin, 275–91. Louvain: Leuven University Press, 1989.

de Jonge, Henk Jan. "The New Testament Canon." In *The Biblical Canons*, edited by Jean-Marie Auwers and Henk Jan de Jonge, 309–19. Leuven: Leuven University Press, 2003.

Dempster, Stephen G. *Dominion and Dynasty: A Biblical Theology of the Hebrew Bible*. Downers Grove, IL: InterVarsity, 2003.

———. "An 'Extraordinary Fact': Torah and Temple and the Contours of the Hebrew Canon, Part I." *Tyndale Bulletin* 48 (1997): 23–56.

Denker, Jürgen. *Die theologiegeschichtliche Stellung des Petrusevangeliums: Ein Beitrag zur Frühgeschichte des Doketismus*. Bern and Frankfurt: Lang, 1975.

Dibelius, Martin. *From Tradition to Gospel*. Cambridge: Clarke, 1971.

Dibelius, Martin, and Hans Conzelmann, *The Pastoral Epistles*. Philadelphia: Fortress, 1972.

David Dickermann, ed. *Karl Barth and the Future of Theology: A Memorial Colloquium Held at the Yale Divinity School, January 28, 1969*. New Haven, CT: YDS Association, 1969.

Dodd, C. H. *According to the Scriptures: The Substructure of New Testament Theology*. London: James Nisbet, 1952.

———. *The Apostolic Preaching and Its Developments*. New York: Harper, 1949.

———. "A New Gospel." *Bulletin of the John Rylands University Library of Manchester* 20 (1936): 56–92.

Dowey Jr., Edward A. *The Knowledge of God in Calvin's Theology*. Grand Rapids: Eerdmans, 1994.

Duff, Jeremy. "P46 and the Pastorals: A Misleading Consensus?" *New Testament Studies* 44 (1998): 578–90.

Dulles, Avery. *The Craft of Theology: From Symbol to System*. New York: Crossroad, 1992.

———. "Scripture: Recent Protestant and Catholic Views." In *The Authoritative Word: Essays on the Nature of Scripture*, edited by Donald K. McKim, 239–61. Grand Rapids: Eerdmans, 1983.

Dumbrell, William J. *Covenant and Creation*. Grand Rapids: Baker, 1984.

Dunbar, David G. "The Biblical Canon." In *Hermeneutics, Authority, and Canon*, edited by D. A. Carson and John D. Woodbridge, 295–360. Grand Rapids: Zondervan, 1986.

Duncan, J. Ligon. "The Covenant Idea in Melito of Sardis: An Introduction and Survey." *Presbyterion* 28 (2002): 12–33.

Dungan, David L. *Constantine's Bible: Politics and the Making of the New Testament*. Philadelphia: Fortress, 2006.

———. "The New Testament Canon in Recent Study." *Interpretation* 29 (1975): 339–51.

Dunkerley, Roderick. "Oxyrhynchus Gospel Fragments." *Harvard Theological Review* 23 (1930): 30–35.

Dunn, James D. G. "Has the Canon a Continuing Function?" In *The Canon Debate*, edited by Lee Martin McDonald and James A. Sanders, 558–79. Peabody, MA: Hendrickson, 2002.

———. "How the New Testament Began." In *From Biblical Criticism to Biblical Faith*, edited by William H. Brackney and C. A. Evans, 122–37. Macon, GA: Mercer University Press, 2007.

———. "The Incident at Antioch (Gal. 2:11–18)." *Journal for the Study of the New Testament* 18 (1983): 3–57.

———. *Jesus Remembered*. Grand Rapids: Eerdmans, 2003.

———. "Pseudepigraphy." In *Dictionary of the Later New Testament and Its Developments*, edited by R. P. Martin and P. H. Davids, 977–84. Downers Grove, IL: InterVarsity, 1997.

———. *Unity and Diversity in the New Testament: An Inquiry into the Character of Early Christianity*. London: SCM, 1990.

Edwards, Jonathan. *The Works of Jonathan Edwards*. Vol. 2, *Religious Affections*. Edited by John E. Smith. New Haven, CT: Yale University Press, 2009.

Edwards, Sarah Alexander. "P75 Under the Magnifying Glass." *Novum Testamentum* 18 (1976): 190–212.

Ehrman, Bart D. *The Apostolic Fathers*. 2 vols. Cambridge, MA: Harvard University Press, 2003.

———. *Forged: Writing in the Name of God—Why the Bible's Authors Are Not Who We Think They Are*. New York: HarperOne, 2011.

———. *Jesus: Apocalyptic Prophet of the New Millennium*. New York: Oxford University Press, 1999.

———. *Lost Christianities: The Battles for Scripture and the Faiths We Never Knew*. New York: Oxford University Press, 2002.

———. *The Lost Gospel of Judas Iscariot: A New Look at Betrayer and Betrayed*. New York: Oxford University Press, 2006.

———. *Lost Scriptures: Books That Did Not Make It into the New Testament*. New York: Oxford University Press, 2003.

———. *The New Testament: A Historical Introduction to the Early Christian Writings*. New York: Oxford University Press, 1997.

———. *The Orthodox Corruption of Scripture*. New York: Oxford University Press, 1993.

Ehrman, Bart D., and M. W. Holmes. *The Text of the New Testament in Contemporary Research: Essays on the Status Quaestionis*. Grand Rapids: Eerdmans, 1995.

Eichrodt, Walter. *Theology of the Old Testament*, vol. 1. Translated by J. A. Baker. Philadelphia: Westminster, 1961.

Elliott, J. K. *The Apocryphal New Testament*. Oxford: Clarendon, 1993.

———. "Manuscripts, the Codex, and the Canon." *Journal for the Study of the New Testament* 63 (1996): 105–22.

Ellis, E. Earle. *The Making of the New Testament Documents*. Leiden: Brill, 2002.

———. "New Directions in the History of Early Christianity." In *Ancient History in a Modern University: Early Christianity, Late Antiquity and Beyond*, edited by T. W. Hillard, R. A. Kearsley, C. E. V. Nixon, and A. M. Nobbs, 1:71–92. Grand Rapids: Eerdmans, 1997.

———. *Paul and His Recent Interpreters*. Grand Rapids: Eerdmans, 1961.

———. "Pseudonymity and Canonicity of New Testament Documents." In *Worship, Theology and Ministry in the Early Church: Essays in Honor of Ralph P. Martin*, edited by M. J. Wilkins and Terence Paige, 212–24. Sheffield: Sheffield Academic, 1993.

Epp, Eldon Jay. "The Codex and Literacy in Early Christianity at Oxyrhynchus: Issues Raised by Harry Y. Gamble's *Books and Readers in the Early Church*." In *Critical Review of Books in Religion 1997*, edited by Charles Prebish, 15–37. Atlanta: American Academy of Religion and Society of Biblical Literature, 1997.

———. "Issues in the Interrelation of New Testament Textual Criticism and Canon." In *The Canon Debate*, edited by Lee Martin McDonald and James A. Sanders, 485–515. Peabody, MA: Hendrickson, 2002.

———. "The New Testament Papyri at Oxyrhynchus in Their Social and Intellectual Context." In *Sayings of Jesus: Canonical and Non-Canonical*, edited by William L. Petersen, 47–68. Leiden: Brill, 1997.

———. "New Testament Papyrus Manuscripts and Letter Carrying in Greco-Roman Times." In *The Future of Early Christianity: Essays in Honor of Helmut Koester*, edited by Birger A. Pearson, A. Thomas Kraabel, George W. E. Nickelsburg, and Norman R. Petersen, 35–56. Minneapolis: Fortress, 1991.

———. "The Oxyrhynchus New Testament Papyri: 'Not Without Honor Except in Their Hometown'?" *Journal of Biblical Literature* 123 (2004): 5–55.

———. "Textual Criticism." In *The New Testament and Its Modern Interpreters*, edited by Eldon Jay Epp and George W. MacRae, 75–126. Atlanta: Scholars Press, 1989.

Epp, Eldon J., and Gordon D. Fee. *Studies in the Theory and Method of New Testament Textual Criticism*. Grand Rapids: Eerdmans, 1993.

Eusebius, *Ecclesiastical History*. Translated by Kirsopp Lake. Loeb Classical Library. Harvard: Harvard University Press, 1926.

Evans, Craig A. "Aspects of Exile and Restoration in the Proclamation of Jesus and the Gospels." In *Exile: Old Testament, Jewish, and Christian Conceptions*, edited by James M. Scott, 299–328. Leiden: Brill, 1997.

———. *Fabricating Jesus: How Modern Scholars Distort the Gospels*. Downers Grove, IL: InterVarsity, 2008.

———. "Jesus and the Continuing Exile of Israel." In *Jesus and the Restoration of Israel*, edited by C. C. Newman, 77–100. Downers Grove, IL: InterVarsity, 1999.

———. "The Scriptures of Jesus and His Earliest Followers." In *The Canon Debate*, edited by Lee Martin McDonald and James A. Sanders, 185–95. Peabody, MA: Hendrickson (2002): 185–95.

Evans, C. Stephen. "Canonicity, Apostolicity, and Biblical Authority: Some Kierkegaardian Reflections." In *Canon and Biblical Interpretation*, edited by Craig Bartholomew, Robin Parry, and Scott Hahn, 147–66. Carlisle: Paternoster, 2006.

———. *The Historical Christ and the Jesus of Faith: The Incarnational Narrative as History.* New York: Oxford University Press (1996): 218–30.

Fackre, Gabriel. "Revelation." In *Karl Barth and Evangelical Theology*, edited by Sung Wook Chung, 1–25. Grand Rapids: Baker, 2006.

Fallon, Francis T., and Ron Cameron. "The *Gospel of Thomas*: A *Forschungsbericht* and Analysis." In *Aufstieg und Niedergang der römischen Welt: Geschichte und Kultur Roms im Spiegel der neueren Forschung*, vol. 2, edited by H. Temporini and W. Haase, 4195–251. Berlin: de Gruyter, 1988.

Farkasfalvy, Denis. "The Papias Fragments on Mark and Matthew and Their Relationship to Luke's Prologue: An Essay on the Pre-History of the Synoptic Problem." In *The Early Church in Its Context: Essays in Honor of Everett Ferguson*, edited by A. J. Malherbe, F. W. Norris, and J. W. Thompson, 92–106. Leiden: Brill, 1998.

———. "'Prophets and Apostles': The Conjunction of the Two Terms before Irenaeus." In *Texts and Testaments: Critical Essays on the Bible and the Early Church Fathers*, edited by W. E. March, 109–34. San Antonio: Trinity University Press, 1980.

Farmer, William R. "Galatians and the Second Century Development of the *Regula Fidei*." *Second Century* 4 (1984): 143–70.

———. "Some Critical Reflections on Second Peter: A Response to a Paper on Second Peter by Denis Farkasfalvy." *Second Century* 5 (1985–1986): 31–46.

Farmer, William R., and D. M. Farkasfalvy. *The Formation of the New Testament Canon.* New York: Paulist, 1976.

Fee, Gordon D. *1 and 2 Timothy, Titus.* Peabody, MA: Hendrickson, 1988.

———. *The First Epistle to the Corinthians.* New International Commentary on the New Testament. Grand Rapids: Eerdmans, 1987.

———. *Papyrus Bodmer II (p66): Its Textual Relationships and Scribal Characteristics.* Salt Lake City: University of Utah Press, 1968.

Fensham, F. Charles. "Common Trends in Curses of the Near Eastern Treaties and Kudurru-Inscriptions Compared with Maledictions of Amos and Isaiah." *Zeitschrift für die alttestamentliche Wissenschaft* 75 (1963): 155–75.

Ferguson, Everett. "The Covenant Idea in the Second Century." In *Texts and Testaments: Critical Essays on the Bible and the Early Church Fathers*, edited by W. E. March, 135–62. San Antonio: Trinity University Press, 1980.

———. "Review of Geoffrey Mark Hahneman, *The Muratorian Fragment and the Development of the Canon*." *Journal of Theological Studies* 44 (1993): 691–97.

Filson, Floyd. *One Lord, One Faith*. Philadelphia: Westminster, 1943.

Finkelberg, Margalit, and Guy G. Strousma, eds. *Homer, the Bible and Beyond*. Leiden: Brill, 2003.

Fiorenza, Elisabeth Schüssler. *Bread Not Stone: The Challenge of Feminist Biblical Interpretation*. Boston: Beacon, 1995.

———. *In Memory of Her: A Feminist Theological Reconstruction of Christian Origins*. New York: Crossroad, 1983.

Fishbane, Michael A. "Varia Deuteronomica." *Zeitschrift für die alttestamentliche Wissenschaft* 84 (1972): 349–52.

Fitzmyer, Joseph A. "'4Q Testimonia' and the New Testament." *Theological Studies* 18 (1957): 513–37.

———. "The Oxyrhynchus Logoi of Jesus and the Coptic Gospel According to Thomas." *Theological Studies* 20 (1959): 505–60.

———. "The Qumran Scrolls, the Ebionites and Their Literature." In *The Semitic Background of the New Testament*, 435–80. Grand Rapids: Eerdmans, 1997.

Flesseman-van Leer, E. *Tradition and Scripture in the Early Church*. Assen: Van Gorcum, 1954.

Folkert, Kendall W. "The 'Canons' of 'Scripture.'" In *Rethinking Scripture: Essays from a Comparative Perspective*, edited by Miriam Levering, 170–79. Albany: State University of New York Press, 1989.

Foster, Paul. "Are There Any Early Fragments of the So-Called Gospel of Peter?" *New Testament Studies* 52 (2006): 1–28.

———. "The Epistles of Ignatius of Antioch and the Writings That Later Formed the New Testament." In *The Reception of the New Testament in the Apostolic Fathers*, edited by Andrew Gregory and C. M. Tuckett, 159–86. Oxford: Oxford University Press, 2005.

———. *The Gospel of Peter: Introduction, Critical Edition and Commentary*. Leiden: Brill, 2010.

———. "The Text of the New Testament in the Apostolic Fathers." In *The Early Text of the New Testament*, edited by Charles E. Hill and Michael J. Kruger. Oxford: Oxford University Press, forthcoming.

———. *The Writings of the Apostolic Fathers*. London: T&T Clark, 2007.

Frame, John M. *The Doctrine of the Knowledge of God*. Phillipsburg, NJ: P&R, 1987.

———. *The Doctrine of the Word of God*. Phillipsburg, NJ: P&R, 2010.

———. *Perspectives on the Word of God: An Introduction to Christian Ethics*. Phillipsburg, NJ: P&R, 1990.

———. "The Spirit and the Scriptures." In *Hermeneutics, Authority, and Canon*, edited by D. A. Carson and John D. Woodbridge, 217–35. Grand Rapids: Zondervan, 1986.

France, R. T. *Matthew: Evangelist and Teacher*. Grand Rapids: Zondervan, 1989.

Freedman, David Noel. *The Unity of the Hebrew Bible*. Ann Arbor: University of Michigan Press, 1991.

Funk, Robert W. *The Five Gospels: What Did Jesus Really Say?* New York: Polebridge, 1993.

———. "The Once and Future New Testament." In *The Canon Debate*, edited by Lee Martin McDonald and James A. Sanders, 541–57. Peabody, MA: Hendrickson, 2002.

Gaffin, Richard B. "The New Testament as Canon." In *Inerrancy and Hermeneutic*, edited by H. M. Conn, 165–83. Grand Rapids: Baker, 1988.

———. "Old Amsterdam and Inerrancy?" *Westminster Theological Journal* 44 (1982): 250–89.

———. *Perspectives on Pentecost*. Phillipsburg, NJ: P&R, 1979.

———. *Resurrection and Redemption*. Phillipsburg, NJ: P&R, 1978.

———. "A Sabbath Rest Still Awaits the People of God." In *Pressing Toward the Mark: Essays Commemorating Fifty Years of the Orthodox Presbyterian Church*, edited by Charles G. Dennison and Richard C. Gamble, 33–51. Philadelphia: Committee for the Historian of the Orthodox Presbyterian Church, 1986.

Gamble, Harry Y. *Books and Readers in the Early Church*. New Haven, CT: Yale University Press, 1995.

———. "Christianity: Scripture and Canon." In *The Holy Book in Comparative Perspective*, edited by Frederick M. Denny and Rodney L. Taylor, 36–62. Columbia: University of South Carolina Press, 1985.

———. "Literacy, Liturgy, and the Shaping of the New Testament Canon." In *The Earliest Gospels*, edited by Charles Horton, 27–39. London: T&T Clark, 2004.

———. *The New Testament Canon: Its Making and Meaning*. Philadelphia: Fortress, 1985.

———. "The New Testament Canon: Recent Research and the Status Quaestionis." In *The Canon Debate*, edited by Lee Martin McDonald and James A. Sanders, 267–94. Peabody, MA: Hendrickson, 2002.

———. "The Redaction of the Pauline Letters and the Formation of the Pauline Corpus." *Journal of Biblical Literature* 94 (1975): 403–18.

Garrow, Alan J. P. *The Gospel of Matthew's Dependence on the Didache*. London: T&T Clark, 2004.

Gavrilyuk, Paul L. "Scripture and the *Regula Fidei*: Two Interlocking Components of the Canonical Heritage." In *Canonical Theism: A Proposal for Theology and the Church*, edited by William Abraham, Jason E. Vickers, and Natalie B. Van Kirk, 27–42. Grand Rapids: Eerdmans, 2008.

Geisler, Norman L., ed. *Inerrancy*. Grand Rapids: Zondervan, 1980.

Geisler, Norman L., and William E. Nix. *From God to Us: How We Got Our Bible*. Chicago: Moody Press, 1974.

Gerhardsson, Birger. *Memory and Manuscript with Tradition and Transmission in Early Christianity*. 2nd ed. Grand Rapids: Eerdmans, 1998.

———. *The Reliability of the Gospel Tradition*. Peabody, MA: Hendrickson, 2001.

Gevirtz, Stanley. "West-Semitic Curses and the Problem of the Origins of Hebrew Law." *Vetus Testamentum* 11 (1961): 137–58.

Gibson, David. "The God of Promise: Christian Scripture as Covenantal Revelation." *Themelios* 29 (2004): 27–36.

Gilmour, Michael J. "Reflections on the Authorship of 2 Peter." *Evangelical Quarterly* 73 (2001): 291–309.

Glover, Richard. "The Didache's Quotations and the Synoptic Gospels." *New Testament Studies* 5 (1958): 12–29.

Gnuse, Robert. *The Authority of the Bible: Theories of Inspiration, Revelation, and the Canon of Scripture.* Mawhaw, NJ: Paulist, 1985.

Goldingay, John. *Models for Scripture.* Grand Rapids: Eerdmans, 1994.

Gonzalez, Catherine. "The Rule of Faith: The Early Church's Source for Unity and Diversity." In *Many Voices, One God: Being Faithful in a Pluralistic World*, edited by Walter Brueggemann and George W. Stroup, 95–106. Louisville: Westminster John Knox, 1988.

Goodspeed, Edgar J. *The Formation of the New Testament.* Chicago: University of Chicago Press, 1926.

Goswell, Greg. "The Order of the Books in the Hebrew Bible." *Journal of the Evangelical Theological Society* 51 (2008): 673–88.

Goulder, Michael D. "Ignatius' 'Docetists.'" *Vigiliae christianae* 53 (1999): 16–30.

———. *Midrash and Lection in Matthew.* London: SPCK, 1974.

Grant, Robert M. *Eusebius as Church Historian.* Eugene, OR: Wipf and Stock, 1980.

———. *The Formation of the New Testament.* New York: Harper & Row, 1965.

———. *Irenaeus of Lyons.* London: Routledge, 1997.

———. "Literary Criticism and the New Testament Canon." *Journal for the Study of the New Testament* 16 (1982): 24–44.

———. *The Secret Sayings of Jesus.* Garden City, NY: Doubleday, 1960.

———. "Tatian and the Bible." In *Studia patristica*, vol. 1 (= TU 63), 297–306. Berlin, 1957.

Green, E. Michael. *2 Peter Reconsidered.* London: Tyndale, 1960.

Gregory, Andrew F. "1 Clement and the Writings That Later Formed the New Testament." In *The Reception of the New Testament in the Apostolic Fathers*, edited by Andrew F. Gregory and C. M. Tuckett, 129–57. Oxford: Oxford University Press, 2005.

———. "The Reception of Luke and Acts and the Unity of Luke-Acts." *Journal for the Study of the New Testament* 29 (2007): 459–72.

———. *The Reception of Luke and Acts in the Period Before Irenaeus.* Tübingen: Mohr Siebeck, 2003.

Gregory Andrew F., and Christopher Tuckett, eds. *The Reception of the New Testament in the Apostolic Fathers.* Oxford: Oxford University Press, 2005.

———. *Trajectories through the New Testament and the Apostolic Fathers.* Oxford: Oxford University Press, 2005.

Grenfell, Bernard P., et al., eds. *The Oxyrhynchus Papyri.* 74 vols. to date. London: Egypt Exploration Society, 1898–.

Grenz, Stanley J., and John R. Franke. *Beyond Foundationalism: Shaping Theology in a Postmodern Context.* Louisville: Westminster John Knox, 2001.

Grindheim, Sigurd. "The Law Kills but the Gospel Gives Life: The Letter-Spirit Dualism in 2 Cor 3:5–18." *Journal for the Study of the New Testament* 84 (2001): 97–115.

Grobel, William K. "How Gnostic Is the Gospel of Thomas?" *New Testament Studies* 8 (1962): 367–73.

Grudem, Wayne. "Scripture's Self-Attestation and the Problem of Formulating a Doctrine of Scripture." In *Scripture and Truth*, edited by D. A. Carson and J. D. Woodbridge, 19–59. Grand Rapids: Baker, 1992.

Gundry, Robert H. *Matthew: A Commentary on His Handbook for a Mixed Church under Persecution.* 2nd ed. Grand Rapids: Eerdmans, 1994.

———. *The Old Is Better: New Testament Essays in Support of Traditional Interpretations.* Tübingen: Mohr, 2005.

Güterbock, Hans Gustav. "Mursili's Accounts of Suppiluliuma's Dealings with Egypt." *Revue hittite et asianique* 18 (1960): 59–60.

Guthrie, Donald. *New Testament Introduction.* Downers Grove, IL: InterVarsity, 1990.

———. *The Pastoral Epistles and the Mind of Paul.* London: Tyndale, 1956.

Habermas, Gary. "Evidential Apologetics." In *Five Views on Apologetics*, edited by Steven B. Cowan, 92–121. Grand Rapids: Zondervan, 2000.

———. "The Personal Testimony of the Holy Spirit to the Believer and Christian Apologetics." *Journal of Christian Apologetics* 1 (1997): 49–64.

Haelst, Joseph van. *Catalogue des papyrus littéraires juifs et chrétiens.* Paris: Publications de la Sorbonne, 1976.

———. "Les origines du codex." In *Les débuts du codex*, edited by Alain Blanchard, 13–36. Turnhout: Brepols, 1989.

Haenchen, Ernst. "Petrus-Probleme." *New Testament Studies* 7 (1961): 187–97.

Hafemann, Scott J. "The Covenant Relationship." In *Central Themes in Biblical Theology: Mapping Unity in Diversity*, edited by Scott Hafemann and Paul House, 20–65. Grand Rapids: Baker Academic, 2007.

———. *Paul, Moses, and the History of Israel: The Letter/Spirit Contrast and the Argument from Scripture in 2 Corinthians 3.* Tübingen: Mohr, 1995.

Hafemann, Scott J., and Paul House, eds. *Central Themes in Biblical Theology: Mapping Unity in Diversity.* Grand Rapids: Baker Academic, 2007.

Hägg, Tomas. "Canon Formation in Greek Literary Culture." In *Canon and Canonicity: The Formation and Use of Scripture*, edited by Einar Thomassen, 109–28. Copenhagen: Museum Tusculanum Press, 2010.

Hägglund, Bengt. "Die Bedeutung der 'regula fidei' als Grundlage theologischer Aussagen." *Studia theologica* 12 (1958): 1–44.

Hagner, Donald A. "The Sayings of Jesus in the Apostolic Fathers and Justin Martyr." In *Gospel Perspectives: The Jesus Tradition Outside the Gospels*, edited by David Wenham, 233–68. Sheffield: JSOT, 1985.

———. *The Use of the Old and New Testaments in Clement of Rome*. Leiden: Brill, 1973.

Hahn, Scott, and Kimberly Hahn. *Rome Sweet Home*. San Francisco: Ignatius, 1993.

Hahneman, Geoffrey Mark. *The Muratorian Fragment and the Development of the Canon*. Oxford: Clarendon, 1992.

———. "The Muratorian Fragment and the Origins of the New Testament Canon." In *The Canon Debate*, edited by Lee Martin McDonald and James A. Sanders, 405–15. Peabody, MA: Hendrickson, 2002.

Haines-Eitzen, Kim. *Guardians of Letters: Literacy, Power, and the Transmitters of Early Christian Literature*. Oxford: Oxford University Press, 2000.

Halverson, John. "Oral and Written Gospel: A Critique of Werner Kelber." *New Testament Studies* 40 (1994): 180–95.

Hanson, Anthony Tyrrell. *The Pastoral Epistles*. Grand Rapids: Eerdmans, 1982.

Hanson, R. P. C. *Origen's Doctrine of Tradition*. London: SPCK, 1954.

———. *Tradition in the Early Church*. London: SCM, 1962.

Harding, Mark. "Disputed and Undisputed Letters of Paul." In *The Pauline Canon*, edited by Stanley E. Porter, 129–68. Leiden: Brill, 2004.

Harnack, Adolf von. *Das Neue Testament um das Jahr 200*. Freiburg: Mohr, 1889.

———. *Der kirchengeschichtliche Ertrag der exegetischen Arbeiten des Origenes*, vol. 1. Leipzig: Hinrichs, 1918.

———. *History of Dogma*, vol. 2. New York: Dover, 1961.

———. *Marcion: Das Evangelium von fremden Gott*. Leipzig: Hinrichs, 1924.

———. *Origin of the New Testament and the Most Important Consequences of a New Creation*. London: Williams & Northgate, 1925.

Harrington, Daniel J. *Jude and 2 Peter*. Collegeville, MN: Liturgical Press, 2003.

———. "The Reception of Walter Bauer's *Orthodoxy and Heresy in Earliest Christianity* During the Last Decade." *Harvard Theological Review* 77 (1980): 289–98.

Harris, James Rendel. *Testimonies*. Cambridge: Cambridge University Press, 1916.

Harris, R. Laird. *Inspiration and Canonicity of the Bible*. Grand Rapids: Zondervan, 1978.

Harris, William V. *Ancient Literacy*. Cambridge, MA: Harvard University Press, 1989.

Harrison, Percy N. *The Problem of the Pastoral Epistles*. London: Oxford University Press, 1921.

Harrisville, Roy A. "What I Believe My Old Schoolmate Is Up To." In *Theological Exegesis: Essays in Honor of Brevard S. Childs*, edited by Christopher Seitz and Kathryn Greene-McCreight, 7–25. Grand Rapids: Eerdmans, 1999.

Hartog, Paul. "Polycarp, Ephesians, and 'Scripture.'" *Westminster Theological Journal* 70 (2008): 255–75.

———. "The 'Rule of Faith' and Patristic Biblical Exegesis." *Trinity Journal* 28 (2007): 65–86.

Harvey, A. E. "'The Workman Is Worthy of His Hire': Fortunes of a Proverb in the Early Church." *Novum Testamentum* 24 (1982): 209–21.

Head, Peter M. "Is P4, P64, and P67 the Oldest Manuscript of the Four Gospels? A Response to T. C. Skeat." *New Testament Studies* 51 (2005): 450–57.

———. "On the Christology of the *Gospel of Peter*." *Vigiliae christianae* 46 (1992): 209–24.

———. "Some Recently Published NT Papyri From Oxyrhynchus: An Overview and Preliminary Assessment." *Tyndale Bulletin* 51 (2000): 1–16.

Heard, Richard. "The ΑΠΟΜΝΗΜΟΝΕΥΜΑΤΑ in Papias, Justin, and Irenaeus." *New Testament Studies* 1 (1954): 122–33.

———. "Papias' Quotations from the New Testament." *New Testament Studies* 1 (1954): 130–34.

Heckel, T. K. *Vom Evangelium des Markus zum viergestaltigen Evangelium*. Tübingen: Mohr, 1999.

Heine, Ronald E. *Origen: Homilies on Genesis and Exodus*. Washington DC: Catholic University Press, 1982.

Helm, Paul. *The Divine Revelation: The Basic Issues*. London: Marshall Morgan & Scott, 1982.

———. "Faith, Evidence, and the Scriptures." In *Scripture and Truth*, edited by D. A. Carson and John D. Woodbridge, 303–20. Grand Rapids: Zondervan, 1983.

Helmer, Christine. "Transhistorical Unity of the New Testament Canon from Philosophical, Exegetical, and Systematic-Theological Perspectives." In *One Scripture or Many?*, edited by Christine Helmer and Christof Landmesser, 13–50. Oxford: Oxford University Press, 2004.

Helmer, Christine, and Christof Landmesser, eds. *One Scripture or Many?* Oxford: Oxford University Press, 2004.

Hendriksen, William. *Ephesians*. Grand Rapids: Baker, 1967.

———. *Exposition of the Gospel According to Matthew*. Grand Rapids: Baker, 1973.

———. *More Than Conquerors*. Grand Rapids: Baker, 1994.

Hengel, Martin. *Die Evangelienüberschriften*. Heidelberg: Winter, 1984.

———. *Die johanneische Frage: Ein Lösungsversuch*. Tübingen: Mohr, 1993.

———. *The Four Gospels and the One Gospel of Jesus Christ*. Harrisburg, PA: Trinity, 2000.

———. *Judaism and Hellenism: Studies in Their Encounter in Palestine During the Early Hellenistic Period*. Philadelphia: Fortress, 1974.

———. *Studies in the Gospel of Mark*. London: SCM, 1985.

———. "The Titles of the Gospels and the Gospel of Mark." In *Studies in the Gospel of Mark*, 64–84. London: SCM, 1985.

Henne, Philippe. "La datation du *canon de Muratori*." *Revue biblique* 100 (1993): 54–75.

Henry, Carl F. H. "Canonical Theology: An Evangelical Appraisal." *Scottish Bulletin of Evangelical Theology* 8 (1990): 76–108.

———. *God, Revelation and Authority*. 6 vols. Waco, TX: Word, 1979.

Herodotus. Translated by A. D. Godley. Loeb Classical Library. Cambridge, MA: Harvard University Press, 1922.

Higgins, A. J. B. "The Non-Gnostic Sayings in the Gospel of Thomas." *Novum Testamentum* 4 (1960): 30–47.

Hilgenfeld, Adolf. *Kritische Untersuchungen über die Evangelien Justin's, der clementinischen Homilien und Marcion's*. Halle: Schwetschke, 1850.

Hill, Charles E. "The Debate over the Muratorian Fragment and the Development of the Canon." *Westminster Theological Journal* 57 (1995): 437–52.

———. "Ignatius and the Apostolate." In *Studia patristica*, vol. 36, edited by M. F. Wiles and E. J. Yarnold, 226–48. Leuven: Peeters, 2001.

———. "Ignatius, 'The Gospel,' and the Gospels." In *Trajectories Through the New Testament and the Apostolic Fathers*, edited by Andrew Gregory and Christopher Tuckett, 267–85. Oxford: Oxford University Press, 2005.

———. "'In These Very Words': Methods and Standards of Literary Borrowing in the Second Century." In *The Early Text of the New Testament*, edited by Charles E. Hill and Michael J. Kruger. Oxford: Oxford University Press, forthcoming.

———. *The Johannine Corpus in the Early Church*. Oxford: Oxford University Press, 2004.

———. "Justin and the New Testament Writings." In *Studia patristica*, vol. 30, edited by Elizabeth Livingstone, 42–48. Leuven: Peeters, 1997.

———. "The New Testament Canon: Deconstructio Ad Absurdum?" *Journal of the Evangelical Theological Society* 52 (2009): 105–6.

———. "Skeat's Thesis, Not Dead Yet? On the Making of P4, P64, and P67." Paper presented at the 2010 meeting of the Society of Biblical Literature, Atlanta, GA.

———. "Was John's Gospel among Justin's Apostolic Memoirs?" In *Justin Martyr and His Worlds*, edited by Sarah Parvis and Paul Foster, 88–94. Minneapolis: Fortress, 2007.

———. "What Papias Said About John (and Luke): A New Papias Fragment." *Journal of Theological Studies* 49 (1998): 582–629.

———. *Who Chose the Gospels? Probing the Great Gospel Conspiracy*. Oxford: Oxford University Press (2010): 226–29.

Hill, Charles E., and Michael J. Kruger, eds. *The Early Text of the New Testament*. Oxford: Oxford University Press, forthcoming.

Hillers, Delbert R. *Covenant: The History of a Biblical Idea*. Baltimore: Johns Hopkins University Press, 1969.

Hodge, A. A. *A Commentary on the Confession of Faith*. Philadelphia: Presbyterian Board of Publication, 1869.

Hodge, C. Wistar. "The Witness of the Holy Spirit to the Bible," *Princeton Theological Review* 11 (1913): 41–84.

Hoffman, Thomas A. "Inspiration, Normativeness, Canonicity, and the Unique Sacred Character of the Bible." *Catholic Biblical Quarterly* 44 (1982): 447–69.

Hoffmann, R. Joseph. *Marcion: On the Restitution of Christianity: An Essay on the Development of Radical Paulinist Theology in the Second Century*. Chico, CA: Scholars Press, 1984.

Holmes, Michael William. "Polycarp's *Letter to the Philippians* and the Writings That Later Formed the New Testament." In *The Reception of the New Testament in the Apostolic Fathers*, edited by Andrew Gregory and Christopher Tuckett, 187–227. Oxford: Oxford University Press, 2005.

Horbury, William. "The Wisdom of Solomon in the Muratorian Fragment." *Journal of Theological Studies* 45 (1994): 149–59.

Horsley, Richard A., Jonathan A. Draper, and John Miles Foley, eds. *Performing the Gospel: Orality, Memory, and Mark*. Minneapolis: Fortress, 2006.

Horton, Michael S. *Covenant and Eschatology: The Divine Drama*. Louisville: Westminster John Knox, 2002.

———. *God of Promise: Introducing Covenant Theology*. Grand Rapids: Baker, 2006.

———. *People and Place: A Covenant Ecclesiology*. Louisville: Westminster John Knox, 2008.

Howard, George. *Paul: Crisis in Galatia*. Cambridge: Cambridge University Press, 1979.

Hübner, Hans. *Biblische Theologie des Neuen Testaments*. Vol. 1, *Prolegomena*. Göttingen: Vandenhoeck & Ruprecht, 1990.

Hughes, Philip Edgcumbe. *A Commentary on the Epistle to the Hebrews*. Grand Rapids: Eerdmans, 1990.

Hunger, Herbert. "Zur Datierung des Papyrus Bodmer II (P66)." *Anzeiger der Österreichischen Akademie der Wissenschaften*, 4 (1960): 12–33.

Hunt, Arthur S. *Catalogue of the Greek Papyri in the John Rylands Library*, vol. 1. Manchester: Manchester University Press, 1911.

Hunter, Archibald M. *The Unity of the New Testament*. London: SCM, 1952.

Hurtado, Larry W. *The Earliest Christian Artifacts: Manuscripts and Christian Origins*. Grand Rapids: Eerdmans, 2006.

———. "The Earliest Evidence of an Emerging Christian Material and Visual Culture: The Codex, the Nomina Sacra, and the Staurogram." In *Text and Artifact in the Religions of Mediterranean Antiquity: Essays in Honour of Peter Richardson*, edited by Stephen G. Wilson and Michael Desjardins, 271–88. Waterloo, ON: Wilfrid Laurier University Press, 2000.

———. *Lord Jesus Christ: Devotion to Jesus in Earliest Christianity*. Grand Rapids: Eerdmans, 2003.

———. "The New Testament in the Second Century: Texts, Collections, and Canon." In *Transmission and Reception: New Testament Text-Critical and Exegetical Studies*, edited by J. W. Childers and D. C. Parker, 3–27. Piscataway, NJ: Gorgias, 2006.

Inge, William Ralph. "Ignatius." In *The New Testament and the Apostolic Fathers*, edited by a Committee of the Oxford Society of Historical Theology, 61–83. Oxford: Clarendon, 1905.

Jacobsen, Anders-Christian, ed. *Religion and Normativity*. Vol. 1, *The Discursive Fight Over Religious Texts in Antiquity*. Aarhus: Aarhus University Press, 2009.

Jaffee, Martin S. "How Much Orality in 'Oral Torah'? New Perspectives on the Composition and Transmission of Early Rabbinic Tradition." *Hebrew Studies* 10 (1992): 53–72.

———. *Torah in the Mouth: Writing and Oral Tradition in Palestinian Judaism*. Oxford: Oxford University Press, 2001.

Jansen, John F. "Tertullian and the New Testament." *Second Century* 2 (1982): 191–207.

Jaubert, Annie. *Homélies sur Josué*. Paris: Éditions du Cerf, 1960.

Jefford, C. N. *The Sayings of Jesus in the Teaching of the Twelve Apostles*. Leiden: Brill, 1989.

Jensen, Peter. *The Revelation of God*. Downers Grove, IL: InterVarsity, 2002.

Jenson, Robert W. *Canon and Creed*. Louisville: Westminster John Knox, 2010.

Jewett, Paul K. *Emil Brunner: An Introduction to the Man and His Thought*. Chicago: InterVarsity, 1961.

Johnson, Luke Timothy. *The First and Second Letters to Timothy*. New York: Doubleday, 2001.

———. *The Letter of James*. Anchor Bible Commentary. New York: Doubleday, 1995.

———. *The Real Jesus: The Misguided Quest for the Historical Jesus and the Truth of the Traditional Gospels*. San Francisco: HarperCollins, 1996.

Johnson, William A. *Bookrolls and Scribes in Oxyrhynchus: Studies in Book and Print Culture*. Toronto: University of Toronto Press, 2004.

———. "Towards a Sociology of Reading in Classical Antiquity." *American Journal of Philology* 121 (2000): 593–627.

Jones, F. Stanley. *An Ancient Jewish-Christian Source on the History of Christianity: Pseudo-Clementine Recognitions 1.27–71*. Atlanta: Scholars Press, 1995.

Jones, Peter R. "1 Corinthians 15:8: Paul the Last Apostle." *Tyndale Bulletin* 36 (1985): 3–34.

———. "The Apostle Paul: Second Moses to the New Covenant Community. A Study in Pauline Apostolic Authority." In *God's Inerrant Word*, edited by J. W. Montgomery, 219–41. Minneapolis: Bethany, 1974.

Jülicher, Adolf. *An Introduction to the New Testament*. London: Smith & Elder, 1904.

Jüngel, Eberhard. *Paulus und Jesus: Eine Untersuchung zur Präzisierung der Frage nach dem Ursprung der Christologie*. Tübingen: Mohr Siebeck, 1962.

Kähler, Martin. *The So-called Historical Jesus and the Historic, Biblical Christ.* Philadelphia: Fortress, 1964.

Kaiser, Walter C. *Recovering the Unity of the Bible: One Continuous Story, Plan, and Purpose.* Grand Rapids: Zondervan, 2009.

Kalin, Everett R. "Early Traditions About Mark's Gospel: Canonical Status Emerges as the Story Grows." *Currents in Theology and Missions* 2 (1975): 332–41.

———. "The New Testament Canon of Eusebius." In *The Canon Debate*, edited by Lee Martin McDonald and James A. Sanders, 386–404. Peabody, MA: Hendrickson, 2002.

———. "Re-examining New Testament Canon History: 1. The Canon of Origen." *Currents in Theology and Missions* 17 (1990): 274–82.

Kannaday, Wayne C. *Apologetic Discourse and the Scribal Tradition: Evidence of the Influence of Apologetic Interests on the Text of the Canonical Gospels.* Atlanta: Society of Biblical Literature, 2004.

Käsemann, Ernst. "Begründet der neutestamentliche Kanon die Einheit der Kirche?" *Evangelische Theologie* 11 (1951): 13–21.

———. "The Canon of the New Testament and the Unity of the Church." In *Essays on New Testament Themes*, 95–107. London: SCM, 1964.

———. *Das Neue Testament als Canon.* Göttingen: Vandenhoeck & Ruprecht, 1970.

———. "The Problem of a New Testament Theology." *New Testament Studies* 19 (1973): 235–45.

———. "The Problem of the Historical Jesus." In *Essays on New Testament Themes*, 15–47. London: SCM, 1964.

Katz, Peter. "The Johannine Epistles in the Muratorian Canon." *Journal of Theological Studies* 8 (1957): 273–74.

Keating, Karl. *Catholicism and Fundamentalism.* San Francisco: Ignatius, 1988.

Keener, Craig S. *The Gospel of John.* Peabody, MA: Hendrickson, 2003.

Kelber, Werner H. *The Oral and Written Gospel: The Hermeneutics of Speaking and Writing in the Synoptic Tradition, Mark, Paul, and Q.* Philadelphia: Fortress, 1983.

Kelber, Werner, and Samuel Byrskog, eds. *Jesus in Memory: Traditions in Oral and Scribal Perspectives.* Waco, TX: Baylor University Press, 2009.

Kelhoffer, J. A. "'How Soon a Book' Revisited: ΕΥΑΓΓΕΛΙΟΝ as a Reference to 'Gospel' Materials in the First Half of the Second Century." *Zeitschrift für die neutestamenliche Wissenschaft und die Kunde der älteren Kirche* 95 (2004): 1–34.

———. *Miracle and Mission: The Authentication of Missionaries and Their Message in the Longer Ending of Mark.* Tübingen: Mohr Siebeck, 2000.

Kelly, J. N. D. *A Commentary on the Epistles of Peter and of Jude.* New York: Harper & Row, 1969.

———. *A Commentary on the Pastoral Epistles.* Peabody, MA: Hendrickson, 1960.

———. *Early Christian Doctrines.* San Francisco: HarperCollins, 1978.

Kelsey, David H. *The Uses of Scripture in Recent Theology.* Philadelphia: Fortress, 1975.

Kenyon, Frederic G. *The Chester Beatty Biblical Papyri: Descriptions and Texts of Twelve Manuscripts on Papyrus of the Greek Bible*, vol. 1. London: Emery Walker, 1933–1937.

Kilpatrick, George Dunbar. *The Origins of the Gospel according to St. Matthew.* Oxford: Clarendon, 1950.

Kim, Young Kyu. "Palaeographical Dating of P46 to the Later First Century." *Biblica* 69 (1988): 248–61.

Kinzig, Wolfram. "καινὴ Διαθήκη: The Title of the New Testament in the Second and Third Centuries." *Journal of Theological Studies* 45 (1994): 519–44.

Kittel, Gerhard, and Herhard Friedrich, eds. *Theological Dictionary of the New Testament.* Translated by Geoffrey W. Bromiley. 10 vols. Grand Rapids: Eerdmans, 1964–1976.

Klausner, Joseph. *From Jesus to Paul.* New York: Macmillan, 1943.

Klijn, A. F. J. *Jewish-Christian Gospel Tradition.* Leiden: Brill, 1992.

Kline, Leslie L. "Harmonized Sayings of Jesus in the Pseudo-Clementine Homilies and Justin Martyr." *Zeitschrift für die neutestamenliche Wissenschaft und die Kunde der älteren Kirche* 66 (1975): 223–41.

Kline, Meredith. *Kingdom Prologue: Genesis Foundations for a Covenantal Worldview.* Overland Park, KS: Two Age Press, 2000.

———. "The Old Testament Origins of the Gospel Genre." *Westminster Theological Journal* 38 (1975): 1–27.

———. *The Structure of Biblical Authority.* 2nd ed. Eugene, OR: Wipf and Stock, 1997.

———. *Treaty of the Great King.* Grand Rapids: Eerdmans, 1963.

Klooster, Fred H. "Internal Testimony of the Holy Spirit." In *Evangelical Dictionary of Theology*, edited by W. Elwell, 564–65. Grand Rapids: Baker, 1984.

Kloppsenborg, John S. "An Analysis of the Pre-Pauline Formula in 1 Cor 15:3b–5." *Catholic Biblical Quarterly* 40 (1978): 351–67.

———. "The Use of the Synoptics or Q in *Did.* 1.3b–2.1." In *The Didache and Matthew: Two Documents from the Same Jewish-Christian Milieu?*, edited by H. van de Sandt, 105–29. Minneapolis: Fortress, 2005.

Knight, George William. *The Pastoral Epistles: A Commentary on the Greek Text.* Grand Rapids: Eerdmans, 1992.

Knox, John. *Marcion and the New Testament: An Essay in the Early History of the Canon.* Chicago: University of Chicago Press, 1942.

Koester, Helmut. *Ancient Christian Gospels: Their History and Development.* London: SCM, 1990.

———. "Apocryphal and Canonical Gospels." *Harvard Theological Review* 73 (1980): 105–30.

———. "The Extracanonical Sayings of the Lord as Products of the Christian Community." *Semeia* 44 (1988): 57–78.

———. "From the Kerygma Gospel to the Written Gospels," *New Testament Studies* 35 (1989): 361–81.

———. *Introduction to the New Testament*. Vol. 2, *History and Literature of Early Christianity*. Philadelphia: Fortress, 1982.

———. *Synoptische Überlieferung bei den apostlischen Vätern*. Berlin: Akademie-Verlag, 1957.

———. "The Text of the Synoptic Gospels in the Second Century." In *Gospel Traditions in the Second Century: Origins, Recensions, Text, and Transmission*, edited by W. L. Petersen, 19–37. Notre Dame: University of Notre Dame Press, 1989.

———. "Written Gospels or Oral Tradition?" *Journal of Biblical Literature* 113 (1994): 293–97.

Köhler, Wolf-Dietrich. *Die Rezeption des Matthäusevangeliums in der Zeit vor Irenäus*. Tübingen: Mohr, 1987.

Kooiman, Willem Jan. *Luther and the Bible*. Philadelphia: Muhlenberg, 1961.

Körtner, Ulrich H. J. "Markus der Mitarbeiter des Petrus." *Zeitschrift für die neutestamenliche Wissenschaft und die Kunde der älteren Kirche* 71 (1980): 160–73.

Köstenberger, Andreas J. "Diversity and Unity in the New Testament." In *Biblical Theology: Retrospect and Prospect*, edited by Scott Hafemann, 144–58. Downers Grove, IL: InterVarsity, 2002.

———. *John*. Baker Exegetical Commentary on the New Testament. Grand Rapids: Baker, 2004.

Köstenberger, Andreas J., L. Scott Kellum, and Charles L. Quarles. *The Cradle, the Cross, and the Crown: An Introduction to the New Testament*. Nashville: B&H Academic, 2009.

Köstenberger, Andreas J., and Michael J. Kruger. *The Heresy of Orthodoxy: How Modern Culture's Fascination with Diversity Has Reshaped Our Understanding of Early Christianity*. Wheaton, IL: Crossway, 2010.

Kraus, Thomas J. "Die Welt der Miniaturbücher in der Antike und Spätantike: Prolegomena und erste methodische Annäherungen für eine Datensammlung." *Studien zum Neuen Testament und seiner Umwelt* 35 (2010): 79–110.

———. "P.Oxy. V 840—Amulett oder Miniaturkodex? Grundsätzliche unde ergänzende Anmerkungen zu zwei Termini." *Zeitschrift für Antikes Christentum* 8 (2004): 485–97.

Kraus Thomas J., and Tobias Nicklas. *Das Petrusevangelium und die Petrusapokalypse*. Berlin: de Gruyter, 2004.

———. eds. *New Testament Manuscripts: Their Texts and Their World*. Leiden: Brill, 2006.

Kreeft, Peter. *Catholic Christianity*. San Francisco: Ignatius, 2001.

Krosney, Herbert. *The Lost Gospel: The Quest for the Gospel of Judas Iscariot*. Hanover, PA: National Geographic Society, 2006.

Kruger, Michael J. "The Authenticity of 2 Peter." *Journal of the Evangelical Theological Society* 42 (1999): 645–71.

———. "The Date and Content of P. Antinoopolis 12 (0232)." *New Testament Studies*, forthcoming.

———. "Early Christian Attitudes Towards the Reproduction of Texts." In *The Early Text of the New Testament*, edited by Charles E. Hill and Michael J. Kruger. Oxford: Oxford University Press, forthcoming.

———. *The Gospel of the Savior: An Analysis of P.Oxy. 840 and Its Place in the Gospel Traditions of Early Christianity.* Leiden: Brill, 2005.

———. "Manuscripts, Scribes, and Book Production within Early Christianity." In *Christian Origins and Classical Culture: Social and Literary Contexts for the New Testament*, edited by Stanley E. Porter and A. W. Pitts. Leiden: Brill, forthcoming.

———. "P.Oxy. 840: Amulet or Miniature Codex?" *Journal of Theological Studies* 53 (2002): 81–94.

———. Review of Stephen C. Carlson, *The Gospel Hoax: Morton Smith's Invention of Secret Mark. Journal of the Evangelical Theological Society* 49 (2006): 422–24.

Krüger, Julian. *Oxyrhynchos in der Kaiserzeit: Studien zur Topographie und Literaturrezeption.* Frankfurt: Peter Lang, 1990.

Kümmel, Werner G. *Introduction to the New Testament.* Nashville: Abingdon, 1973.

———. *The New Testament: The History of the Investigation of Its Problems.* Nashville: Abingdon, 1972.

———. "Notwendigkeit und Grenze des neutestamentlichen Kanons." *Zeitschrift für Theologie und Kirche* 47 (1960): 277–313.

Küng, Hans. *The Council in Action: Theological Reflections on the Second Vatican Council.* Translated by Cecily Hastings. New York: Sheed and Ward, 1963.

———. *Infallible? An Unresolved Inquiry.* Edinburgh: Continuum, 1994.

Kürzinger, Josef. *Papias von Hierapolis und die Evangelien des Neuen Testaments.* Regensburg: Pustet, 1983.

Kuyper, Abraham. *Encyclopedia of Sacred Theology: Its Principles.* New York: Scribner, 1898.

Laato, Timo. "Justification According to James: A Comparison with Paul?" *Trinity Journal* 18 (1997): 47–61.

Ladd, George Eldon, *Rudolf Bultmann.* Downers Grove, IL: InterVarsity, 1964.

———. *A Theology of the New Testament.* Grand Rapids: Eerdmans, 2001.

Lake, Kirsopp, trans. *The Apostolic Fathers.* 2 vols. London: William Hienemann, 1919.

Lampe, G. W. H. "Scripture and Tradition in the Early Church." In *Scripture and Tradition*, edited by Frederick William Dillistone, 21–52. London: Lutterworth, 1955.

Lane, William L. "Covenant: The Key to Paul's Conflict with Corinth." *Tyndale Bulletin* 33 (1982): 3–29.

Lange, Armin. "Oracle Collection and Canon: A Comparison Between Judah and Greece in Persian Times." In *Jewish and Christian Scripture as Artifact and*

Canon, edited by Craig A. Evans and H. Daniel Zacharias, 9–47. London: T&T Clark, 2009.

Lea, Thomas D. "Pseudonymity and the New Testament." In *New Testament Criticism and Interpretation*, edited by David Alan Black and David S. Dockery, 535–59. Grand Rapids: Zondervan, 1991.

Leaney, A. R. C. *The Letters of Peter and Jude*. Cambridge: Cambridge University Press, 1967.

Leipoldt, Johannes. *Geschichte des neuetestamentlichen Kanons*. Leipzig: Hinrichs Buchhandlung, 1907.

Lemcio, Eugene E. "Ephesus and the New Testament Canon." *Bulletin of the John Rylands University Library of Manchester* 69 (1986): 210–34.

———. "The Unifying Kerygma of the New Testament." *Journal for the Study of the New Testament* 33 (1988): 3–17.

———. "The Unifying Kerygma of the New Testament, pt 2." *Journal for the Study of the New Testament* 38 (1990): 3–11.

Lieberman, Saul. *Hellenism in Jewish Palestine*. 2nd ed. New York: Jewish Theological Seminary, 1962.

Lienhard, Joseph T. *The Bible, the Church, and Authority*. Collegeville, MN: Liturgical Press, 1995.

Lierman, John. *The New Testament Moses*. Tübingen: Mohr Siebeck, 2004.

Lightfoot, John B. *The Apostolic Fathers*. 2 vols. London: Macmillan, 1889.

———. *Essays on the Work Entitled Supernatural Religion*. London: Macmillan, 1889.

———. *St. Paul's Epistle to the Philippians*. Peabody, MA: Hendrickson, 1995.

Lindemann, Andreas. *Paulus im ältesten Christentum: Das Bild des Apostels und die Rezeption der paulinischen Theologie in der frühchristlichen Literatur bis Marcion*. Tübingen: Mohr Siebeck, 1979.

Linnemann, Eta. "Echtheitsfragen und Vokabelstatistik." *Jahrbuch für evangelikale Theologie* 10 (1996): 87–109.

Lints, Richard. *The Fabric of Theology: A Prolegomenon to Evangelical Theology*. Grand Rapids: Eerdmans, 1993.

Litfin, Bryan. "The Rule of Faith in Augustine." *Pro ecclesia* 14 (2005): 85–101.

Little, Paul. *Know What and Why You Believe*. Minneapolis: World Wide Publications, 1980.

Llewelyn, S. R. "The Development of the Codex." In *New Documents Illustrating Early Christianity*. Vol. 7, *A Review of the Greek Inscriptions and Papyri Published in 1982–83*, edited by S. R. Llewelyn and R. A. Kearsley, 249–56. North Ryde, NSW: Macquarie University Ancient History Documentary Research Center, 1994.

Lohfink, Norbert. "Über die Irrtumlosigkeit und die Einheit der Schrift." *Stimmen der Zeit* 174 (1964): 31–42.

Loisy, Alfred. *The Gospel and the Church*. Translated by Christopher Home. London: Isbister, 1903.

Lowe, Malcolm, and David Flusser. "Evidence Corroborating a Modified Proto-Matthean Synoptic Theory." *New Testament Studies* 29 (1983): 25–47.

Ludlow, Morwenna. "'Criteria of Canonicity' and the Early Church." In *The Unity of Scripture and the Diversity of Canon*, edited by John Barton and Michael Wolter, 69–93. Berlin: de Gruyter, 2003.

Lührmann, Dieter. "Abendmahlsgemeinschaft? Gal 2:11ff." In *Kirche: Festschrift für Günther Bornkamm*, edited by Dieter Lührmann and Georg Strecker, 271–86. Tübingen: Mohr, 1980.

———. "Gal 2, 9 und die katholischen Briefe: Bemerkungen zun Kanon und zur regula fidei." *Zeitschrift für die neutestamenliche Wissenschaft und die Kunde der älteren Kirche* 72 (1981): 65–87.

———. "P.Oxy. 2949: EvPet 3–5 in einer Handschrift des 2/3 Jahrhunderts." *Zeitschrift für die neutestamenliche Wissenschaft und die Kunde der älteren Kirche* 72 (1981): 216–26.

———. "P.Oxy. 4009: Ein neues Fragment des Petrusevangeliums?" *Novum Testamentum* 35 (1993): 390–410.

Luijendijk, AnneMarie. *Greetings in the Lord: Early Christians in the Oxyrhynchus Papyri*. Cambridge, MA: Harvard University Press, 2008.

Lundhaug, Hugo. "Canon and Interpretation: A Cognitive Perspective." In *Canon and Canonicity: The Formation and Use of Scripture*, edited by Einar Thomassen, 67–90. Copenhagen: Museum Tusculanum Press, 2010.

Luther, Martin. "The Misuse of the Mass." In *Luther's Works*. Vol. 36, *Word and Sacrament II*, edited by A. R. Wentz, 127–230. Philadelphia: Fortress, 1959.

———. "Prefaces to the New Testament." In *Luther's Works*. Vol. 35, *Word and Sacrament I*, edited by E. Theodore Bachmann, 357–411. Philadelphia: Fortress, 1960.

Maccoby, Hyam. *The Mythmaker: Paul and the Invention of Christianity*. London: Weidenfeld and Nicholson, 1986.

Madrid, Patrick. "*Sola Scriptura*: A Blueprint for Anarchy." In *Not By Scripture Alone: A Catholic Critique of the Protestant Doctrine of Sola Scriptura*, edited by Robert A. Sungenis, 1–30. Santa Barbara: Queenship, 1997.

———, ed. *Surprised by Truth*. San Diego: Basilica, 1994.

Maier, Gerhard. *Die Johannesoffenbarung und die Kirche*. Tübingen: Mohr (1981): 96–107.

Manson, Thomas Walter. "The Gospel of St. Matthew." In *Studies in the Gospels and Epistles*, edited by Matthew Black, 68–104. Edinburgh: T&T Clark, 1962.

Massaux, Édouard. *Influence de L'Évangile de Saint Matthieu sur la littérature chrétienne avant Saint Irénée*. Lueven: Lueven University Press, 1986.

———. "Le texte du Sermon sur la Montagne de Matthieu utilisé par Saint Justin." *Ephemerides theologicae lovanienses* 28 (1952): 411–48.

Mara, Maria Grazia. *Évangile de Pierre: Introduction, text critique, traduction, commentaire, et index*. Paris: Éditions du Cerf, 1973.

Marshall, I. Howard. *Biblical Inspiration*. London: Hodder & Stoughton, 1982.

———. *A Critical and Exegetical Commentary on the Pastoral Epistles*. International Critical Commentary. Edinburgh: T&T Clark, 1999.

———. *The Epistles of John*. Grand Rapids: Eerdmans, 1978.

———. *The Gospel of Luke*. Grand Rapids: Eerdmans, 1978.

———. *I Believe in the Historical Jesus*. Grand Rapids: Eerdmans, 1977.

———. *New Testament Theology*. Downers Grove, IL: InterVarsity, 2004.

———. "Orthodoxy and Heresy in Earlier Christianity." *Themelios* 2 (1976): 5–14.

Martin, Ralph P. *2 Corinthians*. Word Biblical Commentary. Waco, TX: Word, 1986.

———. *James*. Word Biblical Commentary. Waco, TX: Word, 1988.

Martin, Victor, and Rudolf Kasser. *Papyrus Bodmer XIV–XV*. 2 vols. Geneva: Bibliotheca Bodmeriana, 1961.

Martyr, Justin. *Apology*. Edited by A. Roberts and J. Donaldson. *The Ante-Nicene Fathers*. 10 vols. 1885. Repr. Peabody, MA: Hendrickson, 1994.

Marxsen, Willi. *Introduction to the New Testament: An Approach to Its Problems*. Philadelphia: Westminster, 1968.

———. *The New Testament as the Church's Book*. Philadelphia: Fortress, 1972.

Mathison, Keith A. *The Shape of Sola Scriptura*. Moscow, ID: Canon, 2001.

Mayeda, Goro. *Das Leben-Jesu-Fragment Papyrus Egerton 2 und seine Stellung in der urchristlichen Literaturgeschichte*. Bern: Paul Haupt, 1946.

Mayor, Joseph B. *The Epistle of St. James*. London: Macmillan, 1892.

———. *The Epistle of St. Jude and the Second Epistle of St. Peter*. London: Macmillan, 1907.

McCallum, Dennis. *Christianity: The Faith That Makes Sense*. Wheaton, IL: Tyndale, 1992.

McCant, Jerry W. "The Gospel of Peter: Docetism Reconsidered." *New Testament Studies* 30 (1984): 258–73.

McCarthy, Dennis J. *Treaty and Covenant*. Rome: Biblical Institute, 1981.

McComiskey, Thomas Edward. *The Covenants of Promise: A Theology of the Old Testament Covenants*. Grand Rapids: Baker, 1985.

McCormack, Bruce L. "The Being of Holy Scripture Is in Becoming: Karl Barth in Conversation with American Evangelicalism." In *Evangelicals and Scripture: Tradition, Authority and Hermeneutics*, edited by Vincent Bacote, Laura C. Miguelez, and Dennis L. Okholm, 55–74. Downers Grove, IL: InterVarsity, 2004.

McCormick, Michael. "The Birth of the Codex and the Apostolic Life-Style." *Scriptorium* 39 (1985): 150–58.

McCown, Chester Charlton. "Codex and Roll in the New Testament." *Harvard Theological Review* 34 (1941): 219–50.

McCue, James. "Orthodoxy and Heresy: Walter Bauer and the Valentinians." *Vigiliae christianae* 33 (1979): 118–30.

McDonald, Lee Martin. *The Biblical Canon: Its Origin, Transmission, and Authority.* Peabody, MA: Hendrickson, 2007.

———. *Forgotten Scriptures: The Selection and Rejection of Early Religious Writings.* Louisville: Westminster John Knox, 2009.

———. *The Formation of the Christian Biblical Canon.* Peabody, MA: Hendrickson, 1995.

———. "Identifying Scripture and Canon in the Early Church: The Criteria Question." In *The Canon Debate*, edited by Lee Martin McDonald and James A. Sanders, 416–39. Peabody, MA: Hendrickson, 2002.

———. "The Integrity of the Biblical Canon in Light of Its Historical Development." *Bulletin for Biblical Research* 6 (1996): 104.

McDonald, Lee Martin, and James A. Sanders, eds. *The Canon Debate.* Peabody, MA: Hendrickson, 2002.

McDowell, Josh. *Evidence That Demands a Verdict*, vol. 1. San Bernardino: Here's Life, 1991.

McGrath, Alister. *Heresy: A History of Defending the Truth.* New York: HarperCollins, 2009.

McKenzie, John L. "The Social Character of Inspiration." *Catholic Biblical Quarterly* 24 (1962): 115–24.

McKenzie, Steven L. *Covenant.* St. Louis: Chalice, 2000.

Meade, David. "Ancient Near Eastern Apocalypticism and the Origins of the New Testament Canon of Scripture." In *The Bible as a Human Witness: Hearing the Word of God Through Historically Dissimilar Traditions*, edited by Randall Heskett and Brian Irwin, 302–21. London: T&T Clark, 2010.

———. *Pseudepigrapha and Canon.* Tübingen: Mohr, 1986.

Meier, John P. "The Inspiration of Scripture: But What Counts as Scripture?" *Mid-Stream* 38 (1999): 71–78.

———. *A Marginal Jew: Rethinking the Historical Jesus*, vol. 1. New York: Doubleday, 1991.

Mendenhall, George E. "Covenant Forms in Israelite Tradition." *Biblical Archaeologist* 17 (1954): 50–76.

———. *Law and Covenant in Israel and the Ancient Near East.* Pittsburgh: The Biblical Colloquium, 1955.

Meredith, Anthony. "Porphyry and Julian Against the Christians." In *Aufstieg und Niedergang der römischen Welt: Geschichte und Kultur Roms im Spiegel der neueren Forschung*, vol. 2, edited by H. Temporini and W. Haase, 1119–49. Berlin: de Gruyter, 1980.

Metzger, Bruce M. *The Canon of the New Testament: Its Origin, Development and Significance.* Oxford: Clarendon, 1987.

———. *An Introduction to the Apocrypha.* New York: Oxford University Press, 1977.

———. "Literary Forgeries and Canonical Pseudepigrapha." *Journal of Biblical Literature* 91 (1972): 3–24.

———. "Patristic Evidence and the Textual Criticism of the New Testament." In *New Testament Studies: Philological, Versional, and Patristic*, 167–88. Leiden: Brill, 1980.

Metzger, Bruce M., and Bart D. Ehrman. *The Text of the New Testament: Its Transmission, Corruption, and Restoration*. 4th ed. Oxford: Oxford University Press, 2005.

Milavec, Aaron. "Synoptic Tradition in the Didache Revisited." *Journal of Early Christian Studies* 11 (2003): 443–80.

Millard, Alan. *Reading and Writing in the Time of Jesus*. New York: New York University Press, 2000.

Mimouni, Simon Claude. *Le judéo-christianisme ancien: Essais historiques*. Paris: Éditions du Cerf, 1998.

Minear, Paul Sevier. *Christians and the New Creation: Genesis Motifs in the New Testament*. Louisville: Westminster John Knox, 1994.

Montgomery, John Warwick. "Lessons from Luther on the Inerrancy of Holy Writ." In *God's Inerrant Word*, edited by John Warwick Montgomery, 63–94. Minneapolis: Bethany, 1974.

———. *History and Christianity*. Downers Grove, IL: InterVarsity, 1965.

———. *The Shape of the Past: A Christian Response to Secular Philosophies of History*. Minneapolis: Bethany, 1975.

Moo, Douglas J. *The Letter of James*. Grand Rapids: Eerdmans, 2000.

Morris, Leon. *The First Epistle of Paul to the Corinthians*. Tyndale New Testament Commentaries. Grand Rapids: Eerdmans, 1975.

———. *The Gospel According to John*. New International Commentary on the New Testament. Grand Rapids: Eerdmans, 1995.

———. *The Gospel According to Matthew*. Pillar New Testament Commentary. Grand Rapids: Eerdmans, 1992.

———. *The Gospel According to St. Luke*. Tyndale New Testament Commentaries. Grand Rapids: Eerdmans, 1974.

Morrison, John D. "Barth, Barthians, and Evangelicals: Reassessing the Question of the Relation of Holy Scripture and the Word of God." *Trinity Journal* 25 (2004): 187–213.

Moule, C. F. D. "The Problem of the Pastoral Epistles: A Reappraisal." *Bulletin of the John Rylands University Library of Manchester* 47 (1965): 430–52.

Mounce, Robert H. *The Book of Revelation*. New International Commentary on the New Testament. Grand Rapids: Eerdmans, 1998.

Mounce, William D. *Pastoral Epistles*. Word Biblical Commentary. Nashville: Thomas Nelson, 2000.

Muller, Richard A. *Post-Reformation Dogmatics*. Vol. 2, *Holy Scripture*. Grand Rapids: Eerdmans, 1993.

Murray, John. "The Attestation of Scripture." In *The Infallible Word*, edited by N. B. Stonehouse and Paul Woolley, 1–54. Philadelphia: Presbyterian and Reformed, 1946.

———. "Calvin and the Authority of Scripture." In *Collected Writings of John Murray*. Vol. 4, *Studies in Theology*, 176–90. Edinburgh: Banner of Truth, 1982.

Murray, Robert. "How Did the Church Determine the Canon of Scripture?" *Heythrop Journal* 11 (1970): 115–26.

Netland, Harold A. "Apologetics, Worldviews, and the Problem of Neutral Criteria." In *The Gospel and Contemporary Perspectives*, edited by Douglas Moo, 138–52. Grand Rapids: Kregel, 1997.

Neyrey, Jerome H. *2 Peter, Jude*. New York: Doubleday, 1993.

Nicole, Roger. "The Canon of the New Testament." *Journal of the Evangelical Theological Society* 40 (1997): 199–206.

———. "The Neo-Orthodox Reduction." In *Challenges to Inerrancy: A Theological Response*, edited by Gordon Lewis and Bruce Demarest, 121–44. Chicago: Moody, 1984.

Nielsen, Charles Merritt. "Polycarp, Paul, and the Scriptures." *Anglican Theological Review* 47 (1965): 199–216.

Nienhuis, David R. *Not by Paul Alone: The Formation of the Catholic Epistle Collection and the Christian Canon*. Waco, TX: Baylor University Press, 2007.

Nissen, Johannes. "Scripture and Community in Dialogue." In *The Biblical Canons*, edited by Jean-Marie Auwers and Henk Jan de Jonge, 651–58. Leuven: Leuven University Press, 2003.

Noble, Paul R. *The Canonical Approach: A Critical Reconstruction of the Hermeneutics of Brevard S. Childs*. Leiden: Brill, 1995.

Nolland, John. *The Gospel of Matthew: A Commentary on the Greek Text*. New International Greek Testament Commentary. Grand Rapids: Eerdmans, 2005.

Oates, John F., Alan E. Samuel, and C. Bradford Welles. *Yale Papyri in the Beinecke Rare Book and Manuscript Library*. New Haven, CT: American Society of Papyrologists, 1967.

Oberlinner, Lorenz. *Kommentar zum ersten Timotheusbrief*. Freiburg im Breisgau: Herder, 1994.

Ogden, Schubert. "The Authority of Scripture for Theology." *Interpretation* 30 (1976): 252.

Ohlig, Karl-Heinz. *Die theologische Begründung des neutestamentlichen Kanons in der alten Kirche*. Düsseldorf: Patmos, 1972.

O'Keefe, John J., and R. R. Reno. *Sanctified Vision: An Introduction to Early Christian Interpretation of the Bible*. Baltimore: Johns Hopkins University Press, 2005.

Oppel, Herbert. *KANΩN. Zur Bedeutungsgeschichte des Wortes und seiner lateinischen Entsprechungen (regula-norma)*. Leipzig: Dietrich'sche Verlagsbuchhandlung, 1937.

Origen, *On First Principles.* Translated by G. W Butterworth. Gloucester, MA: P. Smith, 1973.

———. *Homilies on Joshua.* Translated by Barbara J. Bruce. Washington, DC: Catholic University Press, 2002.

Osborn, Eric Francis. *Justin Martyr.* Tübingen: Mohr Siebeck, 1973.

———. "Reason and the Rule of Faith in the Second Century AD." In *The Making of Orthodoxy,* edited by Rowan Williams, 40–61. Cambridge: Cambridge University Press, 1989.

Osiek, Carolyn. *The Shepherd of Hermas.* Minneapolis: Fortress, 1999.

Outler, Albert C. "Origen and the *Regula Fidei.*" *Second Century* 4 (1984): 133–41.

Overbeck, Franz. *On the Christianity of Theology.* Translated by John Elbert Wilson. San Jose, CA: Pickwick, 2002.

Owen, John. "The Divine Original: Authority, Self-Evidencing Light, and Power of the Scriptures." In *The Works of John Owen.* Vol. 16, *The Church and the Bible,* edited by William H. Goold, 297–421. Repr. Edinburgh: Banner of Truth, 1988.

Pack, Roger A. *The Greek and Latin Literary Texts from Greco-Roman Egypt.* 2nd ed. Ann Arbor: University of Michigan Press, 1967.

Packer, J. I. *Fundamentalism and the Word of God.* Grand Rapids: Eerdmans, 1992.

———. *God Has Spoken: Revelation and the Bible.* Grand Rapids: Baker, 1993.

Pagels, Elaine. *Beyond Belief: The Secret Gospel of Thomas.* New York: Random House, 2003.

Parker, David. *New Testament Manuscripts and Their Texts.* Cambridge: Cambridge University Press, 2008.

Parsons, Mikeal C. "Canonical Criticism." In *New Testament Criticism and Interpretation,* edited by David Alan Black and David S. Dockery, 255–94. Grand Rapids: Zondervan, 1991.

Parsons, Patricia J., Alan K. Bowman, R. A. Coles, Nikolaos Gonis, eds. *Oxyrhynchus: A City and Its Texts.* London: Egypt Exploration Society, 2007.

Parvis, Sara, and Paul Foster, eds. *Justin Martyr and His Worlds.* Minneapolis: Fortress, 2007.

Patterson, Stephen J. *The Gospel of Thomas and Jesus.* Sonoma, CA: Polebridge, 1993.

Peckham, John C. "The Canon and Biblical Authority: A Critical Comparison of Two Models of Canonicity." *Trinity Journal* 28 (2007): 229–49.

Pelikan, Jaroslav, and Valerie R. Hotchkiss, eds. *Creeds and Confessions of Faith in the Christian Tradition.* 4 vols. New Haven, CT: Yale University Press, 2003.

Penner, Myron B. *Christianity and the Postmodern Turn: Six Views.* Grand Rapids: Brazos, 2005.

Perkins, Pheme. "Gnosticism and the Christian Bible." In *The Canon Debate,* edited by Lee Martin McDonald and James A. Sanders, 355–71. Peabody, MA: Hendrickson, 2002.

Perrin, Nicholas. *Thomas: The Other Gospel*. Louisville: Westminster John Knox, 2007.

Petersen, William L. "The Genesis of the Gospel." In *New Testament Textual Criticism and Exegesis, Festschrift J. Delobel*, edited by Adelbert Denaux, 33–65. Leuven: Leuven University Press, 2002.

——, ed. *The Gospel Traditions of the Second Century: Origins, Recensions, Text, and Transmission*. South Bend, IN: Notre Dame University Press, 1989.

——. "Textual Evidence of Tatian's Dependence upon Justin's ΑΠΟΜΝΗΜΟΝΕΥΜΑΤΑ." *New Testament Studies* 36 (1990): 512–34.

——. "Textual Traditions Examined: What the Text of the Apostolic Fathers Tells Us About the Text of the New Testament in the Second Century." In *The Reception of the New Testament in the Apostolic Fathers*, edited by Andrew Gregory and Christopher Tuckett, 29–46. Oxford: Oxford University Press, 2005.

——. "What Text Can New Testament Textual Criticism Ultimately Reach?" In *New Testament Textual Criticism, Exegesis, and Early Church History: A Discussion of Methods*, edited by Barbara Aland and Joël Delobel, 136–52. Kampen: Kok Pharos, 1994.

Picirilli, Robert E. "Allusions to 2 Peter in the Apostolic Fathers." *Journal for the Study of the New Testament* 33 (1988): 59.

Pieper, Francis. *Christian Dogmatics*. 4 vols. St. Louis: Concordia, 1950–1957.

Pinnock, Clark H. *Set Forth Your Case*. Chicago: Moody, 1971.

Piper, Ronald A. "The One, the Four, and the Many." In *The Written Gospel*, edited by Markus Bockmuehl and Donald A. Hagner, 254–73. Cambridge: Cambridge University Press, 2005.

Plantinga, Alvin. "Two (or More) Kinds of Scripture Scholarship." In *"Behind" the Text: History and Biblical Interpretation*, edited by Craig Bartholomew, C. Stephen Evans, Mary Healy, and Murray Rae, 19–57. Grand Rapids: Zondervan, 2003.

——. *Warrant: The Current Debate*. New York: Oxford University Press, 1993.

——. *Warrant and Proper Function*. New York: Oxford University Press, 1993.

——. *Warranted Christian Belief*. New York: Oxford University Press, 2000.

Porter, Calvin L. "Papyrus Bodmer XV (P75) and the Text of Codex Vaticanus." *Journal of Biblical Literature* 81 (1962): 363–76.

Porter, Stanley E. *The Criteria for Authenticity in Historical-Jesus Research*. Sheffield: Sheffield Academic, 2000.

——. "Pauline Authorship and the Pastoral Epistles: Implications for Canon." *Bulletin for Biblical Research* 5 (1995): 105–23.

——. "When and How Was the Pauline Canon Compiled? An Assessment of Theories." In *The Pauline Canon*, edited by Stanley E. Porter, 95–127. Leiden: Brill, 2004.

Powell, Mark E. "Canonical Theism and the Challenge of Epistemic Certainty." In *Canonical Theism: A Proposal for Theology and the Church*, edited by William J.

Abraham, Jason E. Vickers, and Natalie B. Van Kirk, 195–209. Grand Rapids: Eerdmans, 2008.

Poythress, Vern S. "Johannine Authorship and the Use of Intersentence Conjunctions in the Book of Revelation." *Westminster Theological Journal* 47 (1985): 329–36.

———. *The Shadow of Christ in the Law of Moses*. Phillipsburg, NJ: P&R, 1991.

Prior, Michael. *Paul the Letter-Writer and the Second Letter to Timothy*. Sheffield: JSOT, 1989.

Provan, Iain. "Canons to the Left of Him: Brevard Childs, His Critics, and the Future of Old Testament Theology." *Scottish Journal of Theology* 50 (1997): 23.

———. "Ideologies, Literary and Critical: Reflections on Recent Writings on the History of Israel." *Journal of Biblical Literature* 114 (1995): 585–606.

Pryor, John W. "Justin Martyr and the Fourth Gospel." *Second Century* 9 (1992): 153–67.

Quinn, Jerome D. "P46—The Pauline Canon?" *Catholic Biblical Quarterly* 36 (1974): 379–85.

Quispel, Gilles. *Makarius, das Thomasevangelium und das Lied von der Perle*. Leiden: Brill, 1967.

Rahner, Karl. *Foundations of Christian Faith: An Introduction to the Idea of Christianity*. New York: Crossroad, 1997.

———. *Inspiration in the Bible*. New York: Herder & Herder, 1961.

Räisänen, Heikki. *Beyond New Testament Theology: A Story and a Program*. London: SCM, 1990.

Ramm, Bernard. *The Witness of the Spirit*. Grand Rapids: Eerdmans, 1959.

Reicke, Bo. *The Epistles of James, Peter, and Jude*. New York: Doubleday, 1964.

Rendtorff, Rolf. *Theologie des Altens Testaments: Ein kanonischer Entwurf*. Neukirchen-Vluyn: Neukirchener Verlag, 1999.

Revell, Ernest John. "The Oldest Evidence for the Hebrew Accent System." *Bulletin of the John Rylands University Library of Manchester* 54 (1971): 214–22.

Reymond, Robert L. *Brunner's Dialectical Encounter*. Philadelphia: Presbyterian and Reformed, 1967.

———. *A New Systematic Theology of the Christian Faith*. Nashville: Thomas Nelson, 1998.

Richards, E. Randolph. "The Codex and the Early Collection of Paul's Letters." *Bulletin for Biblical Research* 8 (1998): 151–66.

———. *Paul and First-Century Letter Writing: Secretaries, Composition, and Collection*. Downers Grove, IL: InterVarsity, 2004.

Ricoeur, Paul. "The 'Sacred' Text and the Community." In *The Critical Study of Sacred Texts*, edited by W. D. O'Flaherty, 271–76. Berkeley: Graduate Theological Union, 1979.

Ridderbos, Herman N. *Bultmann*. Philadelphia: Presbyterian and Reformed, 1960.

———. "The Canon of the New Testament." In *Revelation and the Bible: Contemporary Evangelical Thought*, edited by C. F. H. Henry, 189–201. Grand Rapids: Baker, 1958.

———. *The Gospel of John*. Grand Rapids: Eerdmans, 1997.

———. *Paul: An Outline of His Theology*. Grand Rapids: Eerdmans, 1975.

———. *Redemptive History and the New Testament Scripture*. Phillipsburg, NJ: P&R, 1988.

Riekert, Stephanus J. P. K. "Critical Research and the One Christian Canon Comprising Two Testaments." *Neotestamentica* 14 (1981): 21–41.

Rist, John. "The Greek and Latin Texts of the Discussion on Free Will in *De Principiis*, Book III." In *Origeniana: premier colloque international des études origéniennes, Montserrat, 18–21 septembre 1975*, 97–111. Bari: Università di Bari, 1975.

Robbins, Gregory Allen. "Eusebius' Lexicon of Canonicity." In *Studia patristica*, vol. 25, edited by E. A. Livingstone, 134–41. Leuven: Peeters, 1993.

Robbins, Vernon K. "The Claims of the Prologues and Greco-Roman Rhetoric: the Prefaces to Luke and Acts in Light of Greco-Roman Rhetorical Strategies." In *Jesus and the Heritage of Israel*, edited by D. P. Moessner, 63–83. Harrisburg, PA: Trinity, 1999.

Roberts, Colin H. "An Early Papyrus of the First Gospel." *Harvard Theological Review* 46 (1953): 233–37.

———. *Manuscript, Society and Belief in Early Christian Egypt*. London: Oxford University Press, 1979.

———. "P Yale 1 and the Early Christian Book." In *Essays in Honor of C. Bradford Welles (American Studies in Papyrology, 1)*, edited by A. E. Samuel, 25–58. New Haven, CT: American Society of Papryologists, 1966.

———. "Two Biblical Papyri in the John Rylands Library, Manchester." *Bulletin of the John Rylands University Library of Manchester* 20 (1936): 219–44.

———. "An Unpublished Fragment of the Fourth Gospel in the John Rylands Library." *Bulletin of the John Rylands University Library of Manchester* 20 (1936): 45–55.

Roberts, Colin H., John W. B. Barns, and Henrik Zilliacus. *The Antinoopolis Papyri*. London: Egypt Exploration Society, 1950.

Roberts, Colin H., and T. C. Skeat. *The Birth of the Codex*. London: Oxford University Press, 1987.

Roberts, J. H., and Andreas B. Du Toit. *Guide to the New Testament*. Vol. 1, *Preamble to New Testament Study: The Canon of the New Testament*. Pretoria: N. G. Kerkboekhandel Transvaal, 1979.

Robertson, O. Palmer. *The Christ of the Covenants*. Phillipsburg, NJ: P&R, 1980.

———. *Covenants: God's Way With His People*. Philadelphia: Great Commission, 1987.

Robinson, James M. *The Secrets of Judas: The Story of the Misunderstood Disciple and His Lost Gospel*. San Francisco: HarperSanFrancisco, 2006.

Robinson, James M., and Helmut Koester. *Trajectories Through Early Christianity.* Philadelphia: Fortress, 1971.

Robinson, John A. T. *Redating the New Testament.* Philadelphia: Westminster, 1976.

Robinson, Thomas Arthur. *The Bauer Thesis Examined: The Geography of Heresy in the Early Christian Church.* Lewiston, NY: Mellen, 1989.

———. "Grayston and Herdan's 'C' Quantity Formula and the Authorship of the Pastoral Epistles." *New Testament Studies* 30 (1984): 282–88.

Rodgers, Peter. "The Text of the New Testament and Its Witnesses Before 200 A.D.: Observations on P90 (P.Oxy. 3523)." In *The New Testament Text in Early Christianity: Proceedings of the Lille Colloquium, July 2000,* 83–91. Lausanne: Éditions du Zèbre, 2003.

Roetzel, Calvin. "The Judgment Form in Paul's Letters." *Journal of Biblical Literature* 88 (1969): 305–12.

Rombs, Ronnie J. "A Note on the Status of Origen's *De Principiis* in English." *Vigiliae christianae* 61 (2007): 23.

Rousseau, Adelin, Bertrand Hemmerdinger, Louis Doutreleau, and Charles Mercier, eds. *Irénée de Lyon: Contre les hérésies, Livre 4,* vol. 2. Texte et traduction. Sources chrétiennes 100. Paris: Cerf, 1965.

Rowe, C. Kavin. "History, Hermeneutics and the Unity of Luke-Acts." *Journal for the Study of the New Testament* 28 (2005): 131–57.

Rowland, Christopher, ed. *The Cambridge Companion to Liberation Theology.* Cambridge: Cambridge University Press, 2007.

Rowley, Harold Henry. *The Unity of the Bible.* London: Carey Kingsgate Press, 1953.

Runia, Klaas. *Karl Barth's Doctrine of Holy Scripture.* Grand Rapids: Eerdmans, 1962.

Sailhamer, John H. *Introduction to Old Testament Theology: A Canonical Approach.* Grand Rapids: Zondervan, 1995.

Sanders, Ed Parish. *Paul and Palestinian Judaism.* Minneapolis: Fortress, 1977.

Sanders, Henry A. "The Beginnings of the Modern Book." *University of Michigan Quarterly Review* 44 (1938): 95–111.

———. *A Third-Century Papyrus Codex of the Epistles of Paul.* Ann Arbor: University of Michigan Press, 1935.

———. "A Third-Century Papyrus of Matthew and Acts." In *Quantulacumque: Studies Presented to Kirsopp Lake,* edited by Robert P. Casey, Silva Lake, and Agnes K. Lake, 151–61. London: Christophers, 1937.

Sanders, James A. "Adaptable for Life: The Nature and Function of Canon." In *Magnalia Dei: The Mighty Acts of God,* edited by Frank Moore Cross, Werner E. Lemke, and Patrick D. Miller Jr., 531–60. New York: Doubleday, 1976.

———. *Canon and Community: A Guide to Canonical Criticism.* Philadelphia: Fortress, 1984.

———. "Canon: Hebrew Bible." In *Anchor Bible Dictionary,* vol. 1, edited by David N. Freedman, 837–52. New York: Doubleday, 1992.

———. "Canonical Context and Canonical Criticism." *Horizons in Biblical Theology* 2 (1980): 173–97.

———. *From Sacred Story to Sacred Text*. Philadelphia: Fortress, 1987.

———. "The Issue of Closure in the Canonical Process." In *The Canon Debate*, edited by Lee Martin McDonald and James A. Sanders, 252–63. Peabody, MA: Hendrickson, 2002.

———. *Torah and Canon*. Philadelphia: Fortress, 1972.

Sarna, Nahum. "Bible." In *Encyclopedia Judaica*, vol. 3, edited by Fred Skolnik. Detroit: Macmillan Reference and Keter, 2006. 832.

Schildgen, Brenda Deen. *Power and Prejudice: The Reception of the Gospel of Mark*. Detroit: Wayne State University Press, 1999.

Schleiermacher, Friedrich. *The Christian Faith*. Edinburgh: T&T Clark, 1928.

Schlink, Edmund. *Ökumenische Dogmatik Grundzüge*. Göttingen: Vandenhoeck & Ruprecht, 1983.

Schneemelcher, Wilhelm, ed. *New Testament Apocrypha*. Translated by R. McL. Wilson. 2 vols. Louisville: Westminster John Knox, 1991.

Schneider, Bernardin. "The Meaning of St. Paul's Antithesis 'The Letter and the Spirit.'" *Catholic Biblical Quarterly* 15 (1953): 163–207.

Schnelle, Udo. *The History and Theology of the New Testament Writings*. Minneapolis: Fortress, 1998.

Schoedel, William R. *Ignatius of Antioch*. Philadelphia: Fortress, 1985.

Schoeps, Hans Joachim. "Ebionite Christianity." *Journal of Theological Studies* 4 (1953): 219–24.

———. *Jewish Christianity: Factional Disputes in the Early Church*. Philadelphia: Fortress, 1969.

Schrage, Wolfgang. "Die Frage nach der Mitte und dem Kanon im Kanon des Neuen Testaments in der neueren Diskussion." In *Rechtfertigung: Festschrift für Ernst Käsemann zum 70*, edited by Johannes Friedrich, Wolfgang Pöhlmann, and Peter Stuhlmacher, 415–42. Tübingen: Mohr Siebeck, 1976.

Schreiner, Thomas. *New Testament Theology: Magnifying God in Christ*. Grand Rapids: Baker Academic, 2008.

Schweitzer, Albert. *The Quest of the Historical Jesus*. New York: Macmillan, 1968.

Schwöbel, Christoph. "The Creature of the Word: Recovering the Ecclesiology of the Reformers." In *On Being the Church: Essays on the Christian Community*, edited by Colin E. Gunton and Daniel W. Hardys, 110–55. Edinburgh: T&T Clark, 1989.

Searle, John R. *Speech Acts: An Essay in the Philosophy of Language*. Cambridge: Cambridge University Press, 1970.

Seitz, Christopher. "The Canonical Approach and Theological Interpretation." In *Canon and Biblical Interpretation*, edited by Craig Bartholomew, Robin Parry and Scott Hahn, 58–110. Carlisle: Paternoster, 2006.

———. *The Goodly Fellowship of the Prophets: The Achievement of Association in Canon Formation.* Grand Rapids: Baker Academic, 2009.

Semler, Johann Salomo. *Abhandlung von freier Untersuchung des Canon.* 4 vols. Halle, 1771–1775. Repr. Gütersloh: Mohn, 1967.

Seters, John Van. *The Edited Bible: The Curious History of the "Editor" in Biblical Criticism.* Winona Lake, IN: Eisenbrauns, 2006.

Shea, Mark. *By What Authority?* Huntington, IN: Our Sunday Visitor, 1996.

Sheler, Jeffrey. "Cutting Loose the Holy Canon: A Controversial Re-Examination of the Bible." *U.S. News & World Report* 15, no. 18 (1993): 75.

Sheppard, Gerald T. "Canon." In *Encyclopedia of Religion*, vol. 3, edited by Lindsay Jones, 62–69. Detroit: Thomson Gale, 1987.

———. "Canon Criticism: The Proposal of Brevard Childs and an Assessment for Evangelical Hermeneutics." *Studia Biblica et Theologica* 4 (1974): 3–17.

———. "Canonization: Hearing the Voice of the Same God Through Historically Dissimilar Traditions." *Ex auditu* 1 (1985): 112.

———. "Canonization: Hearing the Voice of the Same God Through Historically Dissimilar Traditions." *Interpretation* 34 (1982): 21–33.

Skarsaune, Oskar. "Justin and His Bible." In *Justin Martyr and His Worlds*, edited by Sara Parvis and Paul Foster, 66–67. Minneapolis: Fortress, 2007.

Skeat, T. C. "A Codicological Analysis of the Chester Beatty Papyrus Codex of the Gospels and Acts (P45)." *Hermathena* 155 (1993): 27–43.

———. "Early Christian Book-Production." In *The Cambridge History of the Bible*, edited by G. W. H. Lampe, 54–79. Cambridge: Cambridge University Press, 1969.

———. "'Especially the Parchments': A Note on 2 Timothy iv.13." *Journal of Theological Studies* 30 (1979): 173–77.

———. "Irenaeus and the Four-Gospel Canon." *Novum Testamentum* 34 (1992): 198.

———. "The Length of the Standard Papyrus Roll and the Cost Advantage of the Codex." *Zeitschrift für Papyrologie und Epigraphik* 45 (1982): 169–75.

———. "The Oldest Manuscripts of the Four Gospels?" *New Testament Studies* 43 (1997): 1–34.

———. "The Origin of the Christian Codex." *Zeitschrift für Papyrologie und Epigraphik* 102 (1994): 263–68.

Skilton, John H. "The Transmission of the Scriptures." In *The Infallible Word*, edited by N. B. Stonehouse and Paul Woolley, 137–87. Philadelphia: Presbyterian and Reformed, 1946.

Smalley, Stephen S. "John's Revelation and John's Community." *Bulletin of the John Rylands University Library of Manchester* 69 (1987): 549–71.

Smith, D. Moody. "John, the Synoptics, and the Canonical Approach to Exegesis." In *Tradition and Interpretation in the New Testament*, edited by Gerald F. Hawthorne and Otto Betz, 166–80. Grand Rapids: Eerdmans, 1987.

———. "When Did the Gospels Become Scripture?" *Journal of Biblical Literature* 119 (2000): 8–9.

Smith, Jonathan Z. "Canons, Catalogues, and Classics." In *Canonization and Decanonization*, edited by Arie van der Kooij and Karel van der Toorn, 295–311. Leiden: Brill, 1998.

Smith, Morton. *Clement of Alexandria and a Secret Gospel of Mark*. Cambridge: Harvard University Press, 1973.

Smith, Terence V. *Petrine Controversies in Early Christianity*. Tübingen: Mohr, 1985.

Smith, Wilfred Cantwell. *What Is Scripture? A Comparative Approach*. London: SPCK, 1993.

Snodgrass, Klyne R. "The Gospel of Thomas: A Secondary Gospel." *Second Century* 7 (1989–1990): 19–38.

———. "Providence Is Not Enough." *Christianity Today* 32 (1988): 33–34.

Snyder, Graydon F. "Hermas' The Shepherd." In *Anchor Bible Dictionary*, vol. 3, edited by David N. Freedman, 148. New York: Doubleday, 1992.

Souter, Alexander. *The Text and Canon of the New Testament*. London: Duckworth, 1954.

Spicq, Ceslas. *Saint Paul: Les Épîtres Pastorales*. 4th ed. Paris: Gabalda, 1969.

Spina, Frank W. "Canonical Criticism: Childs Versus Sanders." In *Interpreting God's Word for Today*, edited by Wayne McCown and James Earl Massey, 165–94. Anderson, IN: Warner, 1982.

Spivey Robert A., and D. Moody Smith. *Anatomy of the New Testament*. New York: Macmillan, 1989.

Sproul, R. C. "The Internal Testimony of the Holy Spirit." In *Inerrancy*, edited by Norman Geisler, 337–54. Grand Rapids: Zondervan, 1980.

———. *Now That's A Good Question!* Wheaton, IL: Tyndale, 1996.

Sproul, R. C., John H. Gerstner, and Arthur W. Lindsley. *Classical Apologetics*. Grand Rapids: Zondervan, 1984.

Stanley, Christopher D. *Paul and the Language of Scripture: Citation Technique in the Pauline Epistles and Contemporary Literature*. Cambridge: Cambridge University Press, 1992.

Stanton, Graham N. "The Fourfold Gospel." *New Testament Studies* 43 (1997): 321–22.

———. *Jesus and Gospel*. Cambridge: Cambridge University Press, 2004.

———. "Jesus Traditions and Gospels in Justin Martyr and Irenaeus." In *The Biblical Canons*, edited by Jean-Marie Auwers and Henk Jan de Jonge, 353–70. Leuven: Leuven University Press, 2003.

Steck, O. H. "Der Kanon des hebraischen Alten Testament." In *Vernunft und Glauben*, edited by Jan Rohls, 231–52. Göttingen: Vandenhoeck & Ruprecht, 1988.

Steenberg, Matthew Craig. "Irenaeus on Scripture, Graphe, and the Status of Hermas." *St Vladimir's Theological Quarterly* 53 (2009): 29–66.

Steinmann, Andrew E. *The Oracles of God: The Old Testament Canon*. St. Louis: Concordia Academic Press, 1999.

Stonehouse, Ned B. *The Apocalypse in the Ancient Church*. Goes: Oosterbaan & Le Cointre, 1929.

———. "The Authority of the New Testament." In *The Infallible Word*, edited by Ned B. Stonehouse and Paul Woolley, 88–136. Philadelphia: Presbyterian and Reformed, 1946.

Stott, John R. W. *The Letters of John*. Grand Rapids: Eerdmans, 1996.

Strack, Hermann L., and Gunter Stemberger. *Introduction to the Talmud and Midrash*. Edinburgh: T&T Clark, 1991.

Strauss, David F. *Die christliche Glaubenslehre in ihrer geschichtlichen Entwicklung und im Kampfe mit der modernen Wissenschaft*. 2 vols. Tübingen: Osiander, 1840.

Strimple, Robert B. *The Modern Search for the Real Jesus*. Phillipsburg, NJ: P&R, 1995.

Stuhlhofer, Franz. *Der Gebrauch der Bibel von Jesus bis Euseb: Eine statistische Untersuchung zur Kanonsgeschichte*. Wuppertal: Brockhaus, 1988.

Stuhlmacher, Peter. *Biblische Theologie des Neuen Testaments*. 2 vols. Göttingen: Vandenhoeck & Ruprecht, 1992, 1999.

———. "Biblische Theologie des Neuen Testaments—eine Skizze." In *Eine Bibel—zwei Testamente. Positionen biblischer Theologie*, edited by Christoph Dohmen and Thomas Söding, 275–89. Paterborn: Schöningh, 1995.

Sundberg, Albert C. "Canon Muratori: A Fourth-Century List." *Harvard Theological Review* 66 (1973): 1–41.

———. "The Making of the New Testament Canon." In *The Interpreter's One-Volume Commentary on the Bible*, 1216–24. Nashville: Abingdon, 1971.

———. "The 'Old Testament': A Christian Canon." *Catholic Biblical Quarterly* 30 (1968): 143–55.

———. "Towards a Revised History of the New Testament Canon." *Studia evangelica* 4 (1968): 452–61.

Sungenis, Robert A., ed. *Not by Scripture Alone: A Catholic Critique of the Protestant Doctrine of Sola Scriptura*. Santa Barbara: Queenship, 1997.

Sweeney, Marvin. "Tanak verses Old Testament: Concerning the Foundation for a Jewish Theology of the Bible." In *Problems in Biblical Theology: Essays in Honor of Rolf Knierim*, edited by Henry T. C. Sun, Keith L. Eades, James M. Robinson, and Garth I. Moller, 353–72. Grand Rapids: Eerdmans, 1997.

Swete, Henry Barclay. *The Akhmîm Fragment of the Apocryphal Gospel of St. Peter*. London: Macmillan, 1893.

Swinburne, Richard. *Revelation: From Metaphor to Analogy*. Oxford: Oxford University Press, 2002.

Talmon, Shemaryahu. "The Crystallization of the 'Canon of Hebrew Scriptures' in the Light of the Biblical Scrolls from Qumran." In *The Bible as Book: The Hebrew Bible and the Judaean Desert Discoveries*, edited by Edward D. Herbert and Emanuel Tov, 5–20. London: The British Library, 2002.

———. "Oral Tradition and Written Transmission, or the Heard and the Seen Word in Judaism of the Second Temple Period." In *Jesus and the Oral Gospel Tradition*, edited by Henry Wansbrough, 121–58. Sheffield: Sheffield Academic, 1991.

Tanner, Norman P., ed. *Decrees of the Ecumenical Councils*. 2 vols. Washington, DC: Georgetown University Press, 1990.

Tavard, George H. *Holy Writ or Holy Church*. New York: Harper, 1959.

Taylor, Charles. "The Oxyrhynchus and Other Agrapha," *Journal of Theological Studies* 7 (1906): 546–62.

Taylor, Vincent. *Formation of the Gospel Tradition*. London: Macmillan, 1933.

Teicher, Jacob L. "The Dead Sea Scrolls—Documents of the Jewish-Christian Sect of the Ebionites." *Journal of Jewish Studies* 2 (1950–1951): 67–99.

Thiede, Carston Peter. "Papyrus Magdalen Greek 17 (Gregory-Aland P64): A Reappraisal." *Zeitschrift für Papyrologie und Epigraphik* 105 (1995): 13–20.

Thielman, Frank. "The New Testament Canon: Its Basis for Authority." *Westminster Theological Journal* 45 (1983): 400–410.

Thiselton, Anthony C. "Canon, Community, and Theological Construction." In *Canon and Biblical Interpretation*, edited by Craig Bartholomew, Robin Parry, and Scott Hahn, 1–30. Carlisle: Paternoster, 2006.

Thompson, John A. *The Ancient Near Eastern Treaties and the Old Testament*. Grand Rapids: Tyndale, 1964.

Thompson, Mark D. "Witness to the Word: On Barth's Doctrine of Scripture." In *Engaging with Barth: Contemporary Evangelical Critiques*, edited by David Gibson and Daniel Strange, 168–97. Nottingham: Apollos/IVP, 2008.

Thornton, Claus-Jürgen. *Der Zeuge des Zeugen: Lukas als Historiker der Paulusreisen*. Tübingen: Mohr Siebeck, 1991.

Thucydides. Translated by Charles Foster Smith. Loeb Classical Library. Cambridge, MA: Harvard University Press, 1980.

Torrance, Thomas F. "The Deposit of Faith." *Scottish Journal of Theology* 36 (1983): 1–28.

———. *God and Rationality*. New York: Oxford University Press, 2000.

———. *Karl Barth: An Introduction to His Early Theology, 1910–1931*. Edinburgh: T&T Clark, 2000.

Tov, Emanuel. *Textual Criticism of the Hebrew Bible*. Minneapolis: Fortress, 1992.

Treat, Jay Curry. "Epistle of Barnabas." In *Anchor Bible Dictionary*, vol. 1, edited by David N. Freedman, 611–14. New York: Doubleday, 1992.

Trebilco, Paul R. *The Early Christians in Ephesus from Paul to Ignatius*. Tübingen: Mohr Siebeck, 2004.

Treu, Kurt. "Neue neutestamentliche Fragmente der Berliner Papyrussammlung." *Archiv für Papyrusforschung* 18 (1966): 25–28.

Trites, Allison. *The New Testament Concept of Witness*. Cambridge: Cambridge University Press, 1977.

Trobisch, David. *Die Entstehung der Paulusbriefsammlung: Studien zu den Anfängen christlicher Publizistik*. Novum testamentum et orbis antiquus. Göttingen: Vandenhoeck & Ruprecht, 1989.

———. *The First Edition of the New Testament*. Oxford: Oxford University Press, 2000.

———. *Paul's Letter Collection: Tracing the Origins*. Minneapolis: Fortress, 1994.

Troeltsch, Ernst. "Historical and Dogmatic Method in Theology." In *Religion in History*, 11–32. Minneapolis: Fortress, 1991.

Tuckett, Christopher. *Nag Hammadi and the Gospel Tradition*. Edinburgh: T&T Clark, 1986.

———. "Thomas and the Synoptics." *Novum Testamentum* 30 (1988): 132–57.

Turner, Cuthbert H. "Marcan Usage: Notes Critical and Exegetical on the Second Gospel V. The Movements of Jesus and His Disciples and the Crowd." *Journal of Theological Studies* 26 (1925): 225–40.

Turner, Eric Gardner. *Greek Manuscripts of the Ancient World*. London: Institute of Classical Studies, 1987.

———. *Greek Papyri: An Introduction*. Oxford: Clarendon, 1968.

———. "Recto and Verso." *Journal of Egyptian Archaeology* 40 (1954): 102–6.

———. "Roman Oxyrhynchus." *Journal of Egyptian Archaeology* 38 (1952): 78–93.

———. "Scribes and Scholars." In *Oxyrhynchus: A City and Its Texts*. Patricia J. Parsons, Alan K. Bowman, R. A. Coles, Nikolaos Gonis, 258–59. London: Egypt Exploration Society, 2007.

———. *The Typology of the Early Codex*. Philadelphia: University of Pennsylvania Press, 1977.

Turner, Henry E. W. *The Pattern of Christian Truth: A Study in the Relations Between Orthodoxy and Heresy in the Early Church*. London: Mowbray, 1954.

Turretin, Francis. *Institutes of Elenctic Theology*. Translated by George Musgrave Giger. Edited by James T. Dennison Jr. 3 vols. Phillipsburg, NJ: P&R, 1992–1997.

Ulrich, Eugene. "The Notion and Definition of Canon." In *The Canon Debate*, edited by Lee Martin McDonald and James A. Sanders, 21–35. Peabody, MA: Hendrickson, 2002.

———. "Qumran and the Canon of the Old Testament." In *The Biblical Canons*, edited by Jean-Marie Auwers and Henk Jan de Jonge, 57–80. Leuven: Leuven University Press, 2003.

Vaganay, Léon. *L'Évangile de Pierre*. Paris: Librairie LeCoffre, 1930.

Vanhoozer, Kevin J. *The Drama of Doctrine: A Canonical-Linguistic Approach to Christian Theology*. Louisville: Westminster John Knox, 2005.

———. *First Theology: God, Scripture and Hermeneutics*. Downers Grove, IL: InterVarsity, 2002.

———. "A Person of the Book? Barth on Biblical Authority and Interpretation." In *Karl Barth and Evangelical Theology*, edited by Sung Wook Chung, 26–59. Grand Rapids: Baker, 2006.

van Peer, Willie. "Canon Formation: Ideology or Aesthetic Quality?" *British Journal of Aesthetics* 36 (1996): 97–108.

Van Til, Cornelius. *Karl Barth and Evangelicalism*. Philadelphia: Presbyterian and Reformed, 1964.

———. *The New Modernism: An Appraisal of the Theology of Barth and Brunner*. Philadelphia: Presbyterian and Reformed, 1947.

van Unnik, Willem C. "De la régle μήτε προσθεῖναι μήτε ἀφελεῖν dans l'histoire du canon." *Vigiliae christianae* 3 (1949): 1–36.

———. "ἡ καινὴ Διαθήκη—A Problem in the Early History of the Canon." In *Studia patristica*, vol. 4 (= TU 79), 212–27. Berlin, 1961.

Vansina, Jan M. *Oral Tradition as History*. Madison: University of Wisconsin Press, 1985.

Verheyden, Jozef. "Assessing Gospel Quotations in Justin Martyr." In *New Testament Textual Criticism and Exegesis, Festschrift J. Delobel*, edited by Adelbert Denaux, 361–78. Leuven: Peeters, 2002.

———. "The Canon Muratori: A Matter of Dispute." In *The Biblical Canons*, edited by Jean-Marie Auwers and Henk Jan de Jonge, 487–556. Leuven: Leuven University Press, 2003.

———. "The Shepherd of Hermas." In *The Writings of the Apostolic Fathers*, edited by Paul Foster, 63–71. London: T&T Clark, 2007.

Via, Dan Otto. "The Right Strawy Epistle Reconsidered: A Study in Biblical Ethics and Hermeneutic." *Journal of Religion* 49 (1969): 253–67.

Vielhauer, Philipp, and Georg Strecker. "Jewish-Christian Gospels." In *New Testament Apocrypha*, vol. 1, edited by Wilhelm Schneemelcher, translated by R. McL. Wilson, 134–78. Louisville: Westminster John Knox, 1991.

Vogels, Walter. "La structure symétrique de la Bible chrétienne." In *The Biblical Canons*, edited by Jean-Marie Auwers and Henk Jan de Jonge, 295–304. Leuven: Leuven University Press, 2003.

Vokes, Frederick E. "The Didache and the Canon of the New Testament." *Studia evangelica* 3 (1964): 427–36.

Vos, Geerhardus. *Biblical Theology*. Edinburgh: Banner of Truth, 1975.

Wachtel, Klaus. "P64/67: Fragmente des Matthäusevangeliums aus dem 1. Jahrhundert?" *Zeitschrift für Papyrologie und Epigraphik* 107 (1995): 73–80.

Wainwright, Geoffrey. "The New Testament as Canon." *Scottish Journal of Theology* 28 (1975): 564.

Wall, Robert W. "Canonical Context and Canonical Conversations." In *Between Two Horizons: Spanning New Testament Studies and Systematic Theology*, edited by Joel Green, 165–82. Grand Rapids: Eerdmans, 2000.

———. "The Jerusalem Council (Acts 15:1–21) in Canonical Context." In *From Biblical Criticism to Biblical Faith*, edited by William H. Brackney and Craig A. Evans, 93–101. Macon, GA: Mercer University Press, 2007.

Wall, Robert W., and Eugene E. Lemcio. *New Testament as Canon*. Sheffield: Sheffield Academic, 1992.

Walton, John H. *Ancient Israelite Literature in Its Cultural Context*. Grand Rapids: Zondervan, 1989.

Wansbrough, Henry, ed. *Jesus and the Oral Gospel Tradition*. Edinburgh: T&T Clark, 2004.

Warfield, Benjamin Breckinridge. *Calvin and Augustine*. Philadelphia: Presbyterian and Reformed, 1956.

———. "The Canonicity of 2 Peter." In *Selected Shorter Writings of Benjamin B. Warfield*, vol. 2, edited by John E. Meeter, 49–79. Nutley, NJ: Presbyterian and Reformed, 1973.

———. "The Formation of the Canon of the New Testament." In *The Inspiration and Authority of the Bible*, 411–16. Philadelphia: Presbyterian and Reformed, 1948.

———. *The Inspiration and Authority of the Bible*. Philadelphia: Presbyterian and Reformed, 1948.

Wasserman, Tommy. *The Epistle of Jude: Its Text and Transmission*. Stockholm: Almqvist & Wiksell, 2006.

Watson, Francis. "Bible, Theology and the University: A Response to Philip Davies." *Journal for the Study of the Old Testament* 71 (1996): 3–16.

———. *Text and Truth: Redefining Biblical Theology*. Grand Rapids: Eerdmans, 1997.

———. *Text, Church and World: Biblical Interpretation in Theological Perspective*. Edinburgh: T&T Clark, 1994.

Watts, Rikki. *Isaiah's New Exodus in Mark*. Grand Rapids: Baker Academic, 2001.

Webb, Robert L. "The Historical Enterprise and Historical Jesus Research." In *Key Events in the Life of the Historical Jesus*, edited by Darrell L. Bock and Robert L. Webb, 9–93. Tübingen: Mohr Siebeck, 2009.

Weber, Max. *The Sociology of Religion*. Boston: Beacon, 1993.

Webster, John B. "Canon and Criterion: Some Reflections on a Recent Proposal." *Scottish Journal of Theology* 54 (2001): 67–83.

———. "'A Great and Meritorious Act of the Church'? The Dogmatic Location of the Canon." In *Die Einheit der Schrift und die Vielfalt des Kanons*, edited by John Barton and Michael Wolter, 95–126. Berlin: De Gruyter, 2003.

———. *Holy Scripture: A Dogmatic Sketch*. Cambridge: Cambridge University Press, 2003.

———. "The Self-Organizing Power of the Gospel of Christ: Episcopacy and Community Formation." In *Word and Church*, 191–210. Edinburgh: T&T Clark, 2001.

Wedderburn, Alexander J. M. *Paul and Jesus: Collected Essays*. Sheffield: JSOT, 1989.

Weingarten, Gene. "Pearls Before Breakfast." *Washington Post*. April 8, 2007.

Weiss, Johannes. *Paulus and Jesus*. Berlin: Verlag von Reuther & Reichard, 1909.

Wenham, David. *Paul: Follower of Jesus or Founder of Christianity?* Grand Rapids: Eerdmans, 1995.

———. "Unity and Diversity in the New Testament." Appendix to George Eldon Ladd, *A Theology of the New Testament*, 684–719. Grand Rapids: Eerdmans, 2001.

Wenham, John W. *Christ and the Bible.* Downers Grove, IL: InterVarsity, 1972.

———. *Redating Matthew, Mark, and Luke: A Fresh Assault on the Synoptic Problem.* Downers Grove, IL: InterVarsity, 1992.

Wescott, Brooke F. *A General Survey of the History of the Canon of the New Testament.* London: Macmillan, 1870.

White, John L. "Introductory Formulae in the Body of the Pauline Letter." *Journal of Biblical Literature* 90 (1971): 91–97.

Whittaker, John. "The Value of Indirect Tradition in the Establishment of Greek Philosophical Texts or the Art of Misquotation." In *Editing Greek and Latin Texts: Papers Given at the Twenty-Third Annual Conference on Editorial Problems, University of Toronto 6–7 November 1987*, edited by John Grant, 63–95. New York: AMS, 1989.

Wilckens, Ulrich. *Die Missionsreden der Apostelgeschichte.* 3rd ed. Neukirchen-Vluyn: Neukirchener Verlag, 1974.

Wilder, Terry L. *Pseudonymity, the New Testament, and Deception: An Inquiry into Intention and Reception.* Lanham, MD: University Press of America, 2004.

Wiles, Maurice F. "Origen as Biblical Scholar." In *The Cambridge History of the Bible: From the Beginnings to Jerome*, edited by Peter R. Ackroyd and Christopher F. Evans, 454–89. Cambridge: Cambridge University Press, 1993.

Wilken, Robert L. *The Christians as the Romans Saw Them.* New Haven, CT: Yale University Press, 1984.

———. "Pagan Criticism of Christianity: Greek Religions and Christian Faith." In *Early Christian Literature and the Classical Intellectual Tradition: In Honorem Robert M. Grant*, edited by William R. Schoedel and Robert L. Wilken, 117–34. Paris: Editions Beauchesne, 1979.

Williams, Daniel H. *Evangelicals and Tradition: The Formative Influence of the Early Church.* Grand Rapids: Baker, 2005.

———. *Receiving the Bible in Faith: Historical and Theological Exegesis.* Washington, DC: Catholic University of America Press, 2004.

———. *Retrieving the Tradition and Renewing Evangelicalism: A Primer for Suspicious Protestants.* Grand Rapids: Eerdmans, 1999.

Williams, Rowan, ed. *The Making of Orthodoxy: Essays in Honor of Henry Chadwick.* Cambridge: Cambridge University Press, 1989.

Witherington, Ben. *The Gospel Code: Novel Claims About Jesus, Mary Magadelene, and Da Vinci.* Downers Grove, IL: InterVarsity, 2004.

Wolterstorff, Nicholas. *Divine Discourse: Philosophical Reflections on the Claim that God Speaks.* Cambridge: Cambridge University Press, 1995.

———. "Tradition, Insight and Constraint." *Proceedings and Addresses of the American Philosophical Association* 66 (1992): 43–57.

Woodbridge, John D. *Biblical Authority: A Critique of the Rogers/McKim Proposal.* Grand Rapids: Zondervan, 1982.

Wooden, R. Glenn. "The Role of the 'Septuagint' in the Formation of the Biblical Canons." In *Exploring the Origins of the Bible: Canon Formation in Historical, Literary, and Theological Perspective*, edited by Craig A. Evans and Emanuel Tov, 129–46. Grand Rapids: Baker, 2008.

Wrede, William. *The Origin of the New Testament.* Translated by James S. Hill. New York: Harper, 1909.

Wright, David F. "Apocryphal Gospels: The 'Unknown Gospel' (Pap. Egerton 2) and the *Gospel of Peter*." In *Gospel Perspectives: The Jesus Tradition Outside the Gospels*, edited by David Wenham, 207–32. Sheffield: JSOT, 1985.

———. "Ebionites." In *Dictionary of the Later New Testament and Its Development*, edited by Ralph P. Martin and Peter H. Davids, 313–17. Downers Grove, IL: InterVarsity, 1997.

Wright, N. T. *Jesus and the Victory of God.* Minneapolis: Fortress, 1996.

———. *The Last Word: Beyond the Bible Wars to a New Understanding of the Authority of Scripture.* San Francisco: HarperSanFrancisco, 2005.

———. *The New Testament and the People of God.* Minneapolis: Fortress, 1992.

Yarbrough, Robert W. "The Date of Papias: A Reassessment." *Journal of the Evangelical Theological Society* 26 (1983): 181–91.

Young, Edward J. *Thy Word Is Truth.* Repr. Edinburgh: Banner of Truth, 1991.

Zahn, Theodore. *Die bleibende Bedeutung des neutestamentlichen Kanons für die Kirche.* Leipzig: Deichert, 1890.

———. *Geschichte des neutestamentlichen Kanons.* Erlangen: Deichert, 1888–92.

Zumstein, Jean. "La naissance de la notion d'Écriture dans la littérature johannique." In *The Biblical Canons*, edited by Jean-Marie Auwers and Henk Jan de Jonge, 371–94. Leuven: Leuven University Press, 2003.

GENERAL INDEX

SCRIPTURE INDEX